AUSTRALIAN INDUSTRIAL RELATIONS

THIRD EDITION

AUSTRALIAN INDUSTRIAL RELATIONS

THIRD EDITION

Professor Stephen J. Deery
Department of Economics
University of Melbourne

Professor David H. Plowman
School of Industrial Relations and Organizational Behaviour
University of New South Wales

McGRAW-HILL BOOK COMPANY Sydney
New York   St Louis   San Francisco   Auckland   Bogotá   Caracas
Hamburg   Lisbon   London   Madrid   Mexico   Milan   Montreal
New Delhi   Oklahoma City   Paris   San Juan   São Paulo   Singapore
Tokyo   Toronto

First published 1980

Reprinted with corrections 1981
Reprinted 1981, 1982, 1983
Second edition 1985
Reprinted 1985, 1987 (twice), 1988, 1989
Third edition 1991

Copyright © 1991 by McGraw-Hill Book Company Australia Pty Limited

Apart from any fair dealing for the purposes of study, research, criticism or review, as permitted under the *Copyright Act*, no part may be reproduced by any process without written permission. Inquiries should be made to the publisher.

Copying for educational purposes
Where copies of parts of this book are made by an educational institution under the *Copyright Act*, and an agreement exists between the Copyright Agency Limited and the relevant educational authority (Department of Education etc.) to pay the fee for such copying, no further fee is due. In the absence of such an agreement, the law requires that records of such copying be kept. In such cases the copyright owner is entitled to claim payment.

**National Library of Australia
Cataloguing-in-Publication data:**

Deery, S. (Stephen).
  Australian industrial relations.

  3rd ed.
  Includes index.
  ISBN 0 07 452688 X.

  1. Industrial relations — Australia. I. Plowman, D. H.
  (David H.). II. Title.

331.0994

Produced by Book Generation Proprietary Limited, Glenroy, Victoria for
  McGraw-Hill Book Company Australia Pty Limited
  4 Barcoo Street, Roseville, NSW 2069
Typeset in Australia by Abb-typesetting Pty Ltd
Printed in Australia by Brown Prior Anderson Pty Ltd

Sponsoring Editor: Rosemary Gibbs
Production Editor: Cathryn Game
Designer: Melissa Gray
Cover Designer: Wildfire Graphics

To Chris, Anna,
Michael, Emily

CONTENTS

xi	Figures
xii	Tables
xv	Preface
xvi	Abbreviations

Part One ■ **THE STUDY OF INDUSTRIAL RELATIONS** 1

Chapter 1 ■ **The study of industrial relations** 3

5	Unitary approach
9	Pluralist approach
12	Marxist approach
15	The labour process
17	Divergence and accommodation
18	The systems model
22	Strategic choice theory
24	The approach used in this book
28	Discussion questions
28	Further reading

Part Two ■ **INDUSTRIAL CONFLICT** 31

Chapter 2 ■ **Industrial conflict** 33

33	The forms of industrial conflict
36	Theories of industrial conflict
49	Strikes
64	Summary
66	Appendices
69	Discussion questions
69	Further reading

Part Three	**THE PARTIES**	71
Chapter 3	**Governments**	73

- 73 Making the rules: auxiliary, regulatory and restrictive functions
- 77 Making the environment
- 82 Administering policy
- 84 The government as employer
- 92 Summary
- 92 Discussion questions
- 93 Further reading

Chapter 4	**The federal tribunal system**	94

- 94 The constitutional context
- 96 Influence of the federal tribunals
- 101 The Australian Industrial Relations Commission
- 118 Federal and state tribunal cooperation
- 119 The Federal Court of Australia (Industrial Division)
- 120 Board of Reference
- 121 Local Industry Boards
- 121 The Industrial Registries
- 123 Summary
- 124 Discussion questions
- 124 Further reading

Chapter 5	**The state tribunal systems**	125

- 125 The states' industrial powers
- 127 State unitary arbitration systems
- 137 Industrial boards
- 142 State dual arbitration and conciliation committee board systems
- 149 Conciliation and Arbitration Boards
- 153 A special case: the Northern Territory
- 154 Summary
- 154 Discussion questions
- 155 Further reading

Chapter 6	**Management**	157

- 158 The goals and functions of management
- 161 Work relations and control strategies
- 164 Corporate strategies and industrial relations
- 171 Market conditions and the management of industrial relations
- 177 Managerial style and attitudes
- 185 Structures for the management of industrial relations
- 188 Summary
- 189 Discussion questions
- 189 Further reading

Chapter 7 ■	**Employer associations**	191
191	Theories of employer associations	
195	Employer associations and bargaining structures	
196	Functions of employer associations	
203	Structure and organisation	
208	National coordination	
209	Unity and disunity	
212	Summary	
212	Discussion questions	
213	Further reading	

Chapter 8 ■	**Trade unions: origins, growth, structure**	214
214	Theoretical explanations of the labour movement	
219	Origins and development	
233	The pattern of Australian unionism	
245	Inter-union cooperation	
251	Summary	
253	Appendix	
258	Discussion questions	
258	Further reading	

Chapter 9 ■	**Trade unions: objectives and activities**	259
259	Union objectives	
260	Why employees join unions	
272	Union methods	
277	Unions and party politics	
281	Union democracy and internal government	
287	Union resources, research and education	
290	Unions and immigrants	
292	Unions and women	
299	Summary	
300	Discussion questions	
300	Further reading	

Part Four ■	**PROCESSES**	303
Chapter 10 ■	**The development of industrial arbitration**	305
305	The strikes of the 1890s and the watershed thesis	
308	Compulsory arbitration	
310	The growth of federal arbitration	
321	The use of conciliation	
326	Legalism	
327	Award enforcement and strike penalties	
329	Economic regulation	
331	The new intervention: the Fraser years	
334	Incorporation: the Accord	
335	Summary	

	336	Discussion questions
	337	Further reading
Chapter 11 ■		**National arbitration** 339
	339	The rationale of national test cases
	340	Standard hours of work
	344	Paid leave
	348	Occupational superannuation
	350	Termination, change and redundancy
	352	National wage determination
	366	Equal pay
	369	Summary
	370	Discussion questions
	371	Further reading
Chapter 12 ■		**Industry award determination** 372
	372	Types of award
	376	Award-making
	383	Award variation
	384	Roping-in awards
	384	The content of awards
	385	Industry wage determination
	401	Summary
	402	Appendix
	405	Discussion questions
	405	Further reading
Chapter 13 ■		**Award restructuring** 407
	408	Pressures for change
	410	The two-tiered wages system
	416	The Structural Efficiency Principle
	420	The ACTU blueprint
	425	Summary
	425	Discussion questions
	426	Further reading
Part Five ■		**CONTEMPORARY TRENDS** 429
Chapter 14 ■		**Workplace industrial relations** 431
	431	The workplace and arbitration
	434	Trade unions and the workplace
	437	Workplace bargaining
	442	Management and workplace industrial relations
	451	Absenteeism and labour turnover
	456	Summary
	457	Discussion questions
	457	Further reading
Chapter 15 ■		**The democratisation of work** 459
	459	Industrial democracy as an issue

462	Work reform in the 1970s
468	New directions in industrial democracy
475	Factors affecting the incidence of worker participation
476	Summary
477	Discussion questions
478	Further reading

Chapter 16 ■ **Women and employment equality** 479

479	Women's occupations and industries
486	Explanations of pay differentials
489	Legislative intervention
495	Equal pay and wage fixation principles
498	Summary
499	Discussion questions
499	Further reading

■ **Index** 501

FIGURES

1.1	Framework of an industrial relations system	27
2.1	Relationship between number of disputes and working days lost, Australia, 1966–89	52
2.2	Industrial disputes and working days lost, Australia, 1913–88	54
3.1	Merchants and Ships Chandlers, Sydney Town, 1852	75
4.1	The federal system	122
5.1	Queensland industrial tribunal system	129
5.2	Western Australian industrial tribunals	135
5.3	The Tasmanian industrial boards system	139
5.4	New South Wales industrial tribunals	144
5.5	South Australian industrial tribunals	146
5.6	Victorian industrial tribunal system	151
6.1	Management style and frames of reference	179
6.2	The interconnections between individualism and collectivism	180
7.1	PATEFA: Organisation and structure	205
8.1	Structure and organisation of the ACTU	249
9.1	The process of individual union choice	263
12.1	Award-making under federal arbitration	381
14.1	ICI Australia's industrial relations strategy	448
14.2	Employee attendance: a process model	453

TABLES

1.1	Three levels of industrial relations activity	24
2.1	Proportion of civilian workforce by sector, 1901, 1982 and 1989	42
2.2	Proportionate changes in select industry workforce, sizes, 1961–71	42
2.3	Distribution of wealth in Australia	48
2.4	Industrial disputes by duration, Australia, 1970–89	55
2.5	Proportion of working days lost in strikes of different length, Australia, 1970–89	55
2.6	Proportion of strikes and working days lost by issue, Australia, 1913–89	57
2.7	Average duration of strikes by issue, Australia, 1977, 1989	58
2.8	Proportion of industrial disputes by industry, Australia, 1913–89	59
2.9	Working days lost per thousand employees by industry, Australia, 1972–88	60
2.10	Proportion of industrial disputes by state, 1913–88	61
2.11	Working days lost per thousand employees by state, Australia, 1967–88	62
2.12	Method of settlement of industrial disputes, Australia, 1989	63
2.13	Industrial disputes, Australia, 1913–89	66–67
2.14	Industrial disputes by industry, Australia, 1988	68
3.1	Employed wage and salary earners, by sector and sex, May 1988	85

3.2	Relative size of public sector employment, 1945–88	85
4.1	Proportion of workforce under awards of tribunals, Australia, 1989	98
4.2	Proportion of workforce under awards of tribunals by state, Australia, May 1985	99
4.3	Proportion of workforce by tribunal jurisdiction, Australia, May 1985	100
4.4	Proportion of employees affected by awards by industry, Australia, May 1985	101
4.5	Panel 8, Industrial Relations Commission	105
4.6	General statement of business of the Commission, 1980–81 to 1986–87	107
4.7	Analysis by subject matter of applications to Industrial Relations Commission to vary awards and agreements 1986–87	108
4.8	Analysis by subject matter of dispute notifications under Section 25 of the Act, 1986–87	110–111
6.1	The shape of company policy variables with respect to overall company strategy (ideal-type cases)	167
6.2	The management style of personnel and industrial relations specialists	181
6.3	Opinions of personnel and industrial relations specialists on industrial relations issues	184
8.1	Membership of Australian trade unions, 1901–89	226
8.2	Membership of Australian trade unions, 1976–88	228
8.3	Groups in the community believed to hold 'too much power'	231
8.4	Trade union industry penetration, August 1988	233
8.5	Trade union occupational coverage, August 1988	234
8.6	Trade union size, June 1989	234
8.7	Trade unions with 50 000 or more members, 1989 and 1979	236
8.8	Trade unions interstate structure, June 1989	243
8.9	Membership figures of ACTU affiliated organisations, 1989	253–257
9.1	Proportion of working days lost by cause, all industries, Australia 1970–89	267
10.1	Composition of federal tribunal 1905–90	322–323
11.1	Wage adjustments under wage indexation, March quarter 1975 to December/March quarters 1981	364
12.1	Single-employer and multi-employer federal awards, 1954–87	374

12.2	Award-making: claims and counterclaims	379
12.3	Subject matter of Metal Industry Awards (Part 1—Wages Employees)	402–404
13.1	Key classification relativity range, national wage case, August 1989	423
13.2	Classification structure: Metal Industry Award	424
14.1	Number of trade unions per workplace	435
14.2	Number of trade unions by workplace size	435
14.3	Union representation across workplaces	436
14.4	Number of unions by frequency of union steward–management meetings	438
14.5	Issues most often discussed at shop steward–management meetings	438
14.6	Amount of say workplace representatives have in plant decision-making	439
14.7	Content of second-tier agreements in the metal industry	441
14.8	Level at which second-tier negotiations were conducted	441
15.1	Attitudes to employee participation	473
15.2	Participative processes in Australian workplaces	474
16.1	Pattern of occupational segregation in Australia	481
16.2	Employed persons: industry by sex, February 1989	481
16.3	Part-time workers as a proportion of all employees, 1970–89	483
16.4	Part-time employees: percentage of age group working part-time, 1989	483
16.5	Conditions of employment by type of work, Victoria, October 1988	485
16.6	Average female earnings as a percentage of average male earnings in selected OECD countries, 1968, 1977 and 1987	498

PREFACE

This is now the third edition of *Australian Industrial Relations*. Much has changed in the field since the previous edition was published in 1985. New issues have emerged while others have receded in importance. Substantial changes have occurred in the relationships between employees, managers and trade unions as the parties have been forced to adapt and respond to new international economic pressures. Industrial relations have become more decentralised and less institutionally determined as policy makers have shifted their attention to workplace issues of efficiency and productivity.

Changes have also occurred in the body of knowledge which has underpinned the study of industrial relations. In this edition we have endeavoured to draw upon and incorporate new conceptual and empirical developments where they could be seen to contribute to a better understanding of this complex area of human interaction. Particular attention has been given to management's role in industrial relations and to the relationship between corporate strategies and industrial relations policies. Moreover, the emphasis on the enterprise and on the restructuring of awards has been reflected in a wider and more thorough analysis of industrial relations activities and arrangements at the workplace. Other chapters have been revised to incorporate new theoretical insights or to record major legislative or organisational developments. It is hoped that these and other changes in both the scope and content of the book will enable *Australian Industrial Relations* to make a continuing contribution to the study and understanding of industrial relations in this country.

We would like to acknowledge the assistance of a number of people in the preparation of this book. Ros Dawson-Marsh, Maria Lane and Marie Kwok typed many drafts with unfailing accuracy and good humour, Rosemary Gibbs was an enthusiastic and energetic editor and Harold Simons managed the production with great professionalism.

ABBREVIATIONS

ABS	Australian Bureau of Statistics
ACEF	Australian Council of Employers' Federations
ACMA	Associated Chambers of Manufacturers of Australia
ACOA	Administrative and Clerical Officers' Association
ACTU	Australian Council of Trade Unions
ALP	Australian Labor Party
AMWU	Amalgamated Metal Workers Union
ASIC	Australian Standard Industry Classification
ATEA	Australian Telecommunications Employees' Association
BCA	Business Council of Australia
CAI	Confederation of Australian Industry
CAR	Commonwealth Arbitration Reports
CONMIA	Council of National Manufacturing Industries of Australia
CPA	Communist Party of Australia
CPA (M-L)	Communist Party of Australia (Marxist-Leninist)
DLP	Democratic Labor Party
EEO	Equal Employment Opportunity
FCU	Federated Clerks' Union
ILO	International Labour Organisation
IRC	Industrial Relations Commission
MTIA	Metal Trades Industries Association
NEA	National Employers' Association
NLCC	National Labour Consultative Council
NWC	National Wage Case
PATEFA	Printing and Allied Trades Employers' Federation of Australia
PKIU	Printing and Kindred Industries Union
SPA	Socialist Party of Australia
TUTA	Trade Union Training Authority
VEF	Victorian Employers' Federation

Part One
THE STUDY OF INDUSTRIAL RELATIONS

There are many approaches to the study of industrial relations. Part 1 surveys the major approaches as well as outlining the framework used in subsequent parts of this book.

CHAPTER 1

The Study of Industrial Relations

There has been considerable debate about what the study of industrial relations should embrace. The many attempts to define the subject have merely served to illustrate the diversity of views held about its exact scope and content. Some have taken a narrow perspective of the subject and have defined it as a study of the institutions of job regulation at the workplace.[1] Others have insisted that industrial relations is only one aspect of the wider issue of class conflict and its study must be located in a comprehensive analysis of contemporary capitalism.[2] Differences of view have affected the range of factors that are seen to warrant inclusion in the study of industrial relations. For those who emphasise the irredeemable nature of conflict between capital and labour, class inequality and the structure and distribution of power, both within the industrial relations context and in the wider society, are seen to be central components in the study of industrial relations. For those who take a narrower institutional analysis of 'job regulation', questions about the structure of ownership and control in industry are regarded as being external to the subject.

It is possible to say, however, that in its broadest sense industrial relations is about the behaviour and interaction of people at work. It is concerned with how individuals, groups, organisations and institutions make decisions that shape the employment relationship between management and labour. Industrial relations includes the study of workers and their unions, employers and their associations, and the institutions

---

1. A. Flanders, *Industrial Relations—What is Wrong with the System? An Essay on its Theory and Future*, Faber & Faber, London, 1965.
2. R. Hyman, *Industrial Relations: A Marxist Introduction*, Macmillan, London, 1975.

established to regulate the relations between the two parties. The role that public policy and the legal framework play in affecting employment conditions is also important. So too is an understanding of the power relations between employers and trade unions within the work environment and the way in which wider political, economic and social factors shape and condition those relations.

Industrial relations is an interdisciplinary study. It draws on a number of established academic disciplines such as economics, sociology, psychology, law, political science and history. At times both the subject matter and the analytical tools of each of those disciplines are relevant to the study of industrial relations problems. But though many disciplines can contribute to an understanding of industrial relations, none of them has exactly the same focus or boundaries as industrial relations. Kochan, Katz and McKersie have pointed out some of the differences:

> Ever since the pioneering work of John R. Commons in the early years of this century, industrial relations theory has consistently stressed the importance of the institutional structure in which labour–management interactions occur. This view argues that, to explain industrial relations processes and outcomes, it is not enough to simply understand the pressures that economic or other environmental forces place on the employment relationship. Rather the patterns, laws, customs, and structures that build up over time and establish what Commons, Veblen, and other social scientists consider to be the institutional features of the relationship exert an independent effect of their own. This is one of the central features that differentiate industrial relations theory from neoclassical economics and many other general theories in the behaviour and social sciences. These other theories view institutional factors as a black box of random forces that need not be considered in predicting behaviour or, in some recent formulations, constraints within which choice and individual maximizing behaviour occur.[3]

Some years ago John Dunlop complained that industrial relations 'had merely been a crossroads where a number of disciplines met'.[4] It is important that industrial relations be seen as a discrete area of study with a central focus. Too much emphasis on behavioural variables might, for example, reduce industrial relations to a branch of psychology, human relations or personnel management. Excessive stress on environmental factors could reduce industrial relations to a branch of economics, law, sociology or political science. Since the relations between employers and employees involve dimensions that cut across all disciplines, a complete analysis of the issues must also reflect their full range and complexity.[5]

It is important to recognise that the study of industrial relations may be approached from a number of perspectives. Different people perceive industrial relations in different ways and often from different and competing theoretical stances. Some who hold to what is known as the

---

3. T. Kochan, H. Katz and R. McKersie, *The Transformation of American Industrial Relations*, Basic Books, New York, 1986, p. 16.
4. J.T. Dunlop, *Industrial Relations Systems*, Holt, Rinehart & Winston, New York, 1958, p. 6.
5. T. Kochan, *Collective Bargaining and Industrial Relations*, Richard Irwin, Homewood, 1980, p. 1.

unitary view of industrial relations see employer–employee relations as essentially harmonious, punctuated only by occasions of temporary conflict. Those who subscribe to the pluralist perspective take the view that conflict is inherent in the employment relationship but that it is manageable and can be contained by an appropriate network of rules and regulations. Others see industrial relations in terms of class conflict between the owners and controllers of capital and those who sell their labour to them. For this reason, as Farnham and Pimlott have pointed out, 'industrial relations becomes both an academic and a political arena where the opposing ideologies and different value systems of individuals and of groups compete not only against one another but also for the minds ... of the uncommitted'.[6]

In the following section we review three separate and distinct approaches to the study of industrial relations. These are identified as the unitary, the pluralist and the Marxist approaches. We then examine the attempts to develop comprehensive theories of industrial relations. Finally, the chapter outlines the approach that will be taken in this book.

Unitary approach

The distinguishing feature that characterises this approach to industrial relations is the assumption that each work organisation is an integrated entity with a common purpose or goal. Industrial relations is seen as being based on mutual co-operation and a harmony of interest between employers and employees. It is assumed that both workers and management share a common objective, which, put simply, is the efficient functioning of the organisation. There is no conflict of interest between those who own capital and those who supply their labour. By definition they are in fact part of the same team. They are joint partners to the common aims of production, profits and pay, which will be shared between all the stake-holders as team members. Fox wrote:

> What pattern of behaviour do we expect from the members of a successful and healthily functioning team? We expect them to strive jointly towards a common objective, each pulling his weight to the best of his ability. Each accepts his place and his function gladly, following the leadership of the one so appointed. There are no oppositionary groups or factions and therefore no rival leaders within the team. Nor are there any outside it; the team stands alone, its members giving allegiance to their own leaders but to no others.[7]

Industrial conflict is seen as temporary or the product of aberrant behaviour, something perhaps induced by troublemakers or poor management or the result of bad communications. Trade unions are seen as unwelcome intruders whose presence upsets the unified and

---
6. D. Farnham and J. Pimlott, *Understanding Industrial Relations*, Cassell, London, 1979, p. xii.
7. A. Fox, 'Industrial sociology and industrial relations', Research Paper 3, HMSO, London, 1966, reprinted in A. Flanders (ed.), *Collective Bargaining*, Penguin, London, 1971, pp. 391–2.

co-operative structure that exists within the organisation. Furthermore, they are judged as being in competition with management for the loyalty of employees. The answer to this problem can be readily identified: 'If you can convince the worker that you are genuinely interested in his welfare, his performance, his tenure of employment, then you will be rewarded with his loyalty, dedication and real interests in the goals of the company.'[8]

Those who hold such views of industrial organisations subscribe to the need for strong leadership in order to achieve commitment to the job and to the organisation itself. The unitary perspective of industrial relations is predominantly managerially oriented. Management's commitment to this view has much to do with the fact that it legitimates authority. As Bendix has argued, the aim is to develop obedience 'so as to neutralise or eliminate the conflict between the few and the many in the interest of a more effective exercise of authority'.[9]

The unitary system has a single source of authority and a single focus of loyalty. And as Fox has noted, 'morale and success are closely connected and rest heavily upon personal relationships'.[10] The earliest application of this unitary framework for analysing industrial relations problems was made by American organisational psychologists who, in particular, tended to 'conceptualise organisations as co-operative systems in which it [was] ... the job of management to integrate the goals of individual workers with those of the organisation'.[11] According to Kochan, these theorists did not deny that conflict could exist within organisations, but claimed that the sources of conflict were interpersonal rather than economic or structural. They stressed the need for managerial strategies to build high commitment, improved comunications and in some cases democratic leadership styles and workplace systems of employee participation. Three broad schools of thought can be identified: scientific management, human relations and neo-human relations.

Scientific management

Many of the early organisational writers were concerned with how management could achieve industrial unity and induce efficient work performance. One of the earliest theories of industrial behaviour was formulated by Frederick Taylor around the turn of the century. His principal interest was to create an industrial climate in which an authentic partnership could be formed between capital and labour. Taylor saw this as being best achieved by increasing the efficiency of the organisation. He proposed that management should study the work that had to be performed in order to ascertain scientifically the 'one best way' of doing each task. The results of such an inquiry would then be turned

---

8. G. Spurling, Managing Director, Mitsubishi Motors Australia, *Australian Financial Review*, 1 June 1982.
9. R. Bendix, *Work and Authority in Industry*, University of California Press, Berkeley, 1956, p. 13.
10. Fox, 'Industrial sociology', p. 392.
11. T. Kochan, 'A review symposium', *Industrial Relations*, vol. 21, no. 1, 1982, p. 117.

into a set of rules, which each worker would have to follow. What was required of the job performer was obedience. Taylor proposed that by maximising the product efficiency of each worker, scientific management would maximise the earnings of workers and employers. As a result 'both sides would take their eyes off the division of the surplus as the all important matter and together turn their attention toward increasing the size of the surplus'.[12] Taylor was confident that by adjusting workers' wages to output, the interests of the worker and the interests of the employer could be made compatible. With appropriate task designs and payment systems sources of conflict could be eliminated. However, little thought was given to the conflict that would arise over the distribution of company earnings into wage and profit shares.

Human relations

The emergence of the human relations school was a reaction to the early efforts of the industrial psychologists who had focused on the individual. Instead, the human relations theorists stressed the importance of the work group. Their emphasis lay not on structuring the appropriate economic incentives but on creating satisfying social relations within work groups. Satisfied workers would be high performers and industrially cooperative. Employees needed to be treated as human beings and managers had to understand their feelings and emotions and create a sense of belonging and personal identification with the organisation. According to Hawkins the key was leadership:

> ... the kind of leadership that would reawaken a genuine sense of 'team spirit' within the enterprise while firmly endorsing the position of management at the head of the 'team'. Conflict would thus be overcome simply by the development of a new *esprit de corps* ...[13]

The emphasis was on creating conditions for corporate unity. Good supervision and good communications would inspire a sense of confidence and commitment to the goals of the organisation. The function of management was to provide a working environment concerned with the emotional and personal needs of individuals within work groups.

The human relations approach owed much to the work of an Australian, Elton Mayo, who during the 1920s and 1930s conducted a series of research studies into the industrial attitudes and behaviour of employees at the Western Electric Hawthorne plant in Chicago. He became the mid-century industrial counterpart of Taylor and, like Taylor, his work and the general approach he propounded became the subject of a great deal of criticism. As Michael Rose has observed, human relations is nowadays widely condemned:

> ... economists have ridiculed its rejection of money as the central motivation of work behaviour; political liberals have attacked its denial of individualism; radicals have raged over its assertions of workers' irrationalism and moral

---

12. K. Hawkins, *Conflict and Change*, Holt, Rinehart & Winston, London, 1972, p. 30.
13. Ibid., p. 32.

dependence on management; industrial managers have discarded its unworkable manipulatory techniques; sociological researchers and theorists of all colours have documented its methodological, theoretical and ideological lapses.[14]

Neo-human relations

From the mid-1950s accumulating industrial research cast doubts on the prescriptive remedies of the human relations theory. The neo-human relations school, which included such writers as Herzberg, McGregor and Likert, argued that the key to understanding industrial behaviour was not to be found in the social needs but in the individual (or egoistic) needs of workers.[15] Emphasis was placed on creating the type of satisfaction that came from the nature of the job itself. Things like interest, challenge and the opportunity for responsibility and self-direction were the real motivations and these had to be built into jobs. Schemes such as job enlargement and job enrichment replaced 'social needs' as the way to unlock the energy of employees and overcome industrial conflict. McGregor, in particular, argued that if companies could tap the higher order need of workers through changes in the organisational structure, thereby promoting employee involvement and participation in decision-making at the job level, this would lead to a congruence of private and organisational goals.[16]

The neo-human relations approach therefore built onto the human relations approach the need for intrinsic work satisfaction. It was said that workers required not only social satisfaction at work (i.e. good informal relations) but also self-esteem and the ability to 'self-actualise'. Some work factors, such as good wages and good working conditions, were regarded only as 'hygiene factors'. If they were not present, dissatisfaction would exist. However, work satisfaction was seen to require more than the presence of these hygiene factors. To be satisfied in employment, workers further required 'satisfier factors', such as status, recognition and interesting work.

The neo-human relations theorists were more sophisticated than their predecessors in their analysis of industrial behaviour, but they shared with them the view that a unity of purpose could be achieved. The solution lay in improving interpersonal relations. The sources of conflict were to be found within the organisation and were amenable to change by the application of appropriate managerial techniques. Conflict could be averted by adding to good communications supportive leadership and good informal relationships, as well as work that was satisfying and rewarding, and with which workers could identify. While a pleasant work environment and satisfactory wage level provided the necessary hygiene factors, job enrichment, job enlargement and job

---

14. M. Rose, *Industrial Behaviour*, Penguin, London, 1978, p. 103.
15. F. Herzberg, *Work and the Nature of Work*, Staples Press, Granada, 1968; D. McGregor, *The Human Side of Enterprise*, McGraw-Hill, New York, 1960; R. Likert, *New Patterns in Management*, McGraw-Hill, New York, 1961.
16. See M. Rose, *Industrial Behaviour* p. 188.

rotation became the necessary methods of reducing boring and repetitive production processes.

The unitary approach to industrial relations, and the policy prescriptions that flow from it, takes a very narrow view of the nature of industrial conflict. It avoids fundamental questions such as the conflict over the distribution of the proceeds of industry, security of employment and the status of labour as a factor of production and the issues of power and control in industrial decision-making. Why then do employers and managers subscribe to a 'unitary' view of industrial organisation when it is so 'at variance with demonstrable facts'?[17] Fox contends that it is because management sees it as an instrument of persuasion and as a technique of seeking legitimation of authority:

> Managers seek to persuade their employees and the public at large that industry is a harmony of co-operation which only fools or knaves choose to disrupt. To the extent that they convince their employees their job is made easier; to the extent that they convince the public they gain sympathy whenever their policies are challenged by their workers... [Moreover] the propagation of the idea that the interests of the rulers and the ruled are identical helps to confer legitimacy upon the regime.[18]

Pluralist approach

In contrast to the unitary concept of industrial organisations, the pluralist approach accepts the inevitability of conflict. It recognises that within organisations there will be a variety of groups with divergent interests, objectives and aspirations. Separate sectional groups will compete with each other to achieve their own goals. While the unitary approach admitted only one source of legitimate power, pluralism points to the possibility of diverse interest groups, sources of loyalty and attachment. In the case of employees this will mean that they will have similar interests to those of other employees in other organisations. By creating horizontal links with groups outside the membership of the organisation, in the form of trade unions, they will develop a loyalty and commitment to leaders other than the management of their own organisation.

The British writer Alan Fox was one of the first to popularise the distinction between the two approaches to industrial relations in his research paper to the Donovan Royal Commission in 1966.[19] His work can be traced to the writings of N. S. Ross, who in 1958 called for a new

> theoretical approach to management which treats the firm as a plural society rather than as the organic unity which most theorists appear hitherto to have represented it to be. The problem of government in a plural society is not to unify, integrate or liquidate sectional groups and their special interests in the

---

17. Fox, 'Industrial sociology', p. 394.
18. Ibid., p. 395.
19. Fox, 'Industrial sociology'.

name of some over-riding corporate existence, but to control and balance the activities of competing groups so as to provide for the maximum degree of freedom of association and action for sectional and group purposes consistent with the general interest of the society as conceived . . .[20]

Fox considered that it was important for management to recognise that there were other legitimate sources of leadership and focuses of loyalty within an organisation, and that they must share their decision-making authority with these competing interest groups. Further, he contended that they should not regard industrial conflict as a pathological deviation from the natural harmony of industry but recognise conflict as inherent in the employment relationship. Rather than trade unions being seen as introducing conflict into industry, they should be viewed as providing an organised and continuous way of expressing the sectional interests that exist.[21] Fox believed that the pluralist framework made more sense of industrial relations and provided management with a better understanding of the severe limitations of their power. He saw it as a necessary basis for

> recognising that co-operation is unlikely to be achieved in modern industry through the attempted manipulation of 'team spirit', 'high morale' and 'loyalty' but needs to be engineered by structural adaptions in work organisations, work roles and work practices and that direct negotiation with work groups is an essential part of this process.[22]

The pluralist approach has provided the theoretical perspective for the great majority of recent academic work in industrial relations, but not all of its adherents necessarily subscribe to Fox's notions. As Hyman observed, the problem with pluralism is that it 'is in no way a homogeneous body of analysis and prescription'.[23] It has been employed as a form of analysis of industrial relations by various writers who attach significance to different elements. Nevertheless, there are perhaps two key components to the pluralist approach.[24] The first component is that power is said to be diffused among the main bargaining groups in such a way that no party dominates the other. In other words, competing forces constrain and check absolute power. While no party is able to achieve all its aspirations completely, both are at least able to succeed partly in their goals. Secondly, the state is regarded as an impartial guardian of the 'public interest' whose role is largely to protect the weak and restrain the power of the strong.

Clegg has been specific in elaborating his conception of pluralism. He sees industrial relations as a process of concession and compromise in which a body of rules restrains the abuse of power and enables all parties to accomplish some gains. He contends that the pluralist approach

---

20. N.S. Ross, 'Organised labour and management: the U.K.', in E.M. Hugh-Jones (ed.), *Human Relations and Management*, North Holland, 1958, pp. 101–2.
21. Fox, 'Industrial sociology', p. 399.
22. Ibid., p. 408.
23. R. Hyman, 'Pluralism, procedural consensus and collective bargaining', *British Journal of Industrial Relations*, vol. 16, no. 1, 1978, p. 16.
24. These have been distilled largely from the work of the 'Oxford School' and the theoretical approach of three of its principal advocates and exponents, Hugh Clegg, Allan Flanders and Alan Fox.

explains why, in the face of intractable industrial conflict, modern societies have remained relatively stable. He says this is due to

> some mechanism at work which binds the competing groups together and holds them back from rending their societies to pieces. For the pluralist this mechanism is the continuous process of concession and compromise.[25]

The pluralist approach also has its critics. One major criticism is that while pluralism accepts the inevitability of conflict it assumes an approximate balance of power among the parties as well as agreement on the rules of the game.[26] The enterprise is characterised as a miniature democratic state. Miliband has argued that no such parallel exists:

> What is wrong with pluralist-democratic theory is not its insistence on the factor of competition but its claim (very often its implicit assumption) that the major organised 'interests' in society, and notably capital and labour, compete on more or less equal terms, and that none of them is therefore able to achieve a decisive and permanent advantage in the process of competition. This is where ideology enters and turns observation into myth.[27]

Hyman and Fryer argue that rather than there being some symmetry in the distribution of power between management and unions, power is heavily weighted towards management. They feel that the starting point for any realistic analysis of industrial relations must be the substantial power imbalance between capital and labour.[28] This derives from the fact that the productive system is, in the main, the private property of a very small minority of the population. As Fox observes:

> From this view, any talk of 'checks and balances', however apt for describing subsidiary phenomena, simply confuses our understanding of the primary dynamics which shape and move society—a useful confusion indeed for the major power-holders since it obscures the domination of society by its ruling strata through institutions and assumptions which operate to exclude anything approaching a genuine power balance.[29]

From this perspective the pluralist approach is open to the criticism that it is as obfuscatory as the unitary approach. Instead of drawing attention to the position of the exploited and to the fundamental nature of class relations, pluralism presents the view that the owners and controllers of capital are simply one of a number of competing interest groups staking out a claim for their legitimate share of the productive wealth. It can be said that the propagation of this view 'becomes another of the conditioning influences which indoctrinate the victims of an exploitive set of economic and social relations into accepting the system'.[30] Certainly by obscuring the real disparity of power in our society it does promote acceptance in the prevailing social structure. By

---

25. H.A. Clegg, 'Pluralism and industrial relations', *British Journal of Industrial Relations*, vol. 13, no. 3, 1975, p. 309.
26. J. Child, 'Comment', in A. Thomson and M. Warner (eds), *The Behavioural Sciences and Industrial Relations*, Gower, London, 1981, p. 26.
27. Quoted in M. Jackson, *Industrial Relations*, Croom Helm, London, 1977, p. 32.
28. R. Hyman and R. Fryer, 'Trade unions', in J.B. McKinlay (ed.), *Processing People: Cases in Organisational Behaviour*, Holt, Rinehart & Winston, 1975, p. 161.
29. A. Fox, *Beyond Contract: Work Power and Trust Relations*, Faber & Faber, London, 1974, p. 274.
30. Ibid.

concealing the great differences of power, the pluralist approach can be criticised for fostering the belief that all parties compete fairly for its rewards thereby helping to legitimise the *status quo*.

A second and related criticism of the pluralist framework is its emphasis on the promotion of rational, efficient and effective conflict management. It is open to the interpretation that it is little more than a sophisticated managerialism aimed at finding ways of containing conflict within a regulatory framework that promotes and maintains order:

> Pluralism could be presented, in fact, as the far-seeing manager's ideology for a future in which those in positions of rule come increasingly under challenge, have to seek new legitimations, and must turn intelligence and patience towards the growing task of winning consent. It becomes the recommended frame of reference most likely to enable managers to pursue their purposes successfully amid the multiple values, the diverse and rising group aspirations, and the shifting power relations of a complex society undergoing an accelerating rate of economic and social change.[31]

Pluralism tends to focus attention on the types of rules, regulations and processes likely to contribute to the best interests of the organisation and which will ensure that pressures to distort them are countered effectively so as to restore and maintain the equilibrium of the system. Its emphasis is on social stability, on compromise and on granting concessions. In short, it is about making rules. Flanders summed up the pluralist approach when he defined industrial relations as the 'study of the institutions of job regulation ... [one which] deals with certain regulated or institutionalized relationships in industry'.[32] Hyman, a strong critic of this approach, has found this unsatisfactory:

> To define industrial relations in terms of rules is to emphasise the relatively defined, stable and regular aspects of employer–worker and management–union relationships; by the same token it is to play down the significance of conflicts of control in the labour market and over the labour process as manifestations of a fundamental and continuous antagonism of interest.[33]

Marxist approach

There is one element of the pluralist perspective that is shared by those who adopt a Marxist approach to industrial relations. This is the recognition of fundamental and inherent conflicts of interest between workers and employers at the workplace. But while the pluralists assert that the conflict of interest is not total and that the parties share at least some common goals, Marxists see worker–management relations as only one aspect of class relations, in which the antagonism of interests between capital and labour at the workplace derive from the nature of class conflict in the capitalist society as a whole. Industry is the arena

---

31. Ibid., p. 282.
32. A. Flanders, *Industrial Relations: What's Wrong with the System?*, Faber & Faber, London, 1965, pp. 10, 16.
33. R. Hyman, 'Pluralism', p. 34.

within which class conflict finds its expression: between the property-owning class and the working class 'there exists a radical conflict of interest, which underlies everything that occurs in industrial relations'.[34] Conflict, then, is not just an industrial phenomenon. It is a reflection of class conflict, which permeates the whole of society. The conflict that takes place at the enterprise level between those who buy labour and those who sell it is seen as a permanent feature of capitalism and an indication of the concentration of economic, social and political power in the hands of those who own and control productive resources. Unlike the pluralists, Marxists see 'industrial relations as an element in the totality of social relations of production'.[35] To say, as the pluralists do, that industrial conflict is inherent in the structure of employment relations is to stop short of a full explanation. They argue that this evades the question of the extent to which an antagonism of interest is generated at the societal level and is embedded in the mode of production within which the employment relationship occur.

Marxists are also critical of the pluralist focus on conflict regulation and rule-making. They feel that by concentrating on how conflict is contained and controlled the pluralists divert attention from the more fundamental issue of why disputes are generated:

> ... the question whether the existing structure of ownership and control in industry is an inevitable source of conflict is dismissed as external to the study of industrial relations.[36]

Undue emphasis is placed on how employers, trade unions and other institutions cope with such conflict and what processes can be implemented to maintain industrial stability.

Marxist writers have paid much greater attention to the notion of power than the pluralists have. This is not surprising, given the pluralists' emphasis on conflict resolution and procedural reform.[37] Marxists see the imbalance of power both within society and at the workplace as central to the nature of industrial relations. This power is exercised in a great variety of ways. Gouldner has observed:

> The rich exercise power, including political power... through a variety of interlocking national associations, councils and committees that act as legislative lobbies and as influences upon public opinion;... through their influence on important newspapers, magazines and television networks, by virtue of their advertising in them or their outright ownership of them... through their extensive and disproportionate membership in the executive branch of the government, their financial contributions to political parties... and through their control of the most important legal, public relations and advertising firms.[38]

At the workplace, those who own the means of production have a power superiority over those who sell their labour for wages. This

---
34. R. Hyman, *Industrial Relations: A Marxist Introduction*, Macmillan, London, 1975, p. 23.
35. Ibid., p. ix.
36. Ibid., p. 22.
37. R. Martin, 'Power', in A. Thomson and M. Warner (eds), *The Behavioural Sciences*, p. 116.
38. A.W. Gouldner, *The Coming of Western Sociology*, Heinemann, London, 1971, p. 300.

reflects itself in a substantial inequality in the distribution of rewards. The weakness of labour in the marketplace is said to be reinforced by the creation of social norms, values and beliefs that tend to sustain the existing distribution of power in industry and inhibit the development of working-class political consciousness.[39] The widespread legitimation and acceptance of class and status stratification and of the hierarchical organisation of work is said to be due to the very power and the facilities available to the property owners to create and maintain favourable social attitudes. This is exercised through the control over 'economic, social and political decision-making; over the content of the mass media and communications; and over the major objectives of the economic system'.[40]

Marxists do not share the pluralist view of the role of the state as a guardian of the 'public interest', dispensing favours to the weak and curbing the excesses of the strong. For them, the state plays an integral role in protecting the interests of the power-holders and maintaining the major structural features of society that are crucial for the power, status and rewards of the owners and controllers of resources. The state's interest lies in developing institutionalised mechanisms for controlling conflict and for achieving social stability. As Miliband has written, 'Governments are deeply involved, on a permanent and institutionalised basis, in that "routinisation of conflict" which is an essential part of the politics of advanced capitalism'.[41] Yet, as he observed, on other occasions

> governments have played a decisive role in defeating strikes, often by the invocation of the coercive power of the state and the use of naked violence; and the fact that they have done so in the name of the national interest, law and order, constitutional government, the protection of 'the public', etc., rather than simply to support employers, has not made that intervention any the less useful to those employers.[42]

Government intervention to protect the 'national interest' is inextricably bound up with sustaining the health and strength of private enterprise. Where economic stability is viewed as an important precondition for a society's material well-being, governments of all political persuasions have an interest in maintaining the 'confidence of industry' and encouraging the accumulation of profit and the generation of investment. They have no stake in challenging the control of business over large and crucially important areas of economic life.

The Marxist approach to industrial relations has been criticised on a number of grounds. It has been argued that, while its focus on the inevitable and polarised class struggle in industry and society between capitalists and the proletariat may have been a valid interpretation of nineteenth-century capitalism, it does not explain the complex

---

39. Martin, 'Power', p. 113.
40. A. Fox, *Beyond Contract*, p. 277.
41. R. Miliband, *The State in Capitalist Society*, Quartet, London, 1969, p. 74.
42. Ibid., p. 74.

economic, political and social conflicts of welfare-state capitalism in the late twentieth century.[43] Some writers have made the point that capital comprises a number of heterogeneous and often competing elements, which belies its monolithic character. Dabscheck has argued, for example, that a concession gained from the state by one fraction of capital may impose additional costs and burdens on, or be at the expense of, other fractions of capital.[44] Such may be the case with tariff protection, which provides aid to some fractions of capital while at the same time increasing the costs of inputs to other owners and controllers of capital. Others have criticised Marxists for their views on the role of the state. Martin has argued that the Marxist analysis underestimates the independence of the state. He feels that the legislative action of labour governments in many cases is more designed to cement political alliances with the industrial wing of the labour movement than to serve the interests of capital.[45]

The labour process

Notwithstanding these criticisms, an important body of contemporary industrial relations literature concerning the labour process is derived from Marxist analysis. Marx first addressed the issue of the labour process in Volume 1 of *Capital*. Essentially he saw the labour process as involving the means by which raw materials are transformed into products through human labour and the use of machinery and other forms of technology. Marx argued that one of the main tasks of management in the capitalist mode of production is to convert a worker's capacity to perform work (labour power) into actual work effort (labour) in order to contribute to profitable production and achieve capital accumulation. Because the labour contract is an open-ended arrangement, the translation of this labour power into labour could only be resolved through the establishment of structures of managerial control. This problem has been summed up more recently by Edwards:

> Workers must provide labour power in order to receive their wages, that is, they must show up for work; but they need not necessarily provide *labour* much less the amount of labour that the capitalist desires to extract from the labour power they have sold. There is a discrepancy between what the capitalist can buy in the market and what he needs for production . . .[46]

With the publication of Braverman's *Labor and Monopoly Capital* in 1974 interest was revived in Marx's analysis of the labour process. Braverman built on Marx's original work by placing it in the context of twentieth-century development. He focused in particular on the emergence of new methods of management control occasioned by the rise of

---

43. D. Farnham and J. Pimlott, *Understanding Industrial Relations*, Cassell, London, 1979, p. 66.
44. B. Dabscheck, 'Of mountains and routes over them: a survey of theories of industrial relations', *Journal of Industrial Relations*, vol. 25, no. 4, 1983, p. 499.
45. Martin, 'Power', pp. 115–16.
46. R. Edwards, *Contested Terrain*, Basic Books, New York, p. 12.

monopoly capitalism. Braverman saw the emergence of scientific management and deskilling of work arising from the use of new technology as important means of exercising control over the labour process. He claimed that there had been a general and progressive deskilling of work in the twentieth century and a long-term trend for jobs to become routinised and increasingly devoid of intrinsic content. Under capitalism, technological change was seen to contain an inherent tendency to degrade craft skills and increase management's control of production. Braverman wrote: 'Machinery offers to management the opportunity to do by wholly mechanical means that which it had previously attempted to do by organisational and disciplinary means'.[47] He argued that the logic of capitalist production was such to inexorably deskill the labour process. Because employees could not be relied on to work in the interest of capital it was therefore necessary to avoid reliance on their skills. The fundamental problem of control could only be resolved through the 'degradation' of work and the removal of knowledge, responsibility and discretion from workers in the actual process of production and their transfer to managerial and supervisory employees. According to Braverman, deskilling allowed increased capitalist control over production because opposed centres of knowledge were destroyed and the labour process was fragmented. It also allowed a considerable cheapening of labour and an increased rate of exploitation.

The unilinear and deterministic nature of Braverman's schema has been the subject of much criticism. Researchers have not been able to find a clear link between different phases of capitalism and phases in the work process. Many have questioned the validity of his insistence on a tendency towards deskilling, his emphasis on consciously intended managerial strategies, his neglect of the varying types of managerial control and the inadequacy of his analysis of the role of the labour movement. It is not the intention here to canvass all the issues raised in the debate on Braverman and the labour process. These are covered thoroughly elsewhere.[48] It is important, however, to point out that labour process theory has continued to provide a valuable integrating concept for research. Indeed, one commentator has recently noted that some of the better Australian industrial relations literature is informed by the labour process perspective.[49]

Perhaps the greatest contribution of Braverman's work has been to refocus scholarly attention on the place of work, and to open, in the words of Paul Sweezy, 'lines of inquiry which have been neglected and which cry out for research and elaboration'.[50] Efforts to construct more adequate models of managerial strategies in industrial relations and to understand better the process and effects of technological change on

---

47. H. Braverman, *Labor and Monopoly Capital*, Monthly Review Press, New York 1974, p. 195.
48. P. Thompson, *The Nature of Work: An Introduction to Debates on the Labour Process*, Macmillan, London, 1983; C. Littler and G. Salaman, 'Bravermania and beyond: recent theories of the labour process', *Sociology*, vol. 16, no. 2, pp. 251–69; S. Wood (ed.), *The Degradation of Work?*, Hutchinson, London, 1982.
49. C. Littler, 'Labour process literature—a review 1974–1986' in K. Hince and A. Williams (eds), *Contemporary Industrial Relations in Australia and New Zealand*, AIRAANZ, Wellington, 1987, p. 59.
50. P. Sweezy, 'Foreword' in H. Braverman, *Labor and Monopoly Capital*, p. ix.

work owe much to the pioneering work of Braverman and to the research debates that have been sparked on the labour process. One of the benefits of this, according to Gospel, has been to widen 'the boundaries of industrial relations to cover technology and work organisation which [are now viewed] not as a given constraint or exogenous variable but as a key element in managerial strategies and in management–labour relations'.[51] At a time when industrial relations teaching and research is increasingly focusing its attention on management strategies, the labour process perspective can be seen as providing an important and relevant conceptual framework.

Divergence and accommodation

It can be seen that there are a number of different approaches or perspectives from which industrial relations institutions, structures and processes can be viewed. Each one has its own analytical framework, its own assumptions about society and its own way of interpreting industrial events. Notwithstanding important areas of incompatibility, the approaches do have a lot in common.[52] Though the Marxist and pluralist perspectives differ in fundamental ways, there is not an unbridgeable chasm between them. Clegg argues that, notwithstanding seemingly different definitions,

> ... the difference between their [Marxist and pluralist] analyses of industrial relations should not be exaggerated. There is much in common between the accounts which they give of both 'western' societies in general and industrial relations in particular. Both Marxists and pluralists are concerned with conflict, and both are concerned with stability. Both regard conflict as inevitable in industrial relations as in other aspects of social life. Both face the problem of explaining how social conflict can persist for long periods without destroying society ... and there is much in common in their answers.[53]

Clegg further notes that pluralists accept (and articulate in their own way) the Marxist theory of economism or incorporation, or institutionalisation that sees unions becoming enmeshed in the institutions and operations of capitalist society. Nor does pluralist philosophy necessarily conflict with the Marxist analysis regarding the inevitability of a proletarian revolution. In the final analysis the divergence between Marxists and pluralists is to be found mainly in attitudes, in particular whether the process of assimilation should be welcomed or regretted and whether social revolution would bring in a better order or a more despotic one.

---

51. H.F. Gospel, 'New managerial approaches to industrial relations: major paradigms and historical perspective', *Journal of Industrial Relations*, vol. 25, no. 2, p. 167.
52. A.N.J. Blain, 'Approaches to industrial relations theory: an appraisal and synthesis', *Labour and Society*, 3(2), 1978, p. 207.
53. H. Clegg, *The Changing System of Industrial Relations in Great Britain*, Blackwell, Oxford, 1979, p. 452.

The systems model

In the 1950s an American industrial relations writer, John Dunlop, sought to develop an 'all-embracing theory' which would provide the subject with a comprehensive framework by which the complex phenomena of industrial relations could be best explained and understood. He was critical of his predecessors for their overly empirical or 'fact-gathering' approach and their lack of emphasis on the development of an explicit theoretical foundation to analyse the subject matter. He complained that:

> Facts have outrun ideas. Integrating theory has lagged far behind expanding experience. The many worlds of industrial relations have been changing more rapidly than the ideas to interpret, to explain and to relate them.[54]

Dunlop developed the concept of an 'industrial relations system' which he saw as offering a theoretical basis for a coherent and distinctive academic discipline. His book, *Industrial Relations Systems* (1958), sought to present a general theory of industrial relations and 'to provide tools of analysis to interpret and to gain understanding of the widest possible range of industrial relations facts and practices'.[55]

Dunlop saw an industrial relations system as an analytical subsystem of the wider society or the 'total social system'. The wider society within which it stood imposed certain external constraints and influences on the system. According to Dunlop, an industrial relations system comprised 'certain actors, certain contexts, an ideology which binds the ... system together, and a body of rules to govern the actors at the place of work and work community'.[56] It is the creation of rules, consisting of procedures for establishing the rules, the substantive rules themselves and the application of these rules in the workplace and the work community that is the major concern or output of the system. The substantive rules refer to the various terms and conditions of employment such as wage rates, hours of work and leave, while the procedural rules refer to the means by which these terms and conditions of employment are made and administered.

Dunlop identified three main groups of 'actors' who take part in the rule-making process. There were first managers and their representatives in supervision, secondly, workers and their spokesmen and thirdly, specialised third-party agencies, concerned with workers, enterprises and their relationships. These groups interact within a number of environmental contexts which play an important part in shaping the rules of an industrial relations system. These contexts include the technological characteristics of the workplace; the market or budgetary constraints which impinge on the actors and the locus and distribution of power in the larger society. These environmental factors can influence the system in a variety of ways. The form of technology used will

---

54. Dunlop, *Industrial Relations Systems*, p. vi.
55. Ibid., p. viii.
56. Ibid., p. 7.

affect the skills of the employees, the ways in which jobs are performed and the concentration or dispersion of the workforce. The market or budgetary constraints can refer to the capacity of industry to pay wage increases. A country's balance of payments situation was seen by Dunlop as a form of market constraint for a national system. The distribution of power in the larger society will affect the power relationship between the actors within the industrial relations sub-system. Governments, by dispensing political favours to interest groups within the system, play an important role in shaping the substantive rules of the system.

Dunlop's industrial relations system is held together by an ideology or commonly shared set of ideas and beliefs. He insisted that 'the ideology of the industrial-relations system is a body of common ideas that defines the ideas which each actor holds towards the place and function of the others in the system'.[57] Dunlop acknowledged that each of the actors in the system may have their own ideology. Nevertheless, in mature industrial relations systems these ideologies would be 'sufficiently compatible and consistent as to permit a common set of ideas which recognize an acceptable role for each other'.[58]

Dunlop's notion of an industrial relations system has become widely adopted both as an analytical framework for academic research and as a device for the teaching of industrial relations. Writers such as Blain, in his account of industrial relations in the airline industry,[59] and Goodman and his colleagues in their study of labour–management relations in the footwear industry,[60] have used system analyses. Gill has also shown how industrial relations teaching can be assisted by the use of the systems approach. He argues that it 'enables the student to reach a deeper understanding of the nature of the system under consideration and provides him ... with a useful classifying device'.[61]

With its emphasis on rule-making and the institutions of job regulation the systems model has provided an important theoretical tool for many pluralists. As one of the leading pluralists, Dunlop saw the rule-making process as performing a number of societal functions including conflict management and the promotion of economic efficiency. Moreover, industrial relations was seen to comprise a set of stable institutions through which the inputs of different goals and interests were transformed into a set of outputs in terms of the procedural and substantive rules of the workplace, the industry and the state. This web of rules underwrote the smooth progress of society. His emphasis on conflict resolution and the attainment of order can largely be explained by his dependence on the ideas of one of the principal analytical sociologists of the post-war period, Talcott Parsons.[62] In fact, Dunlop adapted the ideas

---

57. Ibid., p. 16.
58. Ibid., p. 17.
59. A.N.J. Blain, *Pilots and Management: Industrial Relations in the U.K. Airlines,* Allen & Unwin, London, 1972.
60. J. Goodman, E. Armstrong, J. Davis and A. Wagner, *Rule Making and Industrial Peace,* Croom Helm, London, 1977.
61. J. Gill, 'One approach to the teaching of industrial relations', *British Journal of Industrial Relations,* vol. 7, no. 2, 1969, p. 270.
62. M. Poole, *Theories of Trade Unionism,* Routledge & Kegan Paul, London, 1981, p. 20.

of Parsons to the study of industrial relations. Parsons held the view that a society was an integrated system, that stability and order were the norm and that the social fabric was cemented by 'shared values'. His concern was to explain how to contain conflict. The essential mechanism for social order and stability, according to him, would be achieved through shared understandings and common values.

Dunlop's concentration on the functional purpose of rules and on the importance of a shared ideology in attaining a source of order in industrial relations has drawn criticism from a number of quarters. Some have charged that *Industrial Relations Systems* pays insufficient attention to the nature of, and forces shaping, conflict. Dunlop's critics feel that this area of industrial relations should receive a more prominent role in research and theorising than is likely from the use of social systems models. Margerison has pointed out that Dunlop's model 'tends to ignore the essential element of all industrial relations, that of the nature and development of conflict itself'. He argues that Dunlop's work 'is more concerned with studying the resolution of industrial conflict than with its generation'.[63] Bain and Clegg also criticise Dunlop's notion of a 'shared ideology' and the implication that an industrial relations system is 'naturally' stable, integrative and self-perpetuating. They suggest that such a concept has conservative implications and that in the study of industrial relations 'the sources of conflict and co-operation, order and instability must have an equally valid claim to problem status'.[64] Certainly Dunlop places little emphasis on the possibility of internal disorder. His industrial relations system is predicated on a congruency of goals. Should workers and managers possess radically divergent beliefs and values, the system would lose its internal balance, order and stability. Dunlop wrote that should there be

> ... no common ideology in which each actor provided a legitimate role for the other; the relationship within such a work community would be regarded as volatile and no stability would be likely to be achieved in the industrial relations system.[65]

Hyman, similarly, takes issue with the systems theory's inadequate treatment of the conflictual elements in union–management relations and its concentration on the unifying elements in industrial relations systems. He is critical of the assumption that 'processes are naturally at work to maintain stability and equilibrium: that the various institutions and procedures are compatible and well integrated; and that conflict is therefore self-correcting'.[66] Hyman dismisses the view that industrial relations is about the maintenance of stability and regularity in industry. Rather, he suggests that greater significance should be attached to the

---

63. C.J. Margerison, 'What do we mean by industrial relations? A behavioural science approach', *British Journal of Industrial Relations*, vol. 7, no. 2, 1969, p. 273.
64. G.S. Bain and H.A. Clegg, 'A strategy for industrial relations research in Great Britain', *British Journal of Industrial Relations*, vol. 12, no. 1, 1974, p. 92.
65. Dunlop, p. 17.
66. Hyman, *Industrial Relations*, p. 11.

way in which industrial conflict challenges the prevailing social structure.

Other critics have claimed that Dunlop's industrial relations system neglects sub-institutional levels of analysis—that it places to much emphasis on institutions and too little attention on the motivations of the participants involved.[67] This omission of behavioural variables is said to hinder our understanding of the processes of job regulation.

Yet despite all its alleged inadequacies and the many criticisms made of it, few industrial relations writers have rejected the notion of systems analysis. In fact, more are inclined to the view that with appropriate modification and development the systems framework can be a useful device for the study of industrial relations. Hyman suggests that it could become a valuable analytical tool if it incorporated 'the existence of *contradictory* processes and forces, and hence treat[ed] instability and stability as of equal significance as "system outcomes" '.[68] He also feels that the systems analysis must be broadened to 'take account of the *sources* as well as the *consequences* of industrial conflict'.[69] Other writers who see the Dunlop model as lacking theoretical relevance have supported the view that it can be used as a valuable teaching method or 'heuristic device for structuring data'.[70] Bain and Clegg argue that Dunlop is best seen as providing the subject with a certain analytical unity. Gill agrees with this assessment. He states that an industrial relations system should be

> ... regarded as a model within which facts may be organised and must not be misunderstood as having predictive values in itself. It is rather a means of ordering a mass of facts relevant to the study of an industrial relations system.[71]

Eldridge likewise regards the concept of an industrial relations system as a valuable pedagogical device. He sees it as particularly useful in analysing industrial conflict because it 'remind[s] us of a whole range of considerations to bear in mind when trying to explain strikes'.[72] In his view Dunlop's emphasis on the nature of interrelations, both within the system and with the environmental features impinging on and interacting with the system, provides an important 'warning against single-factor explanations of social phenomena'.[73]

Notwithstanding these assessments, it is generally agreed that Dunlop's work does not constitute a theory of industrial relations. The concepts in his book cannot be used to specify, construct or operationalise dependent or explanatory variables. As Lewin has observed: '*Industrial Relations Systems* provides no basis for rejecting alternative

---

67. S.J. Wood, A. Wagner, E.G.A. Armstrong, J.F.B. Goodman and J.E. Davis, 'The "industrial relations system" concept as a basis for theory in industrial relations', *British Journal of Industrial Relations*, vol. 13, no. 3. 1975. pp. 298–300.
68. Hyman, *Industrial Relations*, p. 12.
69. Ibid.
70. Bain and Clegg, p. 92.
71. Gill, p. 269.
72. J.E.T. Eldridge, *Industrial Disputes*, Routledge & Kegan Paul, London, 1968, p. 23.
73. Ibid.

hypotheses, treatments or interpretations of the data. In short, it does not offer predictions which can be empirically confirmed or refuted'.[74]

Strategic choice theory

The inability of the Dunlop model to capture fully the determinants of the changing character of American industrial relations in the 1980s led three writers, Kochan, Katz and McKersie, to propose an alternative explanatory framework which they termed the strategic choice theory. They argued that Dunlop's systems approach was seriously flawed because it neglected the independent and discretionary role of the actors in forming both the procedural and substantive rules of the bargaining system. Kochan, Katz and McKersie took the view that 'industrial relations practices and outcomes were shaped by the interactions of environmental forces *along with* the strategic choices and values' of employers, employees, trade unions and governments.[75] In their opinion, the developments in American industrial relations since the 1970s had resulted largely from fundamental changes in managerial values and strategies. Innovations in human resource management practices were seen as providing the principal source of dynamism. In light of this, it was suggested that a revised theory of industrial relations should incorporate a wider and more sophisticated concept of the role of managerial strategies, structures and policies in employment-related matters.

As part of this reconceptualisation, Kochan, Katz and McKersie pointed to the need to understand the shift in the distribution of decision-making power and authority over industrial relations issues within the managerial hierarchy. In the United States, they found that traditional industrial relations specialists had lost power both to human resource managers and to line managers as top executives demanded greater organisational innovation in managing employees and stressed the need to achieve a more symmetrical relationship between broad business strategies and industrial relations practices within the firm. This, they suggested, had important theoretical implications for the study of industrial relations. It meant that the scope of the subject had to be broadened to include the strategic decisions of business pertaining to such matters as marketing and production, acquisition and divestiture, and the form and location of financial responsibility within the organisation. Many decisions that had an impact on industrial relations processes and outcomes took place, as Kochan, Katz and McKersie pointed out, beyond the functional level of industrial relations in the firm and

---

74. D. Lewin, 'Industrial relations as a strategic variable', in M.M. Kleiner et al. (eds), *Human Resource Management and the Performance of the Firm*, IRRA, Madison, Wisconsin, 1988, p. 4.
75. T.A. Kochan, H.C. Katz and R.B. McKersie, *The Transformation of American Industrial Relations*, Basic Books, New York, 1986, p. 5.

often 'well above both the collective bargaining process and, in some cases, the level of most industrial relations staff'.[76]

This broader conception of the institutional framework of industrial relations led the authors to develop a typology that featured three main levels of industrial relations activity: the strategic, policy and workplace levels. This framework, as shown in Table 1.1, divides the activities of management, labour and government into three tiers. Although each of these tiers is deemed to be relevant to the three main actors in the industrial relations system, the authors are predominantly interested in explaining management's industrial relations activity.

Kochan, Katz and McKersie acknowledge that the three-tier framework 'does not constitute a fully developed new theory of industrial relations' but they contend that it has a number of distinct analytical advantages.[77] Firstly, the framework recognises the interrelationships between activities at the different levels of the system; secondly, it is able to consider the effects that various strategic decisions exert on the different actors in the system, and thirdly, it focuses analysis on the formal as well as the informal relationships at the workplace. Perhaps, most important of all, the authors claim that:

> Since activities both above and below the traditional level of collective bargaining and personnel policy making have become increasingly important, industrial relations researchers can no longer isolate the workplace and strategic levels into separate fields of inquiry any more than practitioners or policy makers can segregate them into independent domains.[78]

Indeed, this multi-levelled perspective and the explicit recognition given to the role of business strategy and managerial values is a major conceptual advance and helps provide important insights into the processes and outcomes of industrial relations. A more complete understanding of labour-management practices does require a consideration both of the environmental forces that impinge on the actors in industrial relations and of the variables that help explain how the actors use the discretion available to them in responding to their environment.

The strategic choice thesis is, however, not without its critics. Hilderbrand claims that the authors overstate the importance of managerial strategies in affecting the character of industrial relations and criticises the evidence for the 'rise of integrated management' as 'sketchy and reflective of casual empiricism'.[79] Strauss has taken issue with the methodology which he describes as a mishmash, relying 'on a range of data, from impressionistic case studies and interviews to quantitative studies that fully conform to the current canons of research orthodoxy'.[80] Perhaps the most systematic analysis of the strategic choice

---

76 Ibid, p. 10.
77 Ibid., p. 19.
78 Ibid., p. 19.
79 G. Hilderbrand, 'Comment: review symposium on the transformation of American industrial relations', *Industrial and Labor Relations Review*, vol. 41, no. 3, 1988, p. 446.
80 G. Strauss, 'Comment', *Industrial and Labor Relations Review*, vol. 41, no. 3, 1988, p. 450.

Table 1.1: *Three levels of industrial relations activity*

Level	Employers	Unions	Government
Long-term strategy and policy-making	Business strategies Investment strategies Human resource strategies	Political strategies Representation strategies Organising strategies	Macroeconomic and social policies
Collective bargaining and personnel policy	Personnel policies Negotiations strategies	Collective bargaining strategies	Labour law and administration
Workplace and individual/ organization relationships	Supervisory style Worker participation Job design and work organization	Contract administration Worker participation Job design and work organization	Labour standards Worker participation Individual rights

Source: T. Kochan, H. Katz and R. McKersie, *The Transformation of American Industrial Relations*, Basic Books, New York, 1986, p. 17.

theory has come from Lewin.[81] He, also, is critical of the research methodology, asserting that:

> ... it is simply not enough to say that there are linkages among corporate level, business unit level, and plant/facility level industrial policies and practices, or to claim that changing managerial values constitute the lynchpin for the theory and practice of strategic industrial relations. Instead, such claims must be tested on data sets obtained from more rigorously constructed research designs that pose specific hypotheses so as better to judge their validity and reliability.[82]

In spite of these criticisms and the obvious need for Australian research to clarify issues relating to the importance of managerial values and business strategies, the concept of strategic choice is clearly relevant to the study of industrial relations in this country.

The approach used in this book

We adopt the view that a systems framework incorporating the notion of strategic choice provides the most useful means of describing and analysing the elements of industrial relations in Australia. It offers an ordered and structured approach to the organisational and institutional features of Australian industrial relations. It also enables both students and practitioners to gain a clearer understanding of the interaction

---

81. D. Lewin, 'Industrial Relations as a strategic variable'.
82. Ibid., pp. 31–32.

between the industrial relations participants, the processes or procedures used to resolve industrial disputes and the nature of the decisions or outcomes found in arbitration awards, collective agreements, parliamentary statutes or custom and practice at the workplace. Australian industrial relations are unique. They are dominated by a complex set of institutions, the tribunals, which now have a history of more than three-quarters of a century. Students cannot hope to make sense of Australian industrial relations until they have a clear idea of how the tribunals are structured and how they work. Because of the existence and importance of the arbitration system, the book must be concerned with the process of rule-making.

This is not to suggest that we see industrial relations as being about conflict regulation or that we are interested in detailing how existing patterns of social relations are stabilised. The study of industrial relations must address the tensions between wealth creation and wealth division. Much of the conflict in industry centres around the division of its product between wages and profits. Of course pay claims are not the only area of conflict. Issues relating to job security, the way in which work is structured and performed, and the exercise and use of managerial prerogatives are also areas of potential conflict. Because the interests of employers and employees are necessarily conflictual, the distribution of power between them is important in determining the allocation of rewards. Power is therefore a critical element in the study of industrial relations. The ability of an individual or group to obtain compliance with their wishes, to overcome or preclude opposition or to gain the acceptance of legitimation of their authority is a crucial consideration in industrial relations. The exercise and use of power takes place not only within the confines of the workplace or work community. It cannot be isolated from the society within which labour–management relations are located. The resources available to the parties in conflict situations are conditioned by factors outside industry.

The approach we take recognises the importance of the wider political, economic, legal, social and technological influences on industrial relations. Industrial relations takes place in a broad historical and social context and this setting will affect the structure and behaviour of the parties, the form and range of dispute-settling procedures that are available to them and the nature and content of the rules that apply in the workplace.

This is not to imply that the outcomes of an industrial relations system can be explained simply by reference to changes in the external environment. The goals, values and strategies of the parties are critical determinants of the character of the work relationship. The independent actions of managers, union leaders and public policy makers affect organisational practices and industrial relations rules or outcomes. Figure 1.1 illustrates the way in which a systems approach can be applied to the study of Australian industrial relations.

The book is divided into five parts. Part 1 covered the various possible approaches to the study of industrial relations. Part 2 looks at the nature of industrial conflict, its causes and the forms that it takes. Part 3 is concerned with the main institutional and organisational features of Australian industrial relations and focuses on the principal participants: governments, federal and state industrial tribunals, management, employer associations and unions. Part 4 deals with the principal forms of party interaction in Australia and the processes by which industrial relations are conducted at the national, industry and enterprise levels. Part 5 examines a number of issues of contemporary importance in Australia. These include industrial democracy, workplace industrial relations, and anti-discrimination.

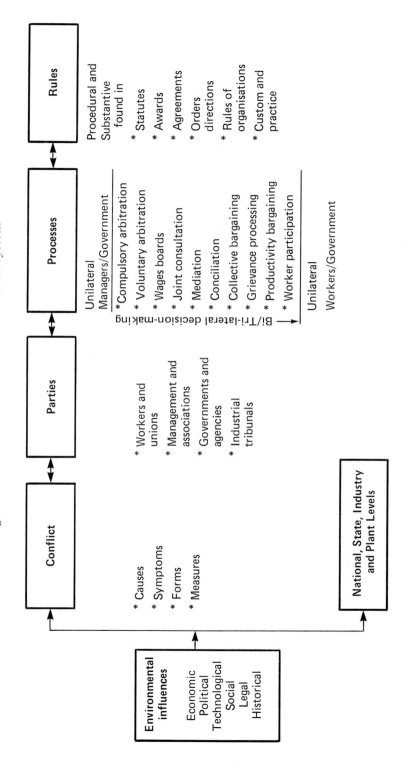

Fig. 1.1: Framework of an industrial relations system

Discussion questions

1. Why are there so many approaches to industrial relations? Do these approaches have anything in common?
2. What do you understand by the term 'industrial relations'?
3. What is meant by the unitary approach?
4. How does Frederick Taylor's theory of industrial behaviour differ from that put forward by the neo-human relations school?
5. Comment on the following statement by Flanders: 'A system of industrial relations is a system of rules'.
6. It has been said that the pluralist approach pays insufficient attention to the real disparity of power that exists in society and in industrial relations. Do you agree?
7. Outline the main elements of the Marxist approach to industrial relations.
8. Discuss the contribution of labour process theory to the understanding of industrial relations.
9. Describe the main components of Dunlop's industrial relations sytem and outline the forms of criticism which have been made of his work.
10. Outline and discuss the strategic choice perspective on industrial relations. In what ways does this perspective help in analysing industrial relations phenomena?

Further reading

Bain, G. and Clegg, H., 'A strategy for industrial relations research in Great Britain', *British Journal of Industrial Relations*, vol. 12, no. 1, 1974.
Blain, A. and Gennard, J., 'Industrial relations theory—a critical review', *British Journal of Industrial Relations*, vol. 8, no. 3, 1970.
Braverman, H., *Labor and Monopoly Capitalism*, Monthly Review Press, New York, 1974.
Bray, M. and Taylor, V. (eds), *Managing Labour? Essays in the Political Economy of Australian Industrial Relations*, McGraw-Hill, Sydney, 1986.
Clegg, H., *The Changing System of Industrial Relations in Great Britain*, Blackwell, Oxford, 1979, Chapter 11.
Craig, A.W.J., 'A framework for the analysis of industrial relations', in B. Barrett, E. Rhodes and J. Beishon (eds), *Industrial Relations and the Wider Society, Aspects of Interaction*, Open University Press, London, 1977.
Dabscheck, B., 'Of mountains and routes over them: a survey of theories of industrial relations', *Journal of Industrial Relations*, vol. 25, no. 4, 1983.
Dunlop, J.T., *Industrial Relations Systems*, Holt, Rinehart & Winston, New York, 1958.
Fox, A., *Beyond Contract: Work, Power and Trust Relations*, Faber & Faber, London, 1974.
Heneman, H.G., 'Towards a general conceptual system of industrial relations: how do we get there?', in G.G. Somers (ed.), *Essays in Industrial Relations Theory*, Iowa State University Press, 1969.

Hyman, R., *Industrial Relations: A Marxist Introduction*, Macmillan, London, 1975.
Hyman, R., 'Pluralism, procedural consensus and collective bargaining', *British Journal of Industrial Relations*, vol. 16, no. 1, 1978.
Kochan, T., Katz, H., and McKersie, R., *The Transformation of American Industrial Relations*, Basic Books, New York, 1986.
Laffer, K., 'Is industrial relations an academic discipline?', *Journal of Industrial Relations*, vol. 16, no. 1, 1974.
Littler, C., 'Labour process literature—a review 1974–1986', in K. Hince and A. Williams (eds), *Contemporary Industrial Relations in Australia and New Zealand: Literature Surveys*, AIRAANZ, Wellington, 1987.
Margerison, C.J., 'What do we mean by industrial relations? A behavioural science approach', *British Journal of Industrial Relations*, vol. 7, no. 2, 1969.
Wood, S.J., et al., 'The Industrial Relations System Concept as a Basis for Theory in Industrial Relations', *British Journal of Industrial Relations*, vol. 13, no. 3, 1975.

Part Two

INDUSTRIAL CONFLICT

Industrial relations are in great measure relations of conflict. If that were not so, they would probably attract little attention. Often, however, the attention paid to conflict in industry goes only to sensational and ephemeral matters. Strikes, in particular, are frequently an occasion for newspaper editorials and ministerial statements. Yet strikes are only a symptom of conflict and only one among a number of symptoms. The pattern and trend of strikes is useful as a provisional geography of stress in industrial relationships but it is no more than that. If industrial conflict is to be understood it is necessary to look at its causes rather than its symptoms. The causes are to be found in the larger structures and processes of economy and society. Conflict also needs to be understood in its institutional context. Many countries, including Australia, have responded to industrial warfare by building institutions which are meant to regulate and control it. The forms of institutional control influence the way in which conflict arises, the way in which it is expressed and the way in which it is resolved, or suppressed.

CHAPTER 2

Industrial Conflict

This chapter examines industrial conflict. The first part of the chapter looks at the various forms conflict may take. The second part reviews the major explanations of industrial conflict. Finally the chapter looks at strikes in Australia.

The forms of industrial conflict

For many people strikes and industrial conflict are synonymous. Removing industrial conflict for them means stopping strikes. 'Good industrial relations' is equated with the absence of strikes. That view is inadequate. It can lead to a confusion between the symptoms of conflict, and to inappropriate policy prescriptions. Industrial conflict may properly be understood only by examining the total range of conflict manifestations and behaviour:

> Complete work stoppages and outbreaks of violence due to industrial disputes are certainly the most dramatic expression of industrial conflict ... But a true understanding of industrial strife ... demands consideration of related, less spectacular manifestations as well. It may even be suggested that the general object of study is not the labour dispute, the strike or the lockout, but the total range of behaviour and attitudes that express opposition and divergent orientations between industrial owners on the one hand and working people and their organizations on the other.[1]

The 'total range of behaviour and attitudes' includes many manifestations of conflict. Some of these are collective and organised; others are

---

1. A. Kornhauser et al. (eds), *Industrial Conflict*, McGraw-Hill, New York, 1954, pp. 12–13.

individual, spontaneous and unorganised. Some forms are overt and easily seen, others are covert. The total range of behaviour includes not only strikes and lockouts, but also peaceful bargaining, work to rules, boycotts, work bans and limitations, political actions, sit-ins, absenteeism, alcoholism, low morale and productivity, material wastage, slackness and inefficiency, go-slows and labour turnover. Dramatic acts of sabotage may also signal work discontents:

> ... materials are hidden in factories, conveyor belts jammed with sticks, cogs stopped with wire and ropes, lorries 'accidentally' backed into ditches. Electricians labour to put in weak fuses, textile workers 'knife' through carpets and farmworkers cooperate to choke agricultural machinery with tree branches.[2]

Hyman has noted that it is useful to apply the same 'industrial conflict' label to such a wide range of behaviour because such 'diverse types of action often appear to reflect similar causes, or to represent alternative response to similar grievances and deprivations'.[3]

Given the many forms of conflict and the covert, individual nature of some of them, it is clear that an equating of industrial conflict with strikes is misleading. An absence of strikes may not mean a lack of conflict. It may merely indicate that the conflict is being expressed in some other (and perhaps more costly) form. Legislation, the use of penal sanctions and other measures which seek to remove strikes without removing their underlying causes, will not remove the conflict itself and may cause one manifestation to be substituted for another. Kerr has noted that in Sweden, where strikes are illegal during the period of a contract, the 'masked strike' takes the place of the open strike.[4] Turner, Clack and Roberts have shown that the sacking of shop stewards in one British car manufacturing firm reduced the amount of strike activity. However, absenteeism, labour turnover and the number of accidents increased sharply.[5] Kuhn has shown that those American companies which imposed tough disciplinary measures on unofficial strikers were successful in reducing the number of strikes, but also succeeded in increasing the number of 'slow downs' in their establishments.[6] Knowles has shown that in British industries where workers are incohesively organised, and where the opportunity cost of strikes may be too great, labour turnover figures are very high compared to other industries.[7] The same author has also argued that trade union expenditure on strikes and on political actions seem to be substitutes for each other and that in British coal-mining, strikes and absenteeism seem to be interchangeable.[8] Scott and others support that finding.[9] Handy has contended that, in the same

---

2. L. Taylor and P. Walton, 'Industrial sabotage: motives and meanings', in S. Cohen (ed.), *Images of Deviance*, Penguin, London, 1971, p. 219.
3. R. Hyman, *Industrial Relations: A Marxist Introduction*, Macmillan, London, 1975, p. 187.
4. C. Kerr, *Labor and Management in Industrial Sociology*, Doubleday, New York, 1964, p. 171.
5. H.A. Turner, G. Clack, and G. Roberts, *Labour Relations in the Motor Industry*, Allen & Unwin, London, 1967.
6. J.W. Kuhn, *Bargaining in Grievance Settlement*, Columbia University Press, New York, 1961, p. 171.
7. K.G.J.C. Knowles, *Strikes: A Study in Industrial Conflict*, Blackwell, Oxford, 1952, p. 210.
8. Ibid., pp. 210–11, 225–6.
9. W.H. Scott, E. Mumford, J.C. McGivering and J.M. Kirkby, *Coal and Conflict*, Liverpool University Press, Liverpool, 1963.

industry, strikes, labour wastage, accidents and absenteeism are used as alternative ways of expressing discontent.[10] Under totalitarian regimes, covert forms of conflict replace open and organised conflict. Neumann has argued that, in Nazi Germany, work grievances took the form of passive resistance:

> The slow-down staged by the German workers [was] certainly not an open or very marked policy, which would spell death for the leaders and concentration camps for the followers. It [consisted of] the refusal to devote all energy to work and sometimes in the determination to give much less than the normal.[11]

Writing about communist East Germany, Bendix noted that worker conflicts

> take the form of production slow-downs, momentary but demonstrative work stoppages, rejection of 'voluntary obligations' or of proposed speed-ups and many others. All these methods have in common that they afford the individual worker a high degree of anonymity and thereby minimise the danger of detection by the Secret Police.[12]

In democratic countries, in those industries where government legislation, professional ethics or public moral pressure place restrictions on strike activity, alternative methods of bringing pressure to bear on management have been employed.[13] In an industrial dispute in some universities, academic staff carried on their normal duties but refused to provide the administration with student results. This made it difficult to plan for subsequent enrolments and courses, flooded the administration with inquiries, and brought pressure from students and employers to bear on the administration. In a hospital dispute, staff treated patients but refused to provide details which would enable the hospital to claim the government medical subsidies it was entitled to. Public transport employees followed a similar procedure by working their normal shifts but refusing to collect fares. For the New York police the 'blue flu', a situation in which all officers report sick on the same day, has provided an effective substitute for the strike. In an industrial dispute in Victoria, police declared their vehicles unroadworthy and were thus unable to carry out their normal patrols.

Clearly, more is involved in resolving and dissipating industrial conflict than strike prevention. There must be a recognition not only of the symptoms of industrial conflict, but also of its causes. This calls for some understanding of the nature and causes of industrial discontent.

---

10. L.J. Handy, 'Absenteeism and attendance in the British coal-mining industry', *British Journal of Industrial Relations*, vol. 6, no. 1, 1969, pp. 27–50.
11. F. Neumann, *Behemoth: The Structure and Practice of National Socialism 1933–1944*, Harper, New York, 1966, p. 344.
12. R. Bendix, *Work and Authority in industry*, Harper, New York, 1963, p. 410.
13. Kerr, *Labour and Management*, p. 171.

Theories of industrial conflict

Many explanations of industrial conflict have been offered. They may be divided into two main categories. One category, of which the Human Relations School is the major exponent, sees industrial harmony as the norm and conflict as a temporary aberration. This approach was considered in Chapter 1. Other explanations see industrial conflict as inevitable in an industrial society. The latter have been grouped under two headings: those which relate industrial conflict to the structure of industry and those which relate industrial conflict to the structure of society itself.

Structural determinants—industrial structure

Under this heading may be grouped a wide range of explanations of industrial conflict. Taken collectively these explanations offer insight into the existence of such conflict and its inevitability. These explanations are grouped together since, explicitly or otherwise, they see the structure of industry as being the major cause of industrial conflict.

Hare distinguishes five main characteristics of industrial work which provide useful reference points for synthesising the contributions of other writers.[14] First, industrial work is a collective activity. It brings 'together many hands, usually into one place of work, and organise[s] them to carry out collectively a common task'. Second, it involves the division of labour which, in its fully developed form, 'means that the process of manufacture is split up into a large number of different operations of a simple character and each operation is performed by a different worker'. Third, industrial work is carried out under control which coordinates and disciplines the workforce. Fourth, industrial work is wage work, performed under conditions of economic insecurity. Workers are dependent on the sale of their labour. Fifth, industrial work is usually carried out for profit: 'one set of persons who own or have control of the instruments of production take the initiative in hiring others to labour for them and seek to make a gain known as profit out of the sale of the product'. These work characteristics give rise to economic, technological, organisational and institutional conflicts.

Economic conflict

Economics is the study of scarcity. Given the ever-present nature of relative scarcity, economic conflict will persist:

> The desires of the parties are more or less unlimited, while the means of satisfaction are limited. Wages can never be as high as workers desire or profits or salaries as high as owners or managers might wish; yet the money available for distribution between the contending claimants is always limited in the short run. The power to make those decisions lying within the orbit of an economic enterprise is also finite. Given the survival of both parties, they must share power in some fashion, and neither can be entirely happy with the

---

14. A.E.C. Hare, *The First Principles of Industrial Relations*, Macmillian, London 2nd ed., 1965, pp. 10–22.

distribution, for, so long as the other has any power at all, it can make unsatisfactory decisions.[15]

In a dynamic society, even if some satisfactory distribution of income and power could be established, forces outside the parties' control—changes in industrial legislation, inflation, changes in wage relativities, devaluation—would upset an established equilibrium. New conflicts emerge in attempts to re-establish some power-sharing, accommodative arrangement. Such arrangements will be short-lived, given further exogenous changes.

Traditionally, the conflict over income distribution has been seen as a contest between wage and profit shares. This conflict has been recognised as one over relative proportions rather than absolute amounts:

> The idea, which is popular with rich men, that industrial disputes would disappear if only the output of wealth were doubled, and everyone were twice as well off, not only is refuted by all practical experience, but is in its very nature founded upon an illusion. For the question is one, not of amounts but of proportions; and men will fight to be paid £30 a week instead of £20, as readily as they will fight to be paid £5 instead of £4, as long as there is no reason why they should be paid £20 instead of £30, and as long as other men who do not work (i.e. shareholders) are paid anything at all ... If the community can afford to pay anything at all to those who do not work, it can afford to pay more to those who do.[16]

On the assumption that increased prices result in increased profits (or at least the ability of management to maintain its profit share), workers' efforts to maintain *real wages* can be accommodated within the wage–profit contest. This dichotomy is, however, complicated by the 'tax bite'—that share of income which goes to governments by way of indirect and direct taxes. The ability of income earners to maintain *real disposable wages* heightens wage discontent and has implications for industrial relations and economic policy. For example, in periods of inflation the ability of workers to maintain the real purchasing power of wages is made more difficult by the fact that wage increases to compensate for price increases are taxed. Thus, unless wage increases of a greater proportion than price increases are gained, real disposable incomes are reduced.

Conflict over wages is a concomitant part of an economic system in which, for most people, the only means of livelihood is the sale of their labour. As high levels of unemployment indicate, there is no assurance that all workers will be able to sell their labour. Even those in employment have little job security. In Australia labour is typically contracted for short periods of time—by the week, day or even the hour. The casual nature of work has been an important source of conflict in some industries. Further, there are few restrictions on the ability of entrepreneurs to close or transfer plants in chasing higher profits or to automate or change the products manufactured. Automation usually results in

---

15. Kerr, *Labour and Management*, pp. 169–70.
16. R.H. Tawney, *The Acquisitive Society*, Fontana, London, 1961, p. 21.

surplus labour while a product change may make an employee's skills superfluous. Little wonder that the sale of labour and the insecurity surrounding this transaction has been viewed as a form of 'wage-slavery':

> The term 'wage-slave', familiar to all who come in contact with the organisations of the workers, expresses more tersely than any other phrase could do the workers' view of [their situation]. The term 'wage' indicates all the complex factors which make the economic circumstances of the worker so uncertain, and 'slavery' the way in which this economic weakness is used to enforce discipline upon unwilling workers.[17]

The provision of unemployment and social security relief has reduced, but not removed, this insecurity and associated conflict.

In a society in which an individual's income determines that person's lifestyle and social status, four areas of wage discontent are important at the individual or occupational levels. This discontent relates to comparative wage deficiencies, absolute wage deficiencies, relative wage deficiencies and comparative relative wage deficiencies.[18] The first of these is the subjective assessment of wages in terms of work input. The other three relate the wage level to the standard of living made possible by that wage level.

Comparative wage deficiency grievances arise when there appears to be little correspondence between the wage received by a group of workers and the effort required to earn it. In most enterprises the heaviest, dirtiest, most unpleasant and most physically demanding tasks tend to be the most poorly paid. Comparisons with what is earned by other occupational groups, whose tasks appear less demanding, require no greater skills and are performed in more congenial physical environments, can aggravate grievances on this ground. Tax structures add a further grievance dimension, as extra effort by way of overtime, to make up wage deficiencies, is taxed.

An *absolute wage deficiency* exists where a worker's wage is insufficient to provide the basic necessities of a healthy life. Contrary to the popular Australian 'lucky country' image, the results of the Commission of Inquiry into Poverty showed 'that there are still large numbers of poor people in this rich country'.[19] More than one tenth of all income units in Australia were found to be 'very poor', that is, had incomes below the 'austere poverty line'. In addition, nearly 8 per cent of all income units were described as 'rather poor', that is, their incomes were less than 20 per cent above the austere poverty line. Thus, 18 per cent of all income units suffered absolute income deficiencies. A disturbing aspect of this situation 'was that there were a quarter of a million dependent children in very poor families, many of them in two-parent families with the father in full employment'.[20] The increased number of unemployed

---

17. Hare, *First Principles*, p. 48.
18. These classifications are based on Hare, ibid., pp. 62–73. However, the nomenclature is not the same.
19. Commission of Inquiry into Poverty, *Poverty in Australia: Interim Report*, AGPS, Canberra, 1974, p. 8.
20. Commission of Inquiry into Poverty, *Poverty in Australia: An Outline*, AGPS, Canberra, 1975, p. 7.

since this survey was taken can be expected to have increased the number and proportion of those in poverty.

Relative wage deficiencies exist where wages are inadequate in terms of the general living standards of the community. The ability to possess a house, a motor car and (colour) television; to be able to entertain, dine out, go to the cinema or the races; to engage in some sport or hobby, and so on, are not essentials of life. However, in a society where such matters are considered the norm, relative wage deficiencies which do not allow for such lifestyles must engender conflict. Given the way consumers are forever being stimulated to new wants and desires by advertising, relative deficiencies will continue to exist.

Comparative relative wage deficiencies relate to wage deficiencies, not relative to general community standards, but rather to what other occupational groups receive. There are both broad and proximate aspects of this deficiency. The broad aspects concern comparisons across the spectrum of wage and salary earners: the disproportionate share of income accruing to select groups such as doctors and lawyers, and to unearned income in the form of rent, interest, shares and speculative investment; the ability of certain groups such as politicians and managers to obtain fringe benefits and tax deductions not generally available; the security and good lifestyle enjoyed by some groups whose work seemingly involves little effort or insecurity. Proximate comparisons compare wage levels, and the standard of living allowed by such wages, to related occupations. Builders' labourers compare their lifestyle to that of bricklayers (and *vice versa*), primary teachers to secondary teachers, secondary teachers to TAFE lecturers, TAFE lecturers to university academics, and so on. Any change in the wage structure of one group brings with it a change in the relative position of other occupational groups. Since comparisons are generally made with income groups receiving salaries which are slightly higher, conflict over 'comparative wage justice' is perpetual.

Technology and conflict

Many conflicts and work grievances relate to the 'technique of industry'. Technology determines the social organisation of the enterprise, the division of labour within the enterprise, and the pattern of change within industry. Typically, workers have had to conform to the requirements of technology.

Woodward has argued that the technological complexity of different forms of production is an important determinant of employer–employee relations. She divides production processes into unit and small batch manufacturing, mass production and process technology:

> The attitudes and behaviour of management and supervisory staff and the tone of industrial relations . . . seemed to be closely related to technology. In firms at the extremes of the scale, relationships were on the whole better than in the middle ranges. Pressure on people at all levels of the industrial hierarchy seemed to build up as technology advanced, became heaviest in assembly line production and then relaxed, so reducing personal conflicts.

Some factors—the relaxation of pressure, the smaller working groups . . . and the reduced need for labour economy— were conducive to industrial peace in process production.[21]

Kuhn has explained differences in fractional bargaining (the presentation of demands unauthorised by the union and supported by unofficial action) in terms of technological differences.[22] He sees fractional bargaining being facilitated in industries with four technological characteristics: technology which 'subjects a large proportion of workers to continued changes in work methods, standards or materials as they work at individually paced jobs'; technology which permits interaction between workers; technology departmentalises the workforce into roughly equal workgroups; technology which 'requires continuous rigidly sequential processing of materials into one type of product'. This last characteristic allows employees to increase the cost of disputes to management. The first two characteristics stimulate fractional bargaining whereas the third characteristic weakens the union's control over work groups.

Certain types of technology not only facilitate or discourage fractional bargaining, but may also in themselves create grievances. This is particularly so of the assembly line production technology, as Walker and Guest have shown.[23] They argue that the monotony, dehumanisation and very limited opportunity of social intercourse associated with this technology are major sources of industrial conflict. Other forms of technology also cause conflict. In evaluating the impact of 'advanced' technology on industrial relations Stettner lists some of the problem areas:

> Nervous strain and mental fatigue are increased by greater noise, faster tempo, lack of control over pace of work, the necessity for constant alertness and close concentration, and the heavy burden of responsibility imposed by awareness of the serious consequences of an error. Boredom is often induced by the monotony of the operation, the lack of interruption and the isolation and reduced opportunity for social intercourse. Many workers derive less satisfaction from their work because of loss of a sense of participation and achievement as the work process is broken down into a series of elementary operations requiring limited skill. Finally, there is a considerable increase in shift work and night work (motivated by the high cost of capital equipment and the importance of avoiding shutdowns) with their obvious drawbacks on family life, social and recreational activities, and disturbance of bodily rhythm.[24]

Since, in the short run, most forms of technology are fixed, conflict over technology is often 'resolved' by an inappropriate means, such as an increase in wages. Since this form of compensation does not remove the underlying source of grievance, conflict must persist.

---

21. J. Woodward, *Management and Technology*, HMSO, London, 1970, p. 18.
22. J.W. Kuhn, *Bargaining in Grievance Settling*, Columbia University Press, New York, 1961.
23. C.R. Walker and R.H. Guest, *The Man on the Assembly Line*, Yale University Press, New Haven, Conn., 1957.
24. L. Stettner, 'The impact of advanced technology on industrial relations', in B. Barrett, E. Rhodes, and J. Beishon (eds), *Industrial Relations and the Wider Society: Aspects of Interaction*, Open University Press, London, 1977, p. 64.

An important feature of industrialised societies, however, is change. As Schumpeter noted, the impulse which keeps the 'capitalist engine in motion' comes from new consumer goods, new methods of production, new markets and new forms of industrial organisation. This 'process of industrial mutation incessantly revolutionises the economic structure from within, incessantly destroying the old one, incessantly creating a new one'.[25]

Such technological change may be a further source of conflict. It displaces labour by machines, changes the power relationships between parties and makes certain groups vulnerable. Thus, even when technological change is designed to reduce unpleasant work, or to reduce the physical exertion required on arduous jobs, conflict may be generated. The disappearance of certain occupations—blacksmiths, coopers, farriers—and the creation of new ones—computer programmers, systems analysts, radiographers, pilots—are related to technological change. For those in threatened jobs, and for the unions covering threatened occupations, insecurity breeds conflict. Demarcation disputes also occur in emerging occupations as unions vie with each other to cover the new workforce.

The mechanisation induced by technological change has resulted in important sectoral shifts in the Australian workforce. This can be seen in Table 2.1, which shows the great decline in the proportion of the workforce in the primary sector (agriculture, timber, fishing, hunting and mining). Largely because of mechanisation, an increase in farm production and a greater extraction of minerals and other resources by a smaller proportion of the workforce has been made possible. Over the period, surplus workers have moved out of rural areas. A lesser reduction has also taken place in the manufacturing industry, thus swelling further the proportion of employees in the tertiary (service) sector.

Table 2.2 shows that even between the population censuses of 1961 and 1971, a decade in which the total workforce increased by 24 per cent, significant occupational shifts took place. Such changes have been influenced, not only by technological change, but also by changes in consumers' tastes and government tariff policies. Workforce growth was being absorbed into the tertiary sector. The proportion of workers who were in primary industries declined. The proportion of workers in the textile, clothing and footwear, wood products and furniture-manufacturing industries also declined.

The workforce growth rate of the total manufacturing industry over the decade was less than one third that of the total workforce. Only one manufacturing industry—paper, paper products and printing—showed a workforce growth rate in excess of the total workforce growth rate. This was attributable to added tariff protection, and increased sales of magazines and journals.

The movements depicted in Tables 2.1 and 2.2 caused relatively little

---

25. J.A. Schumpeter, *Capitalism, Socialism and Democracy*, Allen & Unwin, New York, 1943, p. 82.

Table 2.1 *Proportion of civilian workforce by sector, 1901, 1982 and 1989.*

Year	Sector		
	Primary %	Secondary %	Tertiary %
1901	24.0	27.0	49.0
1982	7.9	20.8	71.3
1989	7.1	16.3	76.6

Sources: Commonwealth Year Book No. 1, 1901–07, p.169; and Labour Statistics, 1982 and 1989.

Table 2.2 *Proportionate changes in select industry workforce sizes 1961–71 (%)*

Textile manufacturing	−85
Agriculture	−20
Clothing and footwear	−14
Forestry	−11
Wood, wood products and furniture	− 4
Mining	− 1
Gas and electricity	4
Total manufacturing	7
Road transport	11
Building and construction	11
Public authorities	16
Food and beverages	19
Shipping	20
Amusements, sport	23
Total workforce growth	24
Chemical products	24
Retail trade	41
Insurance	45
Education	55
Health	61
Banking	107
Paper, paper products and printing	290
Real estate and property	375

Sources: 1976 Labour Statistics, Canberra, 1977, pp.10–11 and Labour Report No. 51, Canberra, 1964, pp.175–6. Because of some alterations in ABS industry classifications in this period the above results should be regarded as indicative rather than definitive of changes over the period.

industrial disputation. This would suggest that labour displacement technology which is introduced gradually and during periods of economic growth and/or full employment is less likely to cause conflict than that which is introduced rapidly and during periods when unemployment is a cause of increased job insecurity. This has been the post-1971 experience in Australia. Automation (the displacement of manual processes by machines) has caused considerable friction in several industries including the one manufacturing industry which had shown relative workforce growth.

The printing industry now has the technical expertise necessary for producing the 'electronic newspaper' which has done away with linotype processes—and printers. Job insecurity has also spread to the banking and insurance industries where cybernation (the replacement of mental processes by computers) has reduced recruitment (and thus, for the unions, membership potential), and promotion possibilities, as well as making retrenchments in the future a distinct possibility. The oversupply of qualified personnel in other growth sectors such as health and education and the decline, since 1971, in the property and real estate workforce as the result of the economic down-turn, have reduced job opportunities and job security in the tertiary sector.

Organisational and institutional conflict

Work is carried out under control. This creates a perpetual opposition of interest between those who manage and those who are managed in establishing 'frontiers of control':

> Most workers endure supervision while they are at work. Many of them build up defences against the supervisor ... While controls [may not be] highly developed in every situation, there is every reason to expect that, in a society where most people have only their labour to sell, a conflict over control will be a feature of the work situation. On the shop floor of many factories the division of labour between the supervisor and the men can be characterised as a 'frontier of control'—management's rights on the one side and those of the worker on the other.[26]

The larger the basic unit of production, the greater the conflict associated with organisational control and the degree of impersonality of the control hierarchy. Bureaucracy, a phenomenon initially identified with public employment, is now common in the private sector. This system of control involves

> ... a clear cut division of integrated activities ... The assignment of roles occurs on the basis of technical qualifications which are ascertained through formalised, impersonal procedures. Within the structure of the hierarchically arranged authority, the activities of 'trained and salaried experts' are governed by general, abstract, clearly defined roles.[27]

Bureaucratic and other forms of enterprise organisation are geared to the requirements of 'enterprise rationality: the logic of getting maximum results at a minimum cost'.[28] Conflict over the frontier of control challenges this 'rationality' and attempts to direct priorities towards employees' work needs. This is clearly seen in the 'effort bargain', the 'struggle over who does what, at what pace, for what price and with whom':

---

26. Huw Beynon, *Working for Ford*, Penguin, London, 1973, p. 131.
27. See A.W. Gouldner, *Patterns of Industrial Bureaucracy*, Free Press, Illinois, 1954, p. 19.
28. J. Barbash, 'The elements of industrial relations', *British Journal of Industrial Relations*, vol. 11, no. 1, 1974, p. 132.

44 / PART TWO INDUSTRIAL CONFLICT

> The issues at stake [in effort bargaining] are management's 'right' to organise the plant as it [thinks] fit and the workers' 'right' to a fair wage, to be without harassment, without speed-ups, without lay-offs, without the sack.[29]

Trade union attempts to replace managerial control by joint regulation should be regarded as an important element in the conflict over control. Fox argues that:

> The public's preoccupation with the unions' economic role in the labour market has meant that an even more important role has been neglected and insufficiently understood. That is the role of union organisation within the workplace itself in regulating managerial authority, i.e. the exercise of management authority in deploying, organising and dismissing the labour force after it has been hired.[30]

Where the 'official' union movement is insufficiently interested or effective in constraining management's implementation of 'enterprise rationality' other media of control emerge. This may be on an informal, individual or group basis, or it may be through a shop floor organisation prepared to act independently of the union hierarchy.[31] Beynon has noted that the emergence, development and activities of shop stewards in some British motor assembly plants were 'woven ... in the backcloth ... of the conflict along the frontier of control'.[32]

An important area of control conflict is that of work output. 'Enterprise rationality' dictates a maximisation of output. On the other hand, market fluctuations, economic instabilities and job insecurity cause workers to place restrictions on output. To workers 'maximising returns makes sense only if you're not going to be maximised into a dole queue'.[33]

Paradoxically, joint regulation, and the 'pursuit of stability, predictability and consistency, [require] work-place unionism ... to apply discipline and control of which management is the prime beneficiary'.[34]

> Trade unionism is about work ... There comes a point where certain individual actions come into direct conflict with the very nature of trade union collectivism. The steward organisation was developed to protect members against management and as such an important part of its function [is] to obtain a degree of internal discipline ... Controlling the membership is part of the steward's job. The nature of the relationship between the union and the employer can mean that the steward rather than the manager disciplines for not working properly.[35]

Though unions and management may have a shared interest in stability and orderliness, the institutional needs of managers and unions

---

29. Beynon, *Working for Ford*, p. 46.
30. A. Fox, *Industrial Sociology and Industrial Relations*, Royal Commission on Trade Unions and Employer Associations, Research Paper 3, HMSO, London, 1966, p. 7.
31. Hence, in the British context, the Donovan Commission reference to the 'two systems of industrial relations'. For a good account of shop floor and information group organisations see 'Controlling the Line' in Beynon, *Working for Ford*.
32. Beynon, *Working for Ford*, p. 190.
33. Ibid., p. 192.
34. Hyman. *Industrial Relations* p. 170.
35. Beynon, *Working for Ford*, p. 140.

ensure that complete harmony and compatibility of interests is not possible. For the most part, methods of antagonistic cooperation, of dealing rather than cooperating with each other, emerge. Conflict is essential to the survival of both parties. As Kerr has noted, the union which is always in agreement with management has ceased to be a union. 'Institutional, like individual, independence is asserted by acts of criticism, of contradiction, of conflict, or competition.'[36]

Other institutional needs may increase conflict. Large establishments generally tend to be multi-union establishments. This may increase the likelihood of inter-union disputes. Unions seeking to establish themselves, to achieve closed shop arrangements, or to increase membership, may engage in disruptive activities to achieve these ends. Ideological conflicts and fractionalism—'the breaking down of institutions into a multitude of elements which may have little overall coherence or inter-relationship'[37]—may also disrupt work. Institutional needs may also cause unions to engage in sympathy strikes in support of other unions. Strikes and other industrial action may be directed against hostile union legislation or in support of Labor Party and ACTU objectives.

One popular explanation of conflict, and in particular of strikes—the 'agitator thesis'—sees them as being the result of the manipulation of trade unionists by 'irresponsible' leaders. Communists and British shop stewards are frequently depicted as such agitators by the Australian press. These opinions have no basis in fact. For example, in testing the hypothesis that communist leadership of the Waterside Workers' Federation was a significant variable in explaining the number of strikes in the stevedoring industry, Bentley was not able to show any definite correlation. Ports with communist leaders did not have worse strike records than other ports. In Sydney, the number of strikes increased with a change to non-communist leadership.[38] Davis has demonstrated that the incidence and effect of British shop stewards in Australia has been considerably exaggerated.[39] This does not mean that militant representatives do not play a part in articulating conflict. However, 'to attribute industrial disputes to agitators . . . is to point to the instrument of conflict rather than its cause'.[40] As Knowles has noted, 'one cannot agitate successfully without widespread grievances'.[41] In this respect, trade union leaders are the 'managers of discontent' rather than its cause:

> Where industrial situations are likely to lead to conflict, they will generally find leaders to organise it anyway; and such leaders are likely to be people of aggressive temperament and also to acquire strong views. The ability of such

---

36. Kerr, *Labour and Management*, p. 170.
37. E. Batstone, The organisation of conflict, in C.M. Stephenson and C.J. Brotherton (eds), *Industrial Relations: A Social Psychological Approach*, Wiles, Chichester, 1979, p. 67.
38. P.R. Bentley, 'Communist trade union leadership and strike incidence, with special reference to the Waterside Workers' Federation, 1950–1966, *Journal of Industrial Relations*, vol. 12, no. 1, March 1970, pp. 88–97.
39. E. Davis, 'A profile of decision-makers in the AMWSU's Victorian Branch', *Journal of Industrial Relations*, vol. 20, no. 2, 1978, pp. 179–90.
40. Hyman, *Strikes*, p. 57.
41. Knowles, *Strikes*, p. xiii.

individuals to create conflict in the absence of circumstances that would induce it anyway seems ... highly marginal.[42]

Structural determinants—social structure

Explanations of industrial conflict under this heading see the structure of society rather than that of industry as being the major determinant of conflict. Two approaches are discussed here: Kerr and Siegel's 'social integration thesis' and the Marxist view of conflict.

In examining the strike records of eleven countries Kerr and Siegel concluded that the strike-proneness of certain industries can be explained in terms of their social isolation:

> The miners, the sailors, the longshoremen, the loggers and, to a much lesser extent, the textile workers form isolated masses, almost a 'race apart'. They live in their own separate communities; the coal patch, the ship, the waterfront district, the logging camp, the textile town. These communities have their own codes, myths, heroes, and social standards. There are few neutrals in them to mediate the conflicts and dilute the mass. All people have their grievances, but what is important is that the members of each of these groups have the same grievances.[43]

These workers, Kerr and Siegel contend, form strong cohesive unions, are more conscious of common grievances, and are removed from many of the social forces deprecating strikes. Conversely, other workers closely integrated with a wider society are likely to associate with workers in different occupations, to belong to clubs and organisations with heterogeneous memberships and to live in multi-industry communities. 'In these communities ... grievances are less likely to coalesce into mass grievances which are expressed at the job level.'

The Australian experience lends some support to the Kerr–Siegel thesis. For example, between 1913 and 1963, nearly 60 per cent of all working days lost through strikes occurred in two industries—mining and stevedoring.[44] During this period the rate of time lost (i.e. working days lost per union member) was 1.06 for all industries in Australia. In the stevedoring industry it was 4.50 and in the mining industry 11.44.

Closer scrutiny, however, would suggest serious weaknesses in this explanation as a general theory of industrial conflict. For example, it leads to the conclusion that the more isolated work communities are, the more strike-prone they are. The Australian mining experience does not support this contention. Metal mining in New South Wales, for example, has had a much lower strike incidence than coal mining, notwithstanding the greater isolation of Broken Hill and the relative proximity of coal mining to urban areas. Further, the Kerr–Siegel view predicts a 'withering away' of strikes as social integration takes place. In both stevedoring and mining the number of working days lost through strikes has

---
42. H.A. Turner, *The Trend of Strikes*, Leeds University Press, 1963, p. 12.
43. C. Kerr and A. Siegel, 'The inter-industry propensity to strike—an international comparison', in Kornhauser et al. (eds), *Industrial Conflict*, pp. 191–2.
44. D.W. Oxnam, 'THe incidence of strikes in Australia', in J.E. Isaac and G.W. Ford (eds), *Australian Labour Relations Readings*, Sun Books, Melbourne, 2nd ed., 1972, p. 33.

remained at the same level over decades despite social changes affecting the industries. A greater weakness of the Kerr–Siegel approach is its inability to explain the increasing number of strikes in industries such as metal manufacturing and construction and in white collar areas of employment.

The Marxist perspective accepts the reality of economic, organisational, institutional and technological conflict. However, conflict is seen as the outcome of broad social, rather than narrow industrial, forces. Industrial conflict is seen as the product of class divisions within society. Hyman, for example, sees conflict as inevitable in British society, in which 7 per cent of taxpayers own 84 per cent of all private wealth and 2 per cent, 55 per cent of total wealth. By contrast, 88 per cent of taxpayers share less than 4 per cent of private wealth, at an average value of $200 in 1966.[45] This inequality is perpetuated from generation to generation:

> The greater a person's wealth, the more profitably he can invest it. In the longer term, not only do the children of the rich inherit parents' wealth; they also enjoy overwhelming advantages within the education system, which further increases their prospects in terms of occupational advance, high salaries and fringe benefits, and social influence and prestige.[46]

The British situation is similar to that in the United States and Australia. In the USA the top 1 per cent of 'spending units' own 32 per cent of wealth, the top 5 per cent, 52 per cent, and the top 10 per cent, 63 per cent of wealth.[47] Table 2.3 indicates the distribution of wealth ownership in Australia in the period 1967 to 1972. This table indicates that 1 per cent of the adult population owned 22 per cent of the private wealth while the poorest 20 per cent of the adult population shared between themselves only 1 per cent of the country's wealth. On the other hand, 80 per cent of the adult population owned less than 30 per cent of all wealth. There was a high correlation between wealth ownership and occupation:

> The average male professional employee has about eight times the probability of being in the top ten per cent of all wealth-holders as the average male worker in the manufacturing sector... It is apparent that in wealth, as in income, employees in predominantly white-collar industries are in the upper echelons ... while those in industries dominated by blue-collar occupations ... are in the lowest proportion of the distribution.[48]

Unfortunately Raskall's survey has not been updated. The evidence, however, suggests an even greater concentration of wealth and a wider chasm between the haves and the have-nots. One source has commented that:

> It is now estimated that 1 per cent of Australians own 25 per cent of private wealth in Australia, while 90 per cent of the population share 40 per cent. In 12 months, the amount needed to get on *Business Review Weekly's* 200 richest list

---

45. Hyman, *Strikes*, p. 84.
46. Ibid.
47. P.L. Raskall, *The Distribution of Wealth in Australia, 1967–1977*, Planning Research Centre, University of Sydney, 1977, p. 45.
48. Ibid., p. 50.

Table 2.3 *Distribution of wealth in Australia*

	Cumulative proportion of individuals %	Cumulative proportion of wealth %
Share of top	1	22.0
	5	45.5
	10	58.5
	15	66.0
	20	72.2
Share of bottom	20	1.0
	30	2.6
	40	4.9
	50	7.9
	60	12.3
	70	18.7
	80	27.8

Source: Philip L. Raskall, *The Distribution of Wealth in Australia 1967–1972*, Planning Research Centre, University of Sydney, 1977, p.29.

has increased from $20 million to $30 million—yet two million Australians still live below the poverty line.[49]

This maldistribution of wealth reinforces economic conflict. It is accompanied by an inequality of power. Raskall has noted that economic wealth is 'convertible into virtually all types of power and influence. Wealth in capitalism is the catalyst where power over others ... is sanctioned and legitimised into authority'.[50]

Wealth, in capitalist society, springs from private control by a few of the means of production. It is this private ownership, and the use of productive resources for private gain, which leads to industrial conflict in the Marxist view. Thus, in commenting on technological conflict, Hyman notes:

> Strictly speaking ... it is not the 'machine' which threatens the workers' security, it is the machine owned and controlled by *someone else*. Technological change as such could in principle be wholly welcome to the worker and to society, allowing more to be produced with less drudgery. It is not inanimate machines that throw men out of work, but the decisions which are taken as to how these machines shall be used. It is because the worker lacks any direct control over these decisions that his desire to establish a right to his job is always a source of conflict.[51]

One important source of discontent, resulting from the separation of the workers from ownership of the means of production, is alienation. This term 'has been used in such a variety of ways [by sociologists] that it comes close to being a shorthand expression for all the socially and

---
49. *Printing Trades Journal*, January 1988, p. 27.
50. P.L. Raskall, *The Distribution of Wealth*, p. iii.
51. Hyman, *Strikes*, p. 91.

psychologically based maladies of modern man'.[52] For Marx and his followers, alienation has a special meaning. Productive or creative labour was a necessary ingredient for self-fulfilment to Marx, for whom work was the 'existential activity of man, his free conscious activity—not a means for maintaining his life but for developing his universal nature'.[53] Under capitalist forms of production, however, the process of self-realisation is frustrated and alienation occurs. Three forms of alienation are identified. First, the worker is alienated from the product he/she helps produce. The worker has little control over the end product. Secondly, the worker is alienated from the means of production. He/she is the servant rather than the owner or master of the productive process. Third, workers are alienated from themselves—self-estrangement. This results from the lack of creative self-expression in organised work. The working class is thus an alienated class.

Since Marxists see the mainspring of conflict as class divisions based on inequalities in private wealth and on private ownership of the means of production, the only effective way of removing alienation and conflict is the creation of the socialist state. Only in the socialist state—which should not be confused with communist countries which represent little more than halfway houses on the road to socialism—will labour be transformed from a coercive to a creative human activity.[54] Since wealth and power elites are not likely to bring about this situation voluntarily, Marxists see the socialist state as the product of revolution.

Strikes

Though strikes are only one manifestation of industrial conflict, their amenability to measurement and their public interest make them the most used index of industrial conflict. This section examines strike trends in Australia.

Strike measurements

From 1913 the Australian Bureau of Statistics has published a wide range of information relating to strikes at the aggregate, state and industry levels. The information includes the number of strikes, the number of working days lost, the duration of disputes, number of workers involved, estimated loss of wages, causes of disputes and methods of settlement.

Since the Bureau's statistics form the basis of strike studies, it is well to note some of the limitations involved in their use. These limitations should qualify the confidence usually placed in statistical conclusions drawn from the use of official figures. Strike statistics relate only to

---
52. W. Faunce, *Problems of an Industrial Society*, McGraw-Hill, New York, 1968, p. 88.
53. Ibid., p. 85.
54. See E. Mandel and G. Novack, *The Marxist Theory of Alienation*, Pathfinder Press, New York, 2nd ed., 1973, pp. 8–11.

those disputes involving stoppages adding up to ten working days or more. Since most strikes are of short duration (two days or less) and since many establishments employ fewer than ten people, strike statistics may well understate the incidence of strikes.[55] A second limitation is that statistics relate only to the establishments where the stoppages occur. Effects on other establishments because of the lack of material, disruption of transport services, power cuts and so on, are not measured. Thus, prolonged strikes in key industries may have employment and production effects which remain unrecorded. On the other hand, multi-industry disputes (for example, the Medibank strike of 1976) are recorded as separate strikes in each of the industries affected. Another limitation is that the classifications used are not detailed enough. Industries with very different industrial characteristics are lumped together: for example, food and tobacco manufacturing, banking and real estate, paper-making and printing, wood and furniture making. Australian strike statistics also include lockouts. Strikes (euphemistically called 'industrial disputes') are defined by the Bureau as 'a withdrawal from work by a group of employees or a refusal by an employer or a number of employers to permit some or all of their employees to work.'[56] Since strike figures are popularly used as an index of worker militancy or intransigence, an increase in the number of lockouts (for example, in attempts by employers to run down stockpiles) could give a distorted view of industrial reality. Subjectivity enters into the collection and classification of strike statistics. For this reason the Bureau's statistics relating to New South Wales and those compiled by the New South Wales Department of Labour show marked variations, notwithstanding the use of similar definitions.

Subjectivity is involved in determining whether a strike represents a new dispute or whether it is part of a previously unresolved dispute. Strikes are classified according to causes. Many strikes are multi-causal, yet must be recorded as having one cause. The imputed cause of the strike is usually the immediate cause of the cessation of work. Often less immediate factors may have been more important. A final limitation is the absence of official statistics before 1913. This makes reliable comparisons with earlier periods difficult, particularly with the strikes of the 1890s, the alleged reason for the introduction of compulsory arbitration.

The use of strike statistics for international comparative studies calls for even greater caution. It has been stressed that industrial conflict is not just about strikes. It has also been noted that under different economic, political and industrial situations alternative forms of conflict are used. Clearly, a comparison based on one index of conflict could be very misleading. In addition, it must be recognised that not all countries use

---

55. In manufacturing, for ecample, 40 per cent of establishments employ less than ten employees. See ABS, *Manufacturing Establishments: Select Items of Data Classified by Industry and Employment Size 1974–1975*, Canberra, 1976, Table 1.
56. See ABS, *Industrial Disputes*, Cat. No. 6322.0.

the same definition of strikes or are as obsessed with quantifying strikes as Australia.[57] In Britain, for example, a strike must either last a full working day, involve ten workers, or lead to a loss of 100 working days or more before it is recorded. In the same country, strikes over non-work issues (for example, political strikes) are not recorded. In the USA a strike must last a full shift and involve at least 1000 employees before being recorded. Sweden does not publish any criteria for defining a strike for statistical purposes.[58] In communist countries strikes do not officially exist. Other export-oriented countries deliberately play down the incidence of strikes:

> The most startling example comes from Sweden. It is estimated that only about half the unofficial strikes are reported ... Furthermore, even if unofficial strikes are reported ... they do not find their way into the official statistics ... Between 1960 and 1969 the number of unofficial strikes reported to the unions from the metal-working industry alone exceeded that presented by the government for the whole of Sweden.[59]

Even if all countries used the same strike measures, and were equally efficient in collecting strike statistics, care would still be required in making meaningful comparisons. It has been shown that some industries are more strike-prone than others. Meaningful comparisons of aggregate data would necessitate an understanding of each country's 'industry mix'. Other variables—the degree of unionisation, political, economic and social conditions—would also be needed before useful comparisons could be made. In the absence of this information, international comparisons of strikes are of little value.

Strike trends in Australia

Two measures are usually employed in evaluating strike trends: the frequency or number of strikes, and the number of working days lost. As can be seen from Figure 2.1, these measures can give very different interpretations of strike trends and severity. It can be seen, for example, that between 1974 and 1981, and after 1983, these measures were negatively related. As the number of strikes decreased between 1974 and 1975, the number of working days lost actually increased. Between 1975 and 1981 the number of strikes increased as the number of working days lost decreased. Which measure is the more appropriate depends on a subjective evaluation of whether a large number of short disputes is more costly than a small number of long disputes. The Donovan Commission argued that the former, because they undermine management confidence, have a greater than proportionate effect on production.[60] On the other hand, Turner has argued that after a certain length of time a strike has a multiplier effect.[61] A prolonged strike in a car component

---

57. For the methods used in collecting strike statistics in Australia, see ibid.
58. G.K. Ingham, *Strikes and Industrial Conflict*, Macmillan, London, 1974, p. 26.
59. Ibid., p. 27.
60. Royal Commission on Trade Union and Employers' Associations, *Report 1965–8*, HMSO, London, 1968, Cmnd 3623.
61. H.A. Turner, *Is Britain Really Strike Prone?*, Cambridge University Press, Cambridge, 1969.

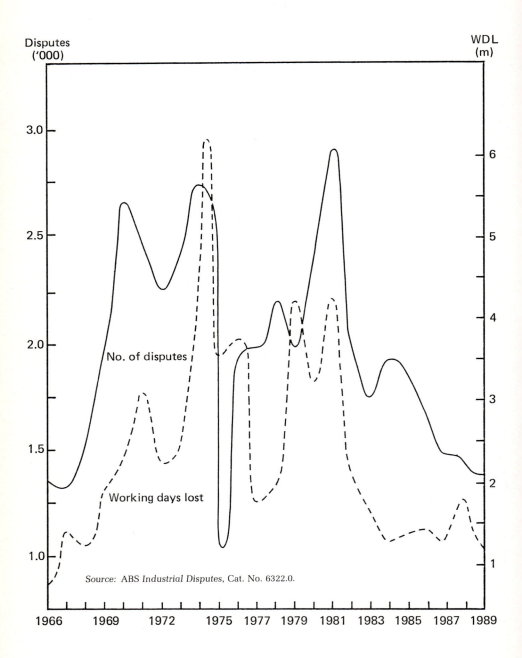

Fig. 2.1: Relationship between number of disputes and working days lost, Australia, 1966–89

Source: ABS Industrial Disputes, Cat. No. 6322.0.

factory, for example, will end up with lost production in car assembly plants once the factory's stocks are run down. Turner postulates a threshold effect. Once this threshold has been crossed a strike will have a greater than proportionate effect on production. In the following analysis both measures are given where possible.

Figure 2.2 shows the pattern of strikes and working days lost in Australia since official statistics were first collected. Five major periods are discernible. The period from 1913 to 1930 was one marked by a small number of strikes accompanied by a large number of working days lost. The average number of strike days per worker involved was high—in excess of twenty days in the years 1917, 1919, 1920 and 1930, and in excess of forty days per worker in 1929 (see App. 2.1). The severity of strikes in the earlier part of this period appears to be related to the influence of the syndicalist movement and to grievances induced by World War I.[62] The strike pattern between 1927 and 1933 is associated with the economic depression of that period. The effect of the depression in terms of both number of strikes and working days lost is self-evident.

The second period is that between 1933 and 1952. During this period the number of strikes showed an upward trend from the lowest strike figure ever recorded (ninety in 1933) to the then record figure of 1627 strikes in 1952. The 1000 strike mark was exceeded for the first time in 1948. During this period, though the number of strikes increased, the number of working days lost was only a small fraction of the earlier period. The pattern began to emerge of a large number of short strikes.

This pattern was the hallmark of the third period, from 1953 to 1966. The number of strikes oscillated around the 1300 mark, and the number of working days lost showed a trend of around 0.7 million days per year. Most strikes were of less than one day's duration.

The period 1966–76 witnessed a resurgence of both the number of strikes and working days lost. An all-time record in both the number of strikes (2809) and working days lost (6.2 million) was established in 1974. This trend was associated with the *de facto* removal of the penal provisions of the arbitration system in 1969 (see Chapter 10), wage demands outside the arbitration system, and wage discontent caused by high rates of inflation. As Table 2.4 and Table 2.5 show, this period was marked by a relative increase in the importance of strikes lasting between five and twenty days and, after 1972, those lasting between twenty and forty days. In the early years of this period strikes lasting two days or less account for more than 70 per cent of all strikes. By 1973 this proportion had fallen to just over half of all strikes. This trend has since been reversed. Since 1978 strikes of two days or less duration have accounted for nearly three-quarters of all strikes.

The strike record for the fifth period, 1976–81, was again one of a large

---

62. For an account of the syndicalist Industrial Workers of the World in Australia during this period see I. Turner, *Industrial Labour and Politics*, ANU Press, Canberra, 1965.

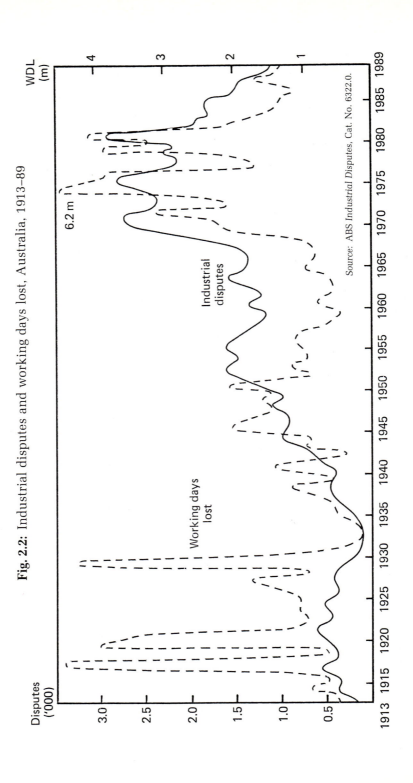

Fig. 2.2: Industrial disputes and working days lost, Australia, 1913–89

Source: ABS Industrial Disputes, Cat. No. 6322.0.

Table 2.4: Industrial disputes by duration, Australia, 1970–89

Length of strike	1970	1971	1972	1973	1974	1975	1976	1977	1978	1979	1980	1981	1982	1983	1984	1985	1986	1987	1988	1989
Up to and including 1 day	1353	1119	1052	998	1165	1092	873	916	1033	947	1075	1273	1011	845	945	920	888	978	939	953
Over 1 to 2 days	465	410	388	437	511	398	370	399	431	370	501	490	413	340	398	357	326	165	192	161
Over 2 and less than 5 days	496	501	480	515	542	436	389	395	424	340	396	509	320	288	319	305	261	159	160	124
5 and less than 10 days	297	243	234	345	329	312	252	212	222	199	235	363	190	166	173	156	132	135	146	86
10 and less than 20 days	99	90	105	182	183	144	120	111	132	140	132	187	82	97	81	75	47	63	49	52
20 days and over	28	35	39	61	79	50	50	57	35	37	62	78	35	45	30	24	21	17	12	16
Total	2738	2398	2298	2538	2809	2432	2054	2090	2277	2033	2401	2900	2051	1781	1946	1837	1675	1517	1498	1392

Source: ABS, *Industrial Disputes*, Cat. no. 6322.0

Table 2.5: Proportion of working days lost in strikes of different length, Australia, 1970–89

Length of strike	1970	1971	1972	1973	1974	1975	1976	1977	1978	1979	1980	1981	1982	1983	1984	1985	1986	1987	1988	1989
Up to and including 1 day	23.6	20.6	21.8	11.7	10.0	11.5	19.5	12.7	16.5	27.5	7.5	6.5	8.4	9.1	14.8	12.9	23.8	28.9	42.8	44.5
Over 1 to 2 days	8.9	8.5	16.7	6.9	10.5	10.9	29.8	16.7	23.2	7.1	23.3	6.5	13.1	8.2	15.5	16.4	10.0	15.1	6.6	6.6
Over 2 and less than 5 days	21.4	14.3	17.9	12.0	11.9	28.3	22.4	23.3	21.1	30.7	14.6	26.5	14.7	13.5	17.1	30.2	10.6	13.2	8.4	11.6
5 and less than 10 days	19.6	17.6	14.9	25.0	50.3	10.8	9.9	14.9	14.5	12.7	13.3	24.8	23.2	17.9	16.2	16.2	16.1	21.6	31.9	10.6
10 and less than 20 days	16.7	36.5	16.4	25.1	6.6	23.4	9.6	15.9	14.9	14.3	14.6	20.8	28.3	14.3	14.7	19.9	29.0	9.6	7.7	16.1
20 days and over	9.8	2.5	12.3	19.3	10.7	15.1	8.9	16.6	9.8	7.7	26.7	14.9	12.3	37.0	21.7	4.4	10.5	11.6	2.5	10.6
Total	100%	100%	100%	100%	100%	100%	100%	100%	100%	100%	100%	100%	100%	100%	100%	100%	100%	100%	100%	100%

Source: ABS, *Industrial Disputes*, Cat. no. 6322.0.

number of short strikes. However, both the number of strikes and the number of working days lost were at a higher plateau than the period 1953–66.

The sixth period is the post-1981 period in which there has been a decline in both strike incidence and working days lost. The period is similar to that of 1953–66 both in terms of the relationship between the number of disputes and working days lost and the incidence of both. Beggs and Chapman have attributed this decline in strike severity to the Accord.[63]

Three features of the recent trends in strikes are worthy of note: the increased proportion of strikes officially classified as being due to wages, hours and leave; the emergence of the manufacturing sector as the dominant strike industry; and the geographic shift in the proportion of strikes away from New South Wales.

Table 2.6 indicates the proportion of strikes and working days lost over various issues. Disputes over managerial policy include matters such as the computing of wages, hours and leave for individuals, disciplinary matters including dismissals, promotion procedures and production quotas. Disputes over physical working conditions include such matters as safety issues, lack of amenities, uncomfortable working conditions and the condition of equipment. Under the trade unionism heading are included disputes over the employment of non-unionists, demarcation and jurisdiction disputes, and sympathy stoppages. It can be seen that between 1913–20 and 1951–60 the proportion of disputes and, to a lesser extent, working days lost, over money issues, decreased. During the same period managerial policy and physical working conditions accounted for an increasing proportion of both strikes and working days lost. By 1953, money issues accounted for only 7.3 per cent of all strikes. Between 1961 and 1982, however, there was an increase in the proportion of strikes over these matters. In addition, the proportion of working days lost over wages and hours was higher in the period 1971–80 than at any other period with the exception of 1913–20. This was the result, not only of the increased number of strikes, but also because strikes over wages were, on average, longer (see Table 2.7). In 1977 the average duration of strikes over wages was 4.9 days, nearly double the length of strikes over each of the other issues recorded. Since 1983 the proportion of strikes and working days lost over wage issues has decreased.

For much of the period in which official strike statistics have been kept, two industries—coal-mining and stevedoring—have collectively accounted for the majority of strikes. Table 2.8 shows that these two industries accounted for approximately 80 per cent of all strikes in each of the decades 1921–30 to 1951–60. The dominance of coal-mining as the leading strike industry is also apparent. Since the 1960s the proportion

---

63. J.J. Beggs and B.J. Chapman, 'Australian Strike Activity in an International Context: 1964–85', Journal of Industrial Relations, vol. 29. no. 2, 1987, pp. 137–48.

Table 2.6: *Proportion of strikes and working days lost by issue, Australia, 1913–89*

Period	Wages, hours and leave	Managerial policy, physical working conditions	Trade unionism	Other
		Strikes %		
1913–20	41.5	40.6	11.8	6.1
1921–30	29.1	48.9	8.8	13.2
1931–40	27.8	46.7	10.9	14.5
1941–50	18.9	50.3	8.4	22.4
1951–60	10.3	60.9	10.5	18.3
1961–70	30.1	53.9	6.8	9.1
1971–80	35.2	50.1	10.2	4.5
1981	36.4	52.8	7.2	3.6
1982	23.3	61.2	9.5	6.0
1983	16.6	61.7	15.4	6.3
1984	14.3	62.7	15.8	7.2
1985	15.4	59.1	17.5	8.0
1986	15.6	62.4	12.8	9.8
1987	29.0	55.1	12.1	3.3
1988	24.4	60.5	12.3	2.9
1989	18.8	61.9	16.3	3.0
		Working days lost %		
1913–20	55.8	12.4	30.8	1.0
1921–30	61.7	22.0	6.8	9.4
1931–40	26.6	39.6	5.3	28.5
1941–50	45.1	32.9	7.7	14.2
1951–60	35.1	43.9	8.9	11.3
1961–70	53.8	28.8	3.8	13.6
1971–80	64.3	17.9	3.9	13.9
1981	77.8	19.5	1.9	6.8
1982	69.2	23.6	3.5	3.7
1983	17.2	75.1	3.3	4.6
1984	30.5	48.7	8.7	12.1
1985	26.9	39.4	16.6	17.0
1986	40.9	43.4	3.4	12.3
1987	60.8	34.7	3.0	1.5
1988	34.3	61.6	2.0	2.0
1989	66.1	26.5	2.7	4.7

Sources: ABS, *Industrial Disputes,* Cat. no. 6322.0 and 6321.0.

(and number) of strikes in the coal industry has dropped markedly and the manufacturing industry has emerged as the strike leading industry. This may be related to the benchmark role of the Metal Trades Award which, after 1952, was used as a vehicle of secondary wage fixing in all industries (see Chapter 12). Bentley attributes the decline of strikes in the coal industry to the emergence of relatively large pockets of

Table 2.7: *Average duration of strikes by issue, Australia, 1977, 1989*

Issue	Average duration (days) 1977	1989
Wages	4.9	1.0
Hours of work	1.6	0.2
Leave provisions	2.4	1.2
Managerial policy	2.6	1.0
Physical working conditions	1.7	0.3
Trade unionism	2.6	0.3
Other	0.7	3.0
All Issues	2.7	0.8

Source: ABS, *Industrial Disputes*, Cat. no. 6322.0 and 6321.0.

unemployment in the industry brought about by the growth of alternative fuels and mechanisation.[64]

Though the proportion of strikes in coal-mining has declined, the number of working days lost in the industry has shown little variation since 1962. Further, though the number of working days lost in the manufacturing industry increased sharply between 1972 and 1974, strike severity still remains higher in the coal-mining industry than any other industry. Table 2.9 shows that the working days lost per thousand employees in coal mining was more than thirty-seven times the national average in 1982 and much higher than the national average in other years.

Appendix 2.2 gives details of the number of strikes in each industry.

The final trend which should be noticed relates to the proportionate change in the number of strikes by state. As can be seen from Table 2.10 New South Wales has been the most strike-prone state. This could be expected, given that coal-mining was centred in that state and that ports in New South Wales handle more vessels than those in any other states. The decline in the number of strikes in coal-mining, the greater industrial diversification of other states (particularly Western Australia) and the increased number of strikes in the manufacturing industry have resulted in a proportionate decrease in the number of disputes in New South Wales. Though New South Wales continues to have more than three times as many strikes as any other state, Table 2.11 indicates that this state compares more favourably with other states in terms of working days lost per employee. In many years, Victorian strikes were more severe. This would indicate that though Victoria has only about one third the number of strikes of New South Wales, they are much longer. This brings us full circle to the choice of the most appropriate measure: working days lost or number of strikes?

---

64. P. Bentley, 'Recent strike behaviour in Australia: causes and responses', *Australian Bulletin of Labour*, Flinders University Institute of Labour Studies, vol. 1, no. 1, September 1974, p. 29.

Table 2.8: *Proportion of industrial disputes by industry, Australia, 1913–89*

Period	Industry				
	Coal-mining[a]	Manufacturing	Construction	Stevedoring[b]	Other[b]
		Strikes %			
1913–20	51	20	3	15	11
1921–30	73	11	3	8	5
1931–40	74	11	2	3	10
1941–50	76	13	1	7	3
1951–60	55	15	5	19	6
1961–65	20	40	12	20	8
1966–70	11	48	16	13	12
1971–75	8	38	12	12	30
1976–81	11	41	9	5	34
1982	11	35	12	4	38
1983	13	31	13	4	39
1984	15	31	8	4	42
1985	14	29	13	5	39
1986	14	37	10	4	35
1987	14	31	14	4	37
1988	20	24	11	4	41
1989	14	17	10	5	55

(a) Includes other mining, 1913–25
(b) Includes other transport, 1913–50 and 1989
Source: ABS, *Industrial Disputes*, Cat. no. 6322.0 and 6321.0.

Strike settlements

Two dominant characteristics stand out in the methods of strike settlement in Australia. First, in most cases work resumes without any form of negotiation. Second, relatively few strikes are settled by industrial tribunals. These traits are highlighted in Table 2.12. The reason why so few strikes are settled by the federal tribunal is that it is ill-equipped to deal with many plant-level grievances. Further, since many strikes are of a short duration, they are not amenable to settlement by tribunals. In many such instances strikes appear to be used as demonstration stoppages to bring grievances to the attention of management, unions and tribunals.

From Table 2.12 it can be seen that in 1988 56 per cent of strikes resulted in work resuming without any negotiations. A further 20 per cent of strikes were settled by negotiations. By way of contrast about 22 per cent of strikes were settled through state and federal tribunals. The state and federal tribunals handled about half of these strikes each. The construction industry exhibits a different strike settlement pattern from the general norm. A higher proportion of disputes is settled by negotiations and by tribunals, while a smaller number of cases end up with work resuming without negotiations.

Though industrial tribunals are not involved in the settlement of many disputes, the evidence would suggest they become involved in

Table 2.9: Working days lost per thousand employees by industry, Australia, 1972–88

Year[a]	Mining		Manufacturing		Construction	Transport and storage; Communication		Other industries[a]	All industries
	Coal	Other	Metal products, machinery and equipment	Other		Stevedoring services	Other		
1972	2 909	1152	1113	533	1037	1990	578	89	435
1973	4 268	2860	1405	889	1119	2705	256	133	552
1974	7 725	2625	4876	1026	3009	6172	1352	194	1273
1975	14 991	1576	2376	674	1255	2581	379	230	717
1976	6 602	3952	1467	1245	1433	2276	1010	292	773
1977	4 145	3182	398	679	591	2625	450	101	336
1978	5 669	2415	1460	747	378	8418	435	74	434
1979	8 220	5752	1886	1112	1100	3724	1138	269	787
1980	23 362	4036	1194	1080	674	2548	353	202	649
1981	10 209	5238	2287	986	1405	2952	970	238	797
1982	9 698	2686	471	505	768	—672—		84	358
1983	3 223	3375	353	186	1269	—485—		42	249
1984	3 913	3745	343	416	503	—372—		91	248
1985	6 898	1931	255	312	666	—432—		71	228
1986	10 773	3328	445	328	458	—135—		72	242
1987	8 902	1069	479	305	773	—217—		69	223
1988	15 543	1777	750	183	725	—177—		85	269

(a) Exclude agriculture, etc. and private households employing staff for the years 1976–83 but included from 1984.
Source ABS, *Industrial Disputes*, Cat. no. 6322.0.

Table 2.10: *Proportion of industrial disputes by state, 1913–88*

Year	NSW %	Vic %	Qld %	SA %	WA %	Tas %
1913	64	15	9	4	4	4
1920	63	10	10	7	8	2
1930	85	3	6	4	1	1
1940	89	6	1	2	1	1
1950	81	3	12	2	1	1
1960	64	9	15	4	4	4
1970	54	16	14	7	6	3
1980	51	13	10	4	15	2
1981	53	13	11	4	12	3
1982	44	13	12	5	21	2
1983	42	13	17	5	17	3
1984	42	11	15	4	21	3
1985	46	14	9	5	19	4
1986	47	15	9	6	15	4
1987	41	15	11	8	16	4
1988	45	13	14	6	15	4

Source: ABS, *Industrial Disputes*, Cat. no. 6322.0.

major strikes. Thus, the 22 per cent of strikes settled through tribunals in 1988 accounted for 52 per cent of the working days lost through strikes in that year. This qualitative importance of industrial tribunals is particulary evident in metal manufacturing, where the federal tribunal was involved in settling disputes which accounted for 72 per cent of working days lost. The traditional benchmark role of the Metal Industry Award may help to explain this phenomenon.

Strike costs

The costs of strikes are difficult to estimate. Official statistics do not indicate production and other losses in establishments. Some costs—such as public inconvenience—have no ready measures. Some figures may overstate costs. A management-induced strike in a factory short on orders may represent a saving rather than a loss. With the exception of perishable commodities, lost production through strikes can usually be made up. Strikes may have very different effects depending on the industry affected, the length of the strike and the timing of the strike. A strike in an essential service such as power generating will have a greater effect than a strike by bowling green curators. A post office strike at Christmas will have a greater social (though not necessarily economic) cost than at other times. Strikes in some public utilities which run at a loss may actually result in a cost saving to taxpayers.[65] Such factors

---

65. See, for example, Hyman, *Strikes*, p. 36.

Table 2.11: *Working days lost per thousand employees by state, Australia, 1967–88*

Period	NSW	Vic.	Qld	SA	WA	Tas	NT	ACT	Aust.
1967	307	94	175	50	22	63			176
1968	373	208	305	133	73	109			261
1969	460	594	442	325	318	81			458
1970	829	409	318	227	413	258			537
1971	1095	542	463	264	192	163			669
1972	503	497	485	143	261	152			435
1973	622	590	509	296	313	1089			552
1974	1462	1757	807	686	656	672			1273
1975	831	910	718	277	253	305			717
1976	827	1051	638	323	623	464			773
1977	308	433	359	65	532	197			336
1978	555	346	536	172	473	261			434
1979	742	1083	679	402	838	439			787
1980	657	792	863	132	446	668			649
1981	1023	863	620	320	548	461			797
1982	381	258	660	101	348	431			348
1983	287	163	176	115	577	478			249
1984	357	132	302	55	256	350	381	88	248
1985	209	236	411	47	187	138	213	159	228
1986	304	240	207	95	272	190	200	55	242
1987	366	172	87	91	213	177	111	143	223
1988	340	214	337	93	299	118	154	112	269

Source: ABS, *Industrial Disputes, Australia* 6322.0.

make accurate estimations of strike costs difficult. Most specialists agree, however, that the economic costs of strikes are greatly exaggerated.[66]

Certainly, compared to other costs, strike costs are insignificant. Absenteeism, for example, is estimated to result in 4 per cent of the workforce being absent from work on any one day.[67] In 1976, a year in which Australian workers averaged half a day on strike, each worker averaged nine and one half days absence from work.[68] Unemployment has resulted in between 6 and 11 per cent of the workforce being unproductive in any one day. On the other hand strikes result in less than 0.2 per cent of possible working days being lost. Industrial accidents, alcoholism and the common cold account for more loss of work than strikes. Wooden notes the insignificance of strike costs relative to absenteeism:

> Non-attendance at work has received considerable attention from researchers, particularly in the fields of organizational behaviour and psychology, presumably because of the chronic nature of the problem and the costs

---

66. See, for example, ibid., pp. 35–41, Kornhauser et al., *Industrial Conflict*, p. 8, and D.W. Oxnam, 'The cost and benefits of industrial conflict', *Economic Activity*, October 1968, pp. 41–7.
67. See Department of Labour, *People and Work*, vol. 3, no. 2, 1977.
68. Mr Macphee, Minister for Productivity, *Australian Financial Review*, 20 September 1977.

Table 2.12: *Method of settlement of industrial disputes, Australia, 1988*

Method of settlement	Mining		Manufacturing			Construction	Transport and storage; Communication	Other industries[a]	All industries	
	Coal	Other	Metal products, machinery and equipment	Other					Total	Per cent
					Number of Disputes					
Negotiation	30	23	31	42		53	40	76	295	19.7
State legislation	n.p.	13	n.p.	21		36	14	32	144	9.6
Federal and joint federal–state legislation	20	9	46	33		31	19	34	192	12.8
Resumption without negotiation	233	98	188	37		40	130	114	840	56.1
Other methods[b]	n.p.	n.p.	n.p.	4		9	3	6	27	1.8
Total	**293**	**143**	**288**	**137**		**169**	**206**	**262**	**1498**	**100.0**
					Working days lost ('000)					
Negotiation	8.2	6.9	12.0	26.4		21.7	9.8	91.1	176.1	10.3
State Legislation	1.9	13.5	11.6	14.1		26.3	3.2	32.1	102.7	6.0
Federal and joint federal–state legislation	445.5	9.7	223.0	28.8		39.3	7.6	34.2	788.2	46.0
Resumption without negotiation	114.0	33.1	62.0	33.8		95.0	54.2	206.3	598.4	34.9
Other methods[b]	13.3	—	0.1	8.9		23.9	0.4	1.9	48.3	2.8
Total	**582.8**	**63.4**	**308.7**	**112.0**		**206.2**	**75.2**	**365.5**	**1713.8**	**100.0**

(a) Comprises agriculture, forestry, fishing and hunting; electricity, gas and water; wholesale and retail trade; finance, property and business services; public administration and defence; community services; and recreation, personal and other services.
(b) Includes mediation, filling the places of workers on strike or locked out and closing down the establishment permanently.
Source: ABS, *Industrial Disputes*, Cat. no. 6322.0.

associated with it. Data collected on a regular quarterly basis by the ABS in the Labour Force Survey indicates that during 1986 just over 213 thousand full-time employees, or 3.8 per cent of the full-time employed workforce, could be expected to be absent from work during any week when they were scheduled to be at work. Assuming an average work year of 45.87 weeks and that, on average, full-time employees are absent for 57.7 per cent of their usual weekly hours, the total number of working days lost by full-time employees during 1986 is 28.8 million. Using data from the 1983 Health Survey this figure can be expanded to account for part-time employees to 29.8 million. This compares with only 2.3 million working days lost on average per year as a result of industrial disputes over the last decade.[69]

Given the relatively small cost of strikes, it is worth considering why they attract such a degree of attention. Clearly, it cannot be because of their cost alone. If this were the case, then the other sources of public cost would attract greater concern. Strikes are distinguished by their unpredictability and challenge to authority. Though absenteeism, labour turnover and other conflict symptoms are more costly than strikes, management can usually predict their incidence and budget accordingly. Strikes, on the other hand, introduce an element of industrial uncertainty. The dramatic challenge of strikes to management and government authority can make them seem to be a threat to the stability of society itself.

Summary

Industrial conflict is as central to industrial relations as scarcity is to economics. Such conflict, it is contended, is an inevitable feature of industrialised societies. It appears in many forms and it would be wrong to see industrial conflict as being synonymous with strikes. Many explanations of conflict have been offered and this chapter grouped these under two forms of structural determinants. The first—industrial structures—pointed to the conflicts which arise from economic, technological, organisational and institutional considerations. The second—social structures—explored the Kerr–Siegel and Marxist explanations of industrial conflict.

Because strikes are amenable to measurement they are the most frequently used index of industrial conflict. Notwithstanding any official *imprimatur*, however, great care should be exercised in using such statistics. The uses of such statistics for cross-country comparisons is of dubious value. The pattern of strike action has undergone marked changes in Australia since official data was first collected in 1913. These changes have occurred in most of the major variables associated with

---

69. M. Wooden, 'The management of labour absence: an inventory of strategies and measures', Working Paper No. 97, National Institute of Labour Studies, 1988.

strikes—their frequency and duration, causes, industry and geographical concentration. Remarkably, given the common perception of compulsory arbitration, only a small proportion of strikes are settled by industrial tribunals. Although strikes can cause inconvenience to some sections of the community, their economic effects can be exaggerated. The common cold accounts for more time lost in any year than do strikes.

Appendix 2.1

Table 2.13: *Industrial disputes, Australia, 1913–89*

		Workers involved ('000)			Working days lost		Estimated loss in wages ($'000)
Year	Number	Directly	Indirectly(a)	Total	Number ('000)	Average days per worker involved	
1913	208	33.2	16.8	50.3	622.6	12.38	576
1914	337	43.1	28.0	71.0	993.2	13.98	1001
1915	358	57.0	24.3	81.3	683.0	8.40	700
1916	508	128.5	42.1	170.7	1644.8	9.64	1890
1917	444	154.1	19.9	174.0	4689.3	26.95	5284
1918	298	42.6	13.9	56.4	539.6	9.56	690
1919	460	100.3	57.3	157.6	4303.7	27.31	5238
1920	554	102.5	53.0	155.6	3587.3	23.06	4741
1921	624	120.2	44.9	165.1	1286.2	7.79	1941
1922	445	100.3	16.1	116.3	858.7	7.33	1503
1923	274	66.1	10.2	76.3	1146.0	15.02	2551
1924	504	132.6	19.9	152.4	918.6	6.03	1835
1925	499	154.6	22.1	176.7	1128.6	6.39	2215
1926	360	80.8	32.3	113.0	1310.3	11.59	2832
1927	441	157.6	43.2	200.8	1713.6	8.54	3353
1928	287	82.3	14.1	96.4	777.3	8.06	1551
1929	259	87.5	17.1	104.6	4461.5	42.65	9139
1930	183	52.0	2.3	54.2	1511.2	27.87	3185
1931	134	34.5	3.1	37.7	246.0	6.53	456
1932	127	29.3	3.6	32.9	212.3	6.45	331
1933	90	27.0	3.1	30.1	112.0	3.72	190
1934	155	47.0	3.9	50.9	370.4	7.28	636
1935	183	44.8	2.5	47.3	495.1	10.46	781
1936	235	57.1	3.5	60.6	497.2	8.21	938
1937	342	92.1	4.1	96.2	557.1	5.79	1014
1938	376	132.5	11.5	144.0	1338.0	9.29	2608
1939	416	143.2	9.6	152.8	459.2	3.00	911
1940	350	178.9	13.7	192.6	1507.3	7.83	3432
1941	567	240.8	7.3	248.1	984.2	3.97	2000
1942	602	1166.2	3.1	169.3	378.2	2.23	912
1943	785	288.0	8.1	296.1	990.2	3.34	2307
1944	941	260.8	15.6	276.4	912.8	3.30	2224
1945	945	299.6	16.3	315.9	2119.6	6.71	5135
1946	869	331.9	16.7	348.5	1947.8	5.59	4580
1947	982	280.7	46.4	327.1	1338.7	4.09	3796
1948	1141	301.0	16.1	317.1	1662.7	5.24	4598
1949	849	260.7	3.9	264.6	1334.0	5.04	5223
1950	1276	391.5	40.2	431.7	2062.9	4.78	8333
1951	1344	380.4	28.2	408.6	873.0	2.14	4512
1952	1627	488.2	17.6	505.7	1163.5	2.30	6880
1953	1459	883.8	12.2	496.0	1050.8	2.12	6675
1954	1490	355.6	14.5	370.1	901.6	2.44	6042

Table 2.13: *Industrial disputes, Australia, 1913–89 (cont'd)*

					Working days lost		
		Workers involved ('000)			Number	Average days per worker	Estimated loss in wages
Year	Number	Directly	Indirectly[a]	Total	('000)	involved	($'000)
1955	1532	424.3	20.3	444.6	1010.9	2.27	6 621
1956	1306	414.6	13.4	428.0	1121.4	2.62	7 934
1957	1103	326.0	11.0	337.0	630.2	1.87	4 617
1958	987	275.6	7.3	282.8	439.9	1.56	3 181
1959	869	229.5	8.0	237.5	365.0	1.54	2 754
1960	1145	592.1	11.2	603.3	725.1	1.20	5 854
1961	815	288.5	11.8	300.4	606.8	2.02	5 448
1962	1183	330.8	23.0	353.9	508.8	1.44	4 244
1963	1250	398.6	14.1	412.7	581.6	1.41	4 992
1964	1334	528.8	16.8	545.6	911.4	1.67	8 561
1965	1346	460.2	14.8	475.0	815.9	1.72	8 198
1966	1273	385.0	9.9	394.9	732.1	1.85	7 302
1967	1340	472.2	11.1	482.3	705.3	1.46	7 263
1968	1713	700.8	19.5	720.3	1079.5	1.50	12 115
1969	2014	1244.0	41.2	1285.2	1958.0	1.52	22 986
1970	2738	1304.2	63.3	1367.4	2393.7	1.75	30 883
1971	2404	1267.7	58.8	1326.5	3068.6	2.31	45 241
1972	2298	1041.2	72.6	1113.8	2010.3	1.80	32 074
1973	2538	758.0	45.0	803.0	2633.4	3.30	45 206
1974	2809	1947.1	57.8	2004.8	6232.5	3.10	128 301
1975	2432	1343.8	54.1	1398.0	3509.9	2.50	95 761
1976	2055	2137.8	52.6	2189.9	3399.2	1.70	114 552
1977	2090	539.4	56.8	596.2	1654.8	2.80	59 674
1978	2277	1011.9	63.7	1075.6	2130.8	2.00	78 404
1979	2042	1818.0	44.9	1862.9	3964.4	2.12	148 614
1980	2429	1108.9	64.0	1172.8	3320.2	2.83	152 022
1981	2915	1175.2	76.6	1251.8	4192.2	3.35	221 779
1982	2060	697.4	25.5	722.9	2158.0	2.99	133 624
1983	1787	444.9	25.4	470.2	1689.4	3.6	—
1984	1965	529.2	31.1	560.3	1253.5	2.2	—
1985	1895	542.3	28.2	570.5	1304.3	2.3	—
1986	1754	671.6	20.1	691.7	1380.7	2.0	—
1987	1517	590.3	18.5	608.8	1209.5	2.0	—
1988	1508	884.1	10.3	894.4	1713.8	1.9	—
1989	1388	705.9	3.3	709.2	1201.8	1.7	—

(a) persons thrown out of work at the establishments where the stoppages occurred but who are not themselves parties to the dispute.
Source: ABS. *Labour Report* and *Industrial Disputes.* Cat. no. 6322.0 and 6321.0.

Appendix 2.2

Table 2.14: *Industrial disputes by industry, Australia, 1988*

Industry	Total number of disputes	Workers involved (directly and indirectly) ('000)	Working days lost	
			Number ('000)	Average days per worker involved
Agriculture, forestry, fishing and hunting	—	—	—	—
Mining	438	155.5	568.6	3.7
Coal	294	122.2	471.2	3.9
Iron ore	99	27.5	70.9	2.6
Other	45	5.8	26.5	4.6
Manufacturing	428	276.5	426.9	1.5
Food, beverages and tobacco	50	13.0	57.3	4.4
Textiles; Clothing and footwear	5	0.7	1.1	1.6
Wood, wood products and furniture	13	1.4	3.5	2.5
Paper and paper products, printing publishing	24	19.2	25.2	1.3
Chemical, petroleum and coal products	22	3.1	7.4	2.4
Metal products, machinery and equipment	290	233.9	309.5	1.3
Other	24	5.1	23.0	4.5
Electricity, gas and water	50	22.2	23.2	1.0
Construction	171	126.7	207.9	1.6
Wholesale and retail trade	56	13.4	39.9	3.0
Transport and storage;	177	42.4	69.9	1.6
Road transport	17	5.0	7.0	1.4
Railway transport	15	11.0	31.2	2.8
Air transport	19	4.4	6.4	1.5
Water transport	3	0.1	0.4	4.0
Transport services				
Stevedoring	68	14.7	13.8	0.9
Other	55	6.8	10.2	1.5
Other transport and storage;	5	0.3	0.8	2.7
Finance, insurance, real estate and business services	20	6.5	17.0	2.6
Public administration and defence	70	134.6	164.5	1.2
Community services	50	105.2	111.4	1.1
Recreation, personal and other services	19	6.1	6.9	1.1
Communication	29	5.4	5.2	1.0
Total	1508	894.4	1641.3	1.8

Source: ABS, *Industrial Disputes*, Cat. no. 6322.0.

Discussion questions

1. Should industrial conflict be regarded as inevitable in an industrial society? Why?
2. What are the causes of industrial conflict?
3. Explain what is meant by 'the frontier of control'. What is the significance of this 'frontier' to industrial conflict?
4. Evaluate the contribution of the Human Relations School to an understanding of industrial conflict.
5. 'Overemphasis on strikes results in an inability to detect the symptoms of conflict other than strike symptoms and inappropriate policy prescriptions.' Discuss.
6. Why are some industries more strike-prone than others?
7. Evaluate the contention that 'the strike is withering away' (Ross and Hartman, p.4).
8. What factors account for strike trends in the period 1970–90?
9. What proportion of strikes are settled by industrial tribunals? How do you account for this proportion?
10. Discuss the contention that strike losses are exaggerated in Australia.
11. Do you consider Australia to be a strike-prone country? Give reasons for your answer.

Further reading

Beggs, J.J. and Chapman, B.J., 'Australian strike activity in an international context 1964–85', *Journal of Industrial Relations*, vol. 29, no. 2, 1987.
Bentley, P., 'Recent strike behaviour in Australia: causes and responses', *Australian Bulletin of Labour*, Flinders University Institute of Labour Studies, vol. 1, no. 1, September 1974, pp. 27–55.
Beynon, H., *Working for Ford*, Penguin, London, 1973.
Blauner, R., *Alienation and Freedom: The Factory Worker and his Industry*, University of Chicago Press, 1973.
Creigh, S., 'Strikes in post-war Australia: a review', *Journal of Industrial Relations*, vol. 27, no. 2, 1985.
Eldridge, J.E.T., *Industrial Disputes*, Routledge & Kegan Paul, London, 1968.
Gouldner, A.W., *Wildcat Strike*, Routledge & Kegan Paul, London, 1955.
Hare, A.E.C., *The First Principles of Industrial Relations*, St Martins Press, New York, 2nd ed., 1966, pp. 1–88.
Hyman, R., *Industrial Relations: A Marxist Introduction*, Macmillan, London, 1975, Ch. 7.
Hyman, R., *Strikes*, Fontana, London, 1972.
Jackson, M.P., *Industrial Relations: A Textbook*, Croom Helm, London, 1977, Chs 7 and 8.
Kerr, C., *Labour and Management in Industrial Society*, Doubleday, New York, 1964.
Knowles, K.G.J.C., *Strikes: A Study in Industrial Conflict*, Blackwell, Oxford, 1972.

Kornhauser, A., et al. (eds), *Industrial Conflict*, McGraw-Hill, New York, 1954.
Kuhn, J.W., *Bargaining in Grievance Settlement*, Columbia University Press, New York, 1961.
Lane T. and Roberts, K., *Strike at Pilkingtons, Fontana, London, 1975.*
Waters, M., *Strikes in Australia*, Allen & Unwin, Sydney, 1982.
Wooden, M., 'The management of labour absence: an inventory of strategies and measures', Working Paper No. 97, National Institute of Labour Studies. 1988.

Part Three

THE PARTIES

There are six main parties in Australian industrial relations: governments, state and federal; the tribunals, state and federal; employers; the employer associations; trade unions; and employees. Governments make and enforce procedural and substantive rules for the workplace, directly determine some aspects of worklife through legislation, and set working conditions and pay as employers in their own right. For the most part, however, Australian governments have left the regulation of industrial conflict and the determining of the substantive rules embodied in awards to independent tribunals, which have the power to intervene in disputes and to settle them, by compulsion, if necessary. The tribunal systems depend for their effectiveness on the grouping of employers and employees into 'registered organisations'. Compulsory arbitration has been especially important in encouraging and protecting trade unions. Care should be taken not to treat the parties as monolithic and homogeneous entities. The state tribunals vary in the extent to which they use arbitration or wages board procedures and in the exact powers they may exercise. The Australian Industrial Relations Commission has come to dominate the arbitration system but is nonetheless restricted in a number of ways, both in the powers it has and in the ways it may use them. There is a great variety of form and purpose among the employer associations and the extent to which they represent employers in different industries. Some are for industrial relations purposes; some are primarily trade associations. Because employers are competitors in business, it is not easy for them to achieve unity of policy in dealing with the trade unions. Similarly, there are different types of trade unions, whose policies and practices, degree of industry penetration, ideological commitment and influence on the system vary greatly.

CHAPTER 3

Governments

Governments are important to Australian industrial relations for a number of reasons. First, governments have at times established substantive rules for the workplace, such as those about leave, working hours and the form in which wages should be paid. Second, governments have set out procedural rules to limit the ways in which employers and employees may conduct their bargaining and disputes. Third, and less specifically, governments help to make the general economic environment of industrial relations through their policies on such matters as incomes, employment, inflation and tariff protection. For support of government activity in those areas, a complex administrative structure has grown up, whose policies and behaviour influence industrial relations and the labour market. Fourth, governments are major shareholders in the economy's resources. Fifth, governments have responsibility for international labour matters. Last, governments employ many people in their own right. The wages and conditions paid to public servants set standards which may affect wages and conditions in private industry.

Making the rules: auxiliary, regulatory and restrictive functions

Government intervention in the labour market in Australia is almost as old as white settlement. The first white settlers were convicts or part of the force that was meant to guard or administer them.[1] The government

---

1. See especially, T.A. Coghlan, *Labour and Industry in Australia*, Macmillan, London, 1918, and J.H. Portus, *The Development of Australian Trade Union Law*, Melbourne University Press, Melbourne, 1958.

exercised a proprietorial right over labour. Yet even in a penal colony, despite all the repressive apparatus of soldiers and the lash, the question of hours and wages arose. The guards and administrators were responsible for that. As they began to acquire land or to engage in trade they also began to demand the use of convict labour. Consequently, convicts were assigned to them to do the work free labourers would have done in England. Competition for labour, and especially for skilled labour, soon developed among these first 'employers'. Some of them began to pay convicts for work and an informal, though primitive, wages structure developed. At times wages rose beyond the level which many employers thought acceptable. Colonial governors responded to that with a series of regulations designed to restrict the amounts which might be paid to various classes of labour and to set the hours of work. As a free labour market grew with the numbers of time-expired convicts and the Australian born, government control extended to cover all types of labour in the colony, particularly through regulations and partly through the ponderous majesty of the *Master and Servants Act* of 1829. This Act attempted to regulate hours of work, wages and the rights and responsibilities of employers and employees. The degree of control afforded management or 'masters' by this Act is indicated in the rules of a company (Fig. 3.1) which considered the conditions resulting from the Act as 'near utopian'.

Direct regulation of hours and wages by government and the unilateral imposition of employment conditions by 'masters' became impractical after the gold rushes of the 1850s. Too many free workers had come into the colonies for rules based on the convict system to be practicable. In any case, transportation of convicts to Australia had already stopped. Nevertheless, the influence of governments on labour relations remained strong. A 'pattern of partnership between government and private institutions'[2] developed, which maintained some of the earlier importance of government in making the rules:

> Undertaking large and increasing programmes of capital formation, governments became the largest employers of labour ... with important influences on wages and labour conditions. Able to attract overseas investment capital, colonial governments carried through ambitious programmes of public formation which required large amounts of labour ... not concerned with product competition, profit and loss, or other commercial considerations, governments could pay a level of wage necessary to attract the labour it needed regardless of the ramifications of such a wage policy in the private sector.[3]

In their competition for labour with private employers, governments early conceded the payment of seven shillings a day for labourers, a rate which did not apply generally until the Harvester Judgment of 1907. In

---

2. N.G. Butlin, 'Colonial socialism in Australia', in H.G.J. Aitken (ed.), *The State and Economic Growth*, Social Science Research Council, New York, 1959, p. 38.
3. P.G. McCarthy, 'The living wage in Australia—the role of government', *Labour History*, no. 18, 1970, p. 4.

Fig. 3.1: Merchants and Ships Chandlers, Sydney Town, 1852

Rules for the Clerical Staff

The owners hereby recognise the generosity of the new labour laws, but will expect a great rise in the output of work to compensate for these near Utopian conditions.

1. Godliness, Cleanliness and Punctuality are the necessities of a good business.
2. On the recommendation of the Governor of this Colony, this firm has reduced the hours of work, and the Clerical Staff will now only have to be present between the hours of 7 a.m. and 6 p.m. on week days.
   The Sabbath is for Worship, but should any Man-of-War or other vessel require victualing, the Clerical Staff will work on the Sabbath.
3. Daily prayers will be held each morning in the Main Office. The Clerical Staff will be present.
4. Clothing must be of sober nature. The Clerical Staff will not disport themselves in raiment of bright colours, nor will they wear hose, unless in good repair.
5. Overshoes and Topcoats may not be worn in the office, but Neck Scarves and Headwear may be worn in inclement weather.
6. A stove is provided for the benefit of the Clerical Staff. Coal and Wood must be kept in the locker. It is recommended that each member of the Clerical Staff bring four pounds of coal, each day, during cold weather.
7. No member of the Clerical Staff may leave the room without permission from Mr Ryder. The calls of nature are permitted, and the Clerical Staff may use the garden below the gate. This area to be kept in good condition.
8. No talking is allowed during business hours.
9. The craving for tobacco, wines or spirits is a human weakness, and as such, is forbidden to all members of the Clerical Staff.
10. Now that the hours of business have been drastically reduced, the partaking of food is allowed between 11.30 a.m. and noon, but, work will not, on any account cease.
11. Members of the Clerical Staff will provide their own pens. A new sharpener is available, on application to Mr Ryder.
12. Mr Ryder will nominate a Senior Clerk to be responsible for the cleanliness of the Main Office and the Private Office, and all boys and Juniors will report to him 40 minutes before Prayers, and will remain after closing hours for similar work. Brushes, Brooms, Scrubbers and Soap are provided by the Owners.
13. The New Increased Weekly Wages are as hereunder detailed:

Junior boys (to 11 years)	1/4
Boys (to 14 years)	2/1
Juniors	4/8
Junior Clerks	8/7
Clerks	10/9
Senior Clerks (after 15 years with the Owners)	21/1

Source: J. Harris, *The Bitter Fight: A Pictorial History of the Australian Labor Movement*, University of Queensland Press, Brisbane, 1970, p. 11.

Victoria, at least, the government also accepted the eight-hour day for those it employed.⁴ Some colonial governments also insisted that employers who tendered for public contracts should 'observe the eight hours a day and pay the ruling rate of wages'.⁵

At the same time, the colonial governments began to regulate the workplace and the labour market, by legislation. Trade union and employer pressure or more general political agitation led governments to make rules both about specific jobs and about the general terms on which all workers were to be employed. A list of the subjects of some of the principal Acts of colonial parliaments before 1900 makes clear the extent of this sort of intervention: coal mines, factory employment and working conditions, chimney sweeps, the hours of shop workers, contractors' debts, workmen's wages, truck payments, trade unions, apprentices and employers' liability. Some of the parliaments also attempted to protect the position of white labour by restricting the entry to the colonies of Chinese workers.

Thus, by 1890, when the first colonial Arbitration Bill was introduced to the South Australian Parliament, there had already been a great deal of government intervention in industrial relations and the labour market.⁶ The first Arbitration Bill was in one sense, therefore, not an innovation. Both before and after the gold rushes, governments had made, or influenced the making of, the substantive rules which established employment standards. What was new about South Australia's Bill, at least in the second half of the century, was that it attempted to make procedural rules.

After the gold rushes, the procedures of bargaining and dispute had been left to the employers and the unions to work out for themselves. They had engaged in direct bargaining, helped by the strike and the lockout. In the 1890s, however, the scale and the intensity of industrial conflict destroyed whatever impartiality there had been in the actions of the state. The governments of the colonies and their judiciaries took the part of the employers and helped to defeat unions. This had several consequences, one of which was the formation of the Labor Party; if the parliament was not impartial then the unions would take a place in parliament to balance or overcome the influence in it of the employers. A second consequence was a move to settle industrial disputes by conciliation and arbitration, in order to avoid the destruction of established society which industrial warfare seemed to threaten.

At this stage governments, both state and federal, began to make procedural rules again. From the 1890s, in the states, and 1904 in the Commonwealth, rule-making has been the job, mostly, of tribunals of one sort or another. The governments made the procedural rules which established the tribunals and the tribunals in turn have made or endorsed most of the substantive rules. Consequently, in the twentieth

---

4. R.A. Gollan, *Radical and Working Class Politics*, Melbourne University Press, Melbourne, 1960, p. 75.
5. P.G. McCarthy, 'The living wage', p. 8.
6. Though introduced in 1890, the Bill was not enacted until 1894.

century, the federal and state systems of conciliation and arbitration have been the main focus of Australian industrial relations. The operation and effect of the tribunals are examined in subsequent chapters.

This brief historical account indicates the three functions of government as rule-maker: its auxiliary function, its regulatory function and its restrictive function.[7]

The auxiliary function is the support that law gives to the autonomous bargaining arrangements, in particular by providing norms and sanctions. The regulatory function supplements the bargaining process by the provision of substantive rules to govern the terms and conditions of employment. It equates with the substantive rule-making function of governments. This regulatory function is held to be inversely proportional to the strength and coverage of the bargaining system.[8]

The restrictive function provides the rules of the game; what is allowed and what is forbidden in the conduct of industrial hostilities. It equates with the government's procedural rule-making function. This function protects the parties from each other. Above all, however, it protects 'what is called the "public", that is the interest of the community, of the consumers, of individuals whose interests may be affected'.[9]

Making the environment

Industrial relations do not happen in some sort of vacuum. They are part of the whole set of relationships and processes that makes up a society and an economy. Industrial relations affect other parts of the society and are affected by them in return. Political instability, class inequalities and tensions, ideological or religious sectarianism, racial violence, or economic insecurity: all these are likely to aggravate the problems of industrial relations. Those general conditions are capable of manipulation, if not of immediate remedy. The extent to which governments are able to manipulate and to remedy will have some direct effect on the level of social and industrial conflict.

Concern with structuring the external environment has been termed 'strategic mediation' to contrast it with the more immediate and direct 'tactical mediation' (conciliation). Kerr writes:

> A strike is not an isolated event, a solitary episode. It occurs within a given social context, a surrounding economic and political environment. The major variations in the incidence of conflict relate ... to the total milieu within which it arises. Strategic mediation is concerned with the manipulation of these situations and thus with factors quite external to the parties themselves. From one point of view, society is a huge mediation mechanism, a means for

---

7. O. Kahn-Freund, 'Industrial relations and the law—retrospect and prospect', *British Journal of Industrial Relations*, vol. 7, no. 3, 1969, pp. 301–16.
8. Ibid., p. 302.
9. Ibid.

settling disagreements between rival claimants—taxpayers and recipients of benefits, buyers and sellers, proponents of opposing political ideologies—so that people may live together in some state of mutual tolerance. Some societies mediate their disagreements through their markets, their courts, their political processes, more effectively than others do. Society in the large is the mediation machinery for industrial as well as other forms of conflict.[10]

An important part of strategic mediation is the government's management of the economy. Inflation, mass unemployment and other economic sickness produce suffering, insecurity and social tension. They make the inequalities endemic to a system based on the private ownership of property more apparent. They also have an important effect on industrial relations, both on relations between capital and labour and on relations between the ranks and grades within those two camps. In the good times, many of the potential sources conflict are not made active. In the hard times they are. Inflation pushes up the cost of living and sets off the demand that wages should be altered continuously so as to prevent a fall in the real incomes of workers. Established wage differentials among groups of workers disappear and are made to reappear by bargaining and disputes. Unemployment results in demarcation disputes as unions attempt to protect job opportunities for their members, or to bring new people into the union to replace others whose jobs have been lost. That happens at the expense of other unionists and of non-unionists, who may well fight back. Recessions reduce promotion possibilities for many people and stop the process of dispersion of grievances through the movement of people to other jobs.

Ideally, an economy would be so structured as to spread the effects of inflation and unemployment equitably across the whole society. Since this is not the case, economic mismanagement by governments has an intensified effect on industrial relations. Where there is inequity in social and economic structures there is a sort of multiplier which increases the burden of economic illness on those who are most likely to seek remedies through trade unions and other pressure groups.

Even in free enterprise societies like Australia and the United States, government actions are decisive in determining the level of economic activity, the levels of inequity and the intensity of attempts to redress the social imbalance:

> The decisive consideration government offers is its role as principal determiner of employment levels, of labour surplus or shortage ... Through arms, space, construction, stock-piling, welfare, and other expenditures that constitute the major components of the national budget and through fiscal and monetary policies that are the critical influences upon employment, price, and wage levels, it is government and businessmen acting in and through government that basically fix workers' standards of living.[11]

---

10. C. Kerr, *Labour and Management in Industrial Society*, Doubleday, New York, 1964, pp. 194–5.
11. M. Ellerman, 'The conservative political consequences of labor conflict ', in Somers (ed.), *Essays in Industrial Relations Theory*, Iowa State University Press, Ames, 1969, p. 166.

Though this statement concerns the United States, the point it makes is also true of Australia.

It is the government that chooses among conflicting economic goals and which establishes economic priorities. If there are both unemployment and inflation in an economy, for example, a government may choose to give the latter priority. That approach is based not only on a suspect economic theory, which suggests a trade-off between rates of unemployment and the rate of inflation, but also on the notion that a 'healthy' level of unemployment will keep the unions in line. The economic merits of such an approach are dubious; the industrial relations consequences of it are appalling. There is the intractable problem of equitable treatment of the unemployed and their families. Their sense of loss and betrayal can only make for long-term social division. Some might argue, in a callous way, that the social cost of unemployment is a reasonable price to pay for the disciplining of the unions. Yet the evidence suggests that the unions will not be thus disciplined. Like other institutions, unions adapt to changed circumstances. As unemployment persists unions learn to live with it—they ignore it, at least as an influence on their bargaining. If a claim seems reasonable, or likely to be won, they will go ahead with it regardless of the reserve arm of the unemployed. Under such circumstances the unemployed bear much for the sake of a negligible social return.

The speed and manner of government response to economic change is as important as the actual content of the response. Rapid growth or a severe economic downturn invite precipitative government action: the immediate removal of subsidies or bounties, large-scale changes in tariffs, sizeable revaluations or devaluations, the hasty destruction of health services and changes to tax structure. Each of these might have some other economic or political merit but they make for poor industrial relations. Gradual change allows for peaceful and rational readjustment of conflicting interests.

It is particularly important that governments deal intelligently and carefully with rapid technological change. Again, employers and employees can adjust more effectively to change which is gradual and controlled. In Australia, governments directly control a number of industries, such as transport and communications, in which there has been persistent technological innovation. Clumsiness in handling those changes has provoked a good deal of industrial strife. Innovation by private employers may also be influenced by government policy on investment and depreciation allowances, interest rates, import controls, loan funds, overseas borrowing and the terms of government contracts. Use of those devices may reduce the conflict brought about by sudden change.

Governments may also contribute to social and economic peace through their efforts to integrate groupings within society:

> To the extent that workers and employers consider themselves primarily citizens with roughly equal status, privileges and opportunity, the sting will be taken out of their relationship. The greater the social mobility, the more

mixed in membership the community's occupational composition, the more accepted the conditions of workers and the greater their participation in general community life ... the less violent will be the industrial conflict in the long run.[12]

Governments control the most important means of making or ending social divisions. The government may create and sustain education systems which allow fully equal opportunities to all children, or they may sustain an elitist system which produces a rigidly stratified society. In its employment practices the government may give the clear impression of fairness and equality or it may, by limiting its recruiting to people of particular social and educational backgrounds, reinforce class divisions and the sort of class conflict which is expressed through industrial strife. Immigration policies may be of a type that encourage assimilation and the enrichment of Australian life, or they may be sources of a new bitterness. At the most general level immigrants need to be given every opportunity to adapt to their new country and become a part of it. They need to learn to speak English, to live scattered throughout the community, to have the same access to good housing and other necessities and to have the same sorts of opportunities to work and to be promoted as any other Australian. In the workplace, the trade qualifications of immigrants need to be recognised. Training and promotion opportunities should not be the special preserve of the older-established ethnic groups. Where immigrant workers are part of a stratum of unskilled, lowly paid workers who have no real future or opportunity but to be exploited, industrial relations will suffer.

In the second half of the twentieth century, governments regulate so much of economic and social life, and in such detail, that they cannot avoid a clear and direct responsibility for the nature of the environment in which industrial relations are conducted. There is no case at all to be made that governments are in some sense neutral or detached from the conflicts of the marketplace. By its choice of political and economic philosophies the government sets limits on what employers and employees can do, determines the content of many of their grievances and directly provokes or suppresses social conflict. If a government is partisan, supports policies which favour one group at the expense of others, then the government makes more difficult the attainment of harmonious industrial relations.

Indeed, there has been in Australia a clear recognition of that central importance of government. In particular there has been recognition of the impact of tax policies in inducing or moderating wage claims. There is also a recognition that real standards depend on the 'social wage' as much as on the actual size of the money wage. Change in the size and effectiveness of social provision by governments, through welfare allocations and educational spending, directly alter the real standards of the

---

12. Kerr, *Labour and Management*, p. 195.

whole community. There is thus a new sense in which the government is an immediate party to industrial relations.

Shareholder

Governments are major shareholders in the Australian economy. They provide much of the essential capital infrastructure for business such as ports, roads, rail and bridges. Many important and essential services are provided by governments, either as monopolies or with the government playing a major role. Such services include health and education, the provision of water, electricity, gas and public transport. Governments actively compete with the private sector in a range of undertakings such as banking, insurance and civil aviation.

These government activities reinforce a number of factors already considered: its role as protector of the public interest; its role as an employer; its role in providing the appropriate environmental context.

International labour matters

In the main, the government's role in international labour matters embraces its functions in relation to the International Labour Organisation (the ILO), of which Australia is a foundation member, and the work of the Organisation for Economic Cooperation and Development (OECD) which Australia joined in 1971.

For most of the period since 1945 the Australian Government has been represented on the ILO's governing body, its 'executive board'. The main work of the Department of Industrial Relations in this field, in consultation with the Department of Foreign Affairs, arises from Australian participation in the various ILO conferences, meetings and committees. Work also arises from the ratification of ILO conventions, as well as from unratified conventions and recommendations, concerning which the Australian Government must provide the ILO with reports on Australian law and practice.

ILO standards have contributed to the introduction of social reform, such as the introduction of the forty-hour working week, equal pay for work of equal value, efforts to eliminate discrimination in employment and occupation, employee participation/industrial democracy and greater job security.

The ILO has a tripartite structure which includes government, trade union and employer association representation. The activities of these representatives are financed by the government. One former Minister for Industrial Relations has noted the benefits of Australian contacts with 'their overseas counterparts', namely 'first-hand knowledge of overseas developments and the ability to put the Australian situation into an international context'.[13]

The interchange of ideas and information is also an important part of

---

13. A. Street (Minister for Employment and Industrial Relations), 'Government responsibilities—government policies', address to 47th ANZAAS Congress, Hobart, 14 May 1976, p. 19.

Australia's involvement in the activities of the OECD Manpower and Social Affairs Committee whose interests are closely related to industrial relations matters.

Administering policy

If the rules which governments make are to be followed, they must be effectively administered. In the states, the responsibility for that rests with the variously named Departments of Labour and Industry. The equivalent Commonwealth Department has been called, successively: Labour and National Service (1940), Labour (1972), Labor and Immigration (1974), Employment and Industrial Relations (1975), Industrial Relations (1978), Employment and Industrial Relations (1982) and Industrial Relations (1986). In 1989 the Department of Industrial Relations employed 750 staff. The Department's role is:

> To assist the Government in achieving its industrial relations and wider economic and social objectives through policies and programs aimed at promoting and assisting the achievement of a competitive, efficient and flexible labour market; providing and maintaining an effective industrial relations system which is fair to all parties; promoting fair wages and conditions for all workers while assisting Australia's economic and industrial performance; fulfilling the role and responsibilities of the Government as an employer to ensure fair and responsible treatment of its workforce; and maintaining a working environment which enables the Department's staff to develop their skills and abilities and contribute to their full potential.[14]

In performing its functions, the Department has a number of responsibilities. These include:

- development, implementation and operation of the Government's industrial relations and incomes policies;
- advice to the Government on industrial relations developments and an active role in dispute prevention and resolution;
- promotion of sound industrial practices including participative management and work practices, together with facilitation of labour market and workplace reform;
- preparation and presentation of the Government's submissions to National Wage Cases and other cases before the Industrial Relations Commission;
- maintenance and development of the Australian industrial relations legislative framework, e.g. the *Industrial Relations Act 1988*;
- ensuring compliance with federal awards by operation of the Arbitration Inspectorate;
- policy on all portfolio legislation;
- preparation and presentation of the Government's submissions to the Remuneration Tribunal in respect of parliamentarians, the judiciary, statutory office holders, departmental heads, etc.;
- the Government's employer role in negotiation and determination of pay

---

14. Department of Industrial Relations, *Annual Report 1988–89*, AGPS, Canberra, 1989, p. 2.

and conditions for Public Service staff and the Australian Defence Force;
- coordination of pay and conditions in all areas of Australian Government Employment to ensure compliance with the Government's national policies;
- servicing the Remuneration, Defence Force Remuneration and Pharmaceutical Benefits Remuneration Tribunals and the Medical Fees and Optometrical Fees Inquiries;
- administration of legislation in respect of Government employees;
- administration of special legislation relating to the stevedoring and coal-mining industries;
- assessment of qualifications for formal recognition of trades skills under the *Tradesmen's Rights Regulation Act 1946*;
- Australia's membership of the International Labour Organisation and the Government's interests in industrial relations issues within the OECD's work program.[15]

The Department consists of five divisions and two discrete branches which report directly to the Secretary.[16]

The Industrial Relations Policy Division is responsible for the development and implementation of wages and employment conditions policies and for the provision of advice about those policies.

The Industrial Relations Development Division is responsible for advising the government of industrial relations developments at the state government, industry and enterprise levels; the development and implementation of industrial relations strategies directed to improving industry performance and the national economy; the administration of certain legislation in the stevedoring and coal-mining industries; and for the federal labour inspection service.

The Australian Government Employment Remuneration and Conditions Division is responsible for the provision of fair and reasonable conditions of employment for public service and Defence Force staff in Australia and overseas, and for ensuring consistent application of the government's wages and industrial relations policies in other areas of Australian Government employment.

The Legislation and Review Division is responsible for the provision of expert policy advice on legal and related issues, the provision of technical and legal support to other areas of the Department, including advocacy services, and for the provision of policy advice and services in relation to Australia's international obligations.

The Corporate Services Branch develops, coordinates and implements management policy and strategies which aim to ensure the efficient administrative functioning of the Department, and provide administrative and portfolio support services.

The Parliamentary Secretariat and Communication Branch provides coordination of the Department's and portfolio agencies' advice and services to the Minister in relation to Cabinet, parliamentary matters,

---

15. Department of Industrial Relations, *Corporate Plan 1988–89*, AGPS, Canberra, 1989, p. 16.
16. See Department of Industrial Relations, *Annual Report 1988–89*, pp. 11–12, 133–7.

ministerial correspondence, appointments and speeches. It also provides secretariat services for key consultative bodies.

The government as employer

Since 1945 the increasingly important role of the government in making social and economic policy and in directly influencing society and the economy has meant that the number of government employees has grown rapidly. Governments are the largest employers in Australia. The number of civilian employees and the proportion of the civilian workforce employed by governments is shown in Table 3.1. In 1989 almost a third of the workforce was to be found in state, federal or local government employment. Table 3.2 shows that the proportion of the total civilian workforce employed by governments has been high in all of the post-World War II period. Clearly, therefore, the governments have a significant direct part in industrial relations as employers in their own right.

Federal, state and local governments employ people in a diverse range of industries and occupations: in the maintenance of the law, through the judiciary, police forces and prisons; in essential services, such as health, education, communications, fire-fighting, electricity, gas, water, sewerage and sanitation; in social services, such as child endowment, immigrant services, unemployment and pensions; in transport and transport services, such as airlines, railways, shipping, buses, customs and port authorities; and in financial services, such as banking and insurance.

In some of these areas, telecommunications for example, the government has a monopoly. In others, such as banking, public services compete with private firms. In still others the government provides the primary service but there are privately owned alternative services which look after a minority of the population. Education and health services are the principal examples of that.

As employers, state and federal governments have devised many different methods of setting the wages and working conditions of their employees. Since the largest and most diverse public employer is the Federal Government, the discussion which follows will concentrate mainly on the Australian Public Service (the Service).

Problems which have followed from the making of arbitrary rules by politicians, the size of public sector employment, the manipulation of Service pay and conditions for the purposes of central economic management, and the substantial voting power of public servants have produced extensive legislation about the management of and employment in the Service. This legislation sets down employment rights and standards, delegates managerial authority away from Parliament, determines procedures for resolving industrial disputes and establishes enough checks to see that government retains ultimate control.

Table 3.1: *Employed wage and salary earners, by sector and sex, May 1988*

Sector	Men ('000)	%	Women ('000)	%	Total ('000)	%
Government						
Aust. Public Service	93.1	2.8	72.5	2.8	156.6	2.8
Other Aust. Govt	184.9	5.5	82.6	3.2	267.3	4.5
State governments	7.6	0.2	7.9	0.3	15.5	0.3
Local governments	111.7	3.3	44.0	1.7	155.7	2.6
Total	1005.9	29.8	738.9	28.7	1744.6	29.3
Private	2373.6	70.2	1836.3	71.3	4209.9	70.7
Total	3379.5	100.0	2575.2	100.0	5954.5	100.0

Source: Department of Finance, *Australian Public Sector Service Statistical Yearbook 1987–88*, AGPS, Canberra, 1989.

Table 3.2: *Relative size of public sector employment, 1945–88*

Year	Total civilian employment* ('000)	Federal government staff ('000)	% of Col. 1	Total government staff (federal, state and local) ('000)	% of Col. 1
1945	1913.7	n.a.	n.a.	525.3	27.4
1950	2546.9	201.3	7.9	662.0	25.9
1955	2803.2	210.3	7.5	736.6	26.3
1960	3126.5	227.0	7.3	798.9	25.6
1965	3604.1	262.8	7.3	906.2	25.1
1970	4340.1	329.4	7.6	1078.7	24.9
1975	4898.7	397.6	8.1	1291.1	26.4
1980	5030.4	397.3	7.9	1530.1	30.4
1983	5167.3	409.2	7.9	1582.2	30.6
1988	5954.5	432.9	7.3	1744.6	29.3

*Full-time employees
Sources: Public Service Board Statistical Yearbooks and Australian Public Sector Service Statistical Yearbook 1987–88.

The employment framework

A number of Acts of Parliament establish the ways in which the terms and conditions of Service employment are to be settled. Most of the Acts cover a specific aspect of employment. Thus the *Superannuation Act* provides a pension scheme for permanent and some long-term 'temporary' staff. The *Commonwealth Employees' Compensation Act* allows compensation for death or injury arising out of government service. The *Commonwealth Employees' Furlough Act* grants long service leave to all full-time Commonwealth employees. The *Crimes Act*, which generally defines offences against the Crown, has a section relating to public servants. Part V makes it an offence for them to disclose information, falsify government records, steal government property, impersonate other officers or obstruct other officers in the performance of their duties. The Act may be used to silence government employees and to prevent any interference with government business by trade unions.[17] The *Public Service Act* establishes mechanisms for resolving disputes between the government and certain designated groups of public servants by way of the Industrial Relations Commission.

As well as these specific Acts, there is a general-purpose *Public Service Act* which affects most areas of government employment. Under this Act the Public Service Commission is made the central personnel authority of the Service, with responsibility for the recruitment, training, supervision and efficiency of public servants. The Act divides the Service into four divisions and sets out the duties and authority of the senior management officers in the Service. Among many other things, the Act also deals with the establishment of salary increment scales, interdepartmental and interservice transfers, promotions, offences, strikes, leave, retirement and the discharging of officers.

Delegation of authority

Parliament has delegated its employer management functions. On the formation of the Commonwealth Public Service on 1 January, 1902, a Public Service Commissioner, who was virtually independent of the government in major aspects of personnel administration, was appointed. The Service then consisted of seven departments and 17,000 employees.[18]

The Commissioner had responsibility for permanent appointments, temporary appointments, appeals, examinations, promotions and remuneration.

This situation was changed by the *Public Service Act 1922* which established the Public Service Board consisting of three Commissioners, to take over the responsibilities of the Public Service Commissioner. The responsibilities of the new Board for personnel management were much the same as those of the former Commissioner. The Board also had responsibility for promoting economies and efficiency.

In 1930 an amendment to the *Public Service Act* led again to a Commission with a single Commissioner. In 1947, by which time the Services employed more than 100,000 in twelve departments, a three-member board was reconstituted. This board continued to operate until 1987 when the Public Service Commission was established.

The purpose of delegating the personnel management functions of the Service is 'to maintain the independence of the recruitment, promotion, discipline and retirement functions from political involvement'.[19] Accordingly, the Commission has been established with independent

---

17. I.G. Sharp, 'The regulation of conditions of government employment', in Isaac, J.E. and Ford, G.W. (eds), *Australian Labour Relations Readings*, Sun Books, Melbourne, 1971, pp. 420–50.
18. Public Service Commissioner, *Annual Report 1987–88*, AGPS, Canberra, 1989, p. 69.
19. Treasurer P. Keating, Economic Statement, 13 May 1987.

statutory responsibility for the policy aspects of recruitment, promotion, dismissal, mobility and retirement of government employees. The Commission consists of a full-time Public Service Commissioner, a Deputy Commissioner and support staff. It has four branches which cater for its major responsibilities: a staffing branch, recruitment branch, staff development branch and selection and placement branch. It also has four special units or sections. These are concerned with equal employment opportunity, information systems, corporate support and secretariat functions, respectively. Unlike its predecessors, the Commission does not have responsibility for pay and conditions. It does not negotiate with public sector unions or get involved with the arbitration of pay claims. These responsibilities now reside with the Department of Industrial Relations. Responsibility for equal employment opportunity, industrial democracy and occupational health and safety programs have also been devolved to department heads.

The Commission is assisted by the Australian Public Service Management Advisory Board. This part-time Board consists of the Commissioner, the Secretaries of a number of nominated departments, a union representative and a private sector management representative. The Board provides a forum for consideration of major management activities affecting the Australian Public Service as a whole, and advises the government in these matters.

The Commission was established at a time of significant Service-wide reorganisation which resulted in the displacement of a number of staff. Its initial preoccupation has been with the fair treatment of these staff, including the large number displaced from the former Public Service Board. Another important area has been that of staff development. The Commission has had an important role in monitoring equal employment opportunities within the Service. It is also active in establishing staff appraisal procedures for the Service and in meeting the challenges of an ageing Service. There has been a decrease in the number of young people recruited. The Service's age profile shows a distinct plateau between the ages of 25 and 38.[20]

There are several reasons why parliament delegates authority to the Public Service Commission. The first is the 'notion that staffing the Civil Service should be a function of an independent agency, the objective being to eliminate political patronage as the basis for appointment and preferment of staff and to promote on merit'.[21] Even if political patronage were not a problem, the amount of work involved in administering a large number of employees spread through the country would make direct parliamentary control impossible. A single board or commission, moreover, prevents the public sector from being

> ... divided into thirty or forty separate distinct sections, each competing against the other, each setting different conditions of employment, each

---

20. Public Service Commissioner, *Annual Report 1987–88*, AGPS, Canberra, p. 8.
21. G.E. Caiden, *Public Employment Compulsory Arbitration in Australia*, Institute of Labour and Industrial Relations, University of Michigan, 1971, p. 37.

offering different opportunities, so that employees in one section doing exactly the same work as employed in others might be treated quite differently, thereby resulting in anomalies and injustice.[22]

The Commission ensures uniformity and standardisation of treatment, impartiality in appeals against the employing authority and a widening of career opportunities from one department or agency to the whole Service.

In establishing employment conditions the Commission attempts— and not entirely unsuccessfully—to steer a middle course between providing fair and enlightened conditions and avoiding extravagant or pace-setting conditions. The Australian Public Service has been a main innovator in allowing flexible working hours and in providing employment opportunities for women, Aborigines and the handicapped.

Industrial relations machinery

Industrial conflict is no more avoidable in public employment than in the private sector. The size of the Service and its complex structure of jobs and classifications, the dual role of the Public Service Commission in making rules and monitoring efficiency, the insecurities created by inflation, the need to maintain some relationship between pay in the Service and pay outside it, the impossibility of completely taking politics out of the Service, and the problems in dealing with many unions, all make for grievances and all demand machinery for dealing with grievances. The machinery takes two forms: the Joint Council of the Australian Public Service, which is a staff–management consultative body, and the arbitration tribunals.

The Joint Council consists of nineteen members. It is chaired by the Secretary of the Department of Industrial Relations. A union representative acts as Deputy Chairperson. Management representatives include the Public Service Commissioner and senior members (Deputy Secretaries and First Assistant Secretaries) of a number of departments. There are a further eight public sector union representatives. The Council may make recommendations on any matter, apart from pay and government policy. As an advisory body the Council's decisions are not binding. Nevertheless, a high proportion of its recommendations have been accepted.[23] The subjects considered by the Council since its meeting in 1947 have ranged from minor conditions of service, such as district allowances and travelling allowances, to the employment of women, and alcoholism and drug dependency.

The first Service arbitration tribunal, the Public Service Arbitrator, was established in 1911. The tribunal was established largely to remove delays in hearing Service grievances because of a congestion of cases before the Court of Conciliation and Arbitration. Since then, other specific tribunals have been established to deal with specific workers or

---

22. Ibid., p. 51.
23. Ibid., p. 59.

industries, including the Academic Salaries Tribunal, the Flight Crew Officers Industrial Tribunal and the Remuneration Tribunal.

Until 1952 the Conciliation and Arbitration Commission and the Public Service Arbitrator had no formal links with each other. In 1952, however, an amendment to the *Public Service Arbitration Act* allowed the Public Service Arbitrator to refer matters to the Commission and allowed appeals from the Arbitrator to the Commission on the grounds of public interest. This appeal system restricted the public sector from going too far ahead of the private in its levels of pay and generosity of conditions. Matters which thus came to the Conciliation and Arbitration Commission were heard by a Full Bench, in the case of an appeal, or the Full Bench plus the Public Service Arbitrator, in the cases referred for consideration.

In 1976 the Report of the Royal Commission on Australian Government Administration recommended the absorption of the Public Service Tribunal into the Conciliation and Arbitration Commission. Legislation repealing the *Public Service Arbitration Act* was enacted in late 1983. On 1 June 1984 Division 1A of the *Conciliation and Arbitration Act* was proclaimed. This provided for the absorption of the jurisdiction of the Public Service Arbitrator within the Conciliation and Arbitration Commission by the creation of a special Public Service Panel.

The *Industrial Relations Act 1988* absorbed the functions of other tribunals into the renamed Industrial Relations Commission.

Ultimate control

The delegation of managerial authority, the resolution of conflict through tribunals, and the formulation of a framework of rules and regulations defining employees' rights and responsibilities, have, to a large degree, depoliticised many aspects of government employment relations. Arbitration has ensured

> equality before an independent third party rather than an unequal contest between a powerful independent central personnel agency—backed by employing authorities and the Commonwealth Government—and weak public employee organisations which [are] unable to strike, speak out on internal issues, or investigate outside conditions, and which are isolated from, and suspected by, the general labour movement. Arbitration has spread results more quickly across the public service than individual and separate negotiations.[24]

The *Public Service Act* and Regulations have provided an orderly, open method of recruitment, promotion, appeals and discipline; have established compensation, leave and superannuation conditions as rights rather than matters dependent on the mood of government of the day; and have removed employees from the uncertainties of authoritarian arbitrary rule. The operations of the Public Service Commission have circumscribed the actions of ministers and permanent heads, and

---

24. Ibid., p. 93.

made direct involvement by government less likely and more politically unacceptable.

However, while they have been prepared to delegate much of their managerial authority and, as employers, to submit to the determinations of tribunals, national governments have not completely relinquished control over their employees. Parliament has reserved to itself important checks which, though rarely used, still make it the ultimate employing authority. In part this is because some aspects of public service employment—in particular the size of the Service and its areas of operation—are not apolitical questions. On such issues it is Parliament, and not the Service, that must answer to the electorate:

> It is only the Government ... which can decide what functions are to be performed by the various departments. The decision is a peculiarly political one, and is affected by the views which any government may hold or the electorate may demand ... Since only the Government can determine these matters, no Government can escape its responsibility for reviewing these functions to determine whether any of them are unnecessary or performed to an undue extent ... Such problems [cannot] be off-loaded on to some entirely non-political body.[25]

Government controls, overt and covert, allow Parliament to be the ultimate arbiter of public service conditions. The members of the Industrial Relations Commission and of the Public Service Commission are government appointees. This gives the government of the day some ability to appoint people who will be likely to act in general agreement with government policy. Rules can be adjusted or made to circumscribe these authorities in the event of their performance being at variance with government wishes. Parliament has further reserved for itself a right of appeal by its ministers against the decisions of these authorities.[26] In addition, all regulations made by the Public Service Commission, the determinations made by the Industrial Relations Commission, must be tabled in both houses of national parliament. During the period of tabling the provisions can be disallowed by parliament. Legislation conferring rights on employees is not immutable. It may be changed to employees' advantage (for example, the provision for an extra week's annual recreation leave in 1974). Conversely it may be altered to the detriment of employees (for example, the enactment of management-initiated retirement has substantially altered the permanent nature of public employment). Government directives to the Public Service Commission, such as those imposing staff ceilings, are another effective form of government control.

The use of all these powers will be coloured not only by the prevailing economic conditions but also by political philosophy. In 1971, Caiden described the Federal Labor Party as

---

25. Speech by R.G. Menzies, recorded in the *Report of the Royal Commission on Australian Government Administration*, AGPS, Canberra, 1976, p. 246.
26. Ministers may appeal against decisions to a full bench of the Industrial Relations Commission.

... a socialist party [that] endorses public ownership of enterprises, enlarged national social services, and by implication the expansion of the federal public service ... It believe[s] the government should be a model employer. It should lead the way in safety measures, workmen's compensation, pension schemes, and increased industrial democracy. It should offer liberal conditions of employment to force other employers to follow suit.[27]

The Liberal–National Party Coalition, on the other hand

had no formulated policy other than its general disposition towards labour and unionism and a vague concept of comparability. It has been concerned to let the system regulate itself without much direction from above. Its main concern has been governmental costs and inflationary pressures. At peak periods of inflationary pressure, it has cut back the employing organ's budgetary allocation, reduced the size of establishments, and delayed, where it could, pay increases.[28]

The contrasting behaviour of the Whitlam and Fraser governments lends support to Caiden. In the three years of Labor Government, from 1972 to 1975, the federal public service grew by more than 50,000 workers and diversified its operations, particularly in health insurance, transport and tertiary education. Local government authorities received unprecedented financial support and became important partners in decentralisation and job-creating programs. Public service conditions, according to private employer submissions to the Royal Commission on Australian Government Administration, became pace-setting.[29] Legislation increased annual leave from three to four weeks, liberalised maternity leave and introduced paternity leave. Union officials were appointed as employee representatives on several boards of management, while in some instances, the employees were allowed to elect their own representatives.[30]

Under the Fraser Government these trends were reversed. Employee representatives on management committees were removed and tight operational budgets imposed.[31] Staff ceilings were enforced, with the result that public service employment fell by more than 10,000 from 1975 to 1977. During this period, as state governments attempted to reduce unemployment and as local governments expanded in the wake of greater financial assistance, total public sector employment increased from 27 per cent to 31 per cent of the civilian workforce. The proportion of total government employees in the Australian Public Service, however, fell from 31 per cent to 26 per cent during this same period. Some of the distinctive (in the sense that the Commission has refused to use them as norms) gains made by employees of the Australian Public Service under Labor were lost. Thus maternity leave was reduced and

---

27. Caiden, *Public Employment*, p. 87.
28. Ibid., p. 89.
29. *Report of the Royal Commission*, p. 280.
30. The Australian Broadcasting Commission, for example.
31. For example, the staff no longer elected a Commissioner, the budget was reduced by 28 per cent and staff by 14 per cent, between 1975 and 1978.

paternity leave abolished.[32] 'Management-initiated retirement' removed the security of tenure once enjoyed by Service employees. In addition, the *Commonwealth Employees' (Employment Provisions) Act 1977* added to the constraints imposed on industrial action by government employees. Thus, the Minister for Industrial Relations said in the second reading speech before Parliament:

> The Bill . . . [will] enable Commonwealth Government employing authorities, in the public interest, to suspend from duty, or in appropriate circumstances dismiss, government employees who have taken industrial action which disrupts the provision of services to the Australian community; and stand down, without pay, government employees who cannot be usefully employed as a result of industrial action taken by fellow government employees, or by workers in private industry . . .

The Hawke Labor Government repealed this Act in 1983. Whatever the extent of consultative and arbitral machinery, governments do finally determine, as their consciences dictate, the conditions under which their employees work. Recent government approaches to matters affecting both the public sector and the general industrial relations environment are covered more fully in subsequent chapters.

Summary

Governments are not neutral in any system of industrial relations. They usually regulate procedural rules and, in many instances, also complement the substantive rule-making processes of tribunals and the parties. As major employers governments are also in a position to establish standards which will flow on to the private sector. Governments can play an important role in minimising industrial relations conflicts through 'strategic mediation'—the ordering of society in such a way as to minimise social and economic conflicts. Governments have created elaborate machinery for the administration of labour policies and the regulation of public employment. Notwithstanding, both areas remain heavily influenced by the political philosophy of the party in government.

Discussion questions

1. Why should governments be regarded as important parties to any system of industrial relations?
2. Explain the machinery which the Federal Government has established for regulating the conditions of employment of its own employees.

---

32. The *Maternity Leave (Government Employees) Act 1973* increased maternity leave to a total of fifty-two weeks, twelve of them on full pay. The Act also allowed one week's paternity leave. In 1978, paternity leave was abolished and paid leave for maternity purposes standardised at twelve weeks, after a twelve-month qualifying period.

3. Explain what is meant by the government's auxiliary, regulatory and restrictive functions in industrial relations.
4. Why have governments found it necessary to establish an elaborate employment apparatus for their own employees?
5. Industrial relations 'are only part of the whole set of relationships and processes which make up a society and an economy'. What is the implication of this statement for government attempts to reduce industrial conflict?
6. Explain the apparatus employed for administering the Federal Government's industrial relations policies.
7. 'Public service employment can never by fully depoliticised.' Discuss the industrial relations implications of this statement.
8. Explain the ways in which the Federal Government maintains ultimate control over conditions of employment of public servants. Why have these controls been thought necessary?
9. Explain the similarities and differences between public sector and private sector arbitration. Account for the differences.

Further reading

Armstrong, E.G., *Industrial Relations: An Introduction*, George Harrap & Co., London, 1969, Ch. 5.

Caiden, G.E., *Public Employment Compulsory Arbitration in Australia*, Institute of Labour and Industrial Relations, University of Michigan, 1971.

Kahn-Freund, O., 'Industrial relations and law—retrospect and prospect', *British Journal of Industrial Relations*, vol. 7, no. 3, 1969.

Keller, B.K., 'The role of the state as corporate actor in industrial relations system', 8th World Congress of the International Industrial Relations Association, Brussels, 1990, vol. 5, pp. 51–67.

Martin, R.M., 'Trade unions and Labor governments in Australia: study of the relation between supporting interests party policy', in C.A. Hughes (ed.), *Readings in Australian Government*, University of Queensland Press, Brisbane, 1968.

McCarthy, P.G., 'The living wage in Australia—the role of government', *Labour History*, no. 18, 1970.

OECD, 'The search for consensus' in *The Role of Institutional Dialogue Between Government, Labour and Employers*, OECD Paris, 1982.

Plowman, D.H., 'Wage determination and the public sector', *Growth* 33, September 1983.

Report of the Royal Commission on Australian Government Administration, AGPS, Canberra, 1976, Section 9.6 and Appendix 4.1.

Trou, T. (ed.), 'Public service labour relations: recent trends and future prospects. A comparative survey of seven industrialised market economy countries'. ILO Geneva, 1987.

CHAPTER 4

The Federal Tribunal System

This chapter examines the structure and organisation of the federal tribunal system. It reviews the Australian Industrial Relations Commission's composition, organisation and role in award/agreement making. The chapter also looks at the role of the Federal Court of Australia (Industrial Division), the Industrial Registries and Boards of Reference. The important position of the Australian Industrial Relations Commission in relation to other industrial tribunals is also examined. Because of the major influence the Australian Constitution has had on the division of industrial powers between federal and state governments and, therefore, on the jurisdiction and operations of federal tribunals, the first part of this chapter looks at the industrial powers of the Federal Government.

The constitutional context

Among the influences at work on the people who made the Australian Constitution were two that were to be especially important in making the Commonwealth—and not the states— dominant in Australian industrial relations. The first was the memory of strikes and lock-outs in the 1890s of a scale and bitterness which threatened the whole fabric of the state. The second was the long political debate about whether the colonies should allow free imports of goods or should set up tariffs to protect local industries.

Though apparently distinct, the two problems were related. How could employers and employees agree about wages if employers had constantly to battle against cheap goods from overseas? A fair wage that would satisfy employees might well price employers' goods out of the market. One of the advantages of a protective tariff might be to allow employers sufficient latitude in settling the price of a product to be able to pay a fair wage. It would be necessary, of course, to make sure that employers did pay the fair wage. The new model protection, indeed, would establish tribunals to define a 'fair wage' and to enforce its payment. Industry would thus thrive and industrial disputes disappear from the land. The Constitution and a number of Acts of the young Commonwealth Parliament created the powers and the institutions which were to make the new protection work.[1] The operation of 'New Protection' is reviewed in Chapter 11.

The Constitution conferred several powers on the Commonwealth, which allowed it to legislate on industrial relations: the industrial power, the incidental power, the trade and commerce power, the defence power and the exclusive power.[2] The most important of these is the industrial power, which lies in section 51 (xxxv) of the Constitution. It allows the Federal Government to make laws with respect to 'conciliation and arbitration for the prevention and settlement of industrial disputes extending beyond the limits of any one State'. This does not allow Parliament to legislate generally about the terms and conditions of employment, only to set up tribunals.[3] Moreover, the tribunals may have jurisdiction only if there is an industrial dispute and the dispute is interstate. Nor does this allow *compulsory* arbitration.

The ability to make arbitration compulsory derives from Section 98 (xxxix), which allows Parliament to legislate on 'matters incidental to the execution of the powers assigned it under the Constitution'. That is to say, Parliament may make laws which will make the exercise of its power effective. Thus the power to legislate for the registration of unions is incidental to the execution of s.51 (xxxv). Similarly, compulsion has been deemed incidental to the power to establish tribunals.

Authority to legislate directly on the terms and conditions of employment for some groups of workers comes from other sections of the Constitution. The defence power 'includes not only a power to prepare for war and to prosecute war, but also power to wind up after a war and to restore conditions of peace'.[4] Throughout the emergency period the government may regulate the workforce, wages, prices and rationing. In peace-time the defence power gives the government control over the wages and conditions of the armed forces and of people engaged in military service and research or in defence projects on Commonwealth property. Further, under s.98 of the Constitution, the Commonwealth may make laws about interstate and international commerce, including the transport services: navigation, shipping and airlines.

---

1. On the 'new protection', see R. Gollan, *Radical and Working Class Politics*, MUP, 1967.
2. See O. de R. Foenander, *Industrial Conciliation and Arbitration in Australia*, Law Book Co., Sydney, 1959, Chapter 1.
3. E.I. Sykes, 'Labour arbitration in Australia', in J.E. Isaac and G.W. Ford (eds), *Australian Labour Relations*, Sun Books, Melbourne, 1971, p.355.
4. Latham, C.J. (1956), *73 Commonwealth Law Reports* (hereafter, CLRO), at p. 176, cited by Foenander, *Industrial Conciliation and Arbitration in Australia*, Law Book Co., Sydney, revised edition 1971, p. 17.

The Federal Government had created several tribunals, such as the Stevedoring, Maritime and Flight Crew Officers tribunals, to determine conditions of employment and resolve industrial disputes in these industries. Most of these tribunals have been absorbed into the newly constituted Australian Industrial Relations Commission.[5]

The government also acquires authority to deal directly in the terms and conditions of employment of some workers from its 'exclusive power'. This largely concerns the public service. The Commonwealth Government may make laws on 'matters relating to any department of the public service the control of which is by this Constitution transferred to the Executive Government of the Commonwealth'. Recent High Court decisions suggest that the Commonwealth foreign affairs powers may be a future source of authority in the area.

The legislation which put the Commonwealth's industrial power into effect was the *Commonwealth Conciliation and Arbitration Act 1904*. The purposes of the Act were:
1. to prevent lock-outs and strikes in relation to industrial disputes;
2. to constitute a Commonwealth Court of Conciliation and Arbitration having jurisdiction for the prevention and settlement of industrial disputes;
3. to provide for the exercise of the jurisdiction of the Court by conciliation with a view to amicable agreement between the parties;
4. in default of amicable agreement between the parties, to provide for the exercise of the jurisdiction of the Court by equitable award;
5. to enable states to refer industrial disputes to the Court, and to permit the working of the Court and of state industrial authorities in aid of each other;
6. to facilitate and encourage the organisation of representative bodies of employers and of employees and the submission of industrial disputes to the Court by organisations, and to permit representative bodies of employers and of employees to be declared organisations for the purpose of this Act;
7. to provide for the making and enforcement of industrial agreement between employers and employees in relation to industrial disputes.

To realise those ambitions the Commonwealth established a Court of Conciliation and Arbitration. The purposes of the original Act may be compared with their most recent formulation given below.

Influence of the federal tribunals

At first the Court of Conciliation and Arbitration attracted little notice. The first President of the Court, indeed, was a judge of the High Court who attended to conciliation and arbitration part-time. Since there were

---

5. The Coal Industry Tribunal, the Remuneration Tribunal and the Committee of Reference for Defence Force Pay have not been absorbed into the Industrial Relations Commission.

no federally registered unions until 1906, he had little to do in 1904 and 1905. The only case which came before him in 1905 concerned the registration of a railwaymen's union. In 1906 the Court made only five awards, all for the maritime industry.

It was the *Excise Tariff Act 1906* which made the federal Court attractive to unions. This Act was the other half of the legislation needed to establish the New Protection. Under the Act employers could apply for a certificate of exemption which would allow them tariff protection against overseas competition. The granting of the certificate depended on employers paying a fair and reasonable wage to their workers. It was Mr Justice Higgins, second President of the Court, who made the first attempt to define the fair wage in the Harvester case of 1907. Higgins' judgment established a basic wage of seven shillings a day. Since that rate was above the minimum rates set down by the existing state tribunals, many unions sought federal registration. The *Excise Tariff Act* was subsequently found by the High Court to be *ultra vires*, but the Court's continued use of the Harvester standard and of the concept of a basic wage continued to attract unions. By 1912, ninety-six unions had registered with the Federal Court.

With the passage of time the federal system has come to dominate conciliation and arbitration in Australia. Nearly 90 per cent of the workforce come under tribunal awards, and nearly a third of the work force come under federal tribunal awards (Tables 4.1 and 4.2).

The great weight of the federal system is seen clearly in comparision with the separate state systems (Table 4.3). The largest of the states, New South Wales, covers only 16 per cent of the male workforce as against 40.0 per cent under federal awards. Nationally. the majority of male workers who are covered by awards are covered by federal awards.

Apart from the attraction of the federal tribunal, which derives from its setting of, successively, the basic wage, the minimum wage and the national wage, there are a number of other reasons for the growth of the federal system. First, the defence, exclusive, trade and commerce powers have placed a large proportion of the workforce under direct federal control. As the largest employer, the government brings about 10 per cent of the total civilian workforce under federal jurisdiction. The trade and commerce powers, in addition, place many large industries under federal control. They include the postal, telecommunications, maritime, stevedoring, tourist, airline, interstate transport, finance and banking industries. The general industry pattern of state and federal awards is shown in Table 4.4.

Another important reason for the growth of the federal system has been the High Court's broad interpretation of s.51 (xxxv) in constitutional test cases. Few people who have wanted to be covered by federal awards, for example, have been disqualified on the constitutional grounds of want of jurisdiction.[6] A dispute, furthermore, has been taken

---

6. P.A. Riach and W.A. Howard, *Productivity and Wage Determination*, Wiley, Sydney, 1973, p. 75.

Table 4.1: *Proportion of workforce under awards of tribunals, Australia, 1989*

	Males %	Females %	Persons %
Federal awards, etc.	40.0	21.6	32.6
State awards, etc.	40.5	63.4	49.8
Unregistered agreements	2.9	2.4	2.6
Award-free	16.6	12.6	15.0
Total	100.0	100.0	100.0

Source: ABS, *Incidence of Awards*, Cat. no. 6315.0.

to exist if some demand has been made and refused. A strike or lock-out is not necessary. The serving of the demand on the other party or parties in more than one state has been sufficient to meet the interstate criterion. And though the High Court has been unpredictable in its interpretation of what constitutes an industry and therefore of what constitutes an industrial dispute, the Act itself has been broad in its definition: '... all matters pertaining to the relations of employers and employees'. With some exceptions, there have not been significant obstacles either to registering federally or having particular matters arbitrated.

The growth of interstate unionism also has been important.[7] The half of Australia's unions which operate in more than one state account for 83 per cent of all unionists. There is a difference to be observed here between male and female workers. Women are predominantly covered by state unions and awards in teaching, nursing, social welfare, the state public services, retailing and clerical work.

Some of these areas have remained under state jurisdiction because, until 1983, it was held by the High Court that employees in occupations such as teaching, nursing and state public services could not engage in industrial disputes within the meaning of s.51(xxxv) because they were not engaged in an industry or in work of an industrial nature. The word 'industrial' was seen to confine the constitutional conception of industrial dispute to disputes in productive industry and organised business carried on for the purpose of making profits. Under this restricted interpretation, unions covering such occupations were not able to obtain federal awards. In the Australian Social Welfare Union Case of 1983 the High Court chose to give a more realistic interpretation to the term 'industrial dispute', namely a dispute between employees and employers about the terms and conditions of employment. This interpretation has given those employees who were formerly not seen as being engaged in an industry the opportunity to seek federal awards. The long-term outcome of the High Court decision may be to increase the dominance of the

---

7. R.J. Hawke, 'The growth of the courts authority', in J.R. Niland and J.E. Isaac (eds), *Australian Labour Economics Readings*, Sun Books, Melbourne, 1975 p. 42.

Table 4.2 Proportion of workforce under awards of tribunals, by state, Australia, May 1985

State	Federal awards			State awards		
	Males (%)	Females (%)	Persons (%)	Males (%)	Females (%)	Persons (%)
New South Wales	36.0	19.9	29.6	45.4	64.4	53.0
Victoria	51.1	26.0	40.8	27.3	59.0	40.3
Queensland	27.8	12.6	21.7	53.7	73.4	61.6
South Australia	43.6	14.8	31.6	40.2	75.6	55.0
Western Australia	23.0	13.7	19.2	53.7	65.1	58.4
Tasmania	45.1	18.1	33.5	39.2	67.2	51.2
Northern Territory	76.3	82.3	78.6	—	—	—
Australian Capital Territory	84.0	90.6	86.8	—	—	—
Australia	40.0	21.6	32.6	40.5	63.4	49.8

Source: ABS, Incidence of Awards, Cat. no. 6315.0.

Table 4.3: *Proportion of workforce by tribunal jurisdiction, Australia, May 1985*

	Proportion		
Tribunal	Males (%)	Females (%)	Persons (%)
Federal tribunals	40.0	21.6	32.6
New South Wales tribunals	15.7	21.7	18.1
Victorian tribunals	7.4	16.1	10.9
Queensland tribunals	8.1	10.8	9.2
Western Australian tribunals	4.7	5.9	5.2
South Australian tribunals	3.5	6.9	4.9
Tasmania tribunals	1.0	2.0	1.4
Other award free	16.6	12.6	15.0

Source: Calculated from ABS, *Incidence of Awards*, Cat. no. 6315.0.

federal tribunals relative to those of the states. Already unions covering teachers, university academics and nurses have been successful in obtaining federal registration which was previously denied them. It would now seem that all employees, other than those working in state government public services, have the potential to come under federal awards.

The potential growth in federal jurisdiction must be balanced by the fact that there has been a decline in the proportion of employees under federal awards (from 39 per cent in 1974 to 32.6 per cent in 1985). This decline is the result of structural changes which have reduced employment in sectors, such as manufacturing, which are covered by federal awards.

A factor influencing the growth of federal jurisdiction has been the fact that it is the federal tribunal that decides whether an award should be a federal or state award. In the past, the Act allowed the federal tribunal to refrain from dealing with a dispute on the grounds that it should be left to a state authority. Federal tribunals rarely disqualified themselves and in some cases attempted to impose federal awards in areas already covered by a state.[8] In addition, the Commission may restrain state tribunals from handling particular disputes (s.128). The question of jurisdiction is all important. In general, since the High Court decision in the *Cowburn Case* of 1926, unions have been required to choose either state or federal awards (see Chapter 10). Where a federal award intends to regulate a matter, it takes priority over clauses touching that matter made in any state award or law. And once a union has chosen federal registration and been granted a federal award it may move back to state jurisdiction only with the permission of the Commission. So far, the Commission has not been willing to allow movement of that sort.

---

8. For example, during recent strikes in New South Wales, the Commission ruled that all refinery workers should come under federal awards. After further protracted action against this ruling, the federal and NSW governments jointly legislated to introduce a tribunal composed of federal and state tribunal personnel.

Table 4.4: *Proportion of employees affected by awards by industry, Australia, May 1985*

Industry	Males Federal (%)	Males State (%)	Females Federal (%)	Females State (%)	Persons Federal (%)	Persons State (%)
Manufacturing						
Food, etc.	25.5	56.3	20.4	69.1	24.1	59.9
Textiles, etc.	56.7	23.0	63.2	30.7	60.8	27.8
Paper and products	45.4	28.8	33.5	44.0	42.1	33.0
Chemicals and products	36.2	32.5	21.3	59.3	31.9	40.3
Metal products	62.3	22.1	49.3	37.3	60.2	24.6
Basic metal products	38.8	46.3	29.1	48.6	38.1	46.4
Fabricated metal products	61.6	17.8	42.1	42.2	57.1	22.8
Transport equipment	80.0	13.6	75.2	20.4	79.3	14.5
Other manufacturing	39.7	41.1	25.2	54.6	36.8	43.8
Total manufacturing	49.5	31.3	39.9	45.1	47.8	34.8
Non-manufacturing						
Mining	53.1	26.2	29.7	27.4	50.8	26.3
Electricity, gas, water	38.6	59.9	44.0	54.3	39.2	59.4
Construction	35.4	38.9	10.8	42.0	31.6	39.4
Wholesale	28.1	33.4	11.8	62.2	23.1	42.3
Retail	30.4	45.8	6.3	80.5	17.9	63.8
Transport and storage	55.3	31.5	47.2	29.7	54.0	31.2
Communication	99.8	—	99.6	—	99.8	—
Finance, property and business services	32.1	28.7	29.1	46.4	30.5	38.0
Public administration and defence	53.4	44.3	64.7	32.3	57.3	40.2
Community services	14.0	72.9	6.9	82.6	9.6	79.0
Recreational services	31.6	46.6	27.3	56.5	29.1	52.4
Total non-manufacturing	42.9	38.9	34.3	46.7	40.3	42.9
Total all industries	40.0	40.5	21.6	63.4	32.6	49.8

Source: ABS, *Incidence of Awards*, Cat. no. 6315.0.

The Australian Industrial Relations Commission

From the time it first established the Commonwealth Court of Conciliation and Arbitration in 1904, the *Conciliation and Arbitration Act* was amended more than seventy times, sometimes in trivial ways, sometimes in ways which have materially altered the structure of the system. Among the most important of the amendments were those of 1956 which divided the functions of the Court between the Australian Industrial Court and the Conciliation and Arbitration Commission. In 1988, following the 1985 Report of the Committee of Review into Australian Industrial Relations Law and Systems (the Hancock Report),[9] the *Conciliation and Arbitration Act* was repealed and the Australian

---

9. Report of Committee of Review, *Australian Industrial Relations Law and Systems*, in three volumes, Australian Government Publishing Service, Canberra, 1985.

Conciliation and Arbitration Commission abolished. The new Act, the *Industrial Relations Act 1988*, established a new commission, the Australian Industrial Relations Commission (the Commission). The Commission attempts to put into effect the objects of the Act, namely:
1. to promote industrial harmony and cooperation among the parties involved in industrial relations in Australia;
2. to provide a framework for the prevention and settlement of industrial disputes by conciliation and arbitration in a manner that minimises the disruptive effects of industrial disputes on the community;
3. to ensure that, in the prevention and settlement of industrial disputes, proper regard is had for the interests of the parties immediately concerned and for the interests (including the economic interests) of the Australian community as a whole;
4. to facilitate the prevention and prompt settlement of industrial disputes in a fair manner, and with the minimum of legal form and technicality;
5. to provide for the observance and enforcement of agreements and awards made for the prevention or settlement of industrial disputes;
6. to encourage the organisation of representative bodies of employers and employees and their registration under the Act;
7. to encourage the democratic control of organisations, and the participation by their members in the affairs of organisations; and
8. to encourage the efficient management of organisations. (s.3)

Composition
The Commission consists of a President, Deputy Presidents and Commissioners (s.8.2). Members of the Commission are appointed by the Governor-General (s.9.1). The President and Deputy Presidents are referred to as Presidential Members. They have the same rank, status precedence, salary and conditions as judges of the Federal Court of Australia and are entitled to be styled 'The Honourable' (ss.9.2, 9.3, 21(1), 21(2)).

Until 1972, all Presidential Members had to have appropriate legal qualifications. This provision now applies only in relation to the President. The Act lays down two requirements for this office: the person must have been a judge of a federal or state court or have been a legal practitioner for at least five years; and the person must be one who in the opinion of the Governor-General is suitable 'because of skills and experience in the field of industrial relations' (s.10.1). The President is responsible for the day-to-day operations of the Commission (s.36) and assigns the members to work in particular industry panels or to deal with particular disputes (ss.27(2), 30(2), 37 and 38). The President has the power to deal with any industrial dispute, even when another Commission member has begun to deal with the matter (s.108). To help coordinate the activies of all members of the Commission the President is required to hold a conference of members 'whenever he considers it desirable to do so but not less frequently than once in each year' (s.39). The President must also make an annual report to the Minister, for presentation to Parliament, on the extent to which the objects of the Act have been achieved (s.49). Provision is made for the appointment of an Acting President when there is a vacancy in the office or during periods when the President is absent from duty or unable to perform duties (s.17).

Deputy Presidents require the same legal qualifications as the President or may be appointed on the basis of experience 'at a high level' in industry or commerce or in the service of unions, employer bodies, government and their agencies. Deputy Presidents may also be appointed on the basis of other qualifications, namely having obtained at least five years previously a degree or equivalent qualification in law, economics or industrial relations, or in 'some other field of study considered by the Governor-General to have substantial relevance of the duties of a Deputy President' (s.10.3). In practice, most Deputy Presidents continue to have legal qualifications. There are currently thirteen Deputy Presidents. Deputy Presidents have charge of industry panels (s.37 (2)) and have special duties in relations to Full Bench cases (see below). When necessary, Acting Deputy Presidents may be appointed for specified periods (s.18).

Commissioners form the bulk of the Commission's membership. There are currently thirty-two Commissioners. They carry out most of the conciliation and arbitration work. The Act requires that Commissioners have 'appropriate skills and experience in the field of industrial relations' (s.10.3). Commissioners are called 'Commissioner' or 'Mr Commissioner' and 'are usually [persons] of proven status, experience and ability in the industrial field and are drawn from the ranks of unions, employers' organisations or government'.[10]

Each member of the Commission is required to 'keep acquainted with industrial affairs and conditions' (s.20). Members have tenured appointments and hold office until they resign or attain the age of 65 (s.16.1). The Governor-General may terminate the commission of a member on the grounds of 'proven misbehaviour or incapacity' (ss.24 and 28(1)). With the consent of the President, Commission members may perform their duties on a part-time basis (s.12.1). Members of the Commission may hold dual appointments with state tribunals, and members of state tribunals may be appointed as a member of the Commission. The duties and powers of members holding conjoint appointments are determined by the President of the Commission and the President of the relevant state authority (ss.13 and 14). Members of the Commission may also hold office as a member of a prescribed Commonwealth or territory tribunal (s.15).

---

10. Department of Labor [sic] and Immigration, *Conciliation and Arbitration in Australia*, AGPS, Canberra, 1975, p. 15.

Organisation

Most of the Commission's work is done by individual members working alone to help the parties bring about a resolution of their differences. There are, however, two important institutions within the Commission: the Full Bench and industry panels. The ability of a single arbiter to take decisions that might have a wide impact on the economy has worried governments ever since the Harvester judgment of 1907. Several amendments have consequently been made to the Act requiring matters of national economic importance to be determined by a Full Bench. A Full Bench consists of at least three members of the Commission, two of whom must be Presidential Members (s.30(2)). The Act reserves the following functions to Full Benches:

1. the making of provision for, or the alteration of, the standard hours of work in an industry;
2. the making of provision for, or the alteration of, rates of wage or the manner in which rates of wage are to be ascertained, on grounds predominantly related to the national economy and without examination of any circumstances pertaining to the work on which, or the industry in which, persons are employed;
3. the making of provision for, or the alteration of, a minimum wage that is to be payable to adults without regard to the work performed or to the industry in which they are employed; or
4. the making of provision in relation to, or the alteration of provision in relation to, annual leave with pay or long service leave with pay. (s.106(1))

Full Benches also have the task of hearing appeals or matters referred to them. The Act provides for appeals to be made against the decisions of a single member of the Commission (s.45), or for a matter to be referred to a Full Bench during the hearing stage (s.107). Either party may appeal against the decision of a Commission member. Alternatively, the Minister may request a review (s.109). If a Full Bench considers that the matter is important in the public interest, it will grant leave to appeal (s.45(2)). An appeal Full Bench may confirm, quash or vary the decision (s.45(7)). In cases where the opinion of a Full Bench is divided, the majority opinion prevails. Where the decision is equally divided, the most senior member's opinion prevails (s.35).

To obviate appeals the Act provides for a referencing system. In this case a request is made to have the matter heard by a Full Bench. The member hearing the case informs the President of the request. The President will refer the matter to a Full Bench if it is considered in the public interest to do so (s.107(2)–(6)). A reference Full Bench may include the member who normally would have heard the matter. Appeal Full Benches do not include the member whose decision is being appealed against.

The panel system dates from 1972. Before then single Commissioners had arbitrated and conciliated in particular industries. The amendments of 1972 required the President to form panels having charge of a

Table 4.5: *Panel 8, Industrial Relations Commission*

Deputy President MacBean	
Commissioner Brown	Banking services
Commissioner Turbet	Brush and broom-making industry
Commissioner Laing	Cemetery operations
	Clerical industry
	Data-processing industry
	Finance and investment services
	Furnishing industry
	Gypsum, plaster board and plaster of paris manufacturing industry
	Health and welfare services
	Health insurance industry
	Insurance industry
	Library services
	Local government administration
	Mannequins and modelling industry
	Photographic industry
	State government administration
	Travel industry
	Water, sewerage and drainage services

number of awards or industries and consisting of a Deputy President and one or more Commissioners. The panel system has been continued under the *Industrial Relations Act* (s.37). In 1989 there were eleven such panels, consisting of two to four members. The panel system is supposed to preserve the development of specialised knowledge among the Commissioners but allow for greater flexibility. Since a number of Commissioners might become familiar with the awards and operations of several industries there will be no delays to proceedings if a single Commissioner becomes ill or is delayed in other cases. The panels make for greater uniformity among awards since Commissioners will be working across a number of industries. The official view is that:

> ...the effect of the panel system has caused the Commission to work more satisfactorily... It [has] the effect of causing a greater mixture of Commissioners and Presidential Members; it creates a situation where more than one person has knowledge of a particular industry and it enables greater flexibility in the use of the Members of the Commission in the resolution of matters brought to it.[11]

The panel system is not completely free of difficulties. Each of the panels must deal with so many industries that adequate specialisation is difficult (see Table 4.5 for the list of a typical panel). Occasional changes of Commissioners from one panel to another also reduces their ability to

---

11. *Nineteenth Annual Report of the President of the Australian Conciliation and Arbitration Commission* (hereafter cited as *Annual Report*, followed by the number of the Report), AGPS, Canberra, 1975, p. 6.

specialise. Another type of problem follows from the fact that workers in one industry may be covered by different panels. On one occasion, for example, vehicle builders received wage increases from Panel 4. Clerks in the same industry, but who were covered by Panel 8, were not given a flow-on to maintain their traditional margin above the builders. The former panel was reconstituted to deal with vehicle building 'in every part thereof'.

As well as working on the panels the members of the Commission have staffed a number of specialist tribunals. Until the 1988 reformulation, Deputy Presidents formed one-person tribunals for the Snowy Mountains area, the maritime industry, the stevedoring industry, the Flight Crew Officers Industrial Tribunal and the Academic Salaries Tribunal. These specialised areas have now been absorbed into the panel system, as well as the functions of the Public Service Arbitrator. The major exception to the panel system is the arrangement for a 'resident' Commissioner for Western Australia, whose jurisdiction has regional rather than industrial boundaries. Two Commissioners also served as Deputy Public Service Arbitrators until that tribunal was abolished.

The purpose of the benches and the panels is to prevent and settle industrial disputes. The word 'dispute' suggests strikes and lock-outs and it is in dealing with large or prolonged strikes that the Commission attracts most public attention. A very small proportion of strikes in Australia, however, are settled by federal tribunals (see Table 2.12) primarily because the predominant type of strike is the twenty-four-hour demonstration stoppage. The bulk of the Commission's work is mundane. It has to do with making awards in settlement of disputes in which no strike or lock-out is contemplated. As we have already noticed, the creation of a dispute need involve no overt conflict. All that is needed is that one party, usually the employer, reject some demand made by another party, usually a union. The bulk of the Commission's work thus largely has to do with 'paper disputes'. Tables 4.6 to 4.8 show the scope of the Commission's work and the subject matter of 'paper disputes'.

Award-making

When a dispute arises the employers or the unions (or a Minister who is aware that there is a dispute) notify the relevant Presidential Member or the Registrar (s.99(1) and (2)). The Registrar notifies the Presidential Member who heads the appropriate panel (s.99(3)). That Member will attempt to conciliate in the matter, or refer it to another Commission member for conciliation, unless 'satisfied that it would not assist the prevention or settlement of the alleged industrial dispute'. In the latter case the dispute will go immediately to arbitration (s.100).

The first part of any proceedings is the finding of a dispute within the meaning of the Act, what the dispute is about, who are the parties and if the Commission has jurisdiction (s.101). The parties are encouraged, and even coerced, to negotiate and to try to resolve their differences. Where the Commission is required to become involved conciliation dominates

Table 4.6: General statement of business of the Commission 1980–81 to 1986–87 [a]

Nature of proceeding	1980–81	1981–82	1982–93	1983–84	1984–85	1985–86	1986–87
Matters lodged							
Applications							
Vary awards/agreements [b]	3145	2397	1273	2981	2528	3926	3795
Certify agreements	7	14	22	13	16	32	60
Declare common rule	32	64	51	99	14	21	15
Set award aside	1	1	nil	nil	nil	nil	nil
Compulsory conference	2	nil	nil	3	7	7	3
Union coverage	10	4	11	7	20	17	12
Appeals from							
Registrar	4	12	7	14	22	14	22
Boards of Reference	4	3	11	7	9	8	8
Full bench matters	170	375	472	345	409	265	306
Notification of dispute [c]	2044	2068	2109	2203	3192	3582	2732
bans and stand downs	12	nil	3	3	nil	2	5
boycott	—	—	nil	nil	4	3	nil
Reference from Registrar	—	—	nil	1	2	1	2
On Commission's own motion	50	2	3	7	4	9	1
Other	—	—	2	nil	nil	1	1
	5480	4942	3964	5683	6228	7895	7000

(a) For year ending 13 August.
(b) See Table 4.7 for details.
(c) See Table 4.8 for details.

Source: Annual Reports of the Australian Conciliation and Arbitration Commission, AGPS, Canberra.

Table 4.7: Analysis by subject-matter of applications to Industrial Relations Commission vary by subject matter of awards and agreements 1986–87

Subject matter	Applications	Awards	Agreements	Variations	Decisions	No further action	Not finalised
Maternity leave	—	—	—	—	—	—	—
Long service leave	—	—	—	—	—	—	—
Over-award payments	—	—	—	—	—	—	—
Employees dismissed	1	—	—	—	—	—	1
Stand down	34	—	—	7	1	9	17
Transfer	1	—	—	—	—	—	1
Special allowance	357	—	—	219	13	6	119
Overtime	17	—	—	11	—	—	6
Conditions	45	—	—	26	2	3	14
Shifts, rosters, etc.	15	—	—	4	2	3	6
Hours	50	—	—	11	2	—	37
Union membership	—	—	—	—	—	—	—
Classifications	121	—	—	42	6	5	68
Public holidays	17	—	—	11	2	—	4
Respondency	96	—	—	48	2	8	38
Service increments	—	—	—	—	—	—	—
Annual leave	21	—	—	3	12	—	6
Sick leave	3	—	—	3	—	—	—
Wages	272	—	6	87	28	4	147
National Wage	1303	—	—	1115	2	5	181
Demarcations	—	—	—	—	—	—	—
Safety provisions	—	—	—	—	—	—	—
Amenities	2	—	—	2	—	—	—
Severance pay	4	—	—	—	2	1	1
Termination, change and redundancy	5	—	—	3	—	—	2
Other	368	48	11	148	18	12	131
Total	2732	48	17	1740	92	56	779

Source: Thirty-first Annual Report of the President of the Australian Conciliation and Arbitration Commission, AGPS, Canberra, 1988, p.8.

the first stages of proceedings. It is the Commission member's responsibility to 'do everything that appears... to be right and proper to assist the parties to agree on terms for the prevention and settlement of the dispute' (s.102(1)). The member may call conferences and preside over them or the parties will confer in the member's absence (s.102(2)). Anyone directed to attend such a conference may be prosecuted for failure to do so (s.119). The main advantage of the conferences is that they allow the parties to make entirely clear what the dispute is or is not about. If, for example, the dispute is a paper dispute about the rejection of a log of claims, not all the clauses of the log will necessarily be in dispute. Conferences are a useful way of reducing a lengthy log of claims to a narrow area of disagreement. Several meetings may subsequently be held in which the Commissioner will try to bring the parties to agreement. This conciliation stage is an important part of the Commission's work. Thus, of the 2199 applications for award variations and dispute notifications finalised by the Commission in 1981–82, only fifty-one cases required arbitration.

The conciliation proceedings are considered as finished under two conditions. The first is when the parties have reached agreement and that agreement has been endorsed by the Commission (s.103(1)(a)). The Commission may endorse the agreement by either making an award in terms of the agreement (a consent award) or by certifying the agreement (s.112 and 115). The second situation is where the Commission member is satisfied that there is no likelihood that an agreement can be reached within a reasonable period (s.103(1)(b)). In this second situation the matter is referred to arbitration. However, even during the arbitration proceedings, conciliation powers may be exercised by the Commission member (s.103(2)).

Failing agreement between the parties, the dispute, or that part of the dispute which is still unresolved, is referred to arbitration (s.104(1)).

The Commission member who exercised conciliation powers may not arbitrate on the matter if any of the parties to the dispute objects (s.105). In cases where one or other of the parties objects, the conciliator makes a report to the relevant Presidential Member 'for the purpose of enabling arrangements to be made for arbitration'. The report includes the matters in dispute, the parties and the extent to which matters in dispute have been settled (s.104(3)). The report may not disclose 'anything said or done in the conciliation proceedings in relations to matters in dispute that remain unsettled' (s.104(4)). During the arbitration proceedings, the parties may not be required to disclose anything said or done during conciliation proceedings unless they agree to do so (s.104(5)). These provisions are designed to ensure that the conciliation process is not frustrated because parties fear that any concessions made, or any information given, will be used adversely against them if agreement cannot be reached. In particular, conciliation proceedings cannot reduce the ambit of the claim unless there is agreement to this effect.

The paper dispute is a legal fiction designed to ensure that the parties have the legal right to tribunal jurisdiction. This constitutional

Table 4.8: Analysis by subject matter of dispute notifications under Section 25 of the Act, 1986–87

Subject matter	Notifications	Awards made	Variations made	No further action needed	Agreements certified	Decisions	Not finalised
Long service leave	3	—	1	—	—	—	2
General logs of claims	357	69	11	12	9	30	226
Total A	360	69	12	12	9	30	228
Maternity leave	1	—	—	—	—	—	1
Over-award payments	18	—	1	3	—	—	14
Dismissals:							
Employees	325	—	6	117	—	44	158
Union representatives	18	—	—	6	—	4	8
Stand down	15	—	—	2	—	1	12
Transfer	16	—	—	2	—	2	12
Demarcations	34	—	—	6	—	1	27
Safety provisions	51	—	—	22	—	3	26
Special allowances	805	—	16	228	—	139	422
Overtime	29	—	—	12	—	—	17
Manning scale	67	—	3	13	—	12	42
Conditions	76	1	3	18	—	4	50
Amenities	6	—	—	3	—	—	3
Shift rosters	34	—	—	15	—	2	17
Hours	48	—	4	13	—	1	30
Union membership	34	—	—	16	—	—	18
Classification	70	—	4	15	—	8	43
Disputes procedures	2	—	—	1	—	—	1

Table 4.8: Analysis by subject matter of dispute notifications under Section 25 of the Act, 1986–87 (Continued)

Subject matter	Notifications	Awards made	Variations made	No further action needed	Agreements certified	Decisions	Not finalised
Public holidays	10	—	1	1	—	1	7
Right of entry	7	—	—	1	—	—	6
Service increments	1	—	—	—	—	—	1
Severance pay	17	—	2	4	—	2	9
Annual leave	10	—	1	3	—	1	5
Payment for time lost	20	—	—	7	—	—	13
Sick leave	7	—	—	1	—	—	6
Wage rates	395	9	18	65	3	31	269
Respondency	—	—	—	—	—	—	—
Termination, Change and Redundancy	4	—	—	—	—	—	4
Other	1279	94	18	303	8	70	786
Total B	3399	104	74	877	11	326	2007
Total A	360	69	12	12	9	30	228
Grand Total	3759	173	86	889	20	356	2235

Source: Thirty-first Annual Report of the President of the Australian Conciliation and Arbitration Commission, AGPS, Canberra, 1988, p.9.

requirement has given rise to the ambit log of claims which is discussed more fully in Chapter 12. While there is ambit, the paper dispute continues and so the parties may utilise the Commission's assistance. To ensure that paper disputes are long, ambit logs of claims are extravagant documents bearing little relationship to everyday realities. During negotiations the union's (or employer's) claims must be more realistic. The difference between what the union is seeking and what the employer is prepared to concede (or *vice versa*) is referred to as the *ambit of the claim*. It is the range between the claim and the response to that claim. This establishes the range within which the Commission may operate. The Commission may award the upper limit of the claim, the lower limit of the claim, any sum in between the two, or may make no variation of the award at all.

Once the ambit of the claim is settled, the Commission will hear submissions from the parties in dispute and from other parties which have been granted permission to intervene. This right of intervention is to protect parties not directly in dispute, but which are likely to be affected by the settlement. Formal statements, documents and the evidence of witnesses under oath may be offered to the Commission. There may also be job inspections and interviews with workers and management on site, in order to help the Commission understand the exact circumstances of the case. In all of this the Commission is obliged to 'act according to equity, good conscience and the substantial merits of the case, without regard to technicalities and legal forms' (s.110(2)(b)). The Act further declares that the Commission'is not bound to act in a formal manner and is not bound by any rules of evidence, but may inform itself on any matter in such manner as it considers just' (s.110(2)(a)). The Commission may 'sit at any place'; conduct its proceedings in private; adjourn to any time or place; refer any matter to any expert; summon witnesses; compel the production of documents and 'generally give all such directions, and do all such things, as are necessary or expedient for the speedy and just hearing and determination' (s.111(1)). The Commission is required to act 'in such manner as it considers appropriate', and to 'carefully and quickly inquire into and investigate the industrial dispute and all matters affecting the merits, and right settlement, of the industrial dispute' (s.110(1)). In order to expedite proceedings, the Commission may determine the periods that 'are reasonably necessary for the fair and adequate presentation of the respective cases' (s.110(3)). In certain circumstances the Commission may require that evidence and arguments be presented in writing rather than orally (s.110(4)). This may help facilitate a speedier outcome.

To help prevent the development of a stiffling legalism in the Commission's procedures, the Act provides that under normal circumstances counsel, solicitors or agents may only represent the parties 'by leave of the Commission and with the consent of all parties' (s.42(3)(a)). That consent is not required when the Commission considers that special circumstances exist which make it desirable that the parties be represented by legal counsel or if 'the Commission is satisfied that the party can only adequately be represented by counsel, solicitor or agent' (s.42(3)(b) and (c)).

This relaxed approach to arbitration is only of relatively recent origin. In the past the federal system was dominated by the archaic rituals of law. 'I never forgot my first experience in an Arbitration Court', one union secretary wrote,

> it was before a Full Bench sitting. The judges were arrayed in wigs and gowns and there was a full exhibition of Court conduct and paraphernalia. My own impression was that it was an awe-inspiring spectacle designed to force its attitudes and decisions, rather than to serve justice in respect of claims put forward on behalf of workers.[12]

The modern procedure helps to prevent arbitration from degenerating into 'a battle of legal wits, bewildering to the representative of the union and utterly incomprehensible to its members, who cannot understand why their dues should be eaten up in some mysterious legal maze'.[13]

In the course of the evidence and argument the parties may wish to refer the dispute to a Full Bench. In some cases where two separate hearings have matters in common, a joint session may be called (s.129). Normally, however, the Commission member will complete the taking of submissions and then make an award.

In determining outcomes the Commission must have regard not only to the interests of the parties in dispute but also to the public interest. This may restrict the Commission's capacity to award terms which would satisfy the disputants. One restriction arises from the operation of wage guidelines which have been in force, in one form or another, since 1975. These guidelines are discussed in Chapter 11. The Commission is also required to take into account 'the state of the national economy and the likely effects on the national economy of any award or order . . . with special reference to likely effects on the level of employment and on inflation' (s.90). To minimise disputes arising from comparative wage justice and similar pressures, the Commission is required to provide, 'so far as is possible and as far as the Commission considers proper, for uniformity throughout an industry. . . in relation to hours of work, holidays and general conditions in the industry' (s.94).

The public interest criterion is also applied to the making of consent awards and to the certification of agreements. The Act encourages the parties to reach their own agreements. The granting of consent awards and the certification of agreements are methods of giving the force of law to contracts reached by the parties themselves. Certified agreements have the same force in law as awards made by the Commission. However, the Commission may not make a consent award unless it believes that award to be in the public interest (s.112). The Commission may not certify an agreement if it considers that agreement not in the public interest, if the agreement is not in settlement of an industrial

---

12. Quoted in K.F. Walker, *Australian Industrial Relations Systems*, Oxford University Press, Melbourne, 1973, p. 86.
13. Ibid.

dispute (and so is outside the Commission's jurisdiction) or if the terms of the agreement are outside the Commission's award-making powers. As already noted, the public interest criterion also results in certain matters—national wage cases, standard hours of work, paid leave— having to be determined by the Full Bench rather than by individual members. It is also possible, in the public interest, to appeal against the decision of a Commission member to a Full Bench.

Having heard all the evidence, the Commission member will normally adjourn proceedings to a date to be determined at which the decision (determination) will be delivered. The matters needing to be determined will be incorporated, with the other matters agreed to by the parties themselves, into an award. The award document usually states the minimum rates of pay and conditions which apply to those bound by it. In some cases awards provide for actual, or paid rates (see Chapter 12). The award has the force of law:

> An award . . . is in the nature of a *legislative act*. It is something which, authorised to be made by statute, is, when made, covered by and made of binding force by the statute, just as is a Governor's regulation or a rule of court, or a municipal by-law. . . Its operation is ordinarily prospective, like any other ordinance, governing future relations and giving rise in appropriate circumstances to new possible rights and obligations.[14]

It is the responsibility of the Industrial Registrar to ensure that awards of the Commission are published and disseminated to the relevant parties as soon as practicable (s.143(3) and (4)). Though an award must specify the period of time for which it is made, it continues to have force until such time as a new award is made dealing with the same matters (s.147 and 148). An award made by the Commission 'is final and conclusive' and 'shall not be challenged, appealed against, reviewed, quashed or called into question in any court' (s.150). Federal awards prevail over state laws and the awards or determinations of state industrial tribunals. Where state laws, awards and determinations are inconsistent with the federal award they are invalid (s.152). An award is not necessarily binding on all parties to the original dispute. Often an interstate log of claims may be served to satisfy the constitutional requirement for an interstate industrial dispute. From this original dispute several localised awards may result, each being in part settlement of the dispute. The award specifies those parties who are respondent to it (s.149). Where the ownership of an enterprise bound by an award changes hands, the new owner is also bound by the award (s.149(d)).

Award enforcement

Once an award is made its terms must be observed by its respondents. To ensure that employers observe award conditions the Act provides for

14. *Commonwealth Law Reports*, vol. 34, pp. 548–9.

the appointment of inspectors. In the course of their duties, inspectors may enter premises, inspect work and records, and interview employees (s.86). Inspectors may also be assigned, at the request of the Commission, to investigate safety issues (s.87). Employers in breach of awards may be prosecuted in the Federal Court of Australia (s.178). Where underpayment has occurred, the Court may order the employer to make up that underpayment for a period of up to six years (s.179(6) and (7)).

One enforcement mechanism against unions is the use of bans clauses. These may be inserted into awards by either a Presidential Member or by a Full Bench (s.125). The Act defines a bans clause to be:

> ...a term of an award (however expressed) to the effect that engaging in conduct that would hinder, prevent or discourage:
> a) the observance of an award;
> b) the performance of work in accordance with the award; or
> c) the acceptance of, or offering for, work in accordance with the award; is to any extent prohibited. (s.4.1)

A problem arises here immediately. A basic concept in Australian award determination is that awards provide minimum and not maximum standards. To deny unions the right to press for over-award conditions is to treat the award conditions as maxima. Mr Justice Higgins made the point as early as 1915:

> It is not necessarily an unjust extortion for a man or class of men... to demand more than the minimum rate for his or their services. It is quite in harmony with the principle of freedom of contract subject to the minimum wage that an employer should seek by extra wages to attract men who, as he thinks, will give him greater speed and efficiency. The device of a minimum wage will soon prove to be a bane instead of a blessing if the position be perverted... I can only say plainly that there is no breach of the award of impropriety in a man refusing his services... unless the employer pay more than the minimum.[15]

Subsequently, however, strikes by unions in support of demands for overaward payments were treated as breaches. As a result the whole system of awards and award enforcement is 'predicated on contradictory premises':

> If the basis of the system is that, failing voluntary agreement by the parties, an independent tribunal is empowered to finally settle the dispute, it would make sense to ensure that the settlement is really final. That is, some means of direct enforcement to preserve the *status quo* arrived at must be available. A refusal to work encouraged by an organisation must lead to disruption of the settlement. This can not be permitted and strikes ought, therefore, to be prohibited. But on closer examination, the above line of argument may be thought to be inapplicable to the peculiar brand of compulsory arbitration found in Australia. The awards made in settlement of a dispute are not final. They merely provide for the minimum conditions that an employee must be granted in his employment in a particular industry. The system is one which

---

15. *Commonwealth Arbitration Reports*, vol. 21, p. 44.

envisages that collective bargaining shall take place. Thus only minima are laid down, leaving the parties free to agree to institute 'over award' conditions. If this is to work adequately, the employees must be left their main bargaining weapon, that is, the power to coerce. So we have come full circle (as is inevitable in a system that is predicated on contradictory premises): prior to award making, there ought to be freedom to strike, then when settlement is made, this right ought not to be available; but because of the nature of the settlement imposed, the power to bargain successfully ought to be available.[16]

Clear though the contradiction has become, the intention of the Act is nevertheless 'to provide for the observance and enforcement of agreements and awards made for the prevention and settlement of industrial disputes' (s.3(e)). If one of the parties to an award believes that it has been breached, the party may give notice of the matter to the Industrial Registrar. A Presidential Member of the Commission shall then attempt to settle the dispute (s.181(4)). There is a 'cooling off' period before penalties may be imposed. That helps

> prevent the harm which may result from having the legally permissible, but industrially indefensible, imposition of penalties when the Arbitrators might well consider them the worst possible thing to happen from an industrial relations point of view.[17]

Where the Presidential Member cannot find a satisfactory solution to the problem, a certificate is issued which allows the aggrieved party to approach the Federal Court (s.183). The Court may impose a maximum penalty of $1000 for a single breach of an award, or $500 for each day in which a breach of an award takes place (s.111(1)(e) and 178(4)).

The Commission is not empowered to deal with wage claims for periods in which employees have been on strike (s.124(1)). It may authorise employers to stand down without pay employees who engage in industrial action (s.126(5)). Should the Commission consider it desirable (or when the prescribed number of union members request it) to 'find out the attitudes of members' of an organisation engaging, or threatening to engage, in industrial disputation, it may order a secret ballot of those members (s.136). If the Commission 'forms the view that the results of the ballot show that the majority. . .were not in favour of the industrial action', union members are not bound by the rules of their organisation to obey their officials' directives (s.140).

One penalty that the Commission can impose in situations where an organisation has contravened the Act, an award or an order is to suspend or cancel that organisation's award in whole or in part (s.187). In August 1989, the Commission cancelled the awards of the Australian Pilots Federation because of its campaign for a 30 per cent wage increase, a campaign ouside the Commission's wages guidelines. This process denied union members their normal entitlements under the award and allowed employers to deal with individual employees rather than the union.

---

16. E.I. Sykes and H.J. Glasbeek, *Labour Law in Australia*, Butterworth, Sydney, 1972, p. 549.
17. Ibid., p. 554.

In the case of union demarcation, the Commission may determine which union may cover the class of employees contested, and require any alteration of union rules to give effect to that determination. The effect could be to give one union exclusive coverage of the contested area (s.118).

The major sanction which can be imposed on a union is to have its registration cancelled. Unless registered, a union does not have a legal identity. It is not recognised by the Commission for bargaining and arbitration purposes. The members of a deregistered organisation are not entitled to the benefits of any award. The union cannot compel its members to pay fees, nor can it sue members for arrears. Importantly, it can not prevent other unions from enrolling it members. The Builders' Labourers Federation was deregistered in the two mainland states in 1984. Its subsequent history attests to the difficulties of non-registered unions being able to operate effectively. The cancellation of registration is a function of the Federal Court of Australia (s.294–8).

Consent awards and agreements

Any discussion of Australian industrial relations must, of course, focus on the federal system of compulsory arbitration and its activity in making and enforcing awards. It is important, though, to avoid any suggestion that the system excludes direct bargaining or is incompatible with it. Compulsory arbitration was not designed to remove direct interaction between the parties. As Walker had noted, the founders of compulsory arbitration hoped it would achieve the 'recognition of collective bargaining, and the more complete organisation of employers and employees', together with the 'regulation of collective bargaining so as to protect the interests of the community'.[18]

Sections 112 and 115 enable the parties to establish employment conditions without resort to arbitration. These sections provide for the making of consent awards and for the certification of agreements. If, before an industrial dispute has been referred to arbitration, the parties reach agreement for the settlement of all or any of the matters in dispute, they may apply for a certified agreement or for a consent award. In the first case the parties make a memorandum of the terms agreed on and request a member of the Commission to certify the memorandum. In the case of a consent award the parties request the Commission member to make an award or order giving effect to their agreement. A consent award or certified agreement has the same force in law as an award determined by the Commission. The Commission must certify the agreement or make the consent award unless the terms of the agreement or award are not in settlement of an industrial dispute, are not considered to be in the public interest, or concern matters which the Commission does not have the power to include in an award.

---

18. K.F. Walker, *Australian Industrial Relations System*, p. 436.

Federal and state tribunal cooperation

The demands of recent wage principles and guidelines (see Chapter 11) have necessitated a high degree of conformity and cooperation between different tribunal systems. It would be impossible for the Australian Industrial Relations Commission to provide a workable wages policy if state tribunals had no regard for the Commission's guidelines, or if the Commission had no regard for state tribunal operations. Legislation in a number of states requires that their tribunals take account of the Commission's wages policy (see Chapter 5). Recent inquiries into industrial relations systems have also advanced the need for greater federal–state coordination and integration, and have made recommendations to that end.[19]

The *Industrial Relations Act* has also addressed itself to this question. We have already noted that the Commission's awards prevail over state laws and awards (s.152). We have also noted some of the comity provisions of the Act—provisions to ensure some rationalisation between tribunals. These provisions enable the Industrial Relations Commission to determine which tribunal system—federal or state—is best suited to deal with a particular issue. The Commission can order a state authority to refrain from hearing a particular dispute (s.128). Conversely, the Commission itself can dismiss a matter on the grounds, *inter alia*, 'that it is being dealt with or is proper to be dealt with by a state industrial authority' (s.111(1)(g)). The Act also seeks to encourage cooperation between the tribunal systems. The President of the Commission, for example, is required to call meetings of the heads of state industrial authorities 'with a view to encouraging cooperation between the members of the Commission and the member of state industrial authorities, and the coordination of the several industrial relations systems in Australia' (s.171). This provision embodies in law what has become common practice over the recent past. The Industrial Registrar is also required to initiate regular meetings of the principal registrars of the state industrial authorities (s.172).

The Act further provides for the head of a state industrial authority to request the President of the Commission to nominate a member to deal with a matter which the state authority is empowered to deal with (s.173). Conversely, the President may refer an industrial dispute to a state authority to be investigated and dealt with (s.174). The Act provides for conjoint appointments. A member of the Commission may also be appointed as a member of a state industrial authority, and *vice versa* (s.13 and 14). There is also provision for joint proceedings, situations in which a member of the Commission exercises conciliation and arbitration functions in the presence of a state authority (s.173). With the

---

19. Report of Committee of Review, *Australian Industrial Relations Law and Systems*, AGPS, Canberra, 1985 (Hancock Report); *Transforming Industrial Relations in New South Wales* (Green paper prepared by J. Niland) Government Printer, Sydney 1989; and *Report of the Committee of Inquiry into the Queensland Conciliation and Arbitration Act* (the Hangar Inquiry), Government Printer, Brisbane, 1988.

consent of the relevant state authority, the President may arrange a joint meeting 'with a view of securing coordination between any awards or orders of the tribunals' (s.176). This provision is particularly useful in situations where the workforce of one establishment or industry comes to work under the awards of different tribunals.

There is a long history of tribunals established under joint federal and state legislation, the most notable being the Coal Industry Tribunal. This tribunal is the result of, and operates under, joint legislation which was enacted by the Commonwealth and states in 1951:

> The present position is that the Coal Industry Tribunal exercises the Commonwealth Conciliation and Arbitration powers over interstate disputes affecting black coal miners in New South Wales, Queensland, Victoria and Tasmania and in addition in New South Wales the Tribunal possesses state industry regulatory powers over intra-New South Wales matters. In New South Wales the Tribunal is assisted by three local coal authorities appointed under the Coal Industries Acts. In Queensland, Victoria and Tasmania the Tribunal is assisted by Boards of Reference...[20]

The *Industrial Relations Act* provides for a Presidential Member of the Commission to exercise powers under New South Wales legislation with respect to industrial disputes in the oil industry in that state (s.177). The practical effect is to provide joint sittings of federal and state tribunal personnel for this industry.

The Federal Court of Australia (Industrial Division)

The 1956 reconstitution of the federal industrial tribunal established the Australian Industrial Court as the judicial arm of the system. In 1976 the Industrial Court became the Industrial Division of the newly created Federal Court of Australia. The Court's work covers such matters as the interpretation and enforcement of awards; offences concerning membership of organisations; secret ballots and union elections; breaches of union rules; and the recovery of wages when employers have not been paying award rates. Thus, in broad terms, the Court's jurisdiction covers award interpretation and enforcement and control over federally registered organisations. The Commission or Registrar may also refer a question of law, arising out of any matter before them, for the opinion of the Court (ss.46 and 82). In such cases the Commission or the Registrar may not make any decision (or must amend any decision) which is inconsistent with the opinion of the Court.

The Industrial Court is the final arbiter on legal questions in the system:

---

20. R. O'Dea, *Industrial Relations in Australia*, West Publishing, Sydney, 1965, p. 78.

... it may declare a state law involved as being inconsistent with an award or order, and ... there is no appeal from any decision of the Industrial Court, except in hard to imagine circumstances where the High Court may grant leave to appeal. Note also that the Industrial Court's power to control the system is complemented by two direct means of controlling awards under the Act. The first is that inspectors may be appointed to report on the state of the award, and the second is that the Commission may direct the Registrar to commence proceedings in the Court for alleged offences against the Act or for recovery of penalties.[21]

Boards of Reference

Many awards provide for the establishment of Boards of Reference to deal with the application of the award. There is no set formula for deciding the membership of the Boards. The Act provides for Boards to consist 'of a person or two or more persons' (s.131(1)(a)). In practice they are made up of one or more representatives of the employers and of the unions, with a Commissioner in the chair. Seemingly, the Act confers a wide role on these Boards: 'the functions of allowing, approving, fixing, determining or dealing with ... a matter or thing that, under the award, may from time to time be required to be ... dealt with' (s.131(1)(b)). Strictly, the Boards may only consider matters arising out of the award but in practice often they deal with matters which would otherwise require a hearing by a member of the Commission. Ideally, by providing an easily available but relatively formal setting for the discussion of grievances, these boards allow a better chance of agreement than there might otherwise be. They also allow a way of settling problems which affect individual workers or which are only local in extent. Boards of Reference also help to work out the host of local conditions which awards can not readily specify.

The Metal Industry Award gives some indication of the scope which Boards of Reference may be given. Under this award, Boards may be established on a regional and occupational basis. There are separate Boards for Melbourne, Adelaide, Newcastle, Port Kembla, Hobart, Launceston and Brisbane, and separate boards for the areas of New South Wales, Queensland and South Australia not covered by the Boards in the main cities. The award also stipulates that Boards shall be established for engineering, blacksmithing, boilermaking, moulding, sheetmetal working, electrical trades, stovemaking, porcelain enamelling, ironworking, storing and packing.[22] Each Board is to be composed of two union representatives and two nominated by the employers' association. If the members of the Board can agree in their choice, they appoint the Chairperson. Otherwise the Commission appoints that person. Decisions are taken on a majority vote with the chairperson having

---

21. Sykes and Glasbeek, *Labour Law*, p. 507.
22. *Metal Trades Award*, 1971, Part 1, s. 40.

a casting vote. Invariably that means the Chairperson makes the decision.

Under the award, the Boards of Reference in the metal industry may deal with:
1. The settlement of disputes on any matters arising out of [the] award.
2. Any proposal made by any of the parties concerned for the regulation of overtime and distribution of work.
3. Matters specifically assigned to them by [the] award.[23]

The last of these includes such matters as the cancellation or suspension of an indenture of apprenticeship, decisions about the suitability of some work for women, work arrangements for women and disputes referred to the Board by the Commission. The Commission may review and alter the decisions of the Board on the application of any party to the award.

The Board's function is supposed to be one of conciliation and mediation.[24] Though this is the case in many industries, it is not the experience of the Metal Industry Boards. The metal industry case is as indicative of the weakness of this arrangement as it is of its scope and possibilities. A practice has developed of the Board rarely meeting. The parties instead send written submissions to the Chairman and then wait for a decision. Few objections have been made to this practice, despite its suspect legality, because it usually had to do with relatively unimportant matters.

Local Industry Boards

Section 130 of the Act allows the establishment of Local Industry Boards. They may be some state industrial authority, which is acting on behalf of the Commission, or may be specially constituted bodies. Where they are specially constituted bodies, Local Industry Boards consist of equal numbers of representative of employers and employees and a convenor, all of whom are appointed by the Commission. The Commission may refer a dispute to a Local Industry Board for investigation and report. On receiving the report the Commission may, with or without hearing further evidence, make an award or order (s.130(2)). The boards thus help the Commission to reach a better informed decision.

The Industrial Registries

The Industrial Registries perform the administrative duties required for the operation of the Commission, such as serving notices and maintaining award records and files. The Act designates the following functions to the Industrial Registry:

---

23. Ibid., s. 40 (h).
24. *Annual Report*, 4, p. 6.

Fig. 4.1: The federal system

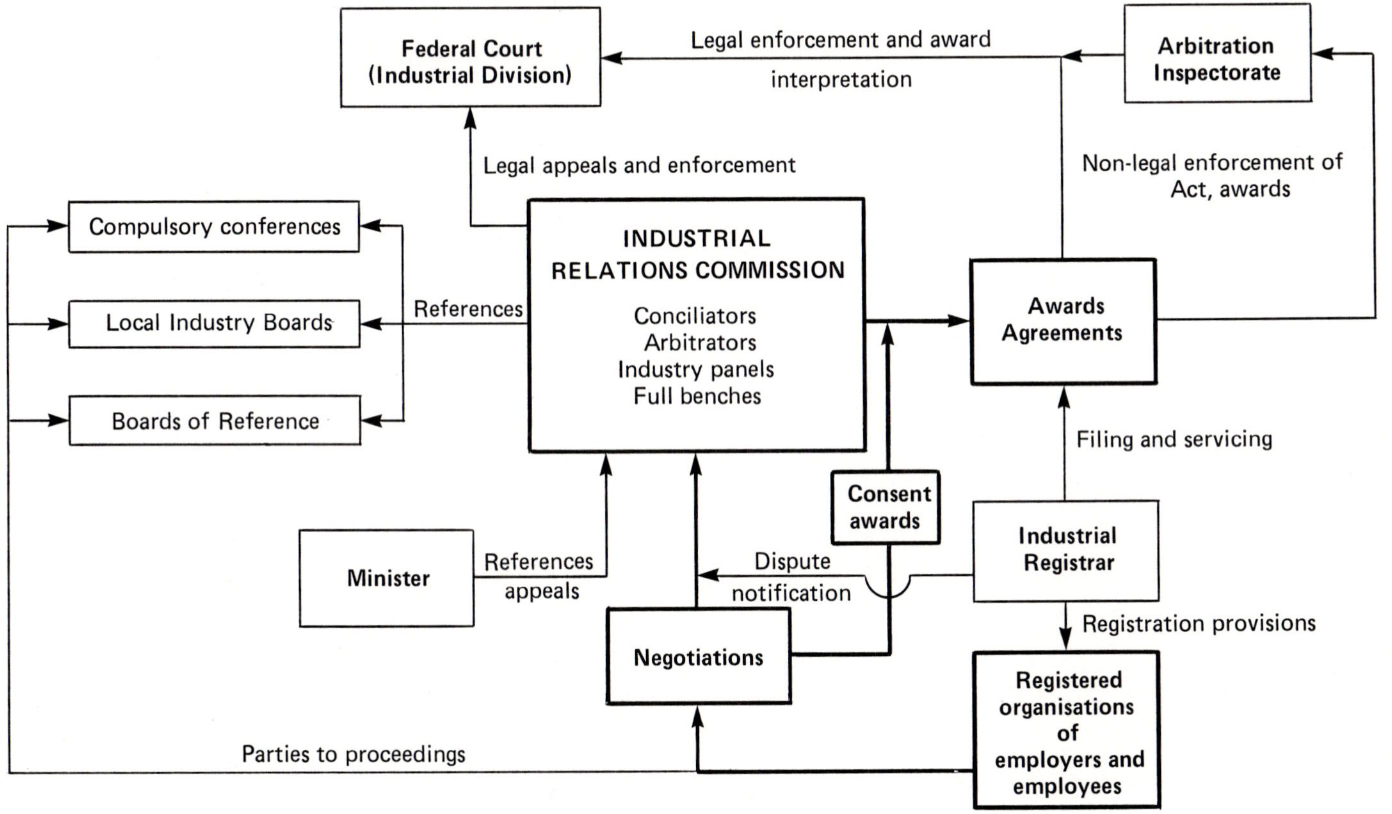

1. to keep a register of organisations;
2. to act as the registry for the Commission and to provide administrative support for the Commission;
3. to provide advice and assistance to organisations in relation to their rights and obligations under the Act; and
4. such other functions as are conferred on the Industrial Registry by this Act (s.63(1)).

As noted previously, one function conferred by the Act is the provision of an award service and the maintenance of an up-to-date list of awards and awards conditions. Another function already alluded to is the role of the Registries in industrial disputes. Parties may notify the Registry of the existence, or impending existence, of a dispute. The Registry will then notify the appropriate Presidential Member and put in train the necessary administrative procedures to have the dispute dealt with promptly. Previously, an important activity of the Registrar was hearing applications for registration. That function is now assigned to a Presidential Member of the Commission (s.189). However, the Registrar continues to have authority regarding certain aspects of registered organisations. For example, it is the Registrar's responsibility to grant exemption from the normal union requirement for elections by secret postal ballot (s.198). It is also the Registrar's duty to determine alterations to union rules to ensure that they conform to the requirements of the Act (s.203). The Registrar must also certify any alterations to the rules of an organisation before those rules take effect (s.205). The Registrar hears applications, together with any objections hereto, for exemptions from the normal requirement that union elections be held by the Australian Electoral Commission (ss.210–14). In the case of a disputed election, the Court may authorise the Registrar to investigate the matter (s.220). The Registrar also issues certificates to employers and employees whose conscientious beliefs do not allow them to be members of employer associations or unions (s.267).

Summary

The federal tribunal system evolved out of Section 51(xxxv) of the Constitution, which limited its jurisdiction to interstate industrial disputes. However, this jurisdiction has been enlarged by other constitutitonal powers, principally the trade and commerce and exclusive powers. Recent High Court decisions would suggest that the foreign affairs powers may be of increasing importance in the future. Despite the constitutional limitations, the federal tribunals are dominant in the area of wages, and nearly 40 per cent of the workforce comes under federal tribunal jurisdiction. Moreover, the recent High Court decisions on what constitutes an industrial dispute may help augment the number of employees under federal awards.

The principal federal tribunal is the Australian Industrial Relations Commission whose members are divided into panels, each of which has responsibility for a number of industries. Most of the Commission's work is undertaken by individual members but certain tasks are performed by Full Benches. The compulsory elements in the system have been downplayed in recent years, and few strikes and paper disputes are settled by arbitration. The Act allows members of the Commission great flexibility in attempting to settle disputes, and legalism and formalities are minimised. While the Commission is responsible for the dispute settlement functions of the system, the Federal Court of Australia (Industrial Division) handles judicial matters such as award interpretation and enforcement. The Arbitration Inspectorate ensures that the minimum standards established by awards are observed while the Industrial Registries attend to the administrative details of the Commissions's activities.

Discussion questions

1. Explain the following terms: Full Bench; Presidential Member; panel; paper dispute.
2. Why is the federal arbitration system more dominant than the state system?
3. Why is the Commission divided into
   (a) Presidential Members and Commissioners and
   (b) panels?
4. 'The whole system of awards and award enforcement is predicated on contradictory premises.' Explain.
5. What are the functions of the Federal Court of Australia?
6. What is the purpose of Boards of Reference?
7. What role is performed by Full Benches?

Further Reading

Annual Reports of the President of the Australian Conciliation and Arbitration Commission and the Industrial Relations Commission.
Dabscheck, B. and Niland, J., *Industrial Relations in Australia*, Allen & Unwin, Sydney, 1981.
Healey, B., *Federal Arbitration in Australia: An Historical Outline*, Georgian House, Melbourne, 1972.
Moore, P., *O'Dea's Industrial Relations in Australia*, West Publishing, Sydney, 1974, Chapters 1 and 2.
Portus, J.H., *Australian Compulsory Arbitration*, Hicks Smith, Sydney, 1971.
Report of the Committee of Review, *Australian Industrial Relations Law and Systems*, AGPS, Canberra, 1985, vol. 2.
Riach, P.A. and Howard, W.A., *Productivity Agreements and Australian Wage Determination*, Wiley, Sydney, 1973.
Sykes, E.I. and Glasbeek, H.J., *Labour Law in Australia*, Butterworth, Sydney, 1972, Part 2.
Walker, K.F., *Australian Industrial Relations Systems*, Oxford University Press, Melbourne, 1971.

CHAPTER 5

The State Tribunal Systems

This chapter examines the structure, composition and operation of the state industrial tribunals. These tribunals may be divided into conciliation and arbitration tribunals (Queensland and Western Australia), wages boards (Tasmania) and hybrid systems incorporating both compulsory arbitration and wages boards (New South Wales, Victoria and South Australia). The special case of the Northern Territory is also examined. The first section of the chapter looks at the importance of state legislation for employment regulation.

The states' industrial powers

Unlike the Federal Government the states are free to legislate directly on employment conditions. This ability to make substantive rules in the parliament has had a substantial influence on industrial conditions. In matters such as the reduction of standard working hours, equal pay for men and women and the extension of annual and long-service leave, state legislation has set standards which have affected conditions in the federal system.

State legislation has been the main vehicle of a progressive reduction in standard working hours. Mr Justice Higgins had discovered the difficulty of reducing hours in the Federal Court. When he cut the standard working week from forty-eight to forty-four hours in the Timber Workers Award of 1920, the Federal Government responded with legislation which created the Full Bench and referred all judgments on hours to it. The Full Bench subsequently put four hours back onto the working week. Labor Government legislation of the forty-four hours however, in

Queensland in 1924 and New South Wales in 1925, made it difficult to maintain the forty-eight hours standard. Consequently, in 1927, the Federal Court again took four hours off the working week. After further legislation in New South Wales, and a proposal for legislation in Queensland, the Court adopted a forty-hour standard in 1947. When the states choose to act in this way it is very difficult for the federal system not to follow suit:

> It would, in the constitutional circumstances, be wrong for this [Arbitration] Court to criticize the exercise by a sovereign State of its powers, and we do not do so. But it is of course very obvious that the New South Wales Act [to reduce standard working hours] did alter very material economic and political factors and did ... present this Court with a *fait accompli* in relation to a substantial section of its industry, and to that extent did affect the freedom with which the Court might have acted.[1]

The states have led the Commonwealth in a similar way on equal pay. From the beginning of the federal system, women had been paid less than men. Men, it was argued, were usually the family breadwinners and thus should receive minimum wages higher than those of women. Despite changes in social attitudes, the fact that women did men's work in wartime and the gradually increasing proportion of women in the workforce, both federal and state tribunals continued to maintain a sex differential in minimum wages. After 1945 women received about 75 per cent of the minimum male rate. In 1958, however, New South Wales legislated for equal pay for work of equal value. The minimum rate for women was to increase to 80 per cent of the state male basic wage by January 1959, and by 5 per cent a year thereafter until the female and male basic wages had become equal in 1963. Other Labor states followed the lead of New South Wales: South Australia in 1965; Tasmania, in relation to its public service, in 1966; and Western Australia in 1968. The federal Commission could not ignore this movement. Two decisions, one in 1969 requiring 'equal pay for equal work', the other in 1972 requiring 'equal pay for work of equal value', gave women full wage parity with men in the federal system by July 1975.

State legislation, together with federal legislation for its own employees, has also provided the federal tribunal with important precedents on annual and long service leave. Thus the Court increased annual leave from seven to fourteen days in 1945 following New South Wales legislation in 1944. New South Wales increased annual leave again, to twenty-one days, in 1958. After several unsuccessful attempts the unions succeeded in having twenty-one days adopted by the federal Commission in 1963. It was a Federal Labor Government which established the four weeks leave standard through legislation for the federal public service in 1974.

Long service leave had been granted in all states between 1951 and 1958. The federal Commission refused to insert clauses granting that

---

1. 59 *CAR*, 589.

sort of leave into its awards on the grounds that the state legislation was adequate and uniform. Since workers covered by federal awards are not excluded from the benefits of state legislation, if there is no intention of a federal award to cover that particular subject, an award by the Commission was unnecessary. In 1963, however, New South Wales made more generous provisions for long service leave and thereby destroyed the uniformity of state legislation. Since then, several federal awards have been made incorporating features of the New South Wales scheme.

State legislation is thus a significant maker of industrial standards. New South Wales has taken the leading part in this process as the only populous state to be administered by Labor Governments for long periods. The alliance between the New South Wales Labor Party and its affiliated unions has thus been a crucial influence on the development and improvement of working conditions in Australia generally. The federal Labor Party, having held office for only ten years since 1949, has not had the same opportunity to influence conditions. In some matters, the federal Labor legislation for its own employees, such as that on maternity and paternity leave, was not followed by similar state legislation. The Commission, therefore, refused to adopt those standards, thus making it easier for a succeeding non-Labor government to dilute or remove the conditions won under Labor.

The importance of state legislation is not confined to its ability to influence federal standards. The states may make substantive rules which supplement, or complement, those made in the state tribunals. The formal tribunals have been partners, not sole agents, in making rules in the state systems. The range of state legislation may be indicated by a list of subjects covered by Acts in the various states: workers' compensation, sex discrimination in employment, trading hours, apprenticeship, health and safety, redundancy and unfair dismissal, employer's liability, superannuation and insurance, rehabilitation, sick leave, public holidays, the employment of minors, aged, infirm and slow workers, payment in kind and industrial diseases.

So far as industrial disputes are concerned, however, the states have not acted directly but have established tribunals. The form of the tribunals varies from state to state. Tasmania uses wages boards. Queensland and Western Australia have compulsory arbitration on the federal model. The other states have hybrid systems in which there are elements of both the wages board and arbitration procedures.

State unitary arbitration systems
Queensland
Following the election of the first Labor Government in more than thirty-five years, and following the Hangar Report on the operation of the *Industrial Conciliation and Arbitration Act*, it is likely that major changes will be made to the Queensland industrial tribunal system.

Unfortunately, the absence of specific details about the nature of those changes makes it difficult to take them into account in this chapter. The following account is based on the existing structure and tribunal operations.

Queensland discarded wages boards in 1912 in favour of compulsory arbitration. Two further Acts, the *Industrial Arbitration Act 1916* and the *Industrial Conciliation and Arbitration Act 1961*, confirmed and extended the state arbitration system which rests on an Industrial Court, an Industrial Commission, Industrial Magistrates, a Chief Inspector and the Industrial Registrar. The Commission, Court and Magistrates have overlapping jurisdiction. The Commission and the Magistrates may determine awards; the Commission has judicial as well as arbitral powers; and all three enforce awards, industrial agreements and the Act.

The Industrial Court consists of one Supreme Court judge, the President, who sits alone except in matters which require a hearing by a Full Industrial Court. In the Full Court two members of the Industrial Commission join the President, despite the fact that they do not usually have legal qualifications. In Full Court hearings, it is the industrial knowledge rather than the legal knowledge of the Commissions which matters most.

The Court has two main jobs: to enforce awards, agreements and the Act; and to act as an appeals Court in matters requiring an interpretation of the law. The Court shares its task of enforcement with the Commission and the Magistrates. The Commission has power to fine employers and unions engaged in lock-outs or strikes and may

> ... make any such order as it deems just and necessary in the nature of a mandatory or restrictive injunction or otherwise to compel compliance with an industrial agreement or award or to restrain a breach thereof or the continuance of any breach.[2]

The Magistrates handle minor breaches which attract penalties of $40 for individuals and $400 for organisations. The Court has jurisdiction over 'proceedings for offences in respect of which imprisonment or a maximum penalty in excess of $400 is provided and proceedings for cancellation or suspension of the registration of an industrial union'. The Court also has the task of deciding matters of legal interpretation. The Commission and the Industrial Registrar may refer matters to the Court and are bound by its opinion. Parties, moreover, may appeal from the Commission or the Magistrates to the Court to decide disputes in law or about jurisdiction. The Court shares this task with the Commission which may 'hear and determine all questions whether of law or fact'.[3]

The Industrial Commission is the main arbitral body in the system. It is composed of non-judicial members appointed for seven years and eligible for reappointment for a further period not exceeding seven years. Commissioners may hold office until the age of 70. No criteria for appointment are laid down but a 'person appointed to be a Commissioner

---

2. *Industrial Conciliation and Arbitration Act, 1961–74* (Qld), s. 102.
3. Ibid., s. 11.

Fig. 5.1: Queensland industrial tribunal system

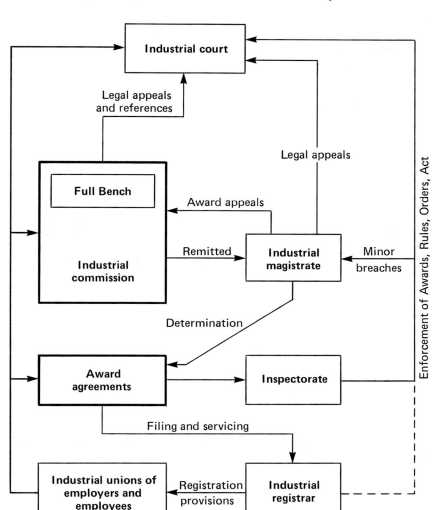

shall not be capable of being a member of the Executive Council or of the Legislative Assembly, and shall not act as a director or auditor or in any other capacity take part in the management of any bank, joint stock company, trade, or business'.[4]

The authority of the Commission is exercised by one Commissioner sitting alone except in those matters requiring a Full Bench hearing.

---

4. Ibid., s. 2.

A Full Bench consists of not fewer than three Commissioners who decide matters on a majority vote. While single Commissioners may refer matters to a Full Bench, and must do so if the determination is likely to affect conditions in awards other than the one under consideration, there are no provisions for appeal against the decisions of a single Commissioner. The powers and jurisdiction of the Commission are extremely wide. The Commission may act in any industrial matter. An 'industrial matter' is very broadly defined by the Act over several paragraphs. It includes, *inter alia*, 'any matter or thing affecting or relating to work done or to be done, or the privileges, rights or duties of employers or employees...' [5] As already noted the Commission's role is both judicial and arbitral.[6] Its judicial power is reinforced by its authority to interpret and enforce awards and agreements. Under Section 28, moreover, the jurisdiction of the Commission 'shall be exclusive of that of the Supreme Court, and of all other Courts whatsoever'. The Commission has power to make a decision 'irrespective of any specific relief claimed or applied for by any party and to give any direction with a view to hearing or determining any matter within its jurisdiction'.[7] It has powers to make common rulings (referred to in the Act as 'general rulings') provided all those affected are given the opportunity of a hearing. Such general rulings obviate the need for a multiplicity of hearings concerning standard hours of work and national wage flow-ons. It has powers to insert trade unions preference clauses in awards, and to determine the male and female basic wage.

While, in the main, the Act constituting the Commission is permissive, in some respects it is prescriptive. Thus it specifies that awards may not contain provisions requiring employees to work more than six days consecutively and that awards for underground work must include permitted intervals for meals and rest, must not exceed six hours per day if the temperature exceeds 28.3 degrees Celsius for a prescribed period, and must provide for proper ventilation. The Act further directs the Commission in a host of other substantive areas of award-making, including overtime provisions, rest pauses, paid holidays, mixed function clauses, unlawful dismissals, annual holidays, sick leave, long-service leave (including provisions for seasonal workers), stand-down provisions, and the employment of apprentices, young workers, juniors and minors.

The Industrial Magistracy is the third main section of the Queensland system. Under the Act 'every Stipendiary Magistrate by virtue of his appointment to that office ... [is] deemed to hold office as an Industrial Magistrate'.[8] Industrial Magistrates are a feature of several state systems, but are not given the industrial power they are in Queensland. As one commentator has noted:

---

5. Ibid., s. 5.
6. Ibid., s. 11.
7. Ibid., s. 13(1).
8. Ibid., s. 42(1).

Industrial Magistrates occupy an important role in the function of Queensland's industrial laws. The importance of their role derives from the width and variety of functions allocated to them by the Act and also arises from the flexibility which they give to the industrial system because of the decentralised way in which Industrial Magistrates are located throughout the State.[9]

Industrial Magistrates in Queensland are unique because not only do they exercise judicial powers, as do their counterparts in other states, but they also exercise arbitral powers; that is, they can determine industrial matters, a job normally reserved for industrial tribunals.

The judicial functions, as we have noted, relate primarily to the enforcement of 'minor' breaches of awards, industrial agreements and the Act. Section 24 of the Act empowers 'Industrial Magistrates to undertake summary proceedings for offences against the Act, for the recovery of wages and other moneys due under awards, for breaches of agreements or awards and for the recovery of union dues'. These proceedings are limited to breaches attracting a maximum fine of $40 in cases involving individuals and $400 in cases involving organisations. This, in effect, means that industrial magistrates may deal with first and second offences. Matters attracting higher fines are usually handled by the Industrial Court.

In addition to their purely judicial functions, the Industrial Commission 'May at any time by order remit to an Industrial Magistrate for investigation and report, or for taking of evidence, or for hearing and *determination* ... any industrial matter'.[10] In addition to matters remitted by the Commission, Industrial Magistrates may originate dispute settlement proceedings outside Brisbane. Determinations by Industrial Magistrates have the same effect as if made by the Commission:

> Every decision of an Industrial Magistrate ... shall be filed in the registry and upon being so filed shall ... become and be a decision of the Commission and shall have operation and effect and be enforceable accordingly.[11]

Industrial Magistrates may also be called on to arbitrate on grievances arising from the stand-down provisions of awards. They may also become involved in the issuing of certificates of conscientious objection against trade union membership, a duty performed by the Industrial Registrar in other arbitration systems.

Operation of the system

Proceedings before the Commission (and Industrial Magistrates) follow the same sort of conventions and rituals as other arbitration systems. As in other systems there is initial emphasis on conciliation. Arbitration is meant to be a last resort. The Queensland Act, in common with most arbitration statutes, requires that

---

9. *Australian Labour Law Report* (hereafter, ALLR), CCH Australia, vol., 3, pp. 13, 163.
10. *Industrial Conciliation and Arbitration Act* (Qld), s. 25(1). (Emphasis added.)
11. Ibid., s. 25(2).

in the course of a hearing, inquiry, or investigation (including any compulsory conference . . .) of any industrial cause, the Commissioner or Industrial Magistrate shall make all such suggestions and do all such things as appear to him to be right and proper for dealing with the cause or bringing about the settlement of the cause by amicable agreement.[12]

In the same spirit the legislation allows consent awards and the registration of industrial agreements. A consent award ensues from the conciliation stage of proceedings and represents a memorandum of the terms agreed on. It is certified by the Commission, filed with the Industrial Registrar and has the same effect as an arbitrated award. Industrial agreements are made outside the system and submitted to the Industrial Registrar for registration. The agreement is then referred by the Registrar to the Commission for its approval. If the Commission considers the agreement 'just and equitable' and not inconsistent with an award or general ruling, the agreement will be approved. The registered agreement is then filed with the Registrar and has the same effect as an award. Those agreements not registered 'are void and of no force or effect'.

The Commission (or Industrial Magistrate) is expected to hear and determine disputes promptly, taking 'such steps as [thought] fit for the prompt prevention or settlement of (a) dispute by conciliation or, if in [the Commission's] opinion reconciliation is unlikely to succeed or has failed, by arbitration'. The Commisson may, however, refuse to proceed with a hearing or to give a determination when the employees are involved in strike activity or fail to comply with the provisions of the Act, award or order of the Commission.

As with most other systems, restrictions are placed on the use of barristers and solicitors. Parties before the Industrial Court may be represented by counsel only with the consent of the parties or by leave of the Court. In proceedings before the Commission or the Industrial Magistrates, legal representation may only be made with the consent of all parties.

Queensland provides a limited appeals system. Appeals in law may be made to the Industrial Court, from the decisions of both the Commission and Industrial Magistrates. Appeals from the award determinations of Industrial Magistrates may also be made to the Commission. In each instance the appeal is conducted by way of a rehearing. However, no provisions exist for appeals from the award decisions of one Commissioner to the Full Bench. In part, such an appeals system may be unnecessary because of the large number of issues which single Commissioners are required to refer to Full Benches for determination.

The Queensland system, like most others, requires the establishment of employer and employee organisations, for which there are elaborate registration requirements. A considerable portion of the Act is devoted to the registration, rules and government of registered organisations. Thus, two of the nine parts of the Act concern industrial unions, as do nearly one-third of the 141 sections of the Act. These provisions set out a

---

12. Ibid., s. 40(1).

host of regulatory minutiae about registration, entitlement to membership, union rules, amalgamation procedures, election procedures, financial accountability, property rights, deregistration and dissolution. The Industrial Registrar ensures that these registration requirements are met.

Western Australia

Western Australia legislated for compulsory arbitration in 1900—the first state to do so. The original Act was repealed and replaced by the *Industrial Arbitration Act 1912* whose long title described it as 'an Act to amend and consolidate the law relating to the Prevention and Settlement of Industrial Disputes by Arbitration, Conciliation and Mediation and for other relative purposes'. This 1912 Act, in amended form, continued to provide the basis for the system until the enactment of the *Industrial Arbitration Act 1979*.

The Western Australian system is similar to the federal system, partly because both the federal and Western Australian Acts were modelled on the New Zealand *Industrial Arbitration Act* of 1894, and, because, unlike the other states, Western Australia has never experimented with a wages board system.

The industrial relations machinery in Western Australia consists of the Western Australian Industrial Commission, which is the arbitral tribunal in the system; the Western Australian Industrial Appeals Court, a judicial body; Industrial Magistrates, who enforce the provisions of awards, agreements and the Act; the Registrar of Industrial Unions; and Industrial Inspectors.

The Industrial Commission is composed of a President, a Chief Industrial Commission, a Senior Commissioner and a number of Commissions. A person may not be appointed as the President unless he or she is qualified to be a judge and is normally addressed as 'Your Honour'. Section 9(3) of the Act requires the person holding the position of Chief Industrial Commissioner to have special qualifications which must be of either a legal, academic or commercial (government) industrial relations character. The Act does not prescribe any qualifications for other members of the Commission. All members are appointed until the age of 65.

The President has power to allocate the work of Commissioners and matters to the Commission in Court Session (see below) but may delegate these powers to the Chief Industrial Commissioner. In addition the Chief Industrial Commissioner is responsible for presenting an annual report relating to the operation of the Act to Parliament. Though the Act differentiates between the Senior Commissioner and Commissioners, it does not appear to place any importance on this distinction. Where a Commissioner is unable to attend to duties because of illness or any other cause an Acting Commissioner may be appointed.

The powers of the Industrial Commission may be exercised either by an individual member, by a Full Bench, or by the Commission in Court Session. Both Full Benches and Court Sessions are constituted by no fewer than three members of the Commission. Full Benches, however, must include the President.

Legal practitioners may only appear when all parties to proceedings give their consent. This is not necessary when a question of law is being argued or likely to be argued. In exercising its jurisdiction the commission is required to act 'according to equity, good conscience, and the substantial merits of the case without regard to technicalities or legal forms'.[13] The Commission is not bound by any rules of evidence 'but may inform itself on any matter in such a way as it thinks just'.[14] In giving judgment the Commission must have regard not only to the interests of disputing parties but also to those of the community. It must therefore take into account the state of the national and Western Australian economies, the capacity of employers in the whole of the industry and the likely economic effects of its decisions on the levels of employment and inflation.

As with other arbitration systems, great emphasis is placed on conciliation and the avoidance of arbitration. A distinctive feature of this system is the provision for final offer arbitration when the parties give their consent. Final offer arbitration is defined for the purposes of the Act as

> arbitration in which an issue is decided by the Commission by awarding, without qualification or amendment, that one of the final proposals made by the parties concerned which, viewed in its entirety is, in the opinion of the Commission, the more or the most reasonable, as the case may be.[15]

The decision of the Commission, before being delivered, must 'be drawn up in the form of minutes which shall be handed down to the parties concerned ... [when] its resources for decision shall be published at the same time'[16] At the appropriate time the parties are entitled to 'speak to matters contained in the minutes'. If necessary the Commission may vary the form of these minutes before they are delivered as the decision of the Commission. Awards of the Commission may not be challenged, appealed against, received, quashed or called in any court on any account whatsoever.

It is mandatory for the Commission's awards to provide for a Board of Reference, which is to consist of a Chairman appointed by the Chief Industrial Commissioner and an equal number of employers' and employees' nominees. Boards of Reference may deal with 'any matter or thing that, under the award, may require to be allowed, approved, fixed or determined'. Boards of Reference may not interpret awards. Matters are decided by majority vote with the Chairman having a casting vote. Decisions of a Board of Reference may be appealed against to the Commission in Court Session.

Appeals may also be made against the decisions of a Commissioner to

---

13. *Industrial Arbitration Act 1919–82* (WA), s. 31(4).
14. Ibid., s. 21(b).
15. Ibid., s. 7(1).
16. Ibid., s. 35(1).

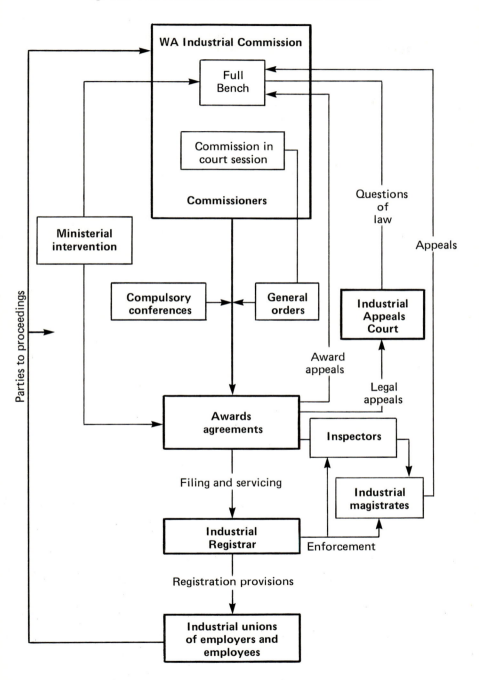

Fig. 5.2: Western Australian industrial tribunals

a Full Bench. Where members of the Full Bench are equally divided on a particular question the President decides the matter. Questions of law are usually dealt with by a Full Bench.

The Commission in Court Session has powers to make General Orders relating to industrial matters including the prescription of a minimum wage for adult employees. A General Order may be made to apply generally to all employees under state awards or limited to designated awards. Thus the Commission in Court Session replicates the Full Bench system in the federal sphere. It is specifically charged with prescribing not only minimum wages but also the minimum conditions as to sick leave, annual leave, long-service leave and such other matters as the WA Trades and Labor Council, the Confederation of WA Industry and the Attorney General may agree. Unless the Commission is satisfied that good reasons exist why it should not do so, it is required, of its own motion, to consider and make, a General Order giving effect to that of a National Wage decision.[17]

The Commission's jurisdiction is both broad—'cognisance of an authority to enquire into any industrial matter and may make an award, order, or declaration relating to any such matter' and restrictive. The Act specifically excludes from the jurisdiction of the Commission what, in the federal system, have been deemed 'management' rather than 'industrial' matters. The Commission 'does not have jurisdiction of any kind'—

> (a) in any matter of the suspension from duty in, discipline in, dismissal from, termination of, or reinstatement in, employment of any employee ... if there is provision, however expressed, by or under any other Act for or in relation to any one or more of the following—
> (i) suspension from duty in that employment;
> (ii) discipline in that employment;
> (iii) dismissal from that employment;
> (iv) termination of that employment.[18]

These provisions exclude most government employees from the Commission's jurisdiction in these areas.

To help overcome problems in industries or situations where some employees are under federal awards and others under state awards, section 23(4) provides that in such instances the federal and WA tribunals may, by agreement between the relevant personnel, jointly determine the matter in dispute.

The Act modifies somewhat the traditional privilege enjoyed by registered unions of employees to have sole right of access to the Commission to the exclusion of individual employees. Section 29(2) enables individuals to refer claims to the Commission concerning alleged unfair dismissal or that they have not been allowed benefits to which they are entitled under their contract of employment. In such cases individuals have an unqualified entitlement to legal representation, a situation

---

17. Ibid., s. 50(1)–(5).
18. Ibid., s. 23(1).

which contrasts with the more usual restrictive approach to legal representation.

Awards and orders of the Commission are enforced by way of Industrial Magistrates. Where an award or order is being contravened the Registrar, an Industrial Inspector, a union, employer organisation or any person may apply to an Industrial Magistrate for the enforcement of the award or order. Magistrates may fine offenders a sum not exceeding $1000 in the case of an employer, union or association or $250 in the case of an individual. Where an employee has been underpaid, the magistrate may order the payment of the unpaid amount for a period up to twelve months before the commencement of proceedings. Decisions of an Industrial Magistrate may be appealed against to a Full Bench of the Commission.

In questions of law the final arbiter in the system is the WA Industrial Appeals Court. This Court consists of three judges nominated by the Chief Justice of WA. The Court has jurisdiction to hear and determine appeals from the President, Full Benches or the Commission in Court Session on 'the ground that the decision is erroneous in law or is in excess of jurisdiction but upon no other ground'.[19]

The operation of the WA arbitration system is predicated on the collective representation of employers and employees. The Act specifies in great detail the requirements for, and duties of, registered unions of employers and employees. The election procedures, financial administration and systems of government of these organisations are spelt out. The Act also provides for the registration of 'industrial associations'— bodies such as the Confederation of WA Industry and the Trades and Labor Council. Part VIA of the Act seeks to protect individuals who do not belong to unions. Individuals committing an offence under this part of the Act are liable to a fine of not less than $400 and not more than $5000. For corporations and organisations fines range between $1000 and $10 000. If the offence is a continuing one a further penalty of not more than $500 per day is provided for.

The Registrar of Industrial Unions, in addition to maintaining the registration files of unions, is also responsible for filing the orders and awards of the Commission and ensuring their publication in the *Industrial Gazette*.

Industrial Boards

A Wages Board was initially established in Victoria in 1896 to

> ... determine the lower price or rate which may be paid to any person for wholly or partly preparing or manufacturing either inside or outside of a factory or work room any particular articles of clothing or wearing apparel or furniture or for bread making or baking ... The Board was limited to the

---

19. Ibid., s. 90(1).

question of wages and those only in the particular trades where sweating was shown to have been rife.[20]

In time the one board evolved into many separate wages boards. Initially they covered the 'sweated' industries but eventually they came to cover most areas of blue- and white-collar employment. The powers of these boards, moreover, were greatly extended so that the designation 'wages boards' became a misnomer. By the time the *Industrial Relations Act 1979* supplanted wages boards in Victoria there were more than 200 separate boards which had an overall power to determine any industrial matter.

Tasmania

In Tasmania wages boards similar to those in Victoria were established and developed by legislation in 1910 and 1920. The system remained stable until the *Industrial Relations Act 1975*, which introduced substantial changes, including an appeals system. The Act also changed the designation of these boards from 'wages boards' to 'industrial boards'. Some seventy-three industrial boards determine awards for employees in the state.

The boards are established by proclamation of the Governor. That requires a submission from both houses of parliament, when parliament is in session. This has the effect of making the Minister for Industrial Relations responsible for deciding which boards should be brought into being; their occupational or industrial coverage; and their geographical jurisdiction. Provision exists for employees not coming under the scope of any special boards. Legislation provides for the jurisdiction of the awards of an industrial board to be extended by proclamation to cover other trades or callings of a similar character.

Industrial boards are composed of an independent chairman appointed by the Minister and an equal number of employer and employee representatives. The number of representatives varies from one to eight from each side, depending on what is considered 'expedient in all circumstances'. The size of each board is prescribed by the Minister. The Act requires that *bona fide* representatives must have had at least twelve months experience in the industry in the previous five years. The system forbids representation by practising barristers and solicitors, except where a board deals only with the legal profession. Union and employer association officials may not number more than half of each side's representatives.

The members of each board are appointed by the Minister. Nominations for boards are permitted from individual employers, representative groups of employers and employees, and organisations of employees and employers. The Minister's powers are not absolute. Where the number of nominations exceeds the number of vacancies to a particular board, the Minister must give public notice of this fact together with a

---

20. ALLR, vol. 1, p. 10 032.

list of his appointments. If employers or employees request it, an election must be held. Representatives are appointed for three years.

Until the 1975 legislative amendments all wages boards in Tasmania were chaired by the one person. The introduction of industrial boards has been accompanied by the appointment of a Chairman of Industrial Boards, a Deputy Chairman and, from 1978, an Assistant Deputy Chairman.

Board procedures

A frequently commented on feature of the wages board system was its informality. Writing of the Victorian system, Hince noted:

> Meetings are conducted with a minimum of formality, an absence of legalism, and in the manner of round table discussions more familiar in the context of a

Fig. 5.3: The Tasmanian industrial boards system

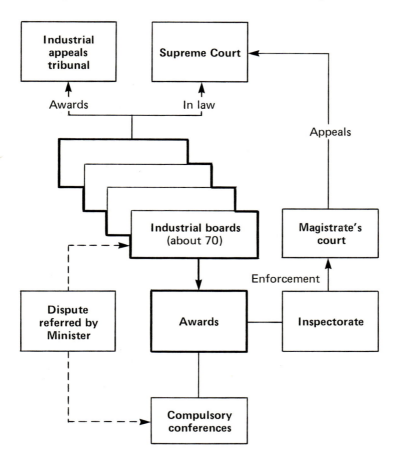

collective bargaining system. The simple procedure of one party moving a motion that a particular course be followed, discussion, and then voting is somewhat analogous to the meeting of a local sports or social club. Decisions of the board are made on each issue by a majority vote of the members present at the meeting. The Chairman, as a member of the board, has a deliberative vote but there is also a provision that the Chairman shall decide any question upon which a majority of members cannot agree.[21]

The Tasmanian legislation is less permissive in the procedural discretion it affords the Chairman. The Act requires that the Chairman (the 'moderator or conciliator-in-chief' in the language of the Tasmanian *Yearbook*) conciliate before resolving any deadlock through arbitration. Thus Section 24(3) requires that, in the absence of a majority vote and before determining any matter.

> ... the chairman shall take such steps as he thinks suitable in the circumstances, whether by adjourning the meeting of the board, by making suggestions, consulting with members of the board, or otherwise, to endeavour to secure that the matter to which the question relates is determined otherwise than by his decision.

The powers of industrial boards are very broad and awards can be made with respect to 'any industrial matter', including rates of pay, hours of work, leave from work, the privileges, rights and duties of employers and employees; conditions of employment, the relations of employers and employees, and age and sex discrimination in employment.

Notwithstanding the wide general powers available to the boards, the Act places restrictions on their powers. Tasmanian legislation prohibits awards from determining the opening or closing hours of an employer's business premises, and from granting superannuation, long-service leave or bonus payments. State legislation is the preferred way of determining the first three of these areas. Bonus payments are over-award conditions which, because of their localised nature, should be outside the scope of industrial boards. Nor are industrial boards, because of the way they are composed, considered appropriate tribunals for resolving demarcation disputes.

An important feature of the state tribunals in comparison with the federal Commission is their ability to make common rules—awards or determinations binding on all employers and employees in the industry covered by the awards. The boards may make common rules within industries and across awards. Section 31 of the *Industrial Relations Act* provides for the Chairman to make an award having the effect of modifying the operations of five or more awards. That sort of common rule is limited to the basic or minimum wage, standard hours of work, paid leave of absence and matters in relation to federal awards.

One peculiarity which may arise as the result of the common rule principle is the impotence of the boards in handling local disputes. This problem has been side-stepped. The Minister has the power to call

---

21. K. Hince, 'Wages Boards in Victoria', *Journal of Industrial Relations*, vol. 7, no. 2, 1965, p. 168.

compulsory conferences of disputing parties presided over by a nominee of the Minister. Orders emanating from compulsory conferences are binding (with a fine of $1000), and may not be appealed against except to the Supreme Court in matters of law.

The *Industrial Relations Act* provides for appeals against awards to an Industrial Appeals Tribunal. This Tribunal consists of a President who must be qualified to hold office as a Supreme Court judge and who must have industrial relations experience, one employer representative and one employee representative. The Tribunal may vary, revoke, remake or reverse any decision of a board or its Chairman. The Act provides that

> the Tribunal shall be guided by the real justice of the matter without regard to legal forms and solemnities, and may direct itself by the best evidence it can procure whether that evidence would be admissible in a court or not.

This appeals system lacks one element found in other systems: the ability of the Minister to refer matters on the grounds of public interest.

Provision is made for inspectors to enforce awards, determinations and industrial legislation (particularly health and safety legislation). These inspectors are appointed under the *Public Service Act* and are subject to the Secretary for Labour. The Secretary is responsible for the administration of the *Industrial Relations Act*. Inspectors have the right to enter any business premises and to inspect wage sheets and other records. Since boards establish minimum standards, enforcement by inspectors necessarily operates only against employers. With the consent of the Minister breaches of awards or of industrial legislation may be prosecuted before a police magistrate.

There are sanctions against strikes and lock-outs. If these concern matters contained in the awards they are deemed illegal. The penalty for taking part in such activities is $5000 in the case of organisations and $2000 in the case of individuals.

A distinctive feature of the boards is that they do not rely on the existence or use of trade unions for their effective operation and the Act imposes limits on trade union representation. The system has not attempted to encourage or regulate trade unions, an important feature of compulsory arbitration legislation. Industrial boards, in fact, seem to operate primarily in areas where union membership concentration is relatively low. The dominant unions have opted for the federal compulsory arbitration system which affords them greater protection and recognition. Thus a higher proportion of Tasmanian employees come under federal awards than in Australia generally.

Though the industrial boards are unlike arbitration tribunals in a number of obvious ways, there are some similarities between them. Since the membership of the boards comes from the employers and employees equally, it is the Chairman's role which decides many matters. Though there is no formal authority for the Chairman to undertake arbitration, because of the constitution of the boards the Chairman does often decide issues by way of the casting vote. The process of award determination is closely analogous to that of compulsory arbitration. There are other similarities too: the emphasis on initial conciliation, the right of appeal, the right of the Minister to intervene, the (limited) separation of judicial and arbitral powers, the power to enforce awards. Awards made by the boards, moreover, are more uniform than might have been expected, given that there are so many boards, each dealing with the special conditions of particular trades and industries. Relative uniformity has been the product of the board's concern to control flow-ons both from one board award to another and from the federal into the state system. The limited number of Chairmen available to conduct the boards and the provision for the Industrial Appeals Court to decide issues from several boards concurrently also help to make for uniformity. Thus, Sykes and Glasbeek have concluded, these conditions

> ... plus the fact that the determination of the wages boards are made for people who work side by side with employees whose conditions are regulated by Federal awards have created an environment in which it is hard to maintain that agreements reached under the scheme are truly the result of conciliation and mediation to settle particular problems. There is an increasing similarity in the effect of wages boards' determinations and arbitral awards, although the machinery employed by the systems is of a contrasting character.[22]

State dual arbitration and conciliation committee board systems

New South Wales and South Australia

New South Wales and South Australia have systems which combine some elements of both compulsory arbitration and wages/industrial boards. Victoria has also recently adopted a dual system. This is described in the next section. South Australia, after an unsuccessful experiment with voluntary arbitration, adopted wages boards on the Victorian model in 1900 and added compulsory arbitration in 1912. Arbitration and the boards worked side by side until 1966 when they were brought into the arbitration machinery and renamed conciliation committees. New South Wales established compulsory arbitration under the *Industrial Arbitration Act 1901*, the *Industrial Disputes Act 1908* and the *Industrial Arbitration Acts* of 1912 and 1940. In 1908 New South Wales also established a number of trade boards, which were similar to wages boards, to help clear away a backlog of cases waiting for arbitration. Like their South Australian counterparts, these boards have also been renamed conciliation committees. Both states thus provide two different types of tribunal, the Industrial Commissions and the conciliation committees. There is no physical separation of judicial and arbitral powers, but when the judicial power is to be exercised, the Commission

---

22. E.I. Sykes and H.J. Glasbeek, *Labour Law in Australia*, Butterworth, Sydney, 1972, p. 673.

in New South Wales reconstitutes itself as a Commission in Court Session, and that in South Australia reconstitutes itself as the Industrial Court.

There is a marked difference between the two states in the composition of their Commissions. In South Australia the President and four Deputy Presidents, all of whom have the status of Supreme Court judges, sit with lay Commissioners. The Commissioners are drawn in equal numbers from among the employers and the unions. The Presidential Members constitute the Industrial Court and the Commissioners act as Chairmen of the conciliation committees. Thus the Court, the Commission and the committees make up a tightly integrated system. By contrast, the members of the Commission in New South Wales all have legal qualifications and the status of Supreme Court judges. No laymen sit on the Commission proper, though a number of Conciliation Commissioners are attached to it as auxiliaries. The main work of the Conciliation Commissioners is to chair conciliation committees. The Commission in Court Session consists of three or more members of the Industrial Commission.

The purposes of the Commissions are similar to those of the Federal Commission, to resolve disputes and to make awards. There are similarities of procedure as well. Initial emphasis is placed on conciliation, legal representation is restricted, consent awards may be made, ministers may intervene in the 'public interest', compulsory conferences are often used, the parties work through registered organisations, appeals are allowed, minimum wage levels are established and awards are enforced. There are inspectors and registries to service the Commissions.

There are, however, a number of differences between the state and federal arbitration procedures. There are no panels in the states, although the work of the conciliation committees does allow a degree of specialisation by the Commissioners. The states may make common rules and they are not confined within the ambit of an industrial dispute. So long as a matter is an industrial matter within the wide meaning of their Acts, the State Commissions may intervene. They may, moreover, award actual rather than minimum rates. In New South Wales the Commission has power to exempt employers from awards if the alternative would be serious unemployment in the industry. The New South Wales Commission, moreover, has a number of powers which go beyond dispute resolution concerning the dissemination of industrial knowledge, the publication of industrial statistics and information, welfare schemes, advice to the government on unemployment, industrial diseases and accidents, reports to the government on prices, parts, sweating in industry, trade monopolies, schemes for better housing, industrial efficiency and productivity; assistance in the establishment of mutual welfare schemes, industrial councils, shop committees, profit-sharing schemes, hostels for women workers and workers' clubs and libraries. Until 1958 the Commission was also responsible for regulating the prices of many commodities. South Australia and New South Wales, largely because of the influence of Labor governments, allow the Commissions

Fig. 5.4: New South Wales industrial tribunals

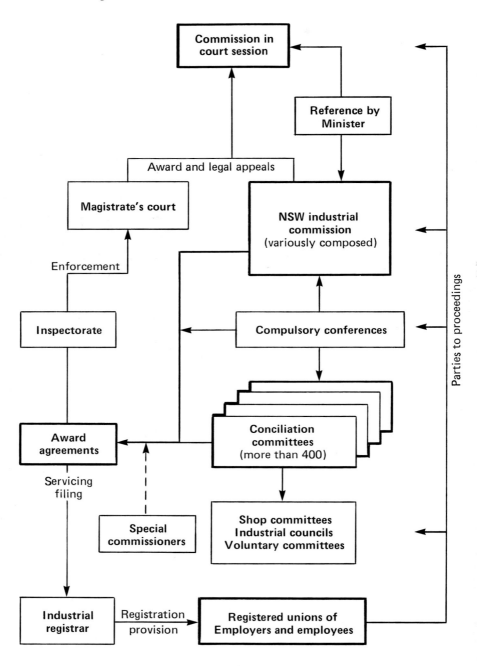

to deal with a number of other matters, which are not covered in the other states or in the federal system. Thus, both Acts require at least three months' notice of redundancy which will follow from technological change; both have measures to prevent sex discrimination in employment; both have provided for equal pay for men and women; and both have provided for reinstatement of workers who have been dismissed unfairly.

The most distinctive activity of the systems in New South Wales and South Australia, however, is in the work of the conciliation committees. These committees are, in effect, wages boards whose determinations may be reviewed by the Industrial Commission in each state. In both states the Industrial Commission has an important influence on the establishment, jurisdiction and dissolution of the committees. In South Australia, the Minister performs these roles on the recommendation of the Full Commission. The Commission itself appoints the chairman and representatives in each committee. In New South Wales the Industrial Commission itself may, of its own motion or on application made to it, establish committees. The New South Wales Commission may also alter the assignment of industries to a particular committee and may dissolve committees. Currently some thirty-six conciliation committees operate in South Australia. In New South Wales they number in excess of 400.

Like the wages boards, conciliation committees consist of an equal number of representatives of employers and employees with an independent chairman. In New South Wales a Senior Conciliation Commissioner and seven Conciliation Commissioners act as chairmen. In South Australia the four lay members of the Industrial Commission are the chairmen. Both systems limit trade union and employer association representation and bar lawyers. In New South Wales representatives 'shall be persons who are or who have been engaged in the industry or calling, or who are acquainted with the working of the industry or calling'. In South Australia, representatives must be 'actual employees' or 'actual employers or managing experts', with the proviso that one employer and employee representative does not have to be an 'actual' employer or employee. This allows registered associations to be represented (as does the 'acquainted with the working . . .' provision in New South Wales). The 'managing experts' provision allows for representation by personnel or industrial relations managers and the like, who themselves are employees in the industry.

In South Australia the Full Commission determines the size of each committee. The President appoints the chairman and selects representatives from those nominated. When there are not enough nominations the President exercises discretion. Similar rules apply in New South Wales.

The Committees in New South Wales have

> . . . a range of award making powers which is akin to that possessed by the Commission. They may fix the lowest prices for work done by employees and the lowest rate of wages to be paid; they may fix the number of hours and

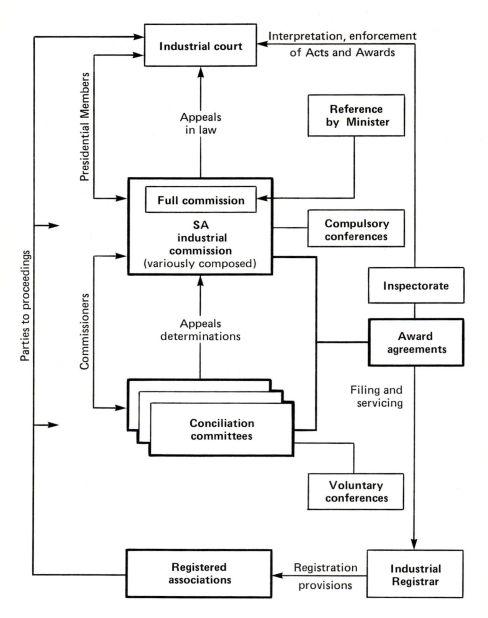

Fig. 5.5: South Australian industrial tribunals

times to be worked for those wages; they may set the ratio of workers to improvers and apprentices; they may award preference in employment; they may determine any industrial matter.[23]

The South Australian committees have much the same authority. Such powers may only be exercised in the area (both industrial and geographical) of each committee's jurisdiction and, in New South Wales, may be taken over at any time by the Industrial Commission. In South Australia, the Industrial Commission has no jurisdiction in the areas covered by conciliation committees. The committees, however, may only settle those matters on which agreement between employers and employees can be reached. Those matters requiring arbitration are referred by the chairman to the Commission where the chairman arbitrates as a Commissioner.

Several distinctive characteristics of the committees in New South Wales are worth noting. First, the Conciliation Commissioners must investigate matters even if employees are on strike. The Federal Commission, in contrast, will generally insist that the employees should go back to work. Second, the Conciliation Commissioner is also authorised to set just and reasonable rates instead of minimum rates. That is useful in allowing the Commissioner to establish over-award payments. The federal system usually sets minimum rates. Special Commissioners are also unique to New South Wales. They are appointed on a stand-by basis and are useful in handling disputes in remote areas or helping to clear away the backlog of cases. Third, special Commissioners are normally used when the Commissioner or committees cannot take charge for some reason. If the Special Commissioner makes a decision or award, it will be binding for a month, by which time the normal machinery will probably be able to handle the matter. Special boards are also set up to handle demarcation disputes. Fourth, the committees are encouraged to delegate their functions to plant level committees and

> ... as far as is consistent with the maintenance of industrial peace [to] deal only with wages and hours of employment, leaving all other matters to shop committees, industrial councils or voluntary committees formed for the purpose of adjusting the industrial relationship of employer and employee.[24]

As well as providing conciliation committees, New South Wales and South Australia allow matters to be appealed against or referred to higher authority. In New South Wales the Commission in Court Session determines appeals about awards, jurisdiction and the interpretation of law. Appeals may be made from any single Commissioner, a Conciliation Commissioner, a Special Commissioner, a compulsory conference, a magistrate's Court or a conciliation committee. As well, members of the Commission may refer matters to the Commission in Court Session for an opinion. The Minister also may refer any award, determination or agreement to the Court Session on the grounds of the public interest. In

---
23. Ibid., p. 684.
24. *Industrial Arbitration Act 1940–68* (N.S.W.), s. 23.

South Australia a distinction is made between appeals concerning awards and appeals concerning interpretation of the law, including questions about jurisdiction. The latter go to the Industrial Court; the former to the Full Commission, which comprises no fewer than three members of the Commission, one of whom must be a Presidential Member.

There are provisions for penalties as well as appeals in both states. Both have an inspectorate to ensure the observance of legislation and awards. Minor breaches of awards, agreements or of legislation are dealt with by magistrates. In South Australia the industrial magistrates are attached to the Industrial Court. Penalties for strikes, lock-outs and the cancellation of a union's registration are dealt with by the Court Session or the Industrial Court. In both states strikes are illegal unless fourteen days notice has been given. In both states strikes by public servants and people employed in essential services are prohibited. Illegal strikes and lock-outs may bring a fine of up to $500 in South Australia and $4000 in New South Wales. Strike penalties, however, are not imposed automatically. Both states protect unions caught up in 'just' strikes provoked by any unjust or unreasonable action by the employers. Thus employers are prevented from using the penal provision to escape their obligation to negotiate in good faith. Proceedings against illegal strikes may only take place after the Industrial Court or the Commission in Court Session has satisfied itself on this point.

Other provisions apply in New South Wales. No union is liable if its officials can show that they made all reasonable attempts to prevent or settle the strike. Alternatively, a strike is not illegal should the union hold a secret ballot on the issue. A majority vote in favour of the strike, if at least two-thirds of the members vote, is sufficient to make the strike legal. Strikes are legal, as well, if the union has deregistered voluntarily. Unions who wish to engage in direct negotiations may voluntarily deregister. In doing so they pass from the Commission's jurisdiction and may use the strike as they wish.

Both states obviously rely on the existence of organisations of employers and employees. The registered organisations are called 'industrial unions of employers and employees' in New South Wales, and 'registered associations' in South Australia. Preference in employment may be granted to unionists in South Australia. In New South Wales the Industrial Commission or the conciliation committees must, on application, insert absolute preference clauses for trade unionists in awards.

Proposed changes

In March 1988 the NSW Government commissioned Professor J. Niland to prepare a Green Paper recommending changes to the industrial relations system. The Green Paper was published in March 1989. Many of its recommendations concerned minor administrative matters, others attempted to give a greater enterprise orientation to the processes of industrial relations.

The government has indicated that a consolidated Industrial Relations Bill will be placed before Parliament in the 1990 autumn session. Key features of the Bill include:
- a unified system which will integrate the Industrial Commission and the Conciliation Commissioner;
- a tribunal structure similar to the South Australian structure;
- provision for the making of enterprise agreements which will override state awards;
- the maintenance of minimum wage, annual leave, long-service leave, sick leave and maternity leave standards under enterprise agreements;
- the 'recognition of association of employees solely for the purposes of making enterprise agreements';
- greater regard for the need for union compliance of awards and legislation;
- the requirement that all awards include grievance procedures;
- the requirement that awards be made for a specific period;
- greater control over union auditing;
- provision for post-entry closed shop arrangements under specified conditions; and
- greater regard for comity provisions between federal and state tribunals.

Conciliation and Arbitration Boards
Victoria
Until recently Victoria had a wages boards system which, in most ways, resembled and operated in a similar manner to the Tasmanian Industrial Boards system. This wages boards system was initiated in 1896 in an attempt to remove sweating from several industries. The present Victorian system, which is the product of the *Industrial Relations Act 1979*, and which commenced operation in November 1981, has retained many of the features of the wages boards system. These boards have been renamed 'Conciliation and Arbitration Boards' and operate in a similar manner to the way wages boards operated. However, several features of the new legislation bring the Victorian system closer to those of New South Wales and South Australia in which boards (called in those states Conciliation Committees) are an adjunct to compulsory arbitration tribunals. These features include the ability of the Victorian Industrial Commission to take charge of any matter normally dealt with by boards, the ability of parties to appeal to the Commission against the determinations of boards, the new dispute settlement role of boards, the ability of the Chairman to arbitrate in dispute matters, the system of registration of industrial agreements, and the recognition of the role of unions and employer organisations.

The linchpin of the system is the Industrial Relations Commission which consists of a President, two Commissioners and as many Chairmen of boards 'as may be necessary'. Currently four Chairmen have charge of about 200 Conciliation and Arbitration Boards.

The President requires legal qualifications for appointment and, as with other Commission members, is appointed to the age of 65. The President is in charge of the day-to-day operations of the Commission and may summon conferences of the members of the Commission to discuss matters relating to the operation of the Act. At least one such conference must be summoned each year. The President is also required to furnish an annual report to the Minister concerning the operation of the Act.

Commissioners are required to have an 'extensive experience of industrial relations'. They may exercise the powers of the Commission by sitting alone or with the President and other Commissioners in which case the Commission in Full Session is constituted.

When sitting alone, the President constitutes the Commission in Court Session. The Commission in Court Session convenes to hear appeals against convictions by a Magistrates' Court for offences under the Industrial Relations and other employment related Acts; any applications by industrial associations requesting a meeting of the relevant Conciliation and Arbitration Board; and appeals concerning factory and shop registrations. The President also hears appeals against the determinations of Commissioners. The Commission in Full Session hears and determines matters relating to the conduct of the boards. It hears applications for the constitution or abolition of a board; the jurisdiction of boards; the interpretation of awards and agreements of boards; matters referred to it by the Minister, a board or chairman; appeals against an award made by a board; appeals against the recognition or non-recognition of an industrial association; and applications to revoke the registration of an industrial agreement. The Commission in Full Session deals with other matters not expressly assigned by the Act to the Commission in Court Session.

Individual Commissioners hear matters assigned them by the President, including industrial disputes or any matters referred by boards to the commission. As with the Commission in Court and Full Session, proceedings before Commissioners are normally in public. The Minister may intervene in any proceedings in the public interest. Barristers, solicitors and paid agents may only take part in the Commission's proceedings (excepting Full Court matters) with the consent of all parties.

The Act directs that in its operations the Commission should proceed informally and 'shall in every case be guided by the real justice of the matter without regard to legal forms and solemnities'[25]

The Conciliation and Arbitration Boards are modelled on the former wages boards. They consist of an equal number of employer and employee representatives and an independent Chairman. Board members

---

25. *Industrial Relations Act 1979–83*, s. 15(1).

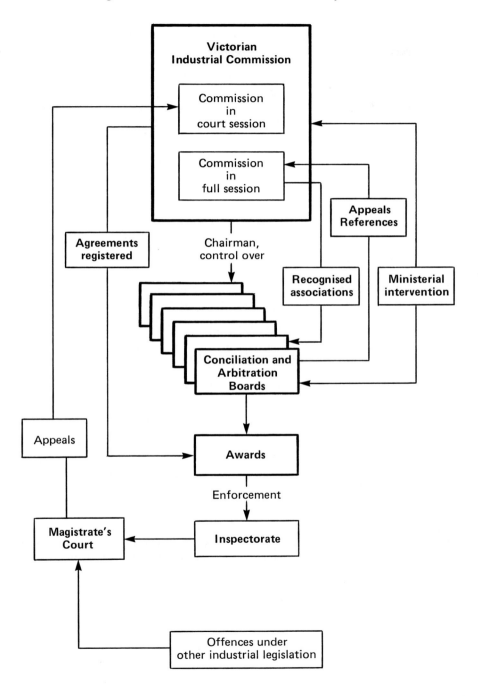

Fig. 5.6: Victorian industrial tribunal system

are appointed by the Commission. The Act stipulates that such members 'shall be *bone fide* and actual' employers and employees, or shall be union or employer association officials.[26] The geographical and trade/occupational jurisdiction of each Board is clearly defined. The Commission may also appoint a General Board to cater for those groups with no special board of their own. This General Board consists of two employer representatives nominated by the Victorian Chamber of Manufactures, two employee representatives nominated by the Victorian Trades Hall Council and the independent Chairman. Lawyers may not take part in Board proceedings except in relation to boards established for the legal profession. A major distinction between the current and previous wages boards system is the ability of the Commission to usurp any of the functions of the boards. This means that any board function may be removed from the round-table casting-vote context to that of a formal arbitration setting.

As with the wages boards, decisions of the Conciliation and Arbitration boards are arrived at by majority decision. Where there is an equality of votes, the Chairman has a casting vote. Boards determine awards and have power to include in such awards matters relating to:
(a) work and days and hours of work;
(b) pay, wages and reward;
(c) privileges, rights and duties of employers and employees;
(d) the mode, terms and conditions of employment and non-employment;
(e) the relations of employers and employees;
(f) industrial disputes;
(g) the employment or non-employment of persons of any particular age;
(h) the demarcation of functions and of employees or class of employees;
(i) the issuing or giving out of any material whatsoever for the purpose of goods being wholly or partly manufactured outside a factory;
(j) questions of what is fair and right in relation to any industrial matter having regard to the interests of the persons immediately concerned and of society as a whole.
(k) the duties and responsibilities of employers upon the introduction of, or decision to introduce, technological changes in the trades in which they are engaged and the notice to be given of termination of services on that ground;
(l) retrenchments and redundancies from any other cause and the notice to be given of termination of services.[27]

Where a board determines an award the parties may appeal against provisions of that award to the Commission in Full Session. Alternatively matters may be referred to the Commission by the board before making an award. Where a matter is likely to affect more than one board

---

26. Ibid., s. 27(3).
27. Ibid., s. 34(1).

(for example a National Wage flow-on to state awards), the Minister may refer that matter to the Commission.

The Conciliation and Arbitration Boards are involved in attempting to settle industrial disputes, a function which did not form part of the activities of the former wages boards. Employers and unions have a duty to notify the registrar of the existence of an industrial dispute. The registrar informs the President and the relevant Board Chairman of the dispute and the latter is required to convene a meeting of the board 'which shall attempt by conciliation to settle the matter of the dispute'.[28] If the board is unable to settle the matter the Chairman 'shall proceed to determine the matter by arbitration'. The board, or its Chairman, may choose to refer the matter to the Commission.

In addition to the determination of awards by boards the Victorian system provides for the registration of industrial agreements. Such agreements are filed with the registrar and, if approved by the Commission, are registered, thus giving it the same force in law as if made by the Commission itself. Unless registered, an industrial agreement 'shall be void and of no force or effect'.[29] In registering such agreements the Commission may impose any conditions or exemptions from its operation as it thinks fit.

Unlike the arbitration system, the former wages boards system did not provide for, or require, the existence of registered organisations. In theory, neither do the present Conciliation and Arbitration Boards. However, to take account of existing realities the present system provides for 'recognised associations'. A recognised association is entitled to nominate people for appointment to the relevant boards, to be kept informed of any board with respect to which it is recognised under the Act, to appear before any board for which it is recognised, and to enter into industrial agreements. Thus the elaborate registration provisions which apply in other systems are not part of the Victorian system. 'Recognised associations' which repeatedly engage in conduct in disregard of the Act may have their recognition revoked by the Commission.

Inspectors are appointed under the Act to ensure the observance of awards and industrial legislation. Proceedings for offences are brought before a Magistrates' Court which consists of a stipendiary magistrate sitting alone. In the Melbourne metropolitan area the Magistrates' Court is called the Metropolitan Industrial Court. The Court has power to recover lost wages for a period of twelve months. Appeals from the Magistrates' Court lie with the Commission in Court Session.

A special case: the Northern Territory

When it granted self-government to the Northern Territory, the Commonwealth retained all the industrial powers granted by the Constitution, except in relation to the employees of the Northern Territory

---

28. Ibid., s. 44(2).
29. Ibid., s. 47(6).

Government. The Territory, therefore, may not establish tribunals to settle industrial disputes or make awards in private employment. The Territory has also inherited three special tribunals to look after the employment conditions of police (under the *Police Administration Act 1978*), firefighters (*Fire Brigades Arbitral Tribunal Ordinance 1978*) and prison officers (*Prisons Ordinance 1950–69*). The first two are composed of a chairman nominated by the Minister, a government nominee and an elected representative of the staff. The tribunals conduct proceedings as they see fit and make decisions on a majority vote. These tribunals resemble wages boards. The Police Tribunal is an arbitration tribunal. The Tribunal is conducted by a member of the Australian Industrial Relations Commission, nominated by its President. He or she is not, however, subject to the procedural constraints of the Commission. Consent agreements may be certified by the Tribunals just as in all the systems.

Summary

State governments do not have the same constitutional limitations as does the Federal Government in the area of industrial relations. This has enabled state governments to legislate for substantive as well as procedural rules. Important employment conditions, such as those relating to workers' compensation and long-service leave, are still regulated primarily by state legislation. State legislation also has been important in improving industrial standards in such areas as shorter standard hours of work and annual leave. All states have legislated to establish industrial tribunals which help establish minimum employment standards and settle industrial disputes. Only Tasmania has not adopted the compulsory arbitration model and still has a wages (industrial) boards system. On the other hand Western Australia is the only state never to have experimented with wages boards. Together with Queensland, which discarded its wages boards in 1912, WA has a unitary arbitration system. New South Wales, South Australia and more recently Victoria have composite systems in which compulsory arbitration is grafted onto the wages boards system. The state systems display a great deal of variation in their structures and procedures, an indication of the differing industrial requirements of each state, their historical conditioning and the political philosophy of the dominant parties in office.

Discussion questions

1. Unlike federal governments, state governments have directly legislated on conditions of employment.
   (a) Why has the Federal Government itself not legislated on conditions of employment?

(b) What impact has state legislation had on conditions of employment?
2. Account for the great differences in structure and operations among the state industrial tribunals.
3. Why are industrial magistrates so important in the Queensland system? Explain the lack of a right of appeal from the determinations of Commissioners in this system.
4. Explain the role of mediators in the Western Australian arbitration system. Does this system establish tribunals with purely arbitral and judicial functions?
5. What are the principles underlying the operations of the wages/industrial boards system? What (a) advantages, (b) disadvantages has this system over compulsory arbitration?
6. Registration of trade unions is a prominent feature of arbitration systems but not of wages/industrial boards. Account for the differences.
7. With reference to the New South Wales and South Australian experiences, how practical is it to combine a wages board system with an arbitration system? What benefits are there in such a dual approach? What problems may be encountered?
8. Though the New South Wales and South Australian systems have many similarities there are also many differences in their structures and operation. Identify these differences.
9. Explain the major enforcement provisions of the state tribunal systems.
10. In what ways do state compulsory arbitration systems differ from the federal arbitration system?

Further reading

Brown, M. and Ferris, R., 'The Industrial Relations Commission of Victoria: a decade of change', *Journal of Industrial Relations*, vol. 31, no. 3, 1989.
Dufty, N.F., 'The genesis of arbitration in Western Australia', *Journal of Industrial Relations*, vol. 28, no. 4, 1986.
Fahey, J.J., 'The NSW Government programme for modernising industrial relations', Department of Industrial Relations and Employment, Sydney, 1989.
Guille, H., 'Industrial relations in Queensland', *Journal of Industrial Relations*, vol. 27, no. 3, 1985.
Hince, K.W., 'Recent developments in the Victorian Wages Boards systems', *Journal of Industrial Relations*, vol. 16, no. 2, 1974.
Molhuysen, P.C., 'The Tasmanian Wages Board system', *Journal of Industrial Relations*, vol. 14, no. 2, 1972.
Niland, J., *Transforming Industrial Relations in New South Wales*, Government Printer, Sydney, 1989.
Plowman, D., 'Recent developments in the Tasmanian Industrial Boards system', *Journal of Industrial Relations*, vol. 21, no. 4, 1979.

Portus, J.H., *Australian Compulsory Arbitration*, Hicks Smith, Sydney, 1971.
Report of the Committee of Inquiry into the Queensland Conciliation and Arbitration Act (the Hanger Inquiry), Government Printer, Brisbane, 1988.
Rimmer, M., 'Transforming industrial relations in New South Wales—a green paper', *Australian Journal of Labour Law*, vol. 2, no. 2, 1989, pp. 188–98.
Shaw, J.W. and Walton, M.J., 'The Niland Report and labour law: a critical response', *Australian Journal of Labour Law*, vol. 2, no. 2, 1989, pp. 197–205.
Sykes, E. and Glasbeek, H., *Labour Law in Australia*, Butterworth, Sydney, 1972, pp. 671–700.
Sykes, E., 'The new Arbitration Act in Queensland', *Journal of Industrial Relations*, vol. 3, no. 3, 1961.
Walker, K. *Australian Industrial Relations Systems*, Oxford University Press, Melbourne, 1970, chs 4 and 12.

CHAPTER 6

Management

Management's role in industrial relations matters has long been neglected as an area of study in Australia. Despite its importance in defining and shaping the form of the employment relationship, management has not attracted the same degree of research attention as have trade unions or industrial tribunals.[1] Recent studies have, however, gone some way to correct this asymmetrical treatment of the key industrial relations actors. Much of this work has had the effect of widening the traditional boundaries of industrial relations by exploring the relationships between business strategies, product and labour markets and the processes of managing industrial relations. In Britain, the focus has tended to be on the strategic choices made by management in relation to the location, control and coordination of collective bargaining.[2] In contrast, in the United States, the union-avoidance behaviour of management in the context of product market strategies has attracted most research attention.[3]

There has also been an upsurge of interest in the managerial function in Australia. This can be explained largely by the more assertive

---

1. J. Purcell, 'The management of industrial relations in the modern corporation: agenda for research', *British Journal of Industrial Relations*, vol. 21, no. 1, March 1983, pp. 1–16; H. Gospel, 'New management approaches to industrial relations: major paradigms and historical perspective', *Journal of Industrial Relations*, vol. 25, no. 2, 1983, pp. 162–76; W. Reitsperger, 'Japanese business strategy and British industrial relations' in B. Wilpert and A. Sorge (eds) *International Perspective on Organizational Democracy*, Wiley, 1984, pp. 153–68.
2. See for example P. Marginson, P. Edwards, R. Martin, J. Purcell and K. Sisson, *Beyond the Workplace*, Blackwell, Oxford, 1988.
3. T. Kochan, R. McKersie and J. Chalykoff, 'The effects of corporate strategy and workplace innovations on union representation', *Industrial and Labor Relations Review*, vol. 39, no. 4, 1986, pp. 487–501; J.J. Lawler and R. West, 'Impact of union-avoidance strategy in representation elections', *Industrial Relations*, vol. 24, no. 3, 1985, pp. 406–20 and T. Kochan, H. Katz and R. McKersie, *The Transformation of American Industrial Relations*, Basic Books, New York, 1986.

approach taken by management to industrial relations matters. Increased international competition has focused greater attention on containing labour costs. Technological changes have required more flexible and adaptable work arrangements. In many of the mature industries in the manufacturing sector, companies have become especially sensitive to price competition. Traditional methods of work, poor job design and inadequate training have all contributed to low productivity. The intensified pressure to improve organisational performance through more innovative employment practices has raised the profile and elevated the status of personnel and industrial relations within Australian firms. Moreover, it has also awakened research interest in their influence on the nature and character of industrial relations. There is now widespread agreement that management cannot be viewed as a passive agent in the formation and structure of employment arrangements in Australia.

Employers possess a degree of choice in the way they may seek to conduct their relations with employees and trade unions. The policies and practices they adopt will be affected by a number of factors, including the type of business strategies used to compete in the market and the values that management may hold about employees. There will, however, be a number of external constraints on managerial discretion. The structure and policies of trade unions and the decisions of tribunals and government impose restrictions on managerial autonomy.

Before exploring some of these matters it is important first to address the issue of business objectives and the function of management. Then the chapter will examine the question of managerial control and look at the possible relationship between corporate strategies and industrial relations policies. The impact of changed market conditions on the character of industrial relations policies will also be discussed, as will the issues of management style and management structure.

The goals and functions of management

It is clear that management's industrial relations objectives can only be understood within the corporation's wider objectives.[4] There has been considerable debate, however, about the exact objectives of modern business organisations—whether they seek to maximise profit, market share, return on capital or a combination of these or other goals. It has been argued that the expansion of joint stock companies and the accompanying contraction of private-owned companies has resulted in the separation of ownership and control and a consequent shift in the nature of the groups who set business objectives.[5] With the decline in the power

---

4. D. MacDonald, 'Management and the labour process in two New South Wales Government organisations' in M. Bray and V. Taylor (eds), *Managing Labour?*, McGraw-Hill, Sydney, 1986, p. 48.
5. A. Berle and G. Means, *The Modern Corporation and Private Property*, Macmillan, New York, 1932; D. Bell, *The End of Ideology*, Collier-Macmillan, New York, 1961 and J.K. Galbraith, *The New Industrial State*, Hamish Hamilton, London, 1967.

of the private owner, control is said to have passed to professional managers who are less preoccupied with the narrow criteria of profitability than their capitalist predecessors. As Aungles and Parker put the argument: 'They will perform their role, not in a total context of profit maximisation but in a wider social context, with a general regard for social responsibility'.[6] Daniel Bell raised the prospect that this new stratum of professional managers would be able to 'judge society's needs in a more conscious fashion . . . on the basis of some explicit conception of the public interest.'[7]

These views have been widely disputed. Although some critics admit that power has shifted from owners to managers, they argue that ownership interests remain dominant and that professional managers pursue goals which are not at variance with those of the wealthy elite in society.[8] Others reject the notion that there has been a separation of ownership from control by pointing to the institutional restructuring of ownership. In Britain, Scott has shown that since the 1960s there has been an increasing concentration of ownership of companies in the hands of large financial institutions such as banks, insurance companies, investment trusts and pension funds.[9] This, he observes, is also the dominant pattern in Australia. As share ownership has become less dispersed, and company boards have come under the influence of this 'constellation of interests', internal managers are constrained from acting independently from the interests of this powerful body of shareholders. These shareholders have predominantly sought high short-term profits and high share prices. Interestingly, it has been observed that this has tended to be at the expense of the longer-run interests of the organisations as they have been less able to plough back earnings into new productive investments.[10]

In most cases, the role of management will be to combine, allocate and utilise productive resources in a way that will assist the organisation to achieve its objectives. Of those resources, labour is probably the most difficult to manage effectively. This is because employers must convert the labour power that they purchase in the market into actual productive labour.[11] Accordingly, there is an indeterminacy that must be resolved within the organisation. The role of management is to realise the full usefulness of labour power; to transform the potential to work into actual productive activity. Management's task is to establish structures of control or methods of consent that elicit cooperation in the pursuit of its objectives.[12] But because the interests of employees will frequently not coincide with the interests of employers, the underlying

---

6. S.B. Aungles and S.R. Parker, *Work, Organisations and Change*, Allen & Unwin, Sydney, 1989, pp. 130–1.
7. D. Bell, *The Coming of Post-Industrial Society*, Heinemann, London, 1974, p. 284.
8. P. Baran and P. Sweezy, *Monopoly Capital*, Penguin, London, 1966 and T. Nichols, *Ownership, Control and Ideology*, Allen & Unwin, London, 1969.
9. J.P. Scott, 'Ownership and employer control' in D. Gallie (ed.), *Employment in Britain*, Blackwell, Oxford, 1988.
10. G.K. Ingham, *Capitalism Divided*, Macmillan, London, 1984.
11. C.R. Littler and G. Salaman, 'Braverman and beyond: recent theories of the labour process', *Sociology*, vol. 16, no. 2.
12. M. Burawoy, *Manufacturing Consent*, University of Chicago Press, Chicago, 1979.

relationship will be conflictual. According to Edwards, that conflict will arise over how work shall be organised, what work pace shall be established, what conditions producers must labour under, what rights workers shall enjoy, and how the various employees of the enterprise shall relate to each other.[13]

Where individuals form unions to utilise their collective power employers will inevitably be forced to adjust employment practices in response to union pressures. In addition, then, to the task of developing policies and techniques designed to influence and control employee behaviour, the firm must pay particular attention to the conduct and outcome of its relations with trade unions. It must do so in order to reduce threats to the continuity of production and so protect its financial interests. Because of the complexities of managing relations with employees and unions, and the array of government regulations and awards that cover employment and work matters, larger firms in particular have recruited specialists to ensure that personnel and industrial relations practices not only conform to legal prescription and award provisions but also are consistent with the broad business objectives of the firm. The need for coherent policies to coordinate the bargaining activities of the organisation and to minimise the uncertainty that often accompanies union–management relations has helped establish a role for personnel and industrial relations specialists.

Indeed, a symbiotic relationship may develop between industrial relations managers and the unions and employees with whom they bargain. As Kochan and Cappelli note: 'The greater the potential threat or cost to the organisation posed by the workforce [or] union . . . the more power the personnel–industrial relations group will be allocated by the organisation'.[14] Batstone's research has tended to confirm this observation.[15] He found in Britain that the development of personnel specialists seemed to reflect the growth of shop stewards. Should the threat posed by the union decline, however, so probably would the power of the personnel–industrial relations unit. On the other hand, as Kochan and Cappelli observe, the personnel and industrial relations group must also continue to perform well in achieving the firm's objectives if it is to maintain power over time. In their opinion, that assessment is likely to be made by more senior managers:

> How well the . . . unit is doing and the acceptability of the strategies used to manage relations with employees, unions, and the government are judgements ultimately made by executives outside of the personnel–industrial relations function. This adds another political dimension to the personnel–industrial role. It must adapt to or influence the perceptions, values, strategies, and judgements of top management and other competing organizational groups in order to preserve its power.[16]

---

13. R. Edwards, *Contested Terrain*, Basic Books, New York, 1979, p. 13.
14. T. Kochan and P. Cappelli, 'The transformation of the industrial relations and personnel function' in P. Osterman (ed.), *Internal Labor Markets*, MIT Press, Cambridge, Mass., 1984, p. 136.
15. E. Batstone, 'What have personnel managers done for industrial relations?', *Personnel Management*, June 1980, pp. 36–9.
16. T. Kochan and P. Cappelli, 'The transformation of industrial relations and personnel function', p. 137.

Work relations and control strategies

It was observed earlier that one of the critical industrial relations functions of management is to obtain a certain level of physical/mental work effort from employees. Management must ensure that employees actually perform the work they are hired to do at the required standard and at the required pace. The difficulty for management is that employment contracts typically are quite open-ended.[17] Lupton and Bowey have made the point that:

> The contract of employment between an employer and an employee hardly ever specifies exactly what the employee undertakes to do during each hour or day of his employment. It is neither possible nor desirable to define every action and sequence of actions precisely, because the employer usually seeks a degree of freedom to direct the workforce to perform tasks which are appropriate to the changing demands of customers, the availability of materials, breakdown of machinery or equipment and so on. And the employee seeks a degree of freedom to respond as he thinks fit. The limits within which these freedoms may be exercised are sometimes written into a contract and sometimes 'understood' but in either case custom and practice will further elaborate what it is reasonable for the employer to demand of the employee and vice versa.[18]

Braverman has argued (see Chapter 1) that management will seek to reduce the imprecision of the exchange relationship by minimising employee discretion or autonomy.[19] Through strict supervision and the fragmentation of jobs into narrowly constituted work tasks, management could achieve compliance with its objectives simply because workers are stripped of the ability to control the conduct of the work they were doing. But as other writers have observed, management is not simply restricted to the use of one type of strategy to control work performance. Nor will they universally rely on a reduced dependence on workers' skills. Where management is sensitive to the labour market position, skills and expectations of different groups of workers it might be expected that it would adopt different strategies towards those groups. Friedman pointed to the use of two broad types of strategy.[20] The first, 'direct control', was similar to that observed by Braverman. It relied on tight supervision and the minimisation of industrial discretion.

The second, 'responsible autonomy', attempted, in Friedman's words 'to harness the adaptability of labour power by giving workers leeway and encouraging them to adapt to changing situations in a manner beneficial to the firm'.[21] To do this, management gave workers status and authority with some degree of responsibility and decision-making power. The latter strategy was applied in particular to more highly skilled, privileged core workers whose knowledge and capacities were essential to secure high long-run profits. Scientific management

---

17. R.K. Brown, 'The employment relationship in sociological theory' in D. Gallie, *Employment in Britain*.
18. T. Lupton and A. Bowey, *Wages and Salaries*, Penguin, London, 1974, p. 72.
19. H. Braverman, *Labor and Monopoly Capital*, Monthly Review Press, New York, 1974.
20. A. Friedman, *Industry and Labour*, Macmillan, London, 1977.
21. Ibid., p. 78.

techniques were, in Friedman's view, inadequate as a means of securing effective control because they ran counter to the organisation's need for some level of creative participation among this core group. On the other hand, Friedman suggested that casual or peripheral workers who were often poorly organised and more expendable were more likely to be subject to a 'direct control' strategy.

The notion of the existence of a variety of alternative management strategies to control the labour process has been developed further by Edwards.[22] Basing his analysis on a study of American companies, he identified three such strategies: simple (hierarchical) control, technical control and bureaucratic control. According to Edwards, each strategy has tended to be predominant in different stages of the development of American business and in different contemporary labour market segments. Simple, personalised control was said to prevail during the competitive capitalist period, principally during the late nineteenth and early twentieth centuries. Workers were subject to the sometimes capricious commands of owners and supervisors. Harsh treatment of workers, however, often provoked militant responses, and after unsuccessful experiments with Taylorism and welfare capitalism employers sought other means of subordination less dependent on personalities and more determined by structural features of the work.

The first of these was technical control, wherein the content and pace of work was determined by plant layout and the imperatives of the production technology. Technical control involved 'designing machinery and planning the flow of work to minimise the problem of transforming labour power into labour as well as to maximise the purely physical based possibilities for achieving efficiences'.[23] Technical control was 'embedded' in technical organisation and work design. It was a form of control not dissimilar from Friedman's notion of direct control where the degree of discretion in work was low. According to Edwards, however, this type of control induced worker militancy, largely provoked by the production-line-type technology, and eventually led employers to design a second structural type of domination: bureaucratic control. Edwards described bureaucratic control as occurring through

> ... the social and organisational structure of the firm ... [being] built into job categories, work rules, promotion procedures, discipline, wage scales, definitions of responsibilities and the like. Bureaucratic control established the impersonal force of 'company rules' or 'company policy' as the basis for control.[24]

Bureaucratic control represented an attempt to attract worker loyalty through positive rewards and through the establishment of a graded hierarchy of benefits available to 'responsible' and 'reliable' workers. Edwards asserted that

> ... bureaucratic control impinged on the behaviour of individual workers in

---

22. R. Edwards, *Contested Terrain*.
23. Ibid., p. 112.
24. Ibid., p. 131.

part by providing strong and systematic incentives to obey company rules, to develop work habits of predictability and dependability, and to internalize the enterprise's goals and values.[25]

In return for compliance, loyalty and commitment, employees were rewarded with job security and protection from retrenchment and personnel policies which provided secure long-term employment opportunities.

Both Friedman and Edwards have suggested that the organisation of the labour process and management's methods of control can be varied. One of the main factors said to influence management's choice is the likely acceptance or resistance of employees. Both writers suggest, for example, that Taylorist techniques which tended to induce dissatisfaction and general organised resistance forced employers to shift policies towards bureaucratic regulation or responsible autonomy. Burawoy has also pointed to the presence of additional factors.[26] State regulation, principally in the form of protective labour legislation, has imposed constraints on managerial discretion and reduced their ability to recognise work relations through coercion. In Burawoy's view:

> Workers must be *persuaded* to co-operate with management. Their interests must be co-ordinated with those of capital ... Not only is the application of coercion circumscribed and regularized, but the infliction of discipline and punishment itself become the object of consent.[27]

The preceding discussion has concentrated largely on the various methods that management might use to control work relationships and organise the process of production. It would be a mistake, however, to believe that management's actions were guided by a simple logic to control labour.[28] As Wood and Kelly have pointed out, the 'tendency to inflate control to the point at which it becomes the central problem of capitalist management is at variance with most analyses of capitalism ... which emphasises the pursuit of profit'.[29] Indeed, in those cases where industrial relations/human resource management policies are formulated by corporate-level managers, there may be little understanding of how the labour process is actually organised and controlled. Greater significance may, in fact, be attached to the degree to which industrial relations arrangements assist with the achievement of the organisation's overall business strategies. Market imperatives, such as product quality or customer service or compliance with delivery dates, may exert more influence over management's relationships with its employees and its workplace requirements. We will now turn to an examination of the linkages between business strategies and industrial relations.

---

25. Ibid., p. 152.
26. M. Burawoy, 'Between the labour process and the state: the changing face of factory regimes under advanced capitalism', *American Sociological Review*, vol. 48, October 1983, pp. 587–605.
27. Ibid., p. 590.
28. C.R. Littler and G. Salaman, 'Braverman and beyond', p. 257.
29. S. Wood and J. Kelly, 'Taylorism, responsible autonomy and management strategy', in S. Wood (ed.), *The Degradation of Work?*, Hutchinson, London, 1982, p. 77.

Corporate strategies and industrial relations

Not all firms will seek to achieve their objectives in the same way. Various approaches can be adopted to obtain a competitive advantage in the marketplace. These, in turn, will have an impact on organisational structures and the management of employees. Porter has identified two main generic business-level strategies which can be used to create and sustain a competitive advantage over competitors.[30] He termed these 'cost leadership' and 'differentiation'. In those cases where organisations choose a cost leadership thrust their aim will be to produce goods and services more cheaply than competitors. This can be realised by either high volume, efficient scale facilities, the pursuit of cost reductions in manufacture and/or the minimisation of expenses in research and development. The characteristics of this approach also include tight financial controls and overhead minimisation. In contrast, a differentiation strategy aims to create a product or service which is perceived as uniquely attractive. It emphasises high product or service quality, reliability or technological superiority. Often firms that pursue this strategy will lead their competitors in innovation and will seek to sell their product at a price premium. Murray has observed that

> ... a product differentiation strategy is viable only if customers, when making purchase decisions, give weight to product attributes other than price ... a firm must be able to build and sustain noticeable differences in its product offerings or in brand image, packaging, pre and post sales service ...[31]

The ability of a firm to differentiate its product will be a function of product characteristics. Relatively homogenous products, such as petroleum and bulk chemicals, offer little scope for differentiation, whereas more complex products, such as computers, electrical goods and motor cars, offer greater scope.[32]

Porter stressed that cost leadership and differentiation were normally inconsistent because differentiation was usually costly. Their joint pursuit could lead to an organisation being 'stuck in the middle' thereby failing to realise the advantage of either strategy and almost surely guaranteeing inferior performance. Furthermore, Porter suggested that cost leadership and product differentiation would imply differing organisational arrangements, control procedures and incentive systems.[33] He also felt that the generic strategies would require different styles of leadership and corporate cultures with different types of people being attracted according to the strategic approach of the business.

Porter's typology has generated considerable academic interest and spawned a body of empirical work which has sought both to apply and to

---

30. M.E. Porter, *Competitive Strategy: Techniques for Analyzing Industries and Competitors*, Free Press, New York, 1980 and M.E. Porter, *Competitive Advantage: Creating and Sustaining Superior Performance*, Free Press, New York, 1985.
31. A. Murray, 'A contingency view of Porter's "Generic Strategies" ', *Academy of Management Review*, vol. 13, no. 3, 1988, p. 394.
32. C.W.L. Hill, 'Differentiation versus low cost or differentiation and low cost: a contingency framework', *Academy of Management Review*, vol. 13, no. 3, 1988, p. 404.
33. M.E. Porter, 1980, *Competitive Strategy*, pp. 40–41.

test his concepts. Although these studies have yielded somewhat contradictory results,[34] Porter's work has provided an important conceptual framework for both organisational theorists and industrial relations writers. Miller, for example, has sought to clarify the relationship between corporate strategies, organisational structures and human resource management environments.[35] He has claimed that there are only a limited number of suitable structures given the pursuit of a particular strategy. In the case of a product differentiator, Miller suggests that innovation would not be facilitated by a mechanistic bureaucratic structure with formal rules and procedures. A high degree of differentiation is likely to require more flexible structures which will enable employee discretion and the collaboration of people with different skills. Power will be decentralised and authority will be based on expertise.[36] On the other hand, organisations that have embraced a cost leadership strategy may require more bureaucratic structures that place emphasis on tight controls, standard procedures, routine operating tasks and a method of coordination effected by rules and hierarchy. According to Miller, power will rest 'in the hands of the top executives and the designers of workflow processes'.[37]

Schuler and Jackson have taken Porter's analysis further and argued that successful implementation of a particular competitive strategy will require certain 'needed role behaviours' at the workplace.[38] They identified three archetypal forms of competitive personnel–human resource management (PHRM) practices based on innovation, quality enhancement and cost reduction. For an organisation pursuing an innovation strategy, the profile of employee 'role behaviour' would include a high degree of creative behaviour, a longer-term focus, a relatively high level of cooperative, independent behaviour, a greater degree of risk-taking and a high tolerance of ambiguity and unpredictability. Schuler and Jackson assert that:

> The implication of pursuing a competitive strategy for innovation for managing people may include selecting highly skilled individuals, giving employees more discretion, using minimal controls . . . [and] making a greater investment in human capital.[39]

Performance appraisals would be more likely to reflect group-based achievements, compensation systems would emphasise internal equity

---

34. See D.C. Hambrick, 'High profit strategies in mature capital goods industries: a contingency approach', *Academy of Management Journal*, vol. 26, 1983, pp. 687–707, and G.G. Dess and P.S. Davis, 'Porter's generic strategies as determinants of strategic group membership and organizational performance', *Academy of Management Journal*, vol. 27, 1984, pp. 467–88 for empirical support of Porter's contention that a commitment to one of the strategies will result in higher performance. Alternatively, two studies which suggest that competitive advantage could be secured through a combination of both low cost and differentiation include R.E. White, 'Generic business strategies, organisational context and performance: an empirical investigation', *Strategic Management Journal*, vol. 7, pp. 217–31 and C.W.L. Hill, 'Differentiation versus low cost', pp. 401–12.
35. D. Miller, 'Configurations of strategy and structure: towards a synthesis', *Strategic Management Journal*, vol. 7, 1986, pp. 233–49.
36. Ibid., pp. 245–6.
37. Ibid., p. 243.
38. R. Schuler and S. Jackson, 'Linking competitive strategies with human resource management practices', *Academy of Management Executive*, vol. 1, no. 3, 1987, pp. 207–19.
39. Ibid., p. 210.

and broad career paths would reinforce the development of a broad range of skills. A quality enhancement strategy would, in Schuler and Jackson's judgement, require somewhat different PHRM practices. Securing employee commitment to quality and continual improvement would necessitate teamwork, flexible job classifications and the incorporation of participative decision-making and responsibility as part of an employee's job description. These practices would 'facilitate quality enhancement by helping to ensure highly reliable behaviour from individuals who can identify with the goals of the organisation and when necessary be flexible and adaptable...'.[40] Finally, in the case of a firm pursuing a cost reduction strategy, the PHRM emphasis is said to be on achieving relatively repetitive and predictable behaviour concerned with maximising quantity rather than quality. This could be facilitated by reducing the room for ambiguity through narrowly defined jobs and work simplification. In the view of Schuler and Jackson, these 'practices maximise efficiency by providing means for management to monitor and control closely the activities of employees'.[41]

Hotz-Hart has also outlined the shape of a number of different policy variables which he suggests would need to be moulded together to implement a particular corporate strategy. He distinguishes two idealised strategies: the first based on innovation and the second on product market consolidation through cost-minimisation. These are illustrated in Table 6.1. The validity of this type of analysis must in the end rest on supporting empirical evidence. In its absence, we are in danger of confusing prescription with practice. Certainly, it is logical to expect that an organisation would seek to integrate its industrial relations/human resource management policies with its corporate strategies if it wants to capitalise fully on market opportunities.[42] But the question remains: do organisations in fact align their industrial relations/human resource managements policies in this way? Are organisational decisions in this area driven by competitive business strategies?

Unfortunately, few studies have systematically sought to test this relationship. Much of the data is based on limited case study samples or is simply anecdotal. The evidence is, therefore, rather sketchy and incomplete. In the United States, Richard Walton has claimed that a growing number of companies are adopting new sophisticated approaches to workforce management where market pressures demand constant innovation and higher product and service quality.[43] He has identified a shift from a 'control' perspective to one more concerned with eliciting worker 'commitment'. Walton shows that in many areas of production, international competition has rendered the control strategy obsolete. He asserts that:

---

40. Ibid., p. 213.
41. Ibid., p. 213.
42. R.R. Collins, 'The strategic contributions of the personnel function', in G. Palmer (ed.), *Australian Personnel Management*, Macmillan, Melbourne, 1988.
43. R. Walton, 'From control to commitment in the workplace', *Harvard Business Review*, March–April 1985, pp. 77–84.

Table 6.1: The shape of company policy variables with respect to overall company strategy (ideal-type cases)

Company strategies	(1) Innovative dynamic	(2) Consolidation of well established position
Policy variables		
Personnel	Activating and developing internal means of improving qualifications: increasing internal mobility; avoiding lay-offs if possible in a downturn	Improving efficiency through work intensification and reduction of labour costs; little training or retraining for new jobs; lay-offs are routine when business declines
Organisation development	Increasing flexibility and adaptability; development towards cooperative and participative structure; teamwork; decentralisation; suggestions from bottom up	Improving control and adjusting layout of work-places; authoritarian, patriarchal leadership; maintaining and reinforcing centralisation; top-down command structure
Competitive behaviour	Aggressive; dynamic through product and process innovation; new ventures	Protective; market closure; reinforcing price competition; streamlining to the most profitable parts
Investment behaviour	In innovation, accepting higher risks, less capital-intensive	Cost optimisation; rationalisation; capital intensification

Source: B. Hotz-Hart, 'Comparative research and new technology: modernisation in three industrial relations systems' in R. Hyman and W. Streeck (eds), *New Technology and Industrial Relations*, Blackwell, Oxford, 1988, p. 68.

A model that assumes low employee commitment and that is designed to produce reliable if not outstanding performance simply cannot match the standards of excellence set by world-class competitors . . . a growing number of manufacturing companies has begun to remove levels of plant hierarchy, increase managers' spans of control, integrate quality and production activities at lower organizational levels, combine production and maintenance operations, and open up new career possibilities for workers.[44]

Piore and Sabel have also detected similar developments.[45] They see production increasingly shifting from standardised goods for mass markets to specialised goods for niche markets. New market strategies have been formed which aim to compete by way of offering product diversity and/or high quality. In turn, this has required the use of more skilled and highly motivated workers, flatter management hierarchies and a correspondingly more participative approach to the management process. Katz and Sabel have provided evidence of this in the motor vehicle industry.[46] Growing international competition has led to mounting pressures to increase the quality of the product and to secure niche markets. These forces have heightened the pressures for technological change and increased the need for flexibility in the use of technology and labour in order to adapt quickly to changing market conditions and opportunities. They argued that there are signs of a movement towards a model of production that turns the principles of mass production upside down:

> Instead of producing a standard car by means of highly specialised resources —workers with narrowly defined jobs and dedicated machinery—the tendency is to produce specialised goods by means of general-purpose resources —broadly skilled workers using capital equipment that can make various models.[47]

Much of this analysis, however, has involved generalisations from a narrow empirical base.[48] Hyman also claims that it exaggerates the coherence and consistency of management strategies.[49] He believes that industrial relations initiatives in most companies are developed in a piecemeal fashion and are more likely to be opportunistic rather than strategically directed: 'In Britain, certainly, it is a familiar comment that managements traditionally 'muddle through' in routine circumstances and respond to problems and crises with *ad hoc* reactions.[50]

This also tends to be the view of others. Purcell and Ahlstrand report that there is little evidence in Britain to indicate that employee relations is considered in strategic management 'and plenty of data to show that it

---

44. Ibid., p. 79.
45. M.J. Piore and C.F. Sabel, *The Second Industrial Divide—Possibilities For Prosperity*, Basic Books, New York, 1984.
46. H. Katz and C.F. Sabel, 'Industrial relations and industrial adjustment in the car industry', *Industrial Relations*, vol. 24, no. 3, 1985.
47. Ibid., p. 298.
48. See J. Phillimore, 'Flexible specialisation, work organisation and skills', *New Technology, Work and Employment*, vol. 4, no. 2, 1989, pp. 79–91.
49. R. Hyman, 'Flexible specialisation: miracle or myth' in R. Hyman and W. Streek (eds.), *New Technology and Industrial Relations*, Blackwell, Oxford, 1988.
50. Ibid., p. 51.

is a stand-alone function'.[51] Similarly, Sisson and Sullivan feel that few organisations in Britain appear to have planned a systematic approach towards industrial relations or possess policies that are integrated or consistent with overall business policies. They assert that the 'vast bulk of British management . . . [do] not appear to have anything that could remotely be called a strategy: most . . . [are] opportunistic or pragmatic in their approach'.[52]

The same picture is revealed in the United States. Nkomo found that less than one in six of the Fortune 500 companies systematically linked their human resource management policies with the overall strategic needs of the organisation.[53] Likewise, in her study of 120 American companies, Christiansen could find little evidence of a fit between long-term corporate goals and labour relations policies.[54] Few companies had an articulated labour relations policy, and most industrial relations staff were slow to embrace change and recognise the relationships between their function and the overall strategic direction of the business. Christiansen's research showed that labour relations specialists were isolated from the centres of critical decision-making. In her view, this was due mainly to 'the natural antipathy between line and staff, the lack of business-oriented strategic outlook on the part of labour staff, and line managers' lack of understanding of the connection between corporate, manufacturing and labour strategies'.[55]

In Australia, Collins has also claimed that few organisations have focused on the current or potential contributions of people of business success. He claims that most Australian managers 'have not had the values, skills or information that would enable them to inject people considerations into their strategic decision-making formulae'.[56] As a consequence, he feels that many companies have missed important opportunities to develop a competitive edge through their employees' behaviour and contributions.

It is, of course, possible to cite exceptions. Deery and Nash provide an example of a metal manufacturing company which developed a set of personnel and industrial relations policies and practices which supported strongly the organisation's product market strategy.[57] Quinlan has also shown that Australia's largest steel producer, BHP, pursued an industrial relations strategy through most of the post-war period which was clearly consistent and well integrated with its business decisions.[58]

---

51. J. Purcell and B. Ahlstrand, 'Corporate strategy and the management of employee relations in the multi-divisional company', *British Journal of Industrial Relations*, vol. 27, no. 3, 1989, p. 399.
52. K. Sisson and H. Sullivan, 'Management strategy and industrial relations: editorial', *Journal of Management Studies*, vol. 24, no. 5, 1987, p. 430.
53. S.M. Nkomo, 'Strategic planning for human resources—let's get started', *Long Range Planning*, vol. 21, no. 1, 1988.
54. E.T. Christiansen, 'Challenges in the management of diversified companies: the changing role of corporate labor relations', *Human Resource Management*, vol. 26, no. 3, 1987.
55. Ibid., pp. 375–6.
56. R.R. Collins, 'The strategic contributions of the personnel function', p. 36.
57. S. Deery and J. Nash, 'Organisational change and the role of personnel and industrial relations management', in G. Palmer (ed.), *Australian Personnel Management*, Macmillan, Melbourne, 1988.
58. M. Quinlan, 'Managerial strategy and industrial relations in the Australian steel industry 1945–1975: a case study', in M. Bray and V. Taylor (eds), *Managing Labour?*, McGraw-Hill, Sydney, 1986.

As a cost minimiser, it followed a classic coercive, control-based industrial relations approach which sought to contain labour costs and protect managerial prerogatives. More recently, in response to the profoundly different product market conditions in the 1980s and the institutional pressures induced by the Steel Industry Plan, BHP seems to have adopted a more cooperative industrial relations approach in order to raise quality performance and lift labour productivity.[59] An even more obvious example of an organisation which has sought to create a synergy between its strategic requirements and its employee relations policies is the newly established Tasmanian-based wheel exporter, Southern Aluminium. It has put into place a set of employment arrangements and industrial relations practices which have been driven explicitly by its operational needs. The high demands placed on the company for product quality and reliability of supply has led to the establishment of multi-skilled production teams, broadly based job classifications and the extensive use of performance-based remuneration systems. The organisational requirements for labour flexibility also led the company to sign a single union agreement with the Federated Ironworkers Association.

In spite of these few examples of corporate fit, there appears to be little general evidence in either Australia or overseas of organisations adopting a strategic approach to industrial relations. There are a number of possible reasons for this operational orientation. One might be the inadequate representation of the personnel and industrial relations function at the executive decision-making level of the organisation and the consequent lack of opportunity to be involved in the formulation of strategic business decisions. Certainly there is evidence to indicate that personnel managers exert very little influence over strategic decisions.[60] Purcell and Ahlstrand have pointed to the fact that in Britain the personnel function and department is isolated from the strategic centre of many large companies.[61] This is most likely to be the case where the internal operating procedures of the company are decentralised and local profit centres have been established. A second reason could lie in the lack of understanding by personnel and industrial relations managers of the goals, performance and plans of the business and an inability to identify the contribution of the function to the successful attainment of business objectives.[62] This position is likely to be reinforced by the attitudes of senior management who often take a limited and narrow view of the potential contribution of the industrial relations role to organisational performance. Deery and Nash have observed that where industrial relations specialists have attempted to adopt a more strategic human resource management perspective and shape organisational

---

59. See D. Macdonald, *Attempted Reforms in Human Resource Management and their Results: A Review of Experiences in Australia and Overseas*, paper commissioned by the Economic Planning and Advisory Council, March 1988.
60. W.W. Hegarty and R.C. Hoffman, 'Who influences strategic decisions?', *Long Range Planning*, vol. 20, no. 2, 1987.
61. J. Purcell and B. Ahlstrand, 'Corporate strategy', p. 403.
62. See E.T. Christiansen, 'Challenge in the management of diversified companies', pp. 376–7.

behaviour through the wider use of training and development programmes, they have frequently faced difficulties in the form of managerial indifference and a lack of disposable resources.[63] Legge has captured the nature of this dilemma for personnel and industrial relations managers

> ... to obtain adequate resources to undertake these tasks, a personnel department requires power which, at present, in many organisations it lacks, precisely because of its inability to convince those who do control resources of its potential contribution. It is the old chicken and egg situation. Until personnel can demonstrate its contribution to organisation success, it will be unable to generate adequate resources for its work, but until it does so, it will be unable to achieve this potential contribution.[64]

Indeed there is some evidence overseas to suggest that line management may have begun to assert greater control over industrial relations issues because of the slowness of the industrial relations and human resource management professional to change. In the United States, Kochan, McKersie and Chalykoff found that workplace innovations in the areas of employee participation, information sharing, quality circles and productivity gain-sharing were positively related to the influence of line managers over industrial relations and human resources management policies.[65] As competitive pressures mounted it was the line managers who first argued for changed work rules and began to find ways of introducing greater flexibility and cooperation into the workplace. In Britain, Purcell and Ahlstrand have observed the growing pressures to devolve the personnel and industrial relations function as organisations have begun to embrace new corporate strategies and business policies which have emphasised local profit centres and greater autonomy for business unit managers.[66] Line managers have argued for the need to make the structures of industrial relations fit the corporate need for profit centre and business unit decentralisation. In their view, this trend towards decentralisation in industrial relations is best explained by changes in the internal operating procedures of the company, not by strategic thinking within industrial relations. In fact, the decentralisation tendencies have often been resisted by functional industrial relations managers.

Market conditions and the management of industrial relations

Much of the impetus for these developments has come from the external environment. Changes in the economic climate have forced management at all levels in organisations to address more seriously those

---

63. S. Deery and J. Nash, 'Organisational change', p. 165.
64. K. Legge, *Power, Innovation and Problem-solving in Personnel Management*, McGraw-Hill, London, 1978.
65. T. Kochan, R. McKersie and J. Chalykoff, 'The effects of corporate strategy and workplace innovations on union representation', *Industrial and Labor Relations Review*, vol. 39, July 1986, pp. 487–501.
66. J. Purcell and B. Ahlstrand, 'Corporate strategy', p. 413.

industrial relations matters relating to the productive and efficient use of labour. Increasing competition combined with greater economic uncertainty have come to characterise the modern marketplace. This has put companies under greater pressure to adapt their organisational structures and production systems. Many of the innovations now taking place in the industrial relations policies and practices of management appear to be due to the changing properties of the product market. In the United States, Lewin is convinced that the new industrial relations initiatives in the area of employee participation, quality circles and quality of working life experiments are principally a reaction to external environmental forces:

> Increasingly, business owners and managers must respond and react to external forces and attempt to match their various production, pricing, distribution, *and industrial relations* decisions to marketplace demands ... Managers of firms are reacting more swiftly to market signals and are behaving more like price takers than price setters ... Because increasing competition typically requires numerous internal adjustments on the part of firms, it would be surprising if changes in firm, business unit and workplace-level industrial relations policies and practices did not occur in the 1980s.[67]

Australian companies have not been exempt from these pressures. The previously over-protected and sheltered manufacturing sector, in particular, is facing severe foreign competition as tariff barriers are scaled down and import restrictions progressively removed. The earlier ability of manufacturing firms to use their positions in largely protected markets either to absorb wage and condition improvements through increasing sales, or to shift the cost of wage increases to consumers through price increases, has been substantially reduced. Weaker product markets and increased price competition, in turn, have led employers to challenge many established practices and make greater efforts to prune costs, improve quality and enhance efficiency. As the then Executive Director of the Business Council of Australia, Mr G. Allen, said in a paper delivered to the Alternatives to Arbitration Conference in 1984:

> We have moved into a new era in terms of our industrial and economic life ... businessmen are coming to apply new tests to industrial relations—compatibility ... with the demands of increased competitiveness. In this they will be looking to see how the system performs in terms of flexibility, costs, commitment, quality and capacity for innovation from enterprises as a whole ...[68]

Certainly, flexibility and adaptability have become key managerial objectives in Australia. Those barriers which have insulated industrial relations practices and procedures from the concerns of economic performance are being gradually removed. Efforts are being made to achieve a greater symmetry between industrial relations practices and

---

67. D. Lewin, 'Industrial relations as a strategy variable', in M.M. Kleiner et al. (eds) *Human Resource Management and the Performance of the Firm*, IRRA, Madison, Wisconsin, 1988, pp. 35–6.
68. G. Allen, 'Management pressures for change and the industrial relations system', paper presented to the Alternatives to Arbitration Conference, October 1984.

outcomes and business performance as organisations see the need to respond more quickly and directly to volatile market conditions. Australian chief executives now appear to be placing a higher level of importance on industrial relations as a means of achieving competitive performance. In a survey of the chief executives of the seventy-eight Business Council of Australia member companies, the National Institute of Labour Studies (NILS) found that the vast majority indicated that employee relations had become a significantly more important function in their enterprises.[69] Despite the prevalence of corporate industrial relations specialists, the chief executives felt it important to play a major role in industrial relations affairs, stating that, on average, they spent 14 per cent of their time on such matters.[70] As a result of the survey information the NILS research team was led to conclude that

> ... chief executives see great merit in improving employee relations within their plants, particularly by involving employees more in decision-making and developing the leadership skills of managers. This indicates that the chief executives of Australia's largest companies are rejecting the confrontational approach to managing their employees and are now seeking to establish structures and processes which will lead to more cooperative relationships between management and employees ... This suggests that the chief executives are in the vanguard of a new era of industrial relations in this country.[71]

But if Australian chief executives are in the vanguard of change it is not a position they appear to share with their site managers. Additional data collected by the NILS research group suggests that management in general still focuses overwhelmingly on containing labour costs rather than generating productivity improvements. The available evidence led to the judgement that: '... managers down the line are still not sufficiently seized with the strategic importance of employee relations ... many Australian managers focus on minimising money wage costs, rather than on maximising outputs by continually adapting work methods and work organisation'.[72] Notwithstanding these comments, it would seem that both chief executives and site managers are in favour of redirecting industrial relations away from the centralised system of arbitration to a setting which is more sensitive to company needs. In this respect there is support for a system that provides greater flexibility and would embody an enterprise focus. The development of site agreements, enterprise unions and company awards was seen as desirable and necessary changes if organisations were to become more competitive and succeed in the world marketplace.

One of the most pressing concerns identified by management was the need to achieve improved utilisation of plant and equipment through

---

69. Business Council of Australia, *Enterprise-based Bargaining Units: A Better Way of Working*, vol. 1, Melbourne, July 1989, p. 74.
70. Ibid., Part A, 'Chief executive survey', p. 4.
71. Ibid., p. 9.
72. Ibid., p. 75.

the more flexible scheduling of working hours. The low utilisation of capital was said to limit productivity and handicap international competitiveness.[73] This argument has been taken up by Professor Helen Hughes, who points out that 'capital invested in building and machinery is used less than 20 per cent of the time available'.[74] Much of the blame for this situation has been attributed to the restrictions imposed by the arbitration system, particularly in the form of its encouragement of uniform hours and shift premia and standard holidays. Despite this, there is evidence to indicate that management is implementing a range of changes.[75] The NILS Workplace Survey showed that 60 per cent of Business Council members had initiated different working hour arrangements over the past three years while a third had successfully changed shiftwork conditions. Over the same period, almost a half had attempted to increase the flexible use of labour through an expansion of the part-time/casual workforce and through the deployment of subcontractors.[76] Changes of this type appear to be associated with the creation of single-employer or enterprise awards. Rimmer found that in 36 per cent of enterprise awards there were more flexible working hours and shift arrangements than in the present award.[77]

Indeed, Rimmer's research points to an important trend in Australian industrial relations: the growth of single-employer or enterprise awards. Between 1974 and 1987 the number of federal single-employer awards almost doubled from 256 to 496.[78] Although many of these awards took the form of supplements or appendices to industry awards, a number contained codes of employment conditions tailored to the specific needs of the enterprise. In general, single-employer awards were found to have higher rates of pay, job classification structures more suited to localised working conditions, and shift systems and hours of work based on the actual production or service needs of the organisation. Rimmer observed that enterprise awards provided 'an opportunity for flexibility upon a wide range of issues—most notably wage rates (wage flexibility) and classifications (functional flexibility)'.[79] He also noted that single-employer awards tended to make more explicit allowance for casual and part-time employment (numerical flexibility) than did industry awards. The incidence of comprehensive enterprise awards tended to be higher in the 'tradeable' goods sector—that is, where organisations produced for export or competed with imports—and seemed to be associated with exposure to international competition in the product market and to a desire to seek flexibility in the labour market. Rimmer concluded that

---

73. Ibid., p. 67.
74. H. Hughes, 'The right to work', *Australian Bulletin of Labour*, vol. 12, no. 4, 1986, p. 236.
75. In August 1987, South Pacific Tyres reached agreement with its thirteen plant unions to raise capital utilisation in its tyre factories by expanding the number of production days from 225 to 309 days a year. Production employees were to work an average of three 12-hour shifts a week. Each sixth week, workers did four 12-hour shifts and in every six-week cycle they worked on one Sunday and three Saturdays. *Business Review Weekly*, 22 January 1988.
76. Business Council of Australia, *Enterprise-based Bargaining Units*, p. 73.
77. Ibid., p. 67.
78. M. Rimmer, 'Enterprise and industry awards', in ibid., Part 3, p. 4.
79. Ibid., p. 17.

there appeared to be a linkage 'between foreign market exposure and the comprehensive formulation of enterprise industrial regulation'.[80]

There is evidence in most industrialised countries that management is seeking to achieve greater flexibility in the organisation of labour. The use of flexibility as a strategy for labour utilisation was first reported by the British writer Atkinson in the mid 1980s.[81] He pointed to management's increasing tendency of break up the labour force into peripheral —and therefore numerically flexible—groups of workers, clustered around a numerically stable core group which conducted the organisation's key firm-specific activities. The core workers obtained job security in exchange for accepting functional flexibility in the form of cross-trade working, reduced craft demarcations, continuous training and new pay arrangements. They tended to be full-time permanent career employees: managers, technical sales staff, quality control staff, technicians and craftsmen. The distinguishing characteristic of this group centred on the fact that their skills could not readily be bought-in. The aim was to establish a stable group of workers who were able to adapt to changes in the level and composition of production.

On the other hand, the periphery accommodated market fluctuation. As demand grew the periphery expanded; as demand slowed the periphery contracted. This contrasted with those at the core where only tasks and responsiblities changed. In the periphery, workers had little job security and less access to career opportunities. They were primarily used to facilitate easy and rapid numerical adjustment to product market uncertainty. The central objective was to render workers disposable rather than adaptable.[82] By and large, the work tended to be more routine and built around a narrow range of tasks. Where jobs were not firm-specific because they were very specialised (for example, systems analysis) or very mundane (for example, office cleaning) firms could resource them from outside using temporary employment agencies, sub-contractors or the self-employed.

Some writers have claimed that the significance of the core–periphery model of employment has been overstated.[83] Others have pointed to the difficulty in obtaining appropriate data from which to measure any trends in this direction and to the problems involved in assessing the coherence of managerial strategies.[84] Although it is not easy to ascertain the extent of functional flexibility in the Australian labour market, there is evidence to suggest that the growth of non-standard employment arrangements has provided firms with the opportunity for numerical flexibility in the face of changing market conditions. For example, in the period 1974–89, part-time employment grew by 105 per cent in

---

80. Ibid., p. 40.
81. J. Atikinson, 'Manpower strategies for flexible organisations', *Personnel Management*, August 1984 and J. Atkinson, 'Flexibility or fragmentation: the UK labour market in the 1980s', *Labour and Society*, vol. 12, no. 1, 1987.
82. R. Hyman, 'Flexible specialisation', p. 56.
83. See A. Pollert, 'The flexible firm: fixation or fact?' *Work, Employment and Society*, vol. 2, no. 3, 1988, pp. 281–316.
84. R. Dore, 'Where we are now: musings of an evolutionist', *Work, Employment and Society*, vol. 3, no. 4, 1989, pp. 425–46.

Australia from 727,400 to 1,492,700 employees. This contrasted with a modest expansion of only 18 per cent in full-time employment.[85] More than 20 per cent of the Australian workforce now occupy part-time jobs. In many areas of the economy, permanent and full-time employment is in rapid retreat. Almost 40 per cent of jobs in the burgeoning Recreation, Personal and Other Services sector are part-time. There has also been a sizeable growth in casual employment as a proportion of total employment over the last five years. In 1987 almost 1.25 million employees or 20 per cent of the Australian workforce was employed on a casual basis.[86] Norris and Dawkins calculate that about a half of these casual workers could be described as 'involuntary casuals'.[87]

The decline of permanent and full-time employment can be seen most vividly in banking and retailing. With the use of computerised technology and the development of new organisational structures, banking employment has taken on a two-tiered or core–peripheral form. At one level, the majority of staff are employed in routine and non-specialised jobs, while at another level the more complex advisory services, including lending, investment and insurance work, are performed by tertiary educated personnel. This division has been made even more apparent by the large increase in employment of part-time workers as tellers and lower-level clerical staff are excluded from the established career structure.[88] Similar developments have been observed in the pattern of employment in retailing. Game and Pringle have shown that management's application of new technologies has led to a reorganisation of work and a growth in the proportion of unskilled jobs in the industry.[89] There has been a major shedding of full-time positions and a switch to casual and part-time staff.

The expansion in the proportion of people who are self-employed must also be seen in the context of corporate objectives to achieve more flexible labour usage. This category of the workforce jumped by 35 per cent in the period 1976–89.[90] Subcontracting has become far more widespread. This form of employment has always been prevalent in the clothing and building industries, but what is new is the contracting-out of entire areas of work which are regarded as peripheral to the core productive activity, such as cleaning, driving and canteen work. The effect of such contracting-out is to save the cost of overheads for an activity which can be bought in cheaply from outside the organisation. Payment need only be made for the contracted number of days and/or services rendered and not for the unproductive time contained in full-time employment.

---

85. Australian Bureau of Statistics, *Labour Force, Australia*, February 1989, Cat. No.6203.0.
86. K. Norris and P. Dawkins 'An analysis of casual employment in Australia', paper presented to ANZAAS Congress, Sydney, May 1988.
87. Ibid., p. 17.
88. Australian Bank Employees Union, Submission to Standing Committee on Science, Technology and the Environment, *High Technology and Employment*, Melbourne 1985, p. 24.
89. A. Game and R. Pringle, *Gender at Work*, Allen & Unwin, Sydney, 1983, pp. 59–68.
90. Australian Bureau of Statistics, *Labour Force, Australia*, February 1989, Cat. No. 6203.0.

In summary, then, there is evidence of a spread of those labour market features which have come to be associated with numerical flexibility.[91] There is also some case study data which suggest that Australian companies are seeking to achieve greater flexibility in the use of skills by reducing the number of job and pay scales and extending the range of functional work responsibilities that individuals can perform. Wider use of consultative arrangements and quality circles as well as other means of 'involving' employees appear to be evident. In addition, therefore, to removing some of their cost rigidities through employing 'untenured' part-time, casual and contract workers, Australian companies seem to be adopting practices aimed at increasing the commitment and willingness of other groups of employees to work more flexibly. This is confirmed by a recent survey of industrial relations and human resource management reforms currently underway in Australian industry. In his review of studies conducted across a number of organisations as diverse as the New South Wales State Rail Authority, Reckitt & Colman, Dulux, Simpson Holdings, Mitsubishi and Hexham Engineering, Duncan Macdonald concluded:

> In response to deteriorating economic conditions and increasing product market competition, especially internationally, many business organisations ... have adopted reforms concerned with their human resource management or employee relationships. These have included the introduction of many forms of employee participation such as consultative committees, autonomous work groups, quality circles and work environment councils. In conjunction with these changes, work organisation has been dramatically altered in a number of cases. Traditional assembly line structures have been replaced with more flexible forms that have given employees more discretion and more responsibility. Increased commitment resulting from these changes and reinforced by personnel practices based around Japanese principles of lifetime employment have, in a number of cases, resulted in increased productivity both in terms of quality and quantity.[92]

Managerial style and attitudes

The character of an organisation's industrial relations policies or strategies will not be determined solely by market pressures or by the form of its business strategies. The conduct of industrial relations will also be influenced by the particular values, beliefs or philosophies held by business founders or owners, chief executive officers or other key decision-makers. These values serve as a filter through which environmental pressures are processed and alternatives are considered.[93] They may, in turn, lead to the development of distinctive managerial styles which

---

91. These developments may of course owe as much to the expansion of those sectors of the economy (particularly the service industries) in which part-time and casual employment have long been used as they do to changes in employer strategies.
92. D. Macdonald, *Attempted Reforms*, p. 1.
93. T. Kochan, H. Katz, and R. McKersie, 'Reply by the authors', *Industrial and Labor Relations Review*, vol. 41, no. 3, 1988, p. 453.

embody particular approaches 'to the problem of motivating and controlling employees, of handling grievances and conducting relationships with organised labour . . .'[94] Management style may also embody a set of guiding principles which form the parameters and provide the signposts for acceptable management action in dealing with employees.[95]

Poole has identified a number of distinctive styles of management. These include directive authoritarian, welfare-oriented paternalism, negotiational constitutionalism and participative.[96] He argues that the first two styles reflect a unitary frame of reference where the enterprise is seen as possessing a unified authority structure with common objectives. In contrast, the second pair are more likely to be associated with a pluralist conception of the firm comprising a coalition of groups with different interests and objectives. This is depicted in Figure 6.1.

Purcell prefers to categorise management style according to two dimensions: individualism and collectivism. Individualism refers to the 'extent to which the firm gives credence to the feelings and sentiments of each employee and seeks to develop and encourage each employee's capacity and role at work'.[97] At one end of the individualism scale are organisations which emphasise employees as a resource and are concerned with developing and nurturing each person's talent and work. Here, careful attention is given to the selection of entrants and there is a focus on internal training, merit-based payment systems, career development and extensive communications. At the other extreme of the continuum are firms that attach a low importance to individualism. They tend to see employees as a commodity—'just numbers'—and pursue more control-oriented, command–obedience industrial relations policies. In between these two positions is a third variant of individualism: paternalism. Here, notions of benevolence and welfare are emphasised as a means of legitimising authority and subordinating lower-level employees.

The second dimension of management style, according to Purcell, is collectivism. This is defined as the extent to which an organisation 'recognises the right of employees to have a say in those aspects of management decision-making which concern them'.[98] There are two ways in which this can be measured. The first refers to the extent, form and level of employee participation while the second relates to the degree of managerial acceptance of collective representation as an alternative authority structure in the organisation. High collectivism would be characterised by an acknowledgement of the legitimacy of unions and a willingness to facilitate representative participation in organisational decisions. At the other extreme, low collectivism could be seen as taking the form of a unitary perspective of management in which industrial

---

94. M. Poole, 'Management strategies and 'Styles' in industrial relations: a comparable analysis', *Journal of General Management*, vol. 12, no. 1, 1986, p. 43.
95. J. Purcell, 'Mapping management styles in employee relations', *Journal of Management Studies*, vol. 24, September 1987, p. 535.
96. M. Poole, 'Management strategies', pp. 43–4.
97. J. Purcell, 'Mapping management styles', p. 536.
98. Ibid., p. 538.

Fig. 6.1: Management style and frames of references

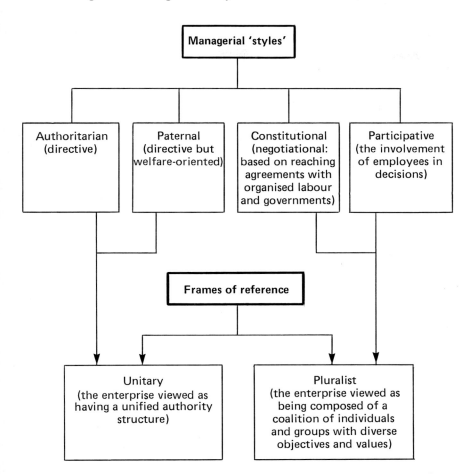

Source: M. Poole, 'Management strategies and "styles" in industrial relations: a comparative analysis', *Journal of General Management*, vol. 12, no. 1, 1986, p. 44.

relations policies would centre on control and the neutralisation of union constraints. The interconnections between the two dimensions of individualism and collectivism are set out in Figure 6.2.

There has been little empirical research on the issue of management style in Australia. Although there has been a number of studies of the attitudes of business executives and personnel officers to industrial relations issues, there have been few attempts to discern the presence of distinctive management styles which might affect the practical conduct

Fig. 6.2: The interconnections between individualism and collectivism

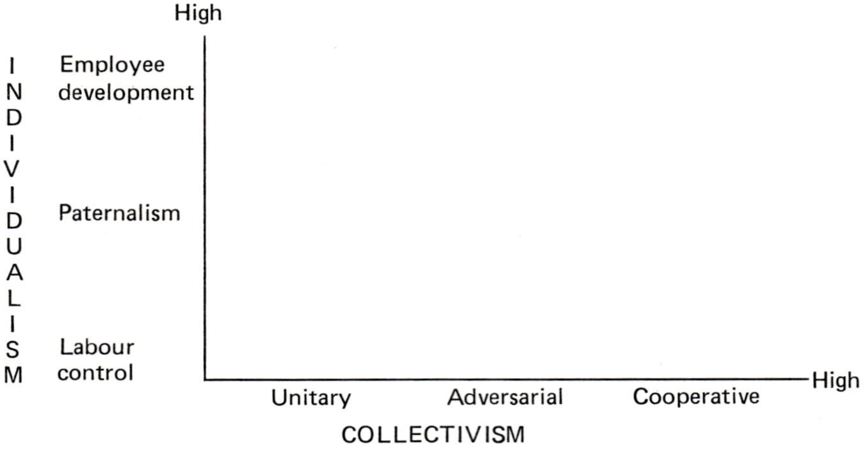

```
                High
 I  Employee
 N  development
 D
 I
 V
 I
 D  Paternalism
 U
 A
 L
 I
 S  Labour
 M  control  ┌─────────────────────────────────────── High
             Unitary      Adversarial      Cooperative
                          COLLECTIVISM
```

Source: J. Purcell, 'Mapping management styles in employee relations', *Journal of Management Studies*, vol. 24, no. 5, 1987, p. 451.

of industrial relations at the workplace.[99] Nevertheless, in a survey of the characteristics and attitudes of Australian personnel and industrial relations practitioners in 1984, Dowling and Deery obtained some relevant information on management style.[100] The classification system adopted for the survey was orginally proposed by Tannenbaum and Schmidt,[101] but was later modified by Sadler and Hofstede[102] as a basis for their research in this field.

Respondents were presented with four standardised descriptions of different types of leadership. These indicated the extent to which the manager of a group of staff sought to involve the staff in the decisions he or she had to make at work. The descriptions imply a continuum from a 'boss-centred' style of leadership at one extreme to 'employee-centred' leadership at the other. As one moves along the continuum from the 'boss-centred' style of leadership, the amount of authority and the degree of control exercised by the manager diminishes, while the amount of freedom exercised by the subordinates increases. These managerial styles can be summarised as:

---

99. See K.F. Walker, 'Attitudes of union leaders and business executives to industrial relations', *Occupational Psychology*, vol. 33, 1959, pp. 157–65; K.F. Walker, 'Attitudes of personnel officers to industrial relations', *Personnel Practice Bulletin*, vol. 17, no. 3, 1961, pp. 17–21 and R. Spillane, 'Attitudes of business executives and union leaders to industrial relations: twenty-three years later', *Journal of Industrial Relations*, vol. 22, no. 3, 1980, pp. 317–25.
100. P.J. Dowling and S.J. Deery, 'The Australian personnel and industrial relations practitioner: a 1984 profile', *Human Resource Management Australia*, vol. 23, 1985, pp. 49–57.
101. R. Tannenbaum and W.H. Schmidt, 'How to choose a leadership pattern', *Harvard Business Review*, March–April 1958.
102. P.J. Sadler and G.H. Hofstede, 'Leadership styles: preferences and perceptions of employees of an international company in different countries', *Mens en Onderneming*, vol. 26, 1972, pp. 43–63.

(a) the 'autocratic' boss, who makes a decision and then *tells* the staff what it is, expecting them to accept it without complaint;
(b) the 'persuasive' boss, who makes a decision and then attempts to *sell* it to the staff;
(c) the 'consultative' boss, who *consults* his or her staff, and takes their views into consideration before reaching a decision; and
(d) the 'participative' boss, who calls a meeting when decisions have to be made and *joins* his or her staff in arriving at a group decision.

Table 6.2 shows the results for preferred, perceived and own management style. The style of management most preferred by the personnel practitioners was the consultative one. Overall, 84 per cent expressed a preference for the consultative or participative management styles, while only 14 per cent expressed a preference for the autocratic or persuasive orientation. The respondents were also asked to indicate which of the four styles most closely corresponded to that of their immediate manager. Many of them saw the management styles of their immediate superiors as somewhat more 'autocratic' than they would have preferred. Thirty-nine per cent classified their immediate managers as 'autocratic' or 'persuasive', but only 14 per cent expressed a preference for those styles.

The personnel and industrial relations specialists were finally asked

Table 6.2: *The management style of personnel and industrial relations specialists* (n = 1398)

	n	%
Preferred management style		
'Tells'	17	1
'Sells'	182	13
'Consults'	686	49
'Joins'	490	35
No reply	23	2
Perceived management style		
'Tells'	251	18
'Sells'	272	20
'Consults'	476	34
'Joins'	212	15
'None of the above'	140	10
No reply	47	3
Own management style		
'Tells'	30	2
'Sells'	253	18
'Consults'	725	52
'Joins'	324	23
'None of them'	44	3
No reply	22	2

Source: P. J. Dowling and S. J. Deery, 'The Australian personnel and industrial relations practitioner: a 1984 profile', *Human Resource Management Australia*, Vol. 23, 1985, p.5.

to indicate which management style they themselves adopted. This pattern of responses closely resembled that for preferred management style. Respondents apparently perceived their own dealings with their subordinates as being far less 'autocratic' in style than those of the immediate superiors to whom they reported. Some 52 per cent indicated that they used a consultative style. It would, of course, be interesting to discover whether the respondents' subordinates shared these perceptions!

The survey also yielded interesting information on the ideological perspectives of personnel and industrial relations practitioners. Deery and Dowling found there was a relatively even balance between those who subscribed to a unitary view of industrial relations and those who adopted a pluralist frame of reference.[103] Forty-five per cent of the respondents, for example, believed that employers and employees shared common objectives and were part of the same team, while 44 per cent considered that industrial conflict was inevitable because of the divergent interests and objectives of the parties. Eleven per cent of the personnel and industrial relations specialists adopted a radical perspective of industrial relations and felt that there was a fundamental conflict of interest between employers and employees which reflected the nature of class conflict in the capitalist society as a whole. The study found that public sector personnel and industrial relations practitioners were more inclined to hold pluralist or radical views of industrial relations than were their private sector counterparts. Similarly, younger-aged respondents were more likely to subscribe to the pluralist or radical perspective than were older respondents.

The personnel and industrial relations practitioners showed a surprising degree of hostility to unions. Sixty-one per cent of the respondents believed that trade unions were not acting in the country's economic interests, while 63 per cent considered that trade unions had too much power.[104] More than a third felt that trade unions had more power than management, and 83 per cent of the personnel and industrial relations practitioners felt that union membership should purely be voluntary. Differences, however, again emerged between the views of private sector and public sector managers to trade unions. Those who worked in the private sector were consistently more hostile.[105]

Deery and Dowling also obtained information on the attitudes of personnel and industrial relations staff to a variety of other issues. This information is contained in Table 6.3. The items listed in that table are identical to those used by Walker in his survey of personnel managers in 1956.[106] The purpose of this was to compare the opinions of the practitioners of the 1980s with those of their predecessors in the 1950s. Table

---

103. S. Deery and P.J. Dowling, 'The Australian personnel manager and industrial relations practitioner: responsibilities, characteristics and attitudes' in G. Palmer (ed.), *Australian Personnel Management*, pp. 15–32.
104. Ibid., pp. 25–6.
105. Ibid., pp. 26–7.
106. See K.F. Walker, *Australian Industrial Relations Systems*, Oxford University Press, Melbourne, 1970, pp. 409–11 and 454–5.

6.3 shows the percentage of respondents who agreed with the items in both the 1984 study and Walker's 1956 study. It also indicates whether there was a statistically significant difference between the attitudes of the two sample groups on each of the fifteen items.

An examination of the data contained in Table 6.3 reveals that, compared with Walker's sample group, the personnel and industrial relations practitioners in the 1984 survey were significantly less inclined to agree with the statements that 'most employers take a real interest in the welfare of their employees' (item 1); that 'most foremen treat their workers fairly' (item 5); and that 'labour usually gets a fair return for the work it does' (item 4). While this might suggest that personnel and industrial relations practitioners in the 1980s did not embrace as strong a managerial ideology as their predecessors, the data also indicate that they were more opposed to union consultation and industrial action. Items 2, 6 and 7 provide information on the different views of trade unions. The 1984 sample is significantly less in favour of any extension of union–management consultation (item 2), a greater percentage of them considering that 'a union can make satisfactory progress without striking' (item 6) and fewer feeling that 'employers and union leaders should see more of each other off the job' (item 7). On the other hand, there was much greater respect for the ability of the average trade union leader (item 9), and the view that unions should restrict their activities to wages and working conditions was less prevalent (item 14).

There is a number of areas in which attitudes appear to have changed very little. For example, both groups of respondents were strongly of the view that 'most employees cooperate with their employer' (item 3), that 'most employees take pride in their work' (item 10), and that 'employers should do more to encourage their employees to make suggestions about their work' (item 12). Furthermore, in both the studies, the overwhelming majority of respondents found little merit in the suggestion that 'industrial relations would be more peaceful without the arbitration system' (item 13). Differences of opinion emerged, however, in relation to the question of incentive payment systems. The 1984 sample was far less convinced that extra pay for extra work was the best way to get more output from workers (item 11).

Finally, the questionnaire sought information on two items (items 8 and 15) which, according to Walker, provided a measure of the respondents' overall socioeconomic ideology.[107] Here it was found that a lower proportion of the personnel and industrial relations practitioners surveyed in 1984 subscribed to the view that 'anyone with ability who is willing to work can get to the top' (item 8). On the other hand, a higher percentage of the 1984 respondents agreed with the statement that 'the difference between the lowest and highest incomes in Australia is too big to be fair' (item 15). This may indicate that personnel and industrial relations practitioners now hold a less conservative socioeconomic

---

107. K.F. Walker, 'Attitudes of union leaders and business executives to industrial relations'.

Table 6.3: *Opinions of personnel and industrial relations specialists on industrial relations issues* (% agreeing)

Items	1984 study (n=1378)	1956 study (n=140)	t-value
1. Most employers take a real interest in the welfare of their employees.	46	57	−2.495*
2. Employers should consult the unions more.	53	75	−5.625*
3. Most employees cooperate with their employer.	78	73	1.273
4. Labour usually gets a fair return for the work it does.	77	85	−2.474*
5. Most foremen treat their workers fairly.	63	81	−5.038*
6. A union could make satisfactory progress without striking.	78	58	4.616*
7. Employers and union leaders should see more of each other off the job.	39	62	−5.322*
8. Anyone with ability who is willing to work can get to the top.	57	78	−5.588*
9. The average union leader has as much ability as the average employer.	43	30	3.163*
10. Most employees take pride in their work.	69	62	1.627
11. Extra pay for extra work is the best way to get more output from workers.	18	47	−6.654*
12. Employers should do more to encourage their employees to make suggestions about their work.	94	96	−1.123
13. Industrial relations would be more peaceful without the arbitration system.	12	12	0.000
14. Unions should restrict themselves to getting fair wages and working conditions for their members and keep out of the management end.	33	58	−5.716*
15. The difference between the lowest and highest incomes in Australia is too big to be fair.	36	30	1.465

*Significant difference at the 0.05 per cent level.

ideology than was the case in the 1950s. Such a conclusion is further supported by the different responses to item 4, where a significantly lower percentage of the 1984 group believed that labour usually got a fair return for the work that it performed.

Poole has suggested that particular national values or ideologies may have a bearing on management styles. He claims that in the USA, for example, a value system based on individualism combined with a strong private enterprise ethos has led to a pronounced unitary perspective to industrial relations and the adoption of aggresive anti-union practices.[108] This view receives support from two American industrial relations writers, Sloan and Witney, who have observed that:

> Our society has historically placed a high premium on property rights. Because of this, and perhaps also because the American soil has nurtured a breed of highly individualistic and aggressive businessmen, employers in this country have accepted unionism through the years approximately as well as nature tolerates a vacuum.[109]

In a study conducted by England in the mid-1970s, quite important differences were found in the 'value' orientations of private sector managers across five different countries including Australia.[110] He concluded that Australian managers could be characterised as placing low values on such concepts as achievement, success, competition and risk. Similarly, organisational growth and profit maximisation were not highly emphasised. This contrasted quite sharply with American managers who, he said, had a high achievement and competence orientation and emphasised traditional organisational goals, such as profit maximisation, organisational efficiency and high productivity.

The effect of cultural values or ideologies on management styles will not, however, be unconstrained. Conditions in both the product market and the labour market will help shape and modify particular management styles. The form and extent of state regulation of industrial relations matters will also be important. So, too, will be the power and influence of trade unions. In addition, Purcell and Ahlstrand have pointed to the effect of corporate structures and to the types of control systems used to manage operating business units. They contend that management's style or approach to industrial relations has been affected by current business practices of portfolio planning and the emphasis on financial control.[111]

Structures for the management of industrial relations

In addition to the choices that an organisation may make about its managerial style, it will also be faced with decisions about the sort of structure it should adopt to bargain with trade unions and to conduct its

---

108. M. Poole, 'Management strategies', p. 47.
109. A.A. Sloan and F. Witney, *Labor Relations*, Prentice Hall, Englewood Cliffs, New Jersey, 1977, p. 3. Another American writer, Bernard Karsh, also made a similar observation. As he put it: 'A note of individualism sounds through the business creed like the pitch in a Byzantine choir', B. Karsh, 'Management ideology and worker co-optation: the United States and Japan', *International Industrial Relations Association*, Sixth World Congress, Kyoto, 1983, vol. 5, p. 86.
110. G.W. England, *The Manager and his Values*, Ballinger, New York, 1975 cited in S.B. Aungles and S.R. Parker, *Work, Organisation and Change*, p. 133–4.
111. J. Purcell and B. Ahlstrand 'Corporate strategy', pp. 404–5.

industrial relations in general. The function of this structure will be to provide a mechanism for establishing and implementing industrial relations strategies and policies.[112] In this context, the organisation must make decisions on two important questions: first, what level of resources should it commit and how many specialist staff should it employ to perform the personnel and industrial relations function, and second, what kind of division of personnel responsibility should take place between the various levels of the organisation.

Resources and staff

Information on the personnel and industrial relations resources of Australian companies is confined to two surveys: that conducted by Deery and Purcell in 1988 of 200 large organisations[113] and the study undertaken by the National Institute of Labour Studies (NILS) of seventy-eight BCA member companies which was also completed in 1988.[114] The Deery and Purcell survey found that the majority of large organisations spent less than ½ per cent of annual sales revenue on the personnel and industrial relations function. Only 7 per cent estimated their annual expenditure to be more than 2 per cent of sales revenue. Generally, the resources appeared to be concentrated at the corporate level. In 91 per cent of cases, companies employed full-time personnel and industrial relations staff at the head office. However, only 47 per cent had personnel and industrial relations staff at the division or business unit level and less than 35 per cent employed them at the establishment level. The NILS survey disclosed a similar picture. Eighty-nine per cent of companies had specialist industrial relations managers, but again the overwhelming majority of these managers were located at the corporate level.[115]

This stands in sharp contrast to the United States of America where staff resources appear to be far more evenly distributed within the organisation. Kochan and Katz report that Conference Board surveys show that about two-thirds of firms have labour relations staff at the plant level, 60 per cent have staff at the division level and almost all firms have staff at the corporate level.[116] Despite the difficulties in drawing comparisons, however, it would not seem that Australian companies on average employ any fewer specialists. In 1977, the 601 firms that responded to the Conference Board survey employed an average of 13.4 labour relations professionals each. In Australia, the 142 respondents to the Deery and Purcell survey employed an average of 26.9 personnel and industrial relations staff.

---

112. T.A. Kochan and H.C Katz, *Collective Bargaining and Industrial Relations*, 2nd ed., Irwin, Homewood, Illinois, 1988, p. 199.
113. S. Deery and J. Purcell, 'Strategic choices in the management of industrial relations in large organisations', *Journal of Industrial Relations*, vol. 31, no. 4, 1989.
114. Both surveys covered large businesses only and the results are therefore not representative of Australian industry in general.
115. Business Council of Australia, *Enterprise-based Bargaining Units*, Part A, 'Chief executive survey', p. 3.
116. T. Kochan and H. Katz, *Collective Bargaining and Industrial Relations*, pp. 199–200.

Another important measure of the importance of the industrial relations function is the presence of a director within the senior management hierarchy. Deery and Purcell found that 46 per cent of the Australian companies surveyed had a main board director wholly or mainly responsible for personnel and/or industrial relations.[117] This would appear to indicate that board-level representation of the personnel function is higher in Australia than it is in Britain. Marginson et al., for example, identified specialist personnel directors in only 34 per cent of British companies with 10 000 or more employees.[118] In the Australian study, 61 per cent of companies in the same size range had a director.

Division of personnel and industrial relations responsibilities

Organisations will normally have a choice as to where they want to locate their specialist personnel and industrial relations staff. In multi-divisional companies, management will have the option of either centralising the function at the corporate level or divesting that responsibility to the division or to the establishment. Where the personnel and industrial relations activities are devolved, line managers might be invested with the primary responsibility of formulating and administering policy. If the NILS study of BCA members can be used as a guide, it would certainly appear that chief executive officers currently have a preference for extending the industrial relations function to line management.[119] In light of this apparent preference for a decentralisation of the industrial relations role, and the evidence in Britain of a downgrading of the corporate personnel department,[120] it is relevant to investigate why some companies employ large numbers of corporate level specialists while others do not.

In their analysis of this question, Deery and Purcell identified several factors that played an important role in explaining differences in the size of the corporate personnel function. In addition to the obvious relationship with company size, the number of establishments that a firm had was positively correlated to head office staffing levels. Organisations with large numbers of establishments possessed more corporate-level specialists in order, it seemed, to maintain and secure industrial relations policies and procedures across the company. Firms whose business activities were concentrated in a single market or closed related markets were more likely to have a larger head office staff than organisations whose activities were spread across a diverse range of industries and businesses. None of the respondents from conglomerate organisations, for example, had a large personnel corporate head office. This group of firms appeared to prefer a decentralised personnel and industrial relations function. In light of their business requirements, they were more likely to need staff who possessed localised knowledge of the

---

117. Deery and Purcell, 'Strategic choices'.
118. P. Marginson, et al., *Beyond the Workplace*, p. 60.
119. Business Council of Australia, *Enterprise-based Bargaining Units*, Part A, 'Chief executive survey', p. 4.
120. See K. Sisson and H. Scullion, 'Putting the personal department in its place', *Personnel Management*, December 1985, pp. 36–9.

operating conditions in those particular markets and activities. They would also be more prone to define industrial relations as an operational matter, one which would be seen as the concern of divisionalised or profit-centre managers. In such circumstances common issues would be less likely to emerge across the whole enterprise.

The study also found that the lower the profit centre and consequently the more decentralised the level of financial accountability, the less likely it was for an organisation to maintain a large head office function. That is, where financial responsibility lay at the division or business unit level or at the establishment—rather than at the enterprise level—it was more probable that the personnel and industrial relations function would be devolved. There exist a number of possible explanations for this relationship. No doubt those responsible for profit performance could be expected to prefer greater control over important aspects of revenues and costs, including labour costs. In addition, these managers could also resent the inclusion of substantial overheads imposed on their budgets by way of a large corporate personnel function.

Finally, the size of the head office personnel department was found to be associated with the bargaining structure in the organisation. Companies which tended to bargain at the enterprise level rather than at the division, business unit or plant level were significantly more likely to be heavily staffed in the corporate office. Correspondingly, those firms with a more decentralised bargaining structure possessed fewer staff resources in personnel and industrial relations at the corporate level. This finding would seem to have important implications for the future. Should multi-divisional enterprises seek to devolve bargaining responsibility to the business unit—where profit centres are increasingly being located—it would exert a downward influence on the staffing levels of corporate personnel departments and raise the functional responsibility of line managers in industrial relations.

Summary

In recent years there has been a burgeoning literature on management's role in industrial relations. As a consequence, there is now a better understanding of the complexity of the tasks involved and of the policies and practices used to design and maintain systems of employment regulation. The labour process theorists did much to propel the subject of management into the academic industrial relations arena. Although this group of writers may have overstated the importance of management's determination to impose control over the workforce, they raised the issue of managerial strategies within a wider business context and showed how these strategies might be specifically related to the industrial relations environment of the workplace.

An appreciation of this wider business context is particularly important. Over the past five years, there have been considerable pressures to change industrial relations practices in Australian organisations.

Mounting international competition has forced many companies to reassess their traditional approach to the organisation and structure of work and to the way in which they have trained, motivated and remunerated their employees. Most personnel and industrial relations managers are now aware of the need to align their procedures and practices more closely with the business requirements of the organisation—in short, to effect a greater symmetry between industrial relations and business strategies. This, however, may not always be easy in an industrial relations environment which contains a diverse range of groups and institutions with their own goals, values and interests. But, as Gowler and Legge have pointed out, the position of personnel and industrial relations managers rests on a paradox; not only must they appear capable of mediating the problems that arise from those conflict of interests, they also require the long-term persistence of such problems to ensure their continued survival.[121]

Discussion questions

1. Outline the different types of managerial control strategies as developed by Braverman, Friedman and Edwards.
2. Why would organisations seek to link their industrial relations policies to overall business strategies?
3. Do you think that organisational decisions in industrial relations are driven by competitive business strategies?
4. Do personnel and industrial relations practitioners take a strategic view of industrial relations?
5. In what way have changed market conditions had an impact on the character of industrial relations policies and practices?
6. To what extent has Australian management achieved numerical and functional flexibility in the use of labour?
7. Is the concept of management style useful in explaining differences in the conduct of industrial relations?
8. Outline the possible reasons why Australian management has tended to concentrate its personnel and industrial relations resources at the corporate level of the organisation.

Further reading

Bray, M. and Taylor, V. (eds), *Managing Labour?*, McGraw-Hill, Sydney, 1986.

Business Council of Australia, *Enterprise-based Bargaining Units: A Better Way of Working*, vol. 1, Melbourne, July 1989.

---

121. D. Gowler and K. Legge, 'Personnel and paradigms: four perspectives on the future', *Industrial Relations Journal*, vol. 17, no. 3, 1986, p. 225.

Collins, R.R., 'The strategic contributions of the personnel function', in G. Palmer (ed.) *Australian Personnel Management*, Macmillan, Melbourne, 1988.
Deery, S. and Purcell, J., 'Strategic choices in the management of industrial relations in large organisations', *Journal of Industrial Relations*, vol. 31, no. 4, 1989.
Edwards, R., *Contested Terrain*, Basic Books, New York, 1979.
Friedman, A., *Industry and Labour*, Macmillan, London, 1977.
Gospel, H., 'New management approaches to industrial relations: major paradigms and historical perspective', *Journal of Industrial Relations*, vol. 25, no. 2, 1983, pp. 162–76.
Marginson, P., Edwards, P., Martin, R., Purcell, J. and Sisson, K., *Beyond the Workplace*, Blackwell, Oxford, 1988.
Porter, M.E., *Competitive Advantage: Creating and Sustaining Superior Performance*, Free Press, New York, 1985.
Purcell, J., 'The management of industrial relations in the modern corporation: agenda for research', *British Journal of Industrial Relations*, vol. 21, no. 1, March 1983, pp. 1–16.
Purcell, J., 'Mapping management styles in employee relations', *Journal of Management Studies*, vol. 24, September 1987.
Purcell, J. and Ahlstrand, B., 'Corporate strategy and the management of employee relations in the multi-divisional company', *British Journal of Industrial Relations*, vol. 27, no. 3, 1989.
Schuler, R. and Jackson, S., 'Linking competitive strategies with human resource management practices', *Academy of Management Executive*, vol. 1, no. 3, 1987, pp. 207–19.
Walton, R., 'From control to commitment in the workplace', *Harvard Business Review*, March–April 1985, pp. 77–84.

CHAPTER 7

Employer Associations

Employer associations are an integral part of any system in which multi-employer bargaining takes place. This chapter examines the role of employer associations in the Australian industrial relations systems. The first part of the chapter examines theories which help in analysing these complex organisations. The second part of the chapter examines the role of employer associations in determining bargaining structures in Australia. Remaining sections of the chapter examine the functions, structures, organisation, national coordination and problems of employer associations respectively.

Theories of employer associations

Employers organise for many purposes: for trade and commercial purposes, for professional purposes and for industrial relations purposes. This chapter is concerned with those organisations with an industrial relations function. These are called 'employer associations' and have been defined to be 'organisations consisting predominantly of employers and whose activities include participating in determining employees' conditions of employment on behalf of members'.[1] It has been estimated that only about a hundred organisations (5 per cent of all employer organisations in Australia) satisfy this definition.[2] Few of these associations are exclusively engaged in industrial relations. Most

---

1. D.H. Plowman, 'Employer associations in New South Wales', *Journal of Industrial Relations*, vol. 24, no. 3, 1982.
2. D.H. Plowman, 'Compulsory arbitration and national employer co-ordination 1890–1980', PhD thesis, Flinders University, 1986, p. 3.

perform trade and professional functions in addition to their industrial relations functions. This evidence would suggest that industrial relations is not the critical factor in employer combinations.

Though there have been many theories developed to explain the origins and development of trade unions, employer associations have not been the subject of widespread research and analysis. Nonetheless, a number of theories or frameworks have been developed to help understand these organisations.

John Commons and the extension of the market

This approach to the study of employer associations is rooted in the product market. In his celebrated work, 'American shoemakers, 1648–1895'[3] Commons traces the different forms of worker and employer combinations which accompanied the various phases of market development. An important factor in the extension of the market was improved transportation and the emergence of manufacturing machinery. The extension of the market results in both the separation of the employer/employee functions, in employees and employers combining in mutually protective organisations, and in those organisations extending the range of members and the geographical areas covered. Though not addressed in the Commons' thesis, a contraction in the product market could be expected to result in a contraction in the role and influence of combinations.

Jackson and Sisson and the three-model approach

These authors suggest three models which help explain the origins and development of employer associations. The first is the defensive model, which sees employers combining against unions. They conclude that this model might explain the origins of associations, but does not offer much insight into their subsequent development.

The second is the procedural or political model. Employers might combine in opposition to unions, but in doing so they help establish bargaining structures which recognise unions in return for unions accepting employers' right to manage. The bargaining structures also help in the establishing of machinery for institutionalising conflict. This model does not help explain the variance in approaches to unions and to bargaining structures adopted by different associations.

The third model, the market or economic model, builds on the political model. Employers organise and cooperate along product lines, and often collude in 'taking wages out of the market'. The model seems to explain the operations of associations in highly competitive markets but not of those in less competitive markets. 'Between them', claim Jackson and Sisson, 'these three models or variants of them would appear

---

3. J.R. Commons, 'American shoemakers, 1648–1895', *Quarterly Journal of Economics*, vol. 24, November 1909.

to supply most of the underlying variables which help to explain the nature and extent of employer organisations'.[4]

Hoxie and countervailing power

The countervailing power thesis, the view that any interest group strives to become as strong and proficient as the interest group with opposing objectives, is a development of the defensive model discussed earlier. However, this thesis seeks to explain not only the origins of associations, but also their organisation and functions. For example, Hoxie, in his study of American unions, sees management developing 'effective counter organisation' in which 'employers parallel the union structure, trade against trade (local, district and national), city against city, state against state, national against national, and federation against federation'.[5] A number of other studies consider countervailing power as an important determinant of employer associations.[6]

McCaffree: associations as adaptive organisations

McCaffree's work leads him to conclude that 'employer associations ... arise exogenously and are purely responsive and adaptive in their development'.[7] In this view, factors in the environment (the rise of trade unions, or industrial legislation requiring a collective employer response), rather than employers' endogenous interests (for example, the capacity to control the labour market and wages) lead to the formation of associations. As the external factors change, so too will the nature, organisation and functions of associations change. He demonstrates this proposition by reviewing the external pressures, and the adaptive responses, of the major employer association in Spokane, Washington. McCaffree considers three 'environmental and exogenous' elements to be crucial in explaining the origins and developments of associations: unions, government regulations and agencies, and trade activities.

Streeck and the new corporatism

Streeck's study of business associations in West Germany leads him to suggest that corporatism, rather than pluralism, is the appropriate framework for understanding employer associations. Though associations may have started out as pluralist 'state-free' organisations, they have been 'drawn by the State into neo-corporatist structures of collective discipline and responsibility'. He notes that peak German associations have continuous associations with the state. The state determines

---

4. P. Jackson and K. Sisson, 'Management and collective bargaining—a framework for an international comparison of employer organisations', Industrial Relations Research Unit, University of Warwick, mimeo, 1975.
5. R.F. Hoxie, Trade Unionism in the United States, Appleton, New York, 1924.
6. See, for example: D.M. Slate, 'Trade union behaviour and the local employers' association', Industrial and Labor Relations Review, vol. 11, no. 1, 1957; J.T. Carpenter, Employers' Associations and Collective Bargaining in New York City, Cornell University Press, Ithaca, New York, 1950; A.G. Taylor, Labour Policies of the National Association of Manufacturers, Arno Press, New York, 1973.
7. K.M. McCaffree, 'A theory of the origin and development of employer associations', Proceedings of the 15th Annual Meeting, IRRA, Pittsburgh, 1962.

much of the agenda and the work cycle of these associations. The state has also devolved a number of public tasks and responsibilities to associations, thereby transforming them, in part at least, into *de facto* state agencies. Recognition and support by the state have become important elements in the status and recruitment capacity of associations. Employer associations have become social partners in the system of governance.[8]

The Australian case

There are three elements which are common to most of the theories described above: the notion of defensive or countervailing organisation against unions; the importance of the product market in bringing cohesion and in determining membership; and the role of the state as a rationale for organisation. It has been argued that countervailing power does not provide a good explanation for the development and operations of Australian employer associations.[9] Though the need to service the activities generated by the State has had an important bearing on Australian employer association developments, in particular the need to form national peak councils, to date these associations have actively sought to preserve their independence and autonomy. They are incorporated into the activities of the state, but cannot be described as corporatist institutions. Thus Streeck's analysis does not provide the appropriate framework for analysing Australian employers' associations. Neither does Commons' extension of the market thesis provide a fruitful framework, partly because most of the transport infrastructure was established before the advent of modern (post-1890) associations and partly because many associations continue to have a state focus. The three-pronged approach of Jackson and Sisson provides only a partial explanation of the Australian experience.

McCaffree's analysis, which sees associations as adaptive institutions and conditioned by the external environment (in particular unions, the state and product markets) does fit the contours of the Australian experience. However, the history of associations in this country would suggest the need to incorporate factors endogenous to associations, as well as exogenous factors. The exogenous factors provide the necessary conditions under which associations are formed and are forced to adapt, but endogenous factors are important determinants of the nature of any change. Such endogenous factors include the calibre, dynamism and personalities of leaders; membership composition; internal authority structures; the range of matters associations chose to devote their attention to; internal stability; resources; and inter-organisational relationships.[10]

---

8. W. Streeck, 'Between pluralism and corporatism: German business associations and the state', paper presented at the IPSA World Congress, Rio de Janeiro, August 1982, mimeo.
9. D.H. Plowman, 'Countervailing power, organisational parallelism and Australian employer associations', *Australian Journal of Management*, vol. 13, no. 3, 1989, pp. 11–27.
10. This is developed further in D.H. Plowman, 'Compulsory arbitration and national employer co-ordination', pp. 588–98.

Employer associations and bargaining structures

There is a body of literature which contends that employer associations have been critical in initiating bargaining structures and in determining the procedural rules, the level and the scope of bargaining. This approach sees employer associations and trade unions entering into historic compromises which lead to the recognition of trade unions in return for union recognition for the right of managers to manage.[11]

A number of factors are cited for employer association interest in initiating (where necessary) and in determining the rules of bargaining;
1. By collectivising grievances trade unions can provide for an orderly processing of those grievances.
2. Orderly processes can help prevent strike losses.
3. Collective agreements 'take wages out of the market'. They provide a floor under wages which makes it more difficult for one employer to take advantage of other employers by undercutting wages.
4. Centralised agreements make it more difficult for unions to pick off employers individually.
5. By recognising and dealing with unions employer associations can pre-empt state intervention.
6. By recognising the rights of management to manage, the 'historic compromise' has enabled employers to neutralise the socialist objectives of unions.
7. In the absence of unions employers still have to institute some form of remuneration system. Unions help institutionalise such systems.
8. Association bargaining means that competitors will reach the same wage settlements, and that competitors will also be shut down in the event of a strike.
9. Multi-employer bargaining makes it easier for employers to collude when it is to their advantage to do so.

The Australian experience suggests little interest in employer associations in developing bargaining structures. They had a minimal and negative role in initiating the bargaining structures (compulsory arbitration) adopted. The procedural rules were determined with scant contribution from associations (see Chapter 10). Unions, rather than employer associations, have been the critical party in determining the level of bargaining. The major area in which associations have been most active is in limiting the range of issues (the substantive rule) over which bargaining takes place.

A major reason for the passive, if not negative, contribution of employer associations was the intervention by the state in the formative period of development and the adoption of compulsory arbitration following the major employer victories in the strikes of the 1890s. Employers resented the state forcing union recognition on employers and in diluting the fruits of victory. Many important associations continued to

---

11. K. Sisson, *The Management of Collective Bargaining: An International Comparison*, Blackwell, Oxford, 1987.

oppose arbitration until the late 1930s, thus leaving it to unions and governments to determine the appropriate arrangements in the formative period.[12] Employer associations became reactive organisations within the bargaining framework. They frequently resorted to the judicial systems in attempts to shape bargaining structures to their own ends. High Court and Supreme Court appeals, however, proved counterproductive after 1914. The employers' major success was to limit the scope of bargaining because of courts' distinction between industrial and management matters. The former can be bargained and arbitrated on, the latter are outside the scope of bargaining.[13]

Interestingly, the last decade has seen a reversal of these traditional roles. In recent years the High Court has jettisoned or substantially softened its previous distinction between 'industrial' and 'management' matters. Employers are increasingly moving, or being forced, into consultative arrangements regarding management practices. On the other hand, the major structural changes which have impacted on the Australian economy have caused a number of employer associations to re-evaluate the received bargaining frameworks. Many have sought to create greater flexibility within this framework (see Chapter 14). Other associations, particularly those associated with the New Right, have called for the complete abolition of the centralised arbitration system.[14]

Functions of employer associations

Employers' organisations do two main jobs. The first is to promote the trade interests of their members and, in particular, to keep a watch on government policies and regulations to see that rather than hurt trade they positively help and encourage it. The second is to take some part in determining the conditions on which members will employ labour. Some organisations have restricted themselves to one or the other of these tasks. It would be unwise, though, to insist too much on a distinction between trade and industrial relations organisations. Some trade bodies, like the Chambers of Manufactures and Commerce, have come to take part in industrial relations and have created departments for that purpose. Other organisations have gone beyond their early preoccupation with strikes and trade unions and now lobby in the trade and commercial interests of their members.

Employer associations provide an extensive range of trade and commercial services to their members. These services may be broken into a number of categories, the most important of which are information,

---

12. D.H. Plowman, 'Employer associations and bargaining structures: an Australian perspective', *British Journal of Industrial Relations*, vol. 26, no. 3, 1988, and 'Employer associations and industrial reactivity', *Labour and Industry*, vol. 1, no. 2, 1988.
13. D.H. Plowman and G. Smith, 'Moulding federal arbitration: the employers and the High Court 1904–1930', *Australian Journal of Management*, vol. 10, no. 4, 1986, pp. 1–30.
14. See D.H. Plowman, 'Economic forces and the New Right: employer matters in 1986', *Journal of Industrial Relations*, vol. 29, no. 1, 1987.

publicity and promotion, finance, education and research, trade regulation and political lobbying. Information services tell members about government grants, tax concessions and subsidies and about sources of supplies, the names of agents representing interstate and overseas manufacturers and the whole range of statutes and regulations which apply to their industry. For this purpose the associations publish trade directories, commercial journals and statistical summaries. The publicity function is served through advertising campaigns, trade fairs and trade delegations to other states and countries. Financial help comes through the provision of credit facilities and bureaux as well as through insurance agencies and cooperatives. Education and research involves an oversight of the formal system of education to see that it meets the needs of industry. For this reason employers are active on apprenticeship boards and the curriculum committees of some tertiary institutions. Some associations provide research funds for outside bodies and some have worked up research facilities of their own. At another level, employer associations take a hand in the business of the industries on which they are based by providing help with purchasing and tendering contracts and through bulk-buying services. Notwithstanding the *Trade Practices Act*, some organisations also regulate competition among their members, particularly by means of territorial franchises. At another level still, employer associations act as the political agents of their members. In the first instance this requires the organisations to lobby Members of Parliament, and to conduct publicity campaigns for or against particular pieces of legislation. The employers consistently demand from governments favourable legislation and regulations on tariffs, bounties, subsidies, sales tax and the like. Many state and federal departments and authorities deal with trade, industry and commerce. The Trade Practices Commission, the Prices Surveillance Authority and the Industries Assistance Commission are among the most important government bodies. Preparing and advocating submissions to them is one of the primary tasks of employer associations.

As well as for those trade purposes, employers combine to conduct industrial relations. Indeed, their need to unite against trade unions has, historically, been an important stimulus to unity among employers who, for other purposes, regard each other as competitors. Such employer combinations usually arose in response to a particular threat and dissolved or became ineffective once the threat has been overcome. The 1869 Royal Commission on the Organisation and Rules of Trade Unions and Other Associations in the United Kingdom offered this description of temporary associations:

> The employers cannot fail to see the advantage which the trade unions, in their conduct of strikes, have in attacking the employer in detail. The strike is with this view directed against a single employer or against the employers in a single district, the workmen on strike being supported by those still in the employment of masters; the intention being, on the first success of the first strike, to take others in succession. To defeat this policy, the employers resort to such expedients as they deem best for their own protection. The ordinary

course of events is to form an association of their own, in which they agree, in the event of a strike against any member of the association, to close down the workshops of all, and in some cases, by a subscription among themselves, to give pecuniary assistance to the employer against whom the strike is directed. These associations are described as being frequently of a temporary character, and dissolve as the contest with the workmen which gave rise to the association comes to an end.[15]

There are many instances in Australian labour history of employer groups arising, or trade associations diversifying, to meet the challenge of trade unions, dispersing once the threat had been dealt with, and reappearing in the next wave of union militancy.[16]

Since 1904, however, that sort of ephemeral organisation has not been satisfactory. Because the *Conciliation and Arbitration Act* gave trade unions some security and made their continuous existence likely, it was necessary to create employer associations whose purpose would be to deal with, rather than attempt to exterminate, trade unions.[17] The complex working of awards has itself made employers' associations necessary. Because unions have tended to be based on occupations rather than industries, there may be in any one industry or firm as many unions as can claim and enforce occupational coverage. Generally, awards are not made to cover a particular enterprise but to cover a particular classification of employee irrespective of the nature of the employer's business. The Metal Industry Award, for example, covers 'the industries and callings [in] engineering, metal working and fabricating industries in all their branches, and all industries allied thereto'. Allied industries include mechanical and electrical engineering, shipbuilding and repairing, porcelain enamelling, safe and strong-room making and repairing, radio, telephone and X-ray manufacture, maintenance and repair, lift and elevator making, kitchenware and watch and clock making, the generation and distribution of electric energy and, for good measure, 'every operation, process, duty and function carried on or performed in or in connection with or incidental to any of the foregoing industries'. The implementation of this award is further complicated by the fact that eight separate unions are respondent to it. Some of those are obvious metal industry unions, such as the Amalgamated Metal Workers' Union, the Australasian Society of Engineers and the Federated Ironworkers' Association, but other unions are based principally in other industries. They include the Australian Glass Workers' Union, the Building Workers' Industrial Union and the National Union of Workers. To all this, the Award adds the difficulty of interpretation of some 345 occupational classifications. As if that were not enough, the Metal Industry Award does not cover all the employees in the industry. More than 220 federal

---

15. Cited in W. Wigham, *The Power to Manage: A History of the Engineering Employers Federation*, Macmillan, London, 1953.
16. D.H. Plowman, 'Industrial legislation and the rise of employer associations, 1890–1906, *Journal of Industrial Relations*, vol. 27, no. 3, 1985, pp. 283–309.
17. G.A. Bennet, 'Industrial relations and the role of the Central Industrial Secretariat and its constituent multi-industry organisations', Central Industrial Secretariat, mimeograph, n.d.

and state Acts, awards, determinations and industrial agreements have application to the metal industry.

Thus, in any one establishment, many awards may be in force simultaneously. Usually, more than one union has coverage of the workforce. It has been estimated that a company employing a thousand workers can expect its employees to be members of between fifteen and twenty unions covered by twelve separate awards. Some of these, moreover, will be state awards and some will be federal awards.

The employers' association serves the purpose of helping its members to find their way about the awards, to know which of them apply to their employees and what particular requirements particular employers must meet. The associations provide advisory services, answer mail and telephone enquiries and, in some cases, publish newsletters. Many associations see this as their most important task and devote most of their resources to it. The need for the service is the greater because most Australian companies are not large enough to be able to support an industrial relations specialist. In the manufacturing industry, for example, only 9 per cent of establishments employ more than a hundred people. More than 40 per cent employ fewer than two people.[18] Even small firms have to deal with award complexity. One small printing firm producing a suburban weekly newspaper in Adelaide emplcyed only twenty workers: a general manager, two reporters, four typist-stenographers, six printing press operators, a foreman, a mechanic, a photo-engraver, a proofreader, two general hands and a truck driver. These workers are members of nine unions, working under four federal awards, two state awards, two industrial agreements and, for the general manager, a private agreement.[19] There are similarities in some of the awards but there are many important differences. The awards, moreover, are constantly changing. Clearly this employer needs the help of an association.

Employers' associations also play an important part in the making of the awards in the first instance. They do this by helping to formulate and direct employers' policies and strategies, by processing logs of claims served by unions on their members, by representing members in negotiations with trade unions, by appearing before industrial tribunals and by attempting to ensure that members enforce the wages and other policies of the association. In the creation of 'disputes', which is necessary to the working of the arbitration system, an employers' association may stand as representative of all its members. The award made in settlement of the dispute names the association as a party bound by the decision and that, in turn, binds the members of the association. Thus, for example, the Metal Industry Award sets out, in a list, the 'Parties Bound' by the Award. These included:

---

18. Australian Bureau of Statistics, *Manufacturing Establishments, Select Items of Data Classified by Industry and Employment Size, 1974–75*, Catalogue no. 8204.1, December 1977, Table 1.
19. D.H. Plowman, 'Employer associations: challenges and responses', *Journal of Industrial Relations*, vol. 20, no. 3, 1978, p. 238.

(iii) Metal Trades Industry Association of Australia, Metal Industries Association, South Australia, Metal Industries Association, Tasmania, and the Australian Chamber of Manufactures and members of such organisations of employers.

Employer associations as political agencies

If the principal immediate responsibilities of employer associations have to do with trade and industrial relations, it is also true that they have a more general purpose and significance, as political agencies. Employer associations are not affiliated directly with political parties. Such has not always been the case. The Victorian Employers' Federation, for example, was established specifically as an extra-parliamentary organisation to coordinate the activities of non-Labor members of parliament, endorse non-Labor candidates and assist by financial, propaganda and other means the election of such candidates. The VEF attempted to perform such a role between 1901 and 1921. An alleged reason why associations do not now directly affiliate with political parties is given in the 1944 Annual Report of the Victorian Chamber of Manufactures. This organisation played an important role in the establishment of the VEF but withdrew from that body in 1905 in protest against the VEF's anti-protectionist policies. The Annual Report notes:

> The Chamber is not a political organisation and has no part or parcel with party politics ... The task of looking after manufacturers' interests involves the Chamber in very close contact with members of the Government. Governments change, and the Government of today may be the Opposition of tomorrow. What would be the position of an organisation which was known to have a decided bias towards one side or the other? ... Working from a strictly neutral ground this factor does not have to be taken into consideration. Whatever Government is in power the Chamber is free and untrammelled to support or oppose legislation purely on its merit with no deference to party organisation.[20]

This reason for non-affiliation is not a convincing one. Certainly such factors have not deterred unions from affiliating with the ALP and non-Labor governments of necessity consult the union movement over labour legislation. Moreover, employer associations have shown a strong and abiding commitment to the political philosophies of the non-Labor parties.

The principal reason why associations do not affiliate is because of the difficulties they face in trying to reach agreement and commitment on policies when so many differing vested interests are at stake. The VCM's disaffiliation from the then political VEF is evidence of this.

The absence of political affiliation should not, however, lead one to assume that employer associations are apolitical. On the contrary. Politics is in large part about the way in which the economy and the industries within it should be organised and controlled. Politics is also

---

20. Victorian Chamber of Manufactures, *Annual Report 1944*, p. 13.

about the way in which governments should use their fiscal, monetary and other powers to regulate economic activity. When employers' associations make demands on governments about the level of tariff protection, the degree of assistance to be given to particular industries, the role of government enterprise, the content of budgets and the nature of industrial relations legislation, they are engaging explicitly in political behaviour. Consider, for example, the report of the VCM's former peak council (the Associated Chambers of Manufactures of Australia) on the opening of its headquarters, Industry House, in Canberra. The *Canberra ACMA Letter* of December 1954 noted that the new building's advantages included, among other things, being 'close to the Hotel Kurrajong, where the great majority of members of the Federal Parliament are accommodated when Parliament is in session'. Active political lobbying, particularly over tariff measures, had been a feature of ACMA ever since its formation in 1904. Indeed the lobbying of manufacturers over tariffs during the first half decade of the new Commonwealth was such as to cause the Speaker in the House of Representatives to protest.[21] Without political lobbying, associations would not be serving their members' interests.

The amount and type of financial support that employers' associations have given to political parties is not clear. Since most employers' associations have not registered under the terms of the *Industrial Relations Act* they do not have to provide audited annual accounts. This has meant that the political contributions of the associations have not come under the same public and judicial scrutiny as those of the trade unions. Nonetheless, though employers do not have the sort of relationship with the Liberal and National Parties that the trade unions have with the Labor Party, there is still close support:

> It would appear that most employers' financial and other support for political parties is done on an informal basis through individuals, firms and sometimes trade associations. The canvassing of such contributions is also usually done through informal recommendations or suggestions of people who hold leadership positions in both employers' organisations and political parties.[22]

Employer associations have also been useful recruiting grounds for non-Labor members of both state and federal parliaments. More than twenty of the Coalition Members of Parliament at the time of the first Fraser Government had been active in employer organisations before entering parliament.[23] In this respect, employer organisations make a human resource contribution to the non-Labor parties which, to some extent, parallels that made by the trade unions to the ALP. One employers' federation has asked its members to consider following the lead of some British companies which had

---

21. H.G. Turner, *The First Decade of the Commonwealth Parliament*, Melbourne, 1911, p. 172.
22. G.W. Ford et al., 'Employer associations: an introduction', in G.W. Ford, J.M. Hearn and R.D. Lansbury (eds), *Australian Labour Relations: Readings*, Macmillan, Melbourne, 3rd ed., 1980, p. 240.
23. See biographical details of Members of Parliament in *Australian Parliamentary Handbook*, 19th ed., Supplement no. 1, AGPS, Canberra, 1976.

... announced that as a means of encouraging their staffs to seek parliamentary election, [they were] prepared to preserve employment rights for periods of up to ten years during which a successful candidate is a member of parliament. By this means, people employed in private industry might seek to enter parliament secure in the knowledge that if unsuccessful at the ballot box either immediately or at subsequent elections within the ten year span, their services with the Company will not be at an end . . . With this innovation people with a private enterprise background will not be discouraged from seeking to get into parliament.[24]

The political opinions of the employers' associations have never been uniform; they do not always act as a united group. On some matters, such as the level of tariff protection to be afforded to manufacturing industry, there are irreconcilable differences of approach among them. It would be foolish, too, to think that employers have always restricted their financial support to the non-Labor parties. That granted, though, some persistent characteristics of employer politics may be identified. First, there is a public commitment to 'free enterprise'. It is sometimes hard to know exactly what that term means but it is usually defined in contrast to some vague notion of state ownership and control of industry. 'Big Government' is not thought to be desirable. Nor is the emphasis which the Labor Party has placed from time to time on the nationalisation of important sectors of the economy such as banking. The employers have wanted as little government interference as possible in the working of industry:

> Industry, if left to his own devices without constant interference from government, will develop and maintain viability within the laws obtaining at any time . . . if those laws are subjected to constant change, and if new laws are continually introduced, then industry's ability to cope is lessened considerably and its confidence undermined, to the detriment of Australia . . . There is the need for politicians to leave industry alone, and we would serve our interest well, if we tried to get this message received and understood by politicians of all political persuasions.[25]

Yet at the same time employers have wanted the sort of government interference which would maintain barriers against the importation of cheap manufactured goods and which would provide subsidies and assistance of many sorts to many industries. This has not been seen as a contradiction to the free-enterprise philosophy. Nor has the persistent demand of the employers for government regulation of trade unions. Compare the plea above for government to leave industry alone with this statement from the same source:

> Two important decisions taken by the Commonwealth Government during the year related to the enactment of legislation under which were established an Industrial Relations Bureau and a National Labour Consultative Council. This [association] supports both these developments, believing as it does that

---

24. Employers' Federation of New South Wales, *Annual Report 1976–77*, p. 8.
25. Ibid.

the Government has the responsibility of maintaining a proper surveillance of the activities of the trade union movement.[26]

Employers have advocated the use of penalties against militant trade unions, legislation to ensure the election of reasonable trade union officials, and the direction of industrial tribunals to take account of the economic effects of wage increases. All this, despite the fact that because of the registration provisions of the *Industrial Relations Act*, Australian unions are among the most stringently regulated in the free world.

Structure and organisation

Two main types of organisation may be identified: single-industry organisations and multi-industry umbrella organisations. As the names indicate, the single-industry associations (for example, the Master Builders' Association, the Australian Maritime Employers' Association, the Australian Hotels Association) take members from specific industries and deal only with the problems of those industries. Multi-industry organisations (for example, the Australian Chamber of Manufactures, the Victorian Employers' Federation) take in individual employers from many industries, as well as single industry associations.

Industry associations

Though industry associations vary in size and cater for different sectional interests, most have the same sort of organisational structure. This consists of a council (often called a board of management), and executive (committee of management) and a secretariat. The members elect the council, which governs the association in general. The council usually elects an executive (president, vice-president, treasurer) to govern the affairs of the association between council meetings. The executive positions are usually honorary. The executive in its turn appoints a secretariat of full-time paid staff who work under the supervision of a director. The secretariat has immediate responsibility for the day-to-day operation of the association.

Though the industry associations tend to be alike in having this form of government, they are unalike in the degree to which they are capable of providing services to their members. This leads to a subdivision of industry associations, according to whether they are autonomous, semi-autonomous or dependent.

Autonomous associations

Autonomous associations are usually to be found in the larger industries such as banking, mining and metal manufacturing. Because of their size and relative wealth, these associations are capable of providing an extensive range of specialist services to their members. They do not need

---

26. Ibid., p. 15.

the help of other organisations. Among the autonomous associations are the Australian Bankers' Association, the Australian Mines and Metals Association and the Metal Trades Industry Association of Australia.

The Printing and Allied Trades Employers' Federation of Australia (PATEFA) is a fairly typical example of an autonomous association. Like most national associations, PATEFA was initially a weak grouping of interstate industry associations.[27] Two major influences had led to its formation in 1925. The first was the establishment of two large unions, the Printing Industry Employees' Union (PIEU) in 1915, and the Amalgamated Printing Trades Employees' Union (APTEU) in 1920. Both these bodies made necessary some interstate cooperation among the employers. The second was the granting of a federal award to the PIEU in 1925. One of PATEFA's first jobs was to deal with federal awards and their administration in the printing industry. At that stage PATEFA acted at the direction of state branches, which retained their autonomy.

PATEFA reconstituted itself in 1971 in a way which strengthened central control. In part, at least, this was a response to the amalgamation of the PIEU and the APTEU in 1966 to form the Printing and Kindred Industries Union (PKIU). With 50 000 members, the PKIU became the sixth largest union in Australia and the eighth largest printing union in the English-speaking world.[28]

The reorganisation of PATEFA brought the formerly autonomous state associations into a single federal organisation with dependent regional branches. The branches retained enough autonomy and staff to deal with needs peculiar to their region, especially those created by state legislation. Key policies, though, are formulated at the national level. Matters such as submission to federal governments, federal award negotiations and industry surveys are handled by the federal office.

The organisational structure of PATEFA is shown in Figure 7.1. National and regional bodies are similarly structured. They have a council, an executive and, under the control of the executive, a secretariat. Each council does some of its work through subcommittees and maintains affiliations with outside bodies. At the national level PATEFA is affiliated with the Confederation of Australian Industry (CAI), the Conference of National Manufacturing Industry Associations (CONMIA) and the International Master Printers' Association (IMPA). At the regional level a number of trade associations such as the Cardboard Manufacturers' Association, the Lithographers' Association and the Wrapping Paper Merchants' Association are affiliated with PATEFA. Another important regional affiliation is the Junior Printing Executives' Association (JPEA). The JPEA is an organisation of young salaried staff in the industry who carry out public relations and training activities. The

---

27. On the history of industrial associations in the printing industry see J.S. Hagan, *Printers and Politics*, ANU Press, Canberra, 1966.
28. Ibid., p. 30.

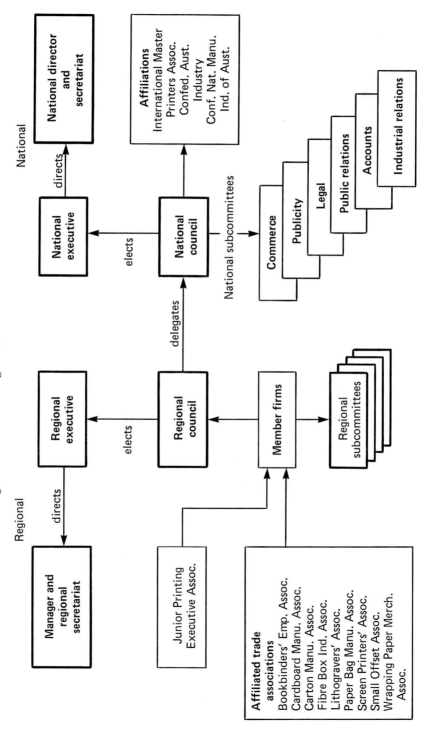

Fig. 7.1: PATEFA: Organisation and structure

JPEA provides extensive educational work for its members and is a useful recruiting source for PATEFA.

The division of PATEFA members into semi-autonomous and affiliated trade associations has advantages. It enables the differing trades to have their own identity but at the same time gives PATEFA enough cohesion to act as the industry mouthpiece. The compartmentalisation of the differing trades reduces the friction which could result from the competing interests of the different groups. Cohesion helps in the promotion of common interests such as the promotion of 'Printed in Australia'. Since the affiliates are all confronted by the same industry union, cohesion is also desirable for industrial relations reasons.

PATEFA owns its own premises, Printing House, and has an income of nearly three million dollars. More than 90 per cent of income comes from membership fees. That sort of wealth allows the association to employ a staff of more than thirty people, some of whom have specialist skills, and to provide a full range of services for members. Over recent years, PATEFA has worked through negotiations with the PKIU over major award changes, participated in the Graphic Arts Award Apprenticeship Conference, conducted a legal struggle with the PKIU over the 'OK card' system of job control, negotiated with the Federal Government and the Industries Assistance Commission on tariffs on imported books and paper and made submissions to a wide range of government enquiries and committees.

Dependent associations

These associations do not employ permanent staff. They rely on another organisation for secretarial and specialist services. An example of this type of association is the South Australian Real Estate Employers' Federation (REEF). This organisation began in 1975 as a response to attempts by two trade unions to recruit salesmen in the industry. By registering with the South Australian Industrial Commission, REEF was able to enter into an industrial agreement with salesmen and then have the agreement made a 'common rule'. REEF has concerned itself entirely with industrial relations, leaving the Real Estate Institute of South Australia (REISA) to carry out the trade activities. Membership of REEF is open to any employer in the real estate business.

REEF is effectively a part-time organisation. It elects a governing council and executive but does not have a full-time secretariat. Instead, REEF's secretariat is vested in the South Australian Employers' Federation (SAEF), which provides a secretary/administrator. SAEF provides other services as well, such as the printing of newsletters, notification of award changes, and representation before award tribunals.

Semi-autonomous associations

Most industry associations lie somewhere between PATEFA and REEF. They employ a full-time staff to administer their business but also use many of the specialist resources of other organisations. In this sort of association the manager is often someone with a legal or an accountancy background who acts as a jack-of-all-trades. The manager keeps members informed of changes in awards and legislation, edits newsletters and journals, acts as publicity officer, provides an advisory service and reference library and represents the association before industrial tribunals.

The Electrical Contractors' Association (ECA) of South Australia is a typical semi-autonomous association. Formed in 1929, the association has about 450 members, or 75–80 per cent of employers in the electrical contracting industry in that state. These members elect a management committee which in turn elects a management executive. The full-time staff consists of a manager, a service officer and two clerical assistants. The management committee breaks itself into subcommittees to deal with contractual and legal matters, industrial and award matters, labour studies, apprenticeship training, education and finance. Much of the work of coordinating, researching and documenting of the activities of the subcommittees falls on the manager. The manager can go for specialist help to the Electrical Contractors' Association of Australia, to the Building Industries Sub-Contractors Association and the Master Builders' Association, as well as to the Chamber of Commerce and Industry and the Metal Trades Industry Association, with whom the ECA is affiliated.

Umbrella organisations

Umbrella organisations take their members from any industry. Technically, only the state employers' federations are open in this way. In practice, however, the chambers of manufactures are similarly catholic in membership. The chambers and employers' federations provide a useful alternative to the dominant employer associations in particular industries. Thus, the Master Builders' Association in each state may not be seen as a helpful body by associations of subcontractors in building. Hostile to the MBA, the subcontractors may go to the employers' federation or a chamber of manufactures for specialist help.

A year after the establishment of the New South Wales Arbitration Court in 1902 the Employers' Federation of New South Wales was set up to help 'employers of all classifications representing commercial, manufacturing and trading interests'. Its inaugural membership included the Sydney Chamber of Commerce. The new Chamber of Manufactures was then a trade association and many of its members also belonged to the Employers' Federation. In 1925 the Chamber of Manufactures became a state-registered union of employers and now competes for members with the Federation.

The Federation, which now has more than 2500 individual members and 115 affiliated associations, has kept to its original charter and has remained an exclusively industrial organisation. Its resources and expertise have been built around the industrial relations requirements of its members. It also keeps a watch on legislation which might affect employment and industrial relations, such as the secondary boycott provisions of the *Trade Practices Act*, and the various Acts and regulations concerning sex discrimination.

The Federation's main work is in award making. In any one year it takes part in more than a thousand cases relating to the making of new awards, variations of existing awards or the resolution of disputes about the implementation of awards. The Federation is the main respondent to about 200 state awards and a co-respondent to another hundred. The Federation watches another 200 or so awards and advises its members of changes in them. On receiving a log of claims from a union, the Federation's industrial officer for the particular industry circulates information to the employers concerned and calls a meeting of them. The industrial officer explains the changes to the meeting, which formulates a policy on the claim. The officer is then left to negotiate on the members' behalf or to represent them before industrial tribunals. Sometimes the Federation contracts to conduct negotiations for organisations which are not members. These have included the Egg Marketing Board, the Maritime Board, the Snowy Mountains Hydro-Electricity Commission, the Public Works Department and several large state-financed projects such as the Shoalhaven Development Project.

The Federation also spends a lot of its effort in disseminating information to its members. It publishes a monthly journal, *The Employers' Review*, which it supplements with regular circulars about award changes. Officers provide an advice and information service by telephone. The usefulness of this to the members is indicated by the fact that more than 60 000 telephone enquiries are received in any one year.

National coordination

National associations of employers have developed in order to deal with federal awards, to ensure that regional differences among state awards are not exploited by the unions, to put the employers' argument at national wage cases and to deal with the ACTU. There are three types of national employer organisations. In the first type, regional umbrella organisations come together to form a national umbrella organisation. Before the formation of the Confederation of Australian Industry, the most important of these were the Associated Chamber of Manufacturers (ACMA) and the Australian Council of Employers' Federations (ACEF). The second type of national organisations brings together state industry associations. PATEFA is that sort of body. Other examples of national industry associations include the Metal Trades Industry Association, the Meat and Allied Trades' Federation of Australia and the Australian Bankers' Association. The third type of national organisation brings together both national industry and national umbrella bodies. The National Employers' Association (NEA) did this from its formation in 1961 until 1978. NEA, which had thirty national organisations of employers on its books worked through the two main committees. The National Employers' Policy Committee implemented the policy made by the members at the general meetings. The National Employers' Industrial Committee made up of experienced industrial officers, looked after national test case proceedings before the Commission.

The functions of NEA were substantially taken over in 1978 by a new body: the Confederation of Australian Industry (CAI). The origins of CAI lie in the formation by ACMA and ACEF in 1972 of a joint industrial relations body, the Central Industrial Secretariat. The success of that venture led to the formation of the CAI in 1978. There are three categories of members: the foundation members, made up of the constituents of ACEF and ACMA; the inaugural members, who were affiliates of NEA and CONMIA and who applied for membership within a specified period after the foundation of the CAI; and ordinary members, which were associations of a 'national character' accepted by the CAI.

The sectional interests of different employer groups have made it difficult for the CAI to represent employers from a position of solidarity. The alleged greater alignment of the CAI with manufacturing interests has caused mining and farming interests to form a potentially rival organisation. Several national organisations have disaffiliated from the CAI including the Australian Hotels Association, the Master Builders' Federation, the National Farmers' Federation, the Federation of Australian Radio Broadcasters, the Australian Retailers' Association and the Metal Trades Industry Association. The National Farmers' Federation has joined the Australian Federation of Employers, a New Right challenge to the CAI. Another potential rival is the Business Council of Australia, formed in 1983 by the merger of Business Roundtable and the Australian Industries Development Association. The Business Council has played an important role in policy debate and has actively represented large companies at national forums. It has commissioned a major review into industrial relations which led to the publication of the influential work, *Enterprise-based Bargaining Units: A Better Way of Working.*[29]

The CAI was dealt a severe blow in 1989 when the Australian Chamber of Manufactures, in effect a reconstitution of the foundation member ACMA, disaffiliated. This move not only reduced the CAI's membership, but also reduced its income by about 40 per cent. Thus, at the time of writing, national employer coordination is in a state of flux with the very existence of the CAI under threat.

Unity and disunity

Despite their record of instability, it is unlikely that employer associations will disappear in the near future. On the contrary, the abiding strength of the trade union movement is likely to demand effective employer organisation. Union amalgamations alone will ensure that

---

29. Business Council of Australia, *Enterprise-based Bargaining Units: A Better Way of Working,* BCA, Melbourne, 1989.

employers do not let their organisations become moribund. The growth in authority of the ACTU and the increasing importance of budget decisions and of legislation whose effects are felt across industry boundaries will help to maintain employer unity. The Confederation of Australian Industry is, in part, a response to those institutional problems. Two other events have had an influence on employers' unity. The first was the election to office of the Labor Party, after nearly a quarter of a century in opposition. Political necessity seemed to offer lessons about the need to suppress rivalries and differences among employers. The second important event was the beginning of serious economic difficulties in the mid 1970s. Inflation and unemployment, and the political struggle over the measures to be taken by the government to deal with them, have made it likely that employers will develop a still more complete public solidarity.

Nonetheless, there are still deep divisions in the ranks of employer associations. Most employer associations have in common the problems of authority. Employers regard their associations as little more than advisory agencies which allow firms to do without specialist industrial relations staff. Employers expect to pay their fees, to receive the services they want and to be left alone to manage their business affairs. They do not expect their associations to direct them and will not, for example, surrender their right to concede a union's demand, in order to avoid a dispute. If an association makes difficulties about that, then there are other associations which might be less restrictive. There is little, in any case, which an association can do to members who will not follow policy.

The making of policy is not made easier by the fact that employers may be competitors. This is true both within and among associations. Members have been wary of common policies and cautious of surrendering any of their autonomy for the sake of the common good. The loyalty of the members is owed to their firms rather than to some larger entity.

Other problems follow from the fact that many Australian industries consist of a few large firms and many small ones. The policies which will suit the large firm will not always suit the small. Voting rights in associations become a problem here too. Should large and small firms have the same voting power? Should they pay the same affiliation fees? Most associations have had to structure their affiliation fees and voting rights to allow for the difference between large and small. Some large companies have found it expedient to employ their own industrial relations specialists and pursue their own policies with little regard for others in the industry.

For most firms the general solution to conflicting policy interests has been to create new associations based on more narrow and particular interests than that of the old. Thus, in the retail trade, large department stores have formed their Retail Traders' Association while other retailers are divided among: the Mixed Business Association, the Retailers' Association, the Shopkeepers' Association, the Milk Vendors'

Association, the Fish Retailers' Association, the Fruit and Vegetable Retailers' Association, the Electrical Retailers' Association, the Retail Timber Merchants' Association and many more. Thus, too, the chemists have registered the following 'industrial unions of employers' in New South Wales: the All Night Chemists' Association, the Pharmaceutical Chemists' Association, the New South Wales Pharmacy Guild, the Extended Hours Pharmacies Guild and the New South Wales Association of Master Pharmacists. The difference between the trade and the industrial relations activities of firms helps account for the proliferation of employer associations. Small shopkeepers are fearful of department stores, retailers of wholesalers, wholesalers of manufacturers, manufacturers of importers. Fragmentation is a natural corollary of market differentiation.

Conflicts of interest among associations make it difficult for them to present a united front either in political lobbying or in important cases before industrial tribunals. One Federal Treasurer has complained of

> ... the inability of Australian business to organise itself in such a way as to make its consultation with Government effective. A strong tendency exists for individual groups to argue for particular benefits, many of which are not in the interests of the community as a whole. There is no one voice, no one group that the Government can consult with.[30]

Public displays of employer disunity on industrial relations policy have made the ACTU's job before the Industrial Relations Commission easier. The employers were divided, for example, about the 1969 Equal Pay Case, in which the ACTU argued that women should have 'equal pay for equal work'. Some manufacturers were experiencing a shortage of labour and were already paying above-award rates to women in order to attract them into the workforce. Other employers, especially those in retailing and banking, vehemently opposed equal pay. The National Employers' Policy Committee steered a middle course between these views by arguing that there should be no change in female rates but that, if there had to be a change, it should follow the limited and restrictive lines of some state legislation. The Metal Trades Association and the Bankers objected, as did the Retail Traders. The Commission was reminded that Mr Robinson, Counsel for the National Employers' Policy Committee, despite his 'grandiose title, ... does not appear for employers generally or private employers generally'. The intensity of the employers' hostility was such that Mr Hawke, the ACTU's advocate, commented that: 'We think at this end of the table that we heard Mr Robinson crying out a moment ago, "Who needs enemies when you have friends like mine" '.[31]

---

30. P. Lynch, *Confederation of Industry News*, vol. 1, no. 1, 1976.
31. F. de Vyver, 'Employers' organisations in the Australian industrial relations system', *Journal of Industrial Relations*, vol. 15, no. 1, 1972, p. 32.

Summary

Though employers combine to form hundreds of employer organisations in Australia, very few of these have any involvement in industrial relations. Those that do are termed 'employer associations'. Few associations have only industrial relations functions. Most also provide trade services for their members. Because of the limited resources available to most associations they affiliate with larger or more specialised employer bodies who are capable of lending assistance when needed. Because many associations have multiple affiliations with organisations which themselves are affiliates of other bodies, a complex maze of interrelationships is established.

Employer associations were formed for three major reasons: to counteract the activities of unions, to represent employers at negotiations and tribunal proceedings, and to offer advisory services concerning awards and industrial legislation. Associations also lobby governments in seeking desirable legislation. Unlike unions they have not persisted with direct political party affiliation.

Two major types of organisational structures can be identified: industry associations and umbrella associations. Depending on the services they provide for members, industry associations can be subdivided into autonomous, semi-autonomous and dependent associations. Both industry and umbrella associations have national organisations. Since 1978 the CAI has attempted to coordinate these national organisations and to provide a counterpart to the ACTU. Such coordination is not easy. Though union activities and hostile legislation may unite employers, the competing interests of different groups tend to have a divisive influence.

Discussion questions

1. What do you understand by the term 'employer associations'? What other forms of employer organisations exist?
2. What factors have led to the formation of employer associations?
3. What are the major activities of employer associations?
4. Distinguish between industry and umbrella organisations. What factors account for the existence of these forms of employer associations?
5. It has been claimed that employer associations are essentially reactive institutions. Do you agree? Give reasons for your answer.
6. What factors account for the difficulty encountered by employer associations in formulating policies and putting these policies into effect?
7. Discuss the role of employer associations in determining the Australian bargaining systems.

8. Several theories have been employed to explain employer associations. Explain the major tenets of these theories. Which theory(ies) best explain(s) the Australian situation?
9. What factors (a) unite employer associations and (b) divide them?
10. Explain the functions of the Confederation of Australian Industry and the Business Council of Australia.

Further reading

Commons, J.R., 'American shoemakers, 1648–1895', *Quarterly Journal of Economics*, vol. 24, November 1909.

Jackson, P. and Sisson, K., 'Management of collective bargaining—a framework for an international comparison of employer organisations', Industrial Relations Research Unit, University of Warwick, mimeo, 1975.

McCaffree, K.M., 'A theory of the origin and development of employer associations', *Proceedings of the 15th Annual Meeting*, IRRA, Pittsburgh, 1962.

Plowman, D.H., 'Employer associations: challenges and responses', *Journal of Industrial Relations*, vol. 20, no. 3, 1978.

Plowman, D.H., 'Employer associations in New South Wales', *Journal of Industrial Relations*, vol. 24, no. 3, 1982.

Plowman, D.H., 'Industrial legislation and the rise of employer associations, 1890–1906, *Journal of Industrial Relations*, vol. 27, no. 3, 1985.

Plowman, D.H., 'Employer associations and bargaining structures: an Australian perspective', *British Journal of Industrial Relations*, vol. 24, no. 3, 1988.

Plowman D.H., 'Employer associations and industrial reactivity', *Labour and Industry*, vol. 1, no. 2, 1988.

Plowman, D.H., 'Countervailing power, organisational parallelism and Australian employer associations', *Australian Journal of Management*, vol. 13, no. 3, 1989.

Plowman, D.H., *Holding the Line: Compulsory Arbitration and National Employer Co-ordination in Australia*, Cambridge University Press, Melbourne, 1989.

Plowman, D.H. and Smith, G., 'Moulding federal arbitration: the employers and the High Court 1904–1930', *Australian Journal of Management*, vol. 10, no. 4, 1986.

Sisson, K., *The Management of Collective Bargaining: An International Comparison*, Blackwell, Oxford, 1987.

Streeck, W., 'Between pluralism and corporatism: German business associations and the state', paper presented at the IPSA World Congress, Rio de Janeiro, August 1982, mimeo.

CHAPTER 8

Trade Unions: Origins, Growth, Structure

Trade unions have existed in Australia for more than a hundred and fifty years. During that time the labour movement has grown from a small collection of mutual benefit societies to a powerful and broadly based organisation which now represents more than three million members. There have been various attempts to explain the rise of unionism in Australia as well as other Western capitalist countries. The first part of this chapter examines a number of theoretical explanations for the emergence of labour movement. Within the context of these theories it then looks at the historical development of trade unions in Australia. The chapter documents their pattern of growth in the nineteenth century, the reverses suffered through the strikes of the 1890s and the subsequent stimulation given to them by the federal and state Arbitration Acts. It then focuses on the more recent experience of membership decline before turning to an examination of the size and structure of Australian unions. Finally, the chapter examines the administrative levels of decision-making within trade unions and the forms of inter-union cooperation provided by the Trades and Labour Councils and the Australian Council of Trade Unions.

Theoretical explanations of the labour movement

There are various explanations for the origins and development of trade unions. Each explanation tends to rest on its own set of assumptions about workers and their motivations, the nature of the economic and political system, and the essential function and behaviour of the labour movement itself. Some labour theorists, for example, insist that the catalyst for unionism lies in the class divisions created by industrial capitalism while others have chosen to emphasise economic self-interest as the driving force for unionisation. A number of other writers have claimed that the emergence of trade unions cannot be understood without reference to the psychological outlook of workers. In contrast to these theories there is also a view in Australia that the formation of unions owes much to the operation of the arbitration system and the sponsorship of the state. Despite the wide variety of labour theories it is possible to classify them under five headings.

Unions as a product of class consciousness

Marx believed that the evolution of industrial capitalism provided the preconditions for the collective organisation of workers. Not only did it throw wage-earners together in large numbers, it also created the deprivations that spurred them to combination.[1] Workers who were brought together by the new factory system and subjected to oppressive working conditions naturally looked to protect themselves, according to Marx, by forming trade unions.[2] The deprivations they suffered were due entirely to the exploitative nature of the economic system itself. Capitalism had created a class of propertyless workers who produced the wealth but shared few of the returns. As Marx explained: '... the labourer works under the control of the capitalist to whom his labour belongs ... [moreover] the product is the property of the capitalist and not that of the labourer, its immediate producer'.[3] Workers were both robbed of the full fruits of their labour and alienated by the nature of the production process.

Furthermore, they were denied economic control and political power. Marx saw capitalism as a system based on antagonistic class interests; class struggle between workers and capitalists was seen as an inevitable feature of the system. Unions were, in his view, the champions and representatives of the working class. They were the vehicle through which workers could protect their wages and working conditions.

But to him, trade unions were more than that. In Marx's opinion, their immediate aim was transcended by a much more significant goal. To quote Martin: 'Their destiny was to provide ... the "lever of proletarian revolution". Their supreme purpose, in other words, was nothing less than the destruction of capitalism'.[4]

Unions as agents of industrial reform

Sidney and Beatrice Webb, the British labour historians and social reformers, agreed with Marx that industrialisation and the creation of a

---

1. R. Hyman, *Marxism and the Sociology of Trade Unionism*, Pluto Press, London, 1971, p. 8.
2. S. Larson and B. Nissen (eds), *Theories of the Labour Movement*, Wayne State University Press, Detroit, 1987, p. 4.
3. K. Marx, *Capital*, vol. 1, Lawrence & Wishart, London, 1974, p. 180.
4. R. Martin, *Trade Unionism*, Clarendon Press, Oxford, 1989, p. 40.

permanent class of wage-earners were the primary factors for the emergence of trade unionism.[5] However, they did not believe that unions were an instrumental force in the revolutionary transformation of capitalism. Rather, they saw unions as the product of a determination by working people to secure a measure of order in their employment relationships with management. The main objective of the labour movement was to maintain and improve the conditions of work of wage-earners. This entailed not only material betterment and job security but also the extension of democratic principles to the workplace.[6] The role of unions, therefore, was protective rather than revolutionary. This protection was effected, according to the Webbs, through a series of rules governing basic employment arrangements. In their view, workers wanted to substitute order in employment relationships for the 'higgling of the market'. The main ways of doing this were through 'the device of restriction of numbers' and 'the device of the common rule'.[7] Although the first method was favoured by craft unions who could restrict entry into the trade by way of apprenticeship ratios, the Webbs emphasised the greater applicability of the common rule:

> ... in the absence of any Common Rule, the conditions of employment are left to 'free competition', this always means, in practice, that they are arrived at by Individual Bargaining between contracting parties of very unequal economic strength. Such a settlement, it is asserted, invariably tends, for the mass of the workers, towards the worst possible conditions of labour—ultimately, indeed, to the barest subsistence level — ... We find accordingly that the Device of the Common Rule is a universal feature of Trade Unionism ...[8]

In order to protect workers from being seriously disadvantaged from the unregulated conditions of the marketplace, unions therefore sought to establish standard rates of pay and conditions of employment in particular trades or across industry in general. The principal methods to achieve this goal were said to be collective bargaining and legal enactment.

Unions as a response to the psychological needs of workers

Whereas the Webbs saw unions primarily as supplying economic protection against the new market forces, Tannenbaum and Hoxie concluded that unions emerged in response to the psychological needs of workers. Tannenbaum believed that unions had formed because of the alienation and loss of community caused by the Industrial Revolution and the subsequent growth of capitalism as a system.[9] He argued that the Industrial Revolution had destroyed the solid moorings of an older way of life and cast workers adrift in a world of wage labour, where jobs were insecure and people became entirely dependent on others for their means of livelihood. It was a world based on competition and economic

---

5. S. and B. Webb, *The History of Trade Unionism*, Longmans, London, 1920.
6. S. Larson and B. Nissen, *Theories of the Labor Movement*, p. 186.
7. S. and B. Webb, *Industrial Democracy*, Longman Green, 1897, p. 560.
8. Ibid., pp. 560–61.
9. F. Tannenbaum, *A Philosophy of Labor*, Alfred Knopf, New York, 1951.

individualism. According to Tannenbaum: 'The symbolic universe that had patterned the ways of men across the ages in village, manor, or guild had disappeared'.[10] In his view, unionism was an unconscious rebellion against the atomization of industrial society. Unions were a repudiation of individualism. They were an attempt to restore the workers' sense of dignity and overcome their loss of community. The union, in Tannenbaum's words:

> ...[returns] to the workers his 'society'. It gives him a fellowship, a part in a drama that he can understand, and life takes on meaning once again because he shares a value system common to others. Institutionally, the trade union movement is an unconscious effort to harness the drift of our time and reorganise it around the cohesive identity that men working together always achieve...It is an unwitting effort to return to the values derived from the past: security, justice, freedom and faith. It is in those values, explicit and inherent, that man had found his human dignity.[11]

Hoxie also claimed that the development of unionism could best be explained in psychological terms.[12] He believed, however, that different groups of workers had different psychological needs and outlooks and that this in turn led to the formation of unions with widely varying functions. Hoxie rejected the notion of a unitary labour movement. Rather, he saw unions as a diverse and heterogenous body of organisations expressing the specific and unique needs of particular workgroups. Hoxie wrote:

> [The union] arises immediately out of the consciousness of the common or group character of those needs and problems; it exists for common action looking to the betterment of the living conditions; it appears primarily as a group interpretation of the social situation in which the workers find themselves, and a remedial program in the form of aims, policies and methods.[13]

In spite of this diversity, Hoxie identified four basic functional types of unionism in the United States of America. These, he classified as: (1) business unionism, (2) friendly or uplift unionism, (3) revolutionary unionism and (4) predatory unionism. The first functional type was essentially characterised by craft-based organisations which were trade-conscious rather than class-conscious and were primarily concerned with improving the economic well-being of their members. Friendly or uplift unions were more idealistic and, in addition to raising the material standards of their members, aspired to elevate the moral, intellectual and social life of the workers. The revolutionary type of union found its ultimate ideal in the socialist state and chose to invoke class political action. The final functional type, predatory unions, were set apart by their actions rather than their objectives. They chose to pursue their goals in a ruthless manner, regardless of ethical or legal codes.

---

10. Extract of F. Tannenbaum, *A Philosophy of Labor*, in S. Larson and B. Nissen (eds), *Theories of the Labor Movement*, p. 226.
11. Ibid., pp. 227–8.
12. R. Hoxie, *Trade Unionism in the United States*, Appleton, New York, 1921.
13. See S. Larson and B. Nissen, *Theories of the Labor Movement*, p. 221.

Unions as defenders of economic self-interest

The most influential theory of the origins and development of the American labour movement was formulated by John Commons and his colleague, Selig Perlman, at the University of Wisconsin.[14] Commons echoed the Webbs' view that the driving force behind unionism was the basic need of employees to protect themselves from the workings of the competitive market.[15] He believed that most individual workers were forced to deal with their employer from a position of unequal bargaining power, and that unions were formed as an instrument to protect job rights and improve the terms and conditions of employment. Unlike the Webbs, however, Commons did not see unions as part of a broader movement to reform and reconstruct the capitalist system. For him, the labour movement was a mechanism for workers to work within, rather than to oppose, the capitalist system. Its purpose was to fulfil an economic function: to advance the job rights of members and to maintain and improve wages and working conditions. In short, unions were viewed as a pragmatic, non-antagonistic interest group competing with others in a pluralist society to enhance the economic well-being of its members.

Perlman drew on much of Commons' work but developed the initial theoretical underpinnings into a far more comprehensive theory, adding a number of distinctive features of his own.[16]

He explained the rise of unionism in terms of the economic attitudes of wage-earners, which he said were 'basically determined by a... consciousness of job scarcity'.[17] The motivating force for unionisation was therefore to be seen in a desire by workers to gain economic security and secure freedom 'from tyranny' on the job. According to Perlman, workers banded together essentially for the purpose of protecting jobs and apportioning available employment opportunities on an equitable basis. He wrote that:

> [Where] opportunity is believed to be limited as in the experience of the manual worker, it then becomes the duty of the group to...assert its collective ownership over the whole amount of opportunity, and, having determined who are entitled to claim a share in that opportunity, undertake to parcel it out fairly, directly or indirectly, among its recognised members, permitting them to avail themselves of such opportunities...only on the basis of a 'common rule'.[18]

Perlman stressed that unions were primarily concerned with basic economic, job-related issues and had to appeal to workers' 'Tom, Dick and Harry idealism' at the workplace.[19] He was highly critical of those on the left who might try to subvert the union movement and commit it to the pursuit of working-class rather than pragmatic sectional goals. Perlman

---

14. Kochan and Katz indeed declared that John Commons was 'The person most deserving of the title Father of U.S. Industrial Relations'. T.A. Kochan and H.C. Katz, *Collective Bargaining and Industrial Relations*, 2nd ed., Irwin, Homewood, Illinois, 1988, p. 425.
15. See J.R. Commons, *Labor and Administration*, Macmillan, New York, 1913.
16. S. Perlman, *A Theory of the Labor Movement*, Augustus M. Kelley, New York, 1949 (originally published 1928).
17. Ibid., p. 6.
18. Ibid., p. 10.
19. Ibid., p. 274.

thus saw trade unions constantly struggling 'against the intellectual who would frame its programs and shape its policies'.[20]

An Australian variant: unions as an offspring of arbitration

The particular relevance to Australia of these theoretical models has been the source of some debate. Howard suggests, for example, that the explanation for the development of Australian unions cannot be derived from international experience and that the evolution of the labour movement in this country does not fit comfortably into any of these accepted theories.[21] He claims that the unions of the nineteenth century may have emerged in response to conventional stimuli but those of the twentieth century developed for quite different reasons. They arose, according to Howard, out of the needs of the arbitral system. In fact, Howard tends to view the experience of the early unions as almost entirely irrelevant. Their swift and almost total demise in the 1890s causes him to question whether they could indeed be defined as unions at all: 'They lacked the resilience, the resources and the self-imposed restraints on growth that a more serious labour movement could have applied. They resembled, in fact, some form of boom phenomenon...'[22]

Howard argues that the birth of the modern labour movement in Australia was due largely to the patronage of the state and to the institutional needs of the conciliation and arbitration system. The newly formed Arbitration Court required unions to enable it to work efficiently and the earliest Registrar created, quickly and without excessive legalism, a body of registered unions. Trade union membership grew from virtually zero to more than half the Australian workforce in the period 1901–21.[23] At the same time the number of unions also doubled. Most of these bodies, according to Howard, could be regarded as 'institution[s] called into existence by the bureaucratic mechanism (the arbitration system) to enhance the functioning of that mechanism'.[24] Indeed, he goes so far as to say that the early trade unions might well have withered away had they not been essential to the bureaucratic needs of the Arbitration Court. Within the context of this theoretical argument it is appropriate, then, to examine the evolution and growth of trade unions in Australia.

Origins and development

The history of the Australian labour movement stretches back to the early nineteenth century, when skilled craftsmen first formed small mutual benefit societies to protect themselves against the adversities of

---

20. Ibid., p. 5.
21. W.A. Howard, 'Australian trade unions in the context of union theory', *Journal of Industrial Relations*, vol. 19, no. 3, September 1977.
22. Ibid., p. 262.
23. Ibid., p. 263.
24. Ibid., p. 255.

illness and unemployment. The principal concern of these organisations lay more in the provision of social welfare benefits than in advancing the economic interests of their members. During the 1830s other organisations were established exclusively for the objective of protecting and improving the conditions of labour. Some were able to employ the strike weapon effectively to secure improvements in their rates of pay but most were at the mercy of the business cycle, which brought violent fluctuations in the price of labour and caused many to collapse in periods of economic recession. As a result, most of these organisations were shortlived and few were able to survive the economic slump of the early 1840s.

1850–60

It was not until the following decade that unions were able to lay claim to any degree of permanency. The discovery of gold in the 1850s greatly assisted their development. It set in motion two powerful forces which were responsible for the emergence of a stable union movement in the second half of the nineteenth century. One was the vast wave of immigrants who swelled the population and provided the country with new settlers sympathetic to the traditions of unionism; and the other was the sustained period of economic prosperity which created conditions of labour shortage and gave workers the bargaining power to form strong organisations. Population growth and the development of secondary industries accentuated the concentration of workers in urban areas and further provided conditions conducive to the growth of trade unions.

Skilled workers were the first to organise. Engineers, stonemasons, carpenters and printers had all formed unions by 1855, and these were followed by plasterers, bricklayers, plumbers and other skilled tradesmen within the next five years. They were all members of craft unions whose strength lay in their ability to control the supply of labour into their particular occupation. By limiting the number of tradesmen competing for jobs—through the enforcement of certain skill requirements only gained through apprenticeships—these unions were able to capitalise quickly on the general scarcity of skilled labour and secure healthy wage increases for their members. With wages rising quickly the unions turned their attention towards shorter hours and the demand for the eight-hour day became the rallying cry for unions during the 1850s. Unions claimed that shorter hours were necessary 'if men were to have the leisure for education and self-improvement'.[25] As Gollan remarked, 'There seemed to be something preordained about the eight hours: eight hours' work, eight hours' rest and eight hours' leisure'.[26] Economic conditions were favourable for the pursuit of such a claim, particularly in the building trades where the gold boom had led to a

---

25. R.A. Gollan, 'The historical perspective', in P.W.D. Matthews and G.W. Ford (eds), *Australian Trade Unions*, Sun Books, Melbourne, 1968, p. 17.
26. Ibid., p. 17.

strong demand for labour and a scarcity of skilled tradesmen. In 1856 the eight-hour day was won; first by the stonemasons and then by other tradesmen in the building industry.

1860–90

Those who had won the eight-hour day during the 1850s, however, had to struggle hard to retain it during the following decade. By the 1860s gold had run out, the economy was depressed and the fight to establish unionism and win improved wages and working conditions proved much more difficult. This was particularly the case for those who were unskilled. Unlike artisans, whose strong bargaining position rested on their limited supply, unskilled workers were exposed to much more intense competition for jobs. Their wages were lower, their hours longer and their organisations virtually non-existent, and it was not until the 1870s and 1880s, when economic conditions became more buoyant, that they were able to achieve significant improvements in their terms of employment.

The first unskilled workers to unionise were those in coal mining. The Hunter River Miners' Protective Association was established in 1860 by miners from various pits around Newcastle. Although there had been intermittent strike action and temporary combinations of workers before that time, miners had lacked a unified body to press for higher 'hewing rates'. The Association's initiation into collective bargaining was a marked success, as only one year after its formation it was able to force mine owners into abandoning their attempt to cut wages throughout the fields. However, the economic climate was not propitious for nascent unions and in 1862 it was crushed after a seven-month strike. Unable to prevent the importation of a steady flow of unemployed strike-breakers, the union was forced to wait for improved business conditions before it could again reassert its collective strength. In 1870 it re-formed and, along with similar unions which had been established in other coalfields in New South Wales, Victoria and Queensland, it was able to win a ten-hour day and a minimum wage within three years. The following year, 1874, twelve local unions formed themselves into the Amalgamated Miners' Association. Within the next decade it had begun to organise all miners throughout Australia in gold, silver, copper and coal, and by 1890 it was able to lay claim to a membership of 25 000, the largest in Australia.

Similar unions of unskilled and semi-skilled workers were established during this period. The Waterside Workers' Federation was formed in 1882 and the Amalgamated Shearers' Union in 1886. Others quickly followed among tanners, agricultural implement workers, ironworkers and bootmakers. The unionisation of unskilled and semi-skilled workers in the 1880s added a new dimension to Australian unionism. These unions were much more militant and class-conscious. Unprotected by the type of limitation that their fellow craft unions could impose on the supply of labour into their trades, they were forced to adopt much more aggressive industrial tactics. Their activities also extended throughout the breadth of Australia and for this reason 'they tended to see themselves as organisations representing a class rather than a trade'.[27] These new organisations brought with them a new spirit of fraternity and purpose. According to W.G. Spence, who played a leading part in organising the miners and shearers:

> Unionism came to the Australian bushman as a religion. It came, bringing salvation from years of tyranny. It had in it that feeling of mateship which he understood already, and which always characterised the action of one 'whole man' to another. Unionism extended the idea, so a man's character was gauged by whether he stood true to Union rules or 'scabbed' it on his fellows.[28]

From 1870 until the late 1880s, Australia experienced a period of sustained economic prosperity. Fed by a burgeoning manufacturing industry and a rich and expanding mining sector, the economy provided a strong base for the growth of unionism. By the mid 1800s, craft unions were firmly established in the building and manufacturing industry, and mass unions were extending their influence through the mining and pastoral sectors of the economy. In 1885 there were more than a hundred unions in existence with a membership nearing 50 000.

During this period unions began to establish machinery to coordinate their activities. The Sydney Trades and Labour Council was formed in 1871 and the Melbourne Trades Hall Council in 1884.[29] Both these organisations began to play an active role in the management of industrial disputes. Unions were obliged to notify these bodies of impending disputes, seek their advice on matters pertaining to the settlement of such disputes, and use their facilities to obtain support from other union organisations in cases of strike action. By the 1890s such councils existed in all capital cities. The success of these bodies led to efforts to coordinate the activities of all unions at a national level. From 1884 onwards intercolonial trade union congresses were held every two years to develop policies for the union movement as a whole on issues such as coloured immigration, factory legislation, workers' compensation and the regulation of apprenticeship training. Parliamentary committees were also formed to lobby members of parliament and secure the passage of legislation that was beneficial to the interests of the union movement.

1890–1900

By the end of the 1880s the trade unions were in a strong position. They had extended their organisation into most trades and industries, and the favourable economic climate and continuing high demand for labour had enabled most workers, both skilled and unskilled, to win substantial improvements in their wages and working conditions. This situation

---

27. Ibid., p. 21.
28. Quoted in I. Turner, *In Union is Strength*, Nelson, Melbourne, 1975.
29. The Melbourne Trade Hall Council actually had its origins in the 1850s, when a committee was formed to build and manage a Trades Hall. However, it was not until 1884 that it assumed the title Trades Hall Council and began to function as a union coordinating body.

was, however, not to last. During the 1890s a number of major strikes in the maritime and pastoral industries resulted in devastating defeats for the union movement. The years of economic prosperity had turned to depression by 1890 and the employers, anxious to offset the earlier gains made by the unions, had embarked on a policy of direct confrontation by asserting their right of 'freedom of contract' with individual employees. As the chairman of the Steamship Owners' Association declared in July 1890:

> All the owners throughout Australia have signed a bond to stand by one another...They are a combined and compact body, and I believe that never before has such an opportunity to test the relative strength of labour and capital arisen.[30]

Between 1890 and 1894 four major strikes were lost in the maritime, pastoral and mining industries, and this resulted in the enforcement of employment conditions unknown since the 1860s.[31] The basic issue in all these disputes was the employers' right of freedom of contract: the right of an employer to negotiate directly with an individual worker instead of the union and the right of an employer to hire whomever he chose, irrespective of whether that person was unionist or not. By 1894 there was no question as to who had won. The employers, aided by a bountiful supply of unemployed 'scab' labour and a sympathetic judiciary and government, had forced the unions into total submission and effectively destroyed their capacity to bargain collectively. The depression had been disastrous for the unions. Many had been dissolved and for those that remained there was little opportunity to resist the offensive mounted against them by the employers. Their industrial strength had been undermined by both widescale unemployment and the forces of the state which had been used to protect 'scab' labour and prosecute and jail strike leaders under archaic laws.

The unions were not slow to learn the lessons of their defeat. Without direct political representation in parliament and a means by which employers could be forced to recognise their organisations, they were ill-equipped to defeat the collective power of the employers. To this end the unions turned their attention towards the formation of their own political party and protection through compulsory arbitration. As early as 1890, after the unsuccessful maritime strike, the New South Wales Defence Committee, which had directed the strike in that state, pointed to the need for political action:

> The rule that unionism must steer clear of politics was a golden rule when there was so much work to be done within our present industrial environments. But that time is drawing to an end, and...before...we can radically improve the lot of the worker we must secure a substantial representation in Parliament. This, then, is over and above all the greatest lesson of the strike,

---

30. I. Turner, *In Union is Strength*, p. 40.
31. See B. Fitzpatrick, *A Short History of the Australian Labor Movement*, Macmillan, Melbourne, 1968, pp. 115–16.

that our organisation must become a means of education and constitutional power.[32]

By 1891 the Labor Party was formed in New South Wales and shortly afterwards in all other states. Priority was placed on the enactment of legislation for the protection of working conditions, the creation of a social welfare system and the restriction of Asian labour. Henceforth the trade unions and the Labor Party 'were to work in close alliance—and a new vision of a working men's Australia, won through the ballot box, began to emerge'.[33] Within twenty years the Labor Party had attained government at the federal level.

1900 to the present day

The unions' interest in compulsory arbitration led to pressure for the establishment of tribunals that would have the power to compel the attendance of both parties at the hearing of a dispute and would have the right to make a legally binding award for the industry or the trade. The labour movement had shown interest in the use of voluntary arbitration since the mid 1880s but it was the great strikes that had convinced them of its necessity.[34] As the federal Labor leader, J.C. Watson, declared in 1903:

> I might mention that about twelve years ago I was not very enamoured of the idea of compulsory arbitration. It seemed to me that considering the class bias which prevailed in the legislatures of those days and bearing in mind that the bias was to some extent reflected in the appointments to the Judicial bench it was not a wise thing for us when we had some chance of winning by means of a strike to hand over to a body in which we were unrepresented the power to determine all the industrial troubles which arose.[35]

Conciliation and arbitration tribunals or wages boards were established in all states during the 1890s and the early 1900s. The Commonwealth Court of Conciliation and Arbitration was formed in 1904 to settle disputes which extended beyond state borders. The development of the state and federal systems of conciliation and arbitration gave unions a degree of stability and security they had lacked until then. The Commonwealth Court, in particular, gave considerable impetus to the growth of unionism. One of its primary objectives was to encourage the organisation of workers. In order to come within the jurisdiction of the Court, unions had simply to register under the *Commonwealth Conciliation and Arbitration Act*. Having done that, they were eligible to obtain a legally enforceable award if they had become involved in an industrial dispute which extended beyond the limits of one state. An 'industrial dispute' became a legal form which did not require unions to

---

32. J.T. Sutcliffe, *A History of Trade Unionism in Australia*, Macmillan, Melbourne, 1967, pp. 162–63.
33. J.Hagan, *The ACTU: A Short History*, Reed, Sydney, 1977, p. 18.
34. Macintyre does point out, however, that labour support for compulsory arbitration was by no means unequivocal. S. Macintyre, 'Neither capital nor labour: the politics of the establishment of arbitration', in S. Macintyre and R. Mitchell (eds), *Foundations of Arbitration*, Oxford University Press, Melbourne, 1989.
35. See J.H. Portus, *Australian Compulsory Arbitration, 1900–1970*, Hicks Smith & Sons, WEA Monographs, Sydney, 1971, p. 5.

waste their resources on long-drawn-out strikes of the sort which had happened before 1900. Compulsory arbitration also helped

> ...by virtue of the fact that the low paid groups of workers who were formerly without union organisation or were workers of weak unions could, by registering under arbitration law, compel their employers to negotiate before an industrial tribunal and thereby obtain wages and conditions comparable to those which the stronger unions had been able to obtain by direct negotiations.[36]

Early decisions of the Court, such as that which established the basic wage in 1907, also encouraged the formation and registration of unions. It helped, too, that because employers had to meet award conditions for unionists and non-unionists alike, there was little incentive to prefer non-union labour or to oppose the extension of union organisation.

Under the shelter of the arbitration system the unions have prospered. From 1901 to 1926 the proportion of the Australian workforce covered by unions grew from 6.1 per cent to 55.2 per cent (Table 8.1). The number of trade unions rose from 198 to 372 over that time. Most of the time since then, with the important exception of the 1930s, unions have covered more than half of the workforce.

Despite the security of the arbitration system, though, the level of union coverage of Australian workers has varied from time to time. Sometimes that has been the result of harsh economic circumstances. During the depression of the 1930s, for example, the proportion of the workforce in unions fell away below 50 per cent. In the early part of that decade unions suffered an absolute loss of members. At other times changes in union coverage followed from changes in the structure of industry. Thus the proportion of workers in unions fell away over the period 1960–70, at a time when there was an expansion of the tertiary and administrative sectors of the economy, sectors in which unions had not traditionally been strong. A subsequent recovery of the rates of union coverage had much to do with the expansion of unions in those areas.

The growth in union membership was assisted greatly by the establishment of closed shop arrangements in the retail, banking and insurance industries in the early 1970s. In addition, the explosion in public sector employment during this period also added substantially to union numbers.[37] Over the subsequent decade the unionisation rate levelled out and, according to the Australian Bureau of Statistics *Trade Union Statistics* series, stayed within a narrow range of 54 to 57 per cent. This apparent stability in union membership rates may, however, be illusionary. Separate data collected by the ABS on trade union members

---

36. See I.G. Sharpe, 'The growth of Australian trade unions: 1907–1969', *Journal of Industrial Relations*, vol. 13, no. 1, 1971, p. 141.
37. Lansbury reported that the staff of the Commonwealth Public Service increased by 13 per cent between 1972 and 1975. R. Lansbury, 'The growth of unionisation of white-collar workers in Australia: some recent trends', *Journal of Industrial Relations* vol. 19, no. 1, 1977, p. 43.

Table 8.1: *Membership of Australian trade unions, 1901–89*

Year	No. of unions	Total members ('000)	Total members as % of total employees		Male members as % of male employees		Female members as % of female employees	
1901	198	97.2	6.1		n.a.		n.a.	
1906	302	175.5	n.a.		n.a.		n.a.	
1911	573	364.7	27.9		n.a.		n.a.	
1916	392	546.6	47.5		55.0		17.2	
1921	382	703.0	51.6		58.0		32.0	
1926	372	851.5	55.2		60.1		36.0	
1931	361	740.8	45.0		47.4		34.7	
1936	356	814.8	44.1		47.2		32.4	
1941	374	1075.6	49.9		53.0		39.1	
1946	362	1284.3	50.8		55.9		37.2	
1951	359	1690.2	60.0		66.0		42.0	
1956	375	1811.4	59.0		66.0		42.0	
1961	355	1894.6	57.0		63.0		41.0	
1966	330	2123.5	54.0		60.0		40.0	
1970	347	2331.4	49.0		56.0		36.0	
1971	351	2452.2	51.0		58.0		38.0	
1972	341	2538.8	52.0		58.0		42.0	
1973	327	2673.6	53.0		59.0		42.0	
1974	326	2777.3	55.0		61.0		44.0	
1975	317	2834.2	56.0		62.0		46.0	
1976	322	2800.0	55.0		61.0		45.0	
1977	324	2797.9	55.0		61.0		46.0	
1978	330	2830.8	56.0		62.0		46.0	
1979	328	2873.6	56.0		61.0		47.0	
1980	325	2955.9	56.0		61.0		47.0	
1981	324	2994.1	56.0		60.0		48.0	
1982	322	3012.4	57.0		62.0		49.0	
1983	319	2985.2	55.0		59.0		48.0	
1984	329	3028.5	55.0		61.0		44.0	
1985*	323	3154.2	57.0	(51)	65.0	(57)	46.0	(43)
1986*	326	3186.2	55.0	(50)	63.0	(56)	44.0	(41)
1987*	316	2140.1	55.0	(49)	63.0	(55)	44.0	(41)
1988*	308	3290.5	54.0	(48)	62.0	(54)	43.0	(40)
1989*	299	3410.3	54.0	(47)	62.0	(52)	44.0	(41)

n.a. = not available
*In the period since 1985 the ABS has collected information on the financial membership of unions. These data are shown in parentheses.
Source: ABS, *Trade Union Statistics Australia*, Cat. no. 6323.

reveal a marked decline in density rates.[38] According to this series, union membership has dropped from 51 per cent of the workforce in 1976 to only 42 per cent in 1988. This information is shown in Table 8.2.

The statistics reveal that in the period 1976–88 trade union membership grew by a meagre 23 000 at a time when the workforce expanded by well over a million and a half employees. The Australian Bureau of Statistics itself observed that, with few exceptions, 'the proportion of employees who are trade union members has fallen in all States, across all age groups, nearly all industries, in both the public and private sector and irrespective of birthplace'.[39]

Explanations for the fall in union membership

There are a number of possible reasons for the downward trend in union membership since the mid-1970s. One of the main factors would seem to be the changing occupational and industrial structure of the Australian workforce. The growth in the proportion of non-manual service sector employees, combined with the significant increase in the female workforce and the expansion of part-time and self-employment, appear to bear some association with the declining membership figures. Another contributing factor could be the increasing unpopularity of unions.[40] In recent years, there has been a relative expansion of employment in those industries and jobs where the propensity to unionise has tended to lowest. For example, in the period 1976–89 total employment grew by almost 1.7 million. More than 85 per cent of this growth occurred in four industries: community services; wholesale and retail trade; finance, property and business services; and recreation, personal and other services. With the exception of community services, only one in four employees in these industries belonged to unions. On the other hand, a number of the traditional strongholds of Australian unionism—such as manufacturing (48 per cent unionisation) and the public sector (68 per cent unionisation)—experienced relative employment decline. Manufacturing, which accounted for 22 per cent of the workforce in 1976, fell to only 16 per cent in 1989.[41] Furthermore, most of the employment growth that occurred in the Australian economy in the 1980s was confined to the private sector whose union density rate (32 per cent) is considerably

---

38. Since 1913 the Australian Bureau of Statistics has published data on trade union membership by way of a series entitled *Trade Union Statistics* (Cat. No. 6323.0). The information is based on membership returns submitted by trade unions. In 1976 the ABS began publishing another series on union membership based on workforce surveys (*Trade Union Members* Cat. No. 6325.0). This series has been produced for the years 1976, 1982, 1986 and 1988. It is generally felt that this series provides a more reliable estimate of union numbers. The *Trade Union Statistics* figures are prone to exaggeration for two reasons. First, individual unions may include in their reported membership unemployed members, members who have retired from the workforce and those who are honorary or unfinancial. Second, people who are members of more than one union may be counted more than once in the totals. It is noteworthy, for instance, that the ACTU itself has tended to rely on the more recent *Trade Union Members* data. See ACTU, *Policy and Strategy Statements, Adopted by ACTU Congress, September 1989*, October 1989.
39. ABS, *Trade Union Members*, 1988, p. 1.
40. D.W. Rawson, *Is Unionism Everywhere in Decline?*, paper delivered to the Australasian Political Studies Association Annual Conference, University of New England, August 1988.
41. ABS, *The Labour Force Australia*, March 1989, Cat. No. 6203.0.

Table 8.2: *Membership of Australian trade unions, 1976–88*

Year	Total members ('000)	Total members as % of total employees	Male members as % of male employees	Female members as % of female employees
1976	2512.7	51	56	43
1982	2567.6	49	53	43
1986	2593.9	46	50	39
1988	2535.9	42	46	35

Source: ABS, *Trade Union Members, Australia*, Cat. no. 6325.0.

lower than that of the public sector. More than 750 000 employees were added to the private sector workforce in the period 1984–8 compared with only 56 000 in the area of public employment.[42]

Workplaces in the burgeoning private sector services area have also tended to be smaller and more decentralised than the traditional manufacturing sector or the public service, and the workforce includes more of those groups which have historically been difficult to organise: managerial, administrative and clerical workers. Overseas research shows that unionisation rates are markedly lower among companies with fewer employees.[43] There is evidence in Australia to indicate that smaller firms are making a disproportionately large contribution to employment generation. The Labour Market Research Centre at Curtin University has shown that firms with 1–20 employees contributed 3.7 times the average rate of net employment generation in the manufacturing sector in Western Australia between 1983 and 1985.[44] In the period 1974/5–82/3 in Australia as a whole the number of large manufacturing enterprise (more than 100 employees) fell by 21 per cent while small firms (less than 100 employees) rose by 13 per cent. The number of persons employed in large firms decreased by 23 per cent over that period. There has also been a rapid increase in the number of small enterprises in services-producing industries which rose by 17 per cent in the period 1983/4–86/7.[45]

The proliferation of non-regular forms of employment—particularly part-time, casual and self-employment—at the expense of traditional full-time continuous jobs has also contributed to the union movement's organisational difficulties. These forms of employment have traditionally been poorly unionised.[46] The marked expansion of these jobs since

42. ABS, *Labour Statistics Australia*, 1988, Cat. No. 6101.0.
43. See A. Booth, 'Estimating the probability of trade union membership: a study of men and women in Britain', *Economica*, vol. 53, February 1986, and G.S. Bain and P. Elias, 'Trade union membership in Great Britain: an individual-level analysis', *British Journal of Industrial Relations*, vol. 23, no. 1, 1985.
44. Labour Market Research Centre *News*, vol. 1, no 3, September 1989.
45. Business Council of Australia, *Bulletin*, May 1989.
46. Deery and De Cieri have estimated that the probability of unionisation is significantly reduced where an individual works part-time or is self-employed. See S. Deery and H. De Cieri, 'Determinants of trade union membership in Australia', Centre for Industrial Relations and Labour Studies, University of Melbourne, Working Paper No. 50, December 1989. There are also major differences between the unionisation rates of casual and permanent employees. In 1988 only 20 per cent of casual workers were union members compared with 47 per cent of permanent workers. ABS, *Trade Union Members Australia*, August 1988, Cat. No.6325.0.

the mid-1970s is quite evident. In the period 1974–89 part-time employment jumped by 105 per cent compared with a modest growth in full-time employment of only 18 per cent. Presently just under 20 per cent of the Australian workforce is employed in part-time jobs. There has also been a substantial rise in casual employment. Norris and Dawkins have estimated that the casual workforce grew from 13.8 per cent of total employees in 1982 to 19.9 per cent in 1987.[47] The number of self-employed rose steeply during the 1970s and early 1980s and presently stands at approximately 10 per cent of the workforce.[48] Australian trade unions have found it difficult to recruit and retain members in these areas of employment. Part of the reason for this would seem to be the high rate of job mobility among part-timers and casuals. Their limited attachment to the labour force may also affect their expectations about the possible utility gains from unionism. In addition, unions themselves may be to blame for the low levels of representation among these types of employees. They may not recruit part-time and casual employees as assiduously as full-time workers because of the relatively higher organisational costs involved.[49]

Changes in the gender composition of the Australian workforce could be associated with the decline in union membership. Women now account for more than 40 per cent of all employees compared with 35 per cent a little more than a decade ago. In the period 1976–89 the number of female employees grew at a rate almost three times as fast as that of male employees.[50] On the other hand, female unionisation rates have been considerably lower than for men (see Table 8.1).[51] There are at least two possible reasons why women might be expected to be less unionised than men. First, the occupational segmentation of the labour market based on gender may assign women to less unionised occupations and industries.[52] Part-time status, lower labour force attachment and employment in smaller-sized business units may explain the differential in union status. Second, the reason may lie in gender-specific tastes for union representation.[53] Women may be less favourably disposed towards unions because they feel that their specific needs are not being addressed and consequently see few advantages in joining a union. Although there would seem to be some evidence to support this second explanation, an assessment of the empirical literature suggests that women are at least as willing as men to join unions. Their lower

---

47. K. Norris, and P. Dawkins, 'An analysis of casual employment in Australia', paper presented to ANZAAS Congress, Sydney, May 1988.
48. The flexible workforce in Australia—comprising part-time and casual employees and the self-employed—has been estimated at just under 2.5 million or approximately one-third of the total workforce. See S. Deery, 'The Australian trade union movement—towards the year 2000', *The Commission for the Future*, Melbourne, 1989, p. 85.
49. A. Booth, 'Estimating the probability of trade union membership', p. 42.
50. ABS, *The Labour Force Australia*, 1989, Cat. No.6203.0.
51. Figures published by the ABS in its *Trade Union Members* series also confirm the quite substantial gender difference.
52. H. Farber, 'The extent of unionisation in the United States' in T.A. Kochan (ed.), *Challenges and Choices Facing American Labor*, MIT Press, Cambridge, Mass., 1986.
53. J. Fiorito and C. Greer, 'Determinants of U.S. unionism: past research and future needs', *Industrial Relations*, vol. 21, Winter 1982.

propensity derives essentially from the jobs and industries in which they work[54]

In addition to changes in the occupational and compositional structure of the workforce another possible factor affecting membership levels could be changes in employee attitudes towards unions. A number of writers have pointed to the downward shift in community support for unions across the industrialised world in general.[55] In Australia, public opinion polls show that unions are seen as being too powerful and their leaders are perceived as being unresponsive to the needs of members. Where such beliefs exist, individuals may be less inclined to join unions.[56] Certainly, the ACTU has shown concern about the poor public image of trade unions and spoken about the need for general publicity initiatives to make unions 'more attractive to members and would-be members'.[57]

One of the standard methods of measuring public attitudes to unions is through national opinion polls. Different polling agencies and academic research teams in Australia have gathered data—if somewhat irregularly—on the public's perceptions of unions for many years. Questions have been asked about union power, the level of confidence that individuals have in unions and about the interests or motives of union officials. The value of this type of data has been widely debated. Some suggest that public opinion polls are little more than a collection of 'top-of-the-head' responses and are poor predictors of behaviour.[58] Others feel that the regular and systematic polling of opinions on trade unions provide a useful indication of overall reactions even if they fail to tap deeper perceptions and understandings of unions.[59]

An indication of Australian attitudes to unions can be seen in Table 8.3. Age polls taken over the period 1971–86 show the extent to which the community believes that unions have 'too much power'. In 1971 somewhat less than half of the respondents believed that trade unions were too powerful. By 1986 almost four out of five Australians nominated the trade unions as excessively powerful—well over twice the proportion of those who selected the next highest group: big business (31 per cent). These figures show a large increase in the assessment of union power over the fifteen-year period. Surveys have also gathered information on the level of confidence that Australians have in unions as institutions and in union officials. In the 1983 Australian Values Study,

---

54. See J. Fiorito and C. Greer, 'Gender difference in union membership, preferences and beliefs', *Journal of Labor Research*, vol. 7, no. 2, 1986.
55. See for example S.M. Lipset, 'Labor unions in the public mind' in S.M. Lipset (ed.), *Unions in Transition*, ICS Press, San Francisco, 1986.
56. Both Kochan and Youngblood et al. have identified the general image of unions as an important factor affecting the unionisation process. T.A. Kochan, 'How American workers view labor unions', *Monthly Labor Review*, April 1979 and S. Youngblood et al., 'The impact of work environment, instrumentality beliefs, perceived labour union image and subjective norms on union voting intentions', *Academy of Management Journal*, vol. 27, no. 3, September 1984.
57. ACTU, *Future Strategies for the Trade Unions Movement*, Melbourne, 1986, p. 17.
58. M. Rosier and T. Little, 'Public opinion, trade unions and industrial relations', *Journal of Occupational Psychology*, vol. 59, 1986.
59. P.K. Edwards and G.S. Bain, 'Why are trade unions becoming more popular? Unions and public opinion in Britain', *British Journal of Industrial Relations*, vol. 26, no. 3, 1988.

Table 8.3: *Groups in the community believed to hold 'too much power'*

Question: 'Some people believe that some groups in the community have too much power while other groups do not have enough power. In general, which of these groups would you say have too much power?'

	1986	1980	1974	1971
Trade unions	78	68	66	49
Big business	31	30	28	24
The press	31	25	24	21
Federal Government	26	25	20	23
Financial institutions	20	*	*	*
State Governments	16	15	13	12
TV channels	15	18	15	10
Public servants	13	7	*	*
Local Government	8	6	8	7
Police	7	6	6	6
The Church	4	6	10	6
Farmers	2	2	*	*

*Indicates group was not included in question. Respondents may provide more than one answer.
Source: The *Age*, 14 October 1986 and 12 August 1974.

more than 75 per cent of the general community and 62 per cent of all union members expressed the view that they did not have very much confidence or had no confidence at all in trade unions.[60] In the same year, the McNair Anderson polling agency in association with Sentry Holdings asked Australians to indicate their confidence in the 'people running' a number of major institutions, including trade unions.[61] The lowest level of confidence was expressed in trade union leaders. Only 6 per cent of those surveyed stated that they had a 'great deal' of confidence in the leaders of trade unions. Even among union members little confidence was expressed in their leadership. More than 45 per cent of union members expressed 'hardly any' confidence in union leaders.[62]

Although Australians appear to have little confidence in unions or their leaders and regard trade unions as too powerful, they seem to have far more favourable attitudes towards union activities and the contribution they have made to living standards. The Australian Values Study survey found that well over half of the respondents strongly agreed or agreed with the statement 'Over the years trade unions have substantially improved the living standards of Australians'.[63] Seventy per cent of unionists and 46 per cent of non-unionists held that view. In an earlier

---

60. *Australian Values Study 1983*, Roy Morgan Research Centre.
61. These institutions included hospitals, universities, law courts, churches, major companies, the government, the press and unions.
62. McNair Anderson, *The Changing Australian*, Sentry Holdings, 1983.
63. Australian Values Study 1983.

study conducted by Rawson just under 70 per cent of the respondents recorded their agreement with the statement that 'unions were good for Australia'.[64] These contradictory attitudes are also evident in trade unionists' attitudes to union power. As Dufty and Mulvey noted: 'Samples of trade unionists...usually reveal a majority who believe unions are too powerful—but unionists seldom if ever believe this of their own unions.'[65]

In Britain, Edwards and Bain have shown that union density and union popularity are related.[66] However, the relationship is inverse: as union density has increased, union popularity has decreased and as union density has decreased, union popularity has increased. They believe that this is consistent with people feeling that unions in general may be too powerful but they themselves need to join a union to seek the benefits of that power. Their multivariate regression results show that net popularity is explained in terms of the volume of strikes and price inflation, with both having an inverse relationship with popularity. The tendency for union popularity to increase in the 1980s was due to the reduction of inflation and the volume of strikes. Unions were seen to cause and were blamed for both inflation and strikes. Edwards and Bain drew the conclusion that the rise in union popularity in Britain may reflect 'weakness and not strength'.[67] It would appear that the more prices rise and the more unions push for wages through strikes and other means, the more employees tend to join them.

Some writers have tended to regard the issue of public perceptions of union power as largely irrelevant to union membership. Kelly, for example, asserts that 'there is no obvious recruitment and membership pay-off for cultivating public opinion. Indeed, insofar as successful recruitment entails industrial action it may damage union standing in public opinion'.[68] Certainly, there is evidence to indicate that employees' perceptions 'of what unions do for their members at the workplace' is a much more important influence on the propensity to organise than their general image of unions in the wider society.[69] On the other hand Deery and De Cieri, using Australian data, found that employees who held a 'negative image' of unions and their leaders were significantly less likely to be unionised.[70]

---

64. See D.W. Rawson, *Unions and Unionists in Australia*, Allen & Unwin, Sydney, 1978.
65. N.F. Dufty and C. Mulvey, *The Sources of Union Power*, Policy Paper No. 11, Australian Institute for Public Policy, 1987, p. 6.
66. P.K. Edwards and G.S. Bain, 'Why are trade unions becoming more popular?'
67. Ibid., p. 324.
68. J. Kelly, 'The decline of trade unionism?', *Industrial Tutor*, vol. 4, no. 7, 1988, p. 16.
69. See T.A. Kochan, 'How American workers view labor unions', and D. Guest and P. Dewe, 'Why do workers belong to trade unions? A social psychological study in the UK electronics industry', *British Journal of Industrial Relations*, vol. 26, no. 2, July 1988.
70. S. Deery and H. De Cieri, 'Determinants of trade union membership in Australia'. There are two possible explanations for this result. First, a negative union image may act as a form of psychological veto mechanism on union membership. Alternatively, and following a different causal path, union members may adopt more favourable attitudes to unions simply through the process of acculturation. The opportunity for unions to communicate and instil their values will obviously be greater when employees are union members.

The pattern of Australian unionism

Industry and occupational coverage

The size of the union presence has varied greatly from industry to industry. In 1988 the industries with the highest proportions of their employees in unions were electricity, gas and water, communications, mining, transport and storage and public administration (Table 8.4). More than 60 per cent of the employees in those industries were union members. At the other end of the scale were agriculture, forestry and fishing, wholesale and retail trade, recreation, personal and other services, and finance, property and business services. In each of these industries less than 30 per cent of the workforce was unionised.

There are also important occupational differences in union density rates (Table 8.5). Drivers and plant and machine operators are three times as heavily unionised as managers and administrators. Among male employees, the highest unionised occupations are drivers, plant and machine operators, para-professionals, tradesmen and clerical workers. Similarly, there is a wide diversity in unionisation rates among female workers. However, in only two occupational categories are union members able to match or outnumber non-unionists.

Union size

By international standards Australia has a large number of trade unions. Most are small. Of the 299 unions in existence at the end of June 1989, 215 had fewer than 5000 members (see Table 8.6). Moreover, the structure and distributional spread of unions has remained relatively stable during the post-war period. Despite the alleged inadequacies of small

Table 8.4: *Trade union industry penetration, August 1988*

	Percentage of all employees unionised in industry		
Industry	Males	Females	Persons
Agriculture, forestry, fishing	13	11	13
Mining	67	19	63
Manufacturing	52	38	48
Electricity, gas and water	82	62	80
Construction	52	11	47
Wholesale and retail trade	21	26	23
Transport and storage	69	35	62
Communication	84	55	76
Finance, property and business services	28	27	28
Public administration and defence	68	48	61
Community services	56	45	49
Recreation, personal and other services	27	26	26
Total	46	35	42

Source: ABS, *Trade Union Members, Australia*, June 1989.

Table 8.5: *Trade union occupational coverage, August 1988*

	Percentage of all employees unionised in occupation		
Occupation	Males	Females	Persons
Managers and administrators	19	17	19
Professionals	39	50	44
Para-professionals	54	48	52
Tradepersons	52	25	50
Clerks	52	26	32
Salespersons and personal service workers	24	33	30
Drivers and plant and machine operators	66	54	64
Labourers and related workers	51	42	48
Total	46	35	42

Source: ABS, *Trade Union Members, Australia*, June 1989.

Table 8.6: *Trade union size, June 1989*

No. of members	No. of unions	% of unions	% of unionists
Under 100	38	12.7	0.1
100– 249	31	10.4	0.2
250– 499	26	8.7	0.3
	95	31.8	0.6
500– 999	41	13.7	0.8
1 000– 1 999	42	14.0	1.7
2 000– 2 999	12	4.0	0.9
3 000– 4 999	25	8.4	2.9
5 000– 9 999	19	6.4	4.1
	234	78.3	10.9
10 000–19 999	19	6.4	7.7
20 000–29 999	12	4.0	8.7
30 000–39 999	10	3.3	10.3
40 000–49 999	6	2.0	7.9
	281	94.0	45.4
50 000–80 000	7	2.3	13.3
80 000 and above	11	2.7	41.3
Total	299	100.0	100.0

Source: ABS, *Trade Union Statistics, Australia*, January 1990.

unions, they have shown remarkable durability. In 1989 72 per cent of all unions had fewer than 5000 members. They had a combined membership of only 232 000 or 7 per cent of the aggregate union membership in Australia in that year. Almost two decades earlier, in 1971, 77 per cent of all unions had fewer than 5000 members. Their combined membership was just over 9 per cent. While the majority of trade unionists belong to a small number of large organisations (see Table 8.7) there has been only a moderate increase in the concentration of union membership. In 1971, for example, there were twelve unions or 4 per cent of all unions with more than 50 000 members. These accounted for 1 250 600 members or 46 per cent of all union members. By 1989, there were eighteen unions with more than 50 000 members. This represented 6 per cent of all unions. Their combined membership was 1 862 000 or 55 per cent of all members.

In contrast to most other Western countries, the concentration of members among the major unions has actually declined. In 1971 the ten largest unions accounted for 38 per cent of the total union membership. In 1989 this figure had dropped slightly to 37 per cent. This differs sharply from overseas experience, where union movements have become more concentrated, either through amalgamations or through the presence of proportionately more members in larger unions.[71] In 1977–8 the ten largest unions in Great Britain accounted for some 62 per cent of the total union membership, in West Germany for 91 per cent, in Sweden for 85 per cent and in the United States of America for 47 per cent.[72]

It is apparent that the structure of Australian trade unionism has remained fairly stable over the past decade and a half. Despite significant changes in the nature of the economy, in the pattern of production and employment, and in the level and impact of technological change, the distributional pattern of Australian trade unions has remained largely unaltered. While there have been quite significant changes in the numbers of trade unions and the concentration of membership in both the United Kingdom and the United States of America, parallel developments have not occurred in Australia. In the United Kingdom, for example, between 1966 and 1979 there was a reduction in the number of trade unions from 622 to 456, a 27 per cent decline.[73] In the same period total union membership increased by 28 per cent.[74] There has been a rapid decline in the number of small unions. In 1966 there were 525 unions with fewer than 5000 members. This had dropped to 354 in 1978, a fall of one-third in the number. A similar, if less dramatic trend has occurred in the USA, a country with some 200 labour unions and employee associations. Chaison observed that between 1956 and 1984 some ninety two union mergers occurred.[75] Certainly, over the past two decades there has been a flurry of merger activity by unions faced with financial difficulties, and membership decline. Between 1975 and 1984 there were forty one cases of union amalgamations or absorptions—a rate of more than four a year.[76] This contrasts quite sharply with the

---

71. J.P. Windmuller, 'Concentration trends in union structure: an international comparison', *Industrial and Labor Relations Review*, vol. 35, no. 1, 1981, p.51.
72. Ibid., p. 50.
73. J. Waddington, 'Trade union mergers: a study of trade union structural dynamics', *British Journal of Industrial Relations*, vol. 26, no. 3, 1988.
74. K. Hawkins, *Trade Unions*, Hutchinson, London, 1981, pp. 93–4.
75. G.N. Chaison, *When Unions Merge*, Lexington Books, Lexington, Mass., 1986.
76. Ibid., p. 32.

Table 8.7: *Trade unions with 50 000 or more members, 1989 and 1979*

Name	Membership (000) 1989	1979
Shop, Distributive & Allied	200.8	145.0
Australian Teachers' Union	173.1	125.4
Australian Public Service Federation*	146.0	—
Amalgamated Metal Workers' Union	131.0	158.5
Federated Miscellaneous Workers	126.1	92.6
Australian Workers' Union	117.5	135.3
Liquor & Allied Ind. Union	111.2	97.5
Transport Workers' Union	98.7	95.1
National Union of Workers	87.1	79.5
Federated Clerks' Union	84.1	99.8
Public Sector Union*	78.5	—
Electrical Trades Union	74.9	66.2
Australian Bank Employees	73.7	67.7
Building Workers (BWIU)	71.1	47.4
Federated Ironworkers' Association	57.6	65.7
Municipal and Shire Council Employees	57.3	50.3
Printing and Kindred Industries Union	50.0	51.7

*Membership figures not available for 1979.
Source: ACTU *Executive Report*, September 1989 and D. W. Rawson and S. Wrightson, *A Handbook of Australian Trade Unions and Employees' Associations* (4th ed.), Research School of Social Sciences, Australian National University, Canberra, 1980.

situation in Australia. In the period between 1970 and 1989 there were only seventeen amalgamations of federally registered unions.[77]

The large number of small trade unions in Australia and the relative stability in the structure of the union movement can be explained by a number of factors. Isaac and Ford have pointed out that the compulsory arbitration system has both encouraged the formation of unions and given them legal protection. Size has been irrelevant to survival in the arbitration system. Unions have neither had to struggle with employers for recognition nor struggle with other unions for membership. Moreover, the doctrine of comparative wage justice and the practice of flow-ons, through which tribunals have passed on gains made by one union almost automatically to members of another, have meant that the less powerful sections of the union movement have not been greatly disadvantaged by their lack of bargaining ability. Small unions have also resisted amalgamation because of 'the desire of particular groups to maintain their independence; the fear of loss of status of officials in the

77. Griffin and Scarcebrook suggest that these data do not adequately capture the extent of merger activity in Australia. They claim that there has been a substantial number of mergers involving a combination of intra-state unions and federal and state unions. See G. Griffin and V. Scarcebrook, 'Trends in mergers in federally registered unions 1904–1986', *Journal of Industrial Relations*, vol. 31, no. 2, June 1989.

smaller unions [and] differences in industrial and political attitudes'.[78]

Union amalgamation

Notwithstanding the presence of a number of factors which have enabled small unions to remain relatively viable, there have been some labour organisations which have actively sought to augment their membership through the means of amalgamation. Before 1972 this was not a particularly difficult legal process. If unions wished to amalgamate, all that was required was for one of them to deregister and for the other organisation to change its eligibility rules in order to cover members of the deregistered body. However, in 1972 new provisions were added to the *Conciliation and Arbitration Act* which made amalgamations much more difficult. They had the effect, as Rimmer observed, of 'reinforcing the general stultifying effect of industrial law upon union structure'.[79]

Under the new provisions an amalgamation proposal had to be submitted to a ballot of the members of each of the organisations involved. An amalgamation would not be approved unless in each ballot, first, at least half of the members on the roll of voters returned their ballot paper on or before the closing date, and second, more than half of the members who recorded formal votes voted in favour of the amalgamation. It was the first of these provisions, namely that each organisation had to record at least a 50 per cent ballot return, that imposed the significant barrier to union amalgamations. Large unions were spared from having to ballot their members in cases where they sought to unite with very much smaller bodies. Under a separate section of the Act a ballot was confined to the smaller organisations where one union held no more than 5 per cent of the membership of the other. There seems little doubt that the 1972 provisions, which were introduced by the McMahon Liberal-Country Party Government, were explicitly designed to prevent union mergers. The legislation followed closely on the heels of the amalgamation of three metal trades unions which formed the Amalgamated Metal Workers' Union, and there was strong support at the time for it to be made retrospective so as to invalidate the merger.[80] It appears to have been well recognised that very few unions could have realistically achieved a 50 per cent ballot return. The failure of the Australian Textile Workers' Union and the Australian Boot Trade Employees' Federation to amalgamate in 1982 was ample evidence of the difficulties of achieving such a ballot return.[81]

Notwithstanding the efforts of the ACTU and the National Labour Consultative Council to have the Act changed, it was not until 1983,

---

78. J.E. Isaac and G.W. Ford (eds), *Australian Labour Relations Readings*, Sun Books, Melbourne, 1971, p. 100.
79. M. Rimmer, 'Long-run structural change in Australian trade unionism', *Journal of Industrial Relations*, vol. 23, no. 3, 1983, p. 327.
80. S. Deery, 'Trade union amalgamation and government policy in Australia', *Australian Bulletin of Labour*, vol. 9, no. 3, 1983.
81. Ibid., pp. 197–9.

after the election of the Federal Labor Government, that the provisions were finally amended. The *Conciliation and Arbitration Amendment Act 1983* eased the voting requirements in relation to organisations which could establish a 'community of interest' in respect to their industrial interests. Organisations that proposed to amalgamate could apply to a Full Bench of the Conciliation and Arbitration Commission for a declaration that the amalgamation was in the public interest and in the industrial interests of those organisations. The Commission was empowered to make the declaration where it was satisfied that the amalgamation would further the objects of the Act and that there was a community of interest between the organisations in respect of their industrial interests. A community of interest was deemed to exist where a substantial number of the members of each of the organisations were:

(a) eligible to become members of the other organisation or each of the other organisations, as the case may be;
(b) engaged in the same work, in aspects of the same work or in similar work;
(c) bound by the same awards;
(d) employed in the same or related work by employers engaged in the same industry; or
(e) engaged in work, or in industries, in respect of which there is a community of interest.

A community of interest was said to prevail where organisations could meet at least one of these criteria. Where unions obtained a declaration from the Commission they were required in an amalgamation ballot to achieve a return of ballot papers from only 25 per cent of members eligible to vote. A simple majority of valid votes had to be cast in favour of the amalgamation. In cases where a community of interest could not be established there were no changes to the voting conditions under which amalgamations could proceed.

In 1985, the (Hancock) Committee of Review into Australian Industrial Relations Law and Systems recommended that measures be taken to reduce the number of registered unions by easing further the voting requirements for amalgamations.[82] Its principal suggestion was that there be no minimum ballot return and that an amalgamation should basically be conditional on a simple majority of votes being cast in favour of the proposal by the membership of each organisation concerned. The Committee also recommended against an explicit community of interest test. The *Industrial Relations Act 1988* made changes to the amalgamation procedures although they were somewhat different from the proposals outlined by the Committee of Review. First, the community of interest test was retained. However, where the Commission issued such a declaration there was no minimum requirement as to the number of votes cast and the amalgamation would succeed if it were

---

82. *Report of the Committee of Review on Australian Industrial Relations Law and Systems*, Vol. 2: *Report*, AGPS, Canberra, p. 463.

approved by a majority of the ballot. Second, in cases where there was no community of interest declared, at least 25 per cent of the members of the organisations must vote, and more than 50 per cent of the members voting must approve the proposed amalgamation (s.246(1)).[83]

These new voting procedures are likely to assist the process of mergers that are now being actively encouraged by the ACTU but which are taking some time to materialise. In 1987, the ACTU Congress endorsed a radical programme involving specific proposals for union amalgamations and a strategy for the reconstruction of the labour movement into seventeen broad industry groupings.[84] Some progress has been made with amalgamations in the public service, telecommunications and maritime industries but none of these has involved major mergers along the lines suggested by the ACTU. In an effort to achieve more fundamental changes, the ACTU Executive announced in 1990 a plan to create a new single union to cover all private sector professional, administrative and clerical workers.[85] To be formed around the Federated Clerks' Union, the new body would be established through a round of amalgamations and membership exchanges with other unions. Notwithstanding this important development, however, there still exists considerable inertia and resistance within the union movement to the ACTU's rationalisation process.

Forms of union organisation

In Australia it is possible to identify four main types of unions: craft unions, occupational unions, industrial unions and general unions. Although that division is overly simple—for few Australian unions fit any of the categories exactly—it does provide a means of distinguishing the broad organisational features of unions.

Craft unions are those that organise workers on the basis of a particular craft or trade, whatever industry they may be employed in. The term 'craft' is commonly used to describe a skilled occupation which recruits and trains workers by means of an apprenticeship system. Australia's earliest trade unions were craft unions which formed among printers, stonemasons, carpenters, plasterers and the like. Over time many of these unions have widened their scope and have taken in semi-skilled and even unskilled workers with the result that they have become more occupationally based.

Occupational unions cover workers who belong to a particular occupational classification or to a related group of occupations. The Australian Foremen Stevedores' Association is an example of the first type while the Printing and Kindred Industries Union contains skilled, semi-skilled and unskilled workers in a group of related occupations. Occupational unions are largely horizontal in form and may include those which have a membership that cuts across industry boundaries, such as

---

83. See the Hon. K.D. Marks, 'Australia's new federal industrial laws—the *Industrial Relations Act 1988* and the *Industrial Relations (Consequential Provisions) Act 1988*', Australian Journal of Labour Law, vol. 2, no. 1, 1989.
84. ACTU, *Future Strategies for the Trade Union Movement*, Melbourne, 1987.
85. The *Age*, 29 March 1990.

the Federated Clerks' Union. The majority of Australian unions are based on one or more specified occupations, and it is usual for their eligibility rules to be framed in terms of the types of occupations or jobs performed.

Industrial unions cover all workers in a particular industry, irrespective of the job they perform. Membership is based purely on the industry rather than on the skill, trade or occupation of the workers. Both manual and non-manual employees are included. They represent a vertical form of organisation. There is no true industrial union in Australia. Unions such as the Australian Bank Employees' Union, the Australasian Meat Industry Employees' Union and the Vehicle Builders' Employees Federation come the closest, as they represent most of the employees in their respective industries.

General unions are those that organise workers regardless of skill, occupation or industry. There are few unions of this type in Australia, although the Australian Workers' Union, one of this country's oldest and largest labour organisations, and the Federated Miscellaneous Workers' Union, can be described as general unions. The Australian Workers' Union covers workers in shearing and rural occupations, construction, water maintenance, sewerage, horse-training, sugar refining, chemicals, and harbour and dock work.

Apart from the preceding typology it is also possible to draw a distinction between manual and white-collar organisations. The earliest trade unions were predominantly blue-collar unions. Those who performed non-manual tasks were fewer in number and were more resistant to unionism. But in the post-war period there has been a significant growth in tertiary or service sector employment and white-collar unions have come to occupy a much more important position in areas such as teaching and nursing and in clerical, administrative and supervisory work. Among the largest white-collar unions are the Shop, Distributive and Allied Employees' Association, the Australian Teachers' Union, the Australian Public Service Federation, and the Federated Clerks' Union. A number of white-collar unions can date their origins back to the last century, although most had their beginnings in the boom conditions after the First World War in the early 1920s.[86] There has been a marked growth in the membership of white-collar unions since the 1970s and as of August 1988 they accounted for just over half the total union members in Australia. Two decades earlier the white-collar share of the unionised workforce was only 28 per cent.[87] Three of the five largest unions in Australia are white-collar and the growth rate of white-collar unions has far outstripped that of their manual counterparts over the last decade.

A long-standing objective of the Australian trade union movement has been to restructure unions along industry lines. The first congress of

---

86. R.D. Williams 'White-collar unions', in P.W.D. Matthews and G.W. Ford (eds), *Australian Trade Unions*, Sun Books, Melbourne, 1968, pp. 150–56.
87. G. Griffin, 'White-collar unionism', p. 27.

the ACTU in 1927 declared as policy the 'closer organisation of the workers by the transformation of the trade union movement from the craft to an industrial basis by the establishment of one union in each industry'.[88] Support for industrial unionism originally came from the revolutionary socialists, who considered that the union movement was too much fragmented and divided by sectional organisations and the spirit of craft unionism. Industrial unions were seen as a means of uniting workers in different occupations, skilled and unskilled, and of providing a vehicle for the eventual overthrow of capitalist society. While many non-socialists have since embraced and supported the concept of industrial unionism, little progress towards that goal has been made over the past fifty to sixty years. Most industries are still covered by a large number of unions. In the late 1970s, Rawson found that up to fifty-five unions had occupational coverage in the various branches of the transport industry, thirty-six in the public service, twenty-three in teaching and twenty-two in manufacturing industry.[89] Although there has been a rationalisation of unions in the teaching profession, few changes have occurred elsewhere.

There are a number of obstacles in the way of industrial unionism. Most of the major unions straddle a number of industries and could not be expected to agree to their own dismemberment. The desire of union hierarchies to preserve their existing positions of power and influence is an important explanation of the rigidity of union structures. So also are ideological and political differences among union leaders. For example, in the metal industry, the different ideological positions taken by the federal leadership of the Amalgamated Metal Workers' Union, the Federated Ironworkers' Association and the Australasian Society of Engineers certainly makes it difficult to envisage their merging into one body. The spirit of craft pride persists, too. That will make any union of the skilled and unskilled difficult.

Nevertheless, in some industries, unions have formed structures to coordinate their activities and prevent the sort of difficulty that arises when unions pursue conflicting courses of action. One such organisation is the Metal Trades Federation. Formed in 1942 by a group of metal trade unions, the Federation has sought to formulate policy on matters of common interest such as award negotiations. It has also established machinery to resolve demarcation and jurisdictional disputes that may arise between its affiliates.[90] Similar bodies exist in the mining, building and transport industries.

Union structure and decision-making

Although organisational and decision-making structures vary from union to union, it is possible to distinguish three separate decision-

---

88. J.S. Hagan, *The ACTU: A Short History*, Reed, Sydney, 1977, p. 18.
89. D.W. Rawson, *A Handbook of Australian Trade Unions and Employee Associations* (3rd ed.), Australian National University, Canberra, 1977.
90. N.F. Dufty, *Industrial Relations in the Australian Metal Industry*, West Publishing, Sydney, 1972, p. 77.

making levels within most unions: the plant, the state or branch and the federal. Almost all large unions in the private sector in Australia are federal or national unions and have branches in two or more states. As Table 8.8 shows, these unions represent more than 80 per cent of trade unionists in Australia.

Plant level

At the plant or shop level it is common for union members to elect one or more shop stewards who act as 'on the job' representatives for the union.[91] Shop stewards are largely concerned with the collection of unions dues, the enrolment of new members and the handling of minor grievances. They also keep watch for breaches of awards or agreements. While the position and functions of shop stewards vary greatly from union to union, they generally play a minor role in the official union organisational structure. Nevertheless, that role seems to have expanded over recent years.[92] In the 1960s Hince was not able to find any union which officially delegated power to shop stewards to resolve 'clearly identifiable breaches of the award'.[93] He observed that the authority to initiate direct action was rarely placed in the hands of shop stewards. It appeared that unions were reluctant to give stewards a positive role in the handling of disputes for fear that it might lead to a diminution of the power and authority of full-time officials. It has not been only individual unions which have sought to constrain the activities of shop stewards and shop committees. The policy of the ACTU towards workplace representatives has been described as 'one of lofty disdain'[94] In 1955 the ACTU Congress resolved that 'There must be greater recognition by the trade unionist that he must accept direction and abide by properly constituted decisions by his union or executive'.[95] In 1961 the ACTU drew up a Charter for Shop Committees which sought to place them firmly under official union control and to deny them a role in regulating wages and conditions of employment. This Charter was re-endorsed at subsequent ACTU biennial congresses and in 1980 it was held that the functions of shop committees should be:

(a) To deal with questions of improvements in shop conditions which affect more than one organisation.
(b) To assist, when requested by the union concerned, to obtain improved shop conditions peculiar to the department in which members of each union work.
(c) To cooperate with other Shop Committees for improvements in general workshop conditions throughout the whole establishment. All matters affecting wage rates and conditions of employment covered by Awards and Agreements shall require final determination by the respective unions concerned.[96]

---

91. In some unions, shop stewards may be appointed by the state branch but this is not a common practice.
92. See M. Rimmer, 'Work place unionism' in B. Ford and D. Plowman (eds), *Australian Unions* (2nd ed.), Macmillan, Melbourne, 1989, pp. 138–42.
93. K.W. Hince, 'Unions on the shop floor', in Isaac and Ford, *Australian Labour Relations*, p. 194.
94. M. Rimmer, 'Work place unionism', p. 136.
95. Quoted in J. Hagan, *The History of the ACTU*, Longman Cheshire, Melbourne, 1981, p. 260.
96. ACTU, *Consolidation of ACTU Policy Decisions 1951–1980*, p. 39.

Table 8.8: *Trade unions interstate structure, June 1989*

Unions operating in:						
1 state	2 states	3 states	4 states	5 states	6 or more	2 or more
168	6	6	10	15	94	131
(56%)	(2%)	(2%)	(3%)	(5%)	(31%)	(44%)
Number of members ('000)						
531.4	18.9	55.9	111.7	186.6	2505.7	2878.9
(16%)	(0.5%)	(2%)	(3%)	(5%)	(73%)	(84%)

Source: ABS, *Trade Union Statistics, Australia*, January 1990.

The Congress also held that shop committees should be subject to the rules and conditions of the respective unions concerned and should 'comply to the procedures determined by the State Labour Council of the ACTU'. In his analysis of the development of shop floor unionism up to 1980, Rimmer concluded that it had been

> ... piecemeal, opportunistic, and—for the most part—circumscribed by official disapproval. Except for a brief interlude during the Second World War, it had never been encouraged to harmonise with central policy objectives of the union movement as a whole, of government, or of tribunals. Unionists at the place of work were to be controlled, not made partners in policy.[97]

Since this time, however, there seems to have been a considerable softening of union attitudes to the role and activities of their workplace representatives. The establishment of new legislative procedures to handle occupational and safety matters at the shop floor and the development of more effective dispute settling procedures within awards have raised the need for a more active, competent and well-informed body of shop stewards and union delegates. But perhaps the most important factor to have strengthened the position of the unions' workplace representatives was the process of second-tier wage negotiations and the subsequent award restructuring arrangements contained in the most recent wage fixation guidelines (see chapter 13).

Notwithstanding these important developments, it should be pointed out that the level of shop-floor organisation and activity in the past has not been insubstantial. Rimmer has observed that shop stewards and committees have played an important negotiating role in wage matters in a number of industries including engineering, metal trades and electricity supply. In the metal trades industry they have been closely integrated into wage negotiations for much of the post-war period.[98] Dufty's study of shop stewards in Western Australia also disclosed a

---

97. M. Rimmer, 'Work place unionism', pp. 138–9.
98. Ibid., pp. 135–6.

surprisingly independent and important role for workplace representatives. While a significant proportion of the shop stewards in his survey felt restrained by union policy to use the established channels, one-third of them reported that they called stop-work meetings without consulting full-time union officials or the executive.[99] Nearly half of the stewards negotiated directly with management at all levels, and there was considerable support for the view that their authority to deal with management should be extended. Dufty found a significant level of shop-floor activity in a range of matters including wages, dismissals and the resolution of demarcation disputes. Benson similarly established the presence of extensive workplace bargaining by shop stewards in the Victorian power industry.[100]

There is no doubt that shop stewards provide an extremely important link in the chain of communication between the rank and file and the full-time officials. While it is true that they have found it difficult to secure an established position in the Australian industrial arena they do, as Dufty remarked:

> ...protect the full-time officials from involvement in numerous petty and day-to-day matters which are important to the individual unionist but which would be time-consuming if dealt with by full-time officials. Without the shop stewards, many more full-time officials would be needed to give the same level of service to the membership as a whole.[101]

Branch level

Except in the case of very small unions, the basic operational level of the typical Australian union is the state branch. The branch is administered by a number of full-time officials, usually consisting of a secretary, assistant secretary and various organisers. As a rule, state branches enjoy a great measure of autonomy in dealing with matters confined to their own state, although it is recognised that they should comply with the rules and policies established by the federal body.

The independence of the state branch, however, may well depend on the organisational structure of the union. Some unions are essentially national bodies and are highly centralised in terms of their activities, resources and decision-making structures. In this type of organisation branches possess limited autonomy. Other federal unions more closely resemble federations of state bodies. They derive their funds and much of their authority from the state affiliates. In these cases there may be a high degree of local autonomy. State bodies would be entitled to call work stoppages without the authority of the federal organisation and may in fact be party to a number of state awards through state registration. Moreover, the ruling in *Moore v. Doyle* has established that state-registered unions have a separate legal existence from their parent organisations, even though they are operationally branches of federal

---

99. N.F. Dufty, 'The shop steward in Western Australia', *Journal of Industrial Relations*, vol. 22, no. 4, 1980, p. 386.
100. J. Benson, 'Workplace union organisation in Australia', *Labour and Industry*, vol. 1, no. 3, October 1988.
101. N.F. Dufty, *Industrial Relations*, p. 91.

unions,[102] Notwithstanding this autonomy, most state affiliates operate as federal branches rather than independent state organisations.

Most of the day-to-day industrial relations problems that the union attends to are dealt with at the state level. The organiser, in particular, is concerned with handling disputes in the workplace. He or she is the full-time official most in contact with the members. It is usual for shop stewards to refer a dispute to the organiser, who will then attempt to resolve the issue with management. Because the largest body of work is handled by the state branch it normally possesses greater administrative resources than any other level of the union hierarchy. This is reflected in the number of full-time officials employed in the state and federal offices. For example, the Amalgamated Metal Workers' Union, one of Australia's largest, has eight federal officials and thirty state officials in New South Wales and seventeen in Victoria. Its rulebook explicitly describes the branch 'as the basic organisation for furthering the interests of the Union and its members'. The Transport Workers' Union devotes even more resources to the state level. It has two federal officials and seventeen state officials in Victoria, sixteen of whom are organisers. New South Wales has an even greater presence of state officials.

Federal level

The supreme governing body of the union is normally the national conference. Usually consisting of the union's state and federal officers and delegates elected from each branch, the national conference meets every two or three years to formulate the union's general policy. Between meetings of the conference the union is managed by a federal executive which is normally elected by the union's entire membership. The federal executive's task is to coordinate national affairs, manage the union's finances and represent the union in federal award negotiations and interstate disputes. The top position in the executive is held by the federal secretary, who is the union's national leader. Most unions also have a federal assistant secretary and a number of federal organisers. The positions of president and vice-president also exist, although they are often not occupied by full-time paid officials.

Inter-union cooperation

Formal cooperation between trade unions exists at two levels in Australia: at the branch level through state Trades and Labour Councils (or Trades Hall Councils) and at the federal level through the Australian Council of Trade Unions (ACTU). Before 1979 there were two other white-collar peak councils, the Australian Council of Salaried and

---

102. The case of *Moore* v. *Doyle* resulted from a dispute in 1968–9 between the federal office of the Transport Workers' Union and the NSW branch of the union, which was registered under the NSW *Industrial Arbitration Act*. At issue was the right of the federal body to force observance of its rules on the state union (branch) in a matter relating to the admission of subcontractors as members. The Australian Industrial Court held that the NSW and federal organisation were separate legal entities and that the NSW body could not be brought within the control of the federal body. Furthermore, the state-registered union was a legal entity separate even from the NSW branch as identified in the rules of the federally registered union.

Professional Associations (ACSPA) and the Council of Australian Government Employee Organisations (CAGEO). In 1979 ACSPA merged with the ACTU, taking most of its affiliates with it, and in 1981 CAGEO completed the process of almost total unification of the union movement at the peak council level.[103]

Trades and Labour Councils

Since the 1870s Trades and Labour Councils have provided machinery through which unions could coordinate their activities at the state level. As well as providing research facilities, legal aid and strike support for unions, these Councils have also assisted their affiliates in award negotiations and have acted as a voice for them on many industrial and political matters. Affiliation is open both to state branches of federal unions and to state unions. Members are represented by delegates, according to the size of their organisations.[104] Through regular meetings of delegates the Councils formulate policy for the affiliated unions in the state. They also provide a means of coordinating and directing the conduct of intrastate disputes. All impending stoppages likely to affect the members of more than one union must be reported to the individual Council's Disputes Committee, which then has the authority to formulate the policy to be followed in the dispute.

The principal full-time officers of the Trades and Labour Councils are the secretary and the assistant secretary, who are elected by the union delegates, and one or more research/industrial officers. The Council is financed by the payment of dues by affiliated unions on a *per capita* basis. In country areas there are provincial Trades and Labour Councils, which act as branches of the main Council in the six capital cities.

The Australian Council of Trade Unions (ACTU)

The ACTU was formed in 1927 after a number of earlier attempts to create a radical One Big Union had failed. It brought together a range of divergent interest groups with competing industrial and political objectives; from those who were imbued with the traditions of craft unionism through to those who wished to see the overthrow of the capitalist system and the consolidation of the union movement into a single class-based organisation. The ACTU succeeded in welding the various constituents of the labour movement together partly because it produced a constitution which managed to offer something both to the socialist supporters of the OBU movement and to those who sought to maintain the system of craft unions and who believed in the sufficiency of compulsory arbitration and of Labor governments. The ACTU's constitution, according to Hagan

---

103. See G. Griffin and V. Giuca, 'Union consolidation: the ACTU mergers' in Ford and Plowman, *Australian Unions*, pp. 145–68.
104. Representation formulae vary among Councils and have been the subject of much acrimony among trade unions. A split took place in the Victorian Trades Hall Council in 1967 on that issue. Some twenty-six unions were suspended from the Council. See D. Plowman, 'Unions in conflict: the Victorian Trades Hall split, 1967–73', *Labour History*, no. 36, 1979, pp. 47–69.

... provided that policy should be made by congress, in which the larger, and more revolutionary unions would have a strong influence; but it left the execution of that policy to the Labour Councils, in which smaller, and more craft based unions predominated.[105]

The ACTU assumed two roles. It presented the unions' case on the basic wage to the Commonwealth Court of Conciliation and Arbitration and it settled interstate industrial disputes. But it also adopted the socialisation of industry as its objective and proclaimed the need to transform the union movement from a craft to an industrial basis by the establishment of industry unions. Its policies and constitution were such that 'Both Labourists and Revolutionaries believed that by dominating the councils of the ACTU they would advance their own causes in their own way'.[106]

Not all unions were enthusiastic about the development of the new peak council. Some, like the Australian Workers' Union, the country's biggest federal union at that time with some 150 000 members, refused to join on the grounds that it was run by 'Red Wreckers'.[107] The AWU also objected to the dominant role which the ACTU constitution gave to the Trades and Labour Councils. The union remained unaffiliated for forty years and did not join the ACTU until 1967, when it was given its own place on the ACTU executive.

Over the years ACTU membership has grown steadily. In 1928 little more than 11 per cent of the unionised workforce belonged to unions affiliated to the ACTU. This figure climbed to 21 per cent in 1936 and then more than doubled over the next two decades to be in excess of 50 per cent by the mid 1950s. During the post-war period of the 1950s and 1960s the ACTU benefited from the significant growth of its affiliates in the burgeoning manufacturing sector. It also gained a host of new members in the late 1960s, including the AWU, and by 1971 was able to claim a membership of 127 affiliates, a jump of more than 30 per cent in four years.[108] By this time it represented more than three-quarters of the unionised workforce. The economic recession of the 1970s, which hit many of the unions that formed the traditional membership base of the ACTU, led to a decline in the proportion of unionists who were within the ACTU. But this trend was reversed by the merger with ACSPA in 1979 and with CAGEO in 1981. In September 1989 the ACTU reported that it had 153 affiliates with a membership of more than 2.7 million members[109] (see Appendix 8.1). It now covers almost 90 per cent of all

---

105. J. Hagan, 'The Australian union movement: context and perspective 1850–1987' in Ford and Plowman, *Australian Unions*, p. 26.
106. J. Hagan, *The History of the ACTU*, p. 443.
107. Ibid., p. 86.
108. D. Rawson, 'The ACTU—growth yes, power no', in K. Cole (ed.), *Power, Conflict and Control in Australian Trade Unions*, 1982, p. 106.
109. These membership figures should be treated with some caution as they are based on information supplied by the affiliates. Since affiliation fees and voting rights are related to membership strength, unions may understate membership figures to reduce affiliation fees or overstate membership figures so as to increase voting rights. At the 1983 Biennial Congress one delegate raised doubts about the accuracy of the membership figure supplied by the Federated Storemen and Packers' Union. He claimed that it had been grossly overstated. See E. Davis, 'The 1983 ACTU Congress: consensus rules OK! *Journal of Industrial Relations*, vol. 25, no. 4, 1983, p. 508.

union members. The influx of a large number of white-collar organisations from both the private and public sectors has changed the character of the ACTU membership. It has now 'ceased to be a federation of manual unions with a few non-manual additions and has come to represent more completely than ever in the past the overall range of trade unionism'.[110]

Those changes have been reflected in the decision-making organs of the ACTU and in the policies and activities it now pursues. The principal policy-making body of the ACTU is the biennial congress. This congress, which consists of delegates from the affiliated unions, the state and provincial Trades and Labour Councils and officers and members of the Executive, meets for five days every two years. It establishes policy on a wide range of matters from working conditions, taxation policy and economic development to Aboriginal affairs, immigration and settlement, and the arts. Between Congresses, the ACTU's supreme governing body is its Executive. The Executive is empowered by the ACTU constitution to 'initiate and deal with all matters affecting the interests of the Trade Union movement as a whole'. However, decisions of the Executive intended to make or alter policy must be endorsed by the state branches. It also has the power to 'intervene in every dispute likely to extend beyond the province of any one State, and to deal with all industrial matters of an interstate character'. The Executive is composed of five full-time officers elected by Congress for six years (president, secretary and three assistant secretaries); six vice-presidents, who are elected by Congress for two years; six state branch representatives, who are elected by the relevant Trades and Labour Council; three female representatives and eighteen industry group representatives. The structure of the ACTU is shown in Figure 8.1. There has been a marked expansion in the size of the ACTU Executive over the last decade. The number of seats has almost doubled from twenty one in 1979 to thirty eight in 1989. The creation of these extra positions has allowed the ACTU to widen its representational coverage among its affiliates and, as a consequence, to enhance its authority and standing within the union movement. Most large unions possess officials on the Executive and there is a careful balance in the representation of the broad factional groupings.

The main function of the ACTU has been to 'formulate and coordinate union policy and union practice on industrial and political matters at the national level'.[111] To this end it appears at Industrial Relations Commission hearings on important issues such as the national wage, working hours, annual leave, equal pay, maternity leave and redundancy protection. The Council's advocate and research officers usually prepare and present cases before the Commission. The ACTU also exercises an important role with respect to interstate disputes. Under its rules, all affiliated unions must notify the ACTU of any pending dispute 'likely to

---

110. D. Rawson, 'The ACTU—growth yes, power no', p. 107.
111. Isaac and Ford, *Australian Labour Relations*, p. 110.

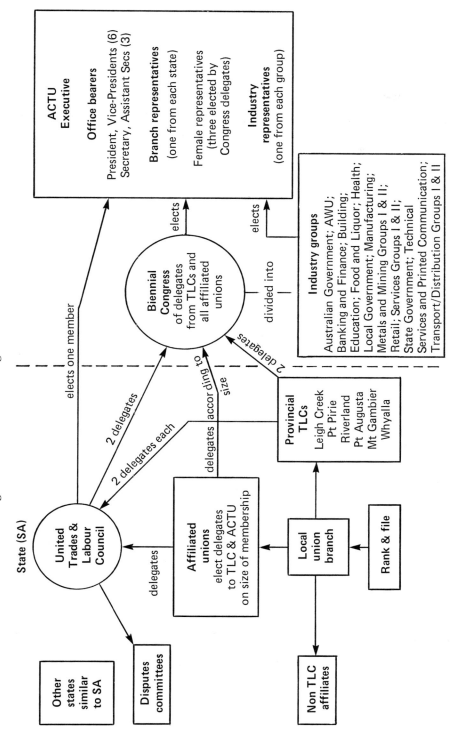

Fig. 8.1: Structure and organisation of the ACTU

extend beyond the limits of any one state before deciding to strike'.[112] On such notification a meeting of the Executive Disputes Committee is convened which then has the authority, along with representatives of the unions involved, to take such action as is deemed necessary to settle the dispute.

As the main voice of the trade unions, the ACTU is frequently consulted by the Federal Government on economic and industrial matters. Since the development of the Accord and the election of the Labor Party to government in 1983, the ACTU has been given an unparalleled opportunity to participate in the processes of national policy-making. It has in effect been elevated to the role of a social partner with government. Through the establishment of a range of tripartite bodies such as the Economic Planning and Advisory Council, the Advisory Committee on Prices and Incomes and the Australian Manufacturing Council, the ACTU has gained an important voice at the level at which important political, economic and social policies are made. In addition to these bodies a formal structure for union–government consultation has existed since 1977 in the form of the National Labour Consultative Council. It was established with the explicit purpose of providing 'a regular and organised means by which representatives of the Commonwealth Government, of employers and employees may consult together on industrial relations and manpower matters of national concern'.[113] Over the years, this has enabled the ACTU to place its views formally before the government on issues such as industrial relations legislation and skills formation and development.

The ACTU's operations are financed through affiliation fees and levies. The peak council has not always found it easy to generate sufficient funds to cover its activities. The reluctance of affiliated unions to agree to higher fees and the internal politics of the organisation have sometimes forced the ACTU into a position of financial difficulty. In 1979, for example, a move to increase affiliation fees from 25c to 75c per head was defeated by a combination of forces led by a number of right-wing unions including the Federated Clerks and the Shop Assistants, who were dissatisfied with their lack of representation on the ACTU Executive. Instead a 41c per member fee was approved. At this time the ACTU was reported to have had to draw $400 000 from its reserves to 'stave off a financial crisis'.[114] The ACTU's financial position was so serious that it needed to strike a special temporary levy on affiliates of 20c per member to remain solvent.[115] In 1981 substantial increases were agreed to and the affiliation fee was raised to $1 per adult member and 90c per junior member.[116] By the 1989 Biennial Congress the affiliation fee had been

---

112. ACTU, *Constitution, Rules and Standing Orders*, 1987.
113. *The National Labour Consultative Council*, Department of Employment and Industrial Relations, undated.
114. The *Age*, 16 June 1979.
115. L. Cupper, 'The 1981 ACTU Congress: consolidation, consensus and cooperation(?)', *Journal of Industrial Relations*, vol. 24, no. 1, 1982.
116. Members of the newly established Australian Government Employees Section agreed to pay an additional 30c levy in order to maintain the level of resources enjoyed in CAGEO. The decision to increase fees averted a deficit for the ACTU, which stood at more than $670 000 for the second half of 1981. The *Age*, 8 September 1981.

lifted to an annual adult rate of $1.32 ($1.10 to the ACTU and $0.22 to the International Fund). The more than five-fold increase in fees in just over a decade has enabled the ACTU to expand its resources to a level where it can now play a leading role in economic policy matters and issues such as superannuation, training, occupational health and safety and the problems of immigrants and women at work. The full-time staff of the ACTU is now close to fifty including twenty-two senior secretariat staff involved in economic research, industrial and legal matters, occupational health and safety and ethnic affairs. The staffing levels are almost double those of the early 1980s.[117]

Summary

Australian unions first emerged among unskilled tradesmen. They were small, exclusive, craft-conscious organisations principally concerned with promoting an 'aristocracy of labour' within the Australian workforce. Broader-based organisations of semi-skilled and unskilled workers did not take root until much later. They were far more dependent on economic conditions for their bargaining strength and as a consequence, generally lacked the capacity to protect their members' interests during times of high unemployment. In their first real test of strength with employers during the 1890s they were soundly beaten and all but wiped out. From this grew a determination to engage the support of the state and the rebirth of unionism in the twentieth century occurred under the protective umbrella of government legislation. This has not been without its implications.

Trade union dependence on government and the conciliation and arbitration system has had an effect on organisational size. Whereas in most other countries, unions have had to build up coercive strength in order to survive and remain industrially effective under collective bargaining, Australian unions have been freed from such pressures. Size and industrial resources are irrelevant for survival because it is ensured through registration. Further, the institution of comparative wage justice and the practice of flow-ons has meant that weak unions often are not greatly disadvantaged by their lack of industrial power. Moreover, governments have been provided with the opportunity of hindering trade union amalgamations when they thought it was politically opportune. Consequently, this has impeded the progress towards union amalgamation and a reduction in the plethora of organisations currently representing wage- and salary-earners in Australia.

Most unions are occupationally based and have shown great resistance to calls for a restructuring of their organisations along industry lines. This has not prevented the growth of industry federations which play an important coordinating role in a number of areas. The main

---

117. See D. Rawson, 'The ACTU—growth yes, power no', p. 119.

operational level of Australian unions is the state branch. There has been a general reluctance to facilitate the decentralisation of power to the shop floor, although the role of shop stewards and shop committees has not been unimportant in the negotiation of wages and other matters. Union coordination exists at both the state level through Trades and Labour Councils and at the federal level through the ACTU. The merger of ACSPA and CAGEO with the ACTU has resulted in the near unification of the union movement at the peak council level and assisted in the process of making the ACTU a dominant force in Australian industrial relations.

Appendix 8.1

Table 8.9 *Membership figures of ACTU affiliated organisations, 1989*

Affiliates	Senior	Junior	Total
A.M.P. Society Staff Association	4 172	—	4,172
Actors Equity of Australia	6 995	—	6 995
Amalgamated Footwear and Textile Workers Union of Australia	30 783	3 032	33 815
Amalgamated Metal Workers Union	116 335	14 694	131 029
Amalgamated Society of Carpenters and Joiners of Australia	10 173	200	10 373
Association of Draughting, Supervisory and Technical Employees	20 039	138	20 177
Association of Foremen and Supervisors	540	—	540
Association of Health Professionals CPS	140	—	140
Association of Professional Engineers Australia	15 076	—	15 076
Association of Professional Scientists of Australia	1 223	17	1 240
Association of Railway Professional Officers of Australia	1 508	—	1 508
The Australasian Meat Industry Employees' Union	40 241	4 072	44 313
Australasian Society of Engineers	26 241	3 709	29 050
Australian Airline Flight Engineers Association	212	—	212
Australian Bank Employees Union	49 115	24 556	73 671
Australian Brushmakers Union	300	55	355
Australian Builders Labourers Federation (W.A.)	5 960	—	5 960
Australian Building Construction Employees & B.L.F. (Qld Branch) Union	6 556	—	6 556
Australian Coal & Shale Employees Federation	11 500	—	11 500
Australian Collieries Staff Association	5 200	—	5 200
Australian Federal Police Association	2 500	—	2 500
Australian Federated Union of Locomotive Enginemen	11 100	—	11 100
Australian Flight Attendants' Association	3 514	—	3 514
Australian Foremen Stevedores Association	912	—	912
Australian Glass Workers' Union	3 462	—	3 462
Australian Government Lawyers Association	589	—	589
The Australian Hairdressers, Wigmakers & Hairworkers Employees' Federation	210	104	314
Australian Institute of Marine & Power Engineers	3 092	—	3 092
The Australian Insurance Employees Union	21 083	2 671	23 754
Australian International Cabin Crew Association	1 690	—	1 690
Australian Licensed Aircraft Engineers' Association	1 823	—	1 823
Australian Nursing Federation	37 290	4 990	42 280

Table 8.9 *Membership figures of ACTU affiliated organisations, 1989 (Continued)*

Affiliates	Senior	Junior	Total
Australian Postal & Telecommunications Union	45 295	3 409	48 704
Australian Postmasters Association	1 261	—	1 261
Australian Public Service Federation	142 289	3 743	146 032
Australian Railways Union	33 542	1 378	34 920
Australian Rope & Cordage Workers Union	278	75	353
Australian Shipping & Travel Officers' Association	3 500	300	3 800
Australian Social Welfare Union	2 250	750	3 000
Australian Stevedoring Supervisors Association	350	—	350
Australian Teachers' Union	173 108	—	173 108
Australian Telecommunications Employees Assoc/Australian Telephone & Phonogram Officers Association	30 210	3 154	33 364
Australian Theatrical & Amusement Employees Association	6 858	—	6 858
Australian Timber Workers Union	13 000	227	13 227
The Australian Tramway & Motor Omnibus Employees' Association	11 115	—	11 115
Australian Transport Officers Federation	17 820	836	18 656
The Australian Workers' Union	110 838	6 698	117 536
Bakery Employees & Salesmens Federation of Australia	6 011	—	6 011
Blind Workers Union (Victoria)	112	2	114
The Breweries & Bottleyards Employees Industrial Union of Workers of W.A.	301	—	301
The Building Workers Industrial Union of Australia	64 900	6 200	71 100
CSIRO Laboratory Craftsmen's Association	310	—	310
CSIRO Officers' Association	2 287	154	2 441
CSIRO Technical Association	1 269	8	1 277
The Clothing & Allied Trades Union of Australia	20 299	8 310	28 609
Coal Miners Industrial Union of Workers, Western Australia	718	8	726
Commonwealth Bank Officers Association	25 594	8 532	34 126
Commonwealth Foremen's Association (APS)	1 100	—	1 100
Commonwealth Works Supervisors' Association	430	—	430
Confectionery Workers Union of Australia	4 814	30	4 844
The Dental Technicians Association of NSW	173	—	173
Disabled Workers Union of W.A.	50	—	50
Electrical Trades Union of Australia	69 901	5 033	74 934
External Plant Officers Association	708	—	708
The Federal Fire Fighters Union	1 014	—	1 014
The Federated Brick, Tile & Pottery Industrial Union of Australia	4 503	197	4 700

Table 8.9 *Membership figures of ACTU affiliated organisations, 1989 (Continued)*

Affiliates	Senior	Junior	Total
Federated Clerks' Union of Australia	69 205	14 921	84 126
Federated Cold Storage & Meat Preserving Employees Union of Australia	7 000	—	7 000
The Federated Council of Academics	6 259	—	6 259
The Federated Engine Drivers & Firemen's Association of Australia	26 058	—	26 058
Federated Furnishing Trades Society	6 700	1 775	8 475
The Federated Gas Employers Industrial Union	3 502	—	3 502
The Federated Ironworkers' Association of Australia	54 090	3 529	57 619
Federated Liquor & Allied Industries Union of Australia	91 012	20 228	111 240
The Federated Millers & Manufacturing Grocers' Employees' Assoc. of A'Asia	3 929	160	4 089
Federated Mining Mechanics Association of Australasia	2 041	39	2 080
The Federated Miscellaneous Workers' Union of Australia	125 379	722	126 101
Federated Municipal & Shire Council Employees' Union of Australia	57 300	—	57 300
Federated Ship Painters & Dockers Union of Australia	1 100	—	1 100
Federated Tobacco Workers Union of Australia (NSW Branch & Federal Office)	1 666	—	1 666
Federated Tobacco Workers Union of Australia (Vic. Branch)	475	—	475
Federation of Australian University Staff Associations	8 059	—	8 059
Firemen & Deckhands Union of NSW	577	—	577
Food Preservers Union of Australia	6 030	—	6 030
Food Preservers Union of Western Australia	1 260	—	1 260
The Funeral & Allied Industries Union of NSW	807	—	807
Gas Industry Salaried Officers Federation	3 718	—	3 718
The Health & Research Employees Association of Australia	33 858	—	33 858
Hospital Employees Federation of Australia	35 192	4 766	39 958
Hunter District Water Board Employees' Association	534	—	534
Independent Teachers' Federation of Australia	21 100	—	21 100
Mannequins & Models Guild of Australia	150	—	150
The Meat Inspectors Association APS	1 710	—	1 710
Medical Scientists Association of Victoria	1 137	70	1 207
Merchant Service Guild of Australia	3 140	—	3 140
The Metropolitan (Perth) Passenger Transport Trust Union of Workers	297	15	312

Table 8.9 *Membership figures of ACTU affiliated organisations, 1989 (Continued)*

Affiliates	Senior	Junior	Total
Municipal Officers' Association of Australia	45 485	2 027	47 512
Musicians Union of Australia	7 133	—	7 133
National Union of Workers	77 200	9 950	87 150
NSW Sales Representatives & Commercial Travellers Guild	1 935	—	1 935
New South Wales Fire Brigade Employees' Union	2 204	1 059	3 263
New South Wales Nurses' Association	26 199	3 812	30 011
New South Wales Public Medical Officers' Association	742	—	742
New South Wales Public Service POA	3 937	—	3 937
Operative Bakers' Union of Victoria	496	115	611
The Operative Painters & Decorators Union of Australia	14 284	800	15 084
The Operative Plasterers & Plaster Workers' Federation	3 560	—	3 560
The Operative Stonemasons Society of Australia	1 020	—	1 020
Pastrycooks, Bakers, Biscuitmakers & Allied Trades Union	1 437	234	1 671
Plumbers and Gasfitters Employees Union of Australia	16 943	—	16 943
Police Association of New South Wales	9 096	57	9 153
Postal Supervisory Officers Association	450	—	450
Printing and Kindred Industries Union	46 317	3 430	49 747
Professional Divers Association of A'Asia	550	—	550
Professional Officers' Association	6 473	—	6 473
Professional Radio and Electronic Institute of Australasia	3 500	300	3 800
Public Sector Union	75 825	2 712	78 537
The Pulp and Paper Workers Federation of Australia	4 000	—	4 000
Queensland Nurses' Union of Employees	10 957	—	10 957
Queensland Professional Officers' Association	10 360	49	10 409
The Real Estate Association of NSW	228	—	228
Salaried Pharmacists Association of W.A.	120	—	120
Seamens Union of Australia	5 866	—	5 866
Secretaries and Managers Association of Australia	1 100	—	1 100
Senior Managers' Assoc. (Postal & Telecommunications Commissions)	250	—	250
Shop, Distributive and Allied Employees' Association	66 787	134 000	200 787
The Slaters, Tilers & Roofing Industry Union of Vic.	813	207	1 020

Table 8.9 *Membership figures of ACTU affiliated organisations, 1989 (Continued)*

Affiliates	Senior	Junior	Total
South Australian Wholesale Softgoods Salesmen & Warehousemens Assoc.	110	36	146
Technical Service Guild of Australia	1 220	—	1 220
Telecommunications Technical Officers Association	771	—	771
Telecommunications, Traffic & Supervisory Officers' Association	189	—	189
Transport Workers Union of Australia	98 710	—	98 710
Trustee Companies' Officers Association	1 040	—	1 040
Union of Christmas Island Workers	300	100	400
Union of Postal Clerks and Telegraphists	4 223	110	4 333
United Firefighters Union of S.A.	802	—	802
United Firefighters Union of Australia Union of Employees — Qld. Branch	850	—	850
United Firefighters Union (Vic. Branch)	2 500	—	2 500
Vehicle Builders' Employees Federation of Australia	33 772	1 228	35 000
Victorian Affiliated Teachers Federation	1 709	—	1 709
Victorian Allied Health Professionals Association	1 050	—	1 050
Victorian Colleges and Universities Staff Association	1 783	750	2 533
Victorian Mothercraft Nurses' & Allied Employees' Association	273	290	563
Victorian Printers Operative Union	1 968	81	2 049
Victorian State Building Trades Union	5 530	—	5 530
W.A. Psychiatric Nurses' Association	650	—	650
Water and Sewerage Employees' Union	4 370	—	4 370
Waterside Workers' Federation of Australia	7 370	—	7 370
West Australian Dental Technicians & Employees Union of Workers	89	33	122
West Australian Fire Brigade Employees' Industrial Union of Workers	712	—	712
West Australian Prison Officers Union of Workers	900	—	900
Wool Brokers' Staffs Association	1 000	500	1 500
Woolclassers Association of Australia	941	213	1 154

Discussion questions

1. Outline and evaluate the theoretical explanations of the labour movement within the context of the evolution of trade unions in Australia.
2. What advantage did skilled workers have over their manual counterparts in forming unions in the nineteenth century?
3. How did the Australian trade union movement respond to the failure of the 1890s strikes?
4. What factors have contributed to the apparent decline in union membership since the mid-1970s?
5. How do you account for the number of small unions in Australia?
6. In what ways has the law affected union amalgamations?
7. Distinguish between craft, occupational, industrial and general unions.
8. What function do shop stewards play in Australian unions and what factors have affected their activities?
9. Explain why the state branch of a federal union is the most active operational level of the organisation.
10. Outline the functions performed by the ACTU and explain why these have expanded over the last decade.

Further reading

Benson, J., 'Workplace union organisation in Australia', *Labour and Industry*, vol. 1, no. 3, October 1988.

Blandy, R., Sloan, J. and Wooden, M., 'Reforming the trade union structure in Australia', *Australian Bulletin of Labour*, vol. 15, no. 5, December 1989.

Cole, K. (ed.), *Power, Conflict and Control in Australian Trade Unions*, Penguin, Melbourne, 1982.

Ewer, P., Higgins, W. and Stevens, A., *Unions and the Future of Australian Manufacturing*, Allen & Unwin, Sydney, 1987.

Ford, B. and Plowman, D. (eds), *Australian Unions* (2nd ed.), Macmillan, Melbourne, 1989.

Frenkel, S.J. and Coolican, A., *Unions Against Capitalism? A Sociological Comparison of the Australian Building and Metal Workers' Unions*, Allen & Unwin, Sydney, 1984.

Griffin, G. and Scarcebrook, V., 'Trends in mergers in federally registered unions 1904–1986', *Journal of Industrial Relations*, vol. 31, no. 2, June 1989.

Hagan, J., *The History of the ACTU*, Longman Cheshire, Melbourne, 1981.

Howard, W.A., 'Australian trade unions in the context of union theory', *Journal of Industrial Relations*, vol. 19, no. 3, September 1977.

Martin, R.M., *Trade Unionism*, Clarendon Press, Oxford, 1989.

Rawson, D.W., *Unions and Unionists in Australia* (2nd ed.), Allen & Unwin, Sydney, 1986.

Sutcliffe, J.T., *A History of Trade Unionism in Australia*, Macmillan, Melbourne, 1967.

CHAPTER 9

Trade Unions: Objectives and Activities

The Australian trade union movement consists of a large and diverse range of organisations. These bodies differ not only in size, structure and organisational strength but also in terms of their objectives, interests and activities. They often hold conflicting political ideologies, pursue varying industrial tactics and serve different interests and roles. This chapter sets out to examine the objectives of Australian unions and the methods they use to achieve their goals. It also explores the question of union democracy and the forms of legal controls that have been instituted to regulate their internal affairs. It then looks at the political affiliations of Australian unions and their financial resources. Finally, the chapter concludes by examining two important groups for whom, until recently, unions have shown little concern: immigrants and women.

Union objectives

The primary objective of a trade union is to improve the well-being of its members. Unions were formed in Australia, as elsewhere, to counter the superior economic power of employers. It was recognised that the market dominance of employers could only be offset by workers acting collectively and establishing organisations to bargain on their behalf. By acting in unity they could limit the power and authority of employers and lessen their dependence on market fluctuations and the arbitrary rule of management. In this way unions could form a countervailing structure of control.

The most important function of a union is to maximise the level of monetary compensation—subject to particular employment constraints—and to raise generally the economic conditions under which work is performed. But trade unions are not simply market bargainers. Workers also combine with each other to influence and control the pace of work, to achieve participation in the processes of managerial decision-making and to secure greater autonomy over their working lives. Not all unions, however, share a common view on the matters that should come within their compass or agree on the methods by which they should achieve their goals. Some hold a narrow and prosaic view of their proper functions, contending that they should confine their activities to the direct and immediate matters of wages and working conditions. Others proclaim far more radical aims and adopt a broader perspective of their role.

In general, the Australian trade union movement has tended to perform its representational function at two levels. At the place of work it has sought to provide a means through which the concerns of employees could be voiced and resolved, and fairer and more equitable employment arrangements could be made and administered. The formation of a system of industrial jurisdiction has thus enabled employee rights to be established and enforced. Outside the enterprise, trade unions have played a role in defending and advancing the overall interests of their members not only as producers but also as consumers and citizens. Invariably they have supplied an important voice for the weakest and often most vulnerable members of the community, acting, according to Kemp, as a 'significant cultural force for the promotion of egalitarian ideas'.[1] The ACTU has described the function of Australian unions in the following way:

> The basic philosophy of the trade union movement has always involved a combination of the pragmatic with the ideal. We support peace as an international objective, the pursuit of membership claims for improvements in wages and working conditions, greater job security, more satisfying employment and a capacity to retire with some income security. In summary the union movement is about reducing inequalities in our society . . . At the same time we seek to make a major contribution to the creation of wealth in the development of the economy.[2]

Why employees join unions

Before we look in detail at the objectives of trade unions it is important first to examine why individuals join unions and what benefits they might expect to derive from union membership. In those situations where individuals exercise choice in this matter it could be expected

---

1. D. Kemp, *Foundations for Australian Political Analysis*, Oxford University Press, Melbourne, 1988, p. 390.
2. ACTU, *Future Strategies for the Trade Union Movement*, Melbourne, 1987, p. (i).

that unions would seek to provide a flow of services which maximise those membership objectives.[3]

The individual decision to join a union may be influenced by a number of factors. An employee could be motivated by instrumental considerations, ideological beliefs or simply by compulsion. Crouch believes that employees make a number of choices about how they will achieve their objectives at work, and union membership will be one of the alternative means available to them.[4] Under such circumstances, the demand for union services may be affected by the price of union membership, the individual's tastes or preferences for union services and the relative attraction of the alternatives. Kochan has suggested that the decision to unionise will be affected by at least three sets of factors: first, dissatisfaction with economic aspects of the job, second, a desire to influence those aspects of the work environment through union-oriented means, and third, a belief that the benefits of unionism outweigh the expected costs.[5]

He postulates that the initial stimulus to unionise will arise out of dissatisfaction with the bread-and-butter aspects of the jobs. Both Farber and Saks[6] and Guest and Dewe[7] have found that dissatisfaction with the supervisory relationship, job content and involvement in work are also important triggers. The second set of determinants influencing the unionisation decision relates to the desire to remedy unsatisfactory working conditions through unions rather than through other more informal, individualistic or employer-initiated participation programmes. The propensity to join unions will finally be affected by an individual's calculation of whether the expected benefits of unionisation outweigh the expected costs. An individual, may of course, be able to secure many of the benefits of unionism without actually joining and bearing the financial costs of membership. Unions provide both public and private goods. Wage improvements, safety conditions and superannuation entitlements apply to all workers irrespective of union membership. The indivisibility of these benefits will allow individuals to a 'free ride' on the public good provided by the union. On the other hand, private goods cannot be consumed without being a union member. In order to make it more attractive for employees to become members, unions may adopt several strategies. First, they can provide a range of services which are additional to their central role and can only be enjoyed by members. They may include credit union facilities, insurance, legal advice or discount purchasing arrangements. A second method of removing the 'free

---

3. See A.J. Oswald, 'The economic theory of trade unions: an introductory survey', *Scandinavian Journal of Economics*, vol. 87, 1985, pp. 160–93 and P.J. Turnbull, 'The economic theory of trade union behaviour: a critique', *British Journal of Industrial Relations*, vol. 26, no. 1, 1988, pp. 99–118.
4. C. Crouch, *Trade Unions: The Logic of Collective Action*, Fontana, London, 1982.
5. T.A. Kochan, 'How American workers view labor unions', *Monthly Labor Review*, April 1979.
6. H. Farber and D. Saks, 'Why workers want unions: the role of relative wages and job characteristics', *Journal of Political Economy*, vol. 88, no. 2, April 1980.
7. D. Guest and P. Dewe, 'Why do workers belong to trade unions? A social psychological study in the UK electronics industry', *British Journal of Industrial Relations*, vol. 26, no. 2, July 1988.

ride' is to make the cost of non-membership unsustainable by reaching closed-shop agreements with employers.

Judgements about the instrumentality or success of unions in improving employment conditions are important in the unionisation decision. It is evident that a union's utility will vary according to the possible range of alternatives an individual has to achieve his or her employment objectives. Professional, well-educated employees may, for example, be less prone than unskilled blue-collar workers to demand union services and require the protection afforded by collective action because of their strong market position and greater mobility across firms and labour markets. The usefulness of a union will also depend, as Crouch notes, on the ease with which the organisation can be used to achieve the individual's objectives.[8] One would expect that those employees whose sex, age, ethnicity or employment status make them readily open to exploitation or discrimination in the labour market would be the most likely to unionise. However, these employees may not be in the best position to secure realisable benefits from unionism. They could be in temporary or casual employment, work in small companies or be employed in a highly competitive sector of the economy where the results of collective action are not easily achievable.

Not all employees will make a rational analysis of the costs and benefits of unionism. Some may simply view trade unions in such an unfavourable light that they will not be motivated to join irrespective of the actual or potential material gains. There are others, of course, who will join because of their commitment to the values or principles of unionism. These employees will join regardless of their work-related conditions. They are ideologically disposed towards unions and join for what Van de Vall calls ideal-collective motives or what Poole calls value-rational reasons.[9] The factors that trigger the individual's unionisation decision may, therefore, be presented as in Figure 9.1.

The empirical evidence in Australia would seem to suggest that employees join unions for instrumental rather than ideological reasons and that, as a consequence, the significance of unions lies largely in their resolution of issues arising directly out of the employment relationship. Martin, for example, has asserted that the majority of Australian unionists 'see the primary purpose of their union as being the protection and improvement of their pay and working conditions'.[10] This view is supported by the work of Rawson[11] and Dufty[12] whose surveys confirm that the majority of unionists do not see their organisation's role as being concerned with struggles around broader social and political matters. On the other hand, Deery and De Cieri found that an individual's

---

8. C. Crouch, *Trade Unions: The Logic of Collective Action*.
9. See B. Klandermans, 'Psychology and trade union participation: joining, acting, quitting', *Journal of Occupational Psychology*, vol. 59, no. 3, 1986.
10. R. Martin, *Trade Unions in Australia*, Penguin, Melbourne, 1980, p. 104.
11. D.W. Rawson, *Unions and Unionists in Australia*, Allen & Unwin, Sydney, 1980, p. 98.
12. N.F. Dufty, 'Conscripts and volunteers', *Australian Bulletin of Labour*, vol. 7, no. 2, 1981, pp. 96–7.

Fig. 9.1: The process of individual union choice

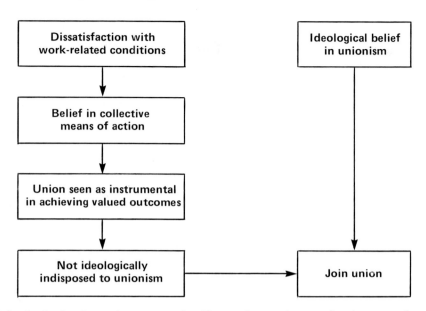

ideological orientation was a significant determinant of union membership.[13] Their results revealed that

> ... certain political and social values were consonant with higher levels of unionisation. The likelihood of union membership was enhanced where individuals held a left political ideology and believed in greater equality in the distribution of wealth in society.[14]

This is not to deny the importance of the union's function in attending to job and work-related issues. Indeed, qualitative research carried out by Australian National Opinion Polls (ANOP) for the ACTU in 1988 disclosed that most unionists saw the function of their organisation in fairly narrow terms.[15] In essence it was 'to look after ... [their] interests—specifically to increase their pay, improve working conditions and protect their jobs'.[16] The report highlighted the importance that many employees placed on the general form of protection offered by the union in circumstances which were often unforeseen. In this sense it was suggested that union membership was 'like insurance and those members who value the protection it confers are most probably motivated in the same way as buyers of life insurance and health insurance, who prefer to be protected against some future threat'.[17]

---

13. S. Deery and H. De Cieri, 'Determinants of trade union membership in Australia', Working Paper no. 50, Centre for Industrial Relations and Labour Studies, University of Melbourne, December 1989.
14. Ibid., p. 19.
15. ANOP, *The Image of the Trade Union Movement in Australia*, Sydney, 1989.
16. Ibid., p. 35.
17. Ibid., p. 37.

It is possible to identify four major objectives which are the primary concern of most unions. These can be categorised as: the provision of direct services to members; improved conditions of employment; organisational security; and political or non-political objectives.

Direct services

Unions provide a range of benefits to their members which are financed directly from union revenue or special levies. Services such as legal aid, taxation advice, mortuary benefits, dental care, education programs and various cultural and recreational activities are among the facilities available to various union members. In the early stages of Australian unionism the main focus had been as much on the provision of mutual benefits to protect members against the adversities of illness and unemployment as it had been on advancing members' economic interests. But these benefits became markedly less important as unions laid greater emphasis on economic and political objectives and placed pressure on governments to supply social services and welfare benefits. With the increased role of the state and the early political success of Australian labour there was a decline in union concern for such organisational activities. The small size of most unions, coupled with their meagre resources, also imposed severe handicaps on the scale of services that could be provided for members.

Over the last decade there has been a discernible growth of interest in the provision of benefit services, particularly among larger organisations. Some unions, like the Australian Bank Employees' Union, have specified in their rules that one of their major objectives is 'to formulate and carry into operation schemes for the industrial, social, recreational and general advancement of members' and 'to establish and maintain clubs and holiday homes for the benefit of members and their families, and to provide scholarships for the children of members and deceased members'. To this end they provide a comprehensive set of services which include a discount purchasing scheme, legal advice for both industrial and personal matters, discount travel facilities, a credit union and the provision of insurance at favourable rates for members. It is not uncommon for unions to furnish members with opportunities to secure cheap housing loans. The Federated Clerks' Union has run a successful cooperative housing scheme for its members since the 1950s. This, along with a wide range of other services, has led the union to describe itself, among other things, as 'a legal and financial umbrella and a social services club'.

It is in the area of financial and general welfare services that much of the activity has occurred. Many larger unions have developed credit union facilities for their members and these have experienced strong growth in the 1970s and 1980s. The provision of insurance has also attracted union attention. Perhaps the most comprehensive is a scheme that was initiated in 1981 by the National Union of Workers (known then as the Federated Storemen and Packers' Union). More than sixty unions now participate in the scheme. Through Labor Union Insurances Pty Ltd

(LUI) members are offered a wide range of cover including life assurance and various types of general insurance such as accident, casualty, home and motor vehicle cover. In 1990 LUI had a premium income of around $3 million, mostly from house and contents cover. It is also not uncommon for unions to form sickness and accident funds for members who become ill or are injured outside working hours. It is normal under these schemes for members to receive additional weekly payments to supplement their social security benefits.

Many unions have mortality or funeral funds which provide the next of kin with cash payments either to defray funeral costs or to alleviate hardship that may arise from the immediate loss of family income. Unemployment registers and the establishment of quasi-employment agencies to help members find jobs have emerged as a union response to increasing difficulties in the labour market.

The growing emphasis on the provision of direct and personal services reflects a pattern of union activities which is likely to expand greatly in the 1990s. While some union leaders see this as part of a general involvement in wider areas affecting the welfare of their members, many others regard it as an essential means to improve the attractiveness of the union for recruitment purposes. The supply of a range of financial services, legal assistance and consumer discounts as well as medical and dental benefits is seen as a way of reversing the decline in union membership numbers.[18] This has been prompted by a belief that workers are becoming more individualistic in their aspirations and are no longer satisfied with trade union action which is limited to collective demands. This view is not confined to Australia.[19] In the United States, the AFL-CIO produced a report in 1985 entitled *The Changing Situation of Workers and Unions* which contained proposals for an array of benefits and services for individuals who did not require a collective bargaining function from unions. In Britain, organisations such as the Electricians' Union (EETPU) have had the label of 'business unionism' attached to their activities as they have emphasised individual services which range from high-technology occupational training to cheap car loans and free legal advice. Their aim has unashamedly been to provide an increasingly sophisticated range of services which will attract new members.

Improved conditions of employment

It can scarcely be denied that the dominant concern of Australian unions is to improve the economic conditions of their members. Claims for higher wages, shorter hours, better annual and long-service leave entitlements, improved physical working conditions and greater job security occupy the central focus of attention for most unions. Through the

---

18. See ACTU, *Policies and Strategy Statements Adopted by ACTU Congress, September 1989*, p. 81.
19. See E. Maire, 'Some signposts for the future of trade unions', *Labour and Society*, vol. 11, no. 2, May 1986.

use of official statistics on the causes of industrial disputes it is possible to identify the issues that have led unions to engage in direct action. These data should be viewed with some caution, because the statistics only record a single factor that precipitated the actual stoppages, and in reality few strikes have one immediate cause. However, they do indicate the type of matter on which Australian unions have been willing to fight. Table 9.1 contains information on the causes of stoppages between 1970 and 1989.

It can be seen from Table 9.1 that the basic economic issues of wages, hours and leave have been the most important causes of time lost between 1970 and 1989. Wages were responsible for just under a half of the total number of working days lost during that period. Matters relating to managerial policy—such as discipline, dismissals, promotion and retrenchments—were also an important cause and accounted for almost 24 per cent of time loss. In fact, in the decade 1980–89 disputes over managerial policy accounted for one-third of working days lost and closely rivalled wages as the dominant cause of lost time.

Wages, hours and leave

As can be seen from Table 9.1, unions' aims for higher living standards manifest themselves most clearly in a demand for higher wages. The principle of 'wage justice' has long been a basic tenet of Australian union philosophy. In practice this is translated into a concern for the maintenance of real wages and an equitable share of national income through the distribution of national productivity growth. Unions have been well aware of the effects of inflation and taxation policies on the purchasing power of wages and salaries, and have framed policies on wage and tax indexation and price control as well as showing concern over interest rates, health care costs and other elements which affect the 'social wage' of their members. Minimum wages have held special significance. The importance attached to the notion of a living wage has endured since the early days of Federation when the Commonwealth Court of Conciliation and Arbitration was called on to set the standard minimum wage payments for the purposes of tariff protection. Union attention has been directed towards ensuring that the minimum wage is set at a level which, according to the ACTU, meets the 'reasonable needs [of working people] determined in the light of standards generally accepted in a progressive community'.[20]

'Equal pay for equal work' has also been a prominent objective, motivated not only by notions of industrial justice but also by the traditional fears of male breadwinners that their wages would be undercut by competition from women. Improvements have been slow and even now are incomplete, despite state legislation during the 1960s and decisions by the Commonwealth Conciliation and Arbitration Commission to give women full wage parity with men by 1975 (see Chapter 11).

---

20. ACTU, *Bulletin*, vol. 3, no. 2(A), 1981, p. 7.

Table 9.1: Proportion of working days lost by cause, all industries, Australia 1970–89 (percentages)

Year	Wages	Hours of work	Leave, pensions, compensation, etc.	Managerial policy	Physical working conditions	Trade unionism	Other causes
1970	63.7	5.1	3.0	12.0	4.6	3.8	7.9
1971	70.8	0.2	1.0	11.0	5.6	4.8	6.6
1972	67.6	0.1	2.3	15.0	3.8	3.9	7.3
1973	66.3	0.8	2.6	14.7	5.8	4.8	5.0
1974	88.3	0.2	0.6	4.5	1.6	2.6	2.2
1975	73.1	0.6	0.3	11.6	2.7	6.0	5.7
1976	18.4	1.5	2.9	15.1	3.4	3.1	55.5
1977	50.5	3.1	2.8	25.5	9.5	4.6	4.1
1978	48.4	1.9	1.2	28.0	5.2	4.4	10.8
1979	52.5	3.0	0.4	12.9	3.9	2.5	24.7
1980	36.0	7.5	15.1	22.9	5.5	3.4	9.6
1981	46.7	24.8	6.3	15.5	4.0	2.0	0.7
1982	48.7	20.5	1.2	16.5	7.0	3.5	3.7
1983	12.2	5.0	4.0	43.5	31.5	3.3	4.6
1984	24.6	5.9	8.4	32.5	16.3	8.7	3.6
1985	23.1	3.8	3.2	24.6	14.9	16.5	13.7
1986	40.0	1.0	10.8	35.6	6.9	3.3	2.4
1987	43.0	1.7	16.1	27.4	7.3	3.0	1.5
1988	29.6	1.8	2.9	52.4	9.2	2.0	2.0
1989	14.7	0.5	7.3	54.0	6.6	6.2	10.7
1970–89	45.9	4.4	4.6	23.8	7.8	4.6	9.1

Source: ABS, Quarterly Summaries of Industrial Disputes.

Reduced working hours has been an historic goal since the struggle for the eight-hour day was waged in the 1850s under the slogan 'eight hours work, eight hours rest and eight hours leisure'. The forty-eight-hour week was first won by the Stonemasons in 1856. Principally through the agency of state Labor governments, the standard working week was reduced to forty-four hours during the 1920s and to forty hours in the late 1940s. The objective of a thirty-five-hour week was adopted by the Australian Council of Trade Unions in 1957. However, it has not been until the early 1980s that concerted union pressure yielded significant concessions in this area.

Paid annual vacations and long-service leave are also important items of interest. The principle of a minimum of four weeks' annual leave has been established, as has the unions claim for an annual leave loading. Long-service leave became an objective among coal-mining unions after World War II and was taken up by most unions shortly afterwards. When it was introduced into the industry in 1949 it was quickly established as a precedent which led most state governments to enact long-service legislation during the 1950s. In both this and other industrial matters, state Labor governments, and in particular those in New South Wales, have taken a leading role in the development of improved conditions of work.

Physical working conditions

Issues relating to physical working conditions and the industrial environment have been traditionally accorded a low priority by most unions. Occupational health and safety was viewed as a matter of marginal concern compared to wages, hours and leave. In recent years there has been a changing emphasis towards ameliorating hazards at the workplace and both the ACTU and individual unions have begun to play a more active role in pressing for improvements in state health and safety legislation and in initiating shop-floor campaigns around health issues. Indeed, in the period 1980–89 disputes over physical working conditions accounted for 11 per cent of total working days lost compared with only 4 per cent in the decade 1970–79.

Superannuation

One of the most recent challenges to be taken up by Australian unions has been that of superannuation. The general failure of the existing company, occupational and industrial superannuation structure to provide adequate retirement benefits for the vast majority of employees prompted both the ACTU and individual unions to campaign strongly for union-administered schemes. The absence of superannuation coverage for many blue-collar and female employees and the lack of portability or adequate vesting rights under most employer-run schemes drew substantial criticism. Restrictions on the portability of cover were seen as the most important deficiency. In 1980, for example, it was suggested that more than half of all employees in superannuation funds would never to able to use their accumulated contributions to finance their retirement because of job changes.[21]

As well as calling for the removal of discrimination against women, part-time and casual employees and improvements in portability rights, the ACTU has sought to achieve either joint management or union control of superannuation funds. One of the first union-run funds was established by the Federated Storemen and Packers' Union (now the National Union of Workers) in 1978 under the name of Labor Union Cooperative Retirement Fund (LUCRF). Although it began operations with only a small number of contributing employers in the skin and hide industry, it has grown substantially. From an initial membership of 700 employees it has increased its coverage to more than 35 000 with assets in excess of $82 million. More than 1100 companies now contribute to the scheme. In 1980, an agreement between the ACTU and the Australian Paper and Pulp Mills created an important precedent for joint union–management participation in the running of superannuation funds. The scheme provided for the fund to be managed by a board of trustees comprising equal numbers of employer and employee representatives who had the right to choose the portfolio managers.

Perhaps the most important breakthrough came in 1984, when, as a result of negotiations in the building industry, employers agreed to pay weekly contributions into a union-run superannuation scheme known as the Building Unions' Superannuation Scheme (BUSS). Within eighteen months it had become the largest private superannuation fund in the country and by September 1989 it had 190 000 members. The scheme is said to have the potential for a membership of more than 250 000 and contributions of more than $100 million per year. It has been suggested that BUSS could accumulate investment capital of up to $8 billion during the next twenty years.[22] The unions' superannuation strategy was given important support by the renegotiated Accord agreement between the Federal Labor Government and the ACTU in 1985. In exchange for ACTU agreement to wage discounting, the government undertook to support union claims for improvements in superannuation amounting to a '3 per cent wage equivalent' at the 1986 National Wage Case. New or improved superannuation schemes were to be implemented over a two-year period. In setting operational guidelines for new superannuation schemes, the government established that control should rest with trustees nominated equally by the members or, where appropriate, unions, and employer representatives. In June 1986 the Conciliation and Arbitration Commission gave its general approval to these arrangements. Since this time the number of employees with superannuation coverage has risen sharply. In 1989, 47 per cent of the Australian workforce received a superannuation benefit compared with only 39.5 per cent in 1984.[23] The proportion of women belonging to

---

21. The *National Times*, 2–8 March 1980.
22. D. Shaw, 'An investment revolution', *Australian Society*, 1986.
23. ABS, *Employment Benefits*, August 1989, Cat. No. 6334.0.

superannuation schemes is still considerably lower (36 per cent) than it is for men (55 per cent) notwithstanding a strong upward trend over the past five years. Union members have a markedly higher entitlement to superannuation benefits than do non-members.[24] The ACTU estimated in 1989 that there were more than 1.5 million members in superannuation funds under joint or sole trusteeship control of unions.[25]

Job security

In addition to matters relating to wages, hours, leave and working conditions, unions are also interested in providing some form of job security for their members. Protection against arbitrary treatment by management has led to a concern for the negotiation of rules on matters such as the selection, promotion, dismissal and discipline of employees. Because of the marked changes in the application of computer technology the issue of employment security has taken on a greater sense of urgency for Australian trade unions. During the 1980s there were a number of attempts to obtain consultation and participation in decisions relating to the planning and introduction of technological change and to limit the scope of management to terminate redundant workers. Major successes were recorded in both the Federal and State jurisdictions during this period.

Organisational security

Despite the considerable protection afforded them by the arbitration system, Australian trade unions have consistently sought to have union security arrangements included in awards and agreements.[26] This has usually been in the form of attempts to make union membership a compulsory condition of employment. The enforcement of compulsory unionism enhances their bargaining strength by enabling them to call on greater numbers in the event of direct action. It also provides them with a larger and more secure source of finance. Frequently compulsory union arrangements are accompanied by employer 'check-off' systems in which the employer automatically deducts the weekly union dues from the employee's wage packet and sends it on to the union concerned.

Although most of the arbitral bodies in Australia lack the power to make it obligatory for an employee to join a union, many collective agreements provide for such conditions.[27] Lesser union security provisions, such as preference clauses, are also prevalent throughout Australian industry. These require employers to give preferential treatment

---

24. In 1988, 60 per cent of unionists were the beneficiaries of superannuation schemes compared with only 28 per cent of non-unionists. ABS, *Trade Union Members Australia*, August 1988, Cat. No. 6325.0.
25. ACTU, *Reports, Policy and Strategy Recommendations, Wages and Taxation*, Biennial Congress, 25–29 September 1989.
26. Australian trade unions are protected against both employer discrimination and competition from rival unions. Once a union is registered under the *Industrial Relations Act*, it has virtually a sole right to organise in its field of employment. Also both federal and state law makes it an offence to dismiss an employee because he or she is a member of a registered trade union.
27. See R.M. Martin, 'Legal enforcement of union security in Australia', in Isaac and Ford (eds), *Australian Labour Relations*, pp. 173–8.

to union members over non-union members in such matters as engagement, promotion and retrenchment.[28] Mitchell has shown, however, that the federal tribunal has always been reluctant to grant preference to unionists in the absence of evidence that an employer has been actively discriminating against union members.[29] In 1989 only 411 federal awards (27 per cent) gave union preference. In most cases this was confined to preference over hiring.[30]

Political or non-industrial objectives

It is possible to draw a distinction between industrial and non-industrial objectives of unions: between those matters relating to issues like wages and working conditions and those that pertain to broader social and political questions not directly affecting employment conditions at the workplace.[31] The direct involvement of unions in issues of a non-industrial nature has evoked a great deal of controversy. There are some who maintain that it is not a legitimate province for trade union action and that political strikes and other forms of industrial action pose a threat to the parliamentary democratic process. This is a view held by a number of unions on the right of the political spectrum. For instance, a past publication of the Victorian Branch of the Federated Clerks' Union stated that unions had 'no mandate from either their members or the public to dictate the nation's health policy, foreign policy or urban development programs'. It acknowledged the right of the union movement 'to take attitudes and express opinions upon political and social questions' but argued that these should be processed through the 'parliamentary system of government ... [and not through] political strikes, bans and limitations'.[32]

This is not the attitude shared by others within the union movement who hold firmly to the view that there can be no limit to their legitimate concerns. The Prime Minister and former ACTU President, Mr Hawke, also has dismissed what he calls the 'mystical dividing line' which supposedly confines industrial action to 'real' industrial issues but excludes it from wider social matters. Hawke asserted that

> The trade union movement has a legitimate concern in any areas that involve the welfare of the working people of this country and those dependent upon them ... we have a responsibility to in fact use our own strength, our accumulated and cohesive strength in a way which will not only assist those who are directly in our ranks but also to assist those who are less fortunate and less privileged than ourselves and less able to look after their own interests.[33]

---

28. There is often a distinction between absolute and qualified preference. In the first case the employer is required to give preference in employment unconditionally, whereas, in the second, 'all other things being equal', the unionist is given preference over the non-unionist.
29. R.J. Mitchell, 'The preference power and the practice of the Federal Industrial Tribunal, 1904–1970', *Journal of Industrial Relations*, vol. 29, no. 1, March 1987.
30. S. Crean and M. Rimmer, *ILO Study on the Adjustment Problems of Trade Unions in Industrialised Markets—Australia*, mimeo, 1989, p. 120.
31. See R.M. Martin, 'The problem of "political" strikes', in W.A. Howard (ed.), *Perspectives on Australian Industrial Relations*, Longman Cheshire, Melbourne, 1984, pp. 17–24.
32. The Federated Clerks' Union of Australia (Victorian Branch), *Political Strikes*, undated, pp. 5–6.
33. R.J. Hawke, 'The changing role of trade unions: past struggles and future directions', in G. Evans, J. Reeves and J. Malbon (eds), *Labor Essays 1981*, Drummond, Melbourne, 1981, p. 10.

In fact union involvement in political and social matters has been a longstanding one. This involvement has ranged from industrial action on issues of foreign policy such as conscription, the Dutch presence in Indonesia, apartheid and the Australian military involvement in Vietnam to matters of domestic concern such as the sacking of the Whitlam Labor government, 'green bans', sandmining on Fraser Island, the boycott of construction work on the Victorian Newport power station and the ban on drilling at Nookanbah in Western Australia in support of the Aborigines.[34] Despite this, it would be incorrect to suggest that the Australian labour movement has been commonly involved in strike action over issues of a non-industrial nature. Indeed the opposite is true. Political stoppages in Australia represent an insignificant fraction of total working days lost. Moreover, with few exceptions intervention has been confined to a small number of unions in the maritime, stevedoring, building and metal industries.

Union methods

Unions employ a variety of techniques to achieve their goals. These may include the processes of conciliation and arbitration, the use of direct negotiations, the application of industrial pressure through strike action or the recourse to political activities. The methods that actually are used will depend largely on the union's assessment of which ones are the most appropriate in the particular circumstances they face. The conditions under which unions operate vary over time and methods which may be advisable in one situation may be completely ill-advised in another. Unions will attempt to exploit fully whatever power or influence they possess in both the industrial and political arenas and the modes of action they adopt will vary according to a number of factors. These may include general economic conditions, the union's information and research capacity, the political persuasions of governments, the union's actual strategic position within the production process and the types of demands which it is pursuing.

In Australia the use of conciliation and arbitration has historically overshadowed the use of collective bargaining. However, this has not inhibited the recourse to direct action. Invariably industrial power has been applied to exert pressure on both employers at the negotiating table and on industrial tribunals when considering union claims. Likewise, unions have made great use of their political affiliations with the Australian Labor Party at both federal and state levels to secure improvements in the terms and conditions of employment. This has been achieved either through Labor government representations to industrial

---

34. Few issues have drawn such widespread publicity as the 'green bans' imposed by the Builders Labourers' Federation in the 1970s. For a description of the union's activities see R.J. Roddenweig, *Green Bans: The Birth of Australian Environmental Politics*, Hale & Iremonger, Sydney, 1978 and J. Mundey, *Jack Mundey: Green Bans and Beyond*, Angus & Robertson, Sydney, 1981.

tribunals or through legislation. Because of this it is impossible to separate clearly the use of one method of action from another as in reality a combination of tactics may be used. The predominance of one form over another is likely to reflect the union's bargaining position and the wider environment in which it is operating.

Conciliation and arbitration

Up until the 1890s the methods used by Australian unions were similar to those of their British predecessors. Collective bargaining in the form of direct negotiations with employers, occasionally supplemented by conciliation and voluntary arbitration, was the principal means through which unions sought to advance the living standards of their members. But the weaknesses of the union organisation and the fragility of collective bargaining were brutally exposed by the strikes of the 1890s. Since the development of the system of conciliation and arbitration in the early part of the twentieth century it has become the major means of fixing the terms of employment and settling disputes. However, the system has not been without its critics. There are those who consider that it unfairly restricts their use of industrial action, that it is over-cautious and pays too much attention to the economic implications of its decisions. Suggestions have been made that union members would be materially better off without arbitration and their interests better served by collective bargaining without any third-party intervention. Some of these criticisms undoubtedly stem from legitimate disappointments with the results achieved but their misgivings rarely reach the state where an organisation would seriously contemplate detaching itself from the system altogether. As one observer commented, 'Sceptics may note the regularity with which today's critics line up for tomorrow's hearing'.[35] Even those unions which have registered an ideological opposition to the system, and which believe that it saps the union movement of its revolutionary potential, have shown little inclination to cut themselves off from arbitration.

In reality few unions could afford to do so. Most simply do not have the organisational resources necessary to actually pursue a policy of collective bargaining. A great number of Australian unions have become accommodated to a system which has required little in the way of coercive strength or industrial power. In particular many weaker unions have been well served by the doctrine of comparative wage justice and the practice of flow-ons. The tribunal's preference for a uniformity of treatment in wages and conditions claims has meant that arbitration has become a major means of spreading the increases made in one sector of the workforce to other sectors. This has often meant that the less powerful and more inactive sections of the union movement have not been greatly disadvantaged by their lack of bargaining ability.

---

35. A. Cunningham, 'Conciliation and arbitration: is there an alternative?' in G. Evans, J. Reeves and J. Malbon (eds), *Labor Essays 1981*, p. 69.

Australian unions have above all taken a pragmatic approach to arbitration. Their preference for it rests largely on an objective assessment that arbitration represents the most profitable course of action for the achievement of their organisational goals. This does not mean that unions have forsaken the use of the strike weapon or do not make use of collective bargaining. Unions have always been prepared to use direct action if they thought they could secure their objectives more effectively by doing so.

Collective bargaining

The process of collective bargaining has always coexisted alongside the operation of arbitration tribunals in Australia. Indeed, as Isaac has noted, 'the founders and early practitioners of compulsory arbitration saw this process not as displacing collective bargaining but as supplementing it whenever negotiations broke down'.[36] One of the chief objects of the *Industrial Relations Act*, which regulates the federal tribunals, is 'to provide a framework for the prevention and settlement of industrial disputes by conciliation and arbitration in a manner that minimizes the disruptive effects of industrial disputes on the community'. In practice, this means that before a tribunal will attempt to settle a dispute by adjudication it will first order the parties to try to resolve their differences by negotiation and will assist them to do so through conciliation. According to the former President of the Australian Conciliation and Arbitration Commission, Sir Richard Kirby, this emphasis on conciliation 'encourages collective bargaining before arbitration becomes necessary'.[37]

In addition to this form of pre-arbitral negotiations, collective bargaining also occurs in the area of over-award payments. Likewise it is evident in the collective negotiations of certified agreements and consent awards, in the area of award variations and in interpretation problems. Unions also continually negotiate with employers over minor matters which may be outside the terms of an award. Almost all these negotiations have, however, taken place under the shadow of an industrial tribunal. With few exceptions, the most notable of which is the metal-mining industries of Broken Hill, they do not occur in lieu of arbitration or in complete independence of the tribunal system. In this way the style and character of collective bargaining is markedly different from that which is practised overseas. It occurs within an environment dominated by arbitration tribunals and its form is more often than not shaped by the operations of those tribunals, sometimes being conducted at its direction and invariably within the framework it lays down. The imprint of the system is also distinguishable because of the possibility of arbitration being used in the event of negotiations breaking down.

---

36. J.E. Isaac, 'Equity and wage discrimination', paper presented to 51st ANZAAS Congress, 12 May 1981, p. 11.
37. R. Kirby, 'Some comparisons between compulsory arbitration and collective bargaining', *Journal of Industrial Relations*, vol. 7, no. 1, 1965, p. 5.

The use of collective bargaining as a method of action has been influenced by a number of factors. Undoubtedly the most important has been the unions' very ability to employ it effectively, for insofar as collective bargaining involves the use of strike action it may not be a realistic possibility for some or may be available only in certain circumstances. The approach of the tribunals themselves has been also an important determinant. In the early years of arbitration unions made little use of collective bargaining. Given their industrial weakness and the success of arbitration in protecting the interests of the lower paid, unions had neither the ability nor the cause to go outside compulsory arbitration. The federal tribunal in particular consolidated the gains won by the nascent union movement and helped to spread those gains more equally through the workforce. The authority of the arbitration system also was strengthened by the willingness of both state and federal governments to assign to the tribunals the power to make social policy and establish industrial standards that were elsewhere imposed directly by governments through legislation. However, during the 1950s and 1960s the generally buoyant economic conditions enabled many trade unions to make greater use of collective bargaining outside the confines of arbitration. The restrictive wages policy of the federal industrial tribunal during this period did little but strengthen the union view that concessions could be best extracted directly from employers.

The relative importance of direct negotiation continued to grow until the mid 1970s when the Arbitration Commission introduced a centralised system of wage indexation (see Chapter 11). The renewed dominance of arbitration was not unaffected by the high levels of unemployment in the Australian economy and the much weakened market position of the trade unions. The breakdown of the wage indexation system in the early 1980s led to a revival in the leadership role of collective bargaining. But this was shortlived. With the imposition of a wages pause in December 1982 and the re-establishment of centralised wage determination in September 1983 the scope for direct negotiation has been severely limited.

Nevertheless, since then the opportunities for collective bargaining at the level of the enterprise have been widened through the introduction, first, of the two-tier wage system in December 1986 and second, by award restructuring via the structural efficiency principle in August 1988. Both decisions of the Commission were aimed at improving efficiency and productivity at the enterprise level by encouraging the negotiation of new work practices and award structures. The form and extent of collective bargaining, however, was closely monitored and controlled and kept within firm guidelines.

Political action

It is obvious that if trade unions are to protect and advance the working and living standards of their members they simply cannot confine their activities to the boundaries of an enterprise or of an industry. The economic well-being of union members is affected not only by their organisation's ability to win improved conditions through direct action or through the arbitration tribunals but by factors ouside the union's immediate control or influence. Governments influence the general economic environment of industrial relations through their policies on such matters as incomes, employment, inflation and tariff protection. They also help shape the institutional framework and set the rules by which employers and unions may conduct their bargaining and resolve their disputes.

Unions have long recognised the central importance of government and for this reason have actively engaged in political as well as industrial action to further their objectives. Two different types of political activity have been undertaken by Australian unions: the first may be described as 'direct' and the second as 'party political'.[38] Direct political action has taken the form of lobbying governments in order to gain favourable consideration of union policies. In this way unions have attempted to influence governments by acting as an external pressure group outside the party political system.[39] Unions may also make direct representations on matters such as skill development and training, budgetary policy, tariff protection, social welfare measures and industrial relations legislation. The national twenty-four-hour strike over changes to the Medibank system of health insurance in 1976 was another example of how unions act as a pressure group in trying to alter government policy which may be seen as having an adverse economic effect on their membership.

Of far greater importance has been the unions' use of party political methods. Since the formation of the Labor Party in the 1890s unions have sought to achieve economic and social improvements through parliamentary means. Until the early 1980s, however, the lack of tenure of Labor governments at both the federal and state level had tended to limit the benefits of this form of political action.

This has changed quite considerably in recent years. Within the framework of the Prices and Incomes Accord, the trade union movement has been able to exercise substantial influence over government economic and social policy. In its original form—as negotiated between the ACTU and the ALP in 1983—the Accord committed the Labor Government to implement a mutually agreed set of policies to improve the 'social wage' and promote economic growth and employment in exchange for wage constraint.[40] Although the Accord has been modified in the light of changed economic circumstances, it has nevertheless continued to provide unions with an important instrument of access to the processes of national policy making. State Labor governments have also been an important route through which many unions have been able to

---

38. R.M. Martin, *Trade Unions in Australia*, p. 114.
39. Because of the union movement's formal ties with the Australian Labor Party at both federal and state levels, and their ability to influence Labor governments from within, their pressure group activities are directed largely towards non-Labor governments.
40. See F. Stilwell, *The Accord . . . and Beyond*, Pluto Press, Sydney, 1986.

secure improved terms and conditions of employment for their members. Job security and occupational health and safety are two such matters where state Labor governments are playing an influential role.

Unions and party politics
The Australian Labor Party (ALP)
As a result of its defeats in the 1890s, the union movement recognised that industrial action alone could not secure the economic and social gains that it had been striving for. The limited achievements of strike action in adverse economic conditions had been painfully demonstrated by the events of those years. For this reason they turned their attention towards parliamentary representation and legislative change. In 1891 the Labor Party was formed in New South Wales and in the other colonies during the following decade. On Federation the Australian Labor Party was created. Since that time the ALP has remained the single most important party representing the interests of Australian trade unionists. Despite the formation of the Communist Party in 1920 and the splintering of the labour movement in the 1950s culminating in the creation of the Democratic Labor Party in 1955, the ALP has retained the allegiance and support of most unions. At present about 60 per cent of unionists belong to unions affiliated with the ALP. Most full-time union officials are members of the party and are able to deliver solid financial support in the form of regular affiliation fees and additional donations at election times. According to Rawson, trade unionists 'tend to regard the Labor Party as being the creation of the unions and therefore subject to their control'.[41]

Although the character of the ALP has changed markedly over the past thirty years because of a widening of the party's support base and an increased prominence of those with professional and middle-class backgrounds among its parliamentary representatives, the historical dominance of the trade unions is still reflected in the ALP's rules and policy-making bodies. As Rawson observes:
> In most States, the rules guarantee that they will have 60 per cent—a clear but not overwhelming majority—of the delegates to the State convention or conference which controls its affairs and which chooses delegates to the Party's national conference and national executive.[42]

However, this numerical supremacy need not necessarily translate into dominance of policy-making. In Cole's view, 'Unions span a broad and diverse political spectrum and rarely produce a sufficiently united front

---
41. D.W. Rawson, 'Unions and politics', in P.W.D. Matthews and G.W. Ford (eds), *Australian Trade Unions*, Sun Books, Melbourne, 1968, p. 177.
42. Ibid., p. 53.

to impose their will on the rest of the party'.⁴³ This is not to underestimate their presence in policy formulation. Union activists occupy positions of authority and influence at most levels within the ALP and a sizeable number of union officials have been elected to parliament as representatives of the party. Indeed, as Rawson has pointed out: 'Had it not been for the union officials, the manual working half of the Australian workforce would have virtually disappeared from the Federal Parliament'.⁴⁴

White-collar unions have been less ready to affiliate with the ALP. They have seen themselves as being more politically neutral than their blue-collar counterparts and have chosen largely to remain formally independent of the party. The ALP itself has not been unconcerned about this lack of support. In 1978 it stated:

> In organisational terms, it is arguable that one of the greatest failures of the ALP has been its inability to attract affiliation in the growth areas of trade unionism, such as the technical, professional and white-collar areas ... the dramatic changes in the composition of the workforce and the structure of trade unions have not been reflected in new affiliations with the ALP. In 1978, the union connection is basically with the blue-collar movement and with a numerically declining sector of the Australian workforce.⁴⁵

The ALP has found it difficult to reverse this trend. In fact, Rawson has predicted that it may not be long before only a minority of unionists are affiliated with the Party.⁴⁶ Over the past two decades the proportion of unionists belonging to ALP-affiliated unions has dropped from about 67 per cent to about 60 per cent. New affiliations have virtually ceased. There are two possible reasons for this. According to Rawson, affiliation with the ALP appears to be unpopular with rank-and-file unionists.⁴⁷ Surveys of union members indicate that only about one in ten favour affiliation with a political party. A second reason could pertain to factional differences within the ALP and to the reluctance of certain political groupings to support affiliations of unions with different political philosophies. For example, moves by two white-collar unions—the Shop, Distributive and Allied Employees' Association and the Federated Clerks' Union—to affiliate with the Victorian branch of the ALP in 1984 were strongly resisted by the left, largely because of the close ties that the unions then had with the National Civic Council and the Democratic Labor Party.

The communist parties

The Communist Party of Australia (CPA) was formed in October 1920 by a small but disparate group of socialists and trade union militants following the success of the Russian Revolution in 1917. The Party's aim

---

43. K. Cole, 'Unions and the Labor Party', in K. Cole (ed.), *Power, Conflict and Control in Australian Trade Unions*, Penguin, Melbourne, 1982, p. 86.
44. D.W. Rawson, *Unions and Unionists*, p. 55.
45. Reported in D.W. Rawson, 'The union connection: trade union affiliation with the Australian Labor Party' in Evans, Reeves and Malbon (eds), *Labour Essays*, pp. 33–4.
46. D.W. Rawson, *Unions and Unionists*, p. 49.
47. Ibid., p. 50.

was initially to mobilise support within trade unions. It sought to build a mass working-class organisation whose purpose would be to replace private ownership of the means of production with public ownership. To this end the CPA organised rank-and-file groups within trade unions in an effort to displace conservative leaderships opposed to their philosophy. Its first success came in 1933 when the Party captured official trade union positions in the Miners' Federation and later success followed in the maritime and stevedoring industries. Its strength grew considerably during the early 1940s. By the end of World War II the CPA held key union positions in a large number of industries, including metals, mining, railways, building, clerical and maritime. The Party reached its zenith during this period. It had won considerable influence with the ACTU, whose 1947 Biennial Congress had adopted many of its policies, and its membership stood at an all-time high of 23 000.[48] Its influence, however, was to be shortlived. By the following year it was in decline, a trend that was to continue through the cold-war period of the 1950s. Opposition groups led by the virulently anti-communist 'Movement' and supported by sections in the ALP who saw their previously dominant position within the unions being clearly threatened by the CPA, gradually wrested back the leadership of many unions from the communists.

The failure of the communist-led coalminers' strike of 1949 and the attempts by the Liberal Government to outlaw the CPA in 1950 drove the Party into a defensive and isolated position, diminished its influence and increasingly divided it over ideology and future strategy.[49] An open rift emerged in the early 1960s between pro-Russian and pro-Chinese factions and in 1964 the latter group left the Party to found the Communist Party of Australia (Marxist-Leninist). During the 1960s both communist parties began to reassert their influence within a number of unions in the maritime, stevedoring, building, mining and railway industries, although by 1968 the CPA was on the verge of another split. The Russian invasion of Czechoslovakia in that year caused sharp divisions of opinion within the party about whether such an action was justified. The decision of the Party's national executive to condemn the Soviet Union led to a pro-Soviet faction eventually leaving the Party in 1971 and forming the Socialist Party of Australia (SPA).

During the 1980s the two numerically strongest communist parties split again. First, in 1983, the SPA expelled its foundation president, Mr Pat Clancy, the Federal Secretary of the Building Workers' Industrial Union, reportedly because of his unwillingness to allow the activities of the union to be directed by the officials of the SPA.[50] Internal dissension and disaffection by other union officials with the policies of the SPA weakened further the Party's position in the building and maritime

---

48. See R.A. Gollan, *Revolutionaries and Reformists*, ANU Press, Canberra, 1975, and W. Higgins, 'Reconstructing Australian communism', in *Socialist Register*, Merlin Press, London, 1974.
49. See P. Deery, 'The 1949 coal strike', unpublished Ph.D. thesis, La Trobe University, Melbourne, 1976.
50. *Tribune*, 19 October 1983, p. 8.

industries, and caused it to lose much of its industrial base. Second, in 1984, twenty-three members of the thirty-two member Victorian CPA state committee resigned. They declared their desire 'to take socialism out of the margins of Australian society' and argued that it was necessary to 'accept the important role that Labor governments can play as a vehicle of radical reform, subject to and sustained by mass pressure'. A new umbrella organisation called the Socialist Forum was established in cooperation with a number of members of the Victorian ALP's socialist-left faction. It has been estimated that the CPA's national membership has now fallen to about 1300.[51] The fragmentation of the Communist Party over the past twenty-five years has consequently restricted quite severely communist influence within the Australian trade union movement.

The Democratic Labor Party (DLP)

Although the Democratic Labor Party was established in 1955 as a breakaway group from the ALP, its origins lie in the Catholic-inspired 'Movement', an organisation formed in 1942 to combat the influence of communists within trade unions. Led by B. A. Santamaria, then deputy director of the National Secretariat of Catholic Action, the Movement's activities were directed towards organising support for the election of anti-communist union officials. By 1945 it had sufficient influence within the ALP to get party endorsement for the creation of ALP Industrial Groups within each union. The Industrial Groups' aims were indentical to those of the Movement's, although they operated more openly and were composed of both Catholic and non-Catholic members. They were, nevertheless, dominated by the Movement.

In 1950 the Industrial Groups had their first major success when they won the leadership of the Victorian branch of the Federated Clerks' Union from the communists. This was followed by an important victory in the Federated Ironworkers' Association when the Industrial Group candidate, Laurie Short, wrested the federal leadership from Ernest Thornton of the CPA in a court-controlled ballot.[52] Within the next three years significant inroads were made into a number of unions including the Federated Clerks' Union, the Federated Ironworkers' Association, the Australian Railways Union and the Amalgamated Engineering Union. At the expense of their Communist opponents, the Industrial Groups had begun to exert a formidable influence within the union movement. By 1953, however, their position was beginning to be questioned in the ALP. To an increasing number of Labor politicians and union leaders, it seemed that the Movement 'was using the Industrial Groups not merely against communist influence in the trade unions, but against non-communists of whom they did not approve, in an attempt to gain control of the union movement as a whole'.[53]

---

51. D.W. Rawson, *Unions and Unionists*, p. 62.
52. R.A. Gollan, *Revolutionaries*, pp. 281–3.
53. I. Turner, *In Union is Strength*, Nelson, Melbourne, 1975, p. 113.

The growing hostility towards the Movement finally resulted in a public denunciation of its activities by the leader of the ALP, Dr Evatt, in 1954, and the formal withdrawal of ALP endorsement for Industrial Groups. This action was followed by the expulsion of a number of ALP members—including leading figures in the Victorian executive prominent in the Movement—who, with other Industrial Group sympathisers, formed the Democratic Labor Party. Since its inception, the DLP has maintained a stringently anti-communist position and, backed by the Movement (which was renamed the National Civic Council in 1957) has with varying degrees of success endeavoured to gain the election of its own party members to union positions. In Victoria, the Party was able to secure the affiliation of a number of prominent unions including the Federated Ironworkers' Union, the Shop, Distributive and Allied Trades Union, the Federated Clerks' Union and the Amalgamated Society of Carpenters and Joiners. However, the subsequent admission of these unions into the Victorian branch of the ALP in 1984–5 and the electoral defeat of many of the officials of the Clerks' Union who had previous associations with the National Civic Council has brought to an effective end the power of the DLP in union affairs in Australia.

Union democracy and internal government

Few issues in industrial relations generate as much public interest as that of trade union democracy. Despite an apparent indifference to the autocratic authority structures of business, there appears to be a commonly held expectation that the internal decision-making processes of trade unions should be conducted along democratic lines. This may be because trade unions attach more importance to it than do other organisations. Stein has argued that the 'trade union is philosophically and traditionally a democratic institution which differs from other types of association, notably the business corporation, in the degree to which it emphasises internal democracy'.[54] It is also clear that the issue of internal democracy is a very important one for Australian trade unions if only because of the vigorous efforts of the Australian parliament to try to enforce it through legislation. Their internal affairs are subject to perhaps the most extensive set of legal provisions of any union movement in the Western world. The forms of public control are clearly laid down:

> How many unions exist; who shall belong to them; how they conduct their business, including their finances; what rules they shall have; and, not the least, how they shall conduct their elections have all been largely and increasingly determined by the state in one of its forms...[55]

---

54. Quoted in M.P. Jackson, *Industrial Relations*, Croom Helm, London, 1977, p. 74.
55. D. Rawson, 'State-controlled union ballots', in B. Ford and D. Plowman (eds), *Australian Unions*, Macmillan, Melbourne, 1983, p. 221.

The way in which Australian trade unions manage their internal affairs has long since passed from being a private matter between the union leadership and its members. Dating back to the earliest days of the Commonwealth conciliation and arbitration system, legislative controls were established to regulate the administration of federally registered unions. Although the measures adopted were initially conceived as providing only a minimal degree of interference in union affairs they have grown significantly to cover now virtually all aspects of union administration including the admission and resignation of members, the method and conduct of elections, decisions relating to industrial action and the financial management of organisations. The conception and development of these public instruments of control have much to do with the nature of the conciliation and arbitration system. It was through federal regulation that many of the excesses of nineteenth-century employer power were curbed and the new representative bodies of workers were formed. But while the state was willing to promote the growth of these new organisations it was not willing to leave them free from public control. Unions were expected to pay a price for state patronage. The government not only sought to remove their ability to strike, it also imposed restrictions on the way in which they conducted their affairs. It was felt that by controlling the internal operations of unions and by ensuring that decisions were made democratically, any possible abuse of power could be minimised. Furthermore, because the system of conciliation and arbitration gave registered unions considerable protection from rival organisations, it meant that dissatisfied members had few opportunities to leave a body which they found unresponsive to their needs and form another. Consequently it was seen to be important that unions should be democratic and that they should be instruments of their members.

However, the state has been rarely impartial in the way in which it has intervened in the internal affairs of trade unions. Legislation that ostensibly has sought to promote internal democracy has more often than not been motivated by other political objectives. Martin has noted that the secret ballot provisions, which were such a political preoccupation until the 1960s,'were introduced less because they might help promote union democracy than because they might help check the rise and influence of communist union officials, in particular, and militant unionists in general'.[56] Moves by the Fraser Government in 1977 to protect the rights of individuals to refuse to join in industrial action and to exclude themselves from union membership through the means of conscientious objection were not inconsistent, for example, with the government's efforts to weaken the labour movement and curb its industrial power.[57] The types of controls that have been enacted to regulate both the

---

56. R.M. Martin, 'Industrial relations', in D.M. Gibb and A.W. Hannan (eds), *Debate and Decision: Political Issues in 20th Century Australia*, Heinemann, Melbourne, 1975, p. 50.
57. See R. Mitchell and S. Rosewarne, 'Individual rights and the law in Australian industrial relations', in K. Cole (ed.), *Power, Conflict and Control in Australian Trade Unions*, Penguin, Melbourne, 1982.

internal administration of unions and their systems of government have been very much affected by the wider party-political process.

Present controls

One of the chief objects of the *Industrial Relations Act* is 'to encourage the democratic control of organisations... and the participation by their members in the affairs of organisations' (s. 3(g)). To achieve this principle a wide range of regulations have been put into place which deal with the membership, elections, industrial action and financial reporting of unions. Before the Industrial Registrar will permit the registration of a union, its constitution and rules must not be undemocratic. Section 196(c) requires that the rules of an organisation 'shall not impose upon applicants for membership, or members, of the organisation, conditions, obligations or restrictions which... are oppressive, unreasonable or unjust'. A second specification, s. 261 protects the rights of individuals to join and not be unjustifiably dismissed from the union. This right is subject to the qualification that a union may refuse admission to persons of 'general bad character'. Once an employee is admitted to membership that person is entitled to remain a member so long as he or she 'complies with the rules of the organisation'. It has been held that the rules of a union must not have the effect of stifling dissent or be designed to curb valid attempts of members to control the organisation. As a consequence, all members are guaranteed access to their organisation's records (s. 268).

Election procedures are perhaps the most extensively regulated of all areas of union government. Various provisions of the *Industrial Relations Act*

> ... prescribe how union leaders may be chosen (election rather than appointment); the type of electoral system to be followed (direct or collegiate system); how members are to vote (secret postal ballots); how often officials may face election (at least every four years); ... and detailed procedures [allow] for the investigation and rectification by the courts of irregularities in union elections. In addition, the courts have power to strike down rules dealing with union elections which are 'oppressive, unreasonable or unjust'.[58]

Under s. 197 unions are required to file detailed rules on how elections are to be held. The Act specifies that union functionaries must be elected (s. 197(1)(a)), that virtually every election for office holders must be by secret postal ballot (s. 198(1)) and that the period for which elected officers may hold office without re-election must not exceed four years (s. 199(1)(a)). All elections to office in federally registered unions must be conducted by the Australian Electoral Commission, unless an exemption is obtained from the Registrar (ss. 210–211). Where a union makes an application for such an exemption, its membership must be notified and members given the opportunity to object. The Act specifies that an exemption will only be granted if the Registrar is satisfied that the union

---

58. A. Boulton, 'Government regulations of the internal affairs of unions', in K. Cole (ed.), *Power, Conflict and Control*, p. 221.

will conduct the election 'in a manner that will afford members .. an adequate opportunity of voting without intimidation' (s. 213(1)(b)).

Provisions in the *Industrial Relations Act* also empower the Commission to call secret strike ballots on any matter relating to an actual or threatened industrial dispute if the Commission 'considers the prevention or settlement of the dispute might by helped by finding out the attitudes of the members' (s. 135(1)(b)). The strike-ballot provisions of the Act appear to have been used in only a small number of cases.[59] Since 1977 individual union members have also been protected against any form of discriminatory action that may be taken against them because of their refusal to join in industrial action. Section 335 makes it an offence for a union to impose a penalty or disability on an employee or encourage or coerce an employer to take action against an employee who has failed to take part in a strike or any other form of industrial action. It is also an offence for an employer to dismiss or threaten to dismiss an employee or otherwise adversely affect that person in his or her employment by reason of their refusal to join in industrial action (s. 334(1)).

Finally, there is a range of provisions dealing with the financial management of unions. Division II of the Act requires, among other things, that unions should keep proper accounting records and ensure that they are audited every financial year; that members have access to certain prescribed information regarding the accounts of the union; that copies of the auditor's report and the audited accounts by presented to the annual general meeting of the union and be supplied to members of the union or published in the union journal and that the annual accounts of the union and the auditor's report should be filed with the Industrial Registrar within fourteen days of the meeting at which the report was presented. These requirements were originally inserted into the *Conciliation and Arbitration Act* in 1977 and 1980 following the Royal Commission into Alleged Payments to Maritime Unions (the Sweeney Report) and the subsequent recommendations of Mr Justice Sweeney.

Democracy and regulation

Insofar as the government has provided a comprehensive set of controls to regulate the internal affairs of unions it is relevant to enquire how effective that regulation can be in attaining democracy. Ever since Michels's classic work *Political Parties* first appeared in English in 1915 there has been a strong body of support for the view that trade unions display few of the characteristics one associates with democratic control.[60] Michels contended that large-scale organisational size and democracy were simply incompatible.[61] Because trade unions, in his opinion,

---

59. See R. McCallum, 'Secret ballots and the Industrial Relations Bureau: old wine in new bottles', in G.W. Ford, J.M. Hearn and R.D. Lansbury (eds), *Australian Labour Relations: Readings*, Macmillan, Melbourne, 3rd ed., 1980, pp. 374–5.
60. See J. Goldstein, *The Government of British Trade Unions*, Allen & Unwin, London, 1952 and R. Martin, 'Union democracy: an explanatory framework', in W.E.J. McCarthy (ed.), *Trade Unions*, Penguin, London, 1972, pp. 188–208.
61. R. Michels, *Political Parties*, Dover, New York, 1959.

found a need to develop bureaucratic structures in order to achieve their objectives they tended to concentrate power at the top of the organisational hierarchy and lessen the influence of the rank and file. An oligarchy was therefore the inevitable result. With the wide range of resources available to them in office, trade union leaders could be expected to pursue policies designed to enhance their own power and status in the organisation and to nullify internal challenges. In Michels' view, the objectives of the organisation would then take on the personal objectives of the exclusive oligarchy rather than those of the membership in general. Leaders would become increasingly interested in the sheer perpetuation of the organisation—in 'union-oriented demands' rather than 'membership-oriented demands'. Michels has not been alone in forming this judgement of union leaders. Herberg has explained the inevitability of oligarchical control in the following way:

> Beginning with the very best of intentions, desirous of power not for its own sake but in order to implement a constructive program, the idealist in office insensibly passes over to an increasingly exclusive absorption in power as such, explained away and justified by all sorts of rationalisations. This is the inescapable logic of power politics, but without power politics there is no administering or running a union.[62]

The absence of rank-and-file participation in union affairs is also said to enhance the power of bureaucratic leaders. The 'pulls of work, family personal leisure activities, and the like severely limit the amount of actual time and psychic energy which the average person may invest in membership groups'.[63] Other writers have drawn similar conclusions about the oligarchical nature of union organisations. Some have argued that the perpetuation of leadership can lead to the adoption of a conservative stance on many issues. Reynolds has written that union leaders 'become more sceptical about the possibility of rapid progress... They tend to become conservative in their demands, to moderate the zeal of the membership and to settle for less than the members think possible'.[64] Lipset also considers that one of the strongest forces militating against democracy of unions is the stability of incumbent leaders. He is of the view that

> Democracy... implies permanent insecurity for those in governing positions—the more truly democratic the governing system, the greater the insecurity. Turnover in office is inherent in the democratic value that demands equal access by all members of the system to positions of power. Thus every incumbent of a high-status position of power must, of necessity, anticipate a loss of position if democratic values are accepted.[65]

---

62. W. Herberg, 'Bureaucracy and democracy in labor unions', in R. Rowan and H. Northrup, *Readings in Labor Economics and Labor Relations*, Irwin, Homewood, Illinois, 1968, p. 240.
63. R. Michels, p. 17.
64. L.G. Reynolds, *Labor Economics and Labor Relations*, Prentice-Hall, Englewood Cliffs, New Jeersy, 1964, p. 65.
65. S.M. Lipset, 'The political process in trade unions: a theoretical statement', in W. Galenson and S. Lipset (eds), *Labor and Trade Unionism*, Wiley, New York, 1960, p. 223.

Certainly in Australia it is not unusual for union leaders to enjoy long periods in office. Incumbencies of up to thirty years are not uncommon.[66] But of course this in itself may not be a sufficient measure of the presence or absence of democracy. It may be more important, as Allen suggests, to look at the objectives and achievements of the union and to examine the extent to which union leaders are fulfilling the ambitions and needs of their members.[67] Warner and Edelstein have made the point that since democracy is a decision-making system based on majority rule, the key issue should be 'whether the system is producing the policies, representatives, and forms of organisation that membership wants'.[68] Should union leaders disappoint, offend or frustrate too many members there is the danger that their position will be at risk. Howard, however, has argued that union democracy involves the decentralisation of authority to rank and file members and that this will not occur without a conscious effort and philosophical commitment on behalf of the union's leadership.[69] On the other hand, Fairbrother contends that the democratic properties of a union can be best seen in 'membership meetings, selecting, mandating and advising delegates, receiving report-backs, and determining policies and union activities'.[70]

Where opportunities exist for participation in the decision-making processes of the organisation and where safeguards guarantee the rights of individuals and minorities to voice dissent and to organise opposition, it would be unreasonable to conclude that democratic control was entirely absent. Moreover, the non-participation and inactivity of most union members in the affairs of their organisation may reflect their satisfaction with the performance of the leadership. Alternatively, as Brooks put it, apathetic members may be simply 'exercising their inalienable right to be indifferent'.[71] Regulation cannot ensure the democratic control of unions. It cannot guarantee membership participation nor prevent bureaucracies. At the most, according to Yerbury

> ... it can supply safeguards against the worst abuses of individual rights and can ensure the observance of those external trappings of democratic procedures which give rank-and-file members the nominal control of the union. Probably, in fact, this is all the Australian regulation attempts to do; the creation of bureaucracies ... is more consistent with the institutionalised machinery of the compulsory arbitration system than genuine rank-and-file control of unions.[72]

---

66. See R. Murray and K. White, *The Ironworkers: A History of the Federated Ironworkers' Association of Australia*, Hale & Iremonger, Sydney, 1982 and B. Fitzpatrick and R. Cahill, *The Seamen's Union of Australia 1872–1972*, Seamen's Union of Australia, Sydney, 1982.
67. V.L. Allen, *Trade Union Leadership*, Longman, London, 1957.
68. M. Warner and J.D. Edelstein, 'The meaning and dimensions of democracy in work-related organisations', *Journal of Industrial Relations*, vol. 20, no. 2, 1978, p. 136.
69. W.A. Howard, 'Democracy in trade unions' in G.W. Ford, J.M. Hearn and R.D. Lansbury (eds), *Australian Labour Relations: Readings* (3rd ed.), Macmillan, Melbourne, 1980.
70. P. Fairbrother, 'Union democracy in Australia: accommodation and resistance', *Journal of Industrial Relations*, vol., 28, no. 2, June 1986, p. 171.
71. G.W. Brooks, *The Sources of Vitality in the Labor Movement*, New York State School of Industrial Relations, Cornell University, Ithaca, NY, 1960, p. 5.
72. D. Yerbury, 'The main characteristics of trade union law in the Australian compulsory arbitration systems', in Isaac and Ford (eds), *Australian Labor Relations*, p. 151.

Despite this, the studies of the internal decision-making processes of Australian unions have tended to draw favourable conclusions about the level of democratic control. Frenkel and Coolican's research into the Amalgamated Metal Workers' Union and the Building Workers' Industrial Union showed that the decision-making power was neither highly concentrated nor particularly centralised and that both bodies provided members with considerable opportunities to participate in union elections and in matters relating to award negotiations and agreements.[73] They observed, however, that the actual level of membership participation in union activities was very low. In a considerably more comprehensive analysis of the democratic procedures of six blue- and white-collar unions, Davis indicated that 'the overriding impression was that democracy rather than oligarchy governed these unions'.[74] Using a battery of measures he concluded that

> ... there were strong pressures for union democracy. These included the provision of rule books, the responsiveness of officials and delegates to members' views, and the wealth of opportunities for members to participate in the affairs of their union.[75]

Union resources, research and education

Resources and research

By international standards, the resources of Australian trade unions are very small.[76] The ACTU has pointed out that this is reflected in the level of service provided for members:

> There are insufficient full-time officials to provide an adequate level of industrial representation... too much reliance tends to be placed upon unpaid, untrained and over-worked lay officials. Very few unions have adequate research staff. Union publications, including those of the ACTU, tend to be remote from the membership, scrappy in terms of presentation and downright boring in terms of content. Few, if any, unions have adequate strike funds. A minority of unions make any attempt to provide any significant level of service, beyond industrial and legal representation.[77]

The revenue base for most trade unions is drawn almost entirely from memberships subscriptions. While some derive income from other sources, such as investments in property, government bonds, and financial securities, in general the amount is quite insubstantial. This reliance on subscriptions is a problem because, with few exceptions, the average Australian unionist pays out very little to finance the activities of his or her organisation. Most subscription rates represent somewhat less than a half of 1 per cent of average annual earnings. Despite the adoption of a proposal at the 1973 ACTU Biennial Congress that all affiliates should raise their minimum subscriptions to a rate equal to

---

73. S.J. Frenkel and A. Coolican, *Unions Against Capitalism*, Allen & Unwin, Sydney, 1984.
74. E.M. Davis, *Democracy in Australian Unions*, Allen & Unwin, Sydney, p. 196.
75. Ibid., pp. 195–6.
76. See ACTU/TDC *Australia Reconstructed*, Mission to Western Europe, AGPS, Canberra, 1987, p. 181.
77. ACTU, *Future Strategies for the Trade Union Movement*, pp. 15–16.

1 per cent of the All Industry average minimum weekly award rate by 1978, very little has been achieved. In 1989, the ACTU again repeated its call that membership fees be set at a level which ensured that satisfactory services could be provided to union members. It warned affiliates 'not to use the prospect of reduced union dues below the 1 per cent level as a recruitment mechanism to undercut other unions'.[78] Nevertheless, unions seem to be unwilling to lift their rates for fear of the disfavour of their existing members and because of the growing competition for new members.

The implications of low subscriptions for Australian unions, however, are clear. The organisations are under-financed and seriously handicapped in their ability to provide adequate services for their members. As Weilgosz observed, this has led to a 'reliance by many unions on part-time, over-worked officials; limited access to specialist advisory services and little attention to important areas such as research and education'.[79] Most unions possess insufficient research facilities. Full-time research officers are a luxury afforded to a select few. In 1975 Niland reported that less than 5 per cent of positions in New South Wales unions were occupied by people 'whose full-time activity was research-related'.[80] Dufty found the figure for Western Australian unions to be about half of that.[81] In 1989 Plowman and Spooner reported that research officers were still only confined to a small number of unions in New South Wales and those unions that did make use of their services displayed 'one or both of two characteristics: a "white collar" or professional membership, and/or a large membership'[82] Callus' research disclosed similar results. He found that 7 per cent of the full-time officials in New South Wales unions were employed as research officers.[83] Of the 188 unions surveyed in 1983–4 not one had established full-time positions in the areas of education, welfare or publicity.

Financial deficiency may be only one part of the problem. The performance of union organisations can also be affected by the way in which they utilise their financial resources. In a study of trade unions in the Australian government employment sector, Moss found that most possessed an unnecessarily high level of liquidity and held an excessively high proportion of their resources in relatively non-productive assets such as cash deposits.[84] It was clear that with better management of idle cash balances and a restructuring of their finances, resources could have been more usefully employed in areas such as research and

---

78. ACTU, *Policies and Strategy Statements Adopted by ACTU Congress*, September 1989, p. 87.
79. J.B. Weilgosz, 'Financial resources of Australian trade unions', *Journal of Industrial Relations*, vol. 16, no. 4, 1974, p. 328.
80. J. Niland, *Collective Bargaining and Compulsory Arbitration in Australia*, UNSW Press, Sydney, 1978, p. 96.
81. N.F. Dufty, 'The operation of Western Australian unions and prospects for collective bargaining', *Journal of Industrial Relations*, vol. 21, no. 1, 1979, p. 71.
82. D. Plowman and K. Spooner, 'Unions in New South Wales' in B. Ford and D. Plowman (eds), *Australian Unions*, p. 114.
83. R. Callus, 'Employment characteristics of full-time union officials in New South Wales', *Journal of Industrial Relations*, vol. 28, no. 3, September 1986.
84. A. Moss, *'The finances of trade unions in the Australian Government sector'*, MBA research report, University of Melbourne, 1983.

education. This is likely to become a pressing issue for unions as they are forced to support more decentralised collective bargaining activities at the workplace level. The ACTU/TDC Mission to Western Europe has pointed out that

> As unions move into negotiating enterprise agreements over integrated development in work and management practices, work organisation and skill formation they will require a wider variety of expertise within their research department.[85]

Union education

The union movement's lack of resources has also hampered the growth of adequate education and training programs. Before the creation of the Australian Trade Union Training Authority (TUTA) in 1975, very few unions showed any interest in education and training. The ACTU did not appoint a full-time education officer until 1970. A feeling that union affairs could best be learned on the job, and that training was of little use for those with practical experience, partly accounted for that. Consequently, the only body of any note to provide for trade union education up until 1975 was the Workers' Education Association of South Australia, which ran free postal courses for unionists in a variety of industrial relations subjects.

The election of the Labor Government in 1972, however, provided trade unions with an opportunity to change this situation. With the strong support of Mr Clyde Cameron, the Minister for Labour and Immigration, the unions secured the establishment of a publicly funded training program. Under the *Trade Union Training Act 1975*, the Australian Trade Union Training Authority was formed and given the job of coordinating and running programs for all Australian unionists. A national residential training centre, the Clyde Cameron College, was built at Albury-Wodonga and all states were given resources to establish training centres in their capital cities. In 1989 TUTA employed 115 full-time and 12 part-time staff and had an annual budget of almost $9 million.[86] Since it began in 1975–6 the number of unionists taking courses each year has increased almost tenfold and in 1988–9 TUTA conducted courses for more than 38 000 unionists from some 173 unions. The courses ranged from basic training in communication skills and grievance handling to more specialised programs on matters such as technological change, award structuring, industry development, skill formation, affirmative action and superannuation. The majority of participants in TUTA courses held either part-time or honorary positions within unions. Of the total number of course participants at regional centres in 1988–9 only 5 per cent were full-time officials. There has been a steady growth in the number of women undertaking TUTA courses and in 1988–9 they comprised 21 per cent of participants in state centre programs. There has been also a marked increase in the participation of

---

85. *Australia Reconstructed*, ACTU/TDC Mission to Western Europe, pp. 192–3.
86. 1988–9 Annual Report of the Australian Trade Union Training Authority.

unionists born in non-English-speaking countries and basic training courses are currently being conducted for Arabic, Vietnamese, Greek and Italian speaking unionists.

Despite these achievements, little over 1 per cent of all trade unionists in Australia participated in TUTA programs during 1989. By way of contrast, the ACTU/TDC Mission to Western Europe found that almost 15 per cent of the Swedish peak council's (LO) membership took part in union education courses each year. They pointed out that the 'scale of the Swedish union's education effort is matched by impressive organisational arrangements. There are at least ten equivalents in Sweden to the Australian Trade Union Training Authority's (TUTA) Clyde Cameron College'.[87]

Unions and immigrants

While Australian trade unions have been slow to attend to the educational needs of their staff and members, they have been even more reluctant and less disposed to meeting the special needs of minority groupings within their organisations. Non-English-speaking immigrants in particular have long been a disadvantaged group within unions. Despite the massive intake of immigrants in the post-war period, Australian unions have yet to adjust their activities to meet the special problems and disabilities experienced by many of these workers.

In the Jackson Committee's inquiry into the manufacturing industry, G. W. Ford found that migrant workers were 'concentrated in those sectors of manufacturing with the worst physical working conditions, the worst pay and the jobs which are physically hard and contain the most menial tasks'. He reported, however, that: 'The unions they must join do not recognise that they require any special consideration'.[88] Ford concluded that immigrants were regarded as a 'problem' by both management and unions alike, with neither group having a clear perception or understanding of their particular difficulties. This was confirmed by Hearn, whose work showed a 'high degree of ignorance among Australian union officials concerning the basic facts about their migrant members—numbers, sex, nationality, etc. . . .[89]

For many unions, the protection afforded them by closed-shop arrangements and check-off systems has meant that they have not needed to develop better communications with immigrants to look after their special needs because they face no threat of a loss of membership. Where, however, organisational survival has depended on the recruitment of immigrant workers, unions have shown a greater willingness to meet their needs, particularly through the appointment of multilingual

---

87. ACTU/TDC, *Australia Reconstructed*, Mission to Western Europe, AGPS, Canberra, 1987, p. 183.
88. See J. Martin, 'Forms of recognition' in A. Curthoys and A. Markus (eds), *Who are Our Enemies?*, Sydney, 1978, p. 200.
89. J.M. Hearn, 'Management participation in trade union leadership' *Journal of Industrial Relations*, vol. 18, no. 2, 1976, pp. 117–18.

officials. Hearn nevertheless found that those officials suffered under no illusions as to the motives for their recruitment to office. As one was reported to have said:

> Look, make no mistake, if they could have done without us they would have. But who else but Greeks could persuade Greeks (mostly women) to join the union? We didn't even work in the industry but we know about unions and, more importantly, could speak English and Greek. It's as simple as this: the union either recruits migrant workers or goes under.[90]

The failure of unions to take responsibility for the disabilities of immigrant workers began to provoke criticism during the early 1970s. In 1973 and 1975 two Migrant Workers' Conferences met in Melbourne and Sydney in an attempt to force 'the trade union movement . . . to stop and take notice of a new reality—the numerical strength of migrant workers, their exploitation, alienation and isolation from union affairs'.[91] The conferences made a series of proposals for union action and support. They included the employment of multilingual people in union offices; that logs of claims should include demands for English-language classes on the job, without loss of pay; and the establishment of child-care centres for immigrant women. As a result of these conferences and pressure from other social action groups, some unions began to use interpreter services and produce multilingual union publications. In 1977 the ACTU Congress adopted an executive recommendation that the government should provide English classes, trained interpreters, social workers and multilingual information to assist unions in dealing with the problems of immigrant workers.[92] At its 1981 Congress the ACTU endorsed a policy calling for greater immigrant participation in union affairs. This was to be facilitated through the appointment and training of immigrants as union representatives, the recruitment of union staff with the specialised skills and knowledge to assist immigrant workers with their industrial problems and the establishment of immigrant worker centres in the major cities and industrial areas. In the same year the ACTU called its first conference on immigrant workers. Almost 250 delegates from forty-five unions were in attendance and policies were formulated on a wide range of matters affecting workers with non-English-speaking backgrounds. Some unions have become particularly sensitive to the needs of their immigrant members. The Victorian branch of the Australian Railways Union, for example, has a number of full-time immigrant organisers, employs bilingual office staff and produces regular multilingual publications. This is as yet far from a common practice among Australian unions. Indeed, the difficulties confronting immigrant workers are seen by most unions as no more than a peripheral area of concern.[93] Despite the fact that 15 per cent of trade

---

90. Ibid., p. 119.
91. J. Martin, 'Forms of recognition', p. 201.
92. M. Quinlan, 'Unions and immigrants: the post Second World War experience' in B. Ford and D. Plowman (eds), *Australian Unions*, p. 207.
93. Ibid., p. 220.

unionists in 1988 were born in non-English-speaking countries[94] there is still little pressure to enforce the provision of English-language training on the job. There is also a reluctance to promote effective participation in union affairs through an expansion of the number of immigrant union representatives. Callus' survey of full-time trade union officials in New South Wales reported that immigrants were still

> ... grossly under-represented in full-time official positions ... no union had migrant full-time officials in numbers that even came close to proportional representation. Even in unions where the majority of members were born in non-English-speaking countries, few migrant officials were to be found. In total, only 4 per cent of full-time officials were born in a country other than Australia or the United Kingdom, and not one secretary in our sample was born in a non-English-speaking country.[95]

Unions and women

Immigrants are not the only minority group within trade unions who have suffered neglect. Although women have constituted a sizeable body of the general union membership for many years, they have found it difficult to stimulate union interest in matters such as equal employment opportunities, sex discrimination, child-care facilities, flexible working hours and paid parental leave.[96] Even in unions where the great majority of members are now women, there has been little evidence of any departure from traditional policies or any attempt to tailor union activities to their specific needs. This is not unassociated with the fact that women have generally played a very restricted role in trade union government and policy formulation, and have been significantly under-represented in full-time executive positions.[97] Moreover, until recently, the lack of pressure placed on unions from within the organisation by women members has allowed them to remain largely inert and unchallenged on issues related to the particular needs and requirements of female workers.

However, since the mid 1970s, there have been some signs of change. With the number of women in the workforce growing at a faster rate than that of men, some unions have seen women as a new and important membership source and have consequently begun to frame policies to

---

94. ABS, *Trade Union Members 1988*, Cat. No. 6325.0.
95. R. Callus, 'Employment characteristics of full-time union officials', p. 415.
96. In 1988 about 35 per cent of the total union membership was female. This compared with a figure of 23 per cent in 1968.
97. In 1981, in a survey of twenty-five ACTU affiliates, Wilkinson found that the representation of women in full-time positions was only half that of their representation in total membership. J. Wilkinson, 'Unions and women workers' in B. Ford and D. Plowman (eds), *Australian Unions*, Macmillan, Melbourne, 1983, pp. 357–8. Callus' study in 1983 showed a similar picture of underrepresentation in NSW unions. Women held only 12 per cent of full-time official positions even though they made up just under 40 per cent of the workforce. There was also a tendency for them to be concentrated in appointed positions such as research and other specialist functions rather than elected positions. R. Callus, 'Employment characteristics of full-time trade union officials', p. 415. In 1985 the ACTU estimated that 11–12 per cent of union officials were women. ACTU, *Strategy Statement on Women's Employment*, Melbourne, 1985.

attract them.[98] Also, and perhaps more importantly, increasing pressure over the past decade from women's activist groups, both within and outside the union movement, has forced a reappraisal of the unions' position on discriminatory practices in the workplace. The formation of the Women's Action Committee in 1970 and the calling of two alternative Trade Union Women's Conferences in 1971 and 1973 brought forward clearly articulated demands for union action on a whole range of issues.[99] This movement ultimately led to the establishment of the ACSPA-sponsored Working Women's Centre in 1975, a body which came to act as an important focal point for research and publicity on matters related to sex discrimination. Along with the ACTU, the Centre was involved in drawing up the Working Women's Charter which was presented to the ACTU Congress in 1977.

The Charter proposed various methods of action to encourage the entry and integration of women into the workforce. It included recommendations on education and training, child-care provisions and protective legislation. It also called for maternity and paternity leave, increased opportunities for part-time work and relaxed shift work arrangements for female workers. Furthermore, attention was directed towards the need to encourage women to stand for union office. With some minor amendments the Charter was adopted by the ACTU Congress. At the same time the ACTU also endorsed a proposal for the setting-up of a conference of women from affiliated unions to plan ways in which the Charter could be effectively implemented. The Conference was empowered to elect a liaison committee to work with the ACTU executive and officers in a campaign of publicity, education and action to achieve the goals of the Charter. This Conference took place in March 1978 and from it emerged agreement that maternity leave and child care would become the immediate priority areas for union action.

As a consequence, in September 1978, the ACTU launched a case for maternity leave with the Conciliation and Arbitration Commission. The claim was for twelve months unpaid leave. It was successful and as a result more than 1.5 million women under federal awards were granted the right to unpaid leave without the loss of any benefits or entitlements of service. There have also been developments in the area of child care with some unions establishing their own crêche facilities. More important, however, have been the consultative arrangements with government which helped to produce an extra 98 000 federally-funded child care places between 1983 and 1989.[100]

Over time the ACTU has come to play a more active role in developing policies specifically related to working women. In 1981 it called its first Women's Conference for the purpose of identifying ways in which unions could encourage greater female participation. It also has

---

98. The proportion of women in the workforce has grown from 28 per cent in 1965 to 40 per cent in 1989. In the period 1976–89 total female employment jumped by 50 per cent while male employment expanded by just 18 per cent. ABS, *The Labour Force*, March 1989, Cat. No. 6203.0.
99. R. Galbally, 'Women, inequality and trade unions', M.A. thesis, La Trobe University, Melbourne, 1979.
100. ACTU, *Policies and Strategy Statements Adopted by ACTU Congress*, September 1989, p. 65.

strengthened its women's policy in the areas of equal employment opportunity, sex discrimination, sexual harassment and the representation of women in union decision-making. Its 1983 Working Women's Charter called on unions to give encouragement to female workers to attend trade union training courses. The Charter stated that where necessary 'positive discrimination in favour of women attending courses should be exercised to redress current imbalances'.[101] In 1989 the ACTU's Working Women's Policy declared that unions should implement affirmative action strategies to increase women's participation at all organisational levels. There are some signs that women are beginning to exercise greater influence in union affairs and are becoming more conspicuous in the various decision-making forums. In 1983 Ms Jenny George became the first woman to be elected to the ACTU Executive. Since then this number had risen to six, including the three designated female representative positions. The number of women delegates attending ACTU Congresses had also increased. Of the 934 delegates at the 1987 Congress, about 160 (or 17 per cent) were female.[102] In 1975 there were a mere twenty-five women in attendance accounting for less than 4 per cent of delegates. Despite these developments, Davis noted at the 1987 ACTU Congress that

> ... there remained frustration (among women delegates) that policies endorsed in the past had been treated lightly by many officials ... [that] few unions had devoted much thought or energy to diminishing the gap between male and female earnings and women remained poorly represented within union hierarchies.[103]

This criticism is not only confined to Australia. Reviewing the practices of unions across a range of industrialised countries, Cook *et al.* pointed to 'an acceptance of the goal of equality for women ... [although] union rhetoric, once women were accepted into membership, was more supportive and egalitarian than was union practice'.[104] Kaplan Daniels has gone even further:

> When only lip service or minor and token changes will serve, unions are generally supportive of women. Where drastic, expensive changes are required to accommodate women's interests—as they are if we are to deal adequately with part-time work, child care, parental leave and vocational training to bring women into the skilled trades—unions all too often agree with employers that such aims are too visionary, costly and impractical.[105]

Female representation in unions

If Australian unions are to respond adequately to women's special needs and demands, and to attract and hold female members, they must be prepared to increase the representation of women in full-time positions.

---

101. ACTU, 'Working women's charter', Decisions of ACTU Congress, September 1983.
102. E. Davis, 'The 1987 ACTU Congress: reconstructing Australia?' *Journal of Industrial Relations*, vol. 30. no. 1, March 1988, p. 127.
103. Ibid., p. 127.
104. A.H. Cook *et al.* (ed.), *Women and Trade Unions in Eleven Industrialised Countries*, Temple University Press, Philadelphia, 1984, pp. 14–15.
105. A. Kaplan Daniels, 'Conclusion' in A.H. Cook *et al.*, ibid., p. 314.

The same factors that handicap women vocationally tend to handicap them in attaining union office. Both American and British research suggest that men who are interested in union office learn political and administrative skills as young union members during the very years when women tend to be home, bearing and raising children.[106] Often, it is only through prolonged involvement in voluntary union work that individuals develop the skills and contacts necessary to make the transition to full-time office. When women re-enter the workforce, they find themselves at a disadvantage, not only because of the double burden of job and home, but because they lack the experience and organising skills. In effect, according to Mayer Wertheimer, 'women who seek to play an active role in their unions must often accept . . . the "triple day" to combine workplace, home and union career'.[107] Few women who carry the triple burden rise to positions of power, even in those unions where women make up a substantial part of the membership. A British study by Stageman of female representation in union branches in the Hull area disclosed that the majority of women holding positions in branches had relinquished the main load of their family responsibilities. The handful of women who had reached upper levels in the union hierarchy 'were all single, childless or with children who had reached their teenage years'.[108] In Wertheimer and Nelson's study of women's participation in a number of New York union branches (locals), they found that home demands, lack of education and consequent doubts of self-confidence inhibited participation in union affairs by women. They also revealed that communications between female rank-and-file members and male union leadership were commonly poor: 'Women especially voice feelings that they are not listened to at meetings, that what they think on issues does not really matter to the union'.[109] Stageman found a considerable number of women who stressed that they experienced a lack of confidence and interest in union participation and knowledge and understanding of the operations of the union.

Two Australian studies have revealed similar findings. A survey by Nolan of female members of the Tasmanian Public Service Association showed that most of the respondents were negatively disposed towards participation in the internal governance of the union. The formal meeting procedures of the union were seen as alien and frustrating. Meetings were difficult to understand and were usually dominated by men. Female members considered that the workplace hierarchy was replicated in the internal operations of the union and because of their low position in that hierarchy they were intimidated at meetings. In summarising her findings, Nolan wrote

---

106. B. Mayer Wertheimer, 'The United States' in A.H. Cook et al., ibid, and E. Heery and J. Kelly, 'Union women: a study of women trade union officers', Department of Industrial Relations, London School of Economics, mimeo, 1988.
107. B. Mayer Wertheimer, 'The United States', pp. 298–9.
108. J. Stageman, 'A study of trade union branches in the Hull area', in A. Cooke and P. Kellner, Hear This, Brother: Women Workers and Union Power, New Statesman, London, 1980, p. 53.
109. B. Mayer Wertheimer and A. Nelson, Trade Union Women: A Study of Their Participation in New York City Locals, Praeger, New York, 1975, p. 154.

The barriers to women's involvement in the Association parallel the impediments to their progress in the workplace and the impediments to women's full societal participation. Personal reasons such as lack of confidence and lack of time were inhibiting factors and Association customs and practices which fail to address the specific needs and experiences of women effectively prevent them from becoming involved. For many of the survey subjects, particularly those at the bottom of the hierarchy, the Association was perceived to mirror the patterns which they already experience and dislike in the workplace: a hierarchical structure, male dominance among staff and officials, absence of true democracy and marginalisation of women's needs and issues.[110]

Griffin and Benson conducted a survey of members of the Victorian branch of the Municipal Officers Association (MOA) to identify barriers to female membership participation in union activities.[111] They found that male respondents aged between 26 and 35 were significantly more likely to hold union positions than female respondents of this age group. This was consistent with Stageman's findings in Britain where she revealed that female officers were older than average, had been in their job longer and had a greater proportion of their children over the age of 18. Griffin and Benson's analysis showed that the main barrier to female participation was their perception of a lack of encouragement by the union to become involved in its internal activities. Family arrangements and a lack of child care were also important impediments.

There are a number of measures that unions can take to increase female participation and bolster their representation in official union positions. First, there may need to be a relaxation of the traditional criteria used for the recruitment of full-time staff. This has tended to place excessive weight on such things as extensive experience of lay office. Because of the pressure of domestic and family commitments, women find it very difficult to invest the (out of working hours) time necessary to develop a lay trade union career.[112] Second, union meetings may need to be timed and located to maximise female participation. Stageman reported that the holding of meetings in work time greatly encouraged participation in union activities.[113] Evening meetings clashed with expectations that women would carry out their household duties. The location of meetings near or at the worksite is also relevant. Third, structural changes can be made to encourage female participation. Seats can be reserved for women on a union's executive and legislative bodies. One of Britain's largest unions, the General, Municipal and Boilermakers Union (GMB), has reserved one-third of national executive seats for women and has introduced a scheme of 'fast tracking' as a device to bring women more quickly into union positions. Another union, the TGWU, allows each of its eleven Regional Women's Advisory Committees to elect a delegate to the TUC and Labour Party Conference. This

---

110. J. Nolan, *What the Women Said*, Hobart, 1984, pp. 30–31.
111. G. Griffin and J. Benson, 'Barriers to female membership participation in trade union activities', *Labour and Industry*, vol. 2, no. 1, 1989.
112. E. Heery and J. Kelly, 'Union women'.
113. J. Stagemen, 'A study of trade union branches', p. 51.

brought the female proportion of its 1987 TUC delegation up to 21 per cent—higher than the proportion of women among its membership.[114] Last, unions may need to recognise that women will often seek to approach and solve industrial issues in a different way from men. Beccalli has sensed an uneasiness among women in trying to imitate the male model of militancy. She writes: 'The women's way is non-bureaucratic and egalitarian, direct and non-hierarchical, dealing immediately, flexibility and humanely with problems without the constraint of set procedures'.[115] Cockburn argues that the majority of female union members may refuse to engage in, or identify with, organised politics within unions because of the 'male' adversarial approach to internal procedure and political action which tends to predominate.[116]

Another issue that may affect both female membership and participation in union activities relates to the goals of unions and the pursuit of issues relevant to women. Female members have distinctive and different problems at work. If such issues as child care, equal opportunity and sexual harassment are not accorded equal importance in union matters it will possibly reinforce women's perceptions that unions are for men and therefore not relevant to them. Women may simply not join trade unions or alternatively they may boycott union activities because of their apparent irrelevance to their day-to-day work experiences.

In the survey by Benson and Griffin of the members of the Victorian branch of the MOA they found that men and women attached priority to quite different issues.[117] Female union members ranked the following eight issues significantly higher than male members: health and safety, job security, child care, sexual harassment, equal opportunity, part-time work, working conditions and social issues. The employment issues most significant to female members of the Tasmanian Public Service Association were the overload of work, sex discrimination, lack of opportunities for training and lack of staff development and promotion opportunities.[118] In a study conducted by a group of management consultants for the British union, the GMB, the results showed that female concerns were principally centred on the difficulty of matching work demands with family responsibilities. Even single women showed anxiety about future difficulties of combining these dual activities. Retraining, health and safety and discrimination were also important issues. The study found that the failure of unions to address these 'gender-related' concerns created disillusionment and a lack of interest in trade unions. In research commissioned by the TGWU in Britain sexual harassment was identified by women as their major concern. The camaraderie among men which cut across all grades was said to make it virtually impossible to make a serious point about sexual harassment.[119]

---

114. 'Working for equality in the unions', *Labour Research*, March 1988, p. 11.
115. J. Beccalli, 'Italy', in A.H. Cook *et al.*, *Women and Trade Unions*, p. 30.
116. C. Cockburn, *Women, Trade Unions and Political Parties*, Fabian Society, London, 1987.
117. J. Benson and G. Griffin, 'Gender differences in union attitudes, participation and priorities' *Journal of Industrial Relations*, vol. 30, no. 2, June 1988.
118. J. Nolan, *What the Women Said*.
119. The *Independent*, 18 October 1988.

Green and Tilly have cited studies in the United States which suggest that issues of social justice and equality and opposition to discrimination may be more important rallying points for the unionisation of women than the traditional 'bread-and-butter' demands based on wages, hours and leave conditions.[120] Unions which have stressed 'fairness' demands —such as respect and dignity, no gender discrimination and pay equity —and emphasised issues like sexual harassment, authoritarianism and health and safety seemed to have had quite high success rates in unionising female workers. Green and Tilly show that unions seeking to organise largely female office and service staff have found it necessary to adopt quite a different issue orientation from that used to recruit men.

This again raises the issue of the adequate representation of women in leadership positions in unions. The implementation of trade union policies on women will depend in a large part on female officials. A survey of the activities of full-time officers (FTOs) in Britain showed that female union officials were considerably more willing than their male counterparts to raise issues of sexuality—particularly child care and sexual harassment—and to integrate women's domestic and paid employment into the collective bargaining agenda.[121] Male FTOs did not rank specific actions to assist women very highly. They were more prepared to promote women's issues where these could be presented as 'traditional' collective bargaining demands, such as higher basic pay, improved working conditions and job security. Overall, Heery and Kelly found that there was 'suspicion of "novel" women's issues such as sexual harassment and provisions to help with child care'.[122] The evidence showed quite clearly that male and female FTOs had different priorities.

The situation confronting Australian unions is clear. Female participation in the workforce is expanding at the same time as the male participation rate is declining. Increasingly, service sector employment, with its higher proportion of female labour, is displacing the largely male-dominated manufacturing sector. If unions are to compensate for the loss of membership in these declining areas of Australian industry it would appear that they must have union officials who will give priority to women's issues. The views of the British researchers, Heery and Kelly, have equal application in Australia: 'In the labour market of the ... [future] what is good for women workers and women trade union members could well prove to be good for trade unions as organisations'.[123] Iola Matthews, the coordinator of the ACTU's Action Program for Women Workers, has made a similar point:

> Attention to women's issues is not just a question of fairness or equal opportunity for the female half of the workforce. Rather, it is linked to ... the very

---

120. J. Green and C. Tilly, 'Service unionism: directions for organizing', IRRA, *Proceedings of 1987 Spring Meeting*, Boston, Mass., 1987.
121. E. Heery and J. Kelly, 'Union Women', p. 75.
122. Ibid., p. 78.
123. Ibid., p. 5.

survival of the union movement ... Women workers are less likely to be unionised than male workers, yet women's employment is the fastest growing sector of the economy.[124]

Summary

Australian unions are largely concerned with advancing the economic interests of their members and with improving their terms and conditions of employment. They have shown a general preference for practical and immediate results and have been less disposed to the pursuit of goals that might seek to change the social order and bring radical political and social reform. Their industrial demands have centred on achieving improvements in wages, hours, leave, superannuation and physical working conditions. More recently job security has become an important agenda item. While political or non-industrial objectives have been viewed as a legitimate concern, few organisations have used industrial action in the pursuit of such matters. Unions have employed a variety of methods to achieve their goals. The most convenient and accessible has been that of conciliation and arbitration, although collective bargaining and more particularly political action have been important instruments. Most unions have maintained close ties to the ALP although some have cast doubts on the effectiveness of direct labour representation in parliament. The lack of commitment of the ALP to revolutionary change led to the emergence of the Communist Party in 1920 but its influence in the union movement has waned significantly since the 1950s. This was not unassociated with the success of the Industrial Groups and the Movement in the early post-war period.

Union democracy has been a contentious issue in Australia, particularly in view of the array of controls that the government has imposed on the internal decision-making processes of unions. The regulation of union affairs has been extensive but in itself has done little to guarantee membership participation or prevent the creation of bureaucracies. Most Australian unions have meagre financial resources for administration. This is mainly due to their dependence on membership subscriptions which have been often insufficient to provide adequate research and education facilities and to enable the establishment of specialist services for minority groups such as migrants. Trade unions have largely neglected the interests of both immigrant and women members. It has been only in recent years, and under substantial pressure from those groups, that unions have begun to formulate policies and initiate action on their specific problems in the workplace.

---

124. I. Matthews, 'Rights of women workers critical to the future of the union movement', ACTU Bulletin, November 1987, p. 25.

Discussion questions

1. Why do employees join unions and what do they expect to achieve from union membership?
2. 'Most Australian trade unions are "limited-purpose" associations, concerned largely with industrial matters related to their members' pay and working conditions.' Comment on the accuracy of this statement.
3. Has there been any trend towards wider union involvement in social and political issues?
4. 'While unions have derived some benefits from their affiliation to the ALP it is difficult to see that they have received value for money.' Critically analyse.
5. In what ways does the state regulate the internal affairs of federally registered unions?
6. Has the government any real business in interfering with the internal decision-making processes of trade unions?
7. To what extent can government regulation be successful in guaranteeing democracy within unions?
8. 'Because of inadequate resources Australian trade unions have been severely handicapped in their ability to provide adequate services for their members.' Discuss.
9. Have Australian unions shown concern for the special needs of their immigrant members?
10. To what extent have unions developed a commitment to advancing the interests of working women?

Further reading

ACTU, *Future Strategies for the Trade Union Movement*, Melbourne, 1987.
ACTU/TDC, *Australia Reconstructed*, ACTU/TDC Mission to Western Europe, AGPS, Canberra, 1987.
Benson, J. and Griffin, G., 'Gender differences in union attitudes, participation and priorities', *Journal of Industrial Relations*, vol. 30, no. 2, June 1988.
Carney, S., *Australia in Accord*, Macmillan, Melbourne, 1988.
Crouch, C., *Trade Unions: The Logic of Collective Action*, Fontana, London, 1982.
Davis, E., *Democracy in Australian Unions*, Allen & Unwin, Sydney, 1987.
Fairbrother, P., 'Union democracy in Australia: accommodation and resistance', *Journal of Industrial Relations*, vol. 28, no. 2, June 1986.
Ford, B. and Plowman, D. (eds), *Australian Unions* (2nd ed.,) Macmillan, Melbourne, 1989.
Frenkel, S.J. (ed.), *Union Strategy and Industrial Change*, New South Wales University Press, Sydney, 1987.
Frenkel, S.J. and Coolican, A., *Unions Against Capitalism?*, Allen & Unwin, Sydney, 1984.

Griffin, G. and Benson, J., 'Barriers to female membership participation in trade union activities', *Labour and Industry*, vol. 2, no. 1, March 1989.

Mitchell, R.J., 'The rise and fall of the preference power: the practice of the Federal Commission, 1970–1987', *Australian Journal of Labour Law*, vol. 1, no. 3, December 1988.

Rawson, D.W., *Unions and Unionists in Australia* (2nd ed.), Allen & Unwin, Sydney, 1986

Part Four

PROCESSES

The formal industrial relations system in Australia depends on a number of mechanisms through which industrial conflict is channelled and regulated. These mechanisms operate to handle issues, such as wage determination, at the national, industry and, less effectively, plant levels. Many of the processes at those levels are routine and predictable. The way in which a wage dispute comes before a particular tribunal, for example, does not vary greatly over time. The "system", however, is not a machine made up of rigid, finite parts which operate in a fixed and predetermined way. There is no sense, in practice, in which the parties must behave in ways set down in some textbook. Just as the parties to it are not monolithic, homogeneous groupings, the processes of the system are complex and variable. No one dispute or case is quite like any other and no period of industrial conflict is quite like any other. Industrial relations are the product of the changing interaction of all the social, economic and political influences on the parties from time to time. Employers, employees and governments adapt and manoeuvre to suit their own needs. In some periods new influences develop, wich as those which follow from technological change or the demand for industrial democracy. The tribunals in turn must adapt their practices in order to deal with the constant but constantly changing conflict of capital and labour.

CHAPTER 10

The Development of Industrial Arbitration

The present system of conciliation and arbitration is very different in a number of important ways from that established at the turn of the century. The study of industrial relations must take account of the ways in which the formal machinery has changed, as well as the processes of interaction between employers and unions. The changes to the formal machinery provide an indication of the economic, societal and political pressures on the arbitration system. Industrial tribunals have not only been expected to control industrial conflict; they themselves have been the subject of control by the legislators.

In this chapter, the major developments in the system of compulsory conciliation and arbitration are traced by reference to the federal tribunal system. The first part of the chapter examines the growth and development of the tribunal system from 1904 to the present time. It then proceeds to examine the contrary trends of tribunal diffusion and integration; the role of conciliation; legalism; award enforcements; economic regulation; the Fraser Government's (1975–83) more assertive intervention; and the Hawke Government's consensus approach in the period 1983–90.

The strikes of the 1890s and the watershed thesis

To many historians, the strikes of the 1890s represent a watershed in Australian industrial relations which separates the pre-strike collective bargaining period and post-strike compulsory arbitration era. A brief history of the development of labour law and employment relations up to these strikes was outlined in Chapter 3.

By the 1890s Australia had inherited British craft unionism. It had also developed its own brand of industry unions which were particularly strong in the rural vocations of shearing and mining. In the period of economic growth (the 'Long Boom') following the gold rushes of the 1850s shearing, mining and maritime unions made successful demands on employers. These unions grew in strength, membership and financial resources. By 1889, however, prosperity had turned to recession, and then to depression. The price of Australia's wool, the country's staple product, plummeted by 36 per cent between 1889 and 1894. Financial disaster followed. The 'bank smash' of 1891 witnessed the collapse of seventeen out of twenty-eight banks operating in Sydney and Melbourne. Forty-one land and finance companies failed in the same two cities while fifty-four out of sixty-four financial institutions which accepted deposits were suspended or failed.[1]

Financial stringencies caused employers to take a harder line with unions. They also sought to replace compulsory unionism with freedom of contract. The two mutually exclusive principles led to a bitter contest. The 'Great Strikes' that followed resulted in near civil war, in the state siding with employers, and in unions being financially ruined. The strikes left a legacy of bitterness. There was also a public perception that the strikes were the cause of economic depression, a reversal of cause and effect.

Following the strikes there was a collapse of any bargaining arrangements. Union membership had fallen to below 5 per cent of the workforce and the victorious employers refused to negotiate with them. Feeling that their defeat had been the result of employers' control of parliaments, unions formed Labor Parties, a move assisted by the introduction of payment to Members of Parliament and by the advent of manhood (and then universal) suffrage. In 1890 the New South Wales Parliament, in which Labor held the balance of power, appointed a Royal Commission to inquire into the strikes of the 1890s.

The Commission reported in May 1891 and recommended the establishment of a State Board of Conciliation and Arbitration. Disputes not settled by the parties ought, in the first instance, to be referred to a Board of Conciliation

> ... constituted by the election of no less than six persons, an equal number from each side. If the Board failed in its task of conciliation then the members of the Board who form the standing portion would constitute a Court of Arbitration and would give a decision.[2]

The Commission carefully considered whether the Board should have compulsory powers. Two aspects of compulsion were considered: whether the Board should be able to compel disputants to appear before it, and the power of the Board to enforce its decisions compulsorily.

---

1. A.G.L. Shaw, *The Economic Development of Australia*, Longman, Melbourne, 5th ed., 1966, pp. 96–102.
2. *Report of the Royal Commission on Strikes*, New South Wales Government Printer, Sydney, 1891, p. 34.

Though the Commission recommended the compulsory reference of disputes to the Board, it was ambivalent about compulsory arbitration and foresaw difficulties in enforcing decisions. It thought that public moral suasion would be the major instrument for ensuring the success of the Board:

> Such an institution, clothed with the authority of the State, would stand before the public as a mediating influence always and immediately available, and public opinion would be adverse to those who, except for very good cause shown, refused to avail themselves of its good offices.[3]

In the final outcome the New South Wales Parliament legislated for the voluntary reference of disputes to the Board. This outcome was similar to that in South Australia whose Parliament had debated the first Bill designed to promote compulsory arbitration in Australia. The Bill was presented by Charles Kingston in 1890 and was strongly opposed by the employer-dominated upper house. When finally enacted in 1894, the Bill had been stripped of any of compulsory elements and provided only for voluntary arbitration.

Neither the New South Wales or South Australian legislation proved effective. Employers now considered that they had less to fear from strikes than did unions. They saw any reference to arbitration as a hindrance to complete triumph. Though unions had been ambivalent about the benefits of compulsory arbitration, their defeat in the Great Strikes and their incapacity to force employers to voluntary arbitration converted them to the virtues of compulsory arbitration. By 1900 compulsory arbitration Bills had been introduced in all mainland parliaments[4] and the newly adopted Constitution provided for the Commonwealth Government to establish industrial tribunals with conciliation and arbitration powers.

The Constitution adopted at Federation was debated during the 1890s. A Victorian delegate, Henry Bournes Higgins, argued for the inclusion of industrial powers to enable authorities to deal with disputes which extended beyond the boundaries of any one state. The majority held that industrial relations ought remain a state matter. To help it deal with interstate disputes the Commonwealth was given very limited industrial powers: the capacity to legislate for the prevention and settlement of industrial disputes extending beyond any one state by way of conciliation and arbitration. Legislation to establish the Commonwealth Court of Conciliation and Arbitration was enacted in December 1904. By then, both Western Australia (1900) and New South Wales (1901) had enacted compulsory arbitration legislation, in the latter case for a seven-year trial period.

---

3. Ibid.
4. The respective dates are: South Australia 1890, Queensland 1894, New South Wales 1899, Victoria and Western Australia 1900.

Compulsory arbitration

The strikes of the 1890s were an important stimulus to the move towards compulsory arbitration. They are not, however, the complete explanation. The first strike associated with the Great Strikes was the Maritime Strike of 1890. This strike took place in Victoria, a state which did not adopt arbitration until 1979. Queensland, the state in which the Shearers' Strike was centred, did not introduce compulsory arbitration until 1916. South Australia also introduced compulsory arbitration in 1916. Western Australia was the one state not afflicted with strikes during the 1890s, a decade of gold discoveries and prosperity, yet it was the first state to provide for compulsory arbitration.

If the strikes were the impetus for union conversion towards, and reliance on, compulsory arbitration, the immediate cause lay with the Labor Parties. Where Labor held the balance of power (New South Wales, Western Australia and the Commonwealth) it was able to use this power to obtain concessions in return for support. In South Australia Labor remained weak and thus not able to implement its industrial policies for many years. In Queensland it had a different problem. There, its position as the outright opposition party 'put out of possibility the fruitful method of "support for concession" pursued in the southern colonies. As a result, legislation to set up industrial courts made a slow start in Queensland'.[5] In Victoria the general weakness of the Labor Party and the domination of the Legislative Council by employer interests resulted in compulsory arbitration legislation being kept off the statute books.[6]

The *Conciliation and Arbitration Act* 1904 and New Protection

The establishment of compulsory arbitration machinery was slow and difficult. In 1901 Edmund Barton formed the first Commonwealth ministry. Labor held the balance of power between the liberal protectionists (thirty-one seats) and the free trade conservatives (twenty-eight seats). In the Senate Labor held eight seats, the protectionists eleven seats and the conservatives seventeen seats.

The Conciliation and Arbitration Bill was introduced by Charles Kingston, Minister for Trade and Customs, on 7 July 1903. A fortnight later he resigned from the Ministry because of the lack of Cabinet support for some clauses he considered essential. Alfred Deakin took over the Bill but it was shelved because of major opposition.

Following his election as Prime Minister in September 1903 Deakin set about winning support for the Arbitration Bill by way of New Protection. 'New Protection' afforded manufacturers protection from overseas competition on condition that they paid fair and reasonable wages. The mechanism for ensuring this was to be the *Excise Tariff Act*. This

---

5. E. Shann, *An Economic History of Australia*, Georgian House, Melbourne, 1930, p. 374.
6. W.G. Spence, *Australia's Awakening: Thirty Years in the Life an Australian Agitator*, Worker Trustees, Sydney, 1909.

would impose not only tariffs on imported manufactures but also an excise on local manufacturers who did not pay fair and reasonable wages. The operation of this system is reviewed in the next chapter.

New Protection had the effect of galvanising Labor and union support, and of splitting employer resistance. Manufacturers wanted protection, even in the form of New Protection. Notwithstanding this support the Arbitration Bill still had a rough passage. It was reintroduced by Deakin on 22 March 1904 and did not become law until December. In the interim Deakin resigned as Prime Minister over a loss of confidence in the House when he insisted on including state rail employees in the provisions of the Bill. Watson formed the first Labor Government in April but resigned in August when amendments limiting union preference were carried by two votes. The Reid ministry which followed itself survived a want of confidence motion by only one vote two months later. The Bill dragged on between the two chambers until 9 December, when it 'practically drifted into law, as to the application and effect of which, very few people had any clear conception'.[7] The chronicler of the first decade of the Commonwealth Parliament captures the high drama surrounding the Bill's passage:

> No legislation, with the exception of the Tariff, has ever produced anything like the mass of heated discussion. It wrecked three Ministries; it embittered the relations of the parties in Parliament; it evoked the antagonisms of the States... The shiftiness, expediency and flat contrariety of much of the voting can never be explained. Edmond Barton dropped it on the question of the inclusion of the servants of the State. Mr Deakin resigned when that provision was carried against him. His successor, Mr Watson, resigned because an amendment was carried which militated against his 'effective protection of unionists'. The Reid–McLean Ministry compromised on this and a good many other matters in order to get into recess. If ever a Bill drifted through Parliament without fully satisfying any or one of the parties, but from sheer exhaustion of debate and a desire to be rid of it, the Commonwealth *Conciliation and Arbitration Act 1904* certainly achieved that distinction.[8]

The *Conciliation and Arbitration Act* imposed the 'historic compromise' found in other bargaining systems (see Chapter 7). Employers were forced to recognise unions, unions to recognise the rights of management. The pioneering nature of the legislation, the fact that the legislation attempts to regulate power relations which change over time, and the 'shiftiness, contrariety and expediency' embodied in the original Act led to that Act being one of the most frequently amended Commonwealth Acts. In 1988 the Act was repealed and replaced by the *Industrial Relations Act*. The provisions of this Act are outlined in Chapter 4.

---

7. H.G. Turner, *The First Decade of the Australian Commonwealth*, Mason Firth & McCutcheon, Melbourne, 1911, p. 73.
8. Ibid., pp. 73–4.

The growth of federal arbitration

The Constitution assigns the regulation of industrial relations to the state legislatures. The federal legislature has the capacity to establish conciliation and arbitration machinery to regulate interstate industrial disputes. As noted in Chapter 3, the Australian Government can also rely on other heads of power to legislate over employment conditions. Under the exclusive powers it can regulate conditions of employment for its own employees. The trade and commerce powers and the foreign affairs powers have also been used to regulate industrial relations (Chapter 3). Nevertheless, the principal power relied on for general regulation of industrial relations during peace time is the industrial power derived from Section 51 (xxxv) of the Constitution. This would suggest that national regulation in the private sector should be rare, and limited to interstate disputes.

Chapter 3 gives statistical evidence which indicates that the scheme envisaged by the Constitution has not worked out in practice. The federal tribunal, the Industrial Relations Commission, has the largest proportion of employees under its jurisdiction of any tribunal, and this notwithstanding the fact that the common rule, which applies to the provisions of state tribunals, cannot apply in the federal jurisdiction (see Chapter 5).

The beginnings of the Commonwealth Court of Conciliation and Arbitration (Arbitration Court) suggested that it would play a subordinate role to state tribunals. It was constituted in 1905 by a part-time member who was also a High Court judge (Mr Justice O'Connor). The Court heard only five cases in that year, three of which it dismissed on the grounds of a lack of jurisdiction. Its workload in 1906 was concerned mainly with issuing certificates of exemption under the *Excise Tariff Act* to employers paying 'fair and reasonable' wages. This was also the case in 1907 when Mr Justice Higgins became President of the Court. By 1907 the Court had such a large number of applications for exemptions under the *Excise Tariff Act* that Higgins decided to determine a general standard on the basis of a major review. The Harvester Judgment, which resulted in minimum wage increases in the order of 27 per cent, is examined in the next chapter. Employers took High Court action against the decision and the *Excise Tariff Act* was declared unconstitutional. The workload of the Court again subdued, and in 1909 it heard only nine cases. Two of these were dismissed, and employers were successful in having prohibitions applied in another three cases. To this time awards of the federal tribunal were restricted to just two industries, the maritime industry and the pastoral industry.

A major factor in this restriction was the active opposition of employers to arbitration. Following the passage of arbitration legislation in New South Wales and at the national level they resorted to legal action against the activities of the Arbitration Courts to frustrate their operations. This was particularly important in New South Wales where the trial legislation was to be reviewed after a seven-year period. So incessant were the employers (and so sympathetic was the New South Wales Supreme Court to their cause) that the President of the Industrial Arbitration Court declared that compulsory arbitration had not been given a fair trial:

> The barque of the *Industrial Arbitration Act* made a brave show with its sails and bunting at its launching ... but since I took the helm the Act has been riddled, shelled, broken fore and aft, and reduced to a sinking hulk. No pilot could navigate such a craft. Do not say, however, that no ship can sail the seas because this one has been so badly built. When an Act is passed which really means what it seems to say, in which 'industrial dispute' means industrial dispute; in which a dispute 'arising between' certain persons does not mean a dispute which must arise between totally different persons; in which legal rights such as the right to strike and lockout are not taken away without anything being given in their place; then, and only then, can the principle of industrial arbitration be really tested, and if it breaks down, be fairly pronounced to have broken down.[9]

If employers were successful in making the New South Wales legislation inoperable because of superior court challenges, they had every reason to believe that they could do the same to the more constitutionally circumscribed Arbitration Court. In 1904 the Central Council of Employers of Australia was formed. Its major charter was to oppose the Conciliation and Arbitration Bill. When unsuccessful, it collected some £5,000 to fight the legislation. Not only did this body succeed in having the *Excise Tariff Act* declared unconstitutional (thereby removing any statutory New Protection), it was also successful in having the scope of federal arbitration severely circumscribed. This was made easy by the High Court's state orientation and its consideration of industrial relations as a state matter.[10]

That situation altered after 1912 with the change in the composition of the High Court. Employer challenges after this time had the contrary effect and served to open up the scope for federal arbitration. Two cases are of particular note in this regard: the *Bootmakers'* case (1910) and the *Builders' Labourers'* case (1914).

In the first of these cases employers challenged the competence of the Arbitration Court to make an award which was inconsistent with the terms of a state law. The High Court ruled in favour of the employers. However, the test of inconsistency adopted was to cause them much heartache, namely the ability to satisfy the requirements of both awards at the same time. Thus, for example, a federal award prescribing a higher minimum wage than a state award or law would not be inconsistent with that state determination since, by obeying the federal award, the parties would also be obeying the state requirements.

The *Builders' Labourers'* case concerned the method of creating an

---

9. 1907 *Arbitration Reports* (NSW), p. 59.
10. See D.H. Plowman, *Holding the Line: Compulsory Arbitration and National Employer Co-ordination in Australia*, Cambridge University Press, Melbourne, 1989 and D.H. Plowman and G. Smith, 'Moulding federal arbitration: the employers and the High Court', *Australian Journal of Management*, vol. 12, no. 2, 1986 for further details of High Court actions against the Arbitration Court at this time.

interstate dispute. The Builders' Labourers' Federation had served a log of claims on employers in five states and claimed that this constituted an interstate dispute. Employers had already successfully opposed such 'paper' disputes in a number of cases. For example, in a previous case the Chief Justice held that section 51 (xxxv) of the Constitution was to 'prevent and settle real industrial disputes, and not to facilitate the creation of fictitious disputes'.[11]

In the *Builders' Labourers* case, Griffith CJ, together with the other remaining original member of High Court (former Prime Minister Barton J) supported the employers' claim. In their view the log of claims did not constitute an interstate dispute, but rather five different sets of disputes which had merely been consolidated into one set of demands. 'If such a joint demand is sufficient', Griffith CJ added, 'it is plain that the whole subject matter of regulation of any and every branch of industry can be taken out of the hands of the States and transferred to the Federal Arbitration Court.[12]

The majority of the High Court held that the paper dispute did consititute a genuine dispute within the meaning of the Constitution.

These two decisions had an important impact on the growth of federal regulation. The second case made it very easy for unions to create interstate disputes merely by expenditure on postage stamps. The *Bootmakers'* case was important because it gave unions an incentive to obtain federal awards. At this time unions were essentially state organisations. Those national organisations that existed were, in the main, federations of state unions. Thus, unless there was a real need to do so, these unions favoured state awards. The *Bootmakers'* case enabled unions to obtain federal awards without having to jettison state awards, a situation which enabled them to pick the eyes out of federal and state awards. As one commentator has noted, the test of legal inconsistency adopted in the *Bootmakers'* case

> ... meant that an employee was entitled to the highest minimum wage and the shortest working week prescribed by either State law or Federal award. Trade unions in their battle for better wages and hours could use political pressure to obtain State legislation, or they could use the machinery under State law and obtain an award or determination fixing minimum hours to be worked per week. Having obtained what they could in the State sphere, they could seek an award in the Federal sphere for higher minimum wages and less ordinary working hours secure in the knowledge that the State standards which had been won could not be reduced by any Federal award which was made.[13]

Thus, by 1914 unions had both the incentive and the means to seek federal awards.

---

11. 16 *CLR* 86.
12. 18 *CLR* 88.
13. J.H. Portus, *Compulsory Arbitration in Australia*, WEA and Law Book Co., Sydney, 1971, pp. 61–2.

The problem of rival shops

The dual system of regulation which resulted was one in which, in the words of Higgins J, unions treated federal and state tribunals as 'rival shops'. This, in Higgins' view, 'involves grave danger to industrial peace, and to the continuity of operations in industries'.[14] It meant that unions could opt out of their federal awards and resort to state awards when it suited, or *vice versa*. Naturally, employers were alarmed by developments and sought both legislative and legal redress.

From 1917 on Premiers' Conferences attempted a political solution. It was proposed that certain industries be assigned to the Commonwealth, and that the rest remain under state control. However, the division of industries was a matter the states and Commonwealth could not agree on. At the 1925 Premiers' Conference Prime Minister Bruce gave the states an ultimatum: agree to some division of authority or he would seek increased Commonwealth industrial powers by way of referendum. This referendum was held in 1926 and was unsuccessful.[15]

The problem of dual arbitration was compounded by a ten-month strike by timber workers in January 1929 and depression. The Bruce Government came to consider economic deterioration as the product, rather than the possible cause, of worsening industrial relations. This view was supported by the Report of the British Economic Mission which enquired into methods of redressing the economic malaise. The Mission claimed that 'a change in the method prevalent in Australia in dealing with industrial disputes appears to us to be essential'.[16]

At the Premiers' Conference of 1929 Bruce threw down the gauntlet to the states: either they referred full industrial powers to the Commonwealth or the Commonwealth would repeal its federal arbitration legislation. None of the states proposed surrendering industrial authority. In August 1929 Bruce introduced the Maritime Industries Bill which provided for the repeal of the *Conciliation and Arbitration Act*. Bruce was forced to an election on the issue. He lost not only government but also his seat of Flinders.

By 1926, the High Court had effectively provided the means of eliminating the use of tribunals as rival shops when it adopted a different test of inconsistency. In that year it heard the *Cowburn* case. Metal industry workers, under the provisions of a federal award, sought the shorter working week provided by New South Wales legislation. The employer (Cowburn) objected and the matter went to court. Had the High Court followed its earlier precedents it would have ruled in favour of the union: a shorter working week under state legislation was not inconsistent with the federal award because by working the shorter week the maximum conditions of both standards had been fulfilled. In this case, however, the High Court chose a different approach. It ruled that if it

---

14. 14 *CAR* 369.
15. See A. Wildavsky, *The 1926 Referendum*, Cheshire, Melbourne, 1958.
16. Commonwealth Parliamentary Debates, 1929, vol. 2, p. 1248.

was the intention of the federal award to 'cover the field', then it would be inconsistent for state legislation or awards also to cover the field.

Once legislation was enacted (in 1928) to declare the intention of federal awards to 'cover the field' for those areas contained in the award, unions were effectively forced to choose between jurisdictions, rather than continue to pick the eyes out of federal and state awards. Problems remained, however, not the least that it continued (and continues) to be possible for different employees in the same workplace to come under the awards of different tribunals. The importance of the *Cowburn* decision was initially overshadowed by depression and employers' last-ditch attempt to remove federal arbitration from the statute books.

Arbitration and the depression

The Scullin Labor Government, which took over from the Bruce Government, was sworn into office on 22 October 1929—one day after the Wall Street market crash which signalled the beginning of the Great Depression. Despite its global character, Australian employers had little difficulty finding the cause of the economic downturn: compulsory arbitration. The New South Wales Employers' Federation considered arbitration a 'greater curse than droughts, prickly pear or any other curse in Australia and had done nothing else but cripple industry'.[17] The New South Wales Chamber of Manufactures also called for the abolition of arbitration, claiming that the 'evil which now obstructs our path to better conditions is without doubt compulsory arbitration. This must be suspended for it has now completely failed us'.[18] The Metal Trades Employers' Association agreed with this sentiment: 'Away with it, and let us get back to the clear, open, economic rings'.[19] Other major groups, such as the Pastoralists' Association, which had traditionally supported arbitration, also now called for its abolition.

Employers claimed that arbitration was the 'cause of depression in general; it reduces output since wages are paid to employees irrespective of their worth; it causes high unemployment, high tariffs, high production costs, industrial chaos and industrial conflict in particular'.[20] Employers were particularly concerned about the system of wage determination which did not incorporate their preferred system of payment by results. Increased competition and a shrinking domestic market forced employers to reduce production costs. They contended that labour productivity could be increased by the use of piecework, incentive schemes and subcontracting systems. Unions strongly objected to these schemes which they saw directed at reducing their bargaining power. The federal tribunal, for its part, claimed that payment by results was widespread and that 'even in the metal trades industries in which organised opposition has been most successful, piece-work largely

---

17. *Employers' Review* (NSW Employers' Federation), 30 August 1930.
18. C.R. Hall, *The Manufacturers: Australian Manufacturing Achievements to 1960*, Angus & Robertson, Sydney, 1971, pp. 401–2.
19. D. Carboch, *The Fall of the Bruce–Page Government*, Cheshire, Melbourne, 1958, p. 192.
20. *Employers' Review*, 30 September 1929.

prevails'.[21] The debate of the 1930s has its modern counterpart today when globally induced economic problems are the order of the day.

Despite their antagonism towards arbitration, employers were successful in having the Arbitration Court reduce real wages by 10 per cent in spite of Labor Government opposition (see Chapter 11). This wage reduction became the linchpin for the Premiers' Plan designed to combat depression. Other forms of payment—pensions, government salaries, interest rates on mortgages and so on—were also reduced by 10 per cent. The wage reduction, which was followed by state tribunals, also led to the federal tribunal becoming the principal wage-setting tribunal.

The wage reduction was restored in 1934 because of the improvement in the economy. Unemployment peaked in 1932 at about 30 per cent of unionists. This level was halved in each of the trienniums between 1932 and 1941 and then halved again in 1942. By the last date it stood at only 1.6 per cent, compared with the historic norm of around 7 per cent.

Economic recovery was accompanied by a remarkable about-face on the part of employers; initially an acceptance that 'the arbitration tree is rooted in the community'; and then a championing of arbitration as the appropriate mechanism for resolving disputes and containing wages. This transformation is typified by the Metal Trades Employers' Association which had previously called for a return 'to the clear, open economic rings'. In 1937 it declared that the 'arbitration system was a sound one and should be a permanent feature of the Australian legal system.'[22] By then there was a labour shortage. Unions pressed for over-award payments and for the forty-hour working week. Employers looked to the Arbitration Court to maintain existing standards or to slow down union gains.

The centralising effect of war

Employers' expedient support for arbitration was strengthened after Australia entered World War II in September 1939. Under the defence powers the role of the Arbitration Court was strengthened. The defence power in fact 'came to replace practically all other powers as the basis of government'.[23]

The major vehicle of regulation was the *National Security Act*. Manpower planning was introduced; limits (of 4 per cent) were placed on private profits; wages and prices were frozen; training requirements of tradesmen were diluted; technical education was used to speed up the apprenticeship system; ceilings were placed on hours of work; new lines of manufacturing were encouraged and some existing ones limited or prohibited; special tribunals were established to regulate dispute-prone

---

21. 28 *CAR* 937.
22. *Metal Trades Journal*, 2 April 1937.
23. G. Sawer, *Australian Federal Politics and the Law 1929–1949*, Melbourne University Press, Melbourne, 1963, p. 10.

areas and the employment of women in the newly established munitions industry.

In 1941 Labor gained office and employers became extremely apprehensive. 'Under the *National Security Act*', the New South Wales Chamber of Manufactures warned, 'the government can take sufficient powers to almost socialise Australia and make us a totalitarian State'.[24] The Chamber also claimed that Labor was using the emergency powers to introduce 'socialism by stealth'.[25]

The National Security (Industrial Peace) Regulations conferred additional powers on the Arbitration Court. It was empowered to declare a common rule for any industry or calling; it was not required to arbitrate within ambit; it could settle intrastate disputes and 'non-industrial' disputes; and its orders could not be challenged on the grounds that it had not engaged in 'conciliation' and 'arbitration'. In short, the regulations sought to remove those limitations which High Court challenges had demonstrated to exist. The Arbitration Court was given a dominant role over state tribunals and its scope increased by the appointment of a number of Conciliation Commissioners.

In its efforts to mobilise the war industries, governments, by executive action, fixed employment standards in those industries which were better than those in other industries. This conflicted with the Arbitration Court's approach based on uniformity and comparability. Employers condemned this government interference with employment standards and registered their support for the arbitration system which they had historically derided. Under the slogan 'Arbitration—not regulation' employers sought the use of arbitration which entitled them to some influence in the determining of awards. In 1944 employers successfully opposed the extension for five years of the war-time powers. In 1946 they also successfully opposed Commonwealth control of conditions of industrial employment.

The reforms of 1947

Despite employers' referendum victories, and Labor's loss of office in December 1949, the course of arbitration was materially changed as a result of the war and depression. The latter had established the Arbitration Court as the dominant wages tribunal. The centralising of national powers which started as a war-time necessity continued in practice for two major reasons. Before the War both the Commonwealth and states levied taxes. During the war the Commonwealth took over the collection and distribution of taxes. The states have permitted that situation to continue, thus increasing the Commonwealth's capacity to regulate the economy. A second major factor has been the increasing national orientation of the economy. These factors have given the federal tribunal an enhanced role, particularly in its role of wages and incomes regulator.

---

24. Chamber of Manufactures of New South Wales, *Annual Report*, 1940.
25. C.R. Hall, *The Manufacturers*, p. 592.

In 1947 the Labor Government introduced major reforms to the Arbitration Court. To that time the tribunal consisted of judges. There were complaints from both unions and employers about the excessive legalities of the system and delays. Arbitration was held to be dominant, while conciliation was neglected. The 1947 changes went a long way to remove the 'judicial character' of the Arbitration Court. They provided for the appointment of sixteen Conciliation Commissioners, each of whom was responsible for the industries or awards assigned by the Chief Commissioner. The role of the judges became essentially judicial—the interpretating and enforcement of awards and union rules. Their industrial work was confined to Full Bench matters involving standard hours of work, the basic wage, paid leave and minimum rates for women. Subject to the provision of appeals and references introduced in 1952, and to the panel system which has induced greater collaboration between members of the tribunal, the 1947 changes provide the basis for the present tribunal structure (see Chapter 4).

From court to commission

The general trend towards laicising the Arbitration Court received a major impetus in 1956 as the result of the High Court judgment in the *Boilermakers'* case. That case centred on whether the Arbitration Court could both make awards (an arbitral act) and enforce those awards (a judicial act). The High Court claimed that the Constitution provided for a separation between the legislative and executive functions of state—parliaments make the law, but leave its enforcement to the police and courts. In the High Court's view, the Arbitration Court could not exercise both judicial and arbitral functions.

To accommodate this view, in 1956 the Commonwealth Court of Conciliation and Arbitration was bifurcated into the Industrial Court (now the Industrial Division of the Federal Court of Australia) and the Conciliation and Arbitration Commission (now the Industrial Relations Commission). The Industrial Court was to exercise the functions of interpreting and enforcing legislation, union rules and awards. The Commission took over the functions of attempting to prevent and settle industrial disputes. Thus, since 1956, the major industrial tribunal has not been a court of law. Some of the former judges of the Arbitration Court were appointed to the Industrial Court, others were appointed to the Conciliation and Arbitration Commission. The latter were designated Presidential Members and soon discarded the wearing of wigs and other judicial robes. Legislation in 1974 provided for the appointment of Presidential Members who were not legally qualified and, for a short period, provided that legally qualified Presidential Members could not use the title 'Mr Justice' or 'Justice'.

Tribunal diffusion and integration

Since 1911 structural changes have been a continuing part of the federal tribunal system. At times these changes have attempted to diffuse or fragment tribunal operations and control; conversely, at other times changes have attempted to integrate and coordinate that control. Structural changes of two types can be identified: those relating to the establishment of competing or complementary tribunals and those relating to internal composition and operations of the Commission.

In 1911 the Public Service Arbitrator was established as a separate tribunal, the first of many separate tribunals to cut into the 'new province' of the Arbitration Court. The Public Service Arbitrator determined employment conditions and settled disputes relating to the federal public service (see Chapter 3). The industrial conflict following the inflation-prone World War I led to other 'tribunals of expediency' being established, namely the Hibble tribunals created under the *Industrial Peace Act 1920*. These tribunals were established to deal with dispute-prone areas. Industrial peace was sought by the provision of more favourable wages and conditions than could be obtained under general tribunal norms. These tribunals acted as safety valves within a system predicated on conformity and uniformity. Over time special tribunals were established for the Snowy Mountains Authority, the stevedoring industry, the maritime industry, the coal industry, for flight crew officers and, more recently, Kurnell Refinery operators in New South Wales. On a different plane specialised tribunals were established to determine conditions of employment for police, firefighters, academics and the defence forces. As noted later, the Women's Employment Board exercised important functions in relation to war-time industries in the period to 1944. The Remuneration Tribunal determines salaries and allowances for the judiciary, parliamentarians and senior officers in the public service.

Other significant structural changes have been designed to overcome constitutional constraints on the Arbitration Court and its successors, particularly in relation to its enforcement functions. Two major changes might be noted. In 1918, in *Alexander's* case, the High Court held that the Arbitration Court was not competent to impose penalties since it was not properly constituted. To 1912 the Court had consisted of a part-time President. Part-time Deputy Presidents (also members of the High Court) assisted after 1912. The Constitution required that members of a court be appointed for life (since changed to age 70). Because of a personal feud between Prime Minister Hughes and Higgins at this time the Act was not altered to provide for full-time appointees. This happened in 1926 when the Court was reconstituted by full-time members for the first time. An interesting development at this time was the appointment of two Deputy Presidents who were non-lawyers, a practice which was discontinued after 1930 but re-established in 1972 (see Table 10.1). Also of interest was the appointment between 1927 and 1935 of a Conciliation Commissioner with extremely limited arbitral functions. The Commissioner was attached to, but was not a member of, the Court. This practice was renewed in 1940 with the appointment of two Conciliation Commissioners under the National Security (Industrial Peace) Regulations. The number of Commissioners had grown to nine by the time of the major changes of 1947.

The second major change on the question of judicial competence was the breaking up of the Arbitration Court into the Industrial Court and the Conciliation and Arbitration Commission. The factors leading to this bifurcation have already been discussed.

Diffusion also took place within the tribunal itself. This, to some extent, necessarily followed from the increase in tribunal personnel as its workload increased. From being the 'one-man part-time band' of 1905-12, the newly created Court of 1926 consisted of five members: a Chief Judge, two judges and two Deputy Presidents. A Conciliation Commissioner was added to this list the following year. By 1946 the number of personnel had grown to fifteen. The Labor reforms of 1947 not only increased the number of personnel but also considerably changed the balance between the judicial and lay members of the Court. By 1948 the number of judges had been reduced from five to three and the number of Commissioners attached to the Court doubled to eighteen (including a Chief Commissioner).

The independent operation of such a large number of tribunal personnel created the possibility of flow-on problems and of a lack of consistency in the handling of similar claims. Employers claimed that the increased size of the Arbitration Court

> ... brought forward, with emphasis, the need for close collaboration between them [Commissioners] ... Any marked diversion, by any one Commissioner, which might be regarded as a general standard for various types of work ... is not conducive to industrial peace, but rather the contrary.[26]

This concern led to attempts at integrating the work of tribunal members. Strategies to accomplish this have included the appeals and referencing mechanisms and the creation of industry panels. An earlier strategy was to assign to Full Benches the determination of general standards.

The use of Full Benches dates back to 1921 when the Hughes Government legislated to provide that standard hours of work be determined by a Full Bench. This legislation was specifically aimed at preventing Higgins from applying generally the forty-four-hour week which he had determined in the *Timber Workers'* case[27] and which he flowed-on to the Engineers Award.[28] Under the Full Bench system employers were successful in having the forty-eight-hour week re-established as the standard.[29] In 1926 the determination of the basic wage also became a Full Bench matter and subsequently the determination of paid leave and minimum wages for women were added to this list. As already noted, the 1947 amendments did not reduce this Full Bench role.

In 1952 the Act was amended to provide for appeals and references to Full Benches. Appeals are a way of attempting to ensure that the decisions individual members do not create general flow-on problems.

---

26. *Employers' Review*, 31 October 1947.
27. 14 *CAR* 84.
28. 15 *CAR* 320.
29. 16 *CAR* 649.

References are designed to obviate appeals by assigning certain matters to Full Benches rather than to individual members of the Commission. The operations of the appeals and referencing systems are outlined in Chapter 4.

The panel system adopted in 1972 was another method of attempting to integrate the work of tribunal members. The panel system also reabsorbed the judges (by 1972 called Deputy Presidents) into the mainstream of tribunal activities by removing the restrictions on their functions which had applied since the 1947 legislation. Deputy Presidents were given charge of panels consisting of a number of Commissioners and having responsibility for a number of specified industries or awards. Under the panel system individual members of the Commission no longer have exclusive authority over a particular industry. Further, the Presidential Member exercises a coordinating role (see Chapter 4).

Since 1972, under the impact of the first wage indexation regime, governments have progressively cut back the autonomy of individual members of the Commission, but in a way which has brought about procedural rather than structural changes. Thus more Deputy Presidents than there are panels have been appointed, enabling certain Deputy Presidents to be isolated to Full Bench matters. The President has been given competence under the Act to take over the handling of any dispute at any stage of arbitral proceedings. Members of panels are expected to 'consult' with the Deputy President. The quest for greater integration has brought about a strengthening in the role of Deputy Presidents and an increase in their membership (see Table 10.1). The government took the opportunity provided by the establishment of the Industrial Relations Commission to remove a Deputy President considered too independent in his approach to Commission activities.

In the post-war period structural changes have also brought about greater integration between the activities of specialised tribunals and the Commission. This is best demonstrated by the way in which the Public Service Arbitrator was gradually incorporated into the Commission. In 1952 the appeals and referencing systems were extended to the Public Service Arbitrator. Deputy Public Service Arbitrators were appointed who were also members of the Commission. The offices of the Public Service Arbitrator were relocated into the same building as the Commission. Employees of major public corporations such as the Commonwealth Banking Corporation, Telecom Australia and Australia Post were transferred from the jurisdiction of the Public Service Arbitrator to the Commission. The transfer of the last two corporations to the jurisdiction of the Commission in 1974 reduced the number of employees under Public Service Arbitrator determinations by 40 per cent. In 1976 the Report of the Royal Commission on Australian Government Administration recommended that the special public sector tribunal be abolished and replaced by a public sector panel within the Commission. The government legislated to this effect in 1984.

Similar integration occurred with most other specialist tribunals.

Thus, for the most part, they consisted of a Deputy President of the Commission and appeals could be made to the Commission. The major exception in this respect has been the Coal Industry Tribunal created under the *National Security Act 1939*. In its 1985 Report, the Committee of Review into Australian Industrial Relations Law and Systems (the Hancock Report) recommended the abolition of all special tribunals (except the Remuneration Tribunal) and their absorption into the Commission. The Report also recommended the abandonment of the 1956 split between the Industrial Court and the Commission by way of dual appointments to both tribunals. In this schema a Labour Court would be created which would be constituted by Deputy Presidents of the Industrial Relations Commission. This model would have followed the South Australian approach (see Chapter 5). Though the 1988 legislation removed special tribunals with the exception of the Remuneration Tribunal, the Committee of Reference for Defence Force Pay and the Coal Industry Tribunal, it did not create a special Labour Court.

The major composition changes of the federal tribunal can be seen in Table 10.1. This indicates a growth in tribunal membership until the bifurcation of the former Arbitration Court in 1956. Since then the membership of the Commission has more than doubled. The impact of the 1926 amendments creating the tribunal as a court in its own right is evident from the changed designations of members. It will also be apparent that for much of its history the tribunal has had members, or persons attached to it, with no arbitral powers. The effect of the 1947 changes in transforming the tribunal from one composed predominantly of judges to a predominantly lay membership is also apparent. It will also be noted, however, that the proportion of Presidential Members has increased over time.

The use of conciliation

A system of *compulsory* arbitration must ultimately rely for its authority on the coercive power of the state. A system, however, which relied only on compulsion of a blatantly authoritarian sort would not be likely to promote industrial harmony in the long run. An arbitration tribunal, like any other institution, requires some degree of consent from the parties involved. For that reason the word 'conciliation' preceded 'arbitration' in the titles of the Act, the former Commonwealth Court of Conciliation and Arbitration and the Australian Conciliation and Arbitration Commission.

Several attempts have been made to minimise the system's reliance on arbitration. These include the provision for consent awards, industrial agreements and Part X agreements. The 1904 Act also provided for Conciliation Committees, consisting of an equal number of employer and employee representatives. The Court had power to refer disputes to these committees. By 1928 the Court also had power to coopt the assistance of Conciliation Commissioners. In that year the Bruce-Page Government

Table 10.1: *Composition of federal tribunal 1905–90*

Year	Pres.[1]	Chief Judge[2]	D.P.[3]	Judges[4]	Senior Com[5]	Con Com[6]	C&A Com[7]	Arb Com[8]	Total
				Commonwealth Court of Conciliation and Arbitration					
1905–12	1[a]	—	—		—		—	—	1[a]
1913–26	1[a]	1	1–3[a]						2–4[a]
1926		1	2	2					5
1927–30		1	1	3		1			6
1931–7		1		2		1			4
1938–9		1		3					4
1940		1		3		2			6
1941–3		1		3		6			10
1944–5		1		4		9			14
1946		1		5		9			15
1947–50		1		3	1		16–18[b]		23–25
1951		1		4	1		18[b]		24
1952		1		6	1		16[b]		24
1953–6		1		6	1		11–12[b]		19–21

Table 10.1: *Composition of federal tribunal 1905–90 — Continued*

Year	Pres.[1]	Chief Judge[2]	D.P.[3]	Judges[4]	Senior Com[5]	Con Com[6]	C&A Com[7]	Arb Com[8]	Total
				Australian Conciliation and Arbitration Commission					
1956	1		4						14
1957–9	1		4	1		2–3	7–8		16
1960–61	1		5	1		3	8		18
1962–9	1		5	1		3	9–11		19–21
1970–72	1		6–7	1		3–4	13–15		23–24
1972	1		8				8	8	25
1973	1		8				19		28
1974–7	1		7				18–22		26–30
1978–9	1		8–9				21–22		31–33
1980–81	1		11				24–25		37–38
1982–3	1		12				22		35
1983–7	1		12				27		40
				Australian Industrial Relations Commission					
1988–90	1		14				31		46

Notes
(1) President. (2) Chief Judge. (3) Deputy Presidents. (4) Judges. (5) Senior/Chief Commissioner. (6) Conciliation Commissioners. (7) Conciliation and Arbitrations Commissioner. (8) Arbitration Commissioners (no conciliation functions).
(a) Part-time appointments
(b) Designated 'Conciliation Commissioner' but had arbitral powers.
The first female members of the Commission were appointed in 1974. Appointees on other duties are excluded from figures.
Sources: 1905–79 Dabscheck & Niland (1981).
1980–88 ACAC President's Annual Reports.

passed legislation which allowed Conciliation Commissioners to act as chairmen of the Conciliation Committees. A Commissioner was empowered to ascertain the majority view of his Committee and draw up an award accordingly. The government hoped that this arrangement would reduce the formality and legalism of the system and its emphasis on arbitration. However, the legislation was quickly challenged before the High Court. In 1931 the Court held the amendments to be unconstitutional, since they enabled a body to settle a dispute by decree, without any hearing between the disputants. According to the High Court this 'was not in any form or shape conciliation or arbitration'.[30] This ruling stopped the development of the Committees. They did not reappear in federal legislation again until the establishment of the Flight Crew Officers' Industrial Tribunal in 1967. A Coordinating Committee established for the stevedoring industry in 1977 resembles the Conciliation Committees in some ways.

Under the National Security (Industrial Peace) Regulations of 1939 the system became what it had been before 1928; there were six Conciliation Commissioners to help the judges. Amendments to the Act in 1947, however, increased the number of Commissioners to fifteen, made them independent of the judiciary, and increased their powers so that they could arbitrate as well as conciliate. In giving Commissioners arbitral powers, the 1947 amendments gave the Commissioners the same problem which had perplexed Presidential Members: how could conciliation be combined with arbitration? Further amendments to the Act in 1956 reintroduced Conciliators whose arbitration power was minimal. Under this legislation the Conciliators could arbitrate only with the consent of the parties in dispute. Three Conciliators were attached to the Commission. They undertook conciliation either at the request of the parties or whenever a Commissioner dealing with a dispute thought that a Conciliator might provide a valuable service. Apart from the appointment of an extra Conciliator, this arrangement continued unchanged until 1972.

In 1972 another set of amendments to the Act attempted to strengthen conciliation. They led instead to the disappearance of the Conciliators. The amendments made the Conciliator a full member of the Commission, with the title of Conciliation Commissioner. The fifteen Commissioners already attached to the Commission were given new functions. Half of them were to be retitled Conciliation Commissioners and would perform, in effect, the tasks of the former Conciliators though with reduced arbitral powers. The other Commissioners were to be retitled Arbitration Commissioners. Their main job was to arbitrate on matters not resolved by conciliation. Each industry panel was to be reconstituted so that it would consist of at least one Presidential Member, one Arbitration Commissioner and one Conciliation Commissioner. Commenting on these changes the President of the Commission wrote:

---

30. O. de R. Foenander, *Industrial Conciliation and Arbitration in Australia*, Law Book Co., Sydney, 1959, p. 2.

> I am happy that any lingering concept that arbitration has some sort of seniority has been dispelled by the new legislation and more particularly by the fact that not only did all the Conciliators elect to become Conciliation Commissioners rather than Arbitration Commissioners but no less than five Commissioners made the same choice. In my view Conciliation and Arbitration always should rank as equal partners with each other.[31]

These new arrangements proved impractical, partly because they did increase the number of matters going to conciliation. The 'present dichotomy', wrote Mr Justice Moore

> has led to a situation where the work load of Commissioners designated as Conciliation Commissioners tends to be greater than that of Arbitration Commissioners both because of the provisions of section 25 (4) which has the effect of sending disputes to Conciliation Commissioners and because parties are more and more resolving their problems by agreement.[32]

The new arrangements had also severely reduced the Commission's flexibility. Before the 1972 amendments it had often happened that a Commissioner or Presidential Member would commence an arbitration during which the parties might request him to conciliate. On the other hand a conciliation might be commenced during which he might be asked to give *ad hoc* arbitration or even, when conciliation was exhausted, be asked to arbitrate formally on all outstanding matters. Under the changed system matters had to be referred from Arbitrator to Conciliator and *vice versa* at different stages of procedures or according to the whims of the parties. Each change from a Conciliator or Arbitrator required a repetition of arguments already made before the other Commissioner.[33] A system of references from Conciliators to Arbitrators to Full Benches had been made possible which did little to resolve industrial disputes speedily. The President recommended a common designation for all Commissioners, with all having the same powers and functions. He wrote

> Many parties do not object to a combination of both conciliation and arbitration by the same person and indeed welcome it particularly if there have been many conferences, which means that the person concerned knows the facts which do not have to be repeated to a newcomer.[34]

The Act was amended in 1973, therefore, to remove the distinction between Conciliation and Arbitration Commissioners. All members of the Commission were given power to conciliate and arbitrate.

Though the administrative arrangements no longer provide for specialists in conciliation, members of the Commission continue to place emphasis on the value of this form of settlement.

---

31. Australian Conciliation and Arbitration Commission, *Annual Report No. 17*, 1972, p. 6.
32. Ibid.
33. Ibid.
34. Ibid

Legalism

A problem related to conciliation is that of the extent to which the system should be influenced by the forms and procedures of law. If compulsion requires the formal authority of the law, conciliation should be evidently more relaxed and informal. The sometimes pompous and anachronistic procedures of law courts are more likely to stifle than to help agreement between employers and employees. Employees in particular are less likely to behave in an accommodating way in an environment which they think of as alien and hostile. For that reason the original Act had stated

> In the hearing and determination of every dispute the Court shall act according to equity, good conscience, and the substantial merits of the case, without regard to technicalities or legal forms, and shall not be bound by any rules of evidence, but may inform its mind on any matter in such manner as it thinks just.[35]

It was inevitable, though, that the appointment of barristers to the status of judges of a Court of Superior Record, would produce, to a large degree, an imitation of the normal court system.

Changes to the Act in 1947 and in 1956 have helped to remove much of the legalism. As already noted the 1947 amendments resulted in the judicial and lay members of the Arbitration Court being given distinct functions. The functions of the judiciary, or Presidential Members, were limited to Full Bench hearings and disputes over matters of law. The bulk of the Court's functions—the settlement of industrial disputes and the making of awards—were placed in the hands of lay Conciliation Commissioners. This went some way in fulfilling the major aims of the legislators:

> First, the bill boldly attempts to grapple with the two outstanding defects of the present procedure. It emphasises informality and expedition in bringing the machinery of conciliation and arbitration into play. It abolishes the cumbrous preliminaries which have tended to prevent the industrial authorities from getting hold of a situation before it crystallises into a dispute. Secondly, when the machinery has been brought into play, the bill substitutes for legal techniques and courts of law the practical decision of experienced and independent laymen who will exercise administrative discretion. When they get hold of a situation, their methods will not be governed by any technical or legal procedures. They will be given wide discretion to take action for the purpose of preventing and settling disputes.[36]

The 1956 amendments were equally far-reaching in their effects. As already noted they resulted in the Arbitration Court being separated into two new tribunals, the Industrial Court and the Conciliation and Arbitration Commission. This arrangement, the Minister hoped, would 'enable proceedings to be conducted with less formality and with less of a litigious atmosphere, which is difficult to keep separate from courts of

---

35. *Conciliation and Arbitration Act 1904*, section 2.
36. Cited by B. Healey, *Federal Arbitration in Australia*, Georgian House, Sydney, 1973, p. 79.

law functioning in the usual way'. Several aspects of the new legislation strengthened this hope. The Presidential Members' duties were restricted to Full Bench issues. The bulk of disputes were to be settled by the lay Commissioners. Conciliators were reintroduced and provision was made for mixed Benches consisting of both judges and laymen. Presidential Members were no longer to wear wigs and robes of office and, for a short period, were not to be designated 'Mr Justice', the title accorded Judges, on appointment.[37] There was a curtailment of access by barristers to conciliation and arbitration hearings. In 1972 the first non-lawyer was appointed as a Presidential Member of the Commission with the title Mr Deputy President.

Award enforcement and strike penalties

However desirable it may be that the parties to industrial disputes should come together willingly in an informal environment to settle their differences, there remains the problem of what should happen if agreement cannot be reached. In the final resort, a third party, the Commission, will arbitrate the matter and hand down a final and enforceable decision. Those who will not accept the decision, subject of course to appeals procedures, must be penalised. Those, at least, are some of the assumptions upon which the working of the federal arbitration tribunals rests.

The 1904 Act imposed heavy penalties for strikes and lock-outs. Unions, it was thought, could not have it both ways; they could either resort to direct bargaining and the use of the coercive weapons of bargaining, or they could place their case in the Court's hands and submit to its decision. This 'either–or' approach conflicted with the Act's wish to encourage bargaining. Gradually, therefore, the overt anti-strike provisions were diluted by legislative amendment. In 1930 the strike provisions were abolished altogether. Thus strikes ceased to be illegal *per se* and other means of enforcement were found: deregistration and, after 1949, the use of penal sanctions.

Amendments to the Act in 1947 declared the Commonwealth Conciliation and Arbitration Court a Superior Court of Record. This allowed the Court to punish for contempt those who disobeyed its orders. Two years later, in response to a coal strike, the Labor Government passed the National Emergency Coal Strike Act. Under this Act some unions were fined and union officials gaoled for contempt of Court. The system of injunctions was rediscovered, making it possible for employers to have penalties imposed on unions by the Arbitration Court (after 1956 the Industrial Court) through contempt of Court proceedings. The system of penalties operated by way of Section 109 and Section 111:

Section 109 gave the Industrial Court power to order compliance with an

---

37. The title was restored after strong objections from the President. See *Annual Report*, No. 17, p. 4.

award which had been breached and to enjoin the commission or continuation of a contravention of the Act or breach of an award. The order could be made so that it remained in force for the duration of the award or any other period the Court decided. If the Court's order was disobeyed s.111 came into play. It recited that the Court was to have the same power to punish contempts of its authority as the High Court of Australia has.[38]

Bans clauses were put into most major awards. Once a bans clause had been inserted into an award its enforcement became the prerogative of the Industrial Court.

A major problem with such injunctions was that employers increasingly showed a propensity to hide behind them rather than to bargain with the unions. As Portus observed, 'penal proceedings which had become a dead letter in arbitration law gradually came into use and a tendency developed to turn to them automatically as a remedy'.[39]

The mechanistic manner in which the Industrial Court used the penal sanctions gradually alienated the bulk of trade unions, including many that supported the system of compulsory arbitration. It was not difficult to depict the Industrial Court as an anti-union institution. For example, the 'cooling-off' period of fourteen days required by the Act before proceedings could be taken was made ineffective, fines were imposed regardless of the merits of the union's case, and the 'Industrial Court's attitudes of righteousness in respect of violations of its authority [was] dramatically illustrated by [the] cases in which the Court did not limit the total number of fines that could be imposed to one'.[40] Where strikes affected more than one employer, the Court declared that each employer was capable of having separate fines imposed. Fines were imposed for each day of a strike. One judge suggested that there was theoretically a separate liability for 'every moment of time that the ban continues'.[41] Invariably the Court fined the unions the maximum amount possible under the Act.

Whatever the legal merits of such Court conduct, the industrial relations implications were bad. In effect, the only way in which those unions whose awards contained bans clauses could obtain more than the minima provided by their awards was to rely on the goodwill of employers, a far cry from the bargaining situation the conciliation and arbitration system was supposed to foster. Any act of coercion to force employers to the bargaining table resulted in fines. Unions increasingly came to believe that the system was merely trying to tame them through impoverishment in a period when boom conditions were increasing the employers' ability to pay increased wages. The gaoling of O'Shea, the Secretary of the Tramways Union, in 1969, for contempt of court, finally brought matters to a head.[42] A national stoppage was averted and O'Shea released, when a lottery winner paid the union's outstanding fines. The

---

38. E.I. Sykes and H.J. Glasbeek, *Labour Law in Australia*, Butterworth, Sydney, 1972, p. 46.
39. J.H. Portus, *Compulsory Arbitration*, p. 93.
40. E.I. Sykes and H.J. Glasbeek, *Labour Law in Australia*, p. 548.
41. Ibid.
42. See ibid, p. 552 for an account of the O'Shea dispute.

Federal Government quickly moved to enact changes. 'The artificiality of legal pedantry and irrelevance of judicial logic to industrial conflict had led to such violent upheaval that changes in the machinery were forced upon the Commonwealth'.[43]

The 1970 amendments to the Act preserved the notion that under certain circumstances particular kinds of actions will be prohibited. However, these amendments have removed the automatic enforcement of awards by a tribunal having no connection with award-making and dispute resolution. The main amendment introduced a more efficient 'cooling off' system outside the control of the Industrial Court. Before the Court may be approached for the imposition of a penalty, notice must be given to the Industrial Registrar. A Presidential Member of the Commission will then be given the task of attempting to settle the dispute. Thus no penal powers may be invoked by the Court unless the Commission has had the opportunity of conciliating and/or arbitrating on the matter. The power to insert bans clauses has been removed from Commissioners and is now vested in Presidential members only. These amendments have forced employers away from using penal sanctions as an automatic remedy.

A more recent development has again highlighted the conflicting assumptions underlying resort to strike action *and* arbitration. This has involved claims by unions for the payment of wages for the period of a strike as a condition for returning to work. In some instances the Commission has made such recommendations to employers. In 1979 the Fraser Government legislated to prevent that sort of settlement and to reassert the incompatibility of strikers seeking recourse to arbitration. Section 25A of the *Conciliation and Arbitration Act*, which commenced operation in October 1979, read:

> The Commission is not empowered to make an award, certify a memorandum of agreement, make a recommendation or take other action, whether by way of conciliation or arbitration, in respect of a claim for the making of a payment to employees in respect of a period which those employees were engaged in industrial action.

The intent of this provision has been retained in the *Industrial Relations Act* 1988 (s.124).

Economic regulation

The constitutional and statutory functions of the Commission relate to the prevention and settlement of industrial disputes. Wage determination is an incidental part of dispute settlement. The Commission fixes wages as part of helping to resolve disputes over wages. However, as well as having industrial effects, wage settlements also have economic effects. Generous wage provisions may result in industrial peace. They

---

43. Ibid., p. 554.

might also result, according to some economists, in unemployment or inflation, and adversely affect government attempts to regulate the economy. Themselves unable directly to regulate wage standards, federal governments have attempted to make the Commission's wages policy conform with the government's economic policy. In this, governments have attempted to influence and restrain the determinations of the Commission.

Some of the restraints placed on the ability of the Commission to break new industrial ground have already been noted. The Full Bench system, in which matters of national economic importance must be handled by at least three members, is one such restraint. The appeals system, which allows a Full Bench to review the determinations of single Commissioners, is another. Similarly the panel system, by forcing Commissioners to consider the impact of their decisions on related awards, has a restraining effect. The requirement that Commissioners consult the appropriate Presidential Member imposes another restraint. Yet another applies to the certification of consent awards. Those consent awards not considered in the public interest are not certified. Awards having undesirable implications for the economy would be considered against the public interest. Award enforcement and penal sanctions have also been used to restrict changes in wages and working conditions to those considered desirable in the 'national interest'.

Notwithstanding these limits on the Commission, federal governments have attempted more direct methods of compelling the Commission to take greater account of the government's views. The Minister is empowered to apply for a Full Bench review of any award made, or memorandum certified, if the award or decision is contrary to the public interest. In addition, the Minister may intervene directly in any case before the Commission. Since its first intervention in a national wage case, in the 1930–31 Basic Wage and Wage Reduction Inquiry, the Commonwealth has been a major participant in such cases. This has been particularly so in the post Word War II period. For most of the period, non-Labor governments have consistently argued against wage increases. During periods of full employment the Commonwealth has considered wage increases inflationary. At other times the Commonwealth has considered that the economy did not have the capacity to pay increased wages and has argued that such wage increases would result in unemployment.

At times the Commonwealth's position and that of the Commission have been diametrically opposed. The Commonwealth, for example, has argued that price stability should be central to the Commission's task. The Commission has argued that the preservation of purchasing power in existing wages should be given greater importance than the preservation of price stability. In this view, the Commission is an industrial tribunal and not an instrument of government economic policy.[44]

---

44. See, for example, 1967 National Wage Case, 110 *CAR* 189.

Given its constitutional limitations, the government cannot force the Commission into accepting its policies. However, the Act does require the Commission to take into account the likely economic effects of its decisions:

> In the performance of its functions the Commission shall take into account the public interest, and for that purpose shall have regard to ... the state of the national economy and the likely effects on the national economy of any award or order that the Commission is considering, or is proposing to make, with special reference to the likely effects on the level of employment and on inflation (s.90).

The new intervention: the Fraser years

Between 1904 and 1975 the Act was amended more than sixty times. Fourteen sets of amendments were enacted under the Fraser Government (1975–81). As the result of greater economic stress and the federal Coalition Government's obsession with trade union militancy, the amendments showed a new trend. Notwithstanding the Constitution, the government attempted to become a more dominant actor in the system and to usurp functions previously reserved for tribunals.

Conflict between the government of the day and industrial tribunals, and the frustration of the former at its industrial impotence, are nothing new. However, previous attempts to bring about government objectives have been by way of changes to tribunals or the creation of new tribunals. Impatience with the slowness of the Court's handling of public service disputes led to the creation of the Public Service Arbitrator, even though the Commonwealth could have directly regulated the conditions of employment of its own employees. Dissatisfaction with the Court's handling of coal industry disputes resulted in the formation of the Hibble Tribunal, a forerunner of the present-day Coal Industry Tribunal. Concern with strikes in particular industries such as the maritime and stevedoring industries, industries in which the government has the constitutional right to legislate directly about employment conditions, resulted in the establishment of the Maritime and Stevedoring tribunals. These were later augmented by the Snowy Mountains and Flight Crew Officers' tribunals. The Full Bench appeals and panels systems have been used to impose some degree of self-regulation on the Commission. Award enforcement and trade union control have been left to the Industrial Court.

The Fraser Government was less prepared to allow the Commission and related tribunals the independence and support they customarily enjoyed. Further, the government was more prepared to regulate directly the employment conditions of its own employees. It restricted negotiations between unions and statutory authorities, and gave itself power to stand down employees affected by industrial disputes and to dismiss employees taking part in strikes. Amendments to the *Social Security Act* removed unemployment benefits from unionists when their union was on strike, even if the strike occurred in establishments outside the unemployed workers' usual place of work. Secondary boycotts were made illegal under the *Trade Practices Act*. The *Conciliation and Arbitration Act* was amended to give the government greater direct involvement. Legislation in 1976 enabled the Minister to apply for a Full Bench review of any award or agreement certified. Earlier legislation enabled the Minister or his representative to take part in any proceedings before the Commission, irrespective of whether the Commonwealth was a party to the dispute. The government's opposition to wage indexation seriously threatened the continuance of the system. The most important changes to the nature of the system, however, were the establishment of the Industrial Relations Bureau and of provisions enabling the government itself to deregister unions and suspend unionists.

The government set up the Bureau to redress what it considered to be an unfair system of award enforcement. Because of the activities of the Arbitration Inspectorate, employers have been forced to observe award prescriptions. However, as seen in a previous section, award enforcement against trade unions has been largely unsuccessful. Since the changes of 1970, to those parts of the Act relating to penal sanctions, only one union has been prosecuted. On the other hand, in one year alone, more than 10 000 employers were forced, either by persuasion or Court action, to rectify breaches of the awards, at a cost of nearly $800 000.[45] The government considered this a one-sided situation. Because employers are reluctant to prosecute unions, and because the Commission has been 'soft' in issuing certificates enabling penal proceedings to be taken to the Industrial Court, the enforcement of awards against unions has been all but dispensed with. Obviously the government was concerned that employers should be forced to observe the minimum requirements of health, safety and other industrial legislation as well as awards, but that the nature of employees' minimum awards was such as to provide for over-award bargaining. Nor did the government accept that the penal disputes of the 1960s which culminated in the *de facto* removal of penal sanctions, established a trend of award nonconformity which was hard to reverse. The Industrial Relations Bureau was expected to make two contributions to ensuring union observance of awards. First, it was to be an instigator in breaches of award proceedings. Second, it was to assist in implementing those provisions of the Act designed to reduce union strength.

The Bureau could instigate proceedings for award breaches on its own initiative. It was obliged to do so, moreover, if requested to by 5 per cent or 250 members of an organisation. The Bureau's more detached position—unlike employers it did not have to continue to work with unions which had been prosecuted—and its resources made it more likely than other parties in the system to take action against unions. The Bureau had

---

45. Commonwealth Arbitration Inspectorate, *Report*, AGPS, Canberra, 1977, p. 32.

to assist and advise individuals or groups experiencing organisational difficulties. Previously, conscientious objectors had to rely on their own resources, but could now turn to the Bureau for assistance. The grounds for conscientious objection were liberalised, conscientious belief being defined to mean 'any conscientious beliefs, whether the grounds for the beliefs are or are not of a religious character and whether the beliefs are or are not part of the doctrine of any religion'.[46] Individuals could refuse to join in industrial action called by their union. The Bureau's task included assisting such individuals. Clearly if unionists are free to determine individually whether to engage in industrial action called by their union, union strategy will be less effective and a potential source of division will be created.

The ability of the Bureau to take a passive role in the system was limited by subtle means. Unlike members of the Commission and ancillary bodies, or Permanent Heads, the Bureau's Director was appointed for a period not exceeding seven years.[47] Reappointment was subject to the government's satisfaction with his performance. The Bureau was forced by various parts of the Act to become involved at the request of individuals, the requisite number of members of an organisation, parties to an award, the Industrial Court or the Industrial Registrar. The Bureau was accountable to the Commonwealth Ombudsman and the *Administrative Decisions (Judicial Review) Act*. This accountability ensured that the Bureau acted when requested to.

Legislation enacted in October 1979 gave the government its most direct role in the enforcement provisions of the system. Under these amendments the government itself would determine the deregistration of unions or suspension of unionists. This was a clear break with the tradition of impartial tribunal inquiries to determine wrong-doing, the extent of guilt and the penalties attaching to guilt. Under the new provisions:

> Where, on application by the Minister, a Full Bench is satisfied that—
> (a) an organisation has been or is, or two or more members of an organisation action have been or are, engaged in industrial action; and
> (b) the industrial action has had, is having, or is likely to have, a substantial adverse effect on the safety, health, or welfare of the community or a part of the community,
> the Full Bench shall make a declaration that it is so satisfied and cause the declaration to be recorded in writing.[48]

Instead of the matter being then handled by the Industrial Court, the government itself could determine whether or not a union was to be deregistered within a period of six months after the Full Bench declaration. Within the same six-month period the government could suspend any of the 'rights, privileges or capacities of the organisation or . . . of any of its members'. The government could determine if, when and under

---

46. *Conciliation and Arbitration Act*, s. 144A.
47. The Act gave the director 'all the powers of, or exercisable by, a Permanent Head under the *Public Service Act 1922*'.
48. *Conciliation and Arbitration Act*, s. 143A(1).

what conditions a deregistered union could be registered again. If the union ceased to comply with the conditions of re-registration it could be deregistered again. These provisions enabled the government to determine penalties without any open inquiry as to the degree of guilt. Further, it enabled the government to suspend individual unionists and thus remove militants from office. The six-month period within which deregistration might take place meant that unions could have been deregistered over incidents not related to the Full Bench hearing. It can also allow the government to make political capital at the expense of good industrial relations. These provisions were used to deregister the Builders' Labourers Federation although they do not form a part of the new Industrial Relations Act. The Hawke Government has abolished the Industrial Relations Bureau.

Incorporation: the Accord

The conflicting economic and industrial relations goals which attach to the Commission's role as a wage moderator have made it the subject of government concern and influence. This is not surprising. Governments must manage the economy and high levels of inflation and/or unemployment may be electoral liabilities. Particularly in periods of cost–push inflation, where prices are propelled by significant wage gains, governments have attempted to influence the Commission's wages policy. The nature and method of influencing the Commission differs according to the economic strategy of the party in office and its relationship with the other parties in the system. As a generalisation it may be said that the Fraser Government attempted to influence the Commission through legislation and *ad hoc* reactive measures which presupposed a divorcing of industrial relations and economic policies. A victim of this approach was the wage indexation system, implemented in the last year of the Whitlam Labor Government (1975) and predicated on an incomes policy which incorporated economic as well as industrial relations goals. The government supporting mechanisms which formed a part of this approach are outlined in Chapter 11.

During its period in opposition (December 1975 to March 1983) the Labor Party refined its incomes policy approach to economic management and at its Federal Conference of 1979 resolved that:

> With the understanding and co-operation of the trade union movement [it would] develop and implement a policy which [would] encompass prices, wages, incomes non-wage incomes, the social wage, taxation reform and elimination of tax avoidance, and which [would] achieve a more equitable distribution of national wealth and income, with the commitment to supporting the maintenance of real wages by quarterly adjustments and the passing on of the benefits of productivity.[49]

---

49. 'The relationship between the Australian Labor Party and the trade unions', ACTU discussion paper, 1980, p. 2.

The Australian Labour Advisory Committee, a joint ALP–ACTU body which drafted the policy, helped ensure 'the understanding and cooperation of the union movement'. The ALP's commitment and acceptance of an incomes policy approach to economic management was spelt out in its proposed method of controlling inflation which considered it necessary 'to develop a general mix of economic policies to bear down on inflation while allowing recovery to proceed'. The ALP's approach rejected the 'inflation first' approach of the Coalition and saw the removal of unemployment as a matter as pressing as reducing inflation. The ALP's 'general mix' included a price control tribunal, amendments to the *Trade Practices Act* to strengthen competition, cuts in taxes and a commitment to maintain real disposal income of lower- and middle-income earners, support for wage indexation, controls over non-wage incomes, and complementary fiscal, monetary and industry policies. The policy added:

> In the context of such prices and incomes policies being implemented and operating effectively, the trade union movement, whilst maintaining its right to seek improvement in workers' living standards will ensure that action to achieve that end is conducted with a full appreciation of the need to avoid exacerbation of inflation.[50]

The ALP and ACTU announced an Accord as a prices and incomes approach to economic management in February 1983. A month later the ALP was elected to government. It then pressed for the reintroduction of wage indexation. It was the linchpin of both its economic and industrial relations policies and in many ways the Commission was faced with a *fait accompli*. It was of the view that indexation had considerable industrial relations and economic merit, and reintroduced wage indexation in September 1983. In doing so the Commission expressly mentioned the Accord as an important factor influencing its decision.

Since this time the Prices and Incomes Accord has been used by the ALP and the ACTU as a mechanism to achieve quite considerable changes in the form and character of the wage fixation system. As economic conditions became more difficult for the government, the Accord provided the negotiation framework for the abandonment of indexation, the reduction of real award rates and the requirement of efficiency and productivity gains in exchange for wage increases. In return, the government stimulated employment, provided tax relief and facilitated the general spread of occupational superannuation. The operation of the Accord is discussed more fully in Chapters 11 and 12.

Summary

The adoption of compulsory arbitration for the settlement and prevention of industrial disputes placed Australian legislators in a pioneering role. The systems adopted early this century have, however, evolved in

---

50. Ibid., pp. 7–9.

response to a range of external and internal pressures. These include changes in the legal and social environment, as well as changes in the power relations between the major parties and in the organisation of work.

Industrial tribunals have sought to regulate and control industrial disputes and the parties in the system. Governments in turn have attempted to regulate and control tribunals. In a situation where the Constitution guarantees a high degree of autonomy for the Commission, government–Commission conflicts have emerged concerning policy accommodation and the appropriate procedures for dispute resolution under differing circumstances.

This chapter has sought to highlight these difficulties by exploring a number of areas in the original Act of 1904. Thus the need to rationalise the dual tribunal systems which have evolved in each state has been a major concern of governments. This is one area in which judge-made law has been of greater significance than parliamentary statutes. The strike prevention attributes of the federal system have had to be modified to take account of industrial relations realities, increased union bargaining power and an extension of the Commission's jurisdiction beyond that of a tribunal handling rare and dramatic national disputes such as the strikes of the 1890s. These modifications have required a reduction in emphasis on arbitration and a greater concern for bilateral settlements aided by conciliation. It also has necessitated less emphasis on the legal aspects of the system. The introduction of lay arbitrators in 1947 and the separation of any judicial functions from the Commission in 1956 laid the basis for the present informal approach in which legalism is a tactic engaged in by the parties rather than an unavoidable aspect of normal proceedings.

The harmonising of the Commission's wages policies with general government policies has also been a source of government concern. Through legislation, and in the case of the Fraser Government, direct and partisan intervention, governments have sought to influence wages policy. The Hawke Government's approach has been less antagonistic and has sought to influence the Commission by way of incorporation.

Discussion questions

1. Why did Australia adopt compulsory conciliation and arbitration?
2. How do you explain initial employers' hostility and subsequent strong support for the conciliation and arbitration system?
3. It has been contended that the High Court of Australia has had as much influence on the jurisdiction and functions of the Industrial Commission as federal and state parliaments. Do you agree? Give reasons for your answer.
4. Explain the importance of the following High Court cases for the

operations of the Industrial Relations Commission: the *Bootmakers'* case 1910, the *Alexander* case 1918, the *Builders' Labourers'* case 1914, the *Cowburn* case 1926, the *Boilermakers'* case 1956.
5. How did the 1947 amendments to the *Conciliation and Arbitration Act* change the composition and operations of the Arbitration Court? What benefits and problems did these changes bring about?
6. At times parliaments have sought to diffuse or decentralise tribunal operations. At other times they have sought to integrate them and remove specialist tribunals. What factors give rise to such actions by governments?
7. Why is it difficult to combine the functions of a conciliator with those of an arbitrator? What measures have been taken to enhance the conciliation functions of the Commission?
8. Why has compulsory arbitration taken on many characteristics of law courts? Are there (a) any advantages and/or (b) any disadvantages in a semi-legal approach to resolving disputes? How has parliament attempted to remove much of the legalism of the system?
9. What measures have been used to enforce award observance on trade unions? What problems arise if unions are compelled to observe award provisions?
10. What distinguishes the 'new intervention' from previous government measures to regulate industrial relations?
11. Outline the main elements and the developments of the ALP–ACTU Accord.

Further reading

Cupper, L. 'Legalism in the Australian Conciliation and Arbitration Commission: the gradual transition', *Journal of Industrial Relations*, vol. 18, no. 4, 1976.
Dabscheck, B., *Arbitrator at Work: Sir William Raymond Kelly and the Regulation of Australian Industrial Relations*, Allen & Unwin, Sydney, 1983.
Dabscheck, B. and Niland, J.R., *Industrial Relations in Australia*, Allen & Unwin, Sydney, 1981, Ch 9.
d'Alpuget, B., *Mediator: A Biography of Sir Richard Kirby*, Melbourne University Press, Melbourne, 1977.
Evatt, H.V., 'History of federal arbitration', *Australian Quarterly*, March 1937.
Healy, B., *Federal Arbitration in Australia: An Historical Outline*, Georgian House, Melbourne, 1972.
Higgins, H.B., *A New Province for Law and Order*, Dawson, London, 1922.
Hutson, J., *Penal Colony to Penal Powers*, AEU, Sydney, 1966.
Mitchell, R. and MacIntyre, S., *Foundations of Arbitration: The Origins and Effects of State Compulsory Arbitration 1890–1914*, Oxford University Press, Melbourne, 1989.
Perlman, M., *Judges in Industry: A Study of Labour Arbitration in Australia*, Melbourne University Press, Melbourne, 1954.
Portus, J.H., *Australian Compulsory Arbitration*, Law Book Co., Sydney, 1979.

Staples, J.F., 'Conciliation and Arbitration Amendment Bill 1979', *Australian Quarterly*, December 1979.
Staples, J.F., 'Uniformity and diversity in industrial relations', *Journal of Industrial Relations*, vol. 22, no. 3, 1980.
Sykes, E.I. and Glasbeek, H.J., *Labour Law in Australia*, Butterworth, Sydney, Book 2.
Walker, K.F., *Australian Industrial Relations Systems*, Harvard University Press, Cambridge, Mass., 1970.

CHAPTER 11

National Arbitration

Federal industrial tribunals become involved in adjudicating disputes about national, industry and enterprise matters. This chapter focuses on the Commission's handling of national test cases, which are designed to provide general standards for awards. Because of their importance, these test cases are heard by Full Benches. The chapter examines the rationale of national test cases and the issues which have become the subject of test cases. These issues include hours of work; paid leave; occupational superannuation; termination, change and redundancy; and national wage determination. The chapter examines the criteria that have evolved in an attempt to find a national wage formula which is industrially acceptable, economically viable and administratively feasible. The chapter also examines national wage criteria designed to bring about equal pay between the sexes.

The rationale of national test cases

A number of problems have come to be seen as national issues requiring settlement at the national level. These include standard hours of work, annual leave, sick leave and long-service leave. They also include the minimum and national wage variations. They have become so important because changes in them affect so many awards. If a union wins some advance in one award, other unions soon want changes to their awards. Thus, one change to an award in order to settle a dispute might trigger scores of other disputes. Since it was the business of the federal tribunal to settle disputes, not to make them, it was necessary to develop some mechanism which would allow many awards to be varied simultaneously. As Mr Justice Higgins explained:

> The awards must be consistent one with the other or else comparisons breed unnecessary restlessness, discontent and industrial trouble. The advantages of system and consistency in the awards are increasingly apparent, as parties, knowing the lines on which the Court acts and understanding its practice, often now makes agreements in settlement of a dispute ... without evidence or argument.[1]

The evolution of 'system and consistency' has given rise to national test cases. These test cases are designed to obviate the many disputes associated with attempts by unions to vary all awards in an uncoordinated way which increase both industrial disputes and the tribunal's workload.

Standard hours of work

At the time of the establishment of the arbitration systems in Australia there was a general impetus towards a forty-eight-hour working week. The working week consisted of six eight-hour days. This became a norm for the federal tribunal in 1913 when Higgins J recognised it as a general standard in Australian industry.[2]

The forty-eight-hour week was again confirmed as a general standard in 1919. In some cases, however, 'where the nature of the trade required it', hours were still set as high as fifty-two per week.[3] In other cases hours of work were reduced where there were 'some strong and distinctive reasons for reductions'.[4] Such distinctive reasons included the needs of building workers 'to follow their job',[5] the rigours of underground work and work associated with smelters[6] and for women (but not men) in the clothing industry for reasons of 'health, efficiency and output'.[7] In 1919, following the tendering of medical evidence claiming that the dusty and shift work conditions of flour millers rendered them 'less healthy and more liable to infection', working hours were reduced in that industry.[8]

The major departure from this piecemeal approach took place in November 1920, by which time a royal commission in New South Wales was reviewing the forty-eight-hour working week. In the *Timber Workers'* case unions sought reduced working hours on similar grounds to the flour millers. Higgins J found 'no exceptional facts in the industry which would justify reduced working hours'.[9] Rather than dismiss the case

---

1. H.B. Higgins, *A New Province for Law and Order*, Dawson, London, 1968 (first published 1922), p. 41.
2. 7 *CAR* 228.
3. H.B. Higgins, *A New Province*, pp. 56–7.
4. 10 *CAR* 185.
5. 7 *CAR* 226.
6. 10 *CAR* 185, 11 *CAR* 636.
7. 13 *CAR* 705–6.
8. 14 *CAR* 27–8.
9. 14 *CAR* 845.

outright, however, he chose to use it as a test case to determine whether a forty-four-hour standard ought be the norm in industries which involved tending machines. The judge invited the views of employers and unions generally, as well as those of the Federal Government. In the end, the timber workers were successful in having working hours reduced. The findings of this case were also used to justify a forty-four-hour working week in the *Engineers'* case which was initiated in the same year.[10]

Concerned by the potential costs associated with any further reductions in working hours, the Hughes Government acted to restrict the ability of Higgins, or any other single member of the tribunal, from altering standard hours of work. The *Conciliation and Arbitration Act* was amended to provide that any changes to hours of work had to be considered by a Full Bench consisting of three judges. Employers were successful in appealing to a Full Bench and in having the timber workers and engineers revert to the forty-eight-hour week.[11]

The next major test case, the 'Main Hours Case', commenced in August 1926. The Full Bench gave judgment the following February. Dethridge CJ held that the conditions of employees generally in the engineering industry, 'in particular, the strain imposed by the nature of work, confinement, monotony and unremitting concentration, so affected the opportunity or capacity for a rational enjoyment of leisure as to warrant a reduction in working hours'. Using this 'leisure test', Dethridge further held that employees working under similar disadvantages in other industries might also be entitled to a reduction in working hours.[12]

This view differed from that of Lukin J, who held that a reduction in working hours was not warranted under any circumstances, and that of Beeby J who held that the forty-four-hour working week should be generally adopted subject to certain exceptions.

Following this case the forty-four-hour working week was established in the metal, glass and printing industries. However, depressed economic conditions resulted in no further successful applications between 1927 and 1933. After 1933 a large number of forty-four-hour week applications were granted, leading the Court to acknowledge in 1937 that 'the general trend in Australia is towards a uniform working week of forty-four hours.[13] By that date both the New South Wales and Queensland parliaments had provided for a forty-four-hour working week for state award employees.

The next major test case was the standard hours inquiry of 1947 to hear union applications for a forty-hour working week.[14] This case resulted in the Commonwealth, all state governments, the ACTU, thirty-seven unions and a large number of employer associations being granted

---

10. 16 *CAR* 649, 16 *CAR* 649.
11. 16 *CAR* 649.
12. 24 *CAR* 755.
13. 37 *CAR* 937.
14. 59 *CAR* 581.

leave to intervene. Unions sought to have eighty-seven awards varied to provide for a forty-hour working week. Before the Court gave its decision the New South Wales Parliament legislated for a forty-hour week and the Queensland Parliament introduced similar legislation. The Victorian Government also legislated for a forty-hour working week for its own employees. Not surprisingly, the Court held that 'no realist for a minute thinks that a rejection by the Court of these cases would bring about industrial harmony or would abate for an instant the demand for the shorter week'. The Court added:

> There is no doubt of the constitutional authority of the States to make industrial laws and to pass Standard Hours Acts . . . It would, in the constitutional circumstances, be wrong for this Court to criticize the exercise by a sovereign State of its powers, and we do not so. But it is of course very obvious that the New South Wales Act did alter very material economic and political factors and did, during the hearing of the case, present this Court with a *fait accompli* in relation to a substantial section of its industry, and to that extent did affect the freedom with which the Court might have acted. We have, as is proper, weighed these facts and they form part of the bases of our judgment.[15]

In the Basic Wage and Standard Hours Inquiry of 1952–3 private employers unsuccessfully sought a return to the forty-four-hour working week. They based their claims on the massive increase in inflation since the shorter working week was introduced in 1947.[16]

At the Basic Wage and Standard Hours Inquiry of 1961 employers sought to increase standard working hours to forty-two per week. The bases of their claims were the need to counter the balance of payments crisis then being experienced, the need to increase productivity and the need to achieve price stability. The Commission rejected the claim.[17]

From the mid-1960s unions pressed for a reduction in working hours. This was done on a sectional, rather than test case, basis. In 1970 the Coal Industry Tribunal provided for a reduction in working hours to 37.5 from August 1970 and then to thirty-five hours from 30 June, 1971. In 1972 a Full Bench of the Commission ratified an agreement in the stevedoring industry providing for a thirty-five-hour working week. Unions in the power generating industry also achieved reduced working hours. In other industries, unions had difficulty getting employer or tribunal agreement to reduced working hours.

In April 1981 the ACTU and metal unions mounted a major test case seeking a reduction in working hours to thirty-five per week. The Commission rejected the claim on the grounds of incapacity to pay. The metal unions then resorted to industrial action in support of reduced working hours. This direct action was a major factor in the abandonment of the wage indexation guidelines in July 1981. The unions were successful in getting a number of large firms to agree to reduce working

---

15. 59 *CAR* 589.
16. 77 *CAR* 477. Inflation was running at 3.8 per cent in 1947. By 1952 it had escalated to 22 per cent.
17. 97 *CAR* 376.

hours. In December 1981 negotiations between metal industry employers and unions led to an agreement to reduce working hours to thirty-eight from March 1982. The metal industry agreement established standards for negotiated award variations in a number of other industries.

In the first national wage case following the abandonment of indexation, that of May 1982, the ACTU sought to have the Commission declare the metal industry agreement a community standard. This would have provided for all awards to be varied to include the gains, including reduced working hours, resulting from the metal industry agreement. The ACTU submitted that the Commission should accept productivity bargaining as an appropriate vehicle for granting reduced working hours in those industries still working the forty-hour week. The Commission rejected this claim and reaffirmed that the 'arbitrated standard is forty hours per week and as such is not in question.[18] This decision still left it open for unions to negotiate changes in working hours with employers.

In December 1982 the Commonwealth Government requested the Commission to introduce a twelve-month wages freeze. The Commission determined that there should be a 'wages pause' for six months and directed that a 'policy of restraint should apply to any proposal for an increase in wages, salaries or allowances, reduction of hours, or improvement in other conditions of employment'. The guidelines introduced at that time provided that:

> Agreements which have been reached by this date to introduce a thirty-eight-hour week may be approved by Full Benches subject to . . . close scrutiny of labour costs. No other applications for a thirty-eight-hour week should be approved nor should any agreement or application for less than thirty-eight hours be approved.[19]

Shortly after the introduction of the 'wages pause' Labor won office. It sought a return to a centralised wages system and to indexation. In September 1983 the Commission concluded the national wage case which introduced new guidelines on wages and standard hours of work. The Commission established thirty-eight hours as a negotiated (but not arbitrated) standard. However, employees seeking a reduction in working hours from forty to thirty-eight had to provide cost offsets. Where employers opposed the claims for shorter working hours, the guidelines provided for the rejection of these claims.[20]

These guidelines remained in force until reviewed in June 1986. At this review the ACTU sought the removal of the requirement that the introduction of the thirty-eight-hour week should only be by consent. It argued that this requirement gave employers a veto right and resulted in some employers refusing to negotiate. The ACTU contended that thirty-eight hours was a general standard, and that it was inequitable to deny

---

18. ACAC, National Wage Decision, 14 May, 1982, Print E9700, p. 45.
19. ACAC, National Wage Decision, 23 December 1982, Print F1600, p. 9.
20. ACAC, National Wage Decision 23 September 1983, Print F2900, p. 31.

this standard to the small proportion of the workforce still working the forty-hour week. After hearing other claims, the Commission decided to relax the hours principle to provide that members of the Commission could arbitrate on claims seeking a thirty-eight-hour week. The principles continued to require cost offsets:

> In dealing with claims for a reduction in standard hours to thirty-eight per week, the cost impact of the shorter week should be minimized. Accordingly, the Commission should satisfy itself that as much as possible of the required cost offset is achieved by changes in work practices.[21]

The hours principles adopted in June 1986 were reaffirmed in August 1988[22] and again in August 1989.[23] In effect, these principles establish thirty-eight hours as the standard for federal awards, other than in exceptional circumstances.

Paid leave

Under the Act disputes relating to paid leave are required to be heard by a Full Bench. As in the areas of wages and hours of work, the practice has arisen of test cases to determine standards to be incorporated into awards. The role of these test cases in determining standards has been augmented by legislation designed to achieve the same end. Several forms of paid leave are considered here: annual leave, sick leave, long-service leave and maternity leave.

Annual leave

Until 1936 there were no legislative or award provisions for annual paid leave. The approach of tribunals is indicated by the Australian Workers' Union case of 1920 in which the Arbitration Court held that annual leave would not be awarded except in cases of consent by the employers or rare 'special cases'.[24]

This situation changed in 1936 when printing unions were successful in having one week paid leave inserted into the Commercial Printing Award.[25] This new benefit was extended to the Metal Trades Award in 1940.[26] Because of the benchmark role of the metal industry award, it was just a matter of time before one week paid annual leave became registered as a general community standard. This the Court did in 1941.[27]

Since that time the New South Wales or Commonwealth legislatures have set the pace and the federal tribunal has responded. In 1944 the New South Wales Parliament enacted the *Annual Holiday Act* which

---

21. ACAC, National Wage Decision, 20 June 1986, Print G3600, p. 39.
22. ACAC, National Wage Decision, 12 August 1988, Print H4000, p. 14.
23. ACAC, National Wage Decision, 7 August 1989, Print H9100, p. 24.
24. 14 *CAR* 222.
25. 36 *CAR* 738.
26. 43 *CAR* 406.
27. 44 *CAR* 178.

granted all workers in that state (excluding those working under federal awards) two weeks paid annual holidays. In the *Metal Trades Annual Leave* case of the following year the federal tribunal adopted two weeks as its annual leave standard.[28]

This remained the accepted standard until 1958. New South Wales again set the pace by amending the *Annual Holiday Act* to give state award employees three weeks paid leave. In 1960 metal unions sought to 'flow on' the New South Wales standard but the Commission resisted on the grounds of economic circumstances.[29] However, in the 1963 *Metal Trades Annual Leave* case the Commission accepted three weeks as the new standard.[30]

During the early 1970s the Commission resisted union attempts to increase the standard to four weeks. Thus, in the 1972 annual leave cases, it rejected an application for a general increase in annual leave entitlements.[31] However, the Commission's capacity to resist union claims was thwarted in the same year when the Federal Government granted its own employees four weeks annual leave. In 1974 the Commission approved an agreement by metal industry employers and unions to vary their award to provide for four weeks annual leave. The New South Wales Act was amended in the same year to provide for four weeks paid annual leave. Other state tribunals also adopted four weeks as their standard at this time.

This standard has remained intact since 1974. The only significant general variation has been the awarding of annual leave loadings to induce workers to take leave. In 1970 a stevedoring industry agreement provided for a loading of 17.5 per cent. This spread to other industries and, by consent, to the metal industry in 1972. In 1974 the Commission granted the loading by arbitration for the first time and it has since become a general standard. It has been justified on two grounds: to compensate workers for additional expenses usually incurred during holidays, and to compensate them for the unavailability of additional income while on leave (for example, lack of overtime). Employers have since unsuccessfully sought to have the loadings removed.

Sick leave

Awards of both federal and state tribunals generally provide that employees who are absent from work due to sickness or injury (other than covered by workers' compensation) are entitled to sick leave with pay. Such provisions have been a part of awards for nearly forty years. Over that period the extent and nature of sick leave provisions have not varied greatly.

Sick leave was first introduced into industrial awards in 1922. Paradoxically, this provision was to minimise costs to employers rather than

---

28. 55 *CAR* 595.
29. 96 *CAR* 206.
30. 103 *CAR* 637.
31. 144 *CAR* 528.

employees. Courts have held that under common law employees hired by the week are entitled to be paid for absences caused by sickness.[32] In order to protect employers against abuse of this common law right, the following clause was inserted into the Engineers Award: 'No employee shall be entitled to payment for non-attendance on the grounds of personal ill-health for more than six days in each year'.[33]

The six days leave equated with one week of work. One week of sick leave continued to be the entitlement for many years. It was expressed in hours rather than days. By the mid-1970s variations had been introduced to provide for increased sick leave entitlement after the first year of employment. The federal standard adopted at this time, namely forty hours of paid sick leave in to the first year and sixty-four hours in each following year, continues to provide the general industry standard. In some industries where employees are exposed to the elements and dangerous conditions, however, more generous provisions may prevail.[34]

Long-service leave

As noted in Chapter 3, where a federal award is silent on a particular matter employees are entitled to the provisions of state legislation. For many years federal awards did not provide for long-service leave. Instead, federal award employees came under provision of state legislation which, until the 1970s, was reasonably uniform. Differing lengths of leave (in most cases thirteen weeks) were provided after twenty years of service. There was further provision for leave after each additional ten years of service, and for a *pro rata* entitlement of payment or untaken leave if employment was terminated after ten years of service.

In 1964 unions in both the metal trades and printing industries made successful applications for long-service leave provisions under their federal awards.[35] In the case of the printing industry a similar application had been denied in 1959.

In both these cases the Commission adopted the standard of thirteen weeks long-service leave for fifteen years service. This was the standard adopted by amendments to the New South Wales legislation in 1963. The same standard was also adopted by other states in 1964.

The Commission has made it clear that the standards adopted in the Metal Trades (Long-service Leave) Award are intended as general standards for other federal awards. The Commission has also directed that long-service leave provisions should not be contained in general conditions awards, but rather in separate awards.

In practice, because of the high degree of uniformity between federal and state awards, not many unions have sought federal long-service leave awards. Thus, in 1989 there were only eighteen such awards.

---

32. See, for example, 1921 *AR(NSW)*44.
33. 16 *CAR* 285.
34. For example, the National Building Traces Construction Award provides for eighty hours of paid sick leave for employees with more than one year of service.
35. 106 *CAR* 412 and 108 *CAR* 740.

These covered the metal, printing, vehicle-building, space-tracking, aircraft and maritime industries. The metal industry long-service leave award continues to provide the benchmark for the other federal long-service leave awards.

In 1976 amendments were made to the previous standards. Employees became entitled to *pro rata* long-service leave after at least ten years service where employment was terminated for any reason. Further, provision was made for continuous employment with related companies to accrue leave entitlements.

Maternity leave

Since the 1970s community attitudes towards women in the workforce have changed. Changed attitudes have been reflected in both legislation and awards, and have resulted in pressure for equal pay (see below), the removal of discrimination and provision of equality of opportunity (see Chapter 16). Another result of changed attitudes (together with labour shortages in the mid-1960s) was that women were no longer required to resign on marriage and married women increasingly participated in the workforce. Similar considerations have also led to the provision of maternity leave.

A major impetus in the development of maternity leave was the Whitlam Government's 1973 *Maternity Leave (Australian Government Employees) Act*. The Act allowed generous maternity and paternity leave for employees of the federal public service or federal public authorities. In summary, the Act provided for up to fifty-two weeks leave for a pregnant employee, including up to twenty weeks leave before the birth. Provision was made for a minimum of twelve weeks paid leave. The maternity leave period was to be counted for service entitlements and public authorities could not discriminate on the ground of pregnancy. There was also provision of paid paternity leave of one week for men.

In the private sector unions did not mount a test case for a number of years and maternity leave was introduced into awards on a piecemeal basis. Thus, in 1977, the Commission inserted maternity leave provisions into the Federal Meat Industry Interim Award. This provided for maternity leave on full pay and the right to return to work without any loss of seniority.

Before the ACTU did mount a test case the Fraser Government amended the *Maternity Leave (Australian Government Employees) Act* in a number of ways. Paternity leave was completely abolished and a qualifying period of twelve months introduced before maternity leave was available. Maternity leave could not begin earlier than six weeks before the expected confinement date and periods of unpaid maternity leave (up to forty weeks) could no longer count as periods of service.

In March 1979 the Commission handed down its decision in the *Maternity Leave* case. The Full Bench supported the concept of maternity leave and provided for private sector awards to incorporate maternity leave conditions similar to those prevailing in the federal public sector. The Bench provided for a maximum of fifty-two weeks unpaid maternity leave for full-time or permanent part-time employees, including a compulsory period of six weeks immediately following confinement. Provision was made for the transfer to a 'safe job' of pregnant women until the commencement of maternity leave in cases where a doctor considered such a transfer necessary. Other entitlements, such as long-service and annual leave, are available to women on maternity leave, though not paid sick leave. The Bench determined that maternity leave would not break the continuity of service of an employee but would not be taken into account in calculating the employee's period of service or as time worked for accumulation purposes (for example, for long-service leave entitlements).

The maternity guidelines adopted in 1979 have continued to provide the basis for award provisions.

Occupational superannuation

Until recently occupational superannuation was not the subject of test cases. A number of factors accounted for this, including full employment, the old age pension and the question of the Commission's jurisdiction over superannuation disputes. The ageing population, the pressures placed on fiscal policy of age pension payouts, a decrease in job security and High Court clarification as to the Commission's jurisdictional competence have all contributed to greater community and union interest in superannuation.

In 1975 the Whitlam Government established a National Superannuation Committee of Inquiry. The Committee's recommendation for the establishment of a national government-sponsored superannuation system was rejected by the Fraser Government. Following this rejection a number of unions pressured employers into establishing or extending superannuation schemes for non-managerial employees. Unions also became actively involved in the implementation and administration of superannuation funds.

Following the return of Labor to government in 1983, the ACTU Congress called for the 'introduction of a national superannuation scheme which is non-discriminatory, portable and which provides protection against inflation'. Unions were urged to pursue, at both the national and industry levels, the extension of superannuation. The ACTU considered that the reintroduction of the centralised wages system in September 1983, and the implementation of the ACTU–ALP Accord provided a facilitative environment for the spread of superannuation. In March 1984 it proposed that 'in line with the view that national productivity increases can be shared through other than increased real incomes, consideration be given to sharing such increases through the provision of genuine superannuation entitlements'.[36]

By 1985 the ACTU had established a four-step plan for ensuring the spread of superannuation:

1. Establish the percentage of wage cost which is the workers' share in national economic growth via a national productivity case in the Commission.
2. Gain Commission endorsement that this amount may be used for bargaining for the creation of new occupational superannuation schemes and the extension and improvement of existing schemes.
3. As far as possible secure Commission endorsement for guidelines within which bargaining should occur, including criteria as to the appropriate form of superannuation schemes.
4. Secure Federal Government agreement to establish, at an appropriate time, a 'national safety-net' superannuation scheme to which employers will be required to contribute where they have failed to become party to an appropriate superannuation scheme.[37]

The signing of the Mark II Accord in September 1985 ensured Federal Government support for this plan. The government agreed to support full indexation in 1985 in return for the ACTU agreeing to defer its productivity claim until 1986.

The ACTU lodged its productivity claim at the national wage case which commenced in February 1986. By then the economy, which had shown a remarkable recovery in 1984 and 1985, had worsened and Australia's balance of payments position deteriorated drastically. This caused the government to remove its full support for superannuation. The Commission's determination, handed down in June 1985, proclaimed: 'In the present economic circumstances, there is a strong case for arguing that productivity growth for the next two years should not . . . be earmarked for distribution to wage and salary earners but as far as possible be devoted to lowering our inflation rate relative to that of our trading partners'.[38]

Despite its rejection of the 4 per cent productivity claim, the Bench did consider the ACTU's '3 per cent wage equivalent' superannuation claim. It determined not to arbitrate on any such claims but rather to 'monitor and regulate any agreements entered into either for new superannuation schemes or improvements to existing schemes'. The Commission varied the indexation guidelines to embody a new superannuation principle. Agreements and consent awards could be made which were to operate from a date to be determined by the Commission and which did not involve the equivalent of wage increases in excess of 3 per cent of ordinary time earnings of employees.[39]

Following this decision the ACTU became active in coordinating a superannuation drive consistent with the new principles. Unions

---

36. ACTU, *The Way Forward: A Positive Plan for 1984 and 1985*, ACTU, Melbourne, 1984.
37. ACTU, *ACTU Executive Decisions March 12–15*, ACTU, Melbourne, 1985.
38. ACAC, National Wage Case Decision, 26 June 1986, p. 22.
39. Ibid., p. 35.

pressed for superannuation improvements in several industries, in many cases by industrial duress. Heightened conflict over superannuation led to this being the major issue in the national wage case which began in November 1986. At this hearing the government argued the need to 'introduce superannuation in a more rational and orderly fashion, without the level of disputation seen in recent times, and in a way consistent with current economic circumstances'. It proposed that the existing principles apply, but that the Commission should be prepared to arbitrate 'on a case-by-case basis where agreements cannot be reached'.[40]

The Commission gave judgment in March 1987 and largely followed the government's proposals. It determined that, as a last resort, it was prepared to arbitrate on superannuation claims. It also determined that in 'any such arbitration the Commission will award new or improved benefits not exceeding the equivalent of 1.5 per cent of ordinary-time earnings, to operate no earlier than 1 January 1988 and no more than a further 1.5 per cent to operate no earlier than 1 January 1989'.[41]

This decision has made it likely that superannuation will 'flow' to all sections of the workforce over time, thus advancing the ACTU goal of universal superannuation coverage. The decision has also provided a basis from which unions will press for further improvements in superannuation coverage. The Accord Mark VI, negotiated between the ACTU and the Hawke Government in February 1990, commits both parties to seeking a further 3 per cent in employer contributions to employees' superannuation entitlements. This claim will be processed at future national wage cases.

Termination, change and redundancy

Rapid technological change and the increased incidence of retrenchment led to a number of cases being argued before the Commission in which unions sought to include provisions in awards for greater consultation regarding changes to work organisation and improved job security. In March 1983 the Commission enjoined three disputes to provide a national test case. In this case the ACTU sought 'significant improvements in three main situations: firstly, on termination of employment, secondly, on the introduction of change by an enterprise, and thirdly, in the event of redundancy'. These 'three situations' led to the national test case being named the *Termination, Change and Redundancy* case. In general terms the ACTU sought to establish in federal awards a right for individual employees not to be unfairly dismissed, a right for individual employees in ordinary termination of employment situations to more notice according to length of service, obligations on employers to notify and consult employees about the introduction of

---

40. ACAC, National Wage Case Decision, 10 March 1987, p. 21.
41. Ibid., p. 21.

new technology and, in redundancy situations, more notice and a right to compensation and assistance for employees made redundant.

The standard contract of employment clause in federal awards allowed an employer to dismiss an employee for any reason whatsoever on giving one week's notice. The clause did not prohibit unfair dismissals. This situation contrasted with that of the States where industrial tribunals had the power to deal with unfair dismissals and to order the reinstatement of those whose dismissal was considered harsh, unjust or unreasonable.

On the first matter, the Bench claimed that, 'subject to capacity and good conduct, it is reasonable for employees and employers to have proper and reasonable expectation of continued employment after a significant period of time which increases with the length of employment'. It added:

> Further, in our opinion the traditional week's notice of termination included in federal awards provides no practical opportunity for those who have been in a particular job for some time to adjust to the proposed change in circumstances, reorganise their lives and seek alternative employment. In particular, in current economic circumstances, one week would not provide sufficient time for many employees to find another job or for employers to find another employee.[42]

The Bench decided to increase the period of notice on the following formula:

Length of service	Period of notice
Less than one year	1 week
Between one and two years	2 weeks
Between two and four years	3 weeks
Four years or more	4 weeks

Employees over the age of 45 were entitled to an additional week's notice after two years of service. In relation to the termination of employment it was held that employers could not terminate the services of an employee 'harshly, unjustly or unreasonably'.

On the issue of consultation over change the Bench determined:

> ... we are prepared to include in an award a requirement that consultation take place with employees and their representatives as soon as a firm decision has been taken about major changes in production, program, organization, structure or technology which are likely to have significant effects on employees.
> We have decided also that the employer shall provide in writing to the employees concerned and their representatives all relevant information about the nature of the changes proposed, the expected effect of the changes on employees and any other matters likely to affect employees. However, we will not require an employer to disclose confidential information.[43]

---

42. ACAC, Termination, Change and Redundancy Case Decision, 2 August 1984, p. 19.
43. Ibid., p. 22.

The Bench further determined that employees made redundant were entitled to compensation by way of severance pay according to the following formula:

Length of service	Severance pay
Less than one year	nil
Between one and two years	4 weeks pay
Between two and three years	6 weeks pay
Between three and four years	7 weeks pay
Four years or more	8 weeks pay.[44]

This decision continues to provide the general standards for federal awards in these areas.

National wage determination

The area of wage determination has historically been one in which tribunals have sought a high degree of uniformity and consistency. The first landmark case in the movement to 'reduce conditions to system, to standardise them, to prevent irritating contrasts' was the *Sunshine Harvester* case of 1907.[45] This case, which resulted in the first federal definition of a 'living' or minimum wage, did not follow from an industrial dispute but from the operation of the *Excise Tariff Act 1906*. This Act protected Australian manufacturers from overseas dumping and competition by means of duties on imported goods. It was the intention of the Act to pass on some of the benefits of protection to employees. Unless 'fair and reasonable' wages were paid, a manufacturer would be liable to a tax which would effectively remove tariff protection from the business. In order to avoid the tax, employers had to produce a certificate showing that they paid fair and reasonable wages. One of the authorities empowered to issue such a certificate was the Commonwealth Court of Conciliation and Arbitration.[46]

The 'needs' criterion

In November 1907 Mr Justice Higgins was appointed President of the Arbitration Court. At that time 112 applications for certificates of exemption under the *Excise Tariff Act* were outstanding. Higgins decided to take one test case and apply its findings universally. Higgins chose the Sunshine Harvester Company because of its size and the large variety of occupations employed there.

The Act had in no way defined a 'fair and reasonable wage'. Higgins formulated his own criteria by attempting to estimate a 'typical' family's expenditure. He arrived at a figure of 7 shillings per working day or 42 shillings per week. In his judgment and subsequent writings, Higgins went to great lengths to justify this sum of 42 shillings as being necessary to satisfy the 'normal needs of the average employee regarded as a

---

44. Ibid., p. 49.
45. See 2 *CAR* 2.
46. Supreme Courts and state industrial authorities also had power to grant certificates of exemption.

human being living in a civilised community'. He placed great weight on the evidence which he took from a butcher, a landlord's agent and nine labourers' wives as to the actual cost of rent and food. On his own admission, these estimates resulted in a weekly expenditure of 32 shillings and 5 pence. Where, then, did the remaining 9 shillings and 7 pence come from? This extra sum compensated for all the other normal family expenditures about which Higgins had not taken evidence, including 'light, clothes, boots, furniture, utensils, rates, life insurance, savings, accident or benefit societies, loss of employment, union pay, books and newspapers, tram or train fares, sewing machine, mangle, school requisites, amusements and holidays, liquor, tobacco, sickness or death, religion or charity'.[47] Clearly, putting a money value on such a list without some sort of empirical evidence made the whole process vague. That, coupled with the loose methodology used in discovering the cost of food and lodging, might have allowed Higgins to arrive at any figure he wished. Possibly that is why he later commented: 'It is a curious fact that there has been little or no attack on the empirical findings of 1907 as to the actual cost of living'.[48]

In his judgment Higgins directed attention to 'the normal *needs* of the average employee regarded as a human being in a civilised society'. This was most important because of Higgins' insistence that his 'needs' component be an irreducible minimum:

> For this purpose it is advisable to make the demarcation as clear and definite as possible between that part of the wages which is for mere living, and that part of wages which is due to skill, or to monopoly or to other considerations. Unless great multitudes of people are to be irretrievably injured in themselves and their families, unless society is to be perpetually in industrial unrest, it is necessary to keep this living wage as a thing sacrosanct beyond the reach of bargaining.[49]

That irreducible, sacrosanct part of the wage, 'for mere living', was subsequently called the 'basic wage'. The dual wages system established by dividing wages into a component needed for 'mere living' and a component to compensate for skills and other factors survived until 1967. National wage determination over that period related, in great measure, to variations of the basic wage.

The mere establishment of the Harvester standard would not have been in itself so significant if Higgins had not used this standard in making other awards.[50] Thus, when disputing parties came before the Court, that approach helped to standardise a significant element of awards. That approach also made the skill component visible, thus making wage relativity comparisons between tradesmen simpler.

The 'needs' component of the basic wage, however, raised a further problem: if needs are to be satisfied over time the basic wage must hold

---

47. Higgins, *A New Province*, p. 3.
48. Ibid., p. 53.
49. Broken Hill case 1909, 3 *CAR*, p. 32.
50. The High Court declared the *Excise Tariff Act* invalid in 1908. It was the Sunshine Harvester Company that challenged the Act.

its real value as the cost of commodities increases. Higgins, however, had no ready means at hand of determining changes in the cost of living. Until 1920, moreover, the Act provided that awards could not be varied during their lifetime. This inevitably meant that changes in the basic wage could not be applied uniformly across awards. The first problem was solved by the production of the 'A' Series Retail Price Index (RPI) in 1912, by the newly created Commonwealth Bureau of Census and Statistics.

The second problem in establishing basic wage uniformity was removed in 1920 by amendments to the Act which allowed awards to be varied at any time. This led to what might be regarded as prototype national wage cases in 1921 and 1922. The 1921 hearing resulted from a number of applications from trade unions that the findings of the Basic Wage Royal Commission (the Piddington Commission) be declared the basic wage. The Commission had been established to inquire into the actual cost of living of an average Australian family. It concluded that the basic wage had lost approximately a third of its value since the Harvester Judgment. The Court decided that the union applications should be joined for one hearing. One advocate was to represent the unions and one for the employers.[51] Higgins rejected the Piddington Commission's findings on the grounds that it had not discovered the cost of living for unskilled workers but of a cross-section of workers whose basic wage was supplemented by margins.

The 1922 hearing brought unions and employers together again to determine the appropriate *mechanism* for future adjustment of the basic wage rate established the previous year. The judgment introduced a system of automatic quarterly adjustments of the basic wage according to movements of the RPI which continued until 1953. But although the mechanics of wage determination changed little, there were important changes in the criteria by which the basic rate was determined. The most important of these concerned the notion of 'capacity to pay'.

Capacity to pay

Although the 'needs' criteria featured prominently in Higgins' rationalisation of the basic wage level established in the *Harvester* case, he did not ignore the possible economic effect of his decision. His reference to 'reputable employers' reassured him that the wage level he established was one that the economy could sustain. Having established the Harvester standard, Higgins did not ensure that its real value was maintained. Had the 'needs' criteria been his paramount consideration, the maintenance of the real basic wage would have received more attention. In fact, it was not until Judge Powers took over the Presidency of the Court that automatic quarterly cost of living adjustments attempted to ensure the maintenance of the purchasing power of the basic wage. Powers added 3 shillings to the prevailing rate to bring the 1921 base rate

---

51. Gas Employees' case, 15 *CAR*, p. 840.

back to the value of the Harvester standard. Nevertheless, the basic wage continued to be regarded and to be promulgated as a 'living wage without any specific regard to the capacity of the economy in general to bear any particular [wage] level'.[52]

The Great Depression, however, forced a revaluation of the procedures. Thereafter the capacity of the economy to pay a given wage remained an important—at times dominant—consideration in wage adjustments. The Commonwealth revised the Act, strengthened the requirement that the Court take into account the likely economic effects of its decisions and made basic wage fixation a Full Bench matter. The government also intervened for the first time at the 1930–31 Basic Wage and Wage Reduction Inquiry. This inquiry acknowledged the usefulness of automatic quarterly cost of living adjustments but did not affirm that the basic wage standard should be an irreducible minimum.

> The 1930–31 judgment was the first to contain [the economic] exposition of a predominant principle of basic wage assessment, namely the principle that the level of wages, and of the basic wage in particular, must be such as the economy can sustain.[53]

In the following year the Court reduced the basic wage by 10 per cent on the grounds of the inability of the economy to pay the existing rate. In its decision the Court said:

> For this Court to fix a basic wage at an amount which would procure an average standard of living for wage-earners such as the Court would gladly see prevailing, would be worse than futile if the nation's income is not large enough to maintain the prescribed standard.[54]

The capacity to pay principle was given even more emphasis in 1934:

> ... whatever family unit is adopted by a wage-fixing body, the power of that body to endow that unit with any desired standard of living depends on the productive capacity of the economy as a whole ... This suggests, that the adoption of a family unit is not necessary, and what should be sought is the independent ascertainment and prescription of the highest basic wage that can be sustained by the total of industry in all its primary, secondary and ancillary forms.[55]

Subsequent basic wage decisions reaffirmed the paramount place of the capacity concept. Thus, in 1937, the Court said, '[The basic wage] is no longer related to the Harvester wage of 1907 with or without the "Powers 3s", but is assessed at the highest amount which the Court thought could be safely prescribed'. Because of the prevailing economic prosperity the Court awarded a 'prosperity loading' ranging from 4 to 6 shillings. This prosperity loading was not to be adjusted quarterly.[56]

However, while the capacity to pay criterion dominated the Court's judgment in the aftermath of the Depression, the concept of a 'living

---

52. Ibid.
53. Basic Wage and Standard Hours Inquiry 1952–53, 77 CAR, p. 489.
54. Ibid., p. 490.
55. Basic Wage Inquiry 1934, 33 CAR, p. 149.
56. Basic Wage Inquiry 1937, 37 CAR, p. 583.

wage' was not lost sight of. Further, notwithstanding the Court's continual insistence on the capacity to pay principle, the automatic adjustment of the basic wage to variations in the RPI provided a mechanism which buttressed a 'needs' view, namely that basic wage determination related to maintaining the purchasing power of that wage. The logical corollary of the capacity to pay principle was that basic wage adjustments on account of one economic index had little merit and would, sooner or later, be challenged. Automatic quarterly adjustments in relation to the RPI had an inbuilt destruction mechanism whose lesson was not fully grasped after the Depression. There was no guarantee that the basic wage produced by means of automatic quarterly adjustments was one that the economy could sustain. This problem became acute in the wool boom that resulted from the Korean War. Large price rises associated with the export trade in wool did little to increase the capacity of domestic producers to pay increased wages without themselves raising prices. An annual inflation rate of 20 per cent in the year ending June 1952 panicked the Court into dropping quarterly cost of living adjustments in 1953. Having done so, the Court was forced to seek some alternative mechanism of basic wage adjustment.

At the Basic Wage and Standard Hours Inquiry of 1952–53 the Court acceded to the employers' request that automatic quarterly cost of living adjustments be discontinued. The Court reviewed the history of the basic wage, claiming that since 1931, at least, capacity to pay had been the dominant principle invoked in determining the 'foundation wage'. This being the case, the Court saw little reason for continuing the existing system:

> The Court finds it impossible to justify the continuance of an 'automatic' adjustment system ... There is no ground for assuming that capacity to pay will be maintained at the same level or that it will rise or fall coincidentally with the purchasing power of money. In other words, the principle or basis of assessment having been economic capacity at the time of assessment, it seems to the Court altogether inappropriate to assume that the economy will continue at all times thereafter to be able to bear the equivalent of that wage, whatever may be its money terms.[57]

Economic indicators

The 1934 Basic Wage Case, which gave primacy to the capacity to pay principle, also raised one of the difficulties inherent in it: 'There is no clear means of measuring the general wage-paying capacity of the total industry of a country. All that can be done is to approximate ...'[58] Working on the assumption that, in an economy whose production was increasing, price changes were a reasonable indication of capacity to pay, the Court had used quarterly adjustments with occasional reviews to ensure that the base rate being indexed was appropriate. Following the 1953 rejection of price index changes as a useful measure of changes

---

57. Basic Wage Inquiry 1953, 77 *CAR*, p. 496.
58. Basic Wage Inquiry 1937, 33 *CAR*, p. 156.

in capacity to pay, the Court was forced to look for some more appropriate measure. The 1953 decision determined that seven indicators would in future be utilised to approximate national capacity to pay: employment, investment, production and productivity, overseas trade, overseas balance of payments, competitive position of secondary industry and retail trade indicators.

Notwithstanding union efforts to restore automatic quarterly cost of living adjustments over the next thirteen years, the Commission refused to reintroduce them. Its approach to national wage cases until 1967, when the basic wage disappeared, may be divided into two phases. From 1953 to 1960, wages were adjusted by reference to the economic indicators. After 1960 the Commission switched to a hybrid system involving annual adjustments on account of price changes with periodic reviews to take account of national productivity.

Initially the Court (and, after 1956, the Commission) conducted basic wage inquiries using the seven economic indicators as reference points. That system, while seeming to have economic merit, did little to make the Commission's assessment anything but a hazy, subjective process. Accurate measures for some indicators were difficult to find and there was an obvious inbred relationship between others that smacked of 'double-counting', which emphasised some indicators at the expense of others. Short- and long-term indicator trends gave conflicting prescriptions. Further, the Commission had little guidance as to how to weight the various indicators, particularly when different indicators showed contrary movements. Even when all indicators showed positive signs, the Commission was inhibited by the inflationary potential of its decisions. Basic wage fixation had, to a large extent, become an ill-defined, value-laden system of wage adjustment based on variables remote from the experience of workers. Little of the guesswork was taken out of the process by the introduction (in 1956) of a system of annual reviews:

> Just as an enterprise can only have its capacity assessed over a period of time and not by fits and starts according to the success or failure of a day's or a week's trading, so Australia as a trading nation can only have its capacity so assessed. A year has been found almost universally to be a sensible and practical period for such a purpose.[59]

The search for a more tangible formula that would maintain the real value of the basic wage, keep that wage within the bounds of economic capacity and reduce the amount of guesswork, resulted in the adoption of the 'prices plus productivity' approach in 1961. In the search for some measure that would encapsulate the seven economic indicators, productivity became, in effect, a surrogate for capacity to pay. This approach seemed to offer some promise of establishing the highest basic wage compatible with economic capacity while also offering some protection against inflation. Wage increases became inflationary only to the extent that their rate of increase exceeded that of national output. If

---

59. Basic Wage Case 1956, 84 *CAR*, p. 161.

wage increases could be maintained within the bounds of national productivity, economic stability was not endangered. This principle appeared to allow for wage increases, thus making it industrially acceptable; it took account of national capacity to pay, thus making it economically viable; and it rested on (apparently) simple measures and mechanisms, thus making it administratively feasible.

The 1961 approach resulted in annual reviews to take account of changes in the Consumer Price Index (CPI). Automatic wage adjustments were not provided for but the basic wage was to be adjusted in line with CPI changes 'unless [the Commission] is persuaded to the contrary by those seeking to oppose the change.'[60] In a fully employed economy the Commission was reverting to an assumption which its predecessor had denounced in 1953, namely, that changes in the price index adequately reflected changes in capacity to pay. In addition, the Commission had neatly passed on to employers the onus for showing that such a capacity did not exist. The about-turn, from post-1953 practice, was justified by the confidence that the new Consumer Price Index inspired in the Commission.

Less frequent test cases on account of productivity were to ensure that the basic wage, annually adjusted to price increases, was set at the highest level the economy could afford. Such was the theory. The practice was rather different. All the parties before the Commission agreed that the workers were entitled to a share in the fruits of productivity. The parties, however, devised separate productivity measurement formulae suiting their own interests.

The total wage

As early as 1961, the Commission had conceded that 'it may be correct that as an overall economic proposition the important and significant thing to be considered in relation to distribution of productivity increases by increased wages is the overall wages paid and not the basic wage'. However, the Commission was cautious in applying this principle since, as a member of the Full Bench reviewing the 1961 *Employers' Total Wage* case noted, the well-entrenched 'concept of the basic wage has been with us for more than fifty years, and is a well-accepted and fundamental feature of the nation's industrial, social and economic life which ... it has served well'.[61] The 1964 *Total Wage* case sought the deletion of the basic wage from Commonwealth awards and the insertion of a wage expressed as a total wage. In its unanimous decision to reject the employers' request the Commission did not entirely reject the concept. Consciously or otherwise, the Commission paved the way for the adoption of the total wage, which was accepted in principle two years later and adopted formally in 1967.

Three immediate factors aided the adoption of the total wage. First,

---

60. Basic Wage and Standard Hours Inquiry 1961, 97 *CAR*, p. 389. These words were subsequently written into the wage indexation guidelines.
61. Ibid., p. 391.

there was no universal agreement about the basic wage. To some it meant the wage of the unskilled employee, to others the lowest wage paid in each industry. Others regarded it as an assessment of a family wage. The Act saw it as part of a wage fixed without regard to the work undertaken; the Commission as the highest universal foundation wage the economy could afford.

A second contributing factor was the blurring of the distinction between the basic and secondary wage for adjustment purposes. The secondary wage (margins) had represented 'a payment awarded above the basic wage for the skill, qualifications and experience required and the arduousness and other like factors involved'. Since skills, qualifications, arduousness and other factors could be expected to vary from occupation to occupation, variation in margins could be expected in different awards. Further, since the skill, experience and training required were not constant, because of technological change, movement of some margins vis-à-vis others could be expected. After World War II it became increasingly common to vary all margins simultaneously, by using the Metal Trades Award as a test case. Thus, this element of wages, which was supposed to allow for industrial and occupational peculiarities and differences, was increasingly determined uniformly through national test cases. Furthermore, those variations of margins increasingly came to be adjusted according to the criteria used in basic wage cases. By 1965 the Commission was seeking to establish what the highest margin possible was, given the capacity of the economy.

The third significant factor was the hearing by the one Bench of both the basic wage inquiries and margins test cases, in 1965 and 1966. Since both wage elements were adjusted in a similar manner, the next obvious step was to determine them simultaneously.

By 1966, the Commission had adopted the total wage in principle. The establishment of the minimum wage in that year provided a continuing means of protecting low-income earnings. The official adoption of the total wage in 1967 was thus a formality.

The movement towards wage indexation

Following the adoption of the total wage in 1967 the Commission envisaged a system in which the total wage would be annually reviewed on general economic grounds. The mechanism of using the Metal Trades Award as the test award continued with some minor modifications. However, in a period of full employment and accelerated inflation, unions became less reliant on annual national wage cases and turned to other ways of obtaining wage increases, particularly industry award variations, work value cases, consent agreements and over-award bargaining. Direct bargaining for pay increases outside the Commission was encouraged by the success of direct action in defeating the penal provisions in 1969 and in frustrating the Commission's attempt to absorb over-award payments in the Metal Trades Award Work Value Inquiry.

National wage pronouncements by the Commission increasingly became preoccupied with the size of wage increases outside the national wage cases. A 3 per cent increase in the total wage in 1969 did not arrest this flow. Neither did the massive 6 per cent increase of the following year. By the 1971–2 national wage case the Commission was voicing alarm:

> Since [1969] there has been a strong and general growth in federal awards and salaries occurring outside national wage cases and in many instances apparently without regard to what was said in those cases ... Whereas the Commission in 1967 was hopeful that the introduction of total wages and annual reviews would bring about greater flexibility and industrial justice, a continuance of what has occurred may require a new approach.[62]

The Commission decided that 'when examining the economic situation, particularly movements in prices and productivity and future trends in productivity, we should have regard to wages and salary movements which have occurred since the national wage case.[63] But that restraint by the Commission only produced greater activity in direct bargaining. The Full Bench gradually lost control over wage-fixing to the point at which national wage case decisions contributed only a small fraction of the overall increase in wage levels. Whereas in the five years preceding the introduction of the total wage, national reviews (basic wage and margins) contributed 85 per cent to award wage increases, in 1967–8 the national wage case contributed only 39.5 per cent. This proportion fell to 28 per cent in 1972–3 and to only 19 per cent in 1973–4.

That movement away from the Commission caused severe economic dislocation. Average earnings increased by 28 per cent for the year ending the first quarter of 1975 and inflation accelerated to 17.7 per cent. Unemployment increased to 5 per cent of the workforce and, notwithstanding massive Labor Government relief measures, showed signs of becoming even worse. Company profits fell from their historic level of 15 per cent of GDP to 11 per cent. Investment slumped. Industrial disputes increased markedly as unions became increasingly concerned with the maintenance of wage relativities. Pressures emerged for some wage determination mechanism which would solve 'the problem of ... the three-tiered wage system whereby the overall movements may come from national wage cases, industry cases and over-award payments'.[64] The mechanism that emerged from the search was wage indexation.

Indexation

Until the introduction of the total wage and the decline in importance of national wage cases, it could be claimed that the Commission was able to impose a wages policy on unions. It successfully sought to control the level of wage increases to ensure that they were compatible with other

---

62. NWC, 1971–2, 143 *CAR*, p. 303.
63. Ibid.
64. National Wage Case Decision, March 1974, 157 *CAR* 307.

economic goals, particularly low levels of inflation and unemployment. Because increases in earnings were dominated by award determination, and because award determination in turn was dominated by national wage cases, the Commission had a lever whereby it could regulate wages in such a way as to ensure that they were with a moderate rate of inflation.[65]

Following the breakdown of its authority from 1967 and the consistent loss of importance of national wage cases as a major source of wage increases, the Commission lost its ability to regulate wages. Unions had demonstrated an ability to operate outside the system and the Commission had lost any enforcement powers it may have had. In such a context it was not possible to institute a wages policy simply because unions were in a position to frustrate such a policy. Not unreasonably, unions argued that if there were to be controls placed on the earnings of unionists, then controls should also be placed on prices and other forms of income. Wage indexation was initially conceived as part of an incomes policy whereby both wage and non-wage forms of income would be regulated. In addition to the Commission's role of regulating wages through a system of indexation, the Labor Government also promised complementary 'supporting mechanisms'. These included the use of the Prices Justification Tribunal to ensure that excessive prices were not charged by certain dominant companies; the observance of the indexation principles in the federal public sector, which at that time had been a pace-setter in employment conditions; government attempts to encourage uniformity and consistency from the multiplicity of state and federal industrial tribunals; intervention in industry cases where necessary to ensure that the parties would not enter into consent agreements in defiance of the indexation guidelines; and ensuring that the other economic policy instruments—fiscal, monetary and external instruments—were compatible with the needs of indexation. During the December 1975 elections tax indexation was added to the list of supporting mechanisms. It can be seen that as a form of incomes policy wage indexation placed as much restraint and commitment on the government as it did on the other parties.

To some extent, the introduction of indexation in 1975 marked a return to the system of wage fixation abandoned in 1953. Automatic quarterly cost-of-living adjustments (ACOLA) had regularly adjusted a significant element of wages (i.e. the basic wage component) to movements of a price index. However, even when the structure of the total wage was taken into account, the wage indexation package was qualitatively different from the ACOLA system. The guidelines established under the indexation principles extended to the other wage tiers—industry awards and over-award payments—which the ACOLA system did not attempt to regulate. Further, unlike the ACOLA system of 1921–53, indexation necessitated overt support from the government if its

---

65. See D. Whitehead, 'The economic crisis in Australia: a non-monetarist view', paper presented to Conference of Economists, Hobart, 1977, mimeograph.

income policy attributes were to be effective. As a minimum wage adjustment mechanism, the ACOLA system was not dependent on government support.

The indexation principles

In administering indexation the Commission set out a number of guidelines which were amended in the light of experience and changing circumstances. These guidelines regulated the periodicity of adjustments, the choice of wage level to be adjusted and the choice of the price index. They also governed the handling of anomalies, allowances, changes in work value and the making of first awards. The original principles set out in April 1975 were revised in May 1976, September 1978, April 1980 and January 1981. The following section summarises the major elements of the indexation principles in the period to July 1981.

Under each set of guidelines the Commission allowed itself enough flexibility to determine the form of indexation in the light of circumstances and the submissions of the parties. After experimenting with plateau indexation between 1976 and 1978 the principles committed the Commission to uniform (though not full) percentage wage adjustments unless very special circumstances existed. This change in approach was a recognition by the Commission of the importance of maintaining existing wage relativities. Its interference with a wage structure which had been accepted as reflecting appropriate wage differentials became a major cause of discontent. The final set of principles (January 1981) established a system whereby the first case in each year would, fairly automatically, grant a wage increase based on 80 per cent of price movements. The residual 20 per cent of the Consumer Price Index (CPI) movement, together with the ensuing six months CPI movement, were to be the subject of a longer second national wage case.

In its original form, the principles committed the Commission to quarterly indexation. In 1978 the principles were changed to provide for six-monthly indexation with hearings in the months of April and October.

The Consumer Price Index was not designed as a measure of the cost of living. Nonetheless its historical use for national wage determination and its industrial acceptability made it the obvious first choice as the price index for wage indexation purposes. A working party was established by the government to devise a more appropriate index. However, this task proved to be very difficult and because of the lack of any common agreement the major parties to national wage cases concurred with the use of the CPI. The form adopted by the Commission was that of the Six Capitals Consumer Price Index. The use of this index had the potential for distorting real earnings from city to city. Employees in cities with CPI increases less than that of the Six Capitals CPI were entitled to real wage increases while the converse was true of other employees. However, the alternative of adjusting wages in relation to the CPIs of the different capital cities would have led to wage relativity problems since employees with similar award classifications would have received varying rates of pay increases according to where they lived.

The establishing of a *prima facie* link between price adjustment and wage movements gave substance to the term 'Indexation'. Such a system ensured the maintenance, or near maintenance, of real wages. In addition to claims for the maintenance of real wages, another consideration at national wage cases has been to ensure that they provide a wage level which is the highest the economy can afford. Earlier in the chapter we reviewed the relevant developments in this area and the use of productivity as a surrogate of economic capacity to pay. The indexation principles provided that 'Each year the Commission [would] consider what increase in total wage or changes in conditions of employment shall be awarded nationally on account of productivity'. Although the guidelines provided for productivity reviews in the period 1975–81, no such cases were held. The ACTU did lodge a claim following the September 1975 national wage case but it was subsequently withdrawn.

The indexation guidelines also provided for wage increases on account of changes in work value. These were defined as 'changes in the nature of work, skill and responsibility required or the conditions under which the work ... [was] performed'. Although the wording of this principle was modified during the course of indexation in order to prevent it from becoming a general vehicle for wage increases, its intention remained the same, namely, to compensate employees for demonstrable changes in the nature of work undertaken. Despite the attempts of the Commission to limit this principle to discrete areas and occupations, a 'work-value wage round' flowed through the system between 1978 and 1980. During this period, a supposedly restrictive and selective principle was transformed into a mechanism for a generalised wage increase.

It was recognised that some mechanism should be provided for resolving disputes over anomalies and other problems which were not capable of being processed under the other principles. Where anomalies or special problems arose, the President of the Commission had the power to refer such matters to a Full Bench for resolution.

One issue that troubled the Commission was the use of comparative wage justice to initiate wage claims.[66] The Commission feared that the use of this nebulous criterion could involve it in hearing a large number of claims which were not based on price or productivity movements. In an attempt to overcome this the Commission introduced the notion of 'inequities' in 1978. Inequities were to be processed in the same way as anomalies and special problems. These were defined to exist where 'employees performing similar work were paid dissimilar rates of pay without good reason'. To prevent inequities becoming a vehicle for widespread wage increases the principle was severely restricted. Four

---

66. Comparative wage justice is the notion that employees who perform the same work should receive the same pay irrespective of where they are employed. If wage increases are granted to one group in the workforce, significant pressures often emerge for a flow-on to other groups on the grounds of maintaining relativities, fairness and equity.

overriding considerations were to apply: the increases sought had to be justified on their merits; there was to be no likelihood of flow-on; the costs were to be negligible and the increases were to be a once-only matter.

Indexation operated between April 1975 and July 1981, during which time eighteen national wage cases were heard. By 1981, however, the pressures on the system were so great that the Commission decided to abandon it. The wage decisions under indexation can be found in Table 11.1.

Decentralisation and the return of indexation

Indexation collapsed in large measure because of the lack of government support following the defeat of Labor in December 1975. The Fraser Government removed the supporting mechanisms which formed a part of the 1975 package, consistently argued for 'zero indexation' and fuelled inflation by way of 'policy-induced' price rises. Paradoxically,

Table 11.1: *Wage adjustments under wage indexation, March quarter 1975 to December/March quarters 1981*

	Quarter		Wage variation	CPI variation
1975	March	Full	3.6%	3.6%
	June	Full	3.5%	3.5%
	September	None		0.8%
	December	Full	0.8% + 5.6%	5.6%
1976	March	Full	3.0% to $125 p.w.	3.0%
		Flat	$3.80 thereafter	
	June	Full	2.5% to $98 p.w.	2.5%
		Flat	$2.50, $98–$166 p.w.	
		Partial	1.5% thereafter	
	September	Full	2.2%	2.2%
	December	Flat	$2.90 for Medibank	6.0%
		Partial	2.8% to $100 p.w.	
		Flat	$2.80 thereafter	
1977	March	Partial	1.9% to $200 p.w.	2.3%
		Flat	$3.80 thereafter	
	June	Partial	2%	2.4%
	September	Partial	1.5%	2.0%
	December	Partial	1.5% to $170 np.w.	2.3%
		Flat	$2.60 thereafter	
1978	March	Full	1.3%	1.3%
	June/Sept	Full	4%	4.0%
1979	Dec/March	Partial	3.2%	4.0%
	June/Sept	Partial	4.5%	5.0%
1980	Dec/March	Partial	4.2%	5.2%
	June/Sept	Partial	3.7%	4.7%
1981	Dec/March	Partial	3.6%	4.5%

Source: ACAC, National Wage Decisions.

the government continued to argue for the retention of indexation at the many wages conferences which were held during this period. But by the time indexation was finally abandoned in 1981 the government was openly espousing a decentralised approach to wage determination. Its rationale was that under a decentralised bargaining system varying market pressures for the products of different industries would result in wages being determined accordingly. It also considered that under a decentralised approach there would be a reduction in the rate of wage increases.

The brief period of decentralisation (August 1981 to December 1982) would suggest that the short-term outcome was not the expected one. In December 1981 unions and employers in the metal trades industry entered a twelve-month agreement which established a (costly) standard for other industries. They provided for an immediate 11.9 per cent wage increase with a further 5.7 per cent increase on 1 July 1982. Standard hours of work were reduced from forty to thirty-eight per week and supplementary payments of $9 a week and tool allowances of a similar magnitude were provided for. Metal industry unions made an undertaking that they would not press for any further claims during the twelve-month period.

This agreement provided a standard which flowed through to other industries. At the May 1982 national wage case, in which the Full Bench supported the Commonwealth's claim for a retention of the decentralised approach, the ACTU presented evidence of the spread of the 'metal industry standard'. It established that more than 80 per cent of employees covered by the sixty largest federal and the ten largest state awards in each state had received the first round of the metal industry agreement. These 120 awards covered nearly half the total workforce. Subsequent ACTU surveys showed that the second round—the mid-term adjustment—was also widespread. By December 1982, when the metal industry agreement was ready to be renegotiated, only one of the federal awards and five of the state awards had not received the mid-term adjustment.

Demonstrating its apparent loss of faith in the decentralised market approach, the government legislated for a twelve-month wage freeze for its employees in December 1982. At the same time it asked the Commission to impose a similar freeze on the private sector. The Commission imposed a six-month 'pause' which was to be reviewed in June 1983. By then Labor had been returned to office and, as part of its social accord (see Chapter 10) it sought the reintroduction of indexation. In September 1983 the Commission awarded full indexation (4.3 per cent) for price movements in the March and June quarters of that year. At the same time the Full Bench brought down a new set of guidelines which built upon the experience of 1975–81.

The first national wage case under these guidelines concluded in April 1984 and resulted in the awarding of full indexation. Further cases concluded in April 1985, November 1985 and June 1986 likewise awarded full indexation. However, by the end of 1986 a deterioration in economic conditions forced the Commission to move away from indexation and to abandon its guidelines. International competition (resulting from the reduction of tariff protection) had also led to a concern for the removal of restrictive work practices and award restructuring. The latter is the concern of Chapter 13.

Equal pay

The national minimum or basic wage has been the principal national issue in the Australian system of industrial relations. Until recently that minimum was the male minimum. Over recent years, however, under the pressure of state legislation, the Commission has been forced to take up the question of equal pay for women workers.

Since the original basic wage was regarded as a family living wage and since marriage was regarded as the 'usual fate of adult men', women were not thought to need as much money as men.[67] Thus in the *Rural Workers'* case 1912, Higgins refused 'equal pay for equal work' and established two principles which provided precedents for the new Arbitration Court. First Higgins did grant equal pay to those occupations where men could be driven out by cheaper female labour.[68] In relation to other women Higgins claimed that, while women had to find their own food, shelter and clothing, they did not have to support a family. Accordingly, he granted women only a proportion (66 per cent in the case of process workers) of the male rate.

In the *Theatrical* case 1917, Mr Justice Powers summed up the philosophy which was to dominate the Court (and the Commission) for the next half century:

> I think it only right to mention that this Court has, since 1912, laid down that women and men should be paid equal wages if women are employed to do a man's work—or where the work done by a woman is of as great a value as the man's work. It is only where the work in question is woman's work—suitable work for women—that the Court awards what it considers the value of the work as women's work; or if the value is less than a living wage for a woman then it allows a living wage for a week's work. This Court allows to men a living wage based on the assumption that the average man has to keep a wife and family of three children whatever the value of the work he does may be. The Court allows a living wage to a woman as a single woman. The single man often gets more than his work is worth, but if single men are paid less than married men the cheaper labour would be employed and they would not make the necessary provisions for marriage.[69]

In 1919 the female basic rate was determined at 54 per cent of the male basic rate.[70] Notwithstanding the shift from the needs to the capacity to pay approach in fixing the male basic wage, this ratio was maintained

---

67. Higgins, *A New Province*, p. 5.
68. See also Clothing Trade Case 1919, 13 *CAR* 702.
69. 11 *CAR* 145–6.
70. Clothing Trades Case 1919.

until the Women's Employment Board took over the task of administering female pay during World War II. The Board fixed female rates (i.e. basic wage and margins) at between 75 and 100 per cent of the male rate. Most women were awarded 90 per cent of the male rate.[71]

The Arbitration Court took back the Board's jurisdiction in relation to female wage fixation in 1944. It assessed the female basic wage for the first time in the 1949–50 basic wage inquiry and set it at 75 per cent of the male basic wage.[72]

This ratio survived until the *Equal Pay* Case of 1969, at which the Commission agreed to introduce equal pay for equal work in four stages:

Date of operation	Amount of female rate
1 October 1969	85 per cent of male rate
1 January 1970	90 per cent of male rate
1 January 1971	95 per cent of male rate
1 January 1972	100 per cent of male rate[73]

Some unions were disappointed and critical of the gradual phasing in of equal pay. They had even greater cause for complaint at the final outcome of the exercise: only 18 per cent of women in the workforce had received equal pay as the result of this equal pay decision.[74] Given the nature of the exercise—equal pay for equal work—such an outcome might have been expected for several reasons. First, precisely what constituted 'equal work' was not defined and by no means clear. In many occupations employers could claim that a sex differential in pay resulted from 'unequal work' (for example, increased responsibility or heavier physical exertion). More importantly, the historical existence of sex pay differentials had resulted in some work processes being exclusively the province of female workers since added costs were imposed in employing men to do work women were capable of doing. In such cases it was difficult to implement any equal pay for equal work concept since no basis for comparing equal work existed. This was not helped by the equal pay principles which stated that 'equal pay should not be provided by application ... where the work in question is essentially or usually performed by females but is work upon which male employees may also be employed'. Thus major areas of female employment—nursing, banking, secretarial services, retailing, kindergarten teaching, hairdressing, air hostessing, etc.—were effectively excluded from any gains as the result of the 1969 equal pay decision. A further limiting factor was that in areas where both men and women did the same work (and thus the equal pay for equal work formula had direct application) the existence of a *male* minimum wage sometimes resulted in equal award rates

---

71. Hutson, *Six Wage Concepts*, p. 115.
72. Basic Wage Inquiry, 1949–50, 68 *CAR* 689 ff.
73. Equal Pay Case 1969, 127 *CAR* 1159.
74. Equal Pay Case 1972, 147 *CAR* 177.

rather than equal pay rates being established. This happened in those awards where particular award classification rates were set below the male minimum wage. The Commission had continued to differentiate between the minimum wage for men and women claiming that the former took into account family considerations.[75] In some awards the male minimum wage was higher than the rate set for some lower job classification which had now been stripped of any sex differentiation. In the Metal Trades Award, for example, the award rate for process workers was 60 cents less than the male minimum wage. This resulted in about 30 000 female workers receiving less than full male parity.[76]

The Equal Pay Case of 1972 resulted in the adoption of the new principle of 'equal pay for work of equal value', that is, 'the fixation of award rates by consideration of the work performed irrespective of the sex of the worker'.[77] This principle required that female rates be determined by work comparisons without regard to the sex of the employees concerned. In this respect the Commission claimed that:

> ... the gap between the level of male and female rates in awards generally is greater than the gap, if any, in the comparative value of work performed by the two sexes because rates for female classifications in the same award have generally been fixed without a comparative evaluation of work performed by males and females'.[78]

This requirement made it possible to compare the work value of predominantly female classifications (for example, typists) with mixed or predominantly male classifications of related areas of work (for example, clerks and administrative assistants).

In addition, provision was made for intra-award work value comparisons:

> ... where the work is performed exclusively by females, it may be necessary to take into account comparisons of work value between female classifications within the award and/or comparisons of work value between female classifications in different awards. In some cases comparisons with male classifications in other awards may be necessary'.[79]

This provision was significant in that it allowed for work performed exclusively by women (for example, air hostesses) to be compared on a work value basis with male classifications in awards having some work affinity (for example, stewards on ships). Again, because of economic considerations, the new principle was phased in, resulting in full parity by 30 June 1975. This new principle has gone some way to removing pay differentials between the sexes. There are still problems, however. In some instances because of union and management opposition to women doing some work, they are denied access to the better-paid classifications within awards. The purpose of anti-sex-discrimination legislation is to

---

75. Ibid., 176.
76. Hutson, *Six Wage Concepts*, p. 127.
77. Equal Pay Case 1972, 147 *CAR* 179.
78. Ibid.
79. Ibid., 180.

limit that sort of situation. The sex differential in minimum wage fixation was finally removed in the 1974 national wage case when the Commission decided that 'a strong case had been made for acceding to the claim for equal treatment of adult male and female workers in respect of the minimum wage ... [demonstrating] not only widespread and deep social support but also the economic viability of the concept'.[80]

Although the 1972 *Equal Pay* case went a long way in removing unequal award rates of pay there are claims that a lack of wage parity continues to exist. In the *Comparable Worth* case of 1986, the Council of Action for Equal Pay argued that the principle of equal pay for work of equal value had not been implemented in the rates of pay for nurses because nursing is a predominantly female occupation for which rates had been set with an historical gender bias based on the needs concept. In the Council's view, the work of nurses and of other female-dominated occupations has traditionally been undervalued for this reason. It argued that the gender bias should be eradicated, and that this could only be achieved by the implementation of the concept of comparable worth.

The Commission found difficulty in both the concept of comparable worth and in its application to Australian conditions. In rejecting the claim it noted, *inter alia*:

> It is clear that comparable worth and related concepts, on the limited material before us, have been applied differently in a number of countries. At its widest, comparable worth is capable of being applied to any classification regarded as having been improperly valued, without limitation on the kind of classification to which it is applied, with no requirement that the work performed is related or similar. It is capable of being applied to work which is essentially or usually performed by males as well as to work which is essentially or usually performed by females. Such an approach would strike at the heart of long-accepted methods of wage fixation in this country and would be particularly destructive of the present wage fixing system. The countries to which we were specifically referred in which the doctrine is applied, namely Canada, the United States of America and the United Kingdom, have very different industrial relations backgrounds from our own. In addition, different approaches have been taken to the doctrine in each of these countries ... in our view the use of the term comparable worth in the Australian context would lead to confusion, and in particular, we believe that it would be inappropriate and confusing to equate the doctrine with the 1972 principle of equal pay for work of equal value. For all these reasons we specifically reject the notion.[81]

Summary

Certain conditions of employment have come to be determined by way of national test cases. The decisions handed down in such cases serve as a guide to all the parties and establish general standards. Because of the

---

80. National Wage Case Decision, March 1974, 157 *CAR* 293.
81. Comparable Worth Case 1984, Print G2250.

importance of such cases they are conducted by Full Benches of the Commission. In practice, the general standards are established by a mixture of legislative and Full Bench processes.

An area in which the Commission has become the dominant tribunal, and one whose decisions tend to be followed by other tribunals, is in that of wage determination. In evolving general wage standards the Commission has institutionalised a number of criteria such as needs, capacity to pay, real wage maintenance and wage equity. Such criteria have reflected not merely prevailing economic forces, but also social and normative forces. Political factors are also important. The ways in which governments have sought to control wages indicate the political nature of national wage cases. In trying to formulate effective wage determination mechanisms the Commission must not only walk the tightrope between industrial feasibility and economic viability but must also satisfy the requirements of political acceptability. The latter determines the degree of support for the Commission's approach and whether or not that approach will form part of an incomes or wages policy.

Discussion questions

1. What is the rationale for having national test cases?
2. The Act requires that certain matters be determined by Full Benches. What matters are required to be heard by a Full Bench? Why?
3. Explain the significance of the 1969, 1972 and 1974 test cases in bringing about wage parity between women and men.
4. Discuss the contention that legislation has been more influential than industrial tribunals in unions' efforts to reduce standard hours of work.
5. Until relatively recently federal awards did not make provision for long-service leave. How do you explain this phenomenon?
6. An employer is considering the introduction of major new technology which is likely to lead to a marked reduction in staff. What are the obligations of the employer towards the company's employees and their unions?
7. Evaluate the contention that the 1907 basic wage was a 'needs' wage.
8. Discuss the statement: 'In national wage cases the Commission has sought that magical formula which would be industrially acceptable, economically viable and administratively feasible.'
9. What is meant by 'capacity to pay'? What methods has the Commission used over the years to determine national capacity to pay? How successful have these measures been?
10. In what ways did the indexation of wages between 1922 and 1953 differ from that under wage indexation between 1975 and 1981?

Further reading

Dabscheck, B. and Niland, J.R., *Industrial Relations in Australia*, Allen & Unwin, Sydney, 1981, Chapter 11.
Higgins, H.B., *A New Province for Law and Order*, Dawson, London, 1968 (first published 1922).
Hughes, B., *Exit Full Employment*, Angus & Robertson, Sydney, 1980.
Hutson, J., *Six Wage Concepts*, AEU, Sydney, 1971.
McGavin, P.A. 'The introduction of wage indexation under the Whitlam Government', *Journal of Industrial Relations*, vol. 27, no. 1, 1985.
Niland, J.R. (ed.), *Wage Fixation in Australia*, Allen & Unwin, Sydney, 1986.
Plowman, D.H., *Wage Indexation: A Study of Australian Wage Issues 1975–1980*, Allen & Unwin, Sydney.
Short, C., 'Equal pay—what happened', *Journal of Industrial Relations*, vol. 28, no. 3, 1986.
Thornton, M., '(Un)equal pay for work of equal value', *Journal of Industrial Relations*, vol. 23, no. 4, 1981.

CHAPTER 12

Industry Award Determination

The last chapter looked at the role of the Full Bench in determining national issues. This Chapter looks at industy-level disputes. Generally, unless they are referred to a Full Bench on the grounds of the public interest, industry disputes are handled by Commissioners from an appropriate Panel.

Most industry disputes are "paper" disputes created for the sake of making and varying awards. An account of the processes of award making is, therefore, essential to an understanding of party interaction and dispute resolution at the industry level. Before explaining these processes, this chapter looks at the nature of industry awards and award proliferation at the workplace. Awards are classified into parent or main awards and dependent or secondary awards. The use of the ambit log of claims in creating disputes is examined along with the mechanisms used to resolve them. Over-award payments and roping-in awards are also briefly examined, as well as the content of awards. Having seen the *processes* employed in award making the second part of the chapter reviews the criteria or *principles* determining award conditions. This is done through an examination of the criteria used in secondary wage determination.

Types of award
Industry and occupational awards

In any one industry many awards will be in force concurrently, depending on the number of unions represented. Often, however, in most industries, one award covers the bulk of employees. Such awards are industry awards, not in the sense that they are restricted in application to any one industry, but rather in the sense that the occupational classifications covered by the award are found mainly in one industry. Thus, the Graphic Arts Award, the Pastoral Award, the Transport Workers' Award and the Metal Industry Award are industry awards in the sense that printing employees, shearers, truck drivers and metal fabricators come under these awards respectively, and in the sense that the occupational classifications of most employees in each of these industries are catered for in each award. However, none of these awards is restricted to its parent industry. Thus a truck driver working for a building firm (rather than a transport firm) will come under the Transport Workers' Award and not a building industry award. The rates of a shearer shearing sheep at an Australian Expo stand will be determined by the Pastoral Award rather than, say, a tourist or entertainment industry award. Similarly the conditions of a maintenance welder working in a brewery will be set by the Metal Industry Award rather than the Liquor Trades Award.

There is, nonetheless, a proliferation of awards within industries, partly because of the multiplicity of craft union awards, such as the Carpenters and Joiners' Award, the Plumbers and Gasfitters' Award and the Professional Engineers' Award. As with the so-called 'industrial' unions, members of 'craft' unions will usually work under the provisions of their own awards irrespective of the industry in which they are employed. Thus, with very few exceptions, awards tend to be occupationally rather than industrially based. The usual situation in most industries is that the bulk of manual workers come under the main award for each industry. Other manual workers, such as maintenance and service employees, will be thinly spread over many unions, each having its own award or, in some instance, some form of consolidated maintenance award. Supervisory, clerical, professional, administrative and management staff will also come under a range of awards, agreements and union coverage.

The brewery industry provides a good example of the pattern of award coverage. One Sydney brewery employs nearly 1500 award workers in manual and non-manual areas. Of the 1200 manual workers, 900 belong to the 'industry' union (the Federated Liquor and Allied Industries Employees' Union) and come under the provisions of the Liquor Trades (Breweries) Award. Two-thirds of the remaining 300 manual workers belong to two unions, one covering boiler stokers and attendants, the other the maintenance of metal kegs. Each of these unions has its own award. The remaining 100 employees are dispersed among twelve other unions and, until recently, came under the provisions of eleven awards. The consolidation of a maintenance employees' agreement for some unions has reduced the number of maintenance awards to six. In the non-manual area there is a similar pattern. The bulk of these 300 employees belong to the Federated Clerks' Union and come under the Clerks' (General) Award. However, the thirty or so who do not come under this award are represented by five unions, each of which has its own award.

Single-employer and multi-employer awards

Until recently most awards were multi-employer awards, that is, they applied across an industry or calling rather than to a particular company or enterprise. Both unions and employer associations found it easier to administer fewer standardised awards. Employers usually opted for multi-employer bargaining in an attempt to ensure that their labour costs were no greater than those of their competition. The federal tribunal's concern with comparative wage justice pressures led it to prefer common awards. In the state systems the application of the common rule ensured a high degree of standardisation.

Recent pressures on the award system, which are discussed in Chapter 13, have given rise to an increase in the number of single employer awards. This is evident from Table 12.1. It will be seen from this Table that in 1954 single-employer awards accounted for only 12 per cent of all awards. This proportion increased to 35 per cent in 1974 and 39 per cent in 1987. By the last date single-employer awards accounted for 55 per cent of private sector federal awards. This trend is likely to continue in the future (see Chapter 13).

Primary and secondary awards

In any industry or occupation there is usually one primary (parent) award. The parent award is usually the pace-setting award for the industry, and secondary awards tend to move in sympathy with it. Thus in journalism, the parent award is the Journalists' (Metropolitan Daily Newspaper) Award, which establishes employment conditions for journalists working on dailies in the state capital cities. A further thirty-one federal awards relate to other journalists working on other newspapers and periodicals. Those awards particularly take into account specific employment peculiarities, such as: locality (Provincial Non-daily Newspaper Award, Regional Daily Newspaper Award); the type of work (Television Award, Commercial Broadcasters' Award); the

Table 12.1: *Single-employer and multi-employer federal awards, 1954–87**

	Private sector		Public sector	Total
	Multi-employer	Single employer		
1954	176	35	90	301
1974	320	256	155	731
1987	405	496	366	1 267

*Excludes single issues and coping-in awards
Source: M. Rimmer, 'Enterprise and industry awards', in Business Council of Australia, *Enterprise-based Bargaining Units: A Bettter Way of Working*, BCA, Melbourne, 1989.

company (Maxwell Newton Pty Ltd Award, Thomson Publications Award); nationality (Foreign Language Award, Jewish Newspapers' Award); agents (Australian Associated Press Agreement, Press Agencies Award); and newspapers (*Canberra Times* Award, *The Independent* Award). The parent award established the standards for the secondary awards which then also take into account the distinctive features of particular situations.

The pattern of parent and dependent awards in journalism is typical of other areas. Thus, there are more than twenty-nine (federal) awards for pilots and flight crew, eight for bank officers, sixteen in the vehicle building industry, more than forty in the truck transport industry, thirty for storemen and packers, twenty-five for clerks, and twelve for the liquor trade industry. Excluding long-service leave awards, federal multi-employer awards may be divided into some fifty to sixty main awards and about three hundred secondary awards.

The existence of parent and dependent awards simplifies the study of award-making and variation since award movements for an industry or occupation largely follow movements in the parent award. The study is further simplified by the very strong links (relativities) among awards, particularly in the area of wages. Very few awards are *sui generis*, that is, not able to be classified with others, because the substantive content of most awards is determined in relation to some benchmark. In areas such as margins for skill, movements in this award have come to influence general wage movements. The Metal Trades Award and, since 1971, the Metal Industry Award have been used as national test cases. Gains in those awards have been transmitted to other awards by way of the 'shunter's law':

> Wages and salaries in Australia tend to move by what may be called 'the shunter's law' or the law of transmitted shock. An upward pressure is generated in one section or location in the economy and rapidly moves with a series of successive thrusts, through other sections or territories... These upward pressures commence in one State, or with margins for skill, or an Arbitration Court decision such as for engineers and then reverberate quickly through other areas.[1]

Award fragmentation and consolidation

Award fragmentation refers to the process whereby industry awards, or multi-employer awards, have the number of respondents reduced as different employers come under the provision of separate awards. The increase in the number of enterprise awards recorded earlier in this chapter has, in large measure, been the result of the breaking up of industry awards into single company or enterprise awards.

Award fragmentation has accelerated since 1970. In 1976 a survey indicated that in the period 1970–75 the number of federal awards increased by 179, or 42 per cent. The survey noted that there were 'very few first-in-the-industry awards made in the period surveyed. The

---

1. K. Stewart, 'Paying your top men', *Rydges*, September 1963.

increases have been caused almost wholly by the fragmentation of wide-coverage awards and, in particular, by the splitting of single-company awards from a parent one'. Over the same period the number of single-establishment agreements grew by 153 per cent. As noted earlier, the trend to enterprise awards can be expected to continue and today about half of the private sector federal awards are single-establishment awards. The trend towards fragmentation has not been universal. Thus, between 1970 and 1983 a number of industries, including the metal trades, food preserving, pastoralism and liquor trades had hardly been affected by award fragmentation. In other industries award consolidation had occurred. This is a situation in which the number of separate awards is reduced as employers are roped into the parent or industry award. This has been the case in the road transport industry. Another area of award consolidation has been the building and construction industry following the determination of the National Building Trades Construction Award in 1975.

Award-making

Several steps are involved in the making of awards. A variety of processes is also available to the parties in settling their paper disputes.

The ambit log of claims

The first step in award-making, at the federal level, is the creation of a dispute, interstate and industrial, which will bring the matter within the Commission's jurisdiction. For that purpose the system has evolved the paper dispute in which a log of claims, created by one party, is rejected by the other. It is easy enough to create an industrial dispute in more than one state, and thus satisfy the constitutional requirements for Commission intervention, but the process creates some problems. If, for example, a union serves a log of claims on employers demanding, *inter alia*, a wage rise of $10 per week and these claims are rejected, then an industrial dispute exists. If, in that year, the union was successful in obtaining a $7 per wage wage increase, the paper dispute would continue to exist in relation to wages since the union's claim has not been met in full. And since the dispute continues in existence, the Commission's jurisdiction may still be invoked. If the union subsequently sought a further wage rise of, say, $8 per week then, in fact, it could only be legally awarded a maximum increase of $3 per week. Once such a sum is awarded, the dispute in relation to wages no longer continues to exist. In order to overcome the constitutional requirement for the existence of a dispute, the union would need to serve another log of claims on employers to raise the upper limit of ambit.

The constant need to regenerate ambit is an expensive nuisance. Since only parties to the dispute are bound by the ensuing award, unions must serve their claims on every individual enterprise they wish to have bound by the award or on every employers' association. The size of that job is indicated by the fact that there are more than 13 000 respondents to the Metal Industry Award, more than 6000 to the pastoral award and more than 1000 in each of the clothing trades, builders' labourers', graphic arts and dry cleaning awards. Each respondent must be sent a printed log of claims by registered or certified mail.

Given these factors it is not surprising that unions attempt to draw up logs of claims which will have long lives and allow award variations for many years.[2] Such logs of claims are called 'ambit logs'. At face value they appear to be ridiculous and extravagant documents which demand ten weeks annual holidays, pay rates of $2000 per week, a thirty-hour standard working week, and so on. Certainly newspapers have a field day when writing about them, but their reports usually fail to mention that they are dealing with an 'ambit log', not a log of real demands which are expected to be met immediately.

No matter how forward-looking an individual union may be, however, sooner or later ambit will be found to be deficient in one or more areas. A union might draw up an ambit log with generous provisions for standard pay, hours, annual leave and other established conditions, only to find new industrial standards being created during the currency of the dispute. Paid study leave and provisions for maternity leave and paternity leave are recent breakthroughs, which may not have been included in an ambit log served many years previously. Thus, no matter how ingenious a union may be, sooner or later it will be forced to create new ambit. However, if the union does not want to serve a completely new ambit log of claims, it may create new ambit in specific areas of an existing log. That process is neither as demanding nor as expensive as serving a full original ambit log. Unlike the original log which may contain more than a hundred pages, the new demands may fit into one or two roneoed pages. To fulfil legal requirements these demands, of course, will need to be served on all respondents to the award.

The first step in the immediate award-making process is thus the creation of a dispute by way of an (ambit) log of claims. The union will serve this log on employers in more than one state, thereby demonstrating the existence of an interstate dispute.[3] Having done so, however, the union may begin to bargain on a state by state, region by region, or employer by employer basis. It is from that piecemeal bargaining that dependent awards often come. Since a wide ambit will have been built into the union's log of claims, it will not expect complete agreement from the employers. The union will, therefore, notify the Industrial Registrar of the existence of an industrial dispute and ask for a date to be fixed for a Commission hearing. The union then notifies employers of the date set.

---

2. The Metal Trades claim served in 1952 still had ambit when supplanted by the Metal Industry Award some twenty years later.
3. The employers, of course, may initiate the dispute by serving a log of claims on the unions.

The counter log of claims

Just as the union officials will have had to discuss tactics, ambit and immediate objectives when creating the dispute, so too employers will need to formulate their own strategies and policies. Under the guidance of their employer association a counter log of claims is prepared, stating the employers' position on each of the union's demands. The association will negotiate on behalf of members, keep them informed of progress and, if necessary, call meetings to consider, and perhaps change, policy.

The union's log of claims and the employers' counter offer establish the ambit or parameters of the dispute. These parameters are important since no determination can be made outside of ambit. To restate a point made above, a Commissioner cannot award a higher wage than that demanded by the union or a lower one than that offered by employers. Legally the Commissioner is constrained by four choices: the employers' offer, the union's demand, somewhere within ambit (i.e. between the employers' offer and the union's demand) or not to vary existing rates. Of course the last choice is not relevant in the making of a first award.

The ambit of the present claim

Having established the ambit of the dispute it is necessary to establish the *ambit of the present claim*. As we have seen, the desire to create a dispute with a long lifetime leads unions to make apparently extravagant terms in their log of claims. A union may demand $1500 per week, eight weeks annual leave, a thirty-hour standard working week, a meal allowance of $15 per meal and twenty-four months fully paid maternity leave. While the uninitiated employer may be very unhappy about the demands, the employer association will calmly put it down to ambit and find out what the union really wants this time around. This usually involves little more than a telephone call by the association's manager to the union counterpart.

The union's immediate claims are usually more restrained than those in the ambit log. If members are on $500 per week and the union considers a 10 per cent wage increase can be justified, it may ask for $580 per week, but expect somewhere in the order of $530 per week. The union will not usually expect any increase in annual leave or reduced working hours but if those claims are in the log the union might well be able to take advantage of gains made by other unions. In the area of maternity leave the union may think it can improve on the national standard (six months unpaid leave after twelve months service) and seek full pay for the compulsory six-week confinement leave period. The union may wish to increase the meal allowance from $5.25 per meal to $5.80 per meal and ask for a $1.20 increase on the grounds of increased costs. The union's claims in the short run are more 'reasonable'. There is, however, a gap between what the union would settle for ($530 per week, standard hours, annual leave and maternity leave, and a $5.80 meal allowance) and what it asks for (its present demands — $580 per week, six weeks fully paid maternity leave, and meal allowance of $6.45).

In formulating the counter log the employer association will look at conditions in other industries. To a large degree the association's task will be to ensure that the new award does not become a benchmark which sets standards for other awards. To the extent that existing benchmarks are beyond the industry's capacity to pay, the association's task will include convincing unions and the Commission of this fact.

In dealing with the hypothetical log of claims set out above the association would strongly oppose any change in annual leave and standard hours. It would suspect their inclusion related primarily to ambit and refuse any claim made. In the area of wages, the employers might feel that, given movements in relativities, economic capacity and other factors, $520 per week would be as high as they would be prepared to go. They might offer $515 per week. Given the recent establishment of the maternity leave provisions and the Full Bench's decision that such leave ought to be incorporated in all federal awards, employers may see no point in simply opposing it. However, to ensure no 'above standard' gains by the unions (and to give them something to 'bargain away' should trade-offs be required), employers might offer less generous provisions than those announced at the maternity leave case—a two-year qualifying period, for example. In the matter of meal allowances employers may feel that, because of their relative insignificance in the total cost structure, they would be prepared to pay the full $6.45 asked by the union in return for wage or other concessions. Their initial offer might be $5.80 per meal.

Thus, at this stage the union's demands and association's counter offer would look something like that contained in Table 12.2.

Clearly, in this situation, a solution or 'match' is possible in most areas since there is an overlap between what the parties want and are willing

Table 12.2: *Award-making: claims and counterclaims*

Area	Existing rate	Unions' claims	Unions' resistance point	Employers' resistance point	Employers' offer
Annual leave	4 weeks	4 weeks	4 weeks	4 weeks	4 weeks
Wages (per week)	$500	$580	$530	$520	$515
Maternity leave	None	Standard plus six weeks full pay	Standard	Standard	Standard but longer qualifying period
Hours	38	38	38	38	38
Meal allowance	$5.25	$6.45	$5.80	$6.45	$5.80

to take. Negotiation and conciliation should thus bring the parties to agree on such matters. Where there is no overlap (for example, in the area of wages), a settlement will have to be achieved either through industrial action, negotiations, conciliation or through arbitration.

Award-making procedures

In determining award matters a wide range of procedures—some formal, other informal—may be used. Very few matters are determined by arbitration. As professionals, officials from employer associations and trade unions need to (and usually do) establish a working relationship with each other. Most matters are determined by consent, a process encouraged by the Commission. Arbitration is more important for primary than secondary awards. Since the secondary awards are usually made by the parties who made the primary award in the first place, the principal elements of the secondary awards are easily settled by consent. Should the parties agree in part or in whole about any of the matters in dispute, the process of certification codifies, formalises and brings into 'the system' the agreed conditions. About 90 per cent of awards are made fully by consent ('consent awards') and few awards need arbitration of any of their clauses.[4]

Often the parties may prefer to negotiate under the direction of a Commissioner. The operations of a prices surveillance tribunal may make employers wary of awards or agreements too far outside the Commission's fold and may induce some degree of 'pseudo arbitration'.[5] 'Rise and fall' clauses in building contracts may also require wage increases to be arbitrated if their costs are to be passed on to the customer.

Alternatively, a Commissioner may take charge of the dispute. The first step will be to call a compulsory conference of the parties. This conference enables the Commissioner (and, if union–association relations are strained, the parties) to find out precisely what is in dispute. Compulsory conferences also may get things started when the parties have been unable, unwilling or too disorganised to do so. Having decided what is in dispute, the Commissioner will usually instruct the parties to confer privately on certain matters and report back at a prearranged date. Such conferences are an integral part of award determination. De Vyver instances the Clothing Trades Award, in which thirty-seven conferences or negotiation sessions were held before the award was finalised.[6] Such conferences do settle many of the matters in dispute. The terms of agreement are incorporated into the award by being certified by the Commission. Conciliation (mediation) is attempted in areas less amenable to settlement. If the parties are close to

---

4. See Portus, 'Inter-industry award fixation under the Commonwealth Act', *Journal of Industrial Relations*, vol. 11, no. 3, 1969.
5. 'Pseudo' or 'quasi' arbitration exists when the parties are tacitly in agreement but desire that such agreement be by arbitration rather than by consent.
6. F.T. de Vyver, 'Conciliation and arbitration in Australia: the case of the Clothing Trades Award', *South Atlantic Quarterly*, vol. 58, no. 3, 1959, p. 460.

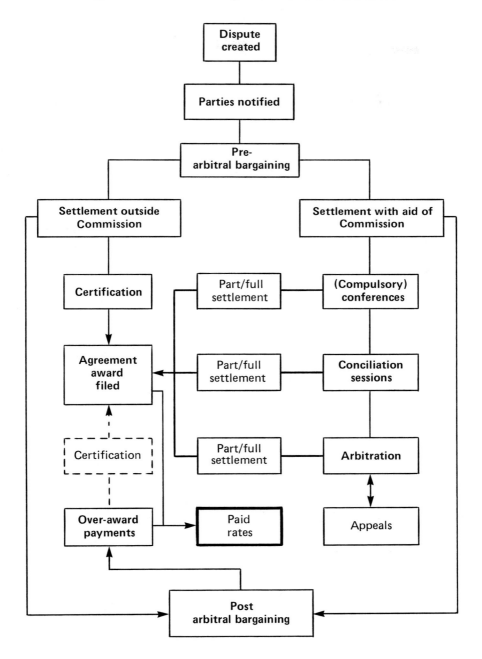

Fig. 12.1: Award-making under federal arbitration

settlement, the Commissioner may direct them to confer again. If satisfied that little is to be gained by further conferences (and if no party objects) the Commissioner will refer outstanding matters to arbitration.

There is an immediate difference in atmosphere and proceedings between the informal discussions and formal arbitration:

> The tone of [conciliation] conferences is informal: no transcripts are taken, smoking is permitted, and first names may be used. Agreement is attempted on many points; in fact many awards are agreed upon completely at such conferences. Some matters, however, may need more formal handling. Then the commissioner, often with agreement of parties, goes into an arbitration session. The tableside conference takes on certain aspects of a court as a stenographer is summoned, the commissioner takes his place on high as a judge might do, cigarettes are extinguished, first names give way to titles, and witnesses are sworn.[7]

The Commissioner's associate formally announces the matter in dispute, union and association representatives 'make their appearances'.[8] The union, as the applicant, puts forward its case. It may call witnesses to give evidence under oath or by affirmation. Such witnesses may be cross-examined by the respondent (employer association). The employers' position is stated and perhaps supported by witnesses or written evidence. The union may cross-examine any employer witness and, as the applicant, has the right of reply.

When each side has presented its case the Commissioner will adjourn proceedings to deliberate on the evidence presented. The Commissioner may, if he or she has not already done so, conduct on-site inspections. Even at this late stage the Commissioner may suggest that the parties should settle the matter by agreement. Should arbitration be necessary, the parties are called back to the Commission when the Commissioner has determined the matters still outstanding. The decision is announced and, usually, the reasons for it. The arbitrated matters are joined to those already settled and filed with the Industrial Registrar.

The appeals system

The arbitrator's decision reflects the Commissioner's notion of what represents the most fair and satisfactory solution, having regard to the evidence, general community standards, knowledge and experience in the field, and prevailing industrial conditions. One (or both) parties, however, may object strongly to the Commissioner's determination and invoke the appeals system. The party objecting proposes to the Commission that the matter is of sufficient public importance to warrant a review by a Full Bench. Should a Full Bench agree that a review is desirable in the public interest, such a review will take place. This review may confirm, modify or overrule the Commissioner's determination.

---

7. Ibid., p. 461.
8. That is, they formally state their names and the capacity in which they appear.

As can be seen from Table 4.6 appeals are not very common. The very existence of an appeals system may make Commissioner's determinations more uniform and thus reduce the number of appeals. However, different conventions govern different industries. In many there is a tacit understanding that the parties will accept the decision: appealing is not considered fair play. In other industries, because of the newness of awards, the pace-setting aspirations of unions, or a Commissioner's reputation for eccentricity, the lodging of appeals is common practice.

Over-award payments

Awards under compulsory arbitration determine minimum rather than actual standards. In negotiating an award binding many employers, a union is placed in a very difficult position, because the capacity to pay of employers in the industry will vary greatly. Should the union be successful in obtaining award rates which only the more productive enterprises can afford, it will only succeed in reducing employment and its own membership. Should award rates be too low, the union is inviting membership dissatisfaction. Thus the union is forced to establish some 'average' award rate which is high enough to appease members, but not so high as to cause short-term unemployment or provoke capital investment to replace labour.

Over-award payments allow union to pitch award rates at the correct average level and then press for higher than award rates in those establishments whose capacity to pay is above average. Over-award payments are also used by employers to attract labour when it is in short supply and to allow them to be more selective at other times. The use of economic capacity to pay criteria in determining the basic, secondary and total wage has also induced unions to press for over-award payments and then use these as evidence of capacity to pay at national and industry hearings. Very few over-award disputes are handled by the Commission (see Table 4.7). However, some over-award agreements are certified. They thus acquire the status of awards. The combination of the over-award payments and award rates is the 'going' or 'paid' rate. In recent years, and no doubt because of indexation, many awards have become paid rates awards by incorporating the former over-award elements into the awards. Such awards determine actual rather than minimum wage levels. As noted in Chapters 11 and 13, over-award bargaining has been constrained by Commission wage guidelines in recent years.

Award variation

The making of an award does not resolve the (paper or legal) dispute that gave rise to it. The dispute exists so long as ambit is not exhausted. Thus parties may vary awards in part settlement of the ongoing paper dispute. Award variations follow the same formal and informal procedures as original award-making, though reopening the dispute is a less tortuous process than that of creating the dispute in the first place. The union applies to the Commission for a hearing and then serves a notice on employers, giving details of the award variation sought and the date of the hearing. In practice often this notice is served only on the employer association or the representatives of the parties who appeared at the original award-making proceedings.

Roping-in awards

Given the Commission's inability to make common rulings, unions are forced to serve their logs of claims on many employers. The enormous task of finding all the employers who should be covered by the award invariably means that unions become aware of the existence of some establishments after the award has been made. Just as the paper dispute mechanism overcomes the constitutional need for the existence of a dispute, so the roping-in device helps overcome the Commission's inability to make common rulings and thus extend the award to enterprises not covered by its provisions.

The case of the Dry Cleaning and Dyeing Industry (consolidated) Award helps illustrate the use of roping-in awards. This award was made in July 1966. At that time the union (the Clothing and Allied Trades Union) had served its log of claims on some 657 employers who became respondents to the award and were listed as such in Schedules A and B of the award. The following year the union wanted to have another 250 employers bound by the award. These employers were served with the original log of claims. The Commission was then asked to settle the dispute by making a roping-in award having the effect of varying the list of respondents in Schedules A and B of the award.[9] A further fifty employers were similarly roped-in four months later.

The content of awards

As noted in Chapter 4, an award is a legal document stating the minimum entitlement and duties of the parties bound by the award. Compared to employment contracts in many other countries Australian awards are extremely comprehensive[10] Awards set out the minimum pay rates for each of the occupational classifications covered, together with the special rates: overtime rates, shift rates and the rates payable for dirt, height, confined space or extreme temperatures. Standard hours of work, meal breaks and allowances, leave entitlement and travelling allowances are all specified in awards. Awards also stipulate whether

---

9. 132 *CAR*, pp. 309–23.
10. F.T. de Vyver, 'Concilliation and arbitration', pp. 473–4.

employment shall be weekly, daily, permanent or casual and cover part-time work and the abandonment and termination of employment. Important awards usually have 'bans clauses' as well as provisions enabling employers to stand down employees when they cannot be gainfully employed, through no fault of the employer. Union rights to enter and inspect premises, to investigate complaints, appoint shop stewards and use notice boards are also provided for. Many awards set out dispute settlement procedures or make provision for Boards of Reference. Medical or first-aid facilities, canteen facilities, washing and sanitary conveniences are also prescribed by awards. Since many terms in any award are not clear in their meaning, there is usually a 'definition' section. Further, the award will list the parties it binds.

The size, scope and content of awards is indicated by Appendix 12.1, which shows the subject matter of Part 1 of the Metal Industry Award.

Industry wage determination

Perhaps the most important part of industry award determination is the establishment of rates for various occupations. An examination of occupational wage rates complements the study of national wage determination covered in the previous chapter and helps to provide a better understanding of the *principles* that the Commission uses in the *processes* of award determination reviewed so far.

Secondary wage criteria

The establishment of an irreducible basic wage common to all employees made necessary a special compensation for workers who had skills or responsibilities beyond those of unskilled labourers. Without a reward for skill it would be difficult to bring young people 'to undergo the necessary training and to make the necessary effort to become efficient craftsmen'.[11]

In the *Builders' Labourers'* case, Higgins J argued that:

> I have to keep steadily in view the recognised practice of treating men of special training or gifts as entitled to higher wages than other workers, and I must do nothing to encourage lads in the idea that they will be as well off in life if they do not apply themselves to the attainment of special skills in industrial work, as if they do so.[12]

The Court evolved the secondary wage, or margin, to meet this need. Margins have been defined as:

> ... minimum amounts awarded above the basic wage to particular classifications of employees for the features attaching to their work which justify

---

11. Gas Employees Case 1919, 13 *CAR*, 461.
12. Builder's Labourers' Case 1913, 7 *CAR*, 210.

payments above the basic wage, whether those features are the skill or experience required for the performance of the work, its particularly laborious nature, or the disabilities attached to its performance.[13]

Higgins' problem of working out a 'fair and reasonable' wage for unskilled workers was relatively simple compared with that of deciding what fair and reasonable margins should be. Writing in 1915, Higgins listed thirty-three 'propositions' used in basic and secondary wage adjustments.[14] Many other criteria have been added to the list. A survey of work-value decisions alone identified fifty-five matters, such as skill and responsibility, which influenced wage rate assessment.[15] Only the most important of the criteria used in setting the secondary wage are discussed here.

Established standards and the Harvester ratio

Higgins freely admitted that the 'Court [was] not expert in the trades or any of them. It cannot attempt to appreciate the nice points of distinction in the higher ranks of labour'.[16] He chose, therefore, to follow the lead of his predecessor, Mr Justice O'Connor, in using existing wage differentials as a guide in setting the secondary wage:

> I think that the safest line to follow for one who is not initiated into the mysteries of the several arts and crafts is to keep close to the distinctions in grade between the employees as expressed in wages by the employers for many years . . . and accepted by the employees.[17]

Higgins departed from O'Connor's practice in that he used existing agreements not to establish actual wage rates but to establish a ratio between the primary (or basic) and secondary wage. The ratio that Higgins settled on in the *Harvester* case was 7:10, that is to say, the unskilled worker received 7 shillings and the skilled worker an extra loading of 3 shillings. The principle that Higgins established in this case was, overtly or covertly, to influence the federal tribunal for many years.

There were, however, a number of problems both in taking existing agreements as a standard and maintaining the Harvester ratio. Existing agreements were not uniform. In the *Builders' Labourers* case, Higgins found that margins for the same classification varied from employer to employer in the same city.[18] Deciding which of the rates to use was not much more than guesswork. Moreover, Higgins was sometimes not satisfied that existing rates were 'fair and reasonable'. He refused to take existing rates for seamen as a guide because their inability to form a union had allowed the employers to depress wage rates.[19] Conversely, in the *Coopers'* case, he found that scarcity of labour had allowed the union

---

13. Metal Trades Award Margins Case 1954, 80 *CAR*, 20.
14. H.B. Higgins, *A New Province for Law and Order*, Dawson, London, 1968 (firt published 1923), London, 1968, pp. 6–15.
15. J. Hutson, *Six Wage Concepts*, AEU, Sydney, 1971, pp. 163–4.
16. Marine Cooks' Case 1908, 2 *CAR*, 77.
17. Ibid., p. 65; and see the *Merchant Service Guild* case 1906, 1 *CAR*, 27.
18. Builders' Labourers' Case 1913, 7 *CAR*, 210.
19. Seamen's Case 1911, 5 *CAR*, 168.

to push rates up unduly.[20] In the *Wool and Basil Workers'* case the Court was concerned that 'custom was not infallible' and that to take existing rates as a guide 'might create and perpetuate injustice'.[21] In the *Actors'* case the problem arose that there was no objective way to measure an actor's skill.[22]

Second, the division of workers into two clear groups, the skilled and the unskilled, proved impossible to maintain. That was partly the result of Higgins' use of a variety of criteria in deciding whether a case for margins could be made: the skills of tradesmen; the exceptional muscular power and training of the shearers; the exceptional heart and physique of gas stokers; the exceptional responsibility of train drivers. The problem with these criteria is that they are relative, not absolute, measures. If one worker receives a special reward for 'exceptional' attributes, it will not be long before others want a proportion of the award for possession of the attribute in 'great', 'some' or 'reasonable' amounts. The pressure thus builds up for the establishment of a continuum of classifications and rewards in which there is no sharp break between the skilled and unskilled. Thus, in varying the Gas Employees Award in 1917, Higgins noted that 'in framing my award of 1913, I had but a few classes of workers to deal with, but in this case I am asked to deal with about seventy-five different classes'.[23] When the Metal Trades Award was first made in 1930 there were twenty margins among 154 classifications. The lowest classification was paid the basic wage. By the time the Commission ceased to use the basic wage there were fifty-three margins among 330 classifications. A contemporary of Higgins summed up the difficulty of awarding margins for skill: 'I do not know of a single occupation that does not require some kind of skill in a sense. It even requires skill to blow one's nose'.[24]

Third, the Court found it difficult to maintain margins in times of unusual economic conditions. Thus, during World War I, the basic wage was increased because of price increases but the secondary wage was not. In 1916 the Merchant Service Guild sought increases in margins to maintain the 'proper' relativities and to allow for price increases, but the Court refused the application on the grounds of the 'violent financial upheaval and widespread uncertainty caused by the Great War'. Higgins considered margins to be 'not so absolutely essential to the commodities necessary for wholesome living'.[25]

The Great Depression also distorted margins. In the Engineers' Award, labourers' wages fell by 8.3 per cent. Margins fell by 33 per cent. Whereas the cuts which the Court had made in the basic wage in 1931 were restored in 1934, it was not until 1937 that secondary wage restoration began. In the *Metal Margins* case of 1937, Mr Justice Beeby accepted the

---

20. Coopers' Case 1918, 12 *CAR*, 427.
21. Wool and Basil Workers' Case 1923, 16 *CAR*, 771.
22. Actors' Case 1924, 19 *CAR*, 795.
23. Gas Employees' Case 1917, 11 *CAR*, 267.
24. Brown, J., President of the South Australian Arbitration Court, *South Australian Industrial Reports*, vol. 1, p. 93.
25. Higgins, *A New Province*, p. 98.

Harvester 7:10 ratio as a standard which should be observed when the economy allowed it. He awarded increases to margins which restored the ratio.[26]

Some members of the Court were reluctant to use the Harvester ratio but nonetheless the ratio continued to be important after World War II. The ratio continued to hold sway in successive important *Metal Trades Award Margins* cases. O'Dea noted that: 'Just as Conciliation Commissioner Mooney could suggest that the court in 1947 had either adopted the 1921 *Engineers*' case ratio of 7:10, or it was a remarkable coincidence, so too one could say the same of the outcome of the 1954 case'.[27] The same might also be said of the 1959 case and of the 1965 case, which was the last metal margins case to be heard before the *de facto* adoption of the total wage. The work-value case of 1967 also produced 'margins', or increments for skill above the minimum wage, which were remarkably consistent with the Harvester ratio. By then, however, the total wage had made margins irrelevant.

Comparative wage justice

As noted earlier, the establishment of one award provides useful benchmarks for establishing the wage rates (or wage relativities) for similar classifications in other awards. The establishment and variation of wage rates in this way, through comparison, has been called the 'doctrine' of comparative wage justice. This doctrine has been taken by the Commission to mean that 'employees doing the same work for different employers or in different industries should by and large receive the same amount of pay irrespective of the capacity of their employers or industry . . .'[28] The Court was convinced of the 'danger to industrial peace involved when men performing the same work, with the same skill, in the same city, are receiving different remuneration'.[29] The territorial application of comparative wage justice quickly enlarged from the same city, to the same state, to the whole nation:

> This Court is not hampered in its action by having to adjust its awards to the interests of any particular State, nor is it hampered by any 'reputable employers' clause; it is authorised to settle disputes as may seem most expedient in the interests of Australia as a whole.[30]

The use of comparative wage justice principles is discernible in the Court's earliest operations. It was there in Mr Justice O'Connor's handling of the *Bagshaw* case of 1906, which established fair and reasonable rates for agricultural implement makers in South Australia.[31] It was also there in the first award determined by Higgins, in which he compared the work of marine cooks and butchers with that of butchers' assistants,

---

26. Metal Trades Award Margins Case 1937, 37 *CAR*, 186.
27. R O'Dea, *Principles of Wage Determination Commonwealth Arbitration*, West, Sydney, 1909, p. 60.
28. Engineering Oil Industry Case 1970, 134 *CAR*, 165.
29. Mining Case 1909, 3 *CAR*, 32.
30. Boot Trades Case 1909, 4 *CAR* 9–10.
31. Bagshaw Case 1906, 1 *CAR* 131.

whose wages were determined by a Victorian wages board.[32] As O'Dea has noticed, comparisons with the metal trades 'possessed from the beginning a special quality'.[33] This was probably because the Harvester Judgment was determined in what was essentially a metal trades industry, and particularly because the judgment established margins for the fitter and metal machinist, whose occupations were to be found in many other industries. Thus, in establishing rates for machinists (operatives) in the footwear industry, Higgins awarded them the same rate as a metal machinist's, claiming that 'there is much general resemblance between the character of the work of such machinists and the work of factory bootmakers'.[34] Few manufacturing industries did not possess some machinist classification, and thus a relativity with the Engineering and, after 1930, the Metal Trades Awards. Other Metal Trades Award classifications proved to be useful benchmarks for unrelated awards. Thus, a nexus was made with the Food Preservers' Award, the tin solderer in this award being compared to the canister maker to the Metal Trades Award.[35] However, it was the fitters' classification in the Metal Trades Award that became most important in the whole relativity structure.

The fitters' classification was the first tradesmen's classification to be assessed for secondary wage rate purposes. It soon became the margins benchmark because fitters were employed in a wide range of industries, and because it could be extended to other classifications which required the same degree of skill and training: millers, borers, slotters, gear cutters, cutting bar drillers, lappers, precision grinders, brass finishers, turners, boiler-makers and metal moulders. In other industries the fitter's rate was applied to tradesmen such as carpenters, coopers, tailors, printing compositors, butchers, and so on. Members of the Court argued that those trades required periods of apprenticeship and training and a degree of manual skill similar to that of the fitter. The establishment of a tradesman's rate in any award in turn provided a benchmark by which the marginal relativities of other classifications within that award could be fixed.

Under the operation of the principle of comparative wage justice, the interlocking relationship between award classifications made the wage structure rigid. Internal award relativities quickly became inflexible. Thus, when the Metal Trades Award varied, pressures mounted for variations to both dependent and related awards. If one award varied, related classifications in other awards would also seek a variation, on the grounds of comparative wage justice with the award already varied. Classifications within awards had then to be varied by the same proportions. Thus comparative wage justice became an important way of

---

32. Marine Cooks' Case 1906, 2 *CAR* 55 ff.
33. O'Dea, *Principles of Wage Determination*, p. 76.
34. Boot Trades Case 1909, 4 *CAR* 1.
35. Food Preservers' Case, 45 *CAR* 343.

transmitting wage gains from one award to another. As Hutson has noted, unions

> ... developed considerable ingenuity in drawing parallels between classifications, while the hunting down of anomalies became, and remains a popular sport. The criterion was of great assistance to weaker unions as it enabled them to gain something from the higher standards obtained by more militant unions.[36]

The logical outcome of that process was for unions to concentrate their resources on achieving marginal variations in one dominant award, from which flow-ons could be expected in other awards. The Metal Trades Award served this purpose. The fitters' rate remained the benchmark classification establishing comparable rates for other skilled tradesmen and hence the marginal differentials between them, semi-skilled and non-skilled workers. This in itself was not as significant as the large number of classifications in the award (more than 330), the award's inter-industry penetration, and the fact that it had by far the largest number of employees working under its provision, more than five times as many as under the next biggest award. The cumulative effect of these factors was that a variation to the Metal Trades Award created comparative wage justice catch-up pressures in more than 300 award classifications and, because of the number of workers already receiving wage changes under the Metal Trades Award, a *prima facie* case of capacity to pay in most industries.

For these reasons, after the 1937 *Metal Trades Margins* case, subsequent cases increasingly took on the appearance of, and became acknowledged as, national test cases, despite initial attempts by the Court to prevent flow-ons. Thus, in the 1947 case the Bench ruled that the decision was 'in settlement of a specific industrial dispute and ... [had] little value as a precedent'.[37] However, within a very short period the Court was forced to acknowledge that 'by consent and by adjudication, the Metal Trades marginal increases are beginning to percolate into other industries'.[38] This fact was highlighted in the 1952 case, in which some twenty unions, eight employer associations, eleven state instrumentalities, six major private employers and three state governments were given permission to intervene. The Commission acknowledged that 'since the principles laid down in the Metal Trades Award form the pattern for quite a large number of awards, the ultimate determination of this dispute has consequences not only to the metal industry but to all industries'.[39]

Following legislative amendments in 1952, which allowed references to be made to Full Benches, all *Metal Trades Margins* cases were handled by them in a way which was explicitly designed to afford general guidance to all authorities.[40] Further, after 1952, the *Metal Trades Margins*

---

36. Hutson, *Six Wage Concepts*, p. 141.
37. Metal Trades Margins Case 1947, 58 *CAR* 1092.
38. Carpenters' Case 1947, 59 *CAR* 959.
39. Metal Trades Margins Case 1952, 73 *CAR* 340.
40. Metal Trades Margins Case 1954, 80 *CAR* 531.

cases were argued on grounds of general economic capacity to pay, not on the specific capacity of the metal trades industry.

As noted in Chapter 11, since the introduction of wage indexation in 1975 the Commission has sought to restrict the use of the comparative wage justice criterion. The definition of an anomaly used in recent wage guidelines, however, comes close to the concept of comparative wage justice.[41]

National, industry and enterprise capacity to pay

The capacity to pay, which increasingly came to dominate marginal wage cases, was the capacity of the *national economy*. Initially, however, margins were determined on the basis of *industry capacity to pay*. The Court, and its successor, have consistently refused to allow *singular profitability*, that is, the profitability of an individual employer or enterprise, to be taken as a basis for award increases.

The rejection of singular profitability as a wage criterion is apparent from the very first award determined by the Court. In this case (1906 *Merchant Service* Case) O'Connor stressed that his obligation under the Act was to award a fair wage and not a 'fair proportion of profits'.[42] In the *Seamen's* case, Higgins set out the relationship between an industry's capacity to pay, community standards and individual employers profitability:

> ... [T]he respondents admit the capacity to pay the additional expenses involved in this claim, and this admission has relieved me of any apprehension as to the effects of increased wages on the financial position of the Companies. At the same time, I do not conceive it to be my duty, under the Act, to make an employer pay more wages if his profits are high for the time being. The Act is not an Act for profit sharing, but for securing peace in industries; and the best way of securing peace is to secure to the man, as far as possible, wages and conditions of life on a level with the current standards of the community. I allow the increase without knowing the profits.[43]

In the *Mining* case of 1909, Higgins outlined his approach to industry wage fixation. As a first step, he established the wage of the unskilled worker. Since this was common to all industries, the amount was predetermined. His next step was to establish the 'proper wage for those possessing extra skill'. The final step was to consider evidence adduced to show why employers ought not be asked to pay such wages.[44] This last step examined the industry's capacity to pay. Similarly in the 1911 *Shearers'* case:

> There is always, according to my system, a further inquiry (beyond unskilled and skilled rates) which may demand — Can the industry (I do not mean the individual employer) bear the wages which would otherwise be fair?[45]

---

41. Employees doing similar work and who are paid dissimilar rates without good reason.
42. Merchant Service Case 1906, 1 *CAR*, 25.
43. Seamen's Case 1911, 5 CAR 164
44. Mining Case 1909, 3 *CAR* 32.
45. Shearers' Case 1911, 5 *CAR* 73.

Since the basic wage was regarded as an irreducible minimum, an industry's inability to pay wages considered fair and reasonable depressed the secondary wage in that industry. It should also be noted that though it was an industry's capacity to pay which was taken into account, in extraordinary circumstances (such as the recession and subsequent depression of the 1920s and early 1930s) individual employers were permitted to pay below award rates so as to reduce possible unemployment.[46] The extensive range of industries under federal jurisdiction, the economic downturn and the transmission of wage increases from one industry to others caused 'the question of the capacity to pay of an industry [to become] interrelated with national capacity and the considerations taken into account in relation to a single industry were placed in the context of their influence on national prosperity'.[47] The wage reductions and dislocation of industry induced by the Great Depression, and the economy's rapid transition thereafter to wartime conditions, seem to have reduced disputes on the grounds of individual or industry capacity to pay. This situation was reinforced by the Court's repeated insistence that it was required 'to have regard not merely to the interests of the parties, but to the interests of the community as a whole, which includes the parties'.

Thus capacity to pay increasingly became a national criterion. The basic wage continued to be adjusted quarterly to take account of cost of living changes, so long as the adjustments remained within the economy's capacity to pay. Periodic reviews on economic grounds altered the basic wage level. Similar inquires at the *Metal Trades Margins* cases reviewed the total economy, rather than the capacity of metal trades industry, and became the basis for adjustment of secondary wages. 'Prosperity' loadings, which took account of high levels of capacity to pay, were also added as flat amounts to either the basic wage or margins, but were not adjusted for changes in the cost of living until that capacity to pay was shown to reflect a long-term change in the condition of the economy. Thus, the 1937 prosperity loading on the basic wage remained unadjustable for price fluctuations until 1950, when it was incorporated into the basic wage for quarterly cost of living adjustments. In that same year a further prosperity loading was made. Similarly the 'war loading' on margins in 1941 was not incorporated into the second wage, for adjustment purposes, until 1952.

Industry profitablility became important again in the late 1960s as, in a situation of over-full employment, unions placed renewed emphasis on overaward bargaining. In formal hearings of claims the unions also began to make much of industry or company profitability. Cases involving General Motors-Holdens, waterside workers, railway employees, steelworkers, clerks, transport workers, the oil industry, Hazelwood Project, Victorian Electricity Commission, NSW electricity generation, the coal industry, dockyard workers and municipal officers, all sought improved

---

46. See, for example, Mt Lyell Case 1921, 15 *CAR* 610.
47. O'Dea, *Principles of Wage Determination*, pp. 178–9.

wages or working conditions on the grounds of singular profitability or industry capacity to pay.[48] Two industry cases (the 1965 *Transport Workers'* case and the 1970 *Engineering Oil Industry* case), and one company case (the 1966 *General Motors-Holden* case) illustrate the principles which have emerged in both areas.

The Transport Workers' Case, 1965

In the *Transport Workers'* case, Commissioner Gough awarded wage increases on grounds including that 'employees whose skill, cooperation and effort were central and vital to the industry should have a share in the benefit they had helped to produce, proportionate to their contribution and consistent with the health and strength of the industry'.[49] An appeals bench overruled this decision, claiming that 'there was ground for the appellants' argument that [the Commissioner] had taken account of some factors not heretofore considered pertinent to the fixation of marginal rates'.[50] The Full Bench concluded that Commissioner Gough was in error in relying on changes in the productivity of the industry in general and the prevailing marginal rates in other countries. The Full Bench argued that the productivity of a single industry should not be divorced from national wage cases. The Full Bench expressed concern, not only about the problem of flow-ons, but also about 'double counting': the use of productivity movements to award increases in both industry and national cases. The *Transport Workers'* case thus reaffirmed the Commission's reluctance to award wage increase on account of an industry's profitability.

The Engineering Oil Industry Case, 1970

In the 1970 *Engineering Oil Industry* case the Commission alluded to a different double counting effect. By then, the growth of over-award payments was an industrial fact of life, which the Commission was forced to live with following its unsuccessful attempt to have them absorbed in the *Metal Trades Work Value* case of 1967. If unions bargained for over-award payments on the grounds of capacity to pay, and sought award increases on the same grounds, then there was double counting.

The dispute in question arose out of the renegotiation of an agreement which had existed in the industry since 1958 and which stipulated actual as distinct from minimum rates; that is, it included provision for over-award payments as part of 'paid' award rates. These over-award payments were based on industry capacity to pay.

The Commission both reaffirmed its general reluctance to use industry or enterprise capacity to pay, and relaxed its principles in order

---

48. GMH Case 1966, 115 CAR, 931; Waterside Workers' Case 1963, 104 *CAR* 208; Railway Traffic Case 1965, 11 *CAR* 553; Steelworkers' Case 1964 (NSW) AR, 350; Clerks' Case (NSW) *IIB*, vol. 20, p. 1033; Transport Workers' Case 1965, 111 *CAR* 553; Engineering Oil Industry Case 1970, 134 *CAR* 159; Hazelwood Project Case 1965, 109 *CAR* 640; State Electricity Commission Case 1964, 106 *CAR* 535; on NSW Electricity Generator, see *AILR* 1973, section 118; Coal Industry Case, 15 *IIIB*, p. 1151; State Dockyard Case 1965, 111 *CAR* 414; Municipal Employees' Case 1964, 108 *CAR* 622.
49. Transport Workers Case 1965, 111 *CAR* 553.
50. Ibid.

to allow it to handle the type of dispute before it. The Commission reasserted its view that:

> The major concept upon which ... National Wage cases rested was that increased prosperity should be shared among employees generally and not confined to employees in the more prosperous industries. This is not a new concept in arbitration in this country which is and always has been based, broadly speaking, on egalitarianism.[51]

If employers in prosperous industries were prepared to grant increased wages, then they were required to do so by way of agreement or over-award payments, and not by way of changes to award rates.

Two exceptions, however, were made to this general rule. First, capacity of an industry or an employer in an industry could be used if the parties to the dispute consented to its use. Second, capacity could be admitted 'to be raised in arbitration if it [had] been the practice of the parties in the past to consider such capacity in negotiations which led to earlier agreements or consent awards'.[52] This latter principle enabled the Commission to determine the issue before it.

Thus the use of industry capacity to pay for award determination can be summed up by saying that, except in the special circumstances outlined above, it is not viewed favourably by the Commission.

The General Motors-Holden Case, 1966

The *General Motors-Holden* case produced a strong restatement by the Commission that the profitability of an individual employer should have no bearing on industry awards. In this case the unions had claimed a company 'prosperity loading' of $6 per week on account of the 'movement and levels of production, productivity and profits of the company [which] had created not only a capacity but an obligation to pay higher rates of wages to the employees whose combined efforts had been responsible in large measure for the company's achievement'.[53] The unions further argued that exceptional profitability had resulted in a rate of increase in stockholders' dividends far in excess of the company's wage increase.

The Full Bench unanimously dismissed the union's application. Commissioner Winter's statement highlighted the Commission's quandary in such cases. He stated that between 1951 and 1965 (excluding 1960 and 1961 for which no figures were published), the company had made after-tax profits in excess of $300 million. The company had asked the Commission to dismiss the union's claims on the grounds that singular profitability was not relevant while enterprise productivity was taken account of at national wage cases. In these cases, employers had consistently argued that, by keeping wage movements in line with average national productivity, firms with low capacity to pay were not unduly threatened, while those with above average productivity were able to

---

51. Engineering Oil Industry Case 1970, 134 *CAR*, 164.
52. Ibid., p. 166.
53. GMH Case 1966, 115 *CAR* 949.

pass on the benefits of that productivity by way of reduced prices. Clearly, in this case, the employers' wage charter had been exposed as trite by a company whose general attitude the Commissioner described as mercenary.[54] Under such circumstances, he felt the employees had a 'moral entitlement to share in the extreme profits being made'.[55] However, he felt the Commission could not order the company to share these profits:

> If the Commission granted the application there is not the slightest doubt that it would be asserted that an anomalous position had been created to the comparative detriment of those employed by other firms in the vehicle manufacturing industry... To single out this firm, which by ethical standards, should of its own volition be either paying its employees higher wages or, in conformity with the economic theory advanced by employers... be reducing its prices, would make havoc of any national principle of wage fixation... the province of industrial arbitration would become chaotic.[56]

Commissioner Winter further asserted that accepting the union's claim in this instance would mean inevitably the 'jettisoning of the doctrine of comparative wage justice'.[57]

Work value

The concept of work value is as old as arbitration itself, since the earliest arbitration cases had been based on some assessment of the nature of the training, skill and responsibility in particular types of work. Once benchmark awards became established, however, work value receded into the background as comparative wage justice became the predominant criterion of secondary wage determination. The inflexibility of a system in which all awards were determined in relation to some other (similarly determined) award, the adoption of the total wage concept, growing concern with overaward payments' contribution to 'wages drift' (a situation in which actual wages increased at a faster rate than award rates) and the wage gains made in the *Professional Engineers' Work Value* case (1961), all contributed to a reawakening of interest in work value.

The extensive use of comparative wage justice led, as we have noticed above, to a rigid wage relativity structure in which changes to margins in one award—in particular the Metal Trades Award—brought about pressures for corresponding changes in other awards. The Commission attempted to rationalise this phenomenon by way of annual national reviews of the economy in which all (total) award wages were simultaneously altered to ensure the highest award rates based upon economic capacity to pay.

That system, however, can turn the principle of comparative wage justice into one of wage injustice, since it can prevent those deserving better treatment, because of changed work circumstances, from receiving

---

54. Ibid., p. 965.
55. Ibid.
56. Ibid., p. 967.
57. Ibid., p. 968.

it. The work value criterion appeared to offer an escape from this impasse by permitting new standards to be established, having regard to changes or new factors in an industry.

Since work value cases could result in (and, in principle, were designed to accommodate) changes in long-established wage relativities, the burden of proof was placed on unions claiming a wage injustice to demonstrate the fact.[58] Possibly to discourage the overuse of such cases, the Commission made the burden of proof onerous, if the *Professional Engineers'* case is any guide:

> It turned out to be the most intensive, extensive and expensive work value case ever held. The case took four-and-a-half years to complete from the serving of the log of claims on employers in January 1957 to the handing down of the decision in June 1961. During the case 26 barristers appeared at various stages, including 8 QCs and the Commonwealth Crown Solicitor. The total cost for the claimant organisation was $200 000, the transcript ran to 11 000 pages and two trips had to be made to the High Court to determine questions of jurisdiction.[59]

Since work value is designed, *inter alia*, to free the system from the constraints of wage relativities, two problems may emerge. In the first place the exercise may unbind existing relativities only to create new relationships having the same inflexibility. A second, and more immediate, problem relates to the possibility of flow-ons to awards with which there is a traditional relationship. If flow-ons do occur, the alleged purpose of the work value exercise has not been achieved. Thus, in any major work value case it becomes important for the Commission to establish the uniqueness of the case under review, to underscore the creation of any new relativities, and to remonstrate against any flow-ons. An examination of the *Professional Engineers' (No. 1)* case and the *Metal Trades Work Value* case (1967) suggests that the Commission has had little success. The latter case also illustrates the problems encountered by the Commission when it is seen to have a duty to act as an economic regulator.

The Professional Engineers' Case, 1961

This case was significant because of its pioneering nature and the stimulus it gave to other work value cases as the result of the substantial salary increases gained. Though the case involved professional engineers employed in both the private and public sectors, this brief review will concentrate on the latter.[60]

The basis of the professional engineers' claim was that their salaries were inappropriate having regard to their status as members of a profession. A strong relativity had existed between the lower ranges of the

---

58. For a very clear statement of the principle see the Merchant Service Case, 48 *CAR* 577.
59. Hutson, *Six Wage Concepts*, p. 161.
60. For a more detailed account of this case see 97 *CAR* 233; O'Dea *Principles of Wage Determination*, Ch. 5; R. O'Dea, 'Some features of the *Professional Engineers'* case, *Australian Economic Papers*, vol. 1, no. 1, September 1962, pp. 57–8; J.R. Kerr, 'Work value', *Journal of Industrial Relations*, vol. 6, no. 1, March 1964, pp. 1–19; J.H. Portus, 'Industry wage fixation under the Commonwealth Act', *Journal of Industiral Relations*, vol. 11, no. 3, November 1969, pp. 201–11.

Professional Division of the Federal Public Service and the Administrative and Clerical Divisions. The original salary structures formulated in 1903 had placed professional officers on virtually the same salary ranges as officers of the Clerical Division. In 1918 greater account was taken of the professional officers' training. The margin between professional officers and clerical officers was increased bringing the former into closer relationship with administrative officers. The professional engineers (who were placed in the lower end of the professional officers' salary ranges) maintained that being assessed in relation to administrative officers prevented the proper assessment of fair and reasonable salaries, given the nature, work value and training of professional engineers. Their case revolved around convincing the Commission that they should be assessed in relation to professional and not administrative standards. This they did in great detail:

> The proceedings were protracted. There was a great deal of evidence, oral, visual and documentary, about 180 witnesses being called, over 600 exhibits tendered and several motion pictures screened. There were several 'on site' inspections. There were lengthy and meticulous addresses. In the result there were placed before the Commission not only the matters relevant to salaries but a detailed analysis or description of the Professional Engineer, the history and development of this profession, its nature, its importance, his status, duties, responsibilities and problems.[61]

This costly and time-consuming exercise was directed at establishing a salary 'which [would] enable all Professional Engineers to maintain a standard of living and a status in keeping with the reasonable needs of a profession.[62] How better to do this than by comparing the training, qualifications and other qualities of professional engineers with those of the recognised professions in the higher regions of professional officers' salary ranges — lawyers, architects, dentists and doctors? This, in short, was a form of comparative wage justice directed at desired, rather than established, relativities. The Commission disavowed such comparisons but was clearly influenced by them. While claiming that the only thing professional engineers and doctors had in common was that both were members of a profession, the relativity claimed by the union between the chartered engineer and the medical officer was tacitly acknowledged. This resulted in salary increases for this group of engineers in excess of 40 per cent.

While the theory and intent of work value cases may be to break existing relativities, it is difficult to conceive of the parties doing so other than by establishing some new comparison and hence relativity. Kerr, however, argued that the *Professional Engineers'* case was a comparison of work value but not of salaries or wage relativities.[63] Since (in relation to men at least) the Commission has always adhered to the principle of equal pay for work of equal value, Kerr's distinction is of little value.

---

61. 97 *CAR* 262.
62. Ibid., p. 265.
63. J.R. Kerr, 'Work value', p. 16.

Even in the *Journalists'* case (1967) — a classification of employees historically considered *sui generis* and thus having no established relativities — there was a great deal of debate about whether journalists should be compared with public servants or teachers, the latter being a more favourable comparison from the journalists' viewpoint. As O'Dea argues, the journalists' case 'clearly shows that in a work value case it is still necessary to apply comparative wage justice in order to find appropriate salary comparisons'.[64] According to Portus, 'there is no distinction between [the] principles [of comparative wage justice or wage relativities] and work value, but work value may be a helpful term to describe the tendency to lay less emphasis in presenting cases on comparison with other industries . . .'[65]

In raising the salary of the professional engineers the Commission was not able to break the existing relativities with clerical and administrative officers, whose wages were restored by agreement to their previous relationship with the professional engineers. Other groups—professional scientists, received salary increases as the professional engineers' gains were transmitted through the public services.

The Metal Trades Work Value Case, 1967

The uncertainty of work value cases — few have paid such rich dividends as the *Professional Engineers'* case — the amount of time and money they take, a preference by some unions for direct bargaining and over-award payments, the tactical difficulties of such cases, the possibility of the downgrading of those classifications deskilled by automation—all these have left work value cases, by and large, as the province of white-collar unions.[66] Few blue-collar unions were keen to engage in such an exercise, least of all those unions respondent to the Metal Trades Award. This award had not had a work value review since 1930 and some key classifications in the award had never been subjected to a non-economic review.[67] The *Metal Trades Work Value* case had the distinction of being initiated by the Commission itself.[68]

Three factors seem to have made the Commission want to hold this work value case. In the first place, a work value study of parent awards was a logical development of the Commission's acceptance of the total wage concept. Second, concern was increasingly being shown with the inadequacy of the Metal Award as a benchmark. Third, the growth of over-award payments indicated that award rates were lagging behind market rates.

The total wage system potentially could ensure greater stability of wage relativities, since all awards would be adjusted uniformly and simultaneously, rather than in a piecemeal fashion. This created the problems associated with 'locking-in' existing injustices, but on the

---

64. O'Dea, *Principles of Wage Determination*, pp. 153–61.
65. Portus, 'Inter-industry award fixation', p. 201.
66. Hutson, *Six Wage Concepts*, p. 174.
67. Metal Trades Case 1930 28 *CAR* 923; and Hutson, *Six Wage Concepts*, p. 166.
68. National Wage Case 1966, 115 *CAR* 121.

positive side, the movement of annual total wage hearings, applicable to all awards, could prevent wage relativity leap-frogging and the 'shunting' of award gains. Stability could be maintained by work value assessments designed to establish up-to-date relativities.

However, so-called 'pure' work value cases cannot be carried out in a vacuum. There must be some reference to a standard. Since the Metal Trades Award provided the traditional standard, as well as the basis for total wage increments at national wage cases, pressures mounted within the Commission to ensure that the standard was appropriately set. Thus, in conducting a work value case for draughtsmen and production planners, Commissioner Clarkson voiced his doubts about using the Metal Trades Award as the yardstick in work value cases. 'Because', he wrote, 'of no reassessment situation, the value of a fitter as a yardstick has deteriorated to the extent that in a work value case such as the Commission is now considering, it is relatively worthless'.[69] Mr Justice Wright concluded similarly:

> I feel deep concern that a period of over thirty years has been allowed to elapse without serious consideration having been given on a work value basis to the structure and level of the marginal setup of the Metal Trades Award. I am very reluctant to continue working percentage additions on the basis of general economic considerations, to a wage pattern which upon deeper examination will probably be revealed as obsolete.[70]

Even more disturbing from the Commission's viewpoint was the increase in over-award payments won by unions outside the Commission. The presence of such over-award payments on a large scale seemed to deny that awards were set at the maximum the economy could sustain, as the Commission claimed at national wage reveiws. Further, the 'wages drift', as economists increasingly came to call this phenomenon, could be regarded as a loss of control over wages by the Commission at a time when the need for wages control or incomes policies was increasingly being stressed. The Vernon Report (published in 1965) saw the presence of over-award payments as a product of full employment, as a threat to economic growth and as a reduction in the status and authority of the Commission's awards.

Increasingly the sentiments of the Commission echoed those of the Vernon Report.[71] The *Metal Trades Work Value* case appears to have been designed to solve the problem. The case was certainly not a pure work value case. The unions merely argued for a restoration of the Mooney Formula, and only seventy award classifications (out of 320) were subjected to any examination. Of these only twenty-six were scrutinised thoroughly. The results of the classifications studied were then extended to the other classifications, which was hardly in keeping with the intention of work value cases.[72] Without giving any coherent reason

---

69. 111 *CAR* 1004.
70. National Wage Case 1966, 115 *CAR* 121.
71. See for example, the *Annual Report*, 10; 114 *CAR*, 65 and 115 *CAR* 227.
72. See O'Dea, *Principles of Wage Determination*, p. 130.

as to how it arrived at its decision, the majority judgment awarded wage increases ranging from $10.50 per week for skilled tradesmen to no increases for non-tradesmen. The wage increases mirrored the pattern of over-award payments. The fitters' rate was increased by $7.40 per week, precisely the average over-award payment claimed for boilermakers (who had the same award rate as fitters) at the 1966 national wage case. The majority decision, moreover, further recommended that the increase be paid out of existing over-award payments.

Both members of the Bench majority hinted strongly that award increases should be paid by way of the absorption of over-award payments. Mr Justice Gallagher, the presiding member, announced:

> ... I wish to make it clear to the unions and to employees themselves so far as the Commission is concerned there is nothing in principle to prevent an employer from using existing over-award payments to offset the increase whether in whole or in part.[73]

Commissioner Winter was even more explicit:

> If the current level of over-award payments be held to express the real value of the work being performed then the level of such payments should be diminished by the amount awarded ... While employers are free to act as they wish concerning the amount of wages they may desire to pay over and above the minimum set by the Commission, it should be made clear that they are under no compulsion to retain over-award payments at their current levels ... By the union's own submission, there should be complete or partial absorption of the current over-award payments in the increases now awarded. Since it is the intention of the Commission that employers may generally apply over-award payments against the increase awarded, these increases are not designed to strain capacity to pay.[74]

The minority decision, by contrast, recommended limited wage increases, acknowledged the likelihood of flow-ons, and did not think absorption possible.

Stunned by the magnitude of the increases (the fitters' wage was raised by nearly 16 per cent and the increased wages bill was estimated at $80 million) the Metal Trades Employers' Association called on its members to absorb over-award payments.[75] The metal unions, backed by the ACTU, took an equally hard line. January and February 1968 witnessed more than 400 strikes (including two national stoppages) in the metal industry, an unprecedented use of penal sanctions and an ACTU threat to call a national strike of all unions. By the end of February the Commission was convinced that absorption was a lost cause. It reconvened the case and made a compromise. Seventy per cent of the award increases were to be granted immediately, with the remaining 30 per cent to be deferred until the national wage case in August.

If the Commission had felt some loss of authority because of over-award payments, the absorption debacle did little to help regain it. The

---

73. 121 *CAR* 680.
74. Ibid., p. 216.
75. Hutson, *Six Wage Concepts*, p. 199.

Commission was not able to contain flow-ons to other industries and came to accept over-award payments.[76] In the 'wage wilderness' that ensued, the Commission increasingly placed emphasis again on industrial relations rather than economic objectives. However, by 1975, industrial peace itself demanded some rationalising of the wages relativity structure and some containment of inflation. Backed by the Labor Government and with hesitant union and employer support, the Commission introduced wage indexation. Under wage indexation, industry wage determination was totally subsumed under the national wage determination processes. Apart from the brief period July 1981 to December 1982, wage determination has been highly centralised (see Chapter 11). More recent national wage judgments have sought the introduction of administered systems of wage flexibility involving national, industry and enterprise bargaining. These developments are reviewed in the next chapter.

Summary

Award-making is at the heart of any system of industrial relations. The federal system, in common with other systems, makes use of a number of processes in the making of awards. These include negotiations, conciliation, mediation, compulsory conferences, arbitration and, on occasion, the appellate process. Though the federal system purports to be one of compulsory arbitration, in practice few awards are determined by arbitration. Those that are so determined are usually primary or parent awards attempting to generate new industrial standards. Thus, though arbitration is quantitatively insignificant, qualitatively it is important. Awards, in the main, determine minimum standards. Over-award payments, when added to award pay, determine the actual or going rate. In several industries there is a trend to paid rates awards through the incorporation of over-award pay into awards.

Over the years the Commission has institutionalised several criteria for determining secondary (or industry) wages. Comparative wage justice and work value have figured prominently, as have established ratios between skilled and unskilled workers. The Commission has generally held that the fruits of productivity increases should be shared by all workers through national wage cases. The profitability of an enterprise has never been considered an appropriate criterion for wage increases for employees of that enterprise though, under special circumstances, the profitability of a specific industry may constitute grounds for an industry wage increase.

---

76. See for example, Australian Conciliation and Arbitraton Commission *Annual Report* No. 12, 1967.

Appendix 12.1

Table 12.3: *Subject matter of Metal Industry Award (Part I — Wages Employees)*

Subject matter	Clause no.	Page no.
Abandonment of employment	6	9
Absence from duty	6	9
Accommodation and conveniences	39	82
Aged and infirm workers	34	68
Air-conditioning allowance NSW and Queensland	8	30
Air-conditioning allowance South Australia	37	74
Annual close down	25	62
Annual leave	25	59
APM Ltd Maryvale site contractors	37	76
Apprenticeship	14	34
Apprenticeship to metal polishing	15	39
Apprenticeship — Additional provisions for specified trades	16	42
Arrangement	2	1
Bereavement leave	26	64
Boards of reference	40	87
Boiling water at meal times	39	82
Broken Hill Proprietary Co. Ltd — Wage rates	8	26
Broken service	24	58
Call back	21	54
Camping allowance	27	65
Casual employment	6	8
Change of residence	27	64
Clothing — Damage to	39	83
Construction allowance Australian Iron & Steel Port Kembla	8	29
Construction allowance BHP Newcastle	8	29
Contract of employment	6	7
Crib time	21	24
Crib time — Holidays and Sundays	22	57
Daylight saving	19	52
Date and period of operation	5	7
Definitions	41	88
Distant work	27	65
Drinking water	39	82
Emergency provisions	38	78
Excess travelling and fares	27	64
Extra rates not cumulative	23	57
Fare allowance — Air-conditioning industry	27	65
Females	12	32
First aid allowance	35	68
First aid attendant	35	68
First aid outfit	35	68
Foundry disability allowance	17	47
Hearing aids — Damage to	39	83
Holidays	22	55

Table 12.3: *Subject matter of Metal Industry Award (Part I — Wages Employees) — Continued*

Subject matter	Clause no.	Page no.
Holidays — Rate for work on	22	56
Holidays — Minimum payment	22	56
Hours of work	18	49
Incidence of award	3	5
Junior males and females	13	33
Juniors — Prohibited occupations	13	34
Jury service	29	66
Latecomers	6	10
Latrobe Valley site contractors SEC Victoria	37	72
Leading hands	8	28
Lift industry allowance	8	28
Lift industry allowance — Melbourne Underground Rail Loop	8	30
Loading on annual leave	25	62
Lockers — Provision of by employer	39	82
MRI Pty Limited	8	26
Maternity Leave	24A	58a
Meal allowance	21	54
Meal allowance — Holidays and Sundays	22	57
Meal breaks	20	53
Melbourne Underground Rail Loop	8	30
Minimum wage	9	31
Miscellaneous provisions	39	82
Mixed functions	11	32
Motor allowance	28	66
Multi-storey buildings — Extra rate for work on	8	28
Multi-storey buildings — Definition	41	93
Multi-storey buildings — Rate for apprentices	14	38
Notice board	33	68
Overtime	21	53
Parties bound	4	6
Part close down, part rostered leave	25	63
Part time employment of female	6	7
Payment for travelling	27	65
Payment of wages	7	10
Piecework and taskwork	10	31
Prescription lenses — Case hardening	39	85
Process worker — Definition	41	94
Prohibited occupations for certain juniors	13	34
Prohibition of bans, limitations or restrictions	6	9
Proportionate leave on termination	25	62
Protective clothing and equipment	39	83
Queensland — Divisional and district allowances	37	69
Queensland — New construction work	37	70
Rest period after overtime	21	53
Rest period after overtime — Holidays and Sundays	22	56
Rest period for females	39	86
Right of entry of union officials	31	66
Saturday — Minimum payment	21	54

Table 12.3: *Subject matter of Metal Industry Award (Part I — Wages Employees) — Continued*

Subject matter	Clause no.	Page no.
Saving	42	98
Seats for females	39	86
Seven day shift workers	22	57
Shift work	19	50
Ship repairing — Definition	41	95
Ship repairing — Extra rate for work on	8	28
Shop stewards	30	66
Sick leave	24	57
Single day absences	24	58
Special exemption	43	99
Special rates	17	44
Special rates not cumulative	17	44
Spectacles — Damage to	39	83
Spread of hours	18	49
Standing by — Rate for	21	54
Standing down of employees	6	8
Statutory declarations	24	58
Sunday — Rate for work on	22	56
Sunday — Minimum payment	22	56
Supplementary payments	8	27
Supersession	44	102
Tasmania Bell Bay Power Station contractors	37	74
Termination of employment	6	8
Time and wage book	32	67
Title	1	1
Tools — Damage to	39	83
Tools — Provision of	39	84
Transport of employees after overtime	21	55
Travelling and board	27	64
Tyree Electrical (Victoria) Pty Ltd — Wage rates	8	26
Victoria — Latrobe Valley site contractors	37	72
Victorian Meatworkers Association — Special rate	17	48
Wage rates — Adults	8	10
Wage rates — Juniors	13	33
Wage rates — Apprentices	14	38
Washing and sanitary conveniences	39	83
Watchman and/or gate keeper	36	69
Wilson Electric Transformer Co. Pty Ltd — Wage rates	8	26
Year of service — Definition	24	59

Discussion questions

1. Distinguish between primary and secondary awards. Why are primary awards so important?
2. How do you account for the growth in single-company awards?
3. What is meant by the terms 'award fragmentation' and 'award consolidation'? Explain why fragmentation and consolidation take place.
4. What is an ambit log of claims? What factors give rise to the use of this device?
5. Explain the process that may be used in award-making. What factors determine the processes used in any particular instance?
6. Discuss the contention of Higgins J. that without a reward for skill it would be difficult to bring young people 'to undergo the necessary training and to make the necessary effort to become efficient craftsmen'.
7. What is the secondary wage? What was the rationale of the secondary wage? Is the concept still a relelvant one in Australian wage determination?
8. What do you understand by the term 'comparative wage justice'? What are the benefits and difficulties resulting from the use of this wage criterion?
9. Why has the federal tribunal determined that productivity increases should be distributed on a national rather than an industry basis?
10. Explain the significance of the *Transport Workers'* case, the *Engineering Oil Industry* case and the *GMH* case for developing and refining the relationship between industry profitability and wage payments.
11. Explain what is meant by the term 'work value'. What role does this criterion play in the wage determination process?
12. Why were the basic wage and secondary wage joined together in 1967?

Further reading

Charles, D., 'Wages and the dispute-setting process', in J. Niland (ed.), *Wage Fixation in Australia*, Allen & Unwin, Sydney, 1986.
Dabscheck, B., 'Tribunals and wage determination: the problem of co-ordination', in J. Niland (ed.), *Wage Fixation in Australia*, Allen & Unwin, Sydney, 1986.
Fells, R.E., *Movement, Phases and Deadlocks: A Study of the Process of Industrial Relations Negotiations*, Industrial Relations Research Centre, University of New South Wales, 1986.
Hince, K., 'Utah and mining unions: a case study of collective negotiations at the company level', *Journal of Industrial Relations*, vol. 22, no. 2, 1980.
Hutson, J., *Six Wage Concepts*, A & U, Sydney, 1971.

Isaac, J.E., 'The meaning and significance of comparative wage justice', in J. Niland (ed.), *Wage Fixation in Australia*, Allen & Unwin, Sydney, 1986.

Isaac, J.E., 'The Arbitration Commission: prime mover or facilitator?', *Journal of Industrial Relations*, vol. 31, no. 3, 1989.

McCallum, R.C. and Smith, G.F., 'Opting out from within: industrial agreements under the *Conciliation and Arbitration Act 1904*', *Journal of Industrial Relations*, vol. 28, no. 1, 1986.

Nieuwenhuysen, J., 'In flexibility is strength: tribunals and the wage fixation process', in J. Niland (ed.), *Wage Fixation in Australia*, Allen & Unwin, Sydney, 1986.

Norris, K., 'Compulsory arbitration and the wage structure in Australia', *Journal of Industrial Relations*, vol. 22, no. 3, 1980.

Provis, C., 'Comparative wage justice', *Journal of Industrial Relations*, vol. 28, no. 1, 1986.

Rowe, L.G., 'Reason, force or compromise: egalitarian wage structure under bargaining and arbitration', *Journal of Industrial Relations*, vol. 24, no. 2, 1982.

Tilling, J. and Wheeler, K., *Toward Collective Bargaining: The Fixed Contract Approach*, Industrial Relations Research Centre, University of New South Wales, 1984.

CHAPTER 13

Award Restructuring

Previous chapters have examined national arbitration and the processes of national wage determination, award-making and variation, and industry wage determination. In recent years the compartmentalising of the different wage tiers—national, industry and over-award—has become less distinct. This has been the product of attempts to implement wages policies since 1975, the obtrusiveness of national wage guidelines into industry/plant award negotiations, and the perceived need to modernise the award system and to facilitate a more flexible and competitive workforce.

This chapter examines developments since 1986 that have led to a modernisation of the award system. Following the first section, which examines the economic and industrial relations pressures to restructure awards, the chapter details attempts in the metal industry to replace the Metal Industry Award with the Metal and Engineering (Federal) Award.

The award provides the employment conditions for more than 400 000 employees in over 10 000 establishments in a multitude of industries. It highlights the inflexibility and anachronism of many Australian awards. It contains more than 340 award classifications and provides for 1800 different award rates of pay. The award classifications are rigid and provide for limited employment and career opportunities. The award gives no consideration to training. Many of its restrictions on labour utilisation add unnecessary labour costs and reduce the industry's competitiveness. There are nine union respondents to the award who negotiate with the Metal Trades Industry Association (MTIA) by way of the Metal Trades Federation of Unions (MTFU).

The metal industry has been important in the award restructuring debate because of the historic benchmark role of the award, because much of the initial impetus for change has come from this industry, and because it has been the basis of the ACTU's 'national blueprint' for award restructuring.

The primary focus of this chapter is on award restructuring at the national and industry levels. Examples of award restructuring at the enterprise or plant level are given in the next chapter, which deals with workplace industrial relations.

Pressures for change

Chapter 11 outlined the wage indexation system that operated from 1975 to 1981 and which sought to contain the escalation of wages. The indexation system was abandoned in July 1981. At the time there was an expectation of a 'resources boom'. This expectation influenced the metal industry negotiations which concluded in December 1981. These resulted not only in major wage gains by the unions, but also in working hours being reduced from forty to thirty-eight per week.

Within weeks of the agreement, unions in many establishments were seeking the introduction of the 'short-time' week. This practice (of dubious legality) provided for employees to be paid for time worked, rather than for a full working week as specified by the award. The resources boom had not eventuated. Instead, an international trade gloom pervaded the industry. Metal employers were squeezed between higher labour costs and shrinking markets. They, and the unions, had failed to react quickly enough to the changed context of wage determination in Australia, in particular the reduction or removal of tariffs; the deregulation of the financial sector including the greater freedom for Australians to invest and relocate industries overseas; the floating of the Australian dollar (and its immediate depreciation by 25 per cent); the decline in commodity prices on which Australia's wealth depended; the greater penetration of manufactured imports; and the constraints placed on economic policy by a large balance of payments deficit.

The impact of the new economic order, one of greater integration with and dependence on international trade, was most felt in the the manufacturing industry and in particular in the metal and engineering sector. Between August 1981 and 1983 nearly 100 000 jobs were lost in this sector.[1] It is estimated that the Amalgamated Metal Workers' Union lost about 60 000 members (about a third of its membership). Other manufacturing-based unions also suffered large membership losses. For these unions survival necessitated a revitalised manufacturing industry.

Metal unions were so concerned about the downturn in heavy engineering that they commissioned a report, at a cost of $100 000, on the

---

1. MTFU National Conference, February 1988, 'Problems confronting the Australian economy: implications for metal workers', p. 3.

industry's problems and future.² The report formed the basis of the unions' submission to the Industries Assistance Commission. It was also the basis of union negotiations with the government which led to the three-year program known as the Heavy Engineering Adjustment Package. This provided for $90 million assistance to the heavy engineering industry. A tripartite Heavy Engineering Board was established to administer the program. To qualify for financial assistance companies were required to reach agreement with relevant unions on changed work practices, the provision for skill formation and the development of consultative arrangements.

In addition to financial assistance, companies were provided with low interest loans for the purchase of new equipment and technology. Unions agreed not to oppose innovation and the introduction of new technologies.

BHP Pty Ltd provided an early example of the potential to harness the new-found need for cooperation between management and labour. In the early 1980s BHP's steel division had suffered severe losses which led to a large number of workers at the Newcastle and Port Kembla smelters being retrenched. By the end of the decade, after-tax earnings of the steel division had exceeded $560 million and BHP had been established as a world leader in bonded steel products.

In December 1986, concern for the viability of the metal and engineering industry led to the MTIA proposing a compact with the metal unions that would seek to change the industrial relations culture of the industry and help make it internationally competitive. This proposal was designed to promote the interests of the industry in five areas: encouraging harmonious industrial relations; creating an environment conducive to investment and commercial viability; increasing employees' disposable income without adding to the industry's costs; developing the skills and capacities of employees; and enhancing the industry's image and reputation for quality products.[3]

In the proposed compact the MTIA recognised the 'need to effect major changes in the current approach to training and career development'. It called for greater labour flexibility, the removal of barriers to enterprise efficiency, better workplace consultation, the establishment of dispute settlement procedures, the restructuring of award classifications, the removal of restrictions on male part-time employment, greater flexibility in working hours, and the merging of unions. Thus the proposed compact canvassed the major areas which came to be associated with award restructuring: training and skill formation, multi-skilling,[4] career structures, award reclassification and broad-banding,[5]

---

2. Metal Trades Federation of Unions, *Heavy Engineering Handbook,* MFTU, Sydney, 1986.
3. Metal Trades Industry Association of Australia, *MTIA Proposals for a Compact with the Metal Unions,* MTIA, Sydney, December 1986.
4. The term *broad-banding* means the bringing together under a single classification or title a number of jobs that were separately or individually classified. It is a reduction in the total number of differently classified jobs within an award or enterprise.
5. The term *multi-skilling* refers to the provision of further training to current employees to enable them to carry out tasks not covered by their present job classification.

consultation, removal of restrictive work practices, dispute settlement procedures and a reduction in job demarcations.

The two-tiered wages system

At this time major changes were being contemplated to the exisiting principles of wage fixation.The rapidly deteriorating balance of payments situation had undermined government support for full indexation. It sought, in particular, the discounting of imported elements in the Consumer Price Index for wage-determining purposes. The government suggested that if this were not done it would undermine the benefits conferred on Australian manufacturing by devaluation. The government obtained ACTU agreement to discounting by undertaking to offset any wage losses through changes to the taxation system. This led the ACTU to propose a two-tiered wage-fixing system, a system that found support from the government and the Confederation of Australian Industry.

In March 1987 the Commission handed down its decision and promulgated guidelines for the operation of the new system. The first tier consisted of general wage increases of $10 per week with provision for a further possible increase of 1.5 per cent six months later. The second tier, with a cap of 4 per cent, was an inducement to unions to engage in workplace restructuring. To this end the Restructuring and Efficiency Principle was introduced. This stated, in part:

> (a) Increases in rates of pay or improvement in conditions of employment may be justified as a result of measures implemented to improve efficiency in both the public and private sectors.
> (i) Changes to work practices and changes to management practices must be accepted as an integral part of an exercise conducted in accordance with this principle.
> (ii) Other initiatives may include action to reduce demarcation barriers, advance multi-skilling, training and retraining, and broad-banding.
> (iii) Changes to working patterns may be necessary...

The Commission identified some of the positive changes it expected to flow from the new principle. These included:
- An examination of restrictive work and management practices in both the public and private sectors to identify areas of inefficiency and to develop means to overcome them;
- The introduction or extension of multi-skilling and broad-banding;
- An acceptance of the concept that the reduction of demarcation barriers may be essential.[6]

This decision marked a major change in the traditional form of national wage determination. Historically the Commission had adjudicated on income distribution. For the first time, a national wage Full

---

6. Australian Industrial Relations Commission, *National Wage Case Decision, March 1987*, Print G6800, p. 13.

Bench awarded wage increases in return for cost offsets from unions.[7] Thus national wage determination had become concerned with the creation, rather than merely the distribution, of income. The decision, in the view of one metal union, 'only created a number of possibilities rather than awarded firm wage adjustments'.[8] It mirrored, in large measure, the MTIA's proposal to increase disposable income without adding to the industry's costs. Further, the decision marked a significant change in the conduct of industrial relations which were characterised by negotiations at the national, industry or sectorial levels. Though the Commission considered that nationally agreed guidelines could assist in the proper processing of enterprise-based restructuring and efficiency exercises, it stressed that 'it [was] primarily at the enterprise level that the objective of this principle [would] be achieved'.

By the end of March 1987 the MTFU had responded to the MTIA's proposal for a compact. It endorsed some of the proposals but sought greater clarification over the substantive aspects of the compact. In April the MTIA provided further information as well as proposals for the implementation of the two-tiered wages system in the metal and engineering industry.[9] The MTIA requested the MTFU to indicate which of a number of proposed variations it was prepared to accept as appropriate trade-offs under the second tier. The areas proposed for trade-offs were changes to hours of work, greater flexibility in annual leave entitlements, tightening of sick leave entitlements, deletion of Melbourne Cup Day as a public holiday, reduction in overtime costs, changes to shift work requirements and payments, greater flexibility in the use of labour, the payment of wages by electronic transfer or cheque, the provision for the part-time employment of men and 'providing that demarcation of work based on union membership, custom or practice or any other artificial basis shall be a breach of the award'.

Despite intense negotiations, the MTFU and the MTIA failed to reach agreement other than on 'longer-term industry issues' which essentially required government sponsorship to promote the industry and for the Australian Council of Employment and Training to provide the basis for training and career development in the metal and engineering industry.[10]

In essence, the MTIA made demands for longer hours and concessions on other award conditions in return for a 3 per cent wage increase (no doubt the latter being an ambit claim). The MTFU made claims for industry development through training and efficiency and sought a 4 per cent wage increase.

A major area of disagreement concerned the proper application of the restructuring and efficiency principle resulting from the two-tiered

---

7. An earlier example of such cost offsets related to the extension of the thirty-eight hour standard working week obtained in the metal industry agreement of December 1981. Unions seeking the thirty-eight hour week had to provide cost offsets.
8. AMWU National Council Paper, 11 March 1987.
9. MTIA, *Proposals for a Compact between MTIA and MFTU: MTIA Response to MTFU Draft Proposals Dated 31 March 1987*, MTIA, Sydney, April 1987.
10. MTIA *Stage 1 of the Compact Between MTIA and MTFU*. MTIA, Sydney, May 1987.

wages system. The employers maintained that wage increases should only follow after unions had conceded changes to employment conditions provided by the Metal Industry Award. The unions maintained that there was enough scope to improve efficiency without trading-off award conditions.

On 12 May 1987 Deputy President Keogh directed the parties to establish a national framework for second-tier wage adjustments and laid down ten rules for the parties to follow. The first of these concerned the matters to be the subject of national-level negotiations. These included some of the matters sought by employers in the compact: procedures for the avoidance of industrial disputes; spread of ordinary hours; flexibility in relation to rostered days off; part-time employment for men; and payment by cheque or electronic funds transfer. The parties were directed to determine the nature of the issues that were to be negotiated at the plant or enterprise level. Among the issues Deputy President Keogh considered warranted discussion were changes in work methods; demarcation barriers; flexibility in the arrangement of working hours; changes in manning levels; training and retraining; unproductive work patterns; guidelines for the use of new technology; consultation procedures; the role of supervision; part-time employment for men; wage payments and the use of contractors.

The national framework was to provide a mechanism for recording plant agreements. Such agreements had to 'result in genuine improvement in efficiency and productivity'. The national organisations were to refer any areas of plant disagreement to the Commission for assistance in resolving the disagreement. To minimise wage relativity leap-frogging problems the Commission was to synchronise wage adjustments resulting from plant negotiations in August 1987.

On 26 May the MTIA and MTFU reported to the Commission. Though each indicated acceptance of the rules, they had been unable to agree as to the full details of a national framework for negotiations. 'Each submitted a proposed approach said to be consistent with the directions of 12 May but which departed in varying degrees from the guidelines laid down in that statement'.[11]

In the final analysis the Commission itself laid down the national framework for continued MTIA and MFTU negotiations. This national framework included a time schedule. Committees comprising representatives of management, workers and relevant unions were to be established at each plant or enterprise no later than 5 June 1987; national-level negotiations were to be completed by 12 June; and the resultant plant agreements were to be put to the Commission on 19 August for award variations as appropriate.

As an aid to the committees the MTIA provided a checklist of fifty-one work practices that could be impediments to efficiency. For its part, the MTFU developed a 'model agreement' as a guide to shop stewards. This

---

11. Australian Industrial Relations Commission, statement by Deputy President Keogh, 28 May 1987, C No. 1180 of 1987.

sought agreement for the removal of inappropriate demarcation lines between similar occupations; for the implementation of consultative committees; the development of company training and retraining programs; the establishment of export targets; the introduction and use of new technology and of management techniques; and the changing of identified work and management practices.[12] The MTFU placed emphasis on the need to form 'negotiating committees for the purpose of reaching agreement on restructuring and efficiency changes at the plant level'.[13]

Under the framework for second-tier negotiations, the MTFU and MTIA were required to negotiate on five nominated matters with the aim of proceeding to agreement on proposed variations to the Metal Industry Award which would facilitate successful negotiations at the plant or enterprise level. A series of discussions and negotiations on these matters were held in June and July before reporting back to Deputy President Keogh on 19 August. At these proceedings the MTFU and MTIA reported that they had agreed on award variations for two of the five matters: flexibility in relation to rostered days off and payment by cheque or electronic funds transfer. They had not reached agreement in the other three areas. They also reported agreement on a matter not included in the national level negotiations framework: the removal of restrictions on the employment of adult apprentices. At the behest of the Commission the unions also agreed that they would not object to the 'one in, all in' overtime provision being prohibited.

Keogh DP arbitrated on the outstanding three issues—disputes procedures, spread of hours and part-time employment for men—thus providing a framework for plant-level negotiations.

By the end of July 1987 nearly a hundred plant agreements had been finalised. This figure increased to 750 in September and to nearly 1800 by December. The majority of these agreements met the framework requirements and were certified by the Commission. On the basis of these agreements the Metal Industry Award was varied to provide for the 4 per cent second-tier wage increase. Since not all workplace negotiations had been finalised, Keogh DP arbitrated on the outstanding cases to reflect the general changes agreed to in other establishments.[14]

Nearly half (47 per cent) of the agreements included provision for training, 40 per cent provided for continuing consultative committees, 23 per cent gave up existing conditions such as tea breaks and canteen subsidies, and 22 per cent provided for new production systems such as total quality control. The majority were modelled on and followed the Keogh national framework.[15]

The second tier promoted workplace changes in other industries.

---

12. MTFU, *Wages Newsletter*, No. 2, June 1987.
13. MFTU, *Wages Newsletter*, No, 3, July 1987.
14. TUTA, 'MTFU delegates semianar: strategies for 1988–89', TUTA, Wodonga, February 1988.
15. Ibid.

Many of the changes or trade-offs appear to be based on the MTIA's fifty-one item 'hit list'. The Department of Industrial Relations estimated that by January 1989 more than 80 per cent of employees covered by awards had received second-tier wage increases. This figure had increased to nearly 100 per cent by the end of that year.[16]

The Department identified changes that had been introduced in five major areas:

1. *Payment methods*

The move to electronic funds transfer was the most common single off-set included in second-tier packages. A number of packages provided for payment by cheque. In some cases automatic pay increments were removed and replaced by increments based on performance.

2. *Flexibility in the use of labour*

There were a considerable number of second-tier decisions which involved award broad-banding, multi-skilling, award restructuring and the development of career paths. In most cases the agreement did not provide much detail on these matters but rather acceptance in principle by the parties. However, in public sector agreements these issues were canvassed at length. Thus, in the case of the Telecom clerical officers' agreement, there was provision for the integration of more than fifty classifications into a single structure of six levels. Multi-skilling was to be achieved through 'flexibility in task rotation across positions, job rotation and training programs and the design of multi-functional jobs'. The Australian Public Service agreement, which covered about 107 000 office-based staff, replaced more than a hundred classifications with a new broad-banded structure of only eight levels.

Many of the agreements had specific provisions for training, both formal and on-the-job. Others provided for the use of part-time and casual labour, others still the use of contract and off-site labour. A large number of awards also provided for a reduction in demarcation barriers. In most instances this involved the establishment of procedures to handle demarcation disputes rather than mechanisms for the elimination of such disputes. In a number of agreements restrictions on staff performing lower-level functions were removed. The removal of demarcation barriers across classifications was detailed in other agreements. A number of agreements incorporated flexible staffing levels. Many of these proposed an outright reduction in staffing levels through natural attrition. Some provided for 'geographic mobility'—the right to move staff from one section to another. Other agreements provided for constant machine production through the reorganisation of work breaks.

3. *Industrial relations procedures*

Many agreements included procedures for avoiding or settling disputes.

---

16. Department of Industrial Relations, *Report on the Operation of the Restructuring and Efficiency Principle*, AGPS, Canberra, April 1990.

In essence, these provided for the maintenance of the *status quo* while discussions continued at the workplace, and then at progressively higher levels; early identification of problems and emphasis on negotiations. A number of agreements provided for the establishment of consultative procedures. Others included provisions for cooperation in the use of new technology.

4. Working time arrangements

A number of agreements contained provisions for a greater spread of working hours. Others had provisions for a reduction of non-productive time (wash-up time, tea breaks, etc). Others still provided for a greater degree of flexibility in scheduling breaks. New shift arrangements were provided for by some agreements, and the strict adherence to starting and finishing times by others. Some agreements contained changes in overtime arrangements, such as the removal of the 'one in, all in, requirements. Flexibility was provided by some agreements for rostered days off, in the Christmas–New Year shut-down period, for public holidays and for annual leave. Other agreements provided for changes to absenteeism and sick leave procedures.

5. Management practices and quality control

A number of agreements contained provisions for revised management practices. These included such matters as improved communication, consultation and information sharing; the devolution of responsibility to technical and professional employees; the reduction in management personnel; changes to management structures; and the computerisation of many management recording functions. Quality control was the subject of agreement in production sectors. The introduction of total quality control programs was the major element of many of these agreements.

Other reports and surveys concerning the Restructuring and Efficiency Principle arrived at broadly similar conclusions.[17] These suggested that generally negotiations had led, or were likely to lead, to improvements in management practices and in the removal of restrictive work practices. There was also general agreement that cost offsets of 4 per cent or more had been achieved and that these were likely to be permanent. There were suggestions of an improvement in the industrial relations climate and a positive attitude by unions.

Despite these positive outcomes, some reservations were expressed. There was concern that there were limitations on any future trade-off exercises, particularly among the most efficient enterprises.

The views of the major parties were enunciated at the June–July

---

17. See, for example, Committee for Economic Development, *How has Business Handled Second-Tier Negotiations?— Survey Results*, Sydney, December 1987; Confederation of Western Australian Industry, *Survey of Second-Tier Wage Negotiations*, CWAI, Perth, October–November 1987; McDonald, T. and Rimmer, M., 'Award restructuring and the second tier', *Australian Bulletin of Labour*, vol. 14, no. 3, 1988; Rimmer, M. and Zappala, J., 'Labour market flexibility and the second tier', *Australian Bulletin of Labour*, vol. 14, no, 4, September 1988.

national wage case in 1988. The ACTU considered that the Restructuring and Efficiency Principle had helped to eliminate inefficient practices and to increase flexibility. It had generated significant organisational and attitudinal change. The ACTU supported the continued operation of a principle aimed at restructuring, but felt that it needed a broader and longer-term scope so as to facilitate award restructuring, skill acquisition and changes to work organisation.

The Confederation of Australian Industry (CAI) argued that there had been many benefits from the principle. It claimed, however, that the principle's emphasis on restrictive work practices had led to a narrow application of changes by unions.

The Commission itself concluded that the March 1987 principles had been 'reasonably successful':

> The proper application of the restructuring and efficiency principle called for a positive approach by trade unions, their members, and individual workers and by employer organisations, their members and individual employers. In the Commission's experience some were inadequate for the task. Many others made positive efforts: the best not only derived benefits which produced immediate efficiency and productivity improvements but also laid the foundation for future improvement.[18]

The Commission introduced the Structural Efficiency Principle, both to facilitate future improvements as well as to reflect post-second tier developments.

The Structural Efficiency Principle

By the beginning of 1988 metal employers and unions had secured government agreement to establish a project team to investigate and recommend solutions to resolve the training and career development problems of the metal and engineering industry. The government agreed to contribute $400 000 per year for three years to the project while the MTIA agreed to contribute $100 000 per year.[19] This represented a major commitment to training in the industry by both the government and the employer organisation.

By then the MTIA was also seeking a major overhauling of the Metal Industry Award and its replacement by a new award to be called the Metal and Engineering Industry Award. The award was to be 'expressed in concise, non-technical language' and to be introduced in three stages, with increasing emphasis on multi-skilling and broad-banding at each stage.

Stage 1 would see the incorporation of a new classification to be known as the 'Mechanical Tradesperson—Special Classification'. This was to meet the need for a higher trade classification and to provide an

---

18. Australian Industrial Relations Commission, *National Wage Case Decision, August 1988*, Print H4000, p. 5.
19. B. Evans, Chief Executive of the MTIA, 'Proposals for award restructuring', address to MTFU conference, 'Issues for 1988', Canberra, February 1988.

appropriate level of remuneration. The new award was to provide for the engagement of adult apprentices and for agreements, to be made at the plant or enterprise level, allowing for the engagement of trainees aged 16 to 18 years under the Australian Traineeship System. It was further proposed that the 349 award classifications be broad-banded to provide for ten new skill levels created to cover both trade and non-trade classifications and for the maximisation of multi-skilling. Both trade and non-trade employees would be required to undertake tasks outside the traditional scope of their classification.

In Stage 2 it was envisaged that there would be a 'refinement of the classification structure by further broad-banding into occupational groups in such a manner as to produce a recognisable career path'. There was also to be the identification and definition of trade streams such as electrical/electronic, mechanical and fabrication. There would be job descriptions for each of the occupational groups in each stream as well as a statement of the education and training requirements for each group. There would also be negotiations over wage levels and vocational training leave.

In the final stage, further refinements would take place, including reductions in the number of occupational groups and in the trade streams.

The provision of trade streams was a recognition of the problems of seeking multi-skilling when a number of unions, each jealous to guard their own membership, was involved. In particular, the Electrical Trades Union made it clear that it was not prepared to allow members of other unions to encroach into its areas of operations. The union was particularly opposed to 'cross-trade multi-skilling'.[20]

The MTFU also sought the establishment of a new award. Its claims, served on the MTIA in April 1988, noted that:

> The central objective of the MTFU is that a new Metal and Engineering (Federal) Award 1988 is operational no later than January 1990. Individual plants would then negotiate an Award Implementation Agreement to move from the old Award to the new Award.[21]

The MTFU evisaged the new award as having about nine basic or generic classifications, each of which would have several sublevels within them and include training requirements. It reaffirmed the view that 'negotiations and work value assessments should be the basis for initiating a career structure in the Award. Central to the career structure should be three trade streams—electrical/electronic, mechanical and metal fabrication'.

Developments in the metal and engineering industry were again overtaken by, and absorbed into, national wage principles. In August 1988 the national wage Bench handed down new wage guidelines that provided for

---

20. ETU, *Metal Industry Restructure: THe ETU Position*, ETU, Sydney, n.d.
21. MTFU National Negotiation Committee, 'THe MTFU claim for wage and award restructuring summary', 14 April 1988.

a Structural Efficiency Principle which would 'be the key element in a new system of wage fixation'. The new principle was to

> provide incentive and scope within the wage fixation system for parties to examine their awards with a view to:
> - establishing skill-related career paths which provide an incentive for workers to continue to participate in skill formation;
> - eliminating impediments to multi-skilling and broadening the range of tasks which a worker may be required to perform;
> - creating appropriate relativities between different categories of workers within the award and at enterprise level;
> - ensuring that working patterns and arrangements enhance flexibility and meet the competitive requirements of the industry . . .[22]

The Commission noted that:

> [it is] not intended that the principle will be applied in a negative cost-cutting manner or to formalise illusory, short-term benefits. Its purpose is to facilitate the type of fundamental review essential to ensure that existing award structures are relevant to modern competitive requirements of industry and are in the best interest of both management and workers.

The Commission did, however, expect that restructuring would be done at 'minimal cost'. The Structural Efficiency Principle, which replaced the Restructuring and Efficiency Principle adopted in March 1987, stated:

> Structural Efficiency
> Increases in wage and salaries or improvement in conditions . . . shall be justified if the union(s) party to an award formally agree(s) to co-operate positively in a fundamental review of the award with a view to implementing measures to improve the efficiency of industry and provide workers with access to more varied, fulfilling and better paid jobs. The measures to be considered should include but not be limited to:
> - establishing skill-related career paths which provide an incentive for workers to continue to participate in skill formation;
> - eliminating impediments to multi-skilling and broadening the range of tasks which a worker may be required to perform;
> - creating appropriate relativities between different categories of workers within the award and at enterprise level;
> - ensuring that working patterns and arrangements enhance flexibility and the efficiency of the industry;
> - including properly fixed minimum rates for classifications in awards, related appropriately to one another, with any amounts in excess of these properly fixed mimimum rates being expressed as supplementary payments;
> - updating and/or rationalising the list of respondents to awards;
> - addressing any cases where award provisions discriminate against sections of the work-force.

Shortly after this decision was handed down, in September 1988, the government sponsored the Metal Industry Mission to the United Kingdom, Sweden and Germany to assist the process of award restructuring.

---

22. Australian Industrial Relations Commission, *National Wage Case Decision, August 1988*, Print H4000, p. 6.

The Mission comprised six representatives from the MTFU, three from the MTIA and three from the Department of Industrial Relations. The mission was charged with the following terms of reference:

> The Mission should examine issues relevant to the restructuring of the Metal Industry Award, and the international competitiveness of the Australian Metal and Engineering Industry. Such issues should include:
> 1. new processes of work and management organisation and their contribution to productivity, international competitiveness and quality assurance;
> 2. associated arrangements in classifications, accreditation, public and private sector training arrangements (and the interface between them) and remunerative incentives for skill acquisition;
> 3. demarcation tensions between unions and the processes for their resolution;
> 4. education/training arrangements which are designed to facilitate the implementation of change in these areas;
> 5. consultation arrangements and participative practices at the plant/enterprise level and their success or otherwise in dealing with these issues;
> 6. the nature of any transitional arrangements entered into to accommodate the above; and
> 7. forms of relevant government involvement (and assistance if any) and their success or otherwise.

The Mission's report to the Minister, entitled *Towards a New Metal and Engineering Industry Award*, provided recommendations regarding each of the terms of reference. It also provided the basis for both the MTIA and the MFTU proposing separate frameworks for the establishment of a new award in December 1988.[23]

In its proposals the MTIA instanced why the Metal Industry Award was 'unsuitable as an instrument to aid in the restructuring process'. It had an excessive number of rigidly defined classifications; its overly prescriptive provisions limited the development of enterprise flexibility; it used complex and legalistic terminology; it did not provide for structured career paths; it had unacceptable wage relativities; and it lacked any training mechanisms. The MTIA envisaged a new classification structure consisting of eight occupational groups (including two groups of trainees and supervisors) and fourteen discrete levels of skill and training. Wage rates were to be determined in respect of each of these levels. The MTIA proposal called for four technical streams: mechanical, fabrication, electrical and electronics.

The MTFU proposal differed in detail rather than in any major way from the MTIA proposal. It proposed that the new award be based on classifications having set educational and training standards. These standards were to be duly accredited and nationally recognised. Within classifications there would be subclassifications based on the progressive acquisition of modules of skill and experience (including limited cross-skilling between engineering streams). The new structure was

---

23. DIR/MTIA/MTFU, *Towards a New Metal and Engineering Industry Award: The Report of the DIR, MTFU and MTIA Mission to UK, Sweden and West Germany, September 1988*, Sydney, 1988.

based on the principle of a career path within each stream, leading from a process worker or tradesperson through to technical officer with a college diploma or experienced engineer.

The ACTU blueprint

The MFTU proposal endorsed, and partly relied on, the ACTU discussion paper entitled *A Draft ACTU Blueprint for Changing Awards and Agreements*. The blueprint was endorsed by the ACTU exective in December 1988 and by a special unions conference in February 1989. The ACTU blueprint, because of the Commission's 'in-principle' acceptance of its basic tenets at subsequent national wage cases, became an important ingredient in the award restructuring exercise. The ACTU recommended that restructuring should proceed after a detailed review of the:
1. structure of the award itself;
2. definitions and classifications;
3. identification of skills exercised in performance of tasks within classifications;
4. relationships between classifications;
5. wage rates applicable to classifications;
6. training needs of industry and employees.

In the ACTU blueprint, the aim of such a review was to establish:
1. a simplified and modern award structure;
2. the removal of obsolete classifications and cover new classifications;
3. a reduction in the number of classifications;
4. the broad-banding of a range of jobs under appropriate single classifications;
5. career paths for all workers within the award;
6. links between training, classifications and wages.

The ACTU blueprint takes a variant of the proposed Metal and Engineering Award as its model and applies it to the building, transport, warehousing, timber, hotel, retail, clerical, vehicle, textile clothing and footwear, furnishing, local government, steel and airlines industries. Its strategy is based on three considerations: higher wage rates for employees on minimum rates awards; the provision of career structures; and the provision of eight or nine skill levels within each award, namely:

1. Basic grade skill, under direct supervision, simple repetitive tasks.
2. Multiple tasks, responsibility for own quality.
3. Operator of mechanical equipment, diagnosis, very limited supervision.
4. More detailed technical knowledge and understanding. Work without supervision, involved with intermediate technology.
5. Trades skill or high skill operative. Completed training equivalent to apprenticeship. Successfully complete 100 or 200 hours of Post Trade Training.

6. Special Class Trade—successfully completed 300 hours of Post Trade Training or equivalent.
7. Advanced Trade—completed Advanced Certificate or 2nd Year of Diploma.
8. Technical Officer—completion of Diploma/Degree.

In February 1989 the national wage Full Bench met to review the Structural Efficiency Principle. The Bench handed down its decision in May. 'Most of the parties and interventors,' the Bench noted, 'informed the Commission of the progress that has been made in the areas they represent'. The Bench added:

> The material indicated that progress is uneven and varies from industry to industry and enterprise to enterprise. It also showed that negotiations are proceeding at different levels and that, in some cases, progress is slow because of disagreement over the agenda and procedure. Preparedness to consider change also appears to vary widely. Progress in some areas is considerable but in the majority is minimal. Notwithstanding that, we are satisfied that the principle as framed in the August 1988 decision can and should facilitate negotiations over a wide range of issues and award areas.[24]

At this case the ACTU submitted that the Commission should approve in principle its national framework or 'blueprint' which would involve restructuring all awards to provide 'consistent, coherent award structures' based on training and skills acquired, and which 'would bear clear and appropriate work value relationships one to another'. The ACTU sought specific endorsement of proposed wage rates spanning the building, metal, warehousing, road transport and clerical industries.

Employers strongly opposed this 'blue-print' approach, claiming that it ignored the distinct needs of different sectors in industry. They also feared that it would result in a rigid system which would reduce the flexibility that formed the rationale of award restructuring. In the final outcome, the Commission endorsed the ACTU proposal (though not the specific wage relationships) because it considered that a national framework would provide a more stable base for on-going award restructuring.

In June 1989 the national wage Bench again reconvened 'to determine whether any wage adjustment should be made having regard to the progress of award restructuring, the tax changes that have been announced, the state of the economy and the extent to which unions are prepared to make the necessary commitments'.[25]

The Commission decided to adjust wage rates between $10 and $15 per week with a second increment to be added six months later. The commencement date of the first increase was to be the date 'on which an award is varied following examination by the Commission of the

---

24. MTFU, *The Metals Engineering Industry Standard: The Next Step. Proposals for Establishing a New Metal and Engineering (Federal) Award*, MTFU, Sydney, December 1988; MTIA and Engineering Employers Association, South Australia, *Award Restructuring in the Metal and Engineering Industry: The Way to Proceed*, MTIA, Sydney, December 1988.
25. ACTU, *Discussion Paper: A Draft ACTU Blueprint for Changing Awards and Agreements*, ACTU, Melbourne, December 1988.

proposals for restructuring and the giving of commitments'. This was intended as a spur to restructuring negotiations. Furthermore, 'the second instalment of the structural efficiency adjustment should only be available if the Commission is satisfied that the principle has been properly implemented and will continue to be implemented effectively'.[26]

At this case the Commission examined the appropriate relativities between awards. Again, it was not prepared to approve the specific relativities sought by the ACTU but did establish a relativity range for 'key classifications'. This relativity range (see Table 13.1) indicates the general acceptance of broad-banding in the metal industry, and union acceptance of appropriate relativities between non-tradespersons and tradespersons in the metal and other industries. The case represented a victory for the ACTU position of a structured or consistent approach between industries. Employers had sought greater flexibility as they had been concerned that the preoccupation with uniformity had inhibited many innovative workplace changes.

Following the national wage cases, negotiations in the metal industry continued with several recourses to the Commission. In March 1990 Deputy President Keogh varied the Metal Industry Award in several important respects. These could be classified under labour flexibility, training, classification structure and transitional arrangements.

The award was varied to enable employers to direct employees to 'carry out such duties as are within the limits of the employee's skill, competence and training' and to 'use such tools and equipment as may be required'. This was in contrast to the former provisions in which employees performed a narrow range of duties defined by their award classification. In addition, more flexible time arrangements have been incorporated into the varied award. Ordinary hours of work 'shall be worked continuously, except for meal breaks, at the discretion of the employer between 6.00 a.m. and 6.00 p.m. provided that the hours are determined by agreement with the majority of employees'. Ordinary hours of work have been extended to ten hours per day. With the agreement of unions and the majority of employees concerned hours may be extended even further, to twelve hours per day. There is provision for greater flexibility with shift work, for continuous operation through the staggering of meal and other breaks, and greater flexibility in the taking of annual leave to minimise disruption to continuity of production.

The amended award states that:

> ... the parties to this award recognise that in order to increase the efficiency, productivity and international competitiveness of industry, a greater commitment to training and skill development is required. Accordingly, the parties commit themselves to:
> (i) developing a more highly skilled and flexible workforce;
> (ii) providing employees with career opportunity through appropriate training to acquire additional skills; and
> (iii) removing barriers to the utilisation of skills acquired.

---

26. Australian Industrial Relations Commission, *National Wage Case Decision, February 1989*, Print H8200, p. 2.

Table 13.1: *Key classification relativity range, national wage case, August 1989*

	% of tradesperson rate
Metal industry worker, grade 4	90–93
Metal industry worker, grade 3	84–88
Metal industry worker, grade 2	78–82
Metal industry worker, grade 1	72–76
Storeman/packer	88–92
Driver, 3–6 tonnes	88–92

Source: Industrial Relations Commission, National Wage Case Decision, August 1989, Print H9100, p. 13.

Employers are required by the award to develop training programs consistent with current and future skill requirements. Vocational skills are to be developed through accredited courses. The relationship between formal qualifications and career advancement is evident from the new award classification structure.

The award variations broad-band more than 340 classifications into fourteen wage groups ranging from engineering/production workers, who have completed one week's induction training, to professional engineers who have completed degress. These groups pivot around the C10 classification, that of the engineering tradesperson. The wage groups, classification titles, minimum training requirements and wage relativities with the enineering tradesperson are indicated in Table 13.2.

In addition to providing for classification broad-banding and the possibilities for multi-skilling the new award places a premium on formal qualifications, some of which (for example the production engineering certificates) are yet to be developed by TAFE. Accredited formal training is regarded as important, not only as part of the skilling process, but also in terms of qualification portability within the industry, and thus the development of career paths. Importantly, the award provides for career development for non-tradespersons as well as tradespersons. Further, with the introduction of adult apprenticeships, there is now greater scope for non-tradespersons to advance into the trades areas.

The award provides for a transition period from March to September 1990 for the implementation of the new award structure. This is to enable all parties to familiarise themselves with the new wage classification and definition structure and for each plant or establishment to apply the new wages and classification system.

The award changes represent the beginning, rather than the end, of the award restructuring exercise in the metal and engineering industry. There is the need to develop the formal courses required for multi-skilling; to provide for the mechanical, fabrication and electrical streams; to provide for subclassifications; to incorporate dispute settlement

Table 13.2: *Classification structure: Metal Industry Award*

Wage group	Classification title	Minimum training requirement	% of C10
C1	Professional engineer	Degree	N/A
	Professional scientist		
C2(b)	Principal technical officer	Diploma	160%
C2(a)	Leading technical officer	5th yr of diploma	150%
	Principal supervisor/trainer/coordinator		
C3	Engineering associate—Level II	Associate diploma	145%
C4	Engineering associate—Level I	3rd yr or assoc. dip.	135%
C5	Engineering technician—Level V	Advanced certificate	130%
	Advanced eng. tradesperson—Level II		
C6	Engineering technician—Level IV	1st yr advanced cert.	125%
C7	Engineering technician—Level III	Post-trade certificate	115%
	Engineering tradesperson—special class Level II		
C8	Engineering Technician—Level II	66% post trade cert.	110%
	Engineering tradesperson—special class Level I		
C9	Engineering technician—Level I	33% post trade cert.	105%
	Engineering tradesperson—Level II		
C10	Engineering tradesperson—Level I	Trade certificate or production eng. cert. III	100%
	Production system employee		
C11	Engineering/production employee—Level IV	Production eng. cert. II	92.4%
C12	Engineering/production employee—Level III	Production eng. cert. I	87.4%
C13	Engineering/production employee—Level II	In-house training	82%
C14	Engineering/production employee—Level I	Up to 38 hours induction training	78%

Source: Australian Industrial Relations Commission, Draft Order, Metal Industry Award 1984—Part 1, 19 March 1990, pp. 16–17.

procedures; to extend further the provisions for labour flexibility; to translate successfully from the old award classification structures to the new; to reduce the potential for demarcations in a multi-union award; and to improve the industrial relations culture in the industry. These, and other challenges, have yet to be overcome.

Summary

The award system that developed under New Protection gave scant regard to international competitiveness. The domestic manufacturing industry was in a cost-plus situation—one in which employers could merely add their margins on to costs in determining product prices. Recourse to the Tariff Board ensured that increased labour costs could be passed onto consumers through higher prices without any consequent loss of business. That situation has changed. In many industries tariff protection has been significantly reduced. Other structural changes, in particular the floating of the Australian dollar and deregulation of the financial sector, have added to the need for Australian manufacturing to be internationally competitive. The employment losses sustained by manufacturing during the 1970s and 1980s gave both employers and unions a rationale for cooperating in changing work methods to make Australian industry more efficient. This endeavour has been facilitated by government activities and by the wage guidelines of the Australian Industrial Relations Commission. A major vehicle for improving work practices has been award restructuring: the development of a more flexible and multi-skilled workforce, the broad-banding of award classifications, the development of training and skill formation modules, and the provision of career structures.

Discussion questions

1. Why have Australian unions and industry become actively involved in award restructuring in recent years?
2. Explain how national wage guidelines have attempted to provide a facilitative environment for award restructuring.
3. What has been the government's role in award restructuring?
4. Explain the ACTU's 'blueprint for changing awards and agreements'. What are the potential benefits and deficiencies of such a blueprint approach to award restructuring?
5. By reference to the metal and engineering experience evaluate the role of the Australian Industrial Relations Commission in award restructuring.
6. What is meant by the terms *broad-banding* and *multi-skilling*? Why are they considered important in the restructuring process?

7. What is the role of formal education in award restructuring and the development of career paths?
8. What are the major impediments to successful award restructuring?
9. What are dispute settlement procedures? Explain their operation and utility.

Further reading

Australian Council of Trade Unions, *Discussion Paper: A Draft ACTU Blueprint for Changing Awards and Agreements*, ACTU, Melbourne, December 1988.
Australian Industrial Relations Commission, *National Wage Case Decision, March 1987*, Print G6800.
Australian Industrial Relations Commission, *National Wage Case Decision, August 1988*, Print H4000.
Australian Industrial Relations Commission, *National Wage Case Decision, February 1989*, Print H8200.
Australian Industrial Relations Commission, *National Wage Case Decision, August 1989*, Print H9100.
Australian Vehicle Manufacturing Industry, *Award Restructuring: Report of the Tripartite Study Mission to Japan, United States, Germany and Sweden*, Melbourne, 1988.
Committee for Economic Development, *How has Business Handled Second-Tier Negotiations?—Survey Results*, Sydney, December 1987.
Confederation of Australian Industry, *Skills Formation and Structural Change*, CAI, Melbourne, December, 1988.
Confederation of Western Australian Industry, *Survey of Second-Tier Wage Negotiations*, CWAI, Perth, October–November 1987.
Dawkins, J.S. (Minister for Employment, Education and Training), *Industry Training in Australia: The Need for Change*, AGPS, Canberra, 1988.
Dawkins J. S. (Minister for Employment, Education and Training), *Improving Australia's Training System*, AGPS, Canberra, 1989.
Department of Industrial Relations, *Labour Market Reform: The Industrial Relations Agenda*, AGPS, Canberra, 1988.
Department of Industrial Relations, *Award Restructuring: Better Jobs Better Future*, AGPS, Canberra, 1989.
Department of Industrial Relations, *Report on the Operation of the Restructuring and Efficiency Principle*, AGPS, Canberra, April 1990.
DIR/MTIA/MTFU, *Towards a New Metal and Engineering Industry Award: the Report of the DIR, MTFU and MTIA Mission to UK, Sweden and West Germany, September 1988*, Sydney, 1988.
Employment and Skills Formation Council, *Guidelines on Women and Award Restructuring*, AGPS, Canberra, 1989.
Grey, I., 'Negotiating structural efficiency: the Maritime Services Board of New South Wales', ACIRRT Working Paper No. 2, University of Sydney, May 1990.
Macken, J.J., *Award Restructuring*, Federation Press, Sydney, 1989.

McDonald, T. and Rimmer, M., 'Award restructuring and the second tier', *Australian Bulletin of Labour*, vol. 14, no. 3, 1988.
Metal Trades Industry Association of Australia, *MTIA Proposals for a Compact with the Metal Unions*, MTIA, Sydney, December 1986.
Metal Trades Industry Association of Australia, *Explanatory Booklet: The Keogh Framework*, MTIA, Sydney, June 1987.
Morris, P, (Minister for Industrial Relations), *Award Restructuring: The Task Ahead*, AGPS, Canberra, 1989.
Rimmer, M. and Zappala, J., 'Labour market flexibility and the second tier', *Australian Bulletin of Labour*, vol. 14, no. 4, September 1988.
State Training Board Victoria, *Award Restructuring: The Challenge and Opportunities for TAFE*, STBV, Melbourne, 1989.
Workplace Change, No. 3, AGPS, Canberra, July 1989.

Part Five

CONTEMPORARY TRENDS

The conduct of workplace industrial relations has emerged as a critical economic issue in Australia. The government's program of micro-economic reform has focused increasing attention on the capacity of industry to become more globally competitive. The need to raise labour productivity and develop more flexible and adaptable forms of work organisation has tended to shift attention to industrial relations at the workplace. In the following chapter we discuss a number of important determinants that have affected the procedures and practices of industrial relations at this particular level. Growing pressures for the democratisation of decision-making within organisations have also been associated with deteriorating economic conditions in Australia and with the need to lift competitive performance. In addition, the demand for greater democracy at work has provoked challenges to the traditional structure of management prerogatives. Both employees and their union representatives have sought to exercise greater influence and control over decisions affecting their employment and their work environment. The renewed interest in industrial democracy has not been unrelated to union initiatives for greater job security and for improved standards of health and safety. Another issue of contemporary economic importance involves female employment. Changing social pressures and the increasing participation of women in the workforce have forced governments to legislate to make it unlawful to discriminate on the basis of sex or marital status. The development of measures to provide more equal opportunities for women has also involved challenges to managerial prerogatives.

CHAPTER 14

Workplace Industrial Relations

Pressures to raise labour productivity and improve efficiency levels in Australia have focused attention on the issue of industrial relations reform at the workplace. There is a widespread belief that major productivity improvements can be achieved through changes in the organisation and structure of work and in the ways in which employees are trained, remunerated and motivated. This chapter first examines the impact of the conciliation and arbitration system on workplace industrial relations and the jurisdictional difficulties that the federal tribunal encounters in handling plant-level disputes. It then examines the structure of unions and the nature of bargaining at the workplace as well as the role and activities of management. Within this context the chapter describes how a number of organisations have sought to restructure their industrial relations arrangements at the workplace. Finally, there is an analysis of the problems of employee turnover and absenteeism.

The workplace and arbitration

In Australia there has been a preoccupation with the study of the formal institutional processes of industrial relations. As a consequence there has been little systematic analysis of the nature, organisation and scope of workplace industrial relations. Important matters such as the processes used to set wages and resolve disputes in different establishments and the practices adopted to manage and motivate individuals or workgroups have not been adequately researched. In a sense this is surprising. The workplace provides the building blocks for our institutional arrangements.[1] The disputes that come before the tribunals for conciliation and arbitration and the issues that are negotiated between unions, managers and employer associations almost all emerge from conflicts that occur at the workplace. This is where capital and labour are brought together to make goods and services. It is where employers and employees fight for control over the labour process and where the amount, type and level of work effort is fixed and regulated. It is also where accommodations are reached and informal agreements are made about how labour power is to be transformed into productive activity.

In spite of the intrinsic importance of the workplace, it is possible to explain this narrow research focus by reference to the institutional arrangements in the country. Australia's system of conciliation and arbitration has tended to limit the scope and reduce the responsibilities of workplace managers and unionists. The room for independent behaviour could be said to have been severely constrained by the dominance of the formal system and the centralising influence of arbitration. Indeed, Rimmer has asserted that the character of Australian workplace industrial relations can best be described as 'structured non-responsibility'.[2] He claims that non-responsibility arises from the structure of industrial relations institutions and the locus of decision-making power. A number of institutional features of Australian industrial relations are said to contribute to this situation. First, multi-unionism at the workplace has fragmented union authority and obstructed union–management relationships. Second, the unwillingness of business organisations to delegate power to industrial relations specialists has contributed to weak industrial relations management at the shopfloor. Third, the nature of awards has militated against workplace involvement in industrial relations matters. In the case of industry awards the provisions are often framed in general terms to suit the lowest common denominators of the industry and make scant allowance for the needs of particular workplaces. Alternatively, where workplaces are covered by multiple awards, setting different standards for different occupational groupings in the same site, a fragmented authority structure may emerge which impedes union–management dealings. Last, the practice of resolving industrial questions by applying general standards may act to restrict the role of workplace managers and unionists to 'implementation and surveillance, devoid of concern for the relationship between pay and job security on the one hand and labour cost control, productivity and the like on the other'.[3]

Littler, Quinlan and Kitay have also pointed to a number of other ways in which the conciliation and arbitration system has affected the charac-

---

1. R. Callus and R. Lansbury, 'Workplace industrial relations', *Labour and Industry*, vol. 1, no. 2, 1988, p. 364.
2. M. Rimmer, 'Research into workplace industrial relations: lessons for Australia from the English experience', *Research into Industrial Relations at the Workplace*, Centre for Industrial Relations Research, University of Sydney, Working Paper No. 1, May 1988, p. 11.
3. Ibid., p. 13.

ter and development of workplace industrial relations.[4] They point out that union shopfloor organisation has received little encouragement from arbitration. In their opinion: 'Tribunals have tended to view shop stewards as an essentially subordinate and minor functionary within the overall policing function performed by unions under arbitration'.[5] It is also suggested that the development of incentive payment systems has been inhibited by the minimum wage floor established by arbitration and that, even where tribunals have permitted the use of such payment systems, they have imposed tight regulations to prevent sweating. Furthermore, the authors assert that the scope of workplace bargaining has been restricted by tribunal and High Court decisions particularly as it relates to the question of managerial prerogatives. Limitations on the ability of tribunals to arbitrate in this area have tended to narrow the boundaries of workplace negotiations.

The limitations of federal jurisdiction

Although the arbitration system has had a profound effect on the conduct of workplace industrial relations, the federal tribunals are poorly equipped to handle disputes that are confined to the single plant. Australia's arbitration system has simply not been designed to deal with them: more often than not, they fall outside the federal Commission's jurisdiction. Such disputes are most unlikely to be interstate in their effect and perhaps unlikely to be 'industrial' in character. The courts have drawn an artificial distinction between 'industrial' and 'managerial' matters, which has placed many plant-level grievances outside the Commission's domain. Some attempts have been made to overcome the problem of jurisdiction, through the argument that plant-level disputes arise out of awards and therefore may be handled by the Commission. That approach has not found much legal support:

> [The High Court's] reasoning was that it was not an interstate dispute and therefore not a matter with which the Commission could deal. The limitation on Federal power in the Australian Constitution to the settlement of interstate industrial disputes precluded the Commissioner from dealing with this intra State dispute and as it was not a matter which had been part of the original interstate ... dispute it could not be part of the award made in settlement of that original dispute. Indeed, it is suggested in the judgment of the High Court that it may be difficult to create an interstate industrial dispute in such a way as to make it possible for an award to be made to confer power on a Commisioner to deal with [such matters].[6]

These limitations on the Commission leave a gap in jurisdiction, because of the reluctance of state tribunals to interfere in disputes

---

4. C. Littler, M. Quinlan and J. Kitay, *Australian Workplace Industrial Relations: Towards a Conceptual Framework*, Centre for Industrial Relations Research, University of Sydney and Labour Studies Program, University of Melbourne, Working Paper No. 8, June 1989.
5. Ibid., p. 17.
6. Mr Justice Moore, commenting on the *Falls* case, in which an employer had challenged a reinstatement order by the Commission. Cited in P.F. Brissenden, *The Settlement of Labour Disputes on Rights in Australia*, Institute of Industrial Relations, University of California, 1966, p. 63.

concerning employees covered by federal awards. To the extent that it does act to settle local disputes, the Commission must depend very much on the agreement of the parties in dispute. Where the parties genuinely desire a mediated or determined solution, and are prepared to convert any determination into 'private' arbitration, federal tribunals and their ancillary machinery can be useful in helping to resolve plant-level disputes. However, where either party wishes to prevent the intervention of the Commission, the Constitution affords a ready means of doing so.

Even if the parties are willing to accept the Commission's help, the generalised level of operation of the tribunal system still hinders the effective handling of plant grievances. As Fisher has noted, the major areas of the Commission's operation, such as national wage cases, annual leave, standard hours and so on, are areas of public debate 'far removed from plant-level relationships and argued by representatives who are ordinarily not known to industrial workers and who are not even representatives of the individual's union. From the management side of the record, the case is equally remote'.[7] According to Fisher, the arbitral systems have also tended to encourage monolithic styles of representation by both unions and employers' organisations for the convenience of Commission processes.

Trade unions and the workplace

The operations of the tribunal system have helped to foster unions that perform competently at the national or industry level but are less effective in handling plant or office-level disputes. Furthermore, the arbitration system has influenced the structural features of trade unionism (see Chapter 8). A multiplicity of craft and occupational unions have been created and sustained. This in turn has led to the establishment of multiple bargaining agents at the workplace. In a speech in 1989, the secretary of the ACTU, Mr Kelty, showed his clear dissatisfaction with these arrangements:

> I have never held the view that union organisation of this country is right. It is not efficient for you as managers in many cases; not efficient for us as unions...it is a ludicrous position that we have in the country so many unions, in so many industries, with so many bargaining agents...There is no place in Australia in the next decade for more than two or three bargaining units in each industry.[8]

At present, most Australian workplaces are covered by multiple unions. A survey of 336 establishments belonging to Business Council of Australia (BCA) member companies disclosed that nearly 80 per cent of the

---

7. W.K. Fisher, 'Plant relationships: the role of the tribunal', *Journal of Industrial Relations*, vol. 14, no. 3, 1965, p. 265.
8. Quoted in R. Blandy, J. Sloan and M. Wooden, 'Reforming the trade union structure in Australia', *Australian Bulletin of Labour*, vol. 15, no. 5, 1989, pp. 370–71.

Table 14.1: *Number of trade unions per workplace*

No. of unions	No. of workplaces	%
0	17	5.1
1	51	15.2
2	44	13.1
3	34	10.1
4	36	10.7
5	37	11.0
6–10	98	29.2
11+	19	5.6
Total	336	100.0

Source: Business Council of Australia, *Enterprise-based Bargaining Units*, Melbourne, 1989, p. 35.

Table 14.2: *Number of trade unions by workplace size*

Workplace	Mean
Less than 50 employees	1.5
50–99 employees	2.2
100–199 employees	3.4
200–499 employees	4.9
500–999 employees	6.2
1000–1999 employees	7.9
More than 2000 employees	10.9

Source: Business Council of Australia, *Enterprise-based Bargaining Units*, Melbourne, 1989, p. 35.

workplaces had employees in two or more unions. More than a third of workplaces had more than six unions, some up to twenty unions. Table 14.1 provides the details of this coverage.

The survey also revealed a clear relationship between workplace size and the number of trade unions present in each workplace. It can be seen from Table 14.2 that those establishments with more than a thousand employees had an average of between eight and eleven unions representing the workforce.

Many of the craft or occupational unions had members spread across a large number of workplaces. Of the 336 workplaces surveyed, the Amalgamated Metal Workers Union (AMWU), for example, had members in 211 plants. It had an average of 76 members in these plants, which represented just 16 per cent of the total union members in those places of work. The Electrical Trades Union (ETU) had an average of only 36 members in the 176 plants in which it was represented. A mere 7.1 per cent of all the union members in those plants belonged to the union. Table 14.3 shows that this situation is not confined to these two unions. Many represented a small number of members in a large number of workplaces. These diseconomies of scale would seem to impose substantial difficulties in the way of unions providing adequate service to their union members, particularly where that membership is dispersed across a diverse range of industries.

Table 14.3: *Union representation across workplaces*

	No. of plants	Membership per plant Average	Average coverage[a]
Amalgamated Metal Workers (AMWU)	211	76	16.1
Electrical Trades Union (ETU)	176	36	7.1
Federated Clerks Union (FCU)	125	35	11.9
Federated Engine Drivers (FEDFA)	88	39	9.2
Australian Workers Union (AWU)	83	150	53.3
Federated Iron Workers (FIA)	76	219	33.7
Transport Workers Union (TWU)	68	49	20.3
Storemen and Packers (FSPU)	63	37	25.2
Australasian Society of Engineers (ASE)	62	56	14.1
Building Workers (BWIU)	57	56	12.5
Assoc of Draughting & Supervisory (ADSTE)	45	49	5.2
Plumbers and Gasfitters (PGEU)	41	12	5.4

[a] The average proportion of employees within each plant represented by each union where a union is present.
Source: Business Council of Australia, *Enterprise-based Bargaining Units*, Melbourne, 1989, p. 36.

The formation of joint union shop committees can often overcome a number of the problems of union fragmentation and provide a stronger and more coordinated system of union representation at the level of the workplace. In the Business Council of Australia's workplace survey, however, only 21 per cent of the multi-union establishments reported the existence of a formal combined union committee.[9] Such structures were more frequent, nevertheless, where the number of unions was large. In those establishments with more than ten unions joint shop committees were present in 35 per cent of plants.

The strength of union representation at the workplace has been the subject of much debate. Some commentators have argued that shop steward activity is very limited compared with the United Kingdom.[10] Certainly the Jackson Committee of Inquiry into manufacturing industry in 1975 could find little evidence of shop organisation. According to the Committee: 'An active shop steward...[was] a rarity'.[11] Others have suggested that the situation is far from uniform and trade union representation at the workplace is far from insignificant.[12] Indeed, Rimmer has detailed the long and continuous history of workplace organisation in the railways, power, shipbuilding, engineering and metal trades industry.[13] Nevertheless, it would appear that Australian unions

---

9. Business Council of Australia, *Enterprise-based Bargaining Units: A Better Way of Working*, BCA, Melbourne, 1989, Part 2, pp. 15–16.
10. O. Foenander, *Shop Stewards and Shop Committees*, Melbourne University Press, Melbourne, 1965.
11. Committee to Advise on Policies for Manufacturing Industries, *Policies for Development of Manufacturing Industry*, vol. 1, AGPS, Canberra, 1975.
12. J. Benson, 'Workplace union organisation in Australia', *Labour and Industry*, vol. 1, no. 3, 1988.
13. M. Rimmer, 'Work place unionism' in B. Ford and D. Plowman (eds), *Australian Unions*, 2nd ed., Macmillan, Melbourne, 1989, pp. 125–136.

generally have been reluctant to allow shop stewards to do little more than assist in a range of minor administrative duties. Benson believes this may be explained by the challenge that strong stewards pose to the authority of full-time officials.[14] A number of writers have suggested that the development of strong shop-floor organisations has similarly been retarded by the attitude of employers who have been reluctant to legitimise the activities of shop stewards and unwilling to incorporate them into plant-level industrial relations.[15] However, recent evidence from the BCA enterprise study indicates that meetings between stewards and management are quite extensive. In 38 per cent of the unionised plants studied, regular and frequent (once a month or more) meetings were held between union stewards and management (see Table 14.4). In almost half of the workplaces with six or more unions regular meetings were held.

The issues most commonly discussed at the shop steward–management meetings are listed in Table 14.5. These were occupational health and safety, pay and conditions of employment, work practices and methods and manning arrangements.

The BCA survey asked plant managers to indicate the extent to which shop stewards had 'a say' over a number of work-related issues. Apart from the initiation of industrial action, shop stewards were only said to have some degree of influence over health and safety issues, dismissals, discipline and redundancy matters. The issues which shop stewards had least influence over were the purchase of new equipment and machinery, hiring, work hours and overtime, the allocation of tasks and fringe benefits. This information is shown in Table 14.6.

Workplace bargaining

The information contained in Tables 14.5 and 14.6 suggests that there is a considerable amount of informal workplace discussion over industrial relations issues. This is particularly the case in establishments characterised by multi-unionism. It would appear that the discussions cover a broad range of issues, although the degree of union influence may be limited to a rather short list of matters. In a study by Benson of workplace negotiations in the electricity generation industry in Victoria, evidence was found of quite extensive bargaining between shop stewards and management.[16] The most frequently negotiated issues were general working conditions, health and safety, staffing and manning levels, pay problems and classifications, overtime and discipline. Indeed he claims that the findings 'are contrary to the conventional wisdom that in a highly centralised system, shop stewards only handle individual grievances and

---

14. J. Benson, ibid, pp. 412–13.
15. See ibid, p. 414.
16. Ibid., pp. 418–20.

Table 14.4: *Number of unions by frequency of union steward–management meetings*

No. of unions	Once a month or more —regular	Once a month or more —irregular	Less than once a month	Never
1	10.3	33.3	33.3	23.1
2	40.0	27.5	22.5	10.0
3	35.3	35.3	26.5	2.9
4	37.1	34.3	25.7	2.9
5	37.8	40.5	16.2	5.4
6–10	48.5	29.9	19.6	2.1
11+1	47.4	42.1	10.5	0.0
Total	38.2	33.2	22.3	6.3

Source: Business Council of Australia, *Enterprise-based Bargaining Units*, Melbourne 1989, Part 2, p. 16.

Table 14.5: *Issues most often discussed at shop steward–management meetings*

	% of companies
Occupational health and safety	41.8
Pay and conditions of employment	30.5
Work practices and methods	25.9
Manning arrangements	20.5
Company performance (profitability)	15.5
Productivity and efficiency	12.3
Company policies and business strategies	11.8
Grievances	10.5
Technological change	10.9
Disciplinary and dismissal issues	9.5
Award interpretation, restructuring and breaches	8.6
Overtime	7.3
Use of contractors	6.4
Hours, flexitime and RDOs	5.5

Source: Business Council of Australia, *Enterprise-based Bargaining Units*, Melbourne, 1989, Part 2, p. 17.

Table 14.6: Amount of say workplace representatives have in plant decision-making

	No say at all %	Very little %	A little %	Quite a lot %	A great deal %
How tasks are allocated	39.2	39.5	16.3	3.9	1.0
Hours of work and overtime	36.8	38.8	15.3	7.5	1.6
Changes in manning levels	28.2	23.6	24.9	14.8	8.5
Pay issues	17.3	30.0	28.7	19.9	4.2
Fringe benefits	43.1	28.6	18.1	8.2	2.0
Initiation of industrial action	3.9	9.4	18.2	39.7	28.7
Health & safety issues	3.6	16.6	30.3	42.0	7.5
Dismissals	17.8	19.5	26.1	26.4	10.2
Major changes in production methods	19.2	29.6	28.3	19.5	3.3
Discipline matters	12.9	19.1	31.0	32.3	4.6
Purchase of new equipment and machinery	52.0	30.4	16.3	1.3	—
Redundancy/rationalisation	21.9	20.2	18.5	26.8	12.6
Who is laid off	30.3	18.9	16.2	23.2	11.4
Who is hired	72.3	20.8	3.6	2.6	0.7

Source: Business Council of Australia, *Enterprise-based Bargaining Units*, Melbourne, 1989, Part 2, p. 17.

minor administrative duties'.[17] Lee has provided additional evidence of the importance of informal workplace bargaining in the coal industry.[18] She shows that bonus payments are wholly negotiated by employee representatives and management at each mine. They reflect productivity and take into account local mining conditions. Such payments make up more than 25 per cent of the average weekly earnings of mine workers.

The introduction of the two-tier wage-fixing system in March 1987 has provided substantial encouragement for workplace bargaining. While the first tier made allowance for national wage increases, the second tier provided for movements of up to 4 per cent under a restructuring and efficiency principle (see chapter 14). In order to obtain such an increase the parties were required to introduce workplace changes that yielded efficiency improvements. Basically, the initiatives were to embrace changes in work and management practices, the reduction of demarcation barriers and measures to facilitate multi-skilling and improved training. The objectives were to be achieved primarily through negotiations and discussions at the enterprise and workplace levels.

Although the Industrial Relations Commission was not always able to achieve this goal, Rimmer and Zappala found that second-tier negotiations in the Metal Industry Award—Australia's largest award—were almost exclusively conducted at the workplace level.[19] This, they suggest, may have been due to the long tradition of strong shop steward organisation in the industry and the Amalgamated Metal Workers' Union's strategy of involvement in industry renewal, which endorsed the concept of greater labour flexibility at the workplace. In their analysis of the content of 1334 metal plant agreements, Rimmer and Zappala identified a considerable range of changes in a number of industrial relations practices. These included methods of avoiding wastage or downtime in the organisation of work, reviews of demarcation barriers, the introduction of more flexible work-time arrangements, initiatives in the areas of communication and consultation, and wider opportunities for supervisors to handle tools. The changes shown in Table 14.7 were found to be most numerous among the plant level agreements.

Data gathered by Deery and Purcell in 1988 on the conduct of second-tier negotiations showed that most large companies in the survey sample carried out the bargaining exercise at the enterprise, division or establishment level.[20] Only 16 per cent of the respondents negotiated second-tier increases at the industry level. This information is shown in Table 14.8.

The study also found that 60 per cent of the negotiations were conducted between company representatives and mixed teams of shop

---

17. Ibid., pp. 418–19.
18. M. Lee, 'The coal industry tribunal; the case for its retention', *Australian Bulletin of Labour*, vol. 15, no. 1, 1988.
19. M. Rimmer and J. Zappala, 'Labour market flexibility and the second tier', *Australian Bulletin of Labour*, vol. 14, no. 4, 1988.
20. The results of the study have not been published. For a description of the research method and a profile of the respondents see S. Deery and J. Purcell, 'Strategic choices in industrial relations management in large organisations', *Journal of Industrial Relations*, vol. 31, no. 4, 1989.

Table 14.7: *Content of second-tier agreements in the metal industry (n=1334)*

Form of change	Plant agreements containing changed practice (%)
Modification to work patterns	86
Review, change or removal of demarcation barriers	49
Reorganisation of work	49
Training and retraining	46
Flexibility in working hours	44
Consultative procedures	41
Dispute settling procedures	40
Changes in role of supervisor	25
Guidelines for introduction and use of new Technology	22
Use of contractors	18

Source: Derived from M. Rimmer and J. Zappala, 'Labour market flexibility and the second tier', *Australian Bulletin of Labour*, vol. 14, no. 4, 1988, pp. 583–7.

Table 14.8: *Level at which second-tier negotiations were conducted (n=121)*

Level of bargaining	Percentage
Industry	16
Enterprise	36
Division or business unit	20
Establishment	28

Source: S. Deery and J. Purcell, 'Factors influencing the conduct of second-tier negotiations', unpublished manuscript, University of Melbourne, 1989.

stewards, employees and union officials. In only 26 per cent of cases were employer associations directly involved in the bargaining process.

The survey revealed a relationship between the size of the corporate personnel department and the location of the second-tier wage negotiations. Firms with large numbers of corporate personnel specialists (10+) showed a greater propensity to centralise their bargaining at the enterprise level than did firms with smaller personnel head offices. Companies with fewer specialists tended to negotiate second-tier arrangements below the enterprise level at the division/business unit or establishment level.[21] It is also relevant to point out that decentralised bargaining was more common in organisations that devolved financial accountability to the division or business unit or the establishment and those that produced goods or services across a wide range of markets.

At a more general level, it would seem that bargaining will become more decentralised as organisations embrace strategies that emphasise

---

21. Ibid., pp. 464–5.

local profit centres and provide greater autonomy for business unit managers. As is evident overseas, these managers will argue that the structures of industrial relations should fit the corporate need for profit centre and business unit decentralisation.[22] Moreover, growing interest in the link between pay and productivity seen in performance-related pay, flexibility and restructuring activities, and the emphasis on individualism and teamwork, has meant that localised initiatives are far more relevant.

Management and workplace industrial relations

The conduct of industrial relations at the workplace will be affected by the policies that are adopted for the management of employees. In framing those policies attention will normally be directed to the development of practices and procedures which assist the organisation to achieve its business objectives. The establishment of orderly systems of dispute resolution and the construction of a work environment in which the organisation can secure employee commitment to its corporate goals will be pre-eminent.

Most large companies in Australia appear to have an established philosophy or policy on the way in which employees are to be managed or treated.[23] According to Brewster, Gill and Richbell such policies provide 'a set of proposals and actions which establishes the organisation's approach to its employees and acts as a reference point for management.[24] They claim that the overriding objective in formalising an industrial relations policy is to assist management establish an ordered and consistent framework for the conduct of industrial relations. This entails the formulation of principles or settled rules of action to which operating management is subject. The industrial relations policy of Mobil Oil Australia provides such an example. According to the company, the aim of its policy is:

> To achieve and maintain a positive industrial relations climate which ensures the commercial viability of Mobil Oil Australia Limited and associated companies and to preserve and protect the rights and dignity of its employees and management and other affected groups.

In terms of its operational elements, the policy outlines the specific responsiblities of line management, the company's approach to dispute settlement and its relations to unions as well as the organisation's attitude to management–employee communications. The following extracts provide the basic components of Mobil Oil's industrial relations policy:

---

22. See J. Purcell and B. Ahlstrand, 'Corporate strategy and the management of employee relations in the multi-divisional company', *British Journal of Industrial Relations*, vol. 27, no. 3, 1989.
23. See S. Deery and J. Purcell, 'Strategic choices in industrial relations management', p. 474.
24. C.J. Brewster, C.G. Gill and S. Richbell, 'Industrial relations policy: a framework for analysis', in K. Thurley and S. Wood (eds), *Industrial Relations and Management Strategy*, Cambridge University Press, Cambridge, 1983, p. 62.

Responsibilities of line management

Line Management has the primary responsibility for day-to-day industrial relations within its immediate area of control. The general principle is that industrial relations matters will be handled by those most closely involved with the issue. However, Line Management will first consult with the Employee Relations Officer or Relations Manager and seek advice as to the manner in which industrial matters should be managed. Decisions taken and postures adopted are at the discretion of the appropriate Line Manager, subject to common law, the industrial agreements and awards binding on the Company and the Oil Industry Industrial Committee (O.I.I.C.) Charter.

Specifically:
1. Line Management should attempt to resolve potential industrial relations problems at the earliest possible stage. Emphasis will be placed on consultation and direct negotiation.
2. Line Management will discuss any proposed change to work practices, procedures or technological change likely to affect employee job security with the Manager Labour Relations before implementation. Prior consultation with the employee's union is an integral part of the Company's policy in these circumstances.

Dispute Settlement

The Company will always be prepared to discuss with an authorized representative of a union, any issue likely to impact on the industrial relations climate. Issues raised with the Company will be handled expeditiously and the Company's reply will be advised promptly.

The Company will attempt to resolve all matters in dispute through direct negotiation with the appropriate union(s) following the established disputes procedure...

Relations with Unions

The Company recognizes that unions are an integral part of the Australian industrial relations system and all employees are expected to be members of the appropriate union in accordance with the industry's agreements.

The Company recognises an employee appointed by his/her union as a shop steward or delegate for the area in which he/she is employed.

He/she is expected to conduct union activities in meal breaks and rest periods except, with management approval, at other times. Union meetings will normally be held outside Company premises except with management approval.

The Company will endeavour to maintain harmonious relations with accredited union officials and will endeavour to ensure that the disputes procedures are followed at all times.

The Company will not unreasonably withhold information, amenities or opportunities that a union officials may seek for the conduct of activities on behalf of employee members of the union.

Management–Employee Communications

Management–employee communications are essential to the maintenance of a positive industrial relations climate.

Communications programmes have been established to increase employees' knowledge and awareness of the Company's activities. To achieve this objective the programme has three major thrusts:

1. to provide information on the Company's activities, plans, policies and philosophy through company publications and presentations.
2. to communicate the need for organisational and technological change to meet our business objectives.
3. to achieve a better flow of information between management and employees to establish a mutual understanding of respective needs. The Company recognizes that change will be most successfully accomplished by establishing a climate of trust through planned advance communication of plans and resolution of potential adverse employee reactions.

The industrial relations policy of an organisation can be seen as a summary of the proposals, objectives and standards that it holds in relation to the management of employees.[25] In larger organisations it has become more common for this to be integrated into a wider corporate plan that places industrial relations within a strategic context and recognises its contribution to the achievement of the firm's medium to long-term goals. It has been submitted that:

> A company's industrial relations policy should form an integral part of the total strategy with which it pursues its business objectives. In this way it will not only define the company's course of action with regard to particular industrial relations issues; it will also reflect the interaction of industrial relations with policies in other areas, such as production, marketing or finance.[26]

At the workplace, such industrial relations policies may seek to maximise the dual objectives of flexibility in the utilisation and deployment of workers and a high degree of commitment, loyalty and participation on the part of individual employees and work groups.[27] Two Australian human resource managers, Bongarzoni and Compton, have claimed that a 'primary ingredient in achieving a firm's objectives is the establishment of an employee relations climate which successfully develops recognition of the shared common purpose among its employees'.[28] They suggest that effective industrial relations within an enterprise will depend on a number of factors, including interesting and challenging work, a fair and equitable reward system, adequate job security, open communications, shared information, effective grievance procedures, and the regular monitoring of the employee relations climate.

Within the American industrial relations context, Kochan and Chalykoff have identified three interrelated dimensions of innovative human resource management at the workplace.[29] The first dimension focuses on the management of conflict and the provision of grievance mechanisms. They assert that innovative organisations normally possess a variety of processes to achieve this goal. These include grievance procedures,

---

25. Ibid., p. 63.
26. See K. Thurley and S. Wood, 'Business strategy and industrial relations strategy' in K. Thurley and S. Wood (eds), *Industrial Relations and Management Strategy*, pp. 198–9.
27. T.A. Kochan and J.B. Chalykoff, 'Human resource management and business life cycles: some preliminary propositons', in A. Kleingartner and C. Anderson (eds), *Human Resource Management in High Technology Firms*, Lexington Books, Lexington, Kentucky, 1917, p. 187.
28. C. Bongarzoni and R. Compton, 'The impact of the macro industrial relations system at the enterprise level' in R. Blandy and J. Niland (eds), *Alternatives to Arbitration*, Allen & Unwin, Sydney, 1986, p. 128.
29. T.A. Kochan and J.B. Chalykoff, 'Human resource management and business life cycles', pp. 187–8.

counselling, appeals, informal meetings and ombudsman services. The second dimension of innovative human resource management involves the rules and principles for organising work and designing jobs. Kochan and Chalykoff indicate that more sophisticated work organisations tend to emphasise relatively few job classifications, the use of work teams as opposed to individual work assignments, compensation systems that set pay on the basis of skill attained rather than the specific job performed on a given day, and the flexible assignment of people to different tasks. The third dimension relates to the extent to which the firm attempts to bring individuals into the decision-making process surrounding their job in order to motivate them better and to improve productivity and product quality through more decentralised organisational decision-making and communications. Within this context they cite the use of quality circles and employee involvement processes.

Few Australian firms have developed such an integrated and innovative set of industrial relations policies and practices at the workplace. Nevertheless, product market pressures and the threat of significant competition have forced many companies to question their existing workplace arrangements and their previous approaches to the management of industrial relations. It is possible to provide a number of examples of this.

Australian Marine Engineering Corporation (Amecon)

Amecon assumed ownership of the former government-owned Williamstown Dockyard in Victoria in 1987. A history of poor management, debilitating work practices, inter-union rivalries and industrial unrest had left the naval dockyard with substantial financial losses and the threat of imminent closure. Following the decision to privatise the dockyard the new owners insisted on radical changes to the workplace industrial relations system in order to raise productivity. One of the most radical was the planned rationalisation of the union structure. Before privatisation the workforce was covered by twenty-three unions, some thirty different awards and more than 400 different work classifications, all strictly demarcated. Through cooperation with the ACTU, Amecon was able to reduce the number of on-site unions to only three— the Amalgamated Metal Workers Union, the Federated Ironworkers Association and the Electrical Trades Union—and reach agreement in June 1988 on an enterprise industrial agreement. This was not achieved without industrial unrest. A picket imposed by the (then) Federated Storemen and Packers' Union, in protest against the union rationalisation scheme, led to the closure of the plant for thirteen weeks.

Productivity became the key objective of the organisation and was seen as the responsibility of both management and the production employees. One of the purposes of the 1988 industrial agreement was to create a demarcation-free and fully flexible work environment which would enable productivity to rise to internationally competitive levels. Eight new skill levels were created for operators and tradespeople, and all employees were provided with a training plan and the opportunity to progress to the highest skill level in their appropriate area within about two years. Skill levels were designed with company requirements in mind, and the job responsibilities of the top-level tradesperson incorporated the training of lower-level employees. Supplementary TAFE training was also provided as part of a skills enhancement program. The overriding intention of this program was 'to enable each person to complete, to the maximum practical extent, whole jobs, i.e. all of the tasks associated with a particular job'.[30] Remuneration was directly related to the level of skill attained.

Another important workplace change was also incorporated in the Industrial Agreement. A Site Consultative Committee was established to assist 'in creating a stable and cooperative environment within the Company' (Clause 30.2.1). The committee comprised the managing director, two other managers and three employee representatives, selected by the unions. It was to serve as a conduit through which management could 'obtain and discuss the views and concerns of the employees' and unions could 'discuss management proposals and the effects of proposed changes on employees'. The agreement also stipulated that the company would provide regular reports on the affairs of the business, including market conditions and prospects, manpower projections and skill requirements, proposed technological changes and contracting arrangements (Clause 30.5.1).

The motive behind these new organisational arrangements was the drive to enhance productivity. Amecon believed that it would not be able to tender successfully for naval contracts unless it raised performance levels to those of its international competitors. Significant productivity achievements have been made. The company recorded a four-fold increase in labour productivity between 1987 and 1990 and partly as a result of this was awarded the ANZAC ship contract for the supply of ten frigates for the Royal Australian Navy and the Royal New Zealand Navy with an option for a further two vessels. The contract was secured by virtue of the internationally competitive price tendered by the company. However, to complete the fixed-price project within budget the company is faced with the challenge of raising productivity by a further 40 per cent by 1992.

Black & Decker

Black & Decker (Australasia) Pty Ltd is a wholly owned subsidiary of the American Black & Decker Corporation, a leading producer of power tools and supplier of household products. In 1986, after a series of disappointing financial results, the parent company dismissed a number of the senior management team and appointed a new managing director. In the space of four years the Australasian operation turned a $5 million loss in 1986 into a $12 million profit. The company was also appointed as

---

30. Australian Marine Engineering Corporation, *Industrial Agreement*, 30 June 1988, p. 73.

a Global Design Centre involved in major research and development work. Over this period the company developed a strategy entitled 'Sustainable Competitive Advantage' which was to be implemented through a program called 'Continuous Improvement'. The manufacturing policy placed a top priority on product quality and its attainment through 'a well-trained, fully involved and motivated workforce'. As a starting point the company gathered the opinions of its employees about a range of matters, including their attitudes to internal communications, feedback on performance, employment practices, management decision-making, the nature of the work, reward systems, employee amenities, opportunities for career development and product quality.

The main findings indicated that the company could do much to improve communications and its general responsiveness to employee suggestions. In addition, it was found that employees were looking for greater feedback on individual performance. Of particular interest to the company was the belief by employees that products were being poorly manufactured and improvements were required. At that time warranty returns were running at 10 per cent and production defect rates for some products at more than 30 per cent. The immediate response of the company was to shut down the production line for two weeks and assign engineers to the task of redesigning the process based on operators' input. Black & Decker used this time to enhance the operator's process skills through training. The company saw this as an opportunity to reinforce the importance of employee input and demonstrate management's willingness to respond positively to employee concerns. Worker participation was highlighted as a crucial factor in achieving total quality control. Black & Decker now closes the production lines early one day a week to enable operators and their supervisors to meet and analyse quality-related statistics for the week's output. Problems are identified and solutions are prepared. Many warranty returns now run at just 0.5 per cent.

Extensive training of the production workforce has become an intrinsic part of the company's total quality program. The company spends more than 3 per cent of its wages and salary bill on training and development. A Worker Career Improvement Program has been introduced under which the company encourages employees to undertake outside education courses in such fields as marketing, computer studies and management. On successful completion of the course the company reimburses the employee 50 per cent of the costs incurred. The purpose of the program is to encourage shopfloor and clerical staff to develop their skills and provide the company with a pool of educated employees with potential for promotion. In 1990 almost 15 per cent of the blue-collar workforce were attending outside courses.

The induction of new employees has become an important feature of Black & Decker's effort to achieve its business objectives. An extensive orientation program has been developed to provide new recruits with a familiarity of the company's products and of the customers it seeks to serve. As part of this program, each new employee is taken through the lifecycle of the product from manufacturing of components to assembly, to storage and distribution and finally to the retail operation. To enhance the impact, the new employee visits each section within the plant and then a retail outlet and participates in customer service. Black & Decker has also sought to effect a 'higher trust' working relationship by removing time-clocks. The practice of clocking on and off was seen as unnecessary and a duty roster is simply maintained. Similarly, time off for personal requirements can easily be obtained subject to reasonable advance notice.

ICI Australia

ICI Australia is a major producer of industrial chemicals, paints and coatings, plastics, commercial explosives and fertilisers and a leading supplier of health care products. The company has been exposed to increasing international competition principally through the progressive lowering of tariff protection. This in turn has affected the character of the organisation's industrial relations policies and human resource management practices. The company has an explicit industrial relations strategy which forms part of its overall business plan. It is based on a rationale that a committed, flexible and skilled workforce can best assist the organisation to achieve its objectives of improved cost and productivity performance and high product quality. The industrial relations strategy comprises five interlocking factors which are depicted in Figure 14.1.

A key element of the strategy has been to strengthen the employer–employee relationship within the organisation. This is to be achieved in a number of ways. The company has embarked on a policy of creating

Fig. 14.1: ICI Australia's industrial relations strategy

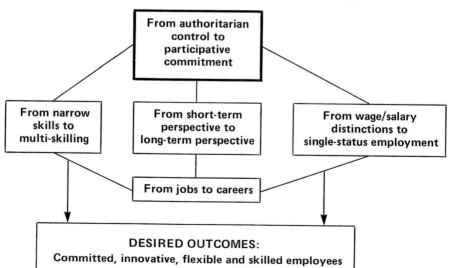

single-status working conditions. Distinctions between management staff and blue-collar workers are being removed in such areas as canteen and parking facilities as well as sick leave entitlements and payment methods. Open-door communication systems have been implemented along with regular shopfloor briefings on factory performance. A greater emphasis is also being placed on performance appraisal within the area of employee remuneration. Cross-skilling for all blue-collar workers has become a priority for the company. A simplified job structure and classification scheme has been adopted with individual operators being paid for the level of skills and knowledge they have obtained. There is a strong focus on training—in 1990 ICI allocated about 5 per cent of its salary budget to the function.

With the diversity of its business activities, ICI has sought to decentralise industrial relations and create more site-specific arrangements tailored to particular business needs. This has led to a number of s. 115 certified agreements. One such agreement has been made with the Federated Ironworkers' Association and covers employees at the ICI Ephedrine plant at Mayfield, New South Wales. In the preface it is stated that:

> This agreement has been designed with the intent of establishing, where practicable, a single set of terms and conditions of employment for all employees (unionised and non-unionised)...The site will be a single-status employment site, pursuing equality of treatment and excellent employee relations amongst a highly skilled and versatile total workforce.[31]

The agreement stipulated that the salaries of all employees would be based on skill level and performance, and that annual reviews and adjustments would take account of skill enhancement, performance assessments and market movements. Similar arrangements have been made in other operating businesses in the ICI group, and the company intends to continue to pursue this approach to workplace industrial relations.

South Pacific Tyres

In 1987 two companies, Dunlop Olympic Tyres and the Goodyear Tire and Rubber Company, merged their operations and formed South Pacific Tyres. The merger was brought about by mounting competitive pressures in the industry and a recognition that future survival depended on greater production efficiencies and substantial injections of investment in new technology. Since the 1960s there had been a marked rationalisation in the number of producers worldwide. No less than twenty-seven tyre companies had closed down between 1982 and 1986.[32] The picture was little different in Australia. In 1965 there were seven manufacturers with a total of twelve separate tyre plants. By 1987 there were only two domestic manufacturers operating from four plants.

---

31. Australian Industrial Relations Commission, *ICI Ephedrine Industrial Agreement, 1989*, Print H8054, p. 2.
32. D. McKerrow and D. Samson, *South Pacific Tyres*, Melbourne Case Library, Graduate School of Management, University of Melbourne, 1990, p. 1.

Over the last decade import penetration had risen from 30 per cent to 46 per cent of the total tyre market. This was largely due to the dramatic reduction in tariff protection, which had fallen from 40 per cent in the late 1970s to 21 per cent in 1990 and was planned to drop to 15 per cent in 1992.

A vital component of the merger agreement was a $200 million investment to be made over five years to upgrade existing plants and build a new high-technology radial truck tyre plant in Somerton, Victoria. This investment was dependent, however, on gaining union and employee agreement to work the new plant to its optimum capacity. The company wanted to raise plant utilisation from a normal operating average of about 230 days per year to the worldwide average of around 340 days per year. A utilisation level in excess of 300 days was deemed as an absolute minimum requirement for the new investment.

Following extensive negotiations with the National Union of Workers and the Amalgamated Metal Workers Union, the company reached an agreement that the Somerton truck tyre plant would operate for 325 days per year. New arrangements encompassed working hours, job progression and training, and a streamlined dispute resolution procedure. The work roster was to allow the plant to operate twenty-four hours a day. The labour force was divided into four groups who worked in twelve-hours shifts over a six-week cycle. Employees averaged thirty-eight hours a week, working three Saturdays and one Sunday in the cycle. Penalty rates were paid on time worked in excess of ten hours in a single shift, on weekend hours and on night shift. The penalty rates lifted the average weekly wage for a thirty-eight hour week to the equivalent of 47.75 hours for day shift workers and 58.75 for night shift workers.

The employment agreement contained a job progression structure that afforded production workers the opportunity of career development. The company provided a range of training programs and activities to improve and extend employees' skills, knowledge and capabilities. Employees were also encouraged to design business plans for their work groups or work shift. Performance goals were to be set in the areas of safety, productivity and material wastage. The involvement of employees in production-related decisions was seen as essential if the company was to implement its newly developed Perfection Strategy. The aim of this strategy was to lift the quality and reduce the cost of the product. The overriding concern was to sell only first-class tyres. If the product did not reach this standard it was to be scrapped. Previously, a 'Blemish' category had existed which was released to the retail network as a second-class product at a reduced price. By excluding this category South Pacific Tyres hoped to raise employee awareness of the need to produce uniformly high-quality products. Scrap levels were to be monitored carefully and employee skills were to be upgraded continuously in the areas of statistical process control and corrective procedures in order to ensure compliance with the increasingly high technical specifications of the product.

In order to minimise possible disruption to the operation of the plant, the parties agreed to the insertion of a disputes avoidance procedure in the Employment Agreement. This contained a three-step procedure for the resolution of grievances. It operated in the following way:

Stage One   Where an employee had a grievance or concern he/she was to discuss the matter with her/his immediate supervisor, who must provide an answer within three days.

Stage Two   In the event of the employee not being satisfied with the answer, the matter was to be taken to the Manufacturing Manager by the Supervisor and the employee. The attendance of the Shop Steward was at the employee's discretion.

Stage Three If the matter was still unresolved, the Manufacturing Manager could request the presence of the Personnel and Industrial Relations Manager, and the Shop Steward may request the presence of senior union officials. If a negotiated settlement cannot be reached within 12 working days the parties can jointly or individually refer the matter to the Industrial Relations Commission.

Throughout all stages of the procedure the parties must avoid the use of stoppages, lockouts or any other bans or limitations on the performance of work.[33] This form of dispute arrangement at South Pacific Tyres seems to be more commonly accepted within Australian industry, although Fells and Mulvey have noted that formal grievance procedures are still the exception rather than the rule.[34] Nevertheless, they indicate that there has been a sharp rise in recent years in the number of awards and agreements containing such procedures.

Absenteeism and labour turnover

Australian companies have only recently recognised the high cost of absenteeism and turnover. With the emphasis on award restructuring and skill formation, and the attendant pressures to invest more heavily in the training of employees, many organisations have found that the retention and full utilisation of labour is critical to the success of these ventures. Estimates have put the loss from unscheduled absenteeism at almost 30 million working days per year.[35] This is more than twenty times the number of days lost through industrial stoppages. In their study of absenteeism in Australia, Crawford and Volard quantified the various causes of temporary 'non-approved work absence'.[36] They calculated that 18.9 per cent of work absences could be attributed to the sickie. The authors stated: 'In others words, for every five days taken off

---

33. South Pacific Tyres, *Employment Agreement*, Somerton Radial Truck Tyre Plant, 1990, Section 8.
34. R.E. Fells and C. Mulvey, 'The Hancock Report and workplace industrial relations', *Journal of Industrial Relations*, vol. 27, no. 4, 1985, p. 539.
35. R. Drago and M. Wooden, 'An empirical study of absence rates: labour–leisure choice, work discipline and workgroup norms', National Institute of Labour Studies, Flinders University, Working Paper No. 101, December 1988, p. 1.
36. B. Crawford and S. Volard, 'Work absence in industrialised societies: the Australian case', *Industrial Relations Journal*, vol. 12, no. 3, 1981.

work by employees throughout Australia we can expect one day to be due to employees consciously deciding not to go to work'.[37]

Employee turnover is no less a problem. In 1989, more than a million Australian workers or almost 14 per cent of the working population voluntarily quit their jobs because of unsatisfactory working conditions or other reasons.[38] In the manufacturing sector this figure was 17 per cent and in the finance, property and business sector it was close to 20 per cent. In some areas of manufacturing, turnover rates in excess of 60 per cent are not exceptional and rates of 100 per cent are not unknown. A recent international study of the motor vehicle industry found that turnover rates among blue-collar workers in Australian companies were seven to eight times higher than those of comparable plants in North America and Europe.[39]

Absenteeism

It is necessary to distinguish between two types of absenteeism; that which is *involuntary* and results from an inability of an employee to work because of sickness or accident, and that which might be termed *voluntary*, where the absence is assumed to arise from an employee's unwillingness to work. In the latter case, the absence may be explained by a host of factors, including the personal characteristics of the employee, the nature of the work, the level of satisfaction and organisational pressures that affect the motivation of the individual to attend work. Steers and Rhodes have incorporated these variables in their process model of employee attendance (see Fig. 14.2).

In their review of the research literature, the authors concluded that:

> ...employee absenteeism reveals a multiplicity of influences on the decision and ability to come to work. These influences emerge both from the individuals themselves (e.g. personal work ethic, demographic factors) and from the work environment (e.g. the job situation, incentive/reward systems, work group norms). Moreover, some of these influences are largely under the control of employees (e.g. organisational commitment) while others are clearly beyond their control (e.g. health)...[In addition] certain factors may facilitate attendance for some employees but not for others. For instance, one employee may be intrinsically motivated to attend because of a challenging job ...Another employee, however, may have a distasteful job (and not be intrinsically motivated) and yet come to work because of other pressures (e.g. financial need). Both employees would attend, but for somewhat different reasons.[40]

Much of the research on absenteeism has sought to identify the association between job satisfaction and motivation to attend work. There has been a view that poorly designed jobs confer frustration and alienation

---

37. Ibid., p. 53.
38. Australian Bureau of Statistics, *Labour Mobility Australia, Year Ended February 1989*, Cat. No. 6209.0.
39. J.F. Krafcik and J.P. MacDuffie, 'The Production System Management Index (PSMX): a user's guide to calculation', International Motor Vehicle Program, MIT, Boston, 1989.
40. R.M. Steers and S.R. Rhodes, 'Major influences on employee attendance: a process model', *Journal of Applied Psychology.*, vol. 63, no. 4, 1978, p. 401.

Fig. 14.2: Employee attendance: a process model

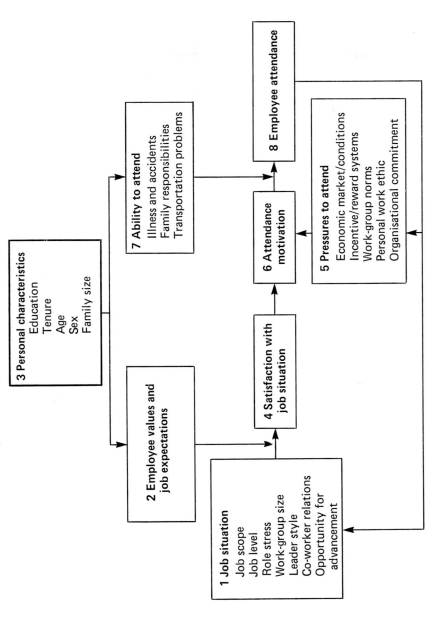

Source: R.M. Steers and S.R. Rhodes, 'Major influences on employee attendance: a process model', *Journal of Applied Psychology*, vol.63, no.4, 1978, p. 393.

resulting in job dissatisfaction and absenteeism. While some studies have established such a link, others have shown that the relationship is at best very weak.[41]

McShane's analysis of the literature nevertheless supports the assumption that employees who are dissatisfied with various aspects of a job are more likely to be absent.[42] In particular, the relationship is strongest in terms of overall satisfaction at work. Studies indicate that satisfaction with supervision, co-workers and pay are associated with lower absenteeism, although satisfaction with promotion is not.[43] Job involvement has also been shown to be correlated with lower frequency of absenteeism. On the other hand, the work of Mowday, Steers and Porter suggests that organisational commitment is likely to be a more stable predictor of absenteeism than either satisfaction or involvement.[44]

Workgroup norms have also been seen as a relevant factor affecting the level of employee absence. In a study of job satisfaction among female assembly line workers, Clegg, Wall and Kemp concluded that group norms were significant determinants of the decision to attend work.[45] Johns and Nicholson suggest that shared understandings emerge in organisations about the legitimacy of absenteeism, and certain customs and practices are established with respect to absence behaviour and its control.[46] Certainly, as De Lorenzo points out:

> ...the prevailing social relations in the work area will determine the extent of absenteeism which is 'permissible'. That is, different supervisors will tolerate differing levels of absenteeism by the way in which they respond to the situation. As a consequence, employees who enter a new work site will acquaint themselves with how many days they can take off and fit into the existing subculture's norms.[47]

In addition, particular attitudes to absenteeism will be formed within particular work groups. There is evidence to indicate that individual employees who do not conform to the group's level of absence—whether that level be high or low—are likely to be ostracised or 'punished' by the other group members.[48] In those cases where the organisational or work group norms are producing a level of absenteeism which is considered unacceptably high by senior management, they may be

---

41. See R.T. Mowday, L.W. Porter and R.M. Steers, *Employee Organisation Linkages: The Psychology of Commitment, Absenteeism and Turnover*, Academic Press, New York, 1982.
42. S.L. McShane, 'Job satisfaction and absenteeism: a meta-analytic re-examination' in M.G. Johns (ed.), *Proceedings of the Annual Conference of the Administrative Sciences Association of Canada*, University of British Columbia, Vancouver, 1983.
43. R.M. Steers and S.R. Rhodes, 'Knowledge and speculation about absenteeism' in P.S. Goodman and R.S. Atkin (eds), *Absenteeism*, Jossey-Bass, San Francisco, 1984.
44. R.T. Mowday, R.M. Steers and L.W. Porter, 'The measurement of organisational commitment', *Journal of Vocational Behaviour*, vol. 14, 1979.
45. C. Clegg, T. Wall and N. Kemp, 'Women on the assembly line: a comparison of main and interactive explanations of job satisfaction, absence and mental health', *Journal of Occupational Psychology*, vol. 60, no. 4, 1987.
46. G. Johns and N. Nicholson, 'The meaning of absence: new strategies for theory and research', in B.M. Staw and L.L. Cummings (eds), *Research and Organisational Behaviour*, vol. 4, 1982, p. 136.
47. M. De Lorenzo 'The extent of leadership influence as a causal explanation of absenteeism', Master of Commerce research report, Department of Economics, University of Melbourne, 1990, p. 25.
48. See Mowday, Porter and Steers, *Employee Organisation Linkages*, p. 95.

forced to 're-negotiate the existing (tacit, informal) agreement concerning existing absence levels'.[49] This may involve changes in supervision, better communication of the company's standards and policies on absenteeism, and greater flexibility for employees to attend to personal matters during the working week. It may also require measures that increase the degree of job satisfaction and enhance the level of organisational commitment.

Employee turnover

Absenteeism and turnover bear an obvious association. They may be viewed respectively as forms of temporary and permanent physical withdrawal from the organisation. Indeed it has been suggested that their relationship can best be expressed by way of a progression-of-withdrawal model. According to this model 'individuals engage in a hierarchically ordered sequence of withdrawal ranging from its most minor form to a complete break from the organization (that is quitting)'.[50] This implies that an individual's job dissatisfaction and/or lack of commitment to the organisation may vary over time as a result of changes in the individual, the job and the organisation. These changes in turn will influence the behavioural decisions made by the individual about his or her physical withdrawal (or non-withdrawal) from the organisation.[51]

Studies that have examined turnover from the psychological perspective have found that a variety of factors are predictive of quitting. Attitudes held towards a job have shown to be important. Dissatisfied employees are more likely to leave as are those who are not strongly committed to their organisation.[52] Demographic characteristics such as age, gender, education and number of dependants are also related to turnover. Age and number of dependants are negatively correlated while education is positively related. Men tend to be less likely to leave than women and married employees are somewhat less prone to quit than unmarried persons.[53] The relationships observed between various demographic or personal characteristics and turnover, nevertheless, are not particularly helpful in terms of managerial intervention. It is one thing to state that increasing age is associated with less turnover but another to state that age causes turnover since of course it cannot. The effect of age on turnover obviously is indirect, perhaps through tenure or through attitudes such as job satisfaction.

The finding of a negative relationship between trade union membership and employee turnover is, however, an issue of direct relevance to management. Research in both Australia and overseas indicates that

---

49. J.K. Chadwick-Jones, N. Nicholson and C. Brown, *Social Psychology of Absenteeism*, Praeger, London, 1986, p. 125.
50. J.G. Rosse and H.E. Miller, 'Relationship between absenteeism and other employee behaviours' in P.S. Goodman and R.S. Atkin (eds), *Absenteeism*, p. 201.
51. G.R. Ferris and K.M. Rowland, 'Tenure as a moderator of the absence–intent to leave relationship', *Human Relations*, vol. 40, no. 5, p. 256.
52. See J.L. Cotton and J.M. Tuttle, 'Employee turnover: a meta-analysis and review with implications for research', *Academy of Management Review*, vol. 11, no. 1, 1986.
53. Ibid., p. 60.

trade unions are associated with significantly lower levels of turnover. Using data from the Australian Longitudinal Survey of the youth labour market, Miller and Mulvey found that trade unions were responsible for a marked reduction in the rate of quits and a considerable increase in the average duration of jobs.[54] Their analysis showed that unions increased job tenure by about 20 per cent. The reasons for this seem to lie in the labour market application of Hirschman's exit-voice paradigm.[55] Unions provide workers with a 'collective voice' through which workplace problems can be aired and made subject to proper managerial consideration. The collective voice is therefore substituted for individual exit behaviour which reduces turnover.

Despite the substantial quantity of theoretical and empirical research on labour turnover, there have been few attempts to develop or test explanatory models within an Australian setting. In a recent study of turnover in the manufacturing industry, Deery and Hintz found that employees were significantly more likely to leave the company when they had low levels of organisational commitment, were given few opportunities to participate in decision-making and suffered from repetitive and monotonous jobs and task overload.[56] The absence of a social support system created among co-workers was also a contributing factor. The research findings indicated that the most effective way of reducing turnover was by increasing the level of organisational commitment. In turn this could best be achieved by promoting participative decision-making and by improving the social and working relationships between co-workers.

Summary

The study of industrial relations at the workplace has been largely neglected in Australia. Consequently, there is an absence of comprehensive information about the nature and conduct of both employer–employee and union–management relations at the shop and office floor. The information that is available, however, suggests that there has been an expansion of activity at this level. There is little doubt that this has been facilitated by changes in the wage fixation principles in the late 1980s which have demanded workplace reforms in exchange for wage increases. Another, and perhaps more important, factor has been the increasing level of domestic and international competition which has forced many companies to address the issues of product quality, reliability of service and delivery performance. This has created the need for more productive and efficient systems of industrial relations at the workplace.

---

54. P. Miller and C. Mulvey, 'The exit/voice model of the labour market: Australian evidence on unionism, job duration, quits and layoffs', discussion paper no. 16, Department of Industrial Relations, University of Western Australia, 1989.
55. A.O. Hirschman, *Exit, Voice and Loyalty*, Harvard University Press, Cambridge, Mass., 1970.
56. S. Deery and P. Hintz, 'The determinants of employee turnover: a test of a causal model', mimeograph, Graduate School of Management, University of Melbourne, 1989.

It is evident that many large companies have developed institutional arrangements at the workplace to manage multiple unionism and other associated issues, and that they in fact engage in extensive discussions and negotiations with union stewards about a full range of industrial relations issues. Much of the second-tier wage negotiations were conducted at the enterprise, business unit or establishment level between company representatives and teams of union officials and shop stewards. In contrast to the management of collective relations with unions and their shopfloor representatives, most Australian companies appear to have neglected the relationship between the organisation and the individual employee. This is reflected in high levels of absenteeism and turnover. In this area there is an obvious need to frame policies that enhance job satisfaction and organisational commitment.

Discussion questions

1. In what ways does the conciliation and arbitration system affect industrial relations activities at the workplace?
2. Why is the federal industrial tribunal limited in its ability to settle plant-level disputes?
3. Is shop steward activity limited in Australian workplaces?
4. Why do business organisations develop industrial relations policies?
5. Have Australian companies formulated more innovative industrial relations approaches at the workplace?
6. How does an organisation reduce voluntary absenteeism?
7. Why has the problem of labour turnover been largely ignored in Australia?
8. Outline the main explanatory variables of turnover.

Further reading

Benson, J., 'Workplace union organisation in Australia', *Labour and Industry*, vol. 1, no. 3, 1988.
Business Council of Australia, *Enterprise-based Bargaining Units: A Better Way of Working*, BCA, Melbourne, 1989.
Callus, R. and Lansbury, R., 'Workplace industrial relations', *Labour and Industry*, vol. 1, no. 2, 1988.
Cotton, J.L. and Tuttle, J.M., 'Employee turnover: a meta-analysis and review with implications for research', *Academy of Management Review*, vol. 11, no. 1, 1986.
Drago, R. and Wooden, M., 'An empirical study of absence rates: labour–leisure choice, work discipline and workgroup norms', National Institute of Labour Studies, Flinders University, Working Paper No. 101, December 1988.

Fells, R.E. and Mulvey, C., 'The Hancock Report and workplace industrial relations', *Journal of Industrial Relations*, vol. 27, no. 4, 1985.

Kochan, T.A. and Chalykoff, J.B., 'Human resource management and business life cycles: some preliminary propositions' in A. Kleingartner and C. Anderson (eds), *Human Resource Management in High Technology Firms*, Lexington Books, Lexington, Kentucky, 1987.

Rimmer, M., 'Work place unionism' in B. Ford and D. Plowman (eds), *Australian Unions*, 2nd ed., Macmillan, Melbourne, 1989.

Rimmer, M. and Zappala, J., 'Labour market flexibility and the second tier', *Australian Bulletin of Labour*, vol. 14, no. 4, 1988.

Steers, R.M. and Rhodes, S.R., 'Major influences on employee attendance: a process model', *Journal of Applied Psychology.*, vol. 63, no. 4, 1978.

CHAPTER 15

The Democratisation of Work

Industrial democracy emerged as an important issue in Australia in the early 1970s. During this period there was considerable activity and experimentation with various forms of employee participation. However, most of the schemes were restricted to fairly modest workplace reforms. They were almost entirely initiated by management and consequently failed to attract the general support of trade unions or their members. This led to a decline of interest in industrial democracy, and it has been only in recent years that it has begun to reappear as an important issue. This chapter traces the development of industrial democracy in Australia, looks at the various forms it has taken and examines the reasons why there has been a resurgence of interest in the subject.

Industrial democracy as an issue

During the early 1970s there was widespread interest in the use and application of various schemes of industrial democracy in Australia. Support for greater employee involvement in the decision-making processes within industry was sustained by a growing belief that employee participation may provide an answer to the lack of job satisfaction and alienation seen to be inherent in many forms of modern work life. The overwhelming weight of evidence collected from research studies of employee involvement schemes demonstrated that satisfaction in work was significantly enhanced when workers were provided with the opportunity to influence decisions within their work organisation. As Blumberg observed at the time:

There is hardly a study in the entire literature which fails to demonstrate that satisfaction in work is enhanced or that other generally acknowledged beneficial consequences accrue from a genuine increase in workers' decision making power.[1]

Others believed that participation at work was an essential ingredient of a democratic society. They pointed to the contradiction of a culture that stressed active participation in the community and political system while at the same time structuring people's working lives in jobs in hierarchical non-democratic organisations.[2] It was argued that non-democratic modes of decision-making could have far-reaching consequences for modern industrial societies.[3] Workers who were deprived of any opportunity to participate in decisions affecting their working lives were likely to be passive, non-involved citizens. A Swedish study on the subject found that:

> ... work which gives limited opportunities for independent control, meaningfulness, and self-actualisation tends to lead to weaker and more passive behaviour in other contexts of life as well—such as social relations, involvement in social activities and the like.[4]

Other research showed that non-involvement in work seemed to discourage involvement in leisure activities.[5] In order to reduce these and other undesirable manifestations of undemocratic work environments, Pateman concluded that 'experience of a participatory authority structure might ... [diminish] tendencies toward non-democratic attitudes in the individual'.[6]

Support for industrial democracy also was evident among sections of management who saw it as enhancing corporate efficiency and productivity, and encouraging industrial harmony and employee motivation; and, therefore, increasing profits. Observations that dull, low-skilled and repetitive jobs resulted in low levels of job satisfaction and productivity generated pressures to reform jobs and create conditions in which workers may have greater variety, autonomy and influence within the workplace. The evolution of views that dated from the Hawthorne experiments of Elton Mayo and the 'Human Relations School', and underwent further refinement in the writings of Maslow, McGregor and Likert,[7] stressed the need to treat workers as 'real human beings' and not as mere appendages to machines. Participative management, open-system organisations, satisfying interpersonal relationships and the fulfilment of 'higher order' needs were all seen as being necessary concomitants of a motivated, loyal, productive and industrially harmonious workforce.

1. P. Blumberg, *Industrial Democracy: The Sociology of Participation*, Constable, London, 1968, p. 123.
2. S. Deutsch and S. Albrecht, 'Worker participation in the United States: Efforts to democratise industry and the economy', *Labour and Society*, vol. 8, no. 3, 1983, pp. 248–9.
3. C. Pateman, *Participation and Democratic Theory*, Cambridge University Press, London, 1970.
4. D. Jenkins, *Job Power*, Penguin, Baltimore, 1974, p. 41.
5. Ibid., p. 42.
6. Pateman, *Participation*, p. 105.
7. A.H. Maslow, *Motivation and Personality*, Harper & Row, New York, 1954; D. McGregor, *The Human Side of Enterprise* McGraw-Hill, New York, 1960; R. Likert, *New Patterns in Management*, McGraw-Hill, New York, 1961.

Interest in industrial democracy was not only confined to liberal political theorists and to management. Many socialists saw the redistribution of power in industry and the institution of a system of self-management as the answer to worker alienation. A commitment to the removal of class differences required the elimination of power inequalities in both the industrial and political settings. The elimination of arbitrary and unchecked authority in industry, and the abolition of rigid superior–subordinate, command–obedience relationships required the democratisation of power at the workplace and the right of employees to govern their own lives. The maxim that 'no man was good enough to be another man's master' expressed a fundamental and longstanding aspiration of many activists in the union movement.[8]

This apparent consensus over the virtues of participation and democratic control was clouded by significant differences both in the meanings attached to the concept and to the particular configurations of power that would be affected by such changes within the organisation. Industrial democracy was used to describe socialist aspirations for self-management on one hand, and limited forms of consultation in which management's right to final decision making remained fully intact, on the other. In most cases management saw industrial democracy simply as a means of increasing organisational efficiency. By perhaps involving workers in decisions about task performance it was thought that they might become more highly motivated to accept organisational goals. Many trade unionists saw industrial democracy in very different terms. In their view participation was to be aimed at restraining the exercise of managerial prerogative and at extending the power and influence of employees over decisions that were previously the right of management. These might range from matters such as the operation of overtime rosters and workflow speeds to such questions as retrenchments, the introduction of new technology and the strategic planning of the organisation.

It is obvious, then, that industrial democracy cannot be viewed as a unitary concept. It can be defined in a wide range of ways and take many different forms. Nevertheless, it is possible to classify its different forms in terms of two properties: the directness of participation and the extent of influence that employees have over organisational decisions.[9] Participation may be direct and entail the immediate personal involvement of organisation members, or it may be indirect and involve some form of employee representation. Direct participation normally takes the form of practices in which individuals or groups in the workplace acquire greater control over their immediate work situation. These practices are largely confined to issues of an on-the-job character. In contrast, the indirect or representative form involves participation in decision-making bodies at various levels within the organisational hierarchy, ranging

---

8. K. Coates and T. Topham, *The New Unionism*, Penguin, London, 1974, p. 231.
9. See H.P. Dachler and B. Wilpert, 'Conceptual dimensions and boundaries of participation in organisations: a critical evaluation', *Administrative Science Quarterly*, vol. 23, 1978, p. 12.

from the board of directors through to workplace joint consultation committees. This brings us to the second property, that of employee influence. The level of influence that organisational members exercise can be located along a continuum from unilateral management control at one extreme—where employees have no influence—to workers' control at the other. In between lie the various forms of information sharing, consultation and joint decision-making. The higher the organisational level at which participation occurs, the greater the potential for employee influence. Walker makes this clear in his distinction between representation in the *government* of the enterprise and representation in the *administration* of the enterprise. He wrote:

> Government of the enterprise, involving broad decisions of strategy and policy, the setting of general objectives and major practical decisions on investment, markets, scale of operations, opening and closing of plants etc., typically take place at the top of the organisation structure, while decisions on administration are taken at various levels of the managerial hierarchy depending on their breadth and other characteristics. The higher the level of decision-making, the more decisions are likely to concern broad policy; the lower the level of decision-making the more likely decisions are to be concerned with the *implementation* of policy.[10]

Work reform in the 1970s

The upsurge of interest in industrial democracy in Australia and elsewhere in the Western world coincided with marked changes in the social and economic environment in many countries. Changes brought about by increasing affluence and higher education quite often led to the development of a questioning and challenging attitude towards traditional authority structures in society. It was thought by many that these changes had also led to the formation of an 'anti-work syndrome' among sections of the young and an intolerance for 'monotonous tasks and undignified subordination'.[11] Some commentators argued that this was manifested in a poor quality of workmanship, 'high turnover and absenteeism and a general declension of commitment and cooperation'.[12] Times of full employment and labour shortages also enhanced the bargaining power of employees and increased their ability to inflict greater economic costs on their employers. The growth of personnel departments within many companies and the development of more systematic and sophisticated attempts to cultivate unity within enterprises reflected a growing awareness of the cost of disputes. There was seen to be a need for management to adjust to a somewhat different power balance between capital and labour. As one businessman was

---

10. K. Walker, 'Concepts of industrial democracy in international perspective', in R.L. Pritchard (ed.), *Industrial Democracy in Australia*, CCH, Sydney, 1977, p. 27.
11. A. Crombie,'Industrial democracy—job satisfaction or social transformation', in R.L. Pritchard (ed.). *Industrial Democracy in Australia*, p. 65.
12. Ibid.

reported to have said when lamenting the general reluctance of employees to accept management's goals and objectives, 'fifteen years ago [when] a man was hungrier he'd finish the job in half the time it now takes'.[13]

Some of these factors were influential in stimulating management's interest in industrial democracy. Their attempts to democratise work clearly represented no idealistic conception; they were but an expendient way of adjusting to changed forces in society. In 1976 the personnel manager of ICI Australia made this clear:

> The current industrial, political, economic and social scenes have changed dramatically during the past few years. No longer do the old concepts and judgements apply. The decision rules have changed. We must now act and respond in ways different to [sic] the old servant–master stance . . . We need to [breathe] new life into our free enterprise system through a willingness to try 'new' approaches.[14]

The pursuit of efficiency, productivity and industrial harmony provided the stimulus for the initiation of new organisational forms of work. As Poole pointed out, participation was seen to facilitate this in a number of ways. It enabled the skills and abilities of workers to be effectively tapped, it reduced workers' resistance to technological change, it raised the level of workers' satisfaction and thereby made for a more contented workforce. Finally it was viewed as an important means for improving industrial relations.[15]

Trade unions in general approached the issue of industrial democracy cautiously. Because the majority of participative arrangements were initiated by management, who surrendered few of their traditional prerogatives, unions tended to regard the schemes 'as a ploy to legitimise management decisions without granting any real power'.[16] They were generally sceptical about the value of most forms of industrial democracy. They saw their industrial role as being more one of improving wages and conditions of employment through the conventional means of arbitration and negotiation. In 1972, after an extensive survey of union attitudes towards industrial democracy, a South Australian Government inquiry into worker participation concluded:

> Unions appear to regard the present adversary system involved in compulsory arbitration as a recognition of the conflict between the interests of the private employer and the worker, and many prefer it to a scheme of worker participation which would emphasise co-operation or co-determination.[17]

There was also a genuine fear that many of the participative schemes were designed to undermine the union's authority and to diminish its power in the workplace. Some unions, moreover, opposed increased

---

13. Jenkins, *Job Power*,.............., p. 10.
14. E.M. Pahlow, 'Employee participation—a decision for disaster or development? Recent experience in ICI', *Journal of the Institution of Engineers, Australia*, January–February 1976, p. 12.
15. M. Poole, *Workers' Participation in Industry*, Routledge & Kegan Paul, London, 1978, p. 56.
16. J.R. Robbins, 'Workers' participation and industrial democracy—variations on a theme', *Journal of Industrial Relations*, vol. 14. no. 4, 1972, p. 435.
17. *Worker Participation in Management, Report of the Committee on Worker Participation in Management: Private Sector*, Adelaide, South Australia, 1973, p. 24.

consultation and cooperation with management because they saw it 'as a betrayal of their traditional confrontation position'.[18] As Gunzburg argued, 'they [did] ... not wish to prop up the capitalist system'.[19]

The form of industrial democracy

With few exceptions, Australia's early experience with industrial democracy was restricted to the modest restructuring of work organisations through job reform schemes and forms of joint consultation, and were almost universally the result of management initiatives. Various schemes of job rotation, job enlargement, job enrichment and the creation of semi-autonomous work groups were initiated in a number of companies in the early 1970s. This type of industrial democracy sought to give workers greater responsibility and involvement in decisions affecting their immediate work situation. Often it involved the redesign of jobs so as to include what were formerly lower-level management functions, such as job planning, quality control and work organisations. Job rotation, which involved the practice of moving workers from one job to another within a defined area of work, sought to give workers a greater variety of tasks to perform and in so doing to reduce the monotony and boredom of being locked into one job. Job enlargement and job enrichment schemes widened the range of activities undertaken by particular operators and delegated a greater degree of responsibility and self-determination to individual workers or work groups. In the case of semi-autonomous work groups, jobs were redesigned so as to enable various tasks to be carried out in small groups. Within these groups, workers were given control over the way in which the job was to be done without any direct supervision from management.

Although these schemes were designed to enhance the degree of personal fulfilment that employees derived from their job, they had a minimal effect on the traditional authority structure of the firm. By their very nature participation was restricted to very low levels of decision-making and was confined to issues of an on-the-job character. They provided employees with little opportunity to affect the existing distribution of power in industry. In effect, these schemes focused 'on the means towards ends already established by management'.[20]

Another form of employee participation that became prevalent among a number of companies was joint consultation. This involved the formation of committees of employer and employee representatives who discussed issues related to working conditions and other enterprise-level matters. Their purpose was often to provide management with formal access to the views and opinions of employees on various matters. By the mid 1970s there had been quite a significant development in the use of joint consultative committees. In 1976 a survey showed that

---

18. D. Gunzburg, *Industrial Democracy Approaches in Sweden*, Productivity Promotion Council of Australia, Melbourne, 1978, p. 15.
19. Ibid.
20. Poole, *Workers' Participation*, p. 59.

almost a quarter of employers interviewed had instituted such committees and that an equal number were proposing to do so.[21] Generally these forms of joint consultation had few decision-making powers, and the consideration of important industrial relations issues were typically considered to be beyond their scope. Trade unions had little control over the election of representatives and in many cases union delegates did not participate.[22] There was little disturbance of the authority structure of the enterprise because employees had few opportunities to exercise any real degree of control or influence over the organisations' objectives or policies. For this very reason these forms of participation failed to attract the widespread support of trade unions.[23] This did not prevent the successful implementation of a number of schemes of joint consultation and job restructuring in Australia. ICI Australia, in particular, was active in seeking to develop more participative forms of management at the shop-floor level. Their experiments with consultative committees at the Osborn Alkali works in South Australia and with semi-autonomous work groups in the company's Welvic plant at Deer Park in Melbourne have been well documented.[24] Other companies, such as Shell, Philips, CSR, Alcan and Simpson Holdings, likewise were among those that became interested in developing systems of employee participation. In 1980 a survey of enterprises in Western Australia showed that almost a third of the respondents practised some form of joint consultation and/or job enrichment schemes. A somewhat smaller proportion made use of semi-autonomous work groups.[25] An interesting finding, however, was that the level of support for employee participation schemes far outweighed the extent of practical application.[26]

The trade union response

With the wider application of participative arrangements in Australian industry in the 1970s the labour movement found it necessary to consider its stance on industrial democracy and to initiate a collective response to these developments. Its initial approach to industrial democracy was characterised by a mixture of hostility and uncertainty. Unlike their European counterparts, Australian unions were slow to develop clear and constructive policies on the subject. It was not until September 1977 that the ACTU was able to formulate a comprehensive policy on industrial democracy. While it did not advocate any one particular form of participation, it endorsed schemes that sought 'a redistribution of

---

21. *Rydges*, October 1976, p. 81.
22. D. Gunzburg, *Employee Participation in Australia Progress Report* AGPS, Canberra, 1980, p. 1.
23. See L. Carlin and J. Leon, 'Employee participation—experiences and attitudes of union officials in WA', *Work and People*, vol. 8, no. 1, 1982.
24. See Pahlow, *Employee Participation*; A. Robinson and G. McCarroll, 'A work group approach at Welvic', *Work and People*, Winter 1976, vol. 2, no. 2, and A. Gibbons and G. McCarroll, 'Welvic revisited', *Work and People*, Autumn–Winter 1978, vol. 4, no. 1–2.
25. L. Carlin and P. Cannon, 'Employee participation—experiences and attitudes of managers in WA', *Work and People*, vol. 7, no. 2, 1981.
26. Vaughan has put forward a number of possible reasons why management may be more predisposed towards participation in theory than they are in practice. E.J. Vaughan, 'Some observations upon the logic of participation', *Journal of Industrial Relations*, vol. 18, no. 3, 1976.

power within the enterprise' and 'an increased say and influence in decision-making' for workers.[27] The ACTU saw industrial democracy as a means of 'equalising power within the workplace' by restricting the prerogatives of management. It adopted the view that, while practices such as consultative committees, job rotation, job enrichment and job enlargement did not in themselves constitute industrial democracy, they were worthwhile developments if they were the result of agreements entered into between employers, unions and their members. The ACTU was less enthusiastic about other practices which it regarded as providing only an illusion of democratic decision-making:

> There are a number of other techniques being employed in Australia which do not provide an increase in the discretionary decision making power of workers but are merely guises for improving the return to owners and consolidating the powers of management elites. Most existing forms of organisational development, management by objectives, employee shareholding schemes, 'improved' communication systems, so-called information-sharing systems, management 'open-door' policies, suggestion box schemes and profit-sharing schemes fall within this category.[28]

The ACTU saw the need for increased government support for industrial democracy. The drafting of appropriate legislation was regarded as a necessary precondition for the successful introduction of democratic decision-making. It called on federal and state governments to legislate for greater industrial democracy through amendments to public service acts, company acts and industrial relations acts. The ACTU held the view that for management prerogatives to be effectively limited, legislation was required to widen the scope of collective bargaining. It declared that:

> The conservative and narrow interpretation of the powers to intervene in managerial matters must be overcome by unions extending their claims under collective bargaining for industrial democracy. Any agreements reached through collective bargaining should be given a legal recognition to provide workers with protection rights in the performance of their duties.[29]

Nevertheless, the ACTU recognised that in the current political and social climate it was quite unlikely that prescriptive legislation of the type it considered necessary would be enacted. It therefore saw a need to stimulate public interest in industrial democracy as a forerunner to legislative change. Subsequent ACTU Congresses reaffirmed the union movement's commitment to industrial democracy and to projects designed to achieve greater equality of power within industry. Guidelines also were issued for unions to follow in order to protect their rights in any negotiations with management in respect to employee participation schemes.

---

27. 'Industry democracy', *Decisions of the Australian Congress of Trade Unions*, 1977.
28. Ibid.
29. Ibid.

A discontinuity of interest

After the initial upsurge in interest in industrial democracy in the period up to the mid 1970s there was a gradual decline in the level of experimentation and diffusion of participative practices in Australia. Ironically this occurred at a time when both the ACTU and the Federal Government had eventually produced policy statements on the subject.[30] While there were a number of reasons that probably contributed to this decline in activity, two factors can be isolated.

First, the participative schemes that were developed in the 1970s by management were formulated during a period of full employment. A concern to reduce labour turnover and absenteeism led to efforts to increase the quality of work life, to reduce monotony and boredom and to achieve an increased commitment to the organisation. The buoyant conditions of the labour market provided employees with considerable opportunities for mobility and allowed them greater scope to express their dissatisfaction of work through quitting. As a result, economic prosperity made employers more receptive to workplace reforms and their emphasis on participative styles of management was not unrelated to the scarcity of labour and to the need to induce greater productive effort from their employees. To some extent, the recession of the late 1970s and early 1980s rewrote the rules of industrial power. Employers were placed in a much stronger position to achieve their objectives and, while they became even more committed to enhancing organisational efficiency, there were increasing doubts that employee participation actually increased job satisfaction or had any tangible effect on productivity.[31] Some programs were dropped because of their lack of success, often due to the resistance by lower-level management to the reforms.

Second, there was little active government support for the promotion of industrial democracy. One of the principal differences between Australia and the countries of Western Europe which have experimented widely with industrial democracy has been that in Australia there has been no legislation either facilitating or prescribing democratic processes of decision-making. Only the Dunstan Labor Government in South Australia in the early 1970s displayed any real initiative in promoting the concept and applicability of industrial democracy in both the private and public sectors. Its appointment in 1972 of a committee to examine the practicability of extending democratic decision-making in industry and its subsequent establishment of a Unit for Quality of Work Life in 1974 were important catalysts for the development of a number of consultative and job reform schemes in that state.[32] However, changes to the government's policy on industrial democracy in 1975 and a marked shift in direction from one which was primarily concerned with

---

30. Department of Productivity, *Commonwealth Government's Policy on Employee Participation*, AGPS, Canberra, 1978.
31. See G.E. O'Brien, 'The success and failure of employee participation—a longitudinal study', *Work and People*, vol. 8, no. 2, 1982.
32. G. Anderson, 'The South Australian initiative' in Pritchard (ed.). *Industrial Democracy*.

minor changes to the organisational structure of the enterprise to one which proposed significant restraints on managerial prerogatives induced a hostile response from management, who claimed that the policy was tantamount to workers' control. This placed the government in a more difficult position in promoting employer initiatives, although its program in the public sector continued to expand various practices of democratic decision-making.

In their assessment of the development of industrial democracy during this period the Australian Government observed:

> ... the changes that did occur at the workplace level during the 1970s were generally neither long-lasting nor well developed. The parties involved lacked information and skills; there was little union involvement; employee participation was treated as distinct and not integrated into the regular management systems; approaches were rarely jointly planned or ongoing, or provided employees with any real influence; and they were often imposed from above, without any commitment on the part of employees.[33]

New directions in industrial democracy

Interest in industrial democracy was revived in the early 1980s. After something of a hiatus in the development of employee participation practices there was a renewed concern for a greater democratisation of decision-making at the workplace. But whereas the earlier forms of participation were introduced by management and largely focused on those forms of employee involvement that were thought to enhance the productive efficiency of the organisation, the new initiatives were distinctively different in character, form and intent. They became largely issue-based and union-initiated. Rather than being centred on job redesign and consultative processes, they concerned substantive workplace issues such as occupational health and safety, disclosure of information, new technology and job protection. Moreover they focused on 'dimensions of participation which [were] ... most directly associated with [the] redistribution of power in organisations'.[34]

The pressure of greater labour involvement in organisational decision-making was not unrelated to the economic recession and the widespread application of microelectronics throughout Australian industry. Both had had a profound impact on job security. The technological revolution in particular led to increasing concern over the issues of deskilling as well as decreased job autonomy and satisfaction. The introduction of new work processes also had important implications for occupational health and safety. The drive by Australian unions to assert greater influence and authority over decisions affecting these matters

---

33. Department of Employment and Industrial Relations, *Industrial Democracy and Employee Participation: A Policy Paper*, AGPS, Canberra, 1986, p. 6.
34. R. Cole, A. Crombie, A. Davies and E. Davis, 'Industrial democracy in Australia 1972–1992: profiting from our experience', *Working Paper No. 2: A Green Paper*, Centre for Continuing Education, ANU, Canberra, August 1983, p. 12.

was paralleled by similar developments overseas. In 1983 Deutsch and Albrecht reported that the growth of interest in industrial democracy in the United States of America was focusing on issues such as:

> ... guaranteeing job protection; controlling ... health and safety hazards caused by the new technology, such as eye strain and low levels of radiation from video display terminal use; protecting workers against deskilling ... and allowing workers and unions to share in the planning and introduction of the new technology.[35]

In Australia industrial democracy increasingly became the subject of arbitration, collective bargaining and legislative action. Rather than being viewed as a separate sphere of activity and as a matter of organisational style, it was seen as an integral part of the conflictual relationship that existed between employers and employees.[36] Perhaps the clearest manifestation of this was seen in the union movement's determination to achieve greater participation in decisions relating to technological and organisational change. In 1981 the ACTU mounted a test case before the Australian Industrial Relations Commission to establish minimum standards of notification, provision of information and consultation for enterprises introducing changes that affected the performance or organisation of work. Following almost three years of hearings the Commission handed down its judgment in the form of the *Termination, Change and Redundancy* decision of 1984. The Commission imposed new obligations on employers retrenching labour and introduced stringent requirements for them to consult employees and unions before initiating major changes to production methods or to the structure of companies.

Although the precise nature of the consultative process was to be determined by the parties, the effect of the decision was to require companies to adopt a more participative and consultative approach to the ongoing management of the enterprise. The award specified that:

> Where an employer has made a definite decision to introduce major changes in production, programme, organisation, structure or technology, that are likely to have significant effects on employees, the employer shall notify the employees who may be affected by the proposed changes and their union or unions ... The employer shall discuss with the employees affected and their union or unions, *inter alia*, the introduction of the changes ... the effects the changes are likely to have on employees, measures to avert or mitigate the adverse effects of such changes on employees and/or their unions in relation to the changes. The discussions shall commence as early as practicable after a definite decision has been made by the employer to make the changes ... For the purposes of such discussion, the employer shall provide in writing to the employees concerned and their union or unions, all relevant information about the changes including the nature of the changes proposed; the expected effects of the changes on employees and any other matters likely to affect employees provided that any employer shall not be required to disclose

---

35. Deutsch and Albrecht, 'Worker participation in the United States', pp. 258–9.
36. R. Cole et al., 'Industrial democracy in Australia 1972–1992', p.3.

confidential information the disclosure of which would be inimical to the employers' interest.

With the election of Labor Governments at both federal and state levels the legislative route also became a more accessible avenue for unions seeking to exercise greater influence over issues like job security and occupational health and safety. Furthermore, with the change of governments and the implementation of different political philosophies, the public sector adopted a pacesetting role in the area of industrial democracy. The Hawke Labor Government made its intentions clear about developing a more participative approach to decision-making in the Australian Public Service.[37] An Industrial Democracy Unit was established in the Office of the Public Service Board to provide advice and assistance to departments on the introduction of more participatory management and to conduct education and training activities to increase awareness of industrial democracy concepts and practices.

The Victorian Labor Government also created an Industrial Democracy Unit in 1983 for the purpose of offering assistance to organisations in both the public and private sectors that were planning to introduce democratic work practices. The establishment of a series of union–management working parties in the public sector proved to be successful in encouraging the development of consultative and participative arrangements for the introduction of new technology.[38] Trade union demands for access to information on investment decisions and for a greater role in processes relating to the strategic planning of organisations were also raised. The Victorian *Transport Act 1983* embodied a number of important developments in this area. It altered radically the forms of decision-making in the various state transport authorities by establishing new consultative mechanisms for unionists to be involved in key strategic, operational and organisational decisions.[39] The Victorian Government released a 'Statement of Industrial Democracy Principles' in May 1985, affirming workers' rights to be informed of, and to participate in, decisions likely to affect them.

Government initiatives in industrial democracy have not only been confined to the public sector. In a major policy discussion paper in 1986 the Federal Government pointed to the urgent need to accelerate the application of participative practices in all workplaces if Australia was to address successfully the problems of productivity and international competitiveness.[40] The government declared that employee participation had become a major priority and that there were compelling arguments on both economic and social grounds for its widespread

---

37. *Reforming the Australian Public Service*, A statement of the Government's intentions, AGPS, Canberra, 1983.
38. S. Edwards, 'Industrial democracy as seen within the general framework of industrial relations in Victoria', Paper presented to seminar organised by Working Environment Branch, Commonwealth Department of Employment and Industrial Relations, September 1983, pp. 5.6.
39. J. Alford, 'Changing power relations in the Victorian Railways' in E. Davis and R. Lansbury (eds), *Democracy and Control in the Workplace*, Longman Cheshire, Melbourne, 1986.
40. Department of Employment and Industrial Relations, Working Environment Branch, *Industrial Democracy and Employee Participation: A Policy Discussion Paper*, AGPS Canberra, 1986.

support.[41] However, it rejected the notion of prescriptive legislation, preferring instead to:

> ... put in place strategies that build on current activities, strategies that emphasise the need to change attitudes; that promote skills, competence and confidence; that develop consensus and tripartite arrangements and that seek to remove legal, industrial relations and other barriers.[42]

To this end the government has made available grants to both employers and unions to support employee participation and industrial democracy research.[43] It has expanded the Industrial Democracy and Employee Participation Cost Subsidisation Program to assist with the practical implementation of participative schemes. In addition, funds have been made available to sponsor the employment of industrial democracy advisors with employer and union bodies. Significant changes in taxation arrangements for employee shareholding schemes have also been put into effect.[44]

Since the mid 1980s the climate for employee participation has become more conducive. Both trade unions and employers have come to recognise the potential benefits that can flow from the democratisation of work in the form of greater enterprise efficiency and productivity. This awareness has been heightened by an acknowledgement of the need to improve international competitiveness. According to the ACTU:

> Industrial democracy is crucial to the maximisation of productivity. It must be harnessed as a force in production based upon the joint commitment of workforce and management ... The most effective expression of industrial democracy is through solving practical problems at the enterprise and workplace levels.[45]

In the view of the ACTU, this will require major changes in management structures and the development of forms of work organisation that encourage innovation, involvement and the greater application of skills and experience. Employers too have been compelled to look more closely at human resource management policies that increase employee involvement in and commitment to work. Gardner, Palmer and Quinlan have claimed that market pressures combined with new production requirements have forced many companies to adopt more participative practices, including quality control circles, improved communication systems and redesigned and more flexible job specifications.[46] They put much of this down to management's increased awareness of the need to raise product quality and reliability. In spite of this, however, there is

---

41. Ibid., p. 15
42. Ibid., p. 11.
43. Confederation of Australian Industry, *Employee Participation: A Guide to Realising Employee Potential and Commitment*, Melbourne, 1987.
44. See Department of Industrial Relations, *Annual Report 1987–88*, AGPS, Canberra, 1989, pp. 23–4.
45. ACTU/TDC Mission to Western Europe, *Australia Reconstructed*, AGPS, Canberra, 1987, p. 135.
46. M. Gardner, G. Palmer and M. Quinlan, 'The industrial democracy debate' in G. Palmer (ed.), *Australian Personnel Management*, Macmillian, Melbourne, 1988.

still little evidence of any widespread application of employee participation in Australia. Research commissioned for the Federal Government's policy discussion paper in 1986 found few cases of participation where workers or their representatives had been able to exert any real degree of influence over major decisions.[47]

Most of the participative practices that were identified involved quality circles, financial participation and information sharing. Typically they were management-initiated and controlled. The research showed that employee involvement schemes were more common in those industries and sectors that employed a large proportion of skilled, male, unionised labour.[48] Nevertheless, there were indications of a growing willingness to consult. According to the research studies:

> In the mining, printing and publishing, and metal industries, for instance, there were a number of cases where management routinely consulted with employees, either directly or through union representatives, on issues such as work allocation, work practices and the use of technology, with benefits to all involved. In other industries, such as retail, food and beverages, and finance, there were few examples of consultation and, where it did occur, it was often perceived by unions as largely irrelevant to employees' immediate concerns.[49]

Overall, the commissioned research revealed a strong tendency for Australian management to defend its prerogatives and resist forms of participation that involved any real sharing of its authority. The study by Gardner *et al.* concluded that 'almost all companies surveyed has resisted changing their management structure to give decision-making powers of any significance to employees'.[50] These findings are not inconsistent with the attitudes expressed about industrial democracy by personnel and industrial relations managers in Australia. In a survey of personnel specialists, Deery and Dowling found a clear preference for those forms of participation that involved little erosion of managerial prerogatives.[51]

It can be seen from Table 15.1 that 66 per cent of the personnel and industrial relations managers considered that there was a need for greater employee participation in their organisations, and 80 per cent agreed that employees should be provided with more information. However, when it came to preferred forms of participation, there were clear indications of a preference for those types of involvement that implied only limited loss of managerial decision-making. For example, while almost three-quarters of the respondents felt that regular meetings between workgroups and their supervisors were an appropriate form of employee participation and 60 per cent were in favour of joint

---

47. B. Ford and L. Tilley (eds), *Diversity, Change and Tradition: The Environment for Industrial Democracy in Australia*, AGPS, Canberra. 1986.
48. Ibid.
49. Department of Employment and Industrial Relations, Working Environment Branch, *Industrial Democracy and Employee Participation*, p. 65.
50. Ibid, pp. 65–6.
51. S. Deery and P.J. Dowling, 'The Australian personnel manager and industrial relations practitioner: responsibilities, characteristics and attitudes' in G. Palmer (ed.), *Australian Personnel Management*, pp. 27–9.

Table 15.1: *Attitudes to employee participation (%)*
(n = 1368)

	Strongly agree 1	Agree 2	Indifferent 3	Disagree 4	Strongly disagree 5	Mean	SD
Desirability of participation							
There is a need for greater employee participation in my organisation	21	45	13	17	4	2.37	1.10
There is a need for the provision of more information to employees	29	51	9	9	2	2.05	0.98
Approval of below board-level types of participation							
Regular meetings between workgroups and their supervisors are an appropriate form of employee participation	16	58	12	13	1	2.25	0.96
Joint consultation committees are an appropriate form of employee participation	8	52	23	14	2	2.51	0.91
Extending collective bargaining is an appropriate form of participation	3	23	29	36	10	3.27	1.01
Board-level participation							
Board-level representation is an appropriate form of employee participation	4	19	16	34	27	3.60	1.18
Worker directors elected through trade unions are an appropriate form of employee participation	2	13	19	38	28	3.78	1.06

Source: S. Deery and P.J. Dowling, 'The Australian personnel manager and industrial relations practitioner' in G. Palmer (ed.), *Australian Personnel Management*, Macmillan, Melbourne, 1988, p.27.

Table 15.2: *Participative processes in Australian workplaces* (n = 335)

Participative process	No. of plants	Percentage of cases
No participation	21	6.3
Feedback procedures only	45	13.4
Frequent employee–management meetings	142	42.4
Formal employee involvement groups but infrequent meetings	27	8.1
Formal employee involvement groups and frequent meetings	100	29.9

Source: Business Council of Australia, *Enterprise-based Bargaining Units*, Melbourne, 1989, Part 2, p.27.

consultative committees, there was little support for an extension of collective bargaining (26 per cent), the development of board-level representation (23 per cent) or the election of worker directors through trade unions (15 per cent) as vehicles for employee participation.

A study conducted in 1988 by the National Institute of Labour Studies (NILS) of 336 workplaces owned by Business Council of Australia member companies disclosed quite low levels of employee influence over the process of management decision-making.[52] The NILS team concluded that real influence over decision-making was best facilitated by a combination of formal employee involvement groups and frequent meetings between employees and management. This combination was present in slightly less than 30 per cent of the workplaces (see Table 15.2).

Financial participation schemes such as employee share ownership and profit-sharing have attracted increased attention over the past five years. Although these schemes have very little to do with the redistribution of organisational power, they are said to enhance employee commitment and raise productivity by providing workers with a financial stake in the company's economic well-being.[53] The NILS study found that just over 20 per cent of non-executive employees participated in share ownership schemes.[54] Profit-sharing arrangements were, however, very uncommon. Deery and Purcell showed that employee shareholding was more commonly found in large companies with a diverse range of business activities (conglomerates).[55] They suggested that these schemes may be viewed by management as a means of identifying employees from different business sectors in a conglomerate organisation with the enterprise at large. Nevertheless, evidence obtained from the ABS Survey of Employment Benefits shows that only 155 000 employees—or just 2.4 per cent of the employed workforce—received

---

52. Business Council of Australia, *Enterprise-based Bargaining Units: A Better Way of Working*, Part 2. 'Employee and industrial relations in Australian companies: a survey of management', (NILS), Melbourne, 1989, p. 27.
53. Department of Industrial Relations, *Sharing Profits and Growth*, AGPS, Canberra, 1988.
54. Business Council of Australia, *Enterprise-based Bargaining Units*, Part 2, p. 27.
55. S. Deery and J. Purcell, 'Strategic choices in industrial relations management in large organisations, *Journal of Industrial Relations*, vol. 31. no. 4, December 1989, pp. 473–4.

shares as an employment benefit in 1989.[56] Although this figure has risen quite sharply since 1985, the incidence of share ownership is skewed towards management and administrative staff. For example, in 1989, 8.2 per cent of managers held shares as an employment benefit compared with just 1.9 per cent of tradespeople and 1.1 per cent of labourers and related workers.[57]

Factors affecting the incidence of worker participation

There has been both a growth of interest and an expansion in the incidence of employee participation practices in Australia since the early 1980s. This can be attributed to two sets of factors. First, the increased application of new technology raised trade union concern about the need to establish employee rights in matters pertaining to job security, organisational change and occupational health and safety. Second, deteriorating economic circumstances combined with greater international competition forced all the parties—government, employers and trade unions—to develop more collaborative approaches to industrial relations in order to improve productivity and organisational efficiency.

Notwithstanding these developments it is clear that the incidence of participation in Australia is still quite uneven; it exists in some companies and establishments but not in others. Democratic work practices have been able to develop and flourish in some workplaces but have not been able to take root and survive in others. There is a range of possible explanations for this. Variations in the incidence of worker participation may be caused by differences in company philosophy or management style, by the degree of environmental stability or predictability that an organisation faces or by the extent of trade union power or influence. The size of the workplace, the ownership of the organisation and the pace and complexity of technology change may also be relevant.[58]

In a recent study, Frenkel sought to identify the most significant factors influencing the presence of worker participation schemes in the Australian metal industry.[59] He found that almost 30 per cent of the 242 plants surveyed have one or more forms of participation in place. The five most common schemes were health and safety committees,

---

56. Australian Bureau of Statistics, *Employment Benefits*, August 1989, Cat. No. 6334.0.
57. A number of Australian companies have a long history of high employee stock ownership. Two of the better known are Fletcher Jones & Staff and Siddons Industries. Fletcher Jones, established in 1944 by the company's Fabian socialist founder, Sir Fletcher Jones, is Australia's largest and oldest employee-owned company. Under the company's share ownership scheme, all the company's 2000 employees have an opportunity to buy shares in the company at a constant price of $1. The company distributes its profits through bonus issues to the 70 per cent of staff who own shares. About 700 of 1600 employees at Siddons Industries own shares in the company and the employee share trust owns about 18.5 per cent of Siddon's issued stock. Accompanying employee shareholding is worker representation on company boards and advisor committees that advise on efficiency and on how to increase production levels.
58. See S.J. Frenkel and D.L Weakliem, 'Worker participation in management in the printing industry', *Journal of Industrial Relations*, vol. 31, no. 4, December 1989.
59. S.J. Frenkel, 'Explaining the incidence of worker participation in management: evidence from the Australian metal industry', *Australian Journal of Management*, vol. 14, no. 2, p. 146.

management–union meetings 'at which company performance/ operations/decisions were discussed', productivity improvement groups, joint negotiating committees and quality circles. The statistical analysis showed that the most important predictor of employee participation schemes was management style. Organisations that were characterised by an open and communicative management style rather than a hierarchical command–obedience approach to industrial relations were significantly more likely to possess one or more forms of worker participation. Moreover, Frenkel's results revealed that the particular management style adopted was 'largely a matter of management choice rather than a product of particular organisational variables and union power'.[60]

A similar—if somewhat more sophisticated—research exercise was carried out by Frenkel and Weakliem in the Australian printing industry.[61] It corroborated the importance of management style. An 'open and participatory style' was found to have a very significant effect on the occurrence and the incidence of quality circles, health and safety committees, joint works committees and informal meetings. Union power— as measured by control over the organisation of work—was also shown to increase the probability of joint works committees, informal meetings and quality circles. With respect to health and safety committees and boards of management, however, work control had no discernible effect.

In addition, the research sought to identify the determinants of the perceived effectiveness of worker participation.[62] Only two variables, management style and union power, were found to have a significant effect. According to Frenkel and Weakliem, their results 'suggest that management's openness is generally the most important factor in establishing participation, but that workers' power is the most important in making it work to achieve union objectives'.[63] Nevertheless, the finding that management style is related to shop stewards' judgments of the effectiveness of participation is not inconsequential. As the writers point out, if union and management objectives for participation were completely at variance, no such relation would be found, as strong unions would thwart or ignore worker participation practices. The results suggest, as Frenkel and Weakliem indicate, that unions must see some benefits in participation, even in the limited forms that currently exist.

Summary

The development of democratic work practices in Australia has lagged behind that of many overseas countries. The often uncompromising attitude of Australian management to the sanctity of its traditional pre-

---

60. Ibid., p. 146.
61. S.J. Frenkel and D.L. Weakliem, 'Worker participation in management in the printing industry'.
62. Evaluations of the effectiveness of the participation schemes were made by union shop stewards rather than management.
63. Ibid., p. 492.

rogatives, combined with trade union disinterest and even active opposition to many forms of direct participation, has imposed quite formidable barriers to workplace reform.

Furthermore, the unwillingness of governments to provide either facilitative or prescriptive legislation for industrial democracy has done little to stimulate experimentation or innovation. The limited forms of participation that emerged in the 1970s produced only cosmetic changes to the processes of organisational decision-making and had very little substance or meaning for the workers involved.

In recent years, the climate has changed. Greater pressures for improved competitiveness and productivity and an emerging awareness of the benefits of employee participation have provided an environment that is much more conducive to industrial democracy. Demands from a better-educated workforce for a greater say in decisions affecting their working life would also seem to be important. Moreover, governments in the 1980s have become much more proactive. Through the passage of legislation and the support for trade union initiatives in the areas of job security, redundancy protection and occupational health and safety, many workers have obtained legal rights to be informed and consulted about a wider range of workplace matters. In some industries and business sectors, management too has identified the importance of developing a more communicative and open style and of enhancing the job skills and work responsibilities of their employees.

Discussion questions

1. 'One of the difficulties encountered in defining the term *industrial democracy* is that it simply means different things to different people.' Discuss.
2. 'Management's interest in industrial democracy is sparked by a genuine concern for the psychological well-being of its employees.' Comment.
3. Describe the early forms of employee participation in Australia.
4. What factors led to the decline of interest in industrial democracy in the mid 1970s?
5. How would you explain the apparent resurgence of interest in industrial democracy in the 1980s?
6. What are the factors that affect the occurrence of employee participation schemes?
7. 'Prescriptive government legislation is essential if Australian workers are to be given any real opportunity to influence decisions within their employment organisations.' Discuss this statement.

Further reading

ACTU/TDC, Mission to Western Europe, *Australia Reconstructed*, AGPS, Canberra, 1987, chapter 5.

Davis, E. and Lansbury, R. (eds), *Democracy and Control in the Workplace*, Longman Cheshire, Melbourne, 1986.

Department of Employment and Industrial Relations, Working Environment Branch, *Industrial Democracy and Employee Participation: A Policy Discussion Paper*, AGPS, Canberra, 1986.

Ford, B. and Tilley, L. (eds), *Diversity, Change and Tradition: The Environment for Industrial Democracy in Australia*, AGPS, Canberra, 1986.

Frenkel, S.J., 'Explaining the incidence of worker participation in management: evidence from the Australian metal industry', *Australian Journal of Management*, vol. 14, no. 2, December 1989.

Frenkel, S.J. and Weakliem, D.L., 'Worker participation in management in the printing industry', *Journal of Industrial Relations*, vol. 31, no. 4, December 1989.

Gardner, M., Palmer, G. and Quinlan, M., 'The industrial democracy debate' in G. Palmer (ed.), *Australian Personnel Management*, Macmillan, Melbourne, 1988.

Wooden, M., 'Employee participation—a practical guide', *Australian Bulletin of Labour*, vol. 16 no. 2, June 1990.

CHAPTER 16

Women and Employment Equality

Over the last two decades there has been a significant change in the profile of the Australian workforce. Women now account for more than 40 per cent of the workforce compared with little more than 25 per cent in 1960. The greater participation of women in paid employment has been a major factor in moves to remedy many of the discriminatory practices that exist in the labour market. This chapter examines the present situation of women in employment in Australia and the possible reasons for gender segmentation in the labour market. It then reviews the recent measures that have been adopted to prevent discrimination on the basis of sex and to promote equal opportunities in employment matters. The role of wage tribunals in establishing equal pay for women is also considered.

Women's occupations and industries

Female employment has expanded rapidly since the mid 1970s. Women accounted for 60 per cent of the growth in total employment between 1976 and 1989. This has resulted in a change in the gender mix of the labour market. In 1976, men accounted for 65 per cent of the workforce. By 1989 this proportion had dropped to less than 60 per cent. By the year 2000 it is predicted that as many women will be working as men in the 20–44 age group.[1] Much of the growth in female employment can be

---

1. M. Anderson and B. Ross, *Labour Force Projections and Tables of Working Life: A Preliminary Investigation*, Paper presented at the 16th Conference of Economists, Surfers Paradise, August 1987.

attributed to the increased participation rate of women with children. At present, nearly a third of women with children under the age of 6 and more than half with children aged between 6 and 11 are working. The picture, according to O'Donnell and Hall, is one where 'there are now more women staying in the labour force without interruption, and more women entering the labour force'.[2]

Much of this expansion in employment has, however, occurred in those occupations, industries and forms of employment in which women have always been overrepresented. Australia has one of the most occupationally segmented workforces of the OECD group of countries. More than 80 per cent of all women are employed in just four occupational groupings. Thirty-three per cent of all female employees work as clerks, 23 per cent are employed as salespersons and personal service workers and 13 per cent are employed as cleaners, factory hands and general labourers. Some 12 per cent are classified as professionals. More than half of all female professionals are school teachers and instructors. The occupational composition of the male labour market is quite different. One of the most stark contrasts relates to managerial positions. In 1989, 14 per cent of all men were managers and administrators compared with little over 6 per cent of all women. Overall, 76 per cent of all managers and administrators are men.[3]

Agrawal has constructed a list of the ten most 'male-dominated' and the ten most 'female-dominated' occupations. Table 16.1 shows systematic differences in the nature of occupations in which males and females are employed. Men are concentrated in particular in trade-related blue-collar jobs while women are predominant in service-oriented white-collar jobs.

Female employment is also concentrated in a small number of industry sectors. Eighty-five per cent of all women in paid employment work in five industry sectors: community services, wholesale and retail trade, finance, property and business services, manufacturing, and recreation, personal and other services. (See Table 16.2.)

Women are segregated both occupationally and industrially. Haig has documented the extent of this occupational segmentation.[4] He has shown, for example, that in 1973, one third of working women were in the jobs that contained less than 2 per cent of the male workforce, and 80 per cent were in jobs that employed 25 per cent of working men. On the other hand, 75 per cent of men were in jobs which employed 10 per cent of the female workforce. Research by Lewis suggests that segregation by both occupation and by industry has decreased over this century, although the rate of decline has slowed down.[5] In contrast, Karmel and MacLachlin argue that gender segmentation has actually increased

---

2. C. O'Donnell and P. Hall, *Getting Equal*, Allen & Unwin, Sydney, 1988, p. 21.
3. ABS, *The Labour Force Australia*, February 1989, Cat. No. 6203.
4. B.D. Haig, 'Sex discrimination in reward for skills and experience in the Australian labour force', *Economic Record*, vol. 58, March 1981.
5. D.E. Lewis, 'The measurement of the occupational and industrial segmentation of women', *Journal of Industrial Relations*, vol. 24, September 1982.

Table 16.1: *Pattern of occupational segregation in Australia*

Jobs most dominated by men	Jobs most dominated by women
1 Mechanics, plumbers etc.	Clerical workers
2 Electricians etc.	Teachers
3 Carpenters etc.	Nurses
4 Bricklayers, plasterers etc.	Stenographers & typists
5 Administrative, executive etc.	Service, sport & recreation
6 Architects, engineers etc.	Barbers, beauticians
7 Road drivers	Waiters, bartenders
8 Farmers & farm managers	Proprietors, shopkeepers etc.
9 Millers, bakers etc.	Artists, entertainers etc.
10 Lifting equipment operators	Housekeepers, cooks etc.

Source: N. Agrawal, 'Sources of inequality between male and female income earners in Australia', Impact Research Centre, University of Melbourne, General Paper No. G-73, 1986, p. 33.

Table 16.2: *Employed persons: industry by sex, February 1989*

	Males %	Females %	Persons %
Agriculture	6.7	4.2	5.7
Mining	2.0	0.0	1.3
Manufacturing	19.9	10.4	16.1
Electricity, gas & water	2.4	0.5	1.6
Construction	11.3	2.4	7.7
Wholesale & retail trade	19.2	23.3	20.9
Transport & storage	7.0	2.6	5.2
Communication	2.3	1.3	1.9
Finance, property & business services	9.3	13.9	11.1
Public administration	4.4	3.9	4.2
Community services	10.3	27.4	17.3
Recreation, personal etc.	5.1	9.8	7.0

Source: ABS, *Labour Force Australia*, February 1989, Cat. No. 6203.0.

slightly over the past twenty years.[6] An examination of the eight occupations that contributed most to segmentation in 1984 disclosed that in only two was there any significant reduction in segmentation. Lewis predicted that occupational segmentation would fall by only 0.5 per cent between 1981 and 2001 while industrial segmentation would fall by 4.5 per cent.[7] This has led Mumford to remark that: '... market mechanisms cannot be relied upon to remove segmentation except in the very long run'.[8]

---

6. T. Karmel and M. MacLachlin, 'Occupation sex segregation — increasing or decreasing', *Economic Record*, September 1988.
7. D.E. Lewis, 'The measurement of occupational and industrial segmentation'.
8. K. Mumford, *Women Working*, Allen & Unwin, Sydney, 1989, p. 30.

Women are also heavily concentrated in part-time employment. They occupy almost 80 per cent of part-time jobs. Forty per cent of all female employees work part-time compared with only 7 per cent of male employees. It can be seen from Table 16.3 that there has been a substantial growth in this form of employment since 1970. In numerical terms, the number of part-time workers almost trebled and, as a proportion of the total workforce, almost doubled. Despite this expansion, part-time employment has constituted a declining proportion of total employment growth: 50 per cent between 1970 and 1975, 45 per cent between 1975 and 1980, 43 per cent between 1980 and 1985 and 35 per cent between 1985 and 1989. This decline has, however, been more marked for men than for women. In the period 1976–85, part-time employment contributed 33 per cent to the total growth in employment of men. This dropped to only 18 per cent between 1985 and 1989. In the last four years, then, 82 per cent of the growth in male employment occurred in the form of full-time jobs. The picture was quite different for women. Between 1976 and 1985 53 per cent of the growth in total employment occurred in the form of part-time employment. This dropped only slightly to 49 per cent in the period 1985–89.

These differences may partly be explained by the period of wage restraint that has occurred since the election of the Hawke Labor Government in 1983. Using simulations based on the ORANI model, Agrawal has shown how cuts in average real wage rates reallocate employment from the non-traded or service sector of the economy to the traded sector and hence towards jobs that tend to be full-time and male-dominated.[9] A fall in labour and other costs leads to an improvement in the price–cost situation of exporters and an expansion of output and employment. Because of the uneven distribution of full-time and part-time workers across industries the growth in the export-oriented agriculture and mining sectors in particular favours full-time employees. Those who work in these industries are less likely to work part-time than those in the service sector (only 2 per cent of miners and 5 per cent of tradesmen and production-process workers, for example, are employed in part-time work). The expansion of these industries also affects men and women differently. The former are the prime beneficiaries because it is they who predominate in the types of occupation and full-time jobs which are the subject of the greatest growth.

Part-time employment also follows a different lifecycle for men and women. For men, the greatest concentration of part-time employment is among the young. There is a substantial decline in part-time work from age 20 onwards and it is not until men reach their late fifties that the proportion working part-time begins to rise. Among women, part-time employment is high among young workers aged 15–19, declines significantly in the next age cohort 20–24, then rises appreciably in the age groups where women marry and have children. (See Table 16.4)

---

9. N. Agrawal, 'The effects of structural change on employment, unemployment and labour force participation', Impact Research Centre, University of Melbourne, General paper No. G-88, 1988.

Table 16.3: *Part-time workers as a proportion of all employees, 1970–89*

Year	Men %	Women %	Total %	Absolute nos (000)
1970	3.1	26.0	10.6	569.7
1975	4.0	31.8	13.6	794.4
1980	5.7	36.0	16.7	1056.2
1985	6.2	37.3	18.2	1206.9
1986	6.7	37.9	18.9	1303.3
1987	7.4	39.2	20.0	1416.9
1988	6.6	37.7	19.0	1373.5
1989	7.4	39.3	20.4	1586.8

Source: Lever-Tracy (1988) and ABS, *Labour Force Australia*, 1988, 1989 Cat. No. 6203.0.

Table 16.4: *Part-time employees: percentage of age group working part-time, 1989*

Age group:	15–19	20–24	25–34	35–44	45–54	55–59	60–64
Males	27	8	4	3	3	7	12
Females	46	17	36	44	44	51	51

Source: ABS, *Labour Force Australia*, February 1989, Cat. No. 6203.0.

Evidence from the United Kingdom indicated that the majority of women who returned to the workforce after a break went into part-time work. Martin and Roberts found that many of them obtained a job with a lower occupational category than held previously.[10] They claimed that part-time work was frequently associated with downward job mobility and skill downgrading. These findings have been corroborated by Dex's study of occupational mobility over the lifecycle.[11] One of her key findings was that women with children tended to transfer from full-time to part-time work and move down to the secondary sector of the labour market. For the majority of women this proved to be an irreversible process. Most women who worked part-time chose not to work full-time and effectively traded off their preferred occupation or status against a job with shorter hours.

Dale's work is also interesting in this context. Her research showed that among employees at a pre-family stage in their life—under the age of 35 with no children—there were fewer women than men in semi-skilled and unskilled jobs.[12] However, for employees who were married with children, the differences were reversed. Women were much more

---

10. J. Martin and C. Roberts, *Women and Employment: A Lifetime Perspective*, HMSO, London, 1984.
11. S. Dex, *Women's Occupational Mobility: A Lifetime Perspective*, Macmillan, London, 1984.
12. A. Dale, 'Occupational inequality, gender and lifecycle', *Work, Employment and Society*, vol. 1, no. 3, September 1987.

likely than men to be doing work classified as semi-skilled or unskilled. Between these two lifecycle changes there was a downward shift for women. By contrast, for men, there was an upward shift, with an increased proportion of men in the professional and intermediate categories compared with the younger age category. Thus during the stage of the lifecycle that incorporated marriage and child-bearing the greatest occupational disparities between men and women appeared, with men consolidating their labour market position through upward mobility, while women lost status.

Much of the downward mobility experienced by women after childbirth is related to a return to part-time jobs. The majority of those who return to paid employment after childbirth look for a job that allows them to combine both childcare and paid work. As a result, these women re-enter the labour market with reduced market power and, because of their position as supplementary wage-earners, are willing to accept lower wages in exchange for a job that fits in with domestic commitments. Generally, women who work part-time are satisfied with the number of hours they work. In 1989 no more than 10 per cent of part-time female workers in Australia expressed a desire to work longer hours.[13] Furthermore, the majority of part-time female workers appear to be satisfied with their working arrangements.[14]

Childcare provisions are, however, crucial to the choices women make. In many cases, part-time work is a forced choice, given the lack of childcare services provided by (or subsidised by) employers or the State. Dex and Shaw have shown that American women are more likely than British women to work during their child-bearing years and they are much more likely to work full-time than are British women.[15] This was largely attributed to the tax deductability of childcare expenses and the greater availability of childcare facilities in the United States. Dex and Shaw established that British women experienced more downward occupational mobility, mainly in association with a longer period away from work and a return to part-time work after childbirth.

For the large number of women who return to work part-time after having children, the future career opportunities are particularly limited. Part-time jobs are often concentrated in lower types and grades of work.[16] They are rarely integrated into career paths and supervisory positions are normally closed to them.[17] It is clear that continuous full-time work seems to be a necessary basis for high attainment in the labour force. In Britain, Elias and Purcell found that part-time female employees were more likely to be segregated in low-status, low-paid

---

13. ABS, *The Labour Force Australia*, February 1989, Cat. No. 6203.0.
14. ABS, *Type and Conditions of Part-time Employment, South Australia*, October 1986, Cat. No. 6203.4.
15. S. Dex and L. Shaw, *British and American Women at Work: Do Equal Opportunity Policies Matter?*, Macmillan, London, 1986.
16. C. Lever-Tracy, 'The flexibility debate: part-time work', *Labour and Industry*, vol. 1, no. 2, June 1988, p. 223.
17. ABS, *Type and Conditions of Part-time Employment, Victoria*, October 1988, Cat. No. 6304.2

Table 16.5: *Conditions of employment by type of work, Victoria, October 1988*

Conditions of employment	Part-time (%)	Casual (%)
Superannuation	31.3	6.9
Award coverage	78.0	49.9
Long-service leave	63.7	8.7
Study leave	25.2	4.3
Career structure	29.8	21.6
Mean hourly rate	$10.76	$9.36
Other characteristics		
Unionisation	35.3	25.2
Proportion with post-secondary school qualification	45.0	25.0

Source: ABS, *Type and Conditions of Part-time Employment, Victoria,* October 1988, Cat. No. 6304.2.

occupations where there was little training and few opportunities to acquire transferable skills or promotion.[18]

Women are also overrepresented in casual employment where the conditions of work tend to be even worse than those that exist in part-time employment. In a recent Australian Bureau of Statistics survey of part-time and casual employees in Victoria—81 per cent of whom were women—it was disclosed that only 6.9 per cent of casual workers were covered by superannuation schemes, less than one in ten were entitled to long-service leave and just over 4 per cent had the right to study leave.[19] Only 21.6 per cent of the casual employees stated that there was a career structure available to them. The survey also showed that very few were unionised. (See Table 16.5).

Women suffer economically not only because their workforce participation is skewed in favour of part-time and casual work. In the area of full-time employment, women's wages are substantially lower than those of men. Bonnell, Dixon and Meagher found that in 1978–79 the average income of a full-year, full-time male worker was nearly 40 per cent higher than that of full-year, full-time female workers.[20] This gap in earnings could not be explained by gender differences in occupations or qualifications. In another study, Chapman and Miller revealed that men received higher hourly wages than women in each of the 140 separate industry-occupation groups they studied (holding constant education, work experience and tertiary qualification).[21] Chapman examined sex

---

18. P. Elias and K. Purcell, 'Women and paid work: prospects for equality' in A. Hunt (ed.), *Women and Paid Work: Issues of Equality,* Macmillan, London, 1988.
19. ABS, *Type and Conditions of Part-time Employment, Victoria.*
20. S. Bonnell, P.B. Dixon and G.A. Meagher, 'A description of income distribution in Australia: 1973/74 to 1981/82', Discussion Paper No. 85–04, Office of the Economic Planning and Advisory Council, 1985.
21. B. Chapman and P. Miller, 'Determinants of earnings in Australia: an analysis of the 1976 census' in K. Hancock, Y. Sano, B. Chapman and P. Fayle (eds), *Japanese and Australian Labour Markets: A Comparative Study,* Australia-Japan Research Centre, Canberra, 1983.

differences in wages within a single occupational group in the Australian Public Service—the clerical and administrative division—and found that even among this homogeneous group, men had an unexplained earnings advantage of between 5 and 7 per cent over women.[22] Chapman and Mulvey sought to explain sex differences in the wages of full-time employees and concluded that: 'If women had been rewarded for their measured human capital levels and other variables, in the same way as men...then, other things being equal, they would have earned...13.07 per cent more than they did earn'.[23] The results, they suggest, 'imply that it is the differential employer treatment of women and men that explains sex differences in wages—measured variable differences between the sexes are seemingly unimportant'.[24]

Explanations of pay differentials

Human capital theory

Why do women earn less than men? The dominant paradigm which has been used to explain the differential between male and female earnings is the human capital theory. According to this theory individuals make decisions about the level of investment they make in themselves by devoting time to study, by gaining skills and securing work experience. Such activities rarely yield immediate benefits but provide a return over time in the form of higher future earnings. An individual's earnings can, therefore, be explained in terms of their level of human capital. It is argued that women often have different expectations from men about their lifetime labour force participation so that they make different investments and accumulate less human capital which in turn gives them lower lifetime earnings. The main difference is that women are said to plan to interrupt their work experience for childbirth.[25]

Studies have shown, however, that no more than half of the earnings gap between the sexes can be explained by human capital variables. The remainder is largely unexplained.[26] British research has suggested that women's wages could be up to 20 per cent higher were it not for the interruptions in work experience related to childbirth.[27] A substantial part of the earnings gap between men and women could be attributed to differences in part-time and full-time job status.[28] It has been indicated

---

22. B. Chapman, 'Sex and location differences in wages in the Australian public service', Australian National University, Centre for Economic Policy Research, Discussion Paper No. 98, 1984.
23. B. Chapman and C. Mulvey, 'An analysis of the origins of sex differences in Australian wages', *Journal of Industrial Relations*, vol. 28, no. 4, December 1986, p. 513.
24. Ibid., p. 505.
25. See S. Dex, 'Gender and the labour market' in D. Gallie (ed.), *Employment in Britain*, Blackwell, Oxford, 1988, p. 284.
26. R. G. Gregory and A. E. Daly, 'Can economic theory explain why Australian women are so well paid relative to their U.S. counterparts?', Australian National University, Centre for Economic Policy Research, Discussion Paper No. 226, February 1990.
27. S. Dex, 'Gender and the labour market', p. 284.
28. B. Main, 'Hourly earnings of female part-time versus full-time employees', Discussion Paper, University of Edinburgh, 1987.

that up to a quarter of the differential can be explained in terms of differences in the number of hours worked.[29] Main estimated that it was possible to close some of the gap in earnings between women in part-time employment—who were much more likely to have interrupted work histories—and men in full-time employment by giving women a continuous record of employment. Nevertheless, a continuous work history only succeeded in closing the gap between women's and men's earnings by a third.

Segmented labour market theories

If the presence of earnings differentials between men and women cannot be explained fully by human capital theory, what other factors may be relevant? Some writers have suggested that the occupational segmentation of the labour market is important. Stewart *et al.* have pointed out that the gender composition of occupations makes a substantial contribution to the determination of income, after 'market' factors have been taken into account.[30] Women tend to be concentrated in occupations that pay relatively lower wages than those in which men are concentrated. There is evidence to indicate that the labour market is segmented and that men and women do not have the same access to particular jobs.

Doeringer and Piore have argued that the characteristics of jobs are determined within a dual labour market.[31] In the primary labour market high wages are paid, employment is stable and promotion prospects are good. The skills and knowledge of workers are highly valued, and companies develop strategies to tie the individual to the firm. The secondary labour market, in contrast, is characterised by jobs with low wages, poor career opportunities, low skill requirements and unstable employment conditions. Doeringer and Piore have suggested that different classes of workers tend to be confined to one or other segment of the labour market, and that those who begin in the secondary market have little prospect of advancing into the primary market because of the limited 'ports of entry' that exist. Women are seen to be confined largely to the secondary or peripheral market with its poor wages, low skill requirements and unstable employment conditions. Moreover, as Dex points out:

> Women were thought to have the necessary attributes which made them a suitable secondary work-force; namely, they are meant to be easily dispensable, they do not value economic rewards highly, they are easily identifiable as a group, they are not ambitious to acquire training or work experience and they are relatively un-unionised and unlikely to develop solidaristic links with their fellow workers.[32]

---

29. See K. Whitfield, 'Disadvantaged groups in the workforce' in G. W. Ford, J.M. Hearn and R.D. Lansbury (eds), *Australian Labour Relations: Readings* (4th ed.), Macmillan, Melbourne, 1987, p. 390.
30. A Stewart, R. M. Blackburn and K. Prandy, 'Gender earnings: the failure of market explanations', in B. Roberts, R. Finnegan and D. Gallie (eds), *New Approaches to Economic Life*, Manchester University Press, Manchester, 1985.
31. P.B. Doeringer and M.J. Piore, *Internal Labor Markets and Manpower Analysis*, Heath, Lexington, Mass., 1971.
32. S. Dex, 'Gender and the labour market', p. 287.

This formulation of the labour market has been criticised as being unacceptably simplistic. A number of writers have pointed to the inaccuracy of locating all women in a unified 'secondary' labour force.[33] In recognition of this, the term *segmented* rather than *dual* has been adopted as a means of providing a more accurate description of the complex set of divisions that exist in the labour market. Researchers have subsequently sought to explain why certain occupations and some sectors of employment are generally confined to men while others are predominantly female. They have also tried to identify the processes of discrimination whereby women are generally excluded from certain types of jobs.

Dale has pointed to the operation of internal labour markets (ILMs) as an important determinant of gender segmentation.[34] She suggests that many firms have created ILMs in which recruitment is located at the bottom level of the organisation and movements up the job hierarchy are provided on the basis of the acquisition of skills and knowledge. Dale argues that the ILM provides the basis of power within the labour market in general. One of the key features of the ILM is the ability of its members to exercise 'social closure': to restrict access to the rewards and opportunities to a limited circle of employees. Jobs that do not fall within the ILM offer no security, promotion and training aspects. They are assigned to the secondary labour market. Many of these jobs are filled with young people, women and ethnic minorities.

An important factor that contributes to the location of many women within the secondary labour market is the process of leaving and re-entering the labour market during family formation. The barriers encountered derive from the exclusionary power of ILMs and the use of 'ports-of-entry' to control access to ILMs. Jobs within an ILM typically include either an implicit or explicit commitment to working hours that may be long and irregular to suit the needs of the employer and, in many organisations, an ability to travel or relocate. Norms and expectations about the primary obligations of married women to their family and children will affect the perceptions of both employers and employees about the ability of women to meet these requirements. Tradition-based assumptions pose very real barriers to re-entry into an ILM for women with children. When women return to work after child-rearing they re-enter the labour market, not only in competition with younger and more recently qualified people, but also in a weak position because of domestic commitments that may limit working hours or travel-to-work time. Women with family responsibilities may have only slight prospects of gaining access to an ILM, and they are likely to turn to the secondary market, with its ready supply of part-time service sector jobs, as the only feasible route back into employment. There is, however, a dearth of higher-level jobs that are constructed on a part-time basis. In a study of

---

33. See, for example, V. Beechey and T. Perkins, *A Matter of Hours: Part-time Employment in Coventry*, Polity Press, Cambridge, 1987.
34. A. Dale, 'Occupational inequality, gender and lifecycle'.

employers of professional and managerial women in Britain, Hirsch, Hutt and Atkinson found that not only were employers opposed to part-time working but also they commonly equated a reduced number of work hours with a reduced capacity for career development and therefore did not expect part-timers to progress in career terms.[35] Jobs within ILMs are not usually constructed on a part-time basis; instead, part-time jobs are normally located in separate labour markets without any career ladders.

Furthermore, women are less likely to receive on-the-job training than men and, when they do, it is likely to be of shorter duration.[36] Often they are not seen by their employer as suitable for training. The ability to gain specific job-related qualifications is often a requirement for progress upwards within an ILM. Moreover, as British research in the banking industry has shown, women are often discouraged from taking the necessary examinations for promotion when at the same time those examinations are regarded as virtually automatic for young male recruits.[37]

Legislative intervention

It can be seen that employers play an important role in structuring pay and employment conditions of men and women. The interdependency between management practices and workforce divisions is evident in relation to the impact of the internal labour market system on those who are included and those who are excluded. The recruitment, training and promotion practices of firms have an important effect on an individual's life chances. In the process of adjudicating between competitive job candidates or in developing criteria for promotion, employers may overtly or covertly treat women less favourably than men. Both anti-discrimination legislation and affirmative action legislative measures have been seen as a necessary and relevant approach to improving the labour market situation of women.

In Australia, anti-discrimination legislation exists at the Commonwealth level and in four states: South Australia, New South Wales, Victoria and Western Australia. In 1984 sex discrimination legislation was enacted by the Federal Parliament.

The Sex Discrimination Act 1984

This legislation sought to give effect to provisions of the ILO Convention 111 relating to the Elimination of All Forms of Discrimination Against Women. When introducing the Sex Discrimination Bill to the Senate, Senator Ryan, in her capacity as Minister assisting the Prime Minister on

---

35. W. Hirsch, R. Hutt and J. Atkinson, *Women, Career Breaks and Re-entry*, IMS Report No. 105, Institute of Manpower Studies, Brighton, Sussex, 1985.
36. P. Elias and B. Main, *Women's Working Lives: Evidence from the National Training Survey*, Institute of Employment Research, University of Warwick, 1982.
37. R. Crompton and G. Jones, *White-collar Proletariat*, Macmillan, London, 1984.

the Status of Women, stated that the primary objective of the legislation was 'to eliminate discrimination on the grounds of sex, marital status or pregnancy in the areas of employment, education, accommodation, the provision of goods, facilities and services, the disposal of land, the activities of clubs and the administration of Commonwealth laws and programs'. The Act also sought to eliminate discrimination involving sexual harassment in the workplace and in educational institutions and to promote recognition and acceptance within the community of the principle of the equality of women.[38]

The Act spelt out a number of offences in relation to sexual discrimination and harassment and established formal machinery for redressing these grievances. These included investigation and conciliation by the Sex Discrimination Commissioner, conciliation and determination by the Human Rights Commission and, if necessary, legal proceedings in the Federal Court.

Two forms of discrimination are identified by the Act: direct and indirect. The first is said to exist where the 'discriminator treats the aggrieved person less favourably than, in the circumstances that are the same or are not materially different, the discriminator treats or would treat a person of the opposite sex'.[39] *Indirect discrimination* is defined as a situation where the discriminator requires the aggrieved person to comply with a requirement or condition:

(a) with which a substantially higher proportion of persons of the opposite sex to the aggrieved person comply or are able to comply;
(b) which is not reasonable having regard to the circumstances of the case; and
(c) with which the aggrieved person does not or is not able to comply.[40]

These may relate, for example, to situations where jobs are said to require applicants of a certain minimum height, notwithstanding the fact that the employee's height does not materially affect that person's job performance, or to certain jobs which require the applicant to demonstrate an ability to lift certain weights which again may have no relevance to the job. These job specifications invariably discriminate in an indirect way against women.

Section 14 of the Act makes it unlawful for an employer to discriminate on the ground of the person's sex, marital status or pregnancy:

(a) in the arrangements made for the purpose of determining who should be offered employment
(b) in determining who should be offered employment; or
(c) in the terms or conditions on which employment is offered.

It is also unlawful for an employer to discriminate against an existing employee on similar grounds in the terms or conditions of employment offered; by denying access to opportunities for promotion, transfer, training or any other employment benefits; dismissal; and 'subjecting

---

38. See *Senate, Parliamentary Debates*, 2 June 1983, pp.1185–7.
39. S.5(1).
40. S.5(2).

the employee to any other detriment'.[41] Such forms of discrimination are also forbidden in other types of employment relationships such as contract work, commission agencies and partnerships.

Employment agencies may not discriminate on the basis of sex, marital basis or pregnancy. It is an offence under the Act to advertise for employees in a discriminatory way. The Act specifically requires registered organisations under the *Industrial Relations Act* (i.e. unions and employer associations) to be non-discriminatory. Such organisations may not refuse membership to applicants on the ground of that person's sex, marital status or pregnancy. Registered organisations may not discriminate against existing members on the grounds of sex.[42] Further, awards may not be made under the *Industrial Relations Act* which are inconsistent with the *Sex Discrimination Act*. Certain exemptions are provided by the Act to the general rule of non-discrimination. Discrimination in employment is permitted, for example, in those cases where the relevant sex is a 'genuine occupational qualification'.[43]

The Act makes it unlawful for employees or prospective employees to be sexually harassed. Such harassment is constituted if an unwelcome sexual advance is made, if there is an unwelcome request for sexual favours, or if unwelcome conduct of a sexual nature is proffered. Harassment also exists where the person to whom the advances are made has reason to believe that the rejection of the advance, or an objection to it, would disadvantage that person's employment opportunities.

The legislation attempts to remedy complaints in a conciliatory and non-legal way. Where necessary, however, matters may be referred to the Federal Court for legal enforcement. The Act provides for the appointment of a Sex Discrimination Commissioner. The Commissioner is required to perform certain functions on behalf of the Human Rights Commission (the Commission) which is the major instrument for implementing the Act. One of the main functions of the Sex Discrimination Commissioner is 'to inquire into alleged infringements...and endeavour by conciliation to effect a settlement of the matters'.[44] Written complaints alleging discrimination may be sent to the Commission by individuals, groups or by a trade union on behalf of members. In conducting inquiries into alleged discrimination the Commissioner has powers to obtain information and documents necessary for processing the complaint. The Commissioner may also direct persons to attend a compulsory conference for the purpose of settling matters in a private and informal setting.

Unlike the conciliation conferences chaired by the Commissioner, inquiries held by the Commission, either on reference from the Commissioner, the Minister or under section 48 of the Act, are normally held in public. In proceedings before the Commission, the parties are entitled

---

41. S.14(2)(d)
42. S.19(1) and 19(2).
43. See S.30 and S.38.
44. S.48(1)(a) and S.49(1)

to legal counsel and the Commission itself may engage counsel to appear and assist it in the performance of its duties. The Commission also may determine 'representative complaints' or class actions where a number of people are affected by particular forms of discrimination.

Kramer has claimed that anti-discrimination legislation of the kind embodied in the *Sex Discrimination Act* serves at least two useful purposes. First, it provides accessible machinery to settle instances of discrimination and second, and perhaps more importantly, 'it establishes a standard of expected behaviour and so attempts to change attitudes and subsequently the behaviour of parties in the labour market'.[45] Mumford is somewhat less sanguine in her assessment of the implications of the Act.[46] She raises several concerns about its effectiveness. In her opinion, the complaint-based system of remedying grievances is inadequate to cope with the widespread discrimination evident in the Australian labour market. Mumford feels that the legislation may only succeed in bringing forward a minority of the most overt cases. Moreover, she contends that it is often very difficult for women to obtain the necessary evidence to prove that they have been discriminated against. In the area of job applications, for example, a woman must establish that she is in a 'comparable position' to a male applicant before she can claim discrimination under the Act. This implies that the woman should have similar education, experience and capabilities to the male applicant. Because of the pronounced occupational and industrial segmentation in the labour market, women may not have acquired the necessary work experience in the traditional male occupations and industries that they require to apply for the jobs. Furthermore, as Mumford points out:

> The enactment of a law does not necessarily mean that the discriminatory practices will stop. If it is in the interests of employers to hold the wages and conditions of a certain group down, employers may evade the law and deliberately discriminate against that group despite the legislation.[47]

Affirmative action

It has already been noted that the main purpose of the sex discrimination legislation is to eliminate direct and indirect forms of discrimination and that its operation is largely based on the redress of individual complaints. As such it has limited ability to remedy a third form of discrimination, *structural* or *systemic discrimination*. This form of discrimination 'is the result of a complex of neutral employment practices, sanctioned by familiarity, which are frequently not recognised as, or intended to be, discriminatory. The effect is not always identified by scrutiny of individual cases but is revealed by scrutiny of statistical

---

45. R. Kramer, 'Discrimination and the development of personnel management' in G. Palmer (ed.), *Australian Personnel Management*, Macmillan, Melbourne, 1988, p. 306.
46. K. Mumford, *Women Working*, p. 101.
47. Ibid, p. 102.

data'.[48] The paucity of women, for example, in managerial or executive positions, and their overwhelming concentration in a small number of occupations such as clerical, sales and secretarial work, is a form of systemic discrimination.

In many countries, notably in Europe and the USA, legislation has sought to redress systemic discrimination and promote equality of employment opportunity (EEO). In Australia, progress has been slower. When Senator Ryan introduced the Sex Discrimination Bill in 1983 she claimed that the time was not yet opportune to include legislative provisions for affirmative action. The Minister made the government's position clear:

> The government will issue a green paper setting out options for further legislation providing for the introduction and implementation of affirmative action programs in employment. Recognising the need for employers, employees, unions and the community generally to be better informed, the government has decided that it is more appropriate to generate public discussion and understanding of the proposals and to have wide-ranging consultation in advance of the introduction of legislation.[49]

The Green Paper

In June 1984 the Commonwealth Government released a Green Paper on affirmative action. The Green Paper pointed to the need to redress the imbalance that existed between the sexes which was manifest in higher unemployment levels for women, a greater vulnerability to technological change, lower participation rates in higher education and a general absence of women in senior employment positions. It suggested that affirmative action programs should be introduced in a number of large companies and tertiary education institutions on a trial basis. The implementation of such programs should proceed through four steps. First, an organisation would prepare a policy statement which was to be issued to the staff outlining the organisation's commitment to such a program. Second, information should be gathered on the positions of women in the organisation, to identify areas where women were underrepresented or from which they were excluded, and to provide a base from which future progress could be measured. Moreover, all employment policies, procedures and practices should be reviewed so as to ensure that they did not directly or indirectly discriminate against women. Third, goals and targets should be set and last, a monitoring or evaluation mechanism should be established to assess whether progress was being made towards achieving equal employment opportunities for women.

In order to assess the difficulties that could arise for employers and for employees in developing such programs, the government invited twenty-eight private sector companies and three tertiary education institutions to participate in a twelve-month voluntary pilot program. The

---

48. R. Dredge and L. Conway, 'Aspects of equal employment opportunity in Australia — Part 1'. *Work and People*, p. 101.
49. *Senate, Parliamentary Debates*, 2 June 1983, p. 1187.

participants in the program received assistance from a special Affirmative Action Resource Unit which was established in the Office of the Status of Women in the Department of the Prime Minister and Cabinet. As a result of the review of the pilot program the government decided to implement a compulsory form of affirmative action for all organisations employing more than a hundred people. This was to commence in 1986, although smaller companies were given until 1989 to meet the legislative obligations.

The Affirmative Action Act 1986

The *Affirmative Action (Equal Employment Opportunity for Women) Act 1986* requires employers to develop and implement an affirmative action program for women and to report to the government annually on its progress. Such a program must ensure that appropriate measures are taken to eliminate discrimination against women in relation to employment matters. In addition, action must be taken to promote equal employment opportunities. These refer to the recruitment procedures and selection criteria for the engagement of employees and to promotion, training and staff development. The Act requires eight steps to be followed in the development and implementation of such a program. These steps are:

(a) issuing a statement by management that an affirmative action program has commenced;
(b) conferring responsibility for the development and implementation of the program on a person with sufficient authority and status within the organisation;
(c) consulting with each trade union having members affected by the program;
(d) consulting with employees and particularly female employees;
(e) collecting and recording statistics and related information about all employees, including the number of employees of either sex and the types of jobs undertaken by, or job classifications of, employees of either sex;
(f) examining all policies in relation to employment matters so as to identify any practices which might discriminate against women and any patterns which might indicate a lack of equality of opportunity for women;
(g) setting objectives and forward estimates in the program; and
(h) monitoring and evaluating the program to assess the achievement of the objectives and forward estimates.[50]

The legislation encourages organisations to gather detailed information about the position of women in their workforce, to establish goals and objectives and to implement strategies to achieve equal employment opportunities. The emphasis is on individuals being treated according to merit rather than gender in matters such as recruitment, promotion and training. As such affirmative action is designed to act before discrimination occurs. This is in contrast to complaint-based types of legislation

---

50. *Affirmative Action (Equal Employment Opportunity for Women) Act 1986*, S.8(1).

which can only deal with discrimination that has already occurred.[51] According to Kramer:

> Affirmative action legislation is based on the philosophy that statistical differences in male and female employment such as the concentration of women in a narrow range of occupations, their lower earnings and poor representation in senior positions in organisations, are mainly the result of discrimination.... The test for the provision of equal employment opportunity is the outcome of selection and promotion procedures which should enable the redistribution of women within the workforce in accordance with their skills and aspirations.[52]

It should be noted that the *Affirmative Action Act* does not prescribe that employers should give preference to women or that organisations be obliged to meet certain quotas. Rather, employers are expected to set targets in order to measure their progress in respect to the recruitment and promotion of women. The only sanction provided in the Act, however, is the power of the director of affirmative action to name in a report to parliament any employer who fails to lodge a report or who fails to provide further information on request.

It is difficult at this stage to assess the effects of the legislation on the labour market position of women. Mumford suggests that it may have some effect in removing discrimination if the discrimination is a consequence of misinformation and/or role stereotyping.[53] The legislation may be important also in raising public awareness of the secondary status of women and in challenging organisations to make more efficient use of their human resources. Nevertheless, in the opinion of O'Donnell and Hall:

> The limitations of the legislation are that while it may make certain individual female job candidates more competitive against certain male candidates in the career and promotion stakes, it can usually do little for low-paid workers in general or for the bulk of women whose chief need may be for low-cost childcare or the paid maternity leave or better wages.[54]

Equal pay and wage fixation principles

Until 1969 the Australian wage fixation system explicitly discriminated against women. Their minimum rates of award pay were deliberately adjusted downwards relative to the pay of men. This was based not only on perceived differences in productivity levels but on the notion of differential 'needs'. Occupations were categorised according to whether they were filled predominantly by men or women. When an occupation was determined to be male, the minimum wage was set so as to support a man, his wife and children 'living in a civilised community'.[55] When the

---

51. K. Mumford, *Women Working*, p. 104.
52. R. Kramer, 'Discrimination and the development of personnel management', p. 308.
53. K. Mumford, *Women Working*, p. 106.
54. C. O'Donnell and P. Hall, *Getting Equal*, pp. 92–3.
55. See R.G. Gregory and R.C. Duncan, 'Segmented labour market theories and the Australian experience of equal pay for women', *Journal of Post Keynesian Economics*, vol. 3, no. 3, 1981, p. 406.

occupation was determined to be female, the minimum wage was set so as to support a single woman. This was fastened at 54 percent of the minimum male wage. The family wage concept effectively precluded women from enjoying the same basic rate as men.[56] In his *Federated Clothing Trades* decision of 1919 Mr Justice Higgins defined the minimum rate for adult women as 'the sum per week necessary to satisfy the normal needs of an average female employee, who has to support herself from her own exertions'.[57] He set a basic rate of 35 shillings per week for women as against 65 shillings per week for men. According to Hunter:

> The family wage structure perpetuated the notion of males as breadwinners, with women's lower earning capacity providing a material basis for their assignment to the domestic sphere. Consequently, more attention was given to maintaining or increasing the value of the male wage, while there was a lack of interest in better wage conditions for women. The unions accepted the family wage as an important measure of protection for male workers and could thus give only half-hearted support to the elimination of the inequalities it involved.[58]

When an occupation was deemed to be predominantly male, women employed in that occupation received the male wage. This acted to preserve the important union principle of 'the same rate for the job'. It was also designed to prevent women from making inroads into male occupations because, in general, it was thought that women were not as efficient as men.[59] Up to World War II, rates of pay for female occupations were generally pegged at 54 per cent of the equivalent male rate. However, with the influx of women into previously male-dominated jobs during the war, the authorities were forced to make adjustments to the relative wage structure. The Women's Employment Board (WEB) was established in 1942 to encourage women into the labour force and to set rates of pay for female workers in jobs where they had not ordinarily been employed and which had not been subjected to arbitrated awards. Where women undertook jobs that were previously classified as male jobs, the Board set wage rates at about 90 per cent of the male equivalent. The differential between the two rates was based on the grounds that women had higher turnover and absenteeism rates and had less physical strength than men. The wage levels set by the WEB, however, covered little more than 10 per cent of the female workforce. The remainder was still subject to the tribunal's 'needs' criterion which prescribed 54 per cent of the male basic rate. Despite widespread discontent, the Arbitration Court refused to depart from this principle, claiming that it 'should not intrude into the field of manpower distribution or regulation by fixing a rate which it would otherwise not fix' in peacetime.[60]

---

56. R. Hunter, 'Women workers and federal industrial law: from Harvester to comparable worth', *Australian Journal of Labour Law*, vol. 1, no. 2, 1988, p. 148.
57. *Federated Clothing Trades* v. *J.A. Archer* (1919) 13 CAR, p. 647.
58. R. Hunter, 'Women workers and federal industrial law', p. 150.
59. R.G. Gregory and R.C. Duncan, 'Segmented labour market theories', p. 407.
60. L. Beaton, 'The importance of women's paid labour: women at work in World War II' in M. Beverage, M. James and C. Shute (eds), *Worth Her Salt: Women at Work in Australia*, Hale & Iremonger, Sydney, 1982, p. 92.

In 1950, following a major basic wage inquiry, the federal tribunal decided that it would raise wages in female occupations to 75 per cent of the male wage equivalent. The primary reason for arriving at this result, according to Hunter, seemed to be the recognition that wartime increases had not generally been cut back to pre-war levels, and that most women in industry were actually receiving around 75 per cent of male wages.[61] Although there were several initiatives by the trade union movement to remove pay discrimination through the 1950s and 1960s, very little changed until 1969 when the Commonwealth Conciliation and Arbitration Commission granted 'equal pay for equal work'. This was introduced in four stages and became fully effective on 1 January 1972 (see Chapter 11). The reasoning behind the tribunal's decision was that employees of equal productivity should be paid an equal wage. However, as Mumford pointed out: 'Since women tend to work in segregated occupations and industries, it was difficult to argue that women were actually performing the *equal work* of men'.[62] Women working in female occupations were completely excluded from the equal pay provisions. In response to this anomaly, the federal tribunal adopted a new principle of 'equal pay for work of equal value' in 1972. Wage increases based on this principle were introduced in three uniform steps over the period to June 1975.

Gregory and Daly have shown that the equal pay initiatives of the federal tribunal between 1969 and 1975 had a considerable effect in narrowing the earnings gap between men and women.[63] The award wage ratio (average female award rates of pay divided by average male award rates of pay) jumped 30 per cent in the period 1969–76. During the preceding nineteen years from 1950 to 1969 the ratio had been almost completely stationary. At the same time the female to male ratio of average weekly earnings increased by a similar amount. In fact, as Gregory and Daly demonstrate, the Australian earnings ratio rose more sharply than any OECD country in the period 1968–77 (see Table 16.6).

The male–female earnings gap closed from 37 per cent in 1968 to just 18 per cent in 1977. Since that time there has been no change in the ratio although Australia in 1987 still had one of the smallest earnings gaps among the Western industrialised nations. These figures underline the importance of the equal pay decisions and the pivotal role that wage–fixing institutions in Australia play in affecting the relative pay levels of men and women.

---

61. R. Hunter 'Women workers and federal industrial law', p. 155.
62. K. Mumford, *Women Working*, p. 34.
63. R.G. Gregory and A.E. Daly, 'Can economic theory explain why Australian women are so well paid relative to their U.S. counterparts?', pp. 6–15.

Table 16.6: *Average female earnings as a percentage of average male earnings in selected OECD countries, 1968, 1977 and 1987*

	1968	1977	1987	Percentage change 1968–77	1977–87
Sweden	.78	.87	.90	11.5	3.5
France	.86 (1972)	.86	.82	0	−4.7
Denmark	.74	.85	.82	14.9	−3.5
Australia	.63	.82	.82	30.2	0
Netherlands	.74	.81	.77 (1986)	9.5	−4.9
Norway	.75	.80	.84	6.7	5.0
New Zealand	.70 (1972)	.79	.79	12.9	0
Germany FR	.69	.73	.73	5.8	0
Great Britain	.54 (1970)	.65	.66	20.3	1.5
Belgium	.67	.70	.74	4.5	6.3
Switzerland	.64	.68	.67	6.3	1.0
United States	.66	.66	.70	0	6.1
Luxembourg	.57	.65	.65	14.0	0
Japan	.43 (1960)	.56 (1975)	.52	28.3	−6.6

Source: R.G. Gregory and A.E. Daly, 'Can economic theory explain why Australian women are so well paid relative to their U.S. counterparts?', Australian National University, Centre for Economic Policy Research, Discussion Paper No. 226, February 1990, p. 2.

Summary

The rapid expansion of female employment in Australia has not been accompanied by a change in the occupational and industrial segmentation of the labour market. Women still tend to be confined to a small range of occupations and industries and are disproportionately concentrated in part-time and casual jobs. Their overrepresentation in part-time jobs is clearly associated with the difficulties of combining child-rearing and paid employment. The asymmetrical domestic workload endured by married women with children also makes it difficult to pursue successful full-time career-oriented employment. Much of the downward occupational mobility experienced by women after child-rearing has been attributed to a shift to part-time work.

These are not the only problems confronting women. Frequently they are discriminated against in the labour market and given less opportunities than men to develop and fully utilise their employment skills. For more than fifty years the wage fixation tribunals employed criteria that explicitly discriminated against women. This has now changed and women currently earn rates of pay which are closer to those of men. Both anti-discrimination legislation and affirmative action legislation have also been enacted recently to promote equality of employment opportunities for women. There are expressions of hope that this will lead to the institution of fairer and more equitable management practices which will enable more women to improve their status in the workforce by, for example, entering better-paid jobs that were once the traditional preserve of men.

Discussion questions

1. How does the labour market position of women differ from that of men?
2. Explain how human capital theory accounts for the differences in male and female earnings.
3. What role do internal labour markets play in shaping the pay and employment opportunities of women?
4. Why is part-time work so frequently associated with downward job mobility for women?
5. Why has the issue of anti-discrimination become important in Australia?
6. Distinguish between direct, indirect and systemic discrimination. Give examples.
7. Outline the main provisions of the *Commonwealth Sex Discrimination Act* of 1984 and evaluate its implications.
8. How does affirmative action legislation promote greater equality of employment opportunity for women?
9. Why have female wages historically been set at a lower rate than male wages?
10. What was the impact of the equal wage decisions on the earnings gap between men and women?

Further reading

Bennett, L., 'Equal pay and comparable worth and the Australian Conciliation and Arbitration Commission, *Journal of Industrial Relations*, vol. 30, no. 4, 1988.

Chapman, B. and Mulvey, C., 'An analysis of the origins of sex differences in Australian wages', *Journal of Industrial Relations*, vol. 28, no. 4, December 1986.

Dale, A., 'Occupational inequality, gender and lifecycle', *Work, Employment and Society*, vol. 1, no. 3, September 1987.

Gregory, R.G. and Daly, A.E., 'Can economic theory explain why Australian women are so well paid relative to their U.S. counterparts?', Australian National University, Centre for Economic Policy Research, Discussion Paper No. 226, February 1990.

Hunter, R., 'Women workers and federal industrial law: from Harvester to comparable worth', *Australian Journal of Labour Law*, vol, 1, no. 2, 1988.

Karmel, T. and MacLachlin, M., 'Occupational sex segregation — increasing or decreasing?', *Economic Record*, September 1988.

Kramer, R., 'Affirmative action: a challenge to Australian employers and trade unions', *Journal of Industrial Relations*, vol. 29, no. 2, 1987.
Mumford, K., *Women Working*, Allen & Unwin, Sydney, 1989.
O'Donnell, C. and Hall, P., *Getting Equal*, Allen & Unwin, Sydney, 1988.
Pittard, M.J., 'Affirmative action programmes for private and public sector employees', *Australian Journal of Labour Law*, vol. 1, no. 1, 1988.
Strachan, G., 'Equal employment opportunity and industrial relations: the path to equality', *Journal of Industrial Relations*, vol. 29, no. 2, 1987.
Williams, C. and Lucas, J., 'Gender and the labour process', *Labour and Industry*, vol. 2, no. 1, 1989.

Index

Aboriginal people, 88, 248, 272
absenteeism, 34–35, 62, 64–65, 415, 431, **451–455**, 457, 462, 467
Academic Salaries Tribunal, 89, 106, 318
accidents, 62, 452
Accord, 56, 250, 269, 276, **334–335**, 348–350, 365
Actors' case (1924), 387
adult apprentices, 413, 417, 423
Advisory Committee on Prices & Incomes, 250
affirmative action, 289, 294, 489, **492–495**, 498
Agrawal, N., 480–482
agreements *see* consent awards & agreements
Ahlstrand, B., 168–171, 185
Alcan, 465
Alexander's case (1918), 318
alienation, 48–49, 215–216, 459, 461
Allen, G., 172
Allen, V.L., 286
Alternatives to Arbitration Conference (1984), 172
Amalgamated Engineering Union, 280
Amalgamated Metal Workers' Union: awards, 198; decision-making, 287; formation, 237; ideology, 241; membership statistics, 236, 253, 408, 435; officials, 245; workplace operations, 435, 440, 445, 450
Amalgamated Shearers' Union, 221
Amalgamated Society of Carpenters & Joiners, 253, 281
ambit, 112, 199, 316, 372, **376–378**, 379–380, 383, 411
Amecon, 445–446
anti-discrimination *see* discrimination in employment
arbitration *see* tribunal system
Arbitration Bills (colonial), 76, 307
Arbitration Commissioners, 322–325
Arbitration Court *see* Federal tribunal system
Arbitration Inspectorate, 82–83, 115, 122, 124, 332
Asian labour, 76, 224

Associated Chamber of Manufacturers of Australia, 201, 208–209
Atkinson, J., 175, 489
Aungles, S.B, 159
Australasian Meat Industry Employees' Union, 240, 253
Australasian Society of Engineers, 198, 241, 253
Australian Bank Employees' Union, 236, 240, 253, 264
Australian Bankers' Association, 204, 208, 211
Australian Builders' Labourers Federation, 117, 253, 312, 385–386
Australian Chamber of Manufactures, 203, 209
Australian Conciliation & Arbitration Commission *see* Federal tribunal system
Australian Council of Employers' Federations (ACEF), 208–209
Australian Council of Employment & Training, 411
Australian Council of Salaried & Professional Associations (ACSPA), 246–247, 252, 293
Australian Council of Trade Unions (ACTU), 214, 245, **246–251**, 252
 ACTU/TDC Mission to Western Europe, 289–290; award restructuring, 408, 410, 416, **420–425**; conditions of employment, 268–270, 341–344, 347–350; education, 289–290; employers' associations &, 208, 210–212; industrial democracy, 465–467, 469–471; membership statistics, 253–257; migrants, 291; national wage cases, 248, 363, 365, 416, 421; objectives, 260, 263; political objectives & activities, 271, 276, 279, 335; resources & research, 251, **287–289**; strikes &, 45, 400; union amalgamation, 237, 239, 241; union popularity, 230; women &, 242–243, 248–249, 254, 293–294, 298; workplace industrial relations, 434, 445
Australian Electoral Commission, 123, 283

501

Australian Federation of Employers, 209
Australian Glass Workers' Union, 198, 253
Australian Hotels Association, 209
Australian Industrial Court see Federal Court of Australia (Industrial Division)
Australian Industrial Relations Commission see Federal tribunal system
Australian Industries Development Association, 209
Australian Labor Party: communists &, 279–280; employers' associations &, 200–202; formation, 76, 224, 306; governments, 15, 125–127, 143, 247 268, 276, 309, 314–317, 319, 327, 467, 470 (See also Hawke government; Whitlam government); incomes policy, 334; industrial arbitration &, 308–309, 314–317, 319, 327; industrial democracy, 467, 470; Industrial Groups, 280–281, 299; public employment &, 90–92; strikes &, 45; trade unions &, 224, 247, 250, 272, 276, **277–278**, 299, 335
Australian Labour Advisory Committee, 335
Australian Manufacturing Council, 250
Australian Mines & Metals Association, 204
Australian Paper & Pulp Mills, 269
Australian Pilots Federation, 116
Australian Public Service: award determination, 397; broad-banding, 414; conditions of employment, 73, **83–92**, 96, 331; equal pay, 126; industrial democracy, 470; industrial relations machinery, 88–89, 310, 318, 331; leave, 126–127, 345, 347; salaries, 318; statistics, 85, 97; wages, 361, 365; women workers, 486
Australian Public Service Association, 240
Australian Public Service Federation, 236, 254
Australian Public Service Management Advisory Board, 87
Australian Railways Union, 254, 280, 291
Australian Retailers' Association, 209–210
Australian Social Welfare Union, 98, 254
Australian Teachers' Union, 236, 240, 254
Australian Traineeship Scheme, 417
Australian Workers' Union, 236, 240, 247, 249, 344
automatic quarterly cost-of-living adjustments (ACOLA), 334, 354–358, **361–362**, 392
automation see technological change
award classifications, 407, 409, 416–417, 419–420, 422–425, 438, 445, 449
award enforcement: government role, 82, 96; national arbitration, 102, **114–117**, 124, 317–318, **327–333**, 361; state systems, 128, 131, 137, 139, 141–144, 146, 148–149, 151, 153, 306–307; workplace, 242
award-making, **376–383**; See also logs of claims appeals, 382–383; bans clauses, 115, 328–329, 385; employers, 208, 316; Federal legislation, 96, 106, 109, 112–116, 332; Federal tribunals, 97, **105–116**, 311–314, 317, 339–340, 342–346, 351–354, 360, 374–376, 385, 434; procedures, 380–382; state systems, 129, 132, 134–137, 139–144, 146, 148–154, 311–314, 341, 374; trade unions, 224, 241, 287
award restructuring, 243, 275, 289, 366, **407–427**, 431, 438, 440–441, 451, 457
awards, 25, 27, 122; See also award enforcement; award-making; award restructuring; consent awards & agreements; Federal & state awards; industry award determination; over-award payments; single-employer & multi-employer awards

content of, 372, **384–385**; employer associations &, 198–199, 201, 204, 206–208, 212; fragmentation & consolidation, 375–376, 445; list of, 123; roping-in, 372, 376, **384**; statistics, 98–101; trade unions, 238, 244–246, 270–271, 274; types of, **372–376**; variation, **383–384**, 413

Bagshaw case (1906), 388
Bain, G.S., 20–21, 232
bans clauses, 115, 328–329, 385
bargaining structures, 191–192, **195–196**; See also enterprise agreements
Barton, Edmund, 308–309, 312
basic wage: Federal tribunals, 97, 317, 319, 342, 350, 353–360; industry award determination, 383, 385–387, 391–392; state systems, 126, 130, 140; trade unions, 225, 247; women, 366–369, 497
Batstone, E., 160
Beccalli, J., 297
Beeby, Mr Justice, 341, 387–388
Beggs, J.J., 56
Bell, Daniel, 159
Bendix, R., 6, 35
Benson, J., 244, 296–297, 437, 440
Bentley, P.R., 45, 57–58
Beynon, H., 44
Black & Decker (Australasia) Pty Ltd, 446–448
Blain, A.N.J., 19
Blueprint for Changing Awards & Agreements (ACTU), 408, **420–425**
Blumberg, P., 459–460
Boards of Reference, 94, 107, 119, **120–121**, 122, 385, 402
Boilermakers' case (1956), 317
Bongarzoni, C., 444
Bonnell, S., 485
Bootmakers' case (1910), 311–312
Braverman, H., 15–17, 161
brewery industry awards, 373
Brewster, C.J., 442
British Economic Mission, 313
broad-banding, 409–410, 414, 416–417, 420, 422–423, 425
Broken Hill, 46, 274
Broken Hill Proprietary Ltd, 169–170, 409
Brooks, G.W., 286
Bruce-Page government, 313–314, 321, 324
Builders' Labourers' case (1913–14), 311–312, 385–386
Builders' Labourers Federation, Australian, 117, 253, 312, 334
Building Unions' Superannuation Scheme (BUSS), 269
Building Workers' Industrial Union, 198, 236, 254, 279, 287
Burawoy, M., 163
Business Council of Australia (BCA), 172–174, 186–187, 209, 434, 436–437, 474

Caiden, G.E., 90–91
Callus, R., 288, 292
Cameron, Clyde, 289
Canada, 369, 452
capacity to pay, 354–358, 366, 370, 379, 383, **390–395**
capitalism: employers, 159, 162–163, 182, 185, 202; industrial conflict, 41, 48–49, 432; industrial democracy, 462–464; industrial relations theories, 3, 12–17; trade unions, 214–216, 218, 223, 241, 246

Index / **503**

career development, 407, 409, 411, 414, 418–420, 422–423, 425, 447–448, 450, 484–485, 488–490, 494–495
Carpenters & Joiners' Award, 373
casual employment, 37, 174, 176–177, 228–229, 262, 269, 385, 402, 414, 485, 498
Central Council of Employers of Australia, 311
Central Industrial Secretariat, 209
certified agreements *see* consent awards & agreements
Chaison, G.N., 235
Chalykoff, J.B., 171, 444–445
Chambers of Commerce, 196, 207
Chambers of Manufactures, 152, 196, 200–201, 203, 207–209, 314, 316
Chapman, B.J., 56, 485–486
check-off systems, 270, 290
chemists' associations, 211
child-care facilities, 291–294, 296–298, 484, 495
Christiansen, E.T., 169
Clancy, Pat, 279
Clarkson, *Commissioner*, 399
class relations: governments, 80; industrial conflict, 49; industrial democracy, 461; management, 182; theories, 3, 5, 11–14, 77; trade unions, **215**, 217–218, 221–222, 224, 246
classifications *see* award classifications
Clegg, C., 454
Clegg, H.A., 10, 17, 20–21
Clerks' (General) Award, 373
closed shop arrangements, 225, 262, 290
Clothing & Allied Trades Union, 254, 384
Clothing Trades Award, 380
Clyde Cameron College (Albury-Wodonga), 289–290
Coal Industry Tribunal, 119, 318, 321, 331, 342
coal mining, 56–60, 63, 68, 76, 83, 221, 268, 279, 327, 392, 440
Cockburn, C., 297
Cole, K., 277–278
collective bargaining: *See also* enterprise agreements
consent awards & agreements, 117; employers, 160; history in Australia, 221, 223, 251, 270, 272–273, **274–275**, 299, 305, 327–328; industrial democracy, 466, 469, 473–474; industry award determination, 377, 380–-381, 398; over-award conditions, 116; overseas theories & experience, 23–24, 157, 216, 218, 259–260, 265, 298; wage indexation, 359–360; workplace, 244, 275
Collins, R.R., 169
Commercial Printing Award, 344
Commissioners (Federal tribunals): functions & powers, 103–106, 320, 322–323, 325, 327, 372, 378, 380, 382
commitment, 444, 448, 455–457, 462, 474
Committee of Review into Australian Industrial Relations Law & Systems, 101, 238, 321
Committee to Advise on Policies for Manufacturing Industries, 290, 436
Commons, John R., 4, 192, 194, 218
Commonwealth Conciliation & Arbitration Act see Conciliation & Arbitration Act
Commonwealth Conciliation & Arbitration Commission *see* Federal tribunal system
Commonwealth Court of Conciliation & Arbitration (1904–56) *see* Federal tribunal system
Commonwealth Industrial Court (1956–73) *see* Federal Court of Australia (Industrial Division)

Commonwealth Public Service *see* Australian Public Service
communism, 35, 45, 49, 51, 247, 277, **278–280**, 281–82, 299
Comparable Worth case (1986), 369
comparative wage justice, 113, 236, 251, 273, 363, 374, **388–391**, 395, 397–398
compulsory arbitration *see* tribunal system
compulsory unionism, 182, 270, 306
conciliation, 96, 102–103, 106, 109, 122, 307, 316–317, **321–326**, 336, 380–382
Conciliation & Arbitration Act (1904): award determination, 120, 391; award enforcement, 327–329; conciliation, 321, 324–325; employers, 198, 311; history, 96, 101, 133, **308–309**, 313, 318–321, 332–333, 336; hours of work, 341; jurisdiction, 100, 224; leave, 344; legalism, 326; national wage determination, 354–355; public sector employment, 89; trade unions, 198, 224, 237–238, 284
Conciliation & Arbitration Boards (Vic.), **149–153**
Conciliation & Arbitration Commission *see* Federal tribunal system
Conciliation Commissioners, 316–319, 321–326, 388
Conciliation Committees, 321, 324
Conciliators, 324–325, 327
conditions of employment: *See also* hours; job security; leave; superannuation; wages; working conditions (physical)
ACTU &, 248; award restructuring, 407, 410, 412–413, 418; employers &, 172, 183, 191; government employment, 73, 331, 361; government regulation, 75–76, 95–96, 310, 316; national arbitration, 98, 341, 343, 350–352, 363, 369, 392; part-time & casual workers, 485; state systems, 127, 136, 140, 152, 154; trade unions &, 215–216, 218, 220–225, 242, 260–264, **265–270**, 271–273, 297, 299; workplace industrial relations, 437–439, 449, 452
Confederation of Australian Industry (CAI), 204, 208–210, 212, 410, 416
Confederation of WA Industry, 136–137
Conference of National Manufacturing Industry Associations (CONMIA), 204, 209
conferences, 380–382, 491
conflict, industrial *see* industrial conflict
conflict resolution *see* dispute settlement
conscientious objectors, 123, 131, 282, 333
consent awards & agreements: *See also* enterprise agreements
award restructuring, 408–409, 412–415; Federal legislation, 113, **117**, 332; Federal tribunals, 122, 330, 342–343, 345, 359, 361, 365; industry award determination, 132, 143, 153–154, 380–383, 394; trade unions, 270, 274; workplace industrial relations, 449–450
Constitution (of Australia), 154, 313, 342, 376, 384; *See also* High Court
Commonwealth industrial relations powers, **94–96**, 97, 109, 123, 126, 154, 307, 310–312, 317–318, 329, 331, 336, 433–434
consultative procedures *see* industrial democracy
Consumer Price Index (CPI), 358, 362, 364, 410
contract workers, 174, 176–177, 314, 412, 438, 441, 446, 491
Cook, A.H., 294

Coopers' case (1918), 386–387
cost of living, 334, 353–358, 361–362, 392
Council of Australian Government Employee Organisations (CAGEO), 246–247, 252
countervailing power, 193–194, 212, 259
Court of Conciliation & Arbitration *see* Federal tribunal system
Cowburn Case (1926), 100, 313–314
craft unions, 216–217, 219–222, **239**, 241, 246–247, 251, 306, 373, 434–435
Crawford, B., 451
Crouch, C., 261–262

Dabscheck, B., 15
Dale, A., 483, 488
Daniels, A. Kaplan, 294
Davis, E., 45, 287, 294
Deakin, Alfred, 308–309
Deery, S., 169–170, 180–182, 184, 186–187, 232, 262–263, 440, 456, 472–475
defence forces, 83, 95, 318, 321
De Lorenzo, M., 454
demarcation barriers, 117, 140, 147, 152, 241, 244, 410–414, 419, 425, 440–441, 445
Democratic Labor Party, 277–278, **280–281**
Department of Foreign Affairs, 81
Department of Industrial Relations, **81–84**, 86–87, 414, 419
Department of the Prime Minister & Cabinet, 494
depression (1930s), 53, 225, **313–316**, 355–356, 387, 392
deskilling, 468–469, 483
Dethridge, *Chief Justice*, 341
Deutsch, S., 469
de Vyver, F.T., 380
Dex, S., 483–484, 487
direct bargaining *see* collective bargaining
discrimination in employment, 81, 127, 140, 145, 262, 269, 292–294, 297–298, 368, 418, 479, **488–495**, 498
dispute settlement:
  ACTU, 250; award restructuring, 409–410, 412–414, 423; employer associations, 199
  Federal tribunal system: constitutional role, 95–98, 100, 123, 307, 310, 329, 336; legislation, 95–98, 100, 102, 123–124, 305, 307, 316–317, 326–327, 329; methods & mechanisms, 109, 116–117, 121–123, 315–316, 318
  government employment, 84, 86; industry level, 372, 376–377, 385, 391; national test cases, 339–340, 363; plant level, 431–434, 441–444, 450–451; state systems, 127–128, 131–136, 140, 143, 147, 149, 152–154; theoretical approaches, 6, 12–14, 19–20, 25; trade unions, 222, 224, 243, 245–247, 273–274
disputes *see* paper disputes; strikes
Doeringer, P.B., 487
Donovan Commission (UK), 9, 51
Dowling, P.J., 180–182
Dufty, N.F., 232, 243–244, 262, 288
Dunlop, John E.T., 4, 18–22
Dunstan government (SA), 467

economic conditions & regulation: *See also* capacity to pay
  ACTU, 247–248, 250–251; award restructuring, 407–408, 410, 421, 425; employer associations, 200–201, 203, 210; employers, 171–172, 182
  Federal tribunals, 305–306, **329–331**, 339, 370, 391

Arbitration Court (to 1956), 315, 330, 341–342, 354–358, 366, 387–388, 391–392; Commission (1956–75), 345, 357–360, 368–369, 395, 399, 401; Commission (1975–90), 102, 104, 113, 315, 329–331, 334–335, 349–350, 361–366
  government as shareholder, 73, **81**; government policy, 73, 77–79, 84, 90, 92; industrial democracy, 462–463, 467–468, 470–471, 475; state tribunals, 134; trade unions, 214–217, **218–219**, 220–223, 225, 235, 251, 260–261, 272–273, 275–277
economic conflict, **36–39**, 47, 64
economic indicators, 356–358
Economic Planning & Advisory Council, 250
economic self-interest, 215, **217–220**, 277, 299
Edwards, P.K., 232
Edwards, R., 15, 160, 162–163
Eldridge, J.E.T., 21
elections, union, 119, 123, 133, 137, **281–284**
Electrical Contractors' Association (ECA) of South Australia, **207**
Electrical Trades Union (ETU), 236, 254, 417, 435, 445
Elias, P., 484–485
employer associations, **191–213**
  award restructuring, 416; Boards of Reference, 120; discrimination, 491; Federal tribunals, 96–97, 102, 122–123, 341; ILO representation, 81; industry award determination, 374, 376, 378–380, 382, 384, 390; national coordination, 191, **208–209**, 250; state tribunal systems, 132, 135, 137–138, 143–146, 148–149, 151–153; workplace industrial relations, 432, 434, 441
employers *see* management
Employers' Federation of NSW, 207–208
Employers' Total Wage case (1961), 358
employment conditions *see* conditions of employment
Engineering Oil Industry case (1970), 393–394
engineers, professional, 373, 395, **396–398**
engineers' awards, 319, 341, 346, 387–389
English language, 80, 290–292
enterprise agreements: award restructuring, 407–408, 411–413, 417; awards, 198, **374**, 375–376; industrial democracy, 464; management, 170, 173–175, 188, 209; national wage determination, 401; New South Wales, 148–149; trade unions, 275, 289; workplace industrial relations, 431–434, **437–442**
equal employment opportunity, 87, 292, 294, 297–298, 479, **493–494**, 498
equal pay, **366–369**
  ACTU, 248; employers' associations &, 211; explanations of differentials, **486–489**; ILO standard, 81; states' industrial powers, 125–126, 145; trade unions, 266; tribunals &, 211, 339, 367–369, 479, 482, **495–497**, 498; work value, 397
Excise Tariff Act (1906), 97, 308–311, 352

Fairbrother, P., 286
Farber, H., 261
Farnham, D., 5
Federal & state awards: comparisons, 136, 140–141, 351; constitution, 97–100, 311; employers, 199, 208; flow-ons, 142, 365; leave provisions, 127; priority, 114; workforce coverage, 97–101, 365
Federal Court of Australia, 490–491
Federal Court of Australia (Industrial Division) [Previously called Commonwealth Industrial Court (1956–73) and Australian Industrial Court

Index / **505**

(1974–77)], 94, 101, 115–117, **119–120**, 122, 124, 317, 319, 321, 326–329, 331–333
Federal Meat Industry Interim Award, 347
Federal-State tribunal relations & comparisons: comity provisions, 149; common rules, 140, 310; *Conciliation & Arbitration Act 1904*, 96; constitutional context, 94, 97–98, 100, 125–126, 154, 336, 434; cooperation, 103, **118–119**, 136; coverage of industries, 100–101; coverage of workforce, **97–100**, 310; discrimination in employment, 145; dual appointments, 103; equal pay, 145, 479; history, **310–316**; leave, 344–346; purposes & procedures, 143; redundancy & technological change, 145; trade unions' role, 141, 214–215, 224–225, 236, 243, 251, 272–275, 299; wage indexation, 361; women &, 98
Federal tribunal system, **94–124**
  [Includes Commonwealth Court of Conciliation & Arbitration (1904–56); Commonwealth Conciliation & Arbitration Commission (1956–74); Australian Conciliation & Arbitration Commission (1974–88); and Australian Industrial Relations Commission (since 1988)]
  See also conciliation; consent awards & agreements; Constitution; Federal Court of Australia (Industrial Division); Federal-State tribunal relations & comparisons; jurisdiction
  appeals, 89, 104, 107, 122, 317, 319–320, 330–331, 341, 381, **382–383**, 393; arbitration function, 102–103, 109, 122, 307, 316–317, 324–325, 336, 380–382, 413; award-making, 94, 106–114, **375–401**; award restructuring, 410–413, 416–418, 420–422, 425; composition, 102–103, 321–323 (*See also* Arbitration Inspectorate; Boards of Reference; Commissioners; Full Bench; Industrial Registrar; Local Industry Boards; Presidential members); employers' associations, 211; equal pay, 126, 266, 366–367, 496–497; government role, 82, 91; history, 88–89, 96–97, 101–102, 125–126, 219, 224–225, 247, **305–336**; industrial democracy, 469; leave, 126–127; legalism, 102, **112–113**, 124, 317, **326–327**, 329, 336; maternity leave, 293; minimum wage, 266; national test cases, **339–371**, 375, 390, 395 (*See also* national wage determination); panel system, 102–106, 122, 124, 317, 319–320, 324, 330–331, 372; public employment, 86, 88–90; special purpose tribunals, 315, 318, 320–321; superannuation, 269; trade unions, 224, 238–239, 247–248, 275, 284–285; wage indexation, 275, 320; workplace industrial relations, 440, 451
Federated Clerks' Union, 236, 239–240, 250, 255, 264, 271, 278, 280–281, 373
Federated Clothing Trades case (1919), 496
Federated Ironworkers' Association, 170, 198, 241, 255, 280–281, 445, 449
Federated Liquor & Allied Industries Employees' Union, 236, 255, 373
Federated Miscellaneous Workers' Union, 236, 240, 255
Federated Municipal & Shire Council Employees' Union, 236, 255
Federated Storemen & Packers' Union *see* National Union of Workers
Federation of Australian Radio Broadcasters, 209
Fells, R.E., 451

female workers *see* women
Fisher, W.K., 434
Flanders, A., 12
flexible working hours, 174, 292–293
Flight Crew Officers Industrial Tribunal, 89, 96, 106, 318, 324, 331
flow-ons: industry award determination, 142, 236, 251, 273, 364, 390, 393, 396, 400–401; Federal arbitration, 319, 364; Federal to state awards, 130, 136, 142, 153; state to Federal, 345
Food Preservers' Award, 389
Ford, G.W., 236–237, 290
Fox, Alan, 5–6, 9–11, 44
Fraser government, 91, 201, 282, 305, 329, **331–334**, 335–336, 347–348, 364–365
freedom of contract, 223, 306
Frenkel, S.J., 287, 475–476
Friedman, A., 161–163
Full Bench (Federal tribunals): functions, **104**, 124, 317, 319, 325

Gallagher, *Mr Justice*, 400
Game, A., 176
Gardner, M., 471–472
Gas Employees Award, 387
General Motors-Holdens case (1966), 392–393, **394–395**
general unions, 239, **240**
George, Jenny, 294
Germany, 35, 193, 235, 418–419
Gill, J., 19, 21
going rate (paid rates), 381, 383, 393
Gollan, R., 220
Goodman, J., 19
Gospel, H.F., 17
Gough, *Commissioner*, 393
Gouldner, A.W., 13
government role in industrial relations, **73–93**, 94–96; *See also* Federal tribunal system; public sector employment
  award determination, 396; award restructuring, 409–411, 416, 418–419, 425; compulsory arbitration, 321–324; conditions of employment, 341, 343–345; economic matters, 104, 330; employers &, 158, 160, 163, 185, 193–197, 200–204, 206, 210–212; history, 306–310, 329–336; industrial democracy, **466–468**, 475, 477; national arbitration, 330–336, 347–350, 355, 361–362, 364–365, 370, 390, 401; theoretical approaches, 10, 14–15, 19, 23–24, 27; trade unions &, 215, 219, 223–224, 243, 250–251, 276; women workers, 484, **489–495**; World War II, 315–316
Gowler, D., 189
Graphic Arts Award, 373
Green, J., 298
green bans, 272
Gregory, R.G., 497–498
Griffith, *Chief Justice*, 312
Guest, D., 261
Gunzburg, D., 464

Hagan, J., 247
Haig, B.D., 480
Hancock Report, 101, 238, 321
handicapped employment, 88
Handy, L.J., 34–35
Hangar Report (Qld), 127

Harvester Judgment (1907), 74, 87, 104, 310, 352–355, **386–388**, 389
Hawke, R.J., 211, 271
Hawke government, 92, 238, 269, 305, 334–336, 343, 348–350, 365, 470–472, 482
Hawkins, K., 7
Hawthorne experiments, 7, 460
Hearn, J.M., 290–291
Heavy Engineering Adjustment Package, 409
Heery, E., 298
Herberg, W., 285
Herzberg, F., 8
Hibble tribunals, 318, 331
Higgins, Henry Bourne: early political career, 307; Harvester Judgment (1907), 97, 310, **352–354**; other Arbitration Court decisions, 115, 125, 313, 318–319, 340–341, 366, 385–389, 391, 496
High Court: Federal Court &, 120, 328; Federal tribunals &, 96–98, 100, 123, 196, 310–313, 316–318, 324, 348, 396; work value cases, 396; workplace bargaining, 433
Hilderbrand, G., 23
Hince, K.W., 139–140, 242
Hirsch, W., 489
Hirschman, A.O., 456
Holz-Hart, B., 166–167
hours: ACTU, 248; award restructuring, 408–409, 411–413, 415, 422; Federal tribunals, 104, 108, 110, 113–114, 312–313, 317, 319, **339–344**, 365, 434; flexible, 174, 292–293; government regulation, 73–76, 81, 88; industrial conflict, 56–58; industry award determination, 377–379, 384, 404; states' industrial powers, 125–126, 130, 140, 145, 147, 152, 154, 313; trade unions &, 220–221, 265, **266–268**, 270, 293, 298–299, 315; women, 340, 483–485, 487–489; workplace industrial relations, 437–439, 441, 450
Howard, W.A., 219, 286
Hoxie, R.F., 193, 216–217
Hughes, Helen, 174
Hughes, W.M., 318–319, 341
human capital theory, 486–487
human relations school, **7–8**, 36, 460; See also neo-human relations school
human resource management see personal & industrial relations management
Human Rights Commission, 490–492
Hunter, R., 496–497
Hutson, J., 390
Hyman, R., 10–12, 20–21, 34, 47–48, 168

ICI Australia, 448–449, 463, 465
immigrants see migrants
indexation see wage indexation
industrial arbitration see tribunal system
Industrial Arbitration Acts, 127–128, 130–134, 136–137, 142, 145, 311
industrial boards see Wages & Industrial Boards
industrial conflict, **31–70**
  See also dispute settlement; economic conflict; organisational & institutional conflict; strikes
  causes of, **36–49**, 64, 266–267, 314, 360, 392, 445; employers, 160, 182, 189, 192; government employment, 88–89, 92; theories of, 3, 5–14, 17–21, 25, 27, **36–49**

Industrial Court see Federal Court of Australia (Industrial Division)
industrial democracy, **459–478**; See also work reform
  award restructuring, 409–410, 412–413, 415, 419; government employment, 87, 91; ILO standard, 81; management &, 161–162, 172, 177–182, 196; neo-human relations approach, 8; pluralist approach, 10–11; trade unions, 216, 260–261, 270, **465–466**; workplace industrial relations, 440–441, 445–448, 450, 456
Industrial Registrar, 94, 106–107, 114, 116, **118–124**, 219, 283–284, 329, 333, 377, 382
industrial relations (study of), **3–29**; See also labour process
Industrial Relations Act (1988), 82, 89, **102–124**, 201, 203, 238, 274, 283–284, 309, 321, 329, 331, 334, 491
Industrial Relations Act (Tas.), 138, 140–141
Industrial Relations Act (Vic.), 138, 149–150, 152–153
Industrial Relations Bill (NSW), 149
Industrial Relations Bureau, 202, 332–334
Industrial Relations Commission see Federal tribunal system
industrial relations management see personnel & industrial relations management
industrial relations policy (national), administration of, 82–84
industrial structure (determinants of conflict), **36–46**, 64
industrial unions, 222, 224–225, **238–241**, 243, 247, 252, 306
industries: See also industrial unions; industry associations; industry award determination; manufacturing industry
  ACTU, 247–249; hours, 341–343; leave, 346–347; state tribunal systems, 143, 145; statistics, 42, 68, 233; strike-proneness, 46–47, 56–60, 63, 65, 331; tribunal jurisdiction, 97–98, 101, 105–106, 313, 392; wages, 365
Industries Assistance Commission (formerly Tariff Board), 197, 206, 409, 425
industry associations, 198–201, **203–207**, 212
industry award determination, 198–199, 359–361, 363, **372–406**, 407–408, 411, 432; See also margins for skills
inequities, 363
inflation: governments &, 73, 78–89, 88, 91, 210; industrial conflict, 53; national arbitration, 330–331, 334–335, 342, 356–357, 359, 361, 364, 401; trade unions, 232, 266, 276
innovation, 165–167, 409, 444
institutional conflict, **43–46**, 64
internal labour markets (ILMs), 488–489
international competition: award restructuring, 366, 408–409, 418–419, 422, 425; industrial democracy, 471, 475; management, 166, 168, 172–175, 189; workplace industrial relations, 445–446, 448, 450, 456
international labour matters, 73, **81–82**
International Labour Organisation (ILO), 81, 83, 489
Isaac, J.E., 236–237, 274

Jackson, P., **192–193**, 194
Jackson Committee, 290, 436
Japanese personnel practices, 177
job satisfaction, 452–455, 457, 459–460, 463, 467–468

Index / **507**

job security, 265, **270**, 277, 297–299, 350, 432, 443–444, 468–470, 475, 477, 488
Johns, G., 454
joint consultation *see* industrial democracy
Joint Council of the Australian Public Service, 88
journalists' awards, **374–375**, 398
jurisdiction (Federal tribunals): disputes, 97–98, 109, 114, 123, 376; growth in, 100, 310, 336; plant-level disputes, 431, **433–434**; public sector, 320; registration, 97, 224; superannuation, 348; work value, 396

Karmel, T., 480
Katz, H.C., 4, 22–23, 168, 186
Kelly, J., 163, 232, 298
Kelty, Bill, 434
Kemp, D., 260
Keogh, *Deputy President*, 412–413, 422
Kerr, C., 34, 45–47, 64, 77–78
Kerr, J.R., 397
Kingston, Charles, 307–308
Kirby, *Sir* Richard, 274
Knowles, K.G.J.C., 34, 45
Kochan, T.A., 4, 6, 22–23, 160, 171, 186, 261, 444–445
Kramer, R., 492, 495
Kuhn, J.W., 34, 40

Labor Party *see* Australian Labor Party
Labor Union Cooperative Retirement Fund (LUCRF), 269
Labor Union Insurances Pty Ltd (LUI), 264–265
Labour Councils *see* Trades & Labour Councils
labour market segmentation *see* segmented labour market theories
labour movement, 15–16, **214–219**, 246–247; *See also* trade unions
labour process, 12, **15–17**, 163, 188, 432
labour turnover, 34, 64, 431, 452, **455–457**, 462, 467, 483–484
leave: *See also* long-service leave; maternity & paternity leave; sick leave
 ACTU, 248; award restructuring, 411, 415, 417, 422; government employees, 86, 89–91; government regulation, 73; industrial conflict, 56–58; industry award determination, 377–379, 384, 402–403; national arbitration, 104, 108, 111, 114, 317, 339, **344–348**, 434; states' industrial powers, 125–127, 136, 140, 149, 154; trade unions &, 265, **266–268**, 270, 298–299; women, 485
Lee, M., 440
Legge, K., 171, 189
Lewin, D., 21–22, 24, 172
Lewis, D.E., 480–481
Liberal & National (Country) Parties, 91, 200–202, 237, 279, 330; *See also* Bruce-Page government; Fraser government
lifetime employment, 177
Likert, R., 8, 460
line managers, 22, 171, 173, 187, 442–443
Lipset, S.M., 285
Liquor & Allied Industries Union, Federated, 236, 253, 373
liquor trades awards, 373
Littler, C., 432–433
living wage, 266, 352, 355–356
Local Industry Boards, **121**, 122

logs of claims, 376–378, 384; *See also* ambit
Long Boom (19th century), 306
long-service leave: Commonwealth employees, 85; national arbitration, 104, 108, 110, 339, **346–347**, 348, 375; states' industrial powers, 125–127, 130, 136, 140, 149, 154; trade unions, 265, 268; women, 485
Lukin, *Mr Justice*, 341
Lupton, T., 161

McCaffree, K.M., **193**, 194
Macdonald, Duncan, 177
McGregor, D., 8, 460
McKersie, R., 4, 22–23, 171
McShane, S.L., 454
Main Hours case (1926), 341
management (employers), **157–171**; *See also* employer associations; industrial democracy; market conditions; personnel & industrial relations management; strategic choice theory; workplace industrial relations
 awards, 114–116, 376–380, 383–386, 388, 391–395, 400–401, 408, 412, 415–416, 421–423, 425; compulsory arbitration, 305–317, 319, 327–329, 332; corporate strategies & industrial relations policies, 157–158, 163, **164–171**, 173, 177, 188–189, 443–444, 447–448, 461; decentralisation, 171, 187–188, 447–448; goals & function, **158–160**, 170, 463; immigrants, 290; industrial conflict, 56–58, 183, 259, 266–267; national test cases, 341–343, 345–346, 348–352, 354, 358, 365, 368; style & attitudes, 158, **177–185**, 475–476; theoretical approaches, **3–27**; women workers, 484, 488–495, 498
manufacturing industry: ACTU, 247; award restructuring, 408, 410, 425; awards, 100–101; employer associations, 197, 199, 202–203, 211; immigrants, 290; industrial conflict, 41–43, 56–61, 63, 68; labour costs, 158; personnel & industrial relations policies, 169–170; tariff protection, 172, 308–309, 352; trade unions, 220, 222, 227–228, 233, 241, 298; wages boards, 137–138; women's employment, 480–481; workplace industrial relations, 447–449, 452, 456; World War II, 315
Margerison, C.J., 20
margins for skills, 353–354, 359–360, 367, 372, 375, 383, **385–386**, 387–393, 395, 397, 399, 401
Marginson, P., 187
Maritime Industries Bill (1929), 313
Maritime Strike (1890), 308
maritime industry tribunal, 96, 106, 318, 331
market conditions: award restructuring, 408; employers, 157–158, 163, 166, 170, **171–177**, 185, 192, 194–195, 314, 445–446, 467; systems model, 18–19; trade unions, 216, 218, 259–260, 262, 275; wages, 365, 398
market development, 166, 168–169, 192, 194
Martin, J., 483
Martin, R.M., 15, 215, 262, 282
Marxist approaches, 5, **12–15**, 17, 64, 215
Maslow, A.H., 460
Master Builders' Association, 207
Master Builders' Federation, 209
maternity & paternity leave, 91–92, 108, 110, 127, 149, 248, 292–294, **347–348**, 377–379, 403, 495
Matthews, Iola, 298

Mayo, Elton, 7, 460
Meat & Allied Trades' Federation of Australia, 208
Medibank strike, 50, 276
Merchant Service case (1906), 391
Merchant Service Guild, 255, 387
Metal Industry Award (to 1971, Metal Trades Award):
  annual leave cases (1940–63), 344–345; as
  benchmark, 344, 359, 375, 389–390, 395, 398–399;
  Boards of Reference, 120–121, 402; classifications
  & margins, **387–392**, 395, 398–399; equal pay, 368;
  industrial conflict, 57, 198–200; industry &
  occupational coverage, 198, 373; long-service
  leave award, 346; parties bound, 199–200;
  respondents to, 377, 398; restructuring (proposed
  Metal & Engineering Award), **407–425**; second-tier
  negotiations, 440; subject matter, 385, **402–404**;
  work value inquiry (1967), 359, 393, 396, **398–401**
Metal Industry Mission to the UK, Sweden &
  Germany, 418–419
Metal Trades Award *see* Metal Industry Award
Metal Trades Employers' Association, 314–315, 400
Metal Trades Federation of Unions (MTFU), 241, 407,
  411–413, 417, 419–420
Metal Trades Industry Association of Australia
  (MTIA), 200, 204, 207–209, 211, 407, 409, 411–414,
  416–417, 419
Michels, R., 284–285
migrants, 76, 80, 220, 222, 224, 248, 251, **290–292**, 488
Miliband, R., 11, 14
Miller, D., 165
Miller, P., 456, 485
Miners' Federation, 279
Mining case (1909), 391
mining industry: *See also* coal mining
  award coverage, 101; employer associations, 203;
  industrial conflict, 46, 60, 63, 68; trade unions,
  221–223, 233, 241, 274, 279, 306; women's
  employment, 481–482
Mitchell, R.J., 271
Mobil Oil Australia, 442–444
Mooney, *Conciliation Commissioner*, 388, 399
Moore, Mr Justice, 325
Moore v. Doyle, 244–245
Moss, A., 288
motivation, 431, 445, 447, 452, 460–461
The Movement, **279–281**, 299
Mowday, R.T., 454
multi-employer awards, 191, **374**
multilingual people & programs, 290–292
multi-skilling, 170, 409–410, 414, 416–418, 423, 425,
  440, 448
Mulvey, C., 232, 451, 456, 486
Mumford, K., 481, 492, 495, 497
Municipal & Shire Council Employees' Union,
  Federated, 236, 255
Municipal Officers Association (MOA), 256, 296–297
Murray, A., 164

national arbitration *see* Federal tribunal system;
  national wage determination
National Building Trades Construction Award, 376
National Civic Council, 278, 281
National Employers' Association (NEA), 208–209
National Employers' Policy Committee, 211
National Farmers' Federation, 209

National Institute of Labour Studies (NILS), 173–174,
  186–187, 474
National Labour Consultative Council, 202, 237, 250
National Security Act (1939), 315–316, 318, 321, 324
National Superannuation Committee of Inquiry, 348
national test cases *See under* Federal tribunal system
National Union of Workers (formerly Federated
  Storemen & Packers' Union), 198, 236, 256, 264,
  269, 445, 450
national wage determination: *See also* flow-ons
  ACTU, 248, 363, 365, 416, 421; award restructuring,
  407, 410–412, 416–417, 420–423; capacity to pay,
  393–394; classification relativity, 423; collective
  bargaining &, 275; constitutional context, 94–95,
  123, 329–330; employer associations, 208, 416,
  421; equal pay, 369; government role, 82, 269,
  330, 334, 336; guidelines, 113, 116, 416–417;
  history, 97, 308–310, 314–316, 339, 342–351,
  352–366, 367–370, 385; hours, 343; *Industrial
  Relations Act 1988*, 104; public interest criterion,
  114; state tribunals, 118; statistics, 108; work
  value, 399–401; workplace industrial relations,
  434, 440
"needs" criterion, **352–354**, 356, 366, 370
neo-human relations school, 8–9
Neumann, F., 35
New Protection, 95, 97, **308–309**, 311, 425
New Right, 196, 209
New South Wales: anti-discrimination legislation, 489;
  chemists' associations, 211; hours of work,
  340–342; industrial conflict, 46, 50, 56, 58, 61–62,
  100; leave, 344–346; oil industry, 119, 318; state
  arbitration system, 97, 125–127, **142–145**, 147–149,
  154, 207, 306–308, 310–311, 313–314
New South Wales Chamber of Manufactures, 314, 316
New South Wales Employers' Federation, 314
Niland, J., 148–149, 288
Nkomo, S.M., 169
Nolan, J., 295–296
Norris, K., 176, 229
Northern Territory, 62, 125, **153–154**

occupational awards *see* industry award determination
occupational health & safety: ACTU, 251; award
  provisions, 115, 332, 385; government
  employment, 87; hours of work, 340; industrial
  democracy, 468–470, 475–477; state systems, 127,
  141; trade unions, 243, 261, 268, 277, 297–298;
  workplace industrial relations, 437–439
occupational unions, 239–240, 434–435
O'Connor, Mr Justice, 310, 386, 388, 391
O'Dea, R., 388–389, 398
O'Donnell, C., 480, 495
Office of the Status of Women, 494
Oil Industry Industrial Committee (OIIC), 100, 119,
  443
Ombudsman, 333
One Big Union, 246
Optometrical Fees Inquiry, 83
Organisation for Economic Cooperation &
  Development, 81–83, 480, 497–498
organisational & institutional conflict, **43–46**, 64
O'Shea, C.L., 328
over-award payments: employers, 211; Federal
  tribunals, 108, 110, 115–116, 332, 359–361;
  industry award determination, 372, 381, **383**,

392–394, 398–401; state systems, 140, 147; trade unions, 274, 315, 328

paid rates, 381, 383, 393
Palmer, G., 471–472
paper disputes, 97–98, 106–112, 123–124, 224, 311–312, 372, **376–384**
Parliament: conditions of employment &, 342; employer associations &, 197, 201–202, 211; industrial arbitration &, 95, 307–309; as public employment authority, 90; trade unions &, 222–223, 271, 276, 281, 299
Parliamentary salaries, 82, 306, 318
Parsons, Talcott, 19–20
part-time workers, 64, 174–177, 227–229, 269, 293–294, 297, 385, 403, 409, 411–414, 482–489, 498
Pastoral Award, 373
Pastoralists' Association, 314
Pateman, C., 460
paternity leave see maternity & paternity leave
payment methods, 411–413, **414**, 449
penal sanctions, 34, 53, 116–117, 128, 141, 148, 223, 282, **327–330**, 332, 359, 400
Perlman, Selig, 218
personnel & industrial relations management, **185–188**; See also workplace industrial relations
business strategies &, 22–24, 157–158, **163–171**, 173, 177, 188–189, 444, 447–448, 461; employer associations &, 199, 210; industrial democracy, 462–463, 471–474; management style & attitudes, 180–184, 472–473; market conditions &, 171–177; state tribunal systems, 145
Pharmaceutical Benefits Remuneration Tribunal, 83
pharmacists' associations, 211
physical working conditions see working conditions (physical)
Piddington Commission, 354
Piore, M.J., 168, 487
Plowman, D., 288
Plumbers & Gasfitters' Award, 373
pluralist approach to industrial relations, 9–12, 178–179, 182, 193, 218
political parties: See also Australian Labor Party; communists; Democratic Labor Party; Liberal & National (Country) Parties
employer associations &, **200–202**, 212; trade unions &, 223–224, **277–281**, 283
political strikes, 271–272, 276
Poole, M., 178–179, 184–185, 262, 463
Porter, M.E., 164–165
Portus, J.H., 328, 398
poverty, 38
Powers, Mr Justice, 354–355, 366
Premiers' Conferences, 313
Premiers' Plan, 315
Presidential members (Federal tribunals), **102–104**, 105–106, 109, 115–116, 123, 154, 231
history, 274, 317, 320–327, 329–330, 363 (See also Higgins, Henry Bourne)
Prices & Incomes Accord see Accord
prices surveillance authorities, 197, 361, 380
Printing & Allied Trades Employers' Federation of Australia (PATEFA), **204–206**, 208
Printing & Kindred Industries Union (PKIU), 204, 206, 236, 239, 256
private enterprise see capitalism

productivity: award restructuring, 412, 416, 419, 422; bargaining, 343, 349, 357–358, 363, 393–395; industrial democracy, 460, 463, 467–468, 471, 474–477; workplace industrial relations, 431–432, 438, 440, 442, 445–446, 448, 456
Professional Engineers' case (1961), 373, 395, **396–398**
profitability, 7, 25, 158–159, 163, 185, 360, 392, 394, 438, 446, 460
protection, tariff see tariff protection
psychological needs of workers, 215, **216–218**
public interest, 113–114, 141, 143, 147, 159, 238, 330, 372, 382
public sector employment: See also Australian Public Service
ACTU, 248–249; award restructuring, 414; industrial democracy, 468, 470; state & territory, 136, 148, 154, 309; trade unions, 227–228, 233, 236, 239, 241, 288; women, 481; work value, 396–398
Public Sector Union, 236, 256
Public Service Arbitrator, 88–89, 106, 318, 320, 331
Public Service Board, 86, 470
Public Service Commission (established 1987), 86–90
Public Service Commissioner (appointed 1902), 86
Purcell, J., 168–171, 178, 180, 185–187, 440, 475

quality control & enhancement: award restructuring, 413, 415, 419; industrial democracy, 462, 464, 471–472, 476; management; 165–166, 168, 170–172, 177; workplace industrial relations, 447, 450, 456
Queensland, 61–62, 125–126, **127–133**, 154, 341–342
Quinlan, M., 169, 432–433, 471–472

Raskall, P.L., 47–48
Rawson, D.W., 232, 241, 262, 277–278
redundancy, 248, 350–352, 477
reform, industrial, **215–216**, 218
Registrar, Industrial see Industrial Registrar
registration, 96–98, 100, 102, 219, 224–225, 282–283, 334
state systems, 128–129, 132–133, 135–136, 144, 146, 148, 153, 244
Remuneration Tribunal, 82–83, 89, 318, 321
restrictive work practices, 407, 409–410, 412–413, 415–416, 418
Restructuring & Efficiency principle, 410–411, 413, 415–416, 418, 440
restructuring awards see award restructuring
Retail Price Index, 354, 356
retail trade associations, 209–211
Reynolds, L.G., 285
Rimmer, M., 174, 237, 243, 432, 436, 440
roping-in awards, 372, 376, **384**
Rose, Michael, 7
Ross, N.S., 9
Royal Commissions: Alleged Payments to Maritime Unions, 284; Australian Government Administration, 89, 91, 320; Forty-Eight Hour Working Week (NSW), 340; Organisation & Rules of Trade Unions (UK), 197–198; Strikes (NSW), 306; Trade Unions & Employers' Associations (UK), 9, 51
Rural Workers' case (1912), 366
Ryan, Senator Susan, 489, 493

sabotage, 34
Sadler, P.J., 180

safety *see* occupational health & safety
Santamaria, B.A., 280
Schuler, R., 165–166
Schumpeter, J.A., 41
scientific management, **6–7**, 16, 161
Scott, J.P., 159
Scott, W.H., 34
Seamen's case (1911), 391
second-tier negotiations *see* two-tiered wages system
secondary awards, 274–275
secondary industries *see* manufacturing industry
secondary wage criteria *see* margins for skills
secret ballots, 119, 123, 148, 282–284
segmented labour market theories, 162, 229, 479–481, **487–489**, 492, 498
self-actualisation, 8
self-employment, 176, 227–229
self-interest, economic, 215, **217–220**, 277, 299
Sex Discrimination Act (1984), **489–492**, 493
sexual harassment, 294, 297–298, 490–491
shearers, 221–222, 240, 306, 308, 373, 391
shift work *see* hours
shop committees, 242–243, 436
Shop, Distributive & Allied Employees' Association, 236, 240, 250, 256, 278, 281
shop floor organisation *see* workplace industrial relations
shop stewards, 242–245, 385, 404, 412, 433, **436–441**, 443, 451, 457, 476
   British, 34, 44–45, 160, 436
Short, Laurie, 280
"shunter's law", 375, 399
sick leave, 399, **345–346**, 348, 404, 411, 415, 449, 451–452
Siegel, A., 46–47, 64
single-employer & multi-employer awards, 191, **374**; *See also* enterprise agreements
Sisson, K., 169, 192–194
skill formation *see* training & retraining
skills, margins for *see* margins for skills
Sloan, A.A., 185
Snowy Mountains area, 106, 208, 318, 331
social structure (determinants of conflict), **46–49**, 64
social wage, 80, 266, 276, 334
Socialist Forum, 280
Socialist Party of Australia (SPA), 279
South Australia, 61–62, 76, 125–126, **142–148**, 149, 154, 206, 307–308, 321, 463, 467, 489
South Pacific Tyres, 449, 451
Southern Aluminium, 170
Spence, W.G., 222
Stageman, J., 295–296
standard hours of work *see* hours
The State *see* government role in industrial relations
state employers' federations, 207
State tribunal systems, 121, **125–156**, 224, 306; *See also* Federal-State tribunal relations & comparisons
Steel Industry Plan, 170
Steers, R.M., 452–454
Stettner, L., 40
stevedoring industry, 46, 56, 59–60, 68, 83, 96–97, 106, 272, 279, 318, 324, 331, 342, 345
Stewart, A., 487
stonemasons, 220–221, 239, 268
strategic choice theory, **22–24**, 157
strategic mediation, **77–78**, 92

Strauss, G., 23
Streeck, W., 193–194
strikes, 33–35, **49–64**, 65–69, 110–111, 462; *See also* bans clauses; penal sanctions; political strikes; strikes of the 1890s
   employer associations &, 195–198; Federal tribunals, 98, 100, 106, 124, 147, 313, 336; government employees, 86; governments &, 14, 77, 96, 331–332; management attitudes, 183; over-award payments, 115–116, 400; penalties, **327–329**; state tribunal systems, 132, 141, 147–148, 307, 311; trade unions, 34, 56–59, 246, 220–225, 232, 272, 274–275, 277, 279, 287
strikes of the 1890s, 76, 94, 195, 214, 219, 223–225, 251, 273, **305–308**, 336
structural efficiency principle, 275, **416–420**, 421–422
structural conflict, **34–46**, 64
subcontractors, 174, 176–177, 314, 412, 438, 441, 446, 491
Sunshine Harvester case *see Harvester* Judgment
superannuation, 85, 89, 127, 140, 251, 261, **268–270**, 289, 299, 335, 339, **348–350**, 485
Sweden, 34, 51, 235, 290, 418–419, 460
Sweeney Report, 284
Sweezy, Paul, 16
Sykes, E.I., 142
systems approach, **18–22**, 24, 27

TAFE, 423, 446
Tannenbaum, F., 216–217
Tannenbaum, R., 180
Tariff Board *see* Industries Assistance Commission
tariff protection: award restructuring, 408, 425; employers, 197, 201–202, 206, 314; establishment of Arbitration Court, 94–95, 97, 266, 308–309, 352; manufacturing industry, 172, 202; in national economy, 276, 314, 366; workplace industrial relations, 448, 450
Tasmania, 61–62, 125–127, **138–139**, 140–142, 149, 154, 170
Tasmanian Public Service Association, 295–297
Taylor, Frederick, 6–7, 162–163
technological change: *See also Termination, Change & Redundancy* cases
   award restructuring, 409, 412–413; employers, 158, 162, 164, 168; government role, 79; industrial conflict &, 37, **39–43**, 47–48, 58, 64; industrial democracy, 461, 463, 468–470, 472, 475; national arbitration, 350–352, 359; state arbitration systems, 145, 152; theoretical approaches, 17–18, 27; trade unions, 235, 270, 289; women, 493; work value, 396, 398; workplace industrial relations, 438–439, 441, 443–444, 446, 449–450
Telecom Australia, 320, 414
Termination, Change & Redundancy cases, 108, 111, 339, **350–352**, 469
Theatrical case (1917), 366
Thornton, Ernest, 280
Timber Workers' case (1920), 125, 319, 340
total wage, **358–359**, 360–361, 363, 383, 388, 395, 398–399
Trade Practices Act, 197, 208, 332, 335
Trade Union Training Authority, 289–290
Trade Union Women's Conferences (1971 & 1973), 293
trade unions, **214–301** *See also* Australian Council of Trade Unions; conciliation & arbitration in

Australia; conditions of employment; elections; general unions; industrial democracy; industrial unions; labour movement; occupational unions; registration; secret ballots; Trades & Labour Councils; training & retraining
  activities, 260–301; amalgamation, 237–239; co-operation (inter-union), 245–251; democracy & internal government, 281–287; direct services, 264–265; Federal level operations, 245; financial resources & management, 281–284; membership, 225–236 (See also compulsory unionism; conscientious objection; trade unions: women members); methods, 272–277; objectives, 259–260; occupational coverage, 233–234; organisational security, 270–271; origins & development, 219–227; politics, 271–272, 275–281; preference clauses, 270–271; public image, 230–232; reasons for joining, 260–272; resources & research, 287–289; size, 233–237; State branches, 244–245; structure & decision-making, 241–242; women members, 294–299; women's employment policies, 292–294
Trades & Labour Councils, 136–137, 214, 222, 243, 245, **246**, 247–249, 252
training & retraining, **289–290**, 299, 407, 409–414, 416–417, 419–425, 431, 440–444, 446–447, 449–451, 470–471, 485–490, 494
Tramways Union, 328
Transport Workers' Award, 373, **393**
Transport Workers' Union, 236, 245, 257
tribunal systems: See also awards; Federal-State tribunal relations & comparisons; Federal tribunal system; State tribunal systems
  employer associations, 195–196, 199, 203, 207–209, 211–212; employers, 157–158, 173–174, 183; government role, 92, 321; history, 76–77, **305–338**; trade unions as offspring, 215, **219**, 236, 251, 282; strike settlement, 59, 61, 65
Turner, H.A., 34, 51
Turner, I., 53
turnover see labour turnover
two-tiered wages system, 243, 275, **410–416**, 440–441, 457

unemployment: employers &, 210; government role, 78–79, 91; industry award determination, 383, 392; national arbitration, 314–315, 330–332, 334–335, 360–361; state tribunal systems, 143; trade unions, 223, 251, 265, 275; women, 493; working days lost, 62
unions see trade unions
unitary frame of reference, 4, **5–9**, 11, 182, 185
United Kingdom: comparable worth, 369; employer associations, 201–202; employers, 157, 159–160, 168–171, 175, 185, 187; industrial conflict, 34, 47, 51; Metal Industry Mission to, 418–419; pluralist approach, 9; shop stewards, 34, 44–45, 160, 436; trade unions, 9, 51, 197–198, 215–216, 232, 235, 265, 273, 292, 295–298, 306; women workers, 483–484, 486, 489
United States of America: comparable worth, 369; employers, 157, 162, 166, 169, 171–172, 184–186, 192–193; government economic role, 78–79; human relations approach, 7; human resource management, 444–445; industrial conflict, 44–45,

47, 51; industrial democracy, 469; labour turnover, 452; multinational corporations, 446; organisational psychologists, 6; strategic choice theory, 22; strikes, 34–35; trade unions, 217–218, 235, 265, 295, 298, 484, 493

Veblen, Thorstein, 4
Vehicle Builders' Employees Federation, 240, 257
Vernon Report (1965), 399
Victoria: anti-discrimination legislation, 489; industrial democracy, 470; industrial disputes, 35, 58, 61–62; part-time & casual workers, 485; public service, 76, 342; state arbitration system, 125, 137–140, **149–153**, 154, 308, 389
Victorian Chamber of Manufactures, 152, 200–201
Victorian Employers' Federation, 200, 203
Victorian Trades Hall Council, 152, 222

wage fixation principles, 243, 410–411, 417–418, 425, 456, 452, **495–498**
wage indexation, 266, 275, 320, 332, 334–335, 343, **359–366**, 383, 391, 401, 408, 410
wage slavery, 38
wages: See also basic wage; comparative wage justice; cost of living; equal pay; national wage determination; real wages; total wage; two-tiered wages system; wage indexation
  employer associations, 192, 195, 199, 203; government employment, 83–84, 86–89, 91; government regulation, 73–76, 78; immigrants, 290; industrial conflict, 37–39, 56–58, 66–67, 267; industrial relations theories, 7–8; industry award determination, 375–380, 384, **385–404**; management, 172, 183, 314–315; state arbitration systems, 138, 140, 147, 152
  trade unions &: history, 220–222, 225; methods, 273, 275; objectives, 260, 265, **266–268**, 270–271, 299; popularity, 232, 261–263; theories, 216, 218; women, 298; workplace negotiations, 242–244, 252
  workplace industrial relations, 431–433, 437, 439, 442, 446
Wages & Industrial Boards, 125, 127–128, 133, **137–142**, 145, 154, 224
wages drift, 395, 399
wages pause, 275, 343, 365
Walker, C.R., 40
Walker, K.F., 117, 182–183, 462
Walton, Richard, 166, 168
Warner, M., 286
Waterside Workers' Federation, 45, 221, 257
Watson, J.C., 224, 309
wealth, 25, 47–48, 159, 260, 263
Webb, Sidney & Beatrice, 215–216, 218
Weilgosz, J.B., 288
Western Australia, 58, 61–62, 106, 125–127, **133–137**, 154, 307–308, 465, 489
Whitlam government: annual leave, 126; dismissal of, 272; maternity leave, 347; Presidential Members, 317; public service, 91; superannuation, 348; unemployment, 360; union education, 289; wage indexation, 334, 361, 364, 401
Williamstown Dockyard (Vic.), 445
Winter, Commissioner, 394–395, 400
women: See also discrimination in employment; equal pay

women: (continued)
  absenteeism & turnover, 454–455; awards, 98–101, 403–404, 485, 491; Boards of Reference, 121; employment equality, **479–499**; government employment, 88; hostels, 143; hours, 340, 483–485, 487–489; management &, 162; occupations & industries, 366–367, 479–486, 495, 498; trade unions, 98, 226–229, 233–234, 248–249, 251, **291–299**, 367–368, 485, 487, 491, 493–494, 496–497; wages, 130, 317, 319, 366–369, 485–489, 492, 495–498; World War II, 316
Women's Employment Board (WEB), 318, 367, 496
Wood, S., 163
Wooden, M., 62, 64
Woodward, J., 39–40
Wool & Basil Workers' case (1923), 387
work practices, restrictive *see* restrictive work practices
work reform, **462–468**; *See also* industrial democracy
work value, 359, 366–369, 373, 386, 388, 393, **395–401**, 417, 421

worker participation *see* industrial democracy
workers' compensation, 85, 127, 154, 222
Workers' Education Association of SA, 289
workforce, 41–42, 64, 95, 97–101, 219, 225–230, 233–234, 247, 315–316, 479–486
working conditions (physical), 8, 56–58, 108, 110, 160, 265, **267–268**, 290, 299; *See also* occupational health & safety
working days lost, 49, 51–53, 55–58, 60–62, 64–68, 266–267
Working Women's Charter (ACTU), 293–294
workplace bargaining *see* enterprise agreements
workplace industrial relations, **242–244**, 252, 260, 414–415, **431–458**; *See also* absenteeism; enterprise bargaining; labour turnover
workplace representatives *see* shop stewards
World War I, 53, 387
World War II, 126, 243, 315–316, 367, 392, 496–497
Wright, Mr Justice, 399

Yerbury, D., 286